WARREN   REEVE

MANAGERIAL
ACCOUNTING

9E

WARREN   REEVE

MANAGERIAL
ACCOUNTING

9E

CARL S. WARREN
Professor Emeritus of Accounting
University of Georgia, Athens

JAMES M. REEVE
Professor Emeritus of Accounting
University of Tennessee, Knoxville

THOMSON

SOUTH-WESTERN

Australia · Brazil · Canada · Mexico · Singapore · Spain · United Kingdom · United States

THOMSON

SOUTH-WESTERN

Managerial Accounting, 9e
Carl S. Warren and James M. Reeve

VP/Editorial Director:
Jack W. Calhoun

Publisher:
Rob Dewey

Executive Editor:
Sharon Oblinger

Developmental Editor:
Steven E. Joos

Assistant Editor:
Erin Berger

Marketing Manager:
Robin Farrar

Sr. Content Project Manager:
Cliff Kallemeyn

Manager of Technology, Editorial:
Vicky True

Associate Manager of Technology:
John Barans

Sr. Technology Project Editors:
Sally Nieman and Robin Browning

Manufacturing Coordinator:
Doug Wilke

Editorial Assistant:
Kelly Somers

Production House:
LEAP Publishing Services, Inc.

Compositor:
GGS Book Services, Inc.

Printer:
RR Donnelley
Willard, OH

Art Director:
Bethany Casey

Infographic Illustrations:
Grannan Graphic Design, Ltd.

Internal Designer:
Grannan Graphic Design, Ltd.

Cover Designer:
Grannan Graphic Design, Ltd.

Cover Images:
Max Dereta/Jupiterimages

Photography Manager:
John Hill

Photo Researcher:
Rose Alcorn

Library of Congress Control Number:
2006934850

For more information about our products, contact us at:

Thomson Learning Academic Resource
Center

1-800-423-0563

Thomson Higher Education
5191 Natorp Boulevard
Mason, OH 45040
USA

The Author Team • • • • • • • • • • • • • • •

Carl S. Warren

Dr. Carl S. Warren is Professor Emeritus of Accounting at the University of Georgia, Athens. For over 25 years, Professor Warren taught all levels of accounting classes. Professor Warren has taught classes at the University of Georgia, University of Iowa, Michigan State University, and University of Chicago. Professor Warren focused his teaching efforts on principles of accounting and auditing. Professor Warren received his doctorate degree (Ph.D.) from Michigan State University and his undergraduate (B.B.A) and masters (M.A.) degrees from the University of Iowa. During his career, Professor Warren published numerous articles in professional journals, including *The Accounting Review, Journal of Accounting Research, Journal of Accountancy, The CPA Journal,* and *Auditing: A Journal of Practice & Theory.* Professor Warren's outside interests include writing short stories and novels, oil painting, playing handball, golfing, skiing, backpacking, and fly-fishing.

James M. Reeve

Dr. James M. Reeve is Professor Emeritus of Accounting and Information Management at the University of Tennessee. Professor Reeve taught on the accounting faculty for 25 years, after graduating with his Ph.D. from Oklahoma State University. His teaching effort focused on undergraduate accounting principles and graduate education in the Master of Accountancy and Senior Executive MBA programs. Beyond this, Professor Reeve is also very active in the Supply Chain Certification program, which is a major executive education and research effort of the College. His research interests are varied and include work in managerial accounting, supply chain management, lean manufacturing, and information management. He has published over 40 articles in academic and professional journals, including the *Journal of Cost Management, Journal of Management Accounting Research, Accounting Review, Management Accounting Quarterly, Supply Chain Management Review,* and *Accounting Horizons.* He has consulted or provided training around the world for a wide variety of organizations, including Boeing, Procter and Gamble, Norfolk Southern, Hershey Foods, Coca-Cola, and Sony. When not writing books, Professor Reeve plays golf and is involved in faith-based activities.

For over 75 years, *Accounting* has been used effectively to teach generations of businessmen and women. As the most successful business textbook of all time, it continues to introduce students to accounting through a variety of time-tested ways. With this edition, we continue our quest to explore new ways to connect the modern student to accounting, a discipline that is challenging and rewarding.

With this quest in mind, we came to you, the teachers of accounting, and asked what works, what doesn't, and what needs improvement. For this edition, we employed many new methods to get closer to instructors who teach the course every day. As always, your responses were thorough and insightful, and through reviews, focus groups, and our ground-breaking Blue Sky Workshops, we've created a contemporary and efficient learning system for today's student and instructor. In fact, our Blue Sky Workshops brought together accounting teachers from all over the country to discuss content, chapter pedagogy, book design, and supplements. For the first time, instructors had input on every aspect of the project, and the effect of their input on this edition is clear. By connecting with those who use the book, *Managerial Accounting, 9e*, delivers everything students and instructors need, with nothing they don't.

The original author of *Accounting*, James McKinsey, could not have imagined the success and influence this text has enjoyed or that his original vision would continue to lead the market into the twenty-first century. As the current authors, we appreciate the responsibility of protecting and enhancing this vision, while continuing to refine it to meet the changing needs of students and instructors. Always in touch with a tradition of excellence but never satisfied with yesterday's success, this edition enthusiastically embraces a changing environment and continues to proudly lead the way. We sincerely thank our many colleagues who have helped to make it happen.

Carl S. Warren

"The teaching of accounting is no longer designed to train professional accountants only. With the growing complexity of business and the constantly increasing difficulty of the problems of management, it has become essential that everyone who aspires to a position of responsibility should have a knowledge of the fundamental principles of accounting."

— James O. McKinsey, Author, first edition, 1929

Connect to Course Content

As the clear leader in pedagogical innovation, *Managerial Accounting, 9e*, introduces the next step in the evolution of accounting textbooks. Through discussions at the Blue Sky Workshops and other instructor interactions, this edition is closer than ever to becoming the "perfect" accounting text.

(NEW!) **Example Exercise**

Based on extensive market feedback, we've developed new Example Exercises that reinforce concepts and procedures in a bold, new way. Like a teacher in a classroom, students follow the authors' example to see how to complete accounting applications as they are presented in the text. This feature also provides a list of Practice Exercises that parallel the Example Exercises, so students get the practice they need.

See the example of the application being presented.

Example Exercise 4-3

objective **3**

Nicolas Enterprises sells a product for $60 per unit. The variable cost is $35 per unit, while fixed costs are $80,000. Determine the (a) break-even point in sales units and (b) break-even point if the selling price were increased to $67 per unit.

Follow My Example 4-3

a. 3,200 units = $80,000/($60 − $35)
b. 2,500 units = $80,000/($67 − $35)

For Practice: PE 4-3A, PE 4-3B

Follow along as the authors work through the example exercise.

Try these corresponding end-of-chapter exercises for practice!

Clear Objectives and Key Learning Outcomes

To help guide students, the authors revised and focused the chapter objectives and developed key learning outcomes related to each chapter objective. All aspects of the chapter content and end-of-chapter exercises and problems connect back to these objectives and related outcomes. In doing so, students can test their understanding and quickly locate concepts for review.

NEW! "At a Glance" Chapter Summary

The "At a Glance" summary grid ties everything together and helps students stay on track. First, the Key Points recap the chapter content for each chapter objective. Second, the related Key Learning Outcomes list all of the expected student performance capabilities that come from completing each objective. In case students need further practice on a specific outcome, the last two columns reference related Example Exercises and their corresponding Practice Exercises. Through this intuitive grid, all the chapter pedagogy links together in one cleanly integrated summary.

5. Compute the break-even point for a business selling more than one product, the operating leverage, and the margin of safety.

Key Points	Key Learning Outcomes	Example Exercises	Practice Exercises
Cost-volume-profit relationships can be used for analyzing (1) sales mix, (2) operating leverage, and (3) margin of safety. Sales mix computes the break-even point for a business selling more than one product. Operating leverage measures the impact of changes in sales on income from operations. The margin of safety measures the possible decrease in sales that may occur before an operating loss results.	• Compute the break-even point for more than one product.	**4-5**	4-5A, 4-5B
	• Compute operating leverage.	**4-6**	4-6A, 4-6B
	• Compute the margin of safety.	**4-7**	4-7A, 4-7B

Provides a conceptual review of each objective.

Creates a checklist of skills to help review for a test.

Directs the student to this helpful new feature!

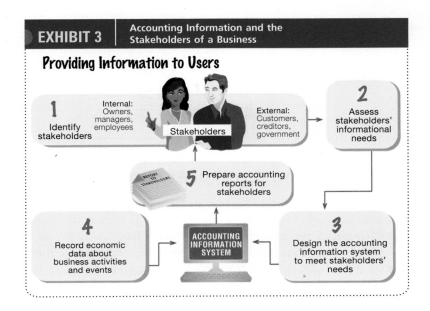

EXHIBIT 3 | Accounting Information and the Stakeholders of a Business

Providing Information to Users

1 Identify stakeholders — Internal: Owners, managers, employees — Stakeholders — External: Customers, creditors, government

2 Assess stakeholders' informational needs

3 Design the accounting information system to meet stakeholders' needs

4 Record economic data about business activities and events

ACCOUNTING INFORMATION SYSTEM

5 Prepare accounting reports for stakeholders

Modern, User-Friendly Design

The internal design has been modified to be both appealing and easy to navigate. Based on student testimonials of what they find most useful, this streamlined presentation includes a wealth of helpful resources without feeling cluttered. To update the look of the material, some Exhibits use computerized spreadsheets to better reflect the changing environment of business. Visual learners will appreciate the generous number of exhibits and illustrations used to convey concepts and procedures.

Always aware of the issues and changes in real world accounting, the colorful and dynamic *Managerial Accounting, 9e,* visually highlights coverage that is designed to help students make the connection between accounting concepts and business practices. Accounting doesn't occur in a vacuum, and the new and improved features found in each chapter make the content come to life.

Improved Chapter Openers

Building on the strengths of past editions, these openers continue to relate the accounting and business concepts in the chapter to the student's life. New for this edition, these openers now employ examples of real companies as well providing invaluable insight into real practice. The following companies are among those that have been incorporated into the chapter openers.

- Google
- Gold's Gym
- Marvel Entertainment
- Electronic Arts
- Fatburger
- The North Face

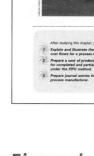
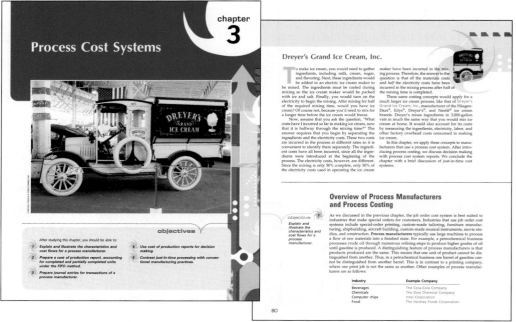

Financial Analysis and Interpretation

The Financial Analysis and Interpretation section in Chapter 13 introduces relevant, key ratios. Students connect with the business environment as they learn how stakeholders will interpret financial reports. This section covers basic analysis tools that students will use again in the Financial Statement Analysis chapter. Furthermore, students get to test their proficiency with these tools through special activities and exercises in the end of the chapter. Both the section and related end-of-chapter material are indicated with a unique icon for a consistent presentation.

Roughly eight out of every ten workers in the United States are service providers.

Comprehensive Real World Notes

Students get a close-up look at how accounting operates in the marketplace through a variety of items in the margins and in the Business Connections boxed features throughout the book. In addition, a variety of end-of-chapter exercises and problems employ real world data to give students a feel for the material accountants see daily. No matter where they are found, elements that use material from real companies are indicated with a unique icon for a consistent presentation. The following companies are among those highlighted in the text.

- AT&T
- Campbell Soup Co.
- Mercedes-Benz
- J.C. Penney Co.
- Hewlett-Packard
- Delta Air Lines
- Ford Motor Co.
- Gillette
- General Electric

Business Connections

RAPID INVENTORY AT COSTCO

Costco Wholesale Corporation operates over 300 membership warehouses that offer members low prices on a limited selection of nationally branded and selected private label products. Costco emphasizes generating high sales volumes and rapid inventory turnover. This enables Costco to operate profitably at significantly lower gross margins than traditional wholesalers, discount retailers, and supermarkets. In addition, Costco's rapid turnover provides it the opportunity to conserve on its cash, as described below.

Because of its high sales volume and rapid inventory turnover, Costco generally has the opportunity to receive cash from the sale of a substantial portion of its inventory at mature warehouse operations before it is required to pay all its merchandise vendors, even though Costco takes advantage of early payment terms to obtain payment dis-

counts. As sales in a given warehouse increase and inventory turnover becomes more rapid, a greater percentage of the inventory is financed through payment terms provided by vendors rather than by working capital (cash).

© DON RYAN/ASSOCIATED PRESS

Integrity, Objectivity, and Ethics in Business

In each chapter, these cases help students develop their ethical compass. Often coupled with related end-of-chapter activities, these cases can be discussed in class or the students can consider them as they read the chapter. These are always indicated with a unique icon for a consistent presentation.

Integrity, Objectivity, and Ethics in Business

THE RESPONSIBLE BOARD

Recent accounting scandals, such as those involving Enron, WorldCom, and Fannie Mae, have highlighted the roles of boards of directors in executing their responsibilities. For example, eighteen of Enron's former directors and their insurance providers have settled shareholder litiga-

tion for $168 million, of which $13 million is to come from the directors' personal assets. Board members are now on notice that their directorship responsibilities are being taken seriously by stockholders.

Connect and Review

Though the presentation of this edition includes many new and improved elements, the traditional tools that have helped students for years remain an integral part of the book.

⊟netsolutions   **Continuing Case Study:** Students follow a fictitious company, NetSolutions, as the example company to demonstrate a variety of transactions. To help students connect to the world of accounting, the NetSolutions transactions are often paired with nonbusiness events to which students can easily relate.

Summaries: Within each chapter, these synopses draw special attention to important points and help clarify difficult concepts.

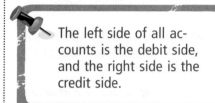

The left side of all accounts is the debit side, and the right side is the credit side.

In the preceding examples, you should observe that the left side of asset accounts is used for recording increases, and the right side is used for recording decreases. Also, the right side of liability and stockholders' equity accounts is used to record increases, and the left side of such accounts is used to record decreases. The left side of all accounts, whether asset, liability, or stockholders' equity, is the debit side, and the right side is the credit side. Thus, a debit may be either an increase or a decrease,

Key Terms: At the end of each chapter, this list of key terms provides page numbers for easy reference.

Self-Examination Questions: Five multiple-choice questions, with answers at the end of the chapter, help students review and retain chapter concepts.

Illustrative Problem and Solution: A solved problem models one or more of the chapter's assignment problems, so that students can apply the modeled procedures to end-of-chapter materials.

Illustrative Problem

Inez Company recently began production of a new product, M, which required the investment of $1,600,000 in assets. The costs of producing and selling 80,000 units of Product M are estimated as follows:

Variable costs:
Direct materials	$ 10.00 per unit
Direct labor	6.00
Factory overhead	4.00
Selling and administrative expenses	5.00
Total	$ 25.00 per unit

Fixed costs:
Factory overhead	$800,000
Selling and administrative expenses	400,000

Students need to practice accounting in order to understand and use it. To give your students the greatest possible advantages in the real world, *Managerial Accounting, 9e,* **goes beyond presenting theory and procedure with comprehensive, time-tested, end-of-chapter material.**

Eye Openers (formerly Discussion Questions): Contains quick concept review questions and single transaction exercises, which are ideal to help students break down concepts into basic parts, ensuring a solid foundation on which to build.

Example Exercises: For Practice Includes two parallel variations of the Example Exercise in the chapter, allowing students to practice the applications the authors illustrated earlier.

Exercises: Completely revised and accompanied by a general topic and a reference to chapter objective.

Problems Series A and B: Completely revised and accompanied by a general topic and a reference to chapter objective.

Special Activities: Focus on understanding and solving pertinent business and ethical issues. Some are presented as conversations in which students can "observe" and "participate" when they respond to the issue being discussed.

Comprehensive Problem: Located after Chapter 7 to integrate and summarize chapter concepts and test students' comprehension.

Financial Statement Analysis Problem: Located in Chapter 14, this problem features the Williams-Sonoma, Inc., 2005 Annual Report, which allows students to engage current, real world data.

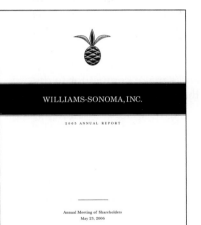

WILLIAMS-SONOMA, INC.

2005 ANNUAL REPORT

Annual Meeting of Shareholders
May 23, 2006

Williams-Sonoma, Inc., Problem

FINANCIAL STATEMENT ANALYSIS

The financial statements for Williams-Sonoma, Inc., are presented in Appendix B at the end of the text. The following additional information (in thousands) is available:

Accounts receivable at February 1, 2004	$ 31,573
Inventories at February 1, 2004	404,100
Total assets at February 1, 2004	1,470,735
Stockholders' equity at February 1, 2004	804,591

Instructions
1. Determine the following measures for the fiscal years ended January 29, 2006, and January 30, 2005, rounding to one decimal place.
   a. Working capital
   b. Current ratio
   c. Quick ratio
   d. Accounts receivable turnover
   e. Number of days' sales in receivables
   f. Inventory turnover

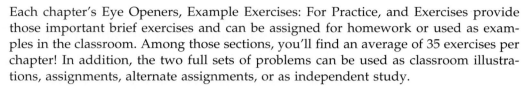

Each chapter's Eye Openers, Example Exercises: For Practice, and Exercises provide those important brief exercises and can be assigned for homework or used as examples in the classroom. Among those sections, you'll find an average of 35 exercises per chapter! In addition, the two full sets of problems can be used as classroom illustrations, assignments, alternate assignments, or as independent study.

While always tied to the chapter content, some of the end-of-chapter material covers special topics like those covered in the book features. Specifically, you'll see

Financial Analysis and Interpretation: After being introduced to key ratios of financial analysis and interpretation in the related section of Chapter 13, students get to test their proficiency through special activities and exercises that frequently feature real company data.

Ethical Dilemmas: Often paired with the scenario presented in the Integrity, Objectivity, and Ethics in Business feature, these exercises and activities put the student in the role of a decision maker faced with a problem to solve.

Real World Applications: These exercises and activities encourage students to speculate about the real-world effects of newly learned material.

In addition to content, the versatile end-of-chapter section also indicates

Communication Items: These activities help students develop communication skills that will be essential on the job, regardless of the fields they pursue.

SA 9-1
Product pricing

Marcia Martinez is a cost accountant for Ascend Inc. Marcus Todd, vice president of marketing, has asked Marcia to meet with representatives of Ascend's major competitor to discuss product cost data. Marcus indicates that the sharing of these data will enable Ascend to determine a fair and equitable price for its products.

> Would it be ethical for Marcia to attend the meeting and share the relevant cost data?

Internet Projects: These activities acquaint students with the ever-expanding accounting-related areas of the Web.

Team Building: Group Learning Activities let students learn accounting and business concepts while building teamwork skills.

SA 8-6
The balanced scorecard and EVA

Internet Project

Group Project

Divide responsibilities between two groups, with one group going to the home page of Balanced Scorecard Collaborative at **http://www.bscol.com**, and the second group going to the home page of Stern Stewart & Co. at **http://www.eva.com**. Balanced Scorecard Collaborative is a consulting firm that helped develop the balanced scorecard concept. Stern Stewart & Co. is a consulting firm that developed the concept of economic value added (EVA), another method of measuring corporate and divisional performance, similar to residual income.

After reading about the balanced scorecard at the bscol.com site, prepare a brief report describing the balanced scorecard and its claimed advantages. In the Stern group, use

Your Time
Your Course
Your Way

Just what you need to know and do NOW.

ThomsonNOW for Accounting is a powerful, fully integrated online teaching and learning system that provides you with the ultimate in flexibility, ease of use, and efficient paths to success to deliver the results you want—NOW!

- Select from flexible choices and options to best meet the needs of you and your students.

- Test and grade student results based on AACSB and AICPA or IMA accreditation standards and a special set of principles of accounting course outcomes.

- Teach and reinforce chapter content through integrated eBooks and Personalized Study Plans.

- Save valuable time in planning and managing your course assignments.

- Students stay mobile with Lectures-to-Go. Available in both audio and video formats, these iPod-ready broadcasts can be downloaded for preparation before class or last-minute reviewing for a test.

- Students connect to real businesses through our Business Connections videos. This collection of films on accounting issues brings the subject alive. Most notably, the new Chapter 1, "Introduction to Managerial Accounting," incorporates a video of the manufacturing operation of Washburn Guitars, a producer of instruments used by many popular artists today.

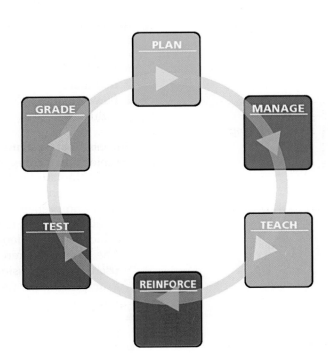

Chapter Changes

1. **Introduction to Managerial Accounting**
   - New chapter introduction to Managerial Accounting begins with a description of managerial accounting that transitions students from financial accounting and outlines the role of the management accountant in the business world.
   - Comprehensive example featuring the Legend Guitar Company grounds the manufacturing processes and provides students with a framework to discuss managerial topics. Objective 2 covers the costs and terminology associated with a manufacturing business, while Objective 3 provides a set of sample financial statements with financial data similar to what students examined in financial accounting.
   - The chapter closes with a description of the other specific uses of managerial accounting information to complete the introduction.
   - New chapter opener features Washburn Guitar. A video tour of the manufacturing process for a specific Washburn Guitar is available through ThomsonNOW.
   - New Integrity, Objectivity, and Ethics in Business discusses developing an ethical framework.
   - New Business Connections discuss grocery plus cards and decisions that can be made from the data they collect.

2. **Job Order Cost Systems** (formerly part of Chapter 1)
   - This chapter continues the Legend Guitar Company from Chapter 1 to provide continuity in the presentation.
   - Washburn Guitar is again featured in the opener with more detail about the manufacturing process of the custom Maya guitar.
   - New Business Connections discusses contingent compensation in the movie industry.

3. **Process Cost Systems** (formerly Chapter 2)
   - Objective 1 compares and contrasts Job Order and Process Costing to help transition students between the two concepts. New Exhibit 1 summarizes this comparison.
   - New comprehensive text example features Frozen Delight Ice Cream Company. In addition, new Exhibit 2 provides a diagram of the ice cream making process, which helps students understand the processes and departments involved.
   - The Example Exercises feature Rocky Springs Bottling Company and can be used in a progression throughout the chapter, providing another comprehensive example of process costing. Yet, they can be assigned independently of each other, providing flexibility in the chapter's coverage.
   - New chapter opener features Dreyer's Grand Ice Cream. A video tour of the manufacturing process for Dreyer's is available through ThomsonNOW.
   - New Integrity, Objectivity, and Ethics in Business discusses DuPont's advocacy for social responsibility.

4. **Cost Behavior and Cost-Volume-Profit Analysis** (formerly Chapter 3)
   - Former objective on the assumption underlying cost-volume-profit analysis now concludes Objective 4 on using CVP and profit-volume chart to improve the flow of the chapter.
   - New chapter opener features NetFlix.
   - New Integrity, Objectivity, and Ethics in Business discusses how pharmaceutical companies create orphan drugs, which target rare diseases, in reference to break-even points.
   - Business Connections features Sirius Satellite Radio's contract with Howard Stern in reference to break-even point.

5. **Variable Costing for Management Analysis** (formerly Chapter 4—Profit Reporting)
   - New title is "Variable Costing for Management Analysis" to reflect the new focus of the chapter on the type of analysis rather than focusing on the method of reporting.
   - A new definition of market segments better defines their characteristics.
   - A new section on Analyzing Contribution Margins introduces Analyzing Market Segments for greater clarity.
   - New Exhibit 11 on Contribution Margin Analysis illustrates the causes for difference between planned and actual contributions margins.
   - New graphic conveys the discrepancy of actual versus planned for both quantity and price/unit cost factors.
   - New chapter opener features Adobe Systems.

6. **Budgeting** (formerly Chapter 5)
   - New Exhibit 2 examines human behavior and budgeting.
   - Computerized budgeting discussion in Objective 2 reflects current business practices.
   - New chapter opener features The North Face.
   - New Business Connections discusses MP3 players.

7. **Performance Evaluation Using Variances from Standard Costs** (formerly Chapter 6)
   - The Example Exercises feature Landon Awards Co., and can be used in a progression throughout the chapter, providing a comprehensive example of using variances. Yet, they can be assigned independently of each other, providing flexibility in the chapter's coverage.
   - Direct Labor and Materials combined in new Objective 3 to integrate related topics. In addition, nonmanufacturing expenses are now covered with direct labor.
   - New terminology is added to reflect other real world considerations. Specifically, nonfinancial performance measure is now defined as a performance measure expressed in unit other than dollars, such as yield, customer satisfaction, or percent on time.
   - New chapter opener features Mini Cooper.
   - New Business Connections contrasts performance evaluation in school with evaluation in the business world.

8. **Performance Evaluation for Decentralized Operations** (formerly Chapter 7)
   - New chapter opener features K2.
   - New Integrity, Objectivity, and Ethics in Business on Shifting Income through Transfer Prices features Glaxo Smith Kline.
   - New Business Connections features Scripps Howard Company in its discussion of ROI.

9. **Differential Analysis and Product Pricing** (formerly Chapter 8)
   - New Exhibit 1 provides a template for using differential analysis to choose between alternatives.
   - The new example of XM Satellite Radio introduces differential analysis to students.
   - Chapter opener features Real Networks.

10. **Capital Investment Analysis** (formerly Chapter 9)
    - Chapter opener features XM Radio.

11. **Cost Allocation and Activity-Based Costing** (formerly Chapter 10)
    - The first three Example Exercises feature the fictitious Morris Company to provide a comprehensive example of the chapter content. They can be assigned in a series or independently.
    - New chapter opener features Coldstone Creamery.
    - Revised Business Connections feature discusses Market Segmentation and features Fidelity Investments.
    - New Integrity, Objectivity, and Ethics in Business feature discusses large government purchases and the use of the False Claims Act in instances where the government and a contractor disagree.
    - New Integrity, Objectivity, and Ethics in Business feature provides an example of students using ABC to help Sommerville, Massachusetts, employ the town's resources effectively.

12. **Cost Management for Just-in-Time Environments** (formerly Chapter 11)
    - Yamaha is now the example company in the section about emphasizing product-oriented layout.
    - Coverage of zero defects section now includes the "six-sigma" improvement system.
    - "Emphasizing Supplier Partnering" has been revised as "Emphasizing Supply Change Management" and covers more electronic means of relaying information about supplies, specifically radio frequency identification devices (RFID) and enterprise resource planning (ERP).
    - Nonfinancial performance usage table has been updated with the latest information.
    - Chapter opener features Precor.
    - Business Connections discusses eliminating nonvalue time and features Northrop Grunman's manufacturing of a B-2 bomber.
    - New Exercise 12-15 covers JIT journal entries.

13. **Statement of Cash Flows** (formerly Chapter 12)
    - Opening section orients the student to the Statement of Cash Flows by building on the discussion in Chapter 1. In addition, new Exhibit 1 examines the Statement of Cash Flows of NetSolutions.
    - New format for the indirect method reflects real world practice.
    - Expanded section on Cash Flows from Operating Activities includes new Exhibit 5 that outlines the adjustment to net income on cash flows and summarizes the affect of changes in current assets and current liabilities on net income as it pertains to cash flows.
    - New chapter opener features Jones Soda Company, as does Exercise 13-16.
    - New Business Connections features Microsoft and Dell's view of cash resources.
    - New Integrity, Objectivity, and Ethics in Business on collecting accounts features Overhill Flowers.
    - Financial Analysis and Interpretation item redefines free cash flows to leave out dividends, which could be considered discretionary, to simplify the presentation.

14. **Financial Statement Analysis** (formerly Chapter 13)
    - Features Williams-Sonoma in the chapter opener and engages Williams-Sonoma's 2005 Annual Report in the end-of-chapter material.
    - Objective 4 on Corporate Annual Reports now discusses internal controls and other auditing issues.
    - New Integrity, Objectivity, and Ethics in Business discusses the results of a CEO survey about corporate ethics.
    - New Business Connections features different investing strategies.

When it comes to supporting instructors, South-Western is unsurpassed. *Managerial Accounting, 9e,* **continues the tradition with powerful printed materials along with the latest integrated classroom technology.**

Instructor's Manual: This manual contains a number of resources designed to aid instructors as they prepare lectures, assign homework, and teach in the classroom. For each chapter, the instructor is given a brief synopsis and a list of objectives. Then each objective is explored, including information on Key Terms, Ideas for Class Discussion, Lecture Aids, Demonstration Problems, Group Learning Activities, Exercises and Problems for Reinforcement, and Internet Activities. Also, Suggested Approaches are included that incorporate many of the teaching initiatives being stressed in higher education today, including active learning, collaborative learning, critical thinking, and writing across the curriculum. Other key features are the following:

- New informational grids relate the Key Learning Outcomes from the new At a Glance grid to the exercises and problems found in the end-of-chapter. These helpful resources ensure comprehensive homework assignments.

- Demonstration problems can be used in the classroom to illustrate accounting practices. Working through an accounting problem gives the instructor an opportunity to point out pitfalls that students should avoid.

- Group learning activities provide another opportunity to actively involve students in the learning process. These activities ask students to apply accounting topics by completing an assigned task in small groups of three to five students. Small group work is an excellent way to introduce variety into the accounting classroom and creates a more productive learning environment.

- Writing exercises provide an opportunity for students to develop good written communication skills essential to any businessperson. These exercises probe students' knowledge of conceptual issues related to accounting.

- Three to five Accounting Scenarios can be used as handouts.

The Teaching Transparency Masters can be made into acetate transparencies or can be duplicated and used as handouts.

Solutions Manual and Solutions Transparencies: The Solutions Manual contains answers to all exercises, problems, and activities that appear in the text. As always, the solutions are author-written and verified multiple times for numerical accuracy and consistency with the core text. New to this edition, there is an expanded end-of-chapter information chart, which includes correlations to chapter objective, level of difficulty, AACSB outcomes, AICPA competencies, time to completion and available software. Solutions transparencies are also available.

Test Bank: For each chapter, the Test Bank includes True/False questions, Multiple-Choice questions, and Problems, each marked with a difficulty level, chapter objective association, and a tie-in to standard course outcomes. Along with the normal update and upgrade of the 1,400 test bank questions, variations of the new Example Exercises have been added to this bank for further quizzing and better integration with the textbook. In addition, the bank provides a grid for each chapter that compiles the correlation of each question to the individual chapter's objectives, as well as a ranking of difficulty based on a clearly described categorization. Through this helpful grid, making a test that is comprehensive and well-balanced is a snap! Also included are blank Achievement Tests and Achievement Test Solutions.

ExamView® Pro Testing Software: This intuitive software allows you to easily customize exams, practice tests, and tutorials and deliver them over a network, on the Internet, or in printed form. In addition, ExamView comes with searching capabilities that make sorting the wealth of questions from the printed test bank easy. The software and files are found on the IRCD.

PowerPoint® and Presentation Transparencies: Each presentation, which is included on the IRCD and on the product support site, enhances lectures and simplifies class preparation. Each chapter contains objectives followed by a thorough outline of the chapter that easily provide an entire lecture model. Also, exhibits from the chapter, such as the new Example Exercises, have been recreated as colorful PowerPoint slides to create a powerful, customizable tool. Selections from the PowerPoint presentation are also available on transparency slides.

JoinIn on Turning Point: JoinIn™ on Turning Point™ is interactive PowerPoint® and is simply the best classroom response system available today! This lecture tool makes full use of the Instructor's PowerPoint® presentation but moves it to the next level with interactive questions that provide immediate feedback on the students' understanding of the topic at hand. As students are quizzed using clicker technology, instructors can use this instant feedback to lecture more efficiently. Adding to the already robust PowerPoint® presentation, JoinIn™ integrates 10–20 questions stemming from the textbook's Example Exercises and Eye Openers and includes a variety of newly created questions. Visit http://www.turningpoint.thomsonlearningconnections.com to find out more!

Instructor Excel® Templates: These templates provide the solutions for the problems and exercises that have Enhanced Excel® templates for students. Through these files, instructors can see the solutions in the same format as the students. All problems with accompanying templates are marked in the book with an icon and are listed in the information grid in the solutions manual. These templates are available for download on www.thomsonedu.com/accounting/warren or on the IRCD.

Tutorial and Telecourse Videos: Nothing brings accounting to life like these media-intensive videos. Each chapter comes alive in two half-hour features that reinforce the concepts presented in the text. Based on the Tutorial Videos, the high-broadcast-quality Telecourse Videos are designed for distributed learning courses.

Product Support Web Site: www.thomsonedu.com/accounting/warren Our instructor Web site provides a variety of password-protected, instructor resources. You'll find text-specific and other related resources organized by chapter and topic. Many are also available on the Instructor's Resource CD-ROM.

Students come to accounting with a variety of learning needs. *Managerial Accounting, 9e,* **offers a broad range of supplements in both printed form and easy-to-use technology. We've designed our entire supplement package around the comments instructors have provided about their courses and teaching needs. These comments have made this supplement package the best in the business.**

Study Guide: This author-written guide provides students Quiz and Test Hints, Matching questions, Fill-in-the-Blank questions (Parts A & B), Multiple-Choice questions, True/False questions, Exercises, and Problems for each chapter. Designed to assist students in comprehending the concepts and principles in the text, solutions for all of these items are available in the guide for quick reference.

Working Papers for Exercises and Problems: The traditional working papers include problem-specific forms for preparing solutions for Exercises, A & B Problems, the Continuing Problem, and the Comprehensive Problem from the textbook. These forms, with preprinted headings, provide a structure for the problems, which helps students get started and saves them time. Additional blank forms are included.

Working Papers Plus: This alternative to traditional working papers integrates selected Practice Exercises, Exercises, Problems, the Continuing Problem, and the Comprehensive Problem from the text together with the narrative and forms needed to complete the solutions. Because the problem narrative is integrated with the solution, the student's work is easy and quick to review—a real plus when preparing for an exam.

Blank Working Papers: These Working Papers are available for completing exercises and problems either from the text or prepared by the instructor. They have no preprinted headings.

 Enhanced Excel® Templates: These templates are provided for selected long or complicated end-of-chapter exercises and problems and provide assistance to the student as they set up and work the problem. Certain cells are coded to display a red asterisk when an incorrect answer is entered, which helps students stay on track. Selected problems that can be solved using these templates are designated by an icon.

 Klooster & Allen General Ledger Software: *(formerly P.A.S.S)* Prepared by Dale Klooster and Warren Allen, this best-selling, educational, general ledger package introduces students to the world of computerized accounting through a more intuitive, user-friendly system than the commercial software they'll use in the future. In addition, students have access to general ledger files with information based on problems from the textbook and practice sets. This context allows them to see the difference between manual and computerized accounting systems firsthand, while alleviating the stress of an empty screen. Also, the program is enhanced with a problem checker that enables students to determine if their entries are correct and emulates commercial general ledger packages more closely than other educational packages. Problems that can be used with Klooster/Allen are highlighted by an icon. The benefits of using Klooster/Allen are that:

- Errors are more easily corrected than in commercial software.
- After the course ends, students are prepared to use a variety of commercial products.
- The Inspector Disk allows instructors to grade students' work.

A free Network Version is available to schools whose students purchase Klooster/Allen GL.

Product Support Web Site: www.thomsonedu.com/accounting/warren. This site provides students with a wealth of introductory accounting resources, including limited quizzing and supplement downloads.

The textbook plays a vital role in the teaching/learning environment, which makes our collaboration with instructors invaluable. For this edition, accounting teachers discussed with us ways to create a more efficient presentation and connect more with students. The result of these discussions can be seen throughout the textbook.

The following instructors participated in our Blue Sky Workshops in 2005 and 2006.

Gilda M. Agacer
Monmouth Univ.

Rick Andrews
Sinclair Comm. College

Irene C. Bembenista
Davenport Univ.

Laurel L. Berry
Bryant & Stratton College

Bill Black
Raritan Valley Comm. College

Gregory Brookins
Santa Monica College

Rebecca Carr
Arkansas State Univ.

James L. Cieslak
Cuyahoga Comm. College

Sue Cook
Tulsa Comm. College

Ana M. Cruz
Miami Dade College

Terry Dancer
Arkansas State Univ.

David L. Davis
Tallahassee Comm. College

Walter DeAguero
Saddleback College

Robert Dunlevy
Montgomery County Comm. College

Richard Ellison
Middlesex County College

W. Michael Fagan
Raritan Valley Comm. College

Carol Flowers
Orange Coast College

Linda S. Flowers
Houston Comm. College

Mike Foland
Southwest Illinois College

Anthony Fortini
Camden Comm. College

Barbara M. Gershowitz
Nashville State Comm. College

Angelina Gincel
Middlesex County College

Lori Grady
Bucks County Comm. College

Joseph R. Guardino
Kingsborough Comm. College

Amy F. Haas
Kingsborough Comm. College

Betty Habershon
Prince George's Comm. College

Patrick A. Haggerty
Lansing Comm. College

Becky Hancock
El Paso Comm. College

Paul Harris
Camden County College

Patricia H. Holmes
Des Moines Area Comm. College

Shirly A. Kleiner
Johnson County Comm. College

Michael M. Landers
Middlesex College

Phillip Lee
Nashville State Comm. College

Denise Leggett
Middle Tennessee State Univ.

Lynne Luper
Ocean County College

Maria C. Mari
Miami Dade College

Thomas S. Marsh
Northern Virginia Comm. College—Annandale

Cynthia McCall
Des Moines Area Comm. College

Andrea Murowski
Brookdale Comm. College

Rachel Pernia
Essex County College

Dawn Peters
Southwest Illinois College

Gary J. Pieroni
Diablo Valley College

Debra Prendergast
Northwestern Business College

Renee A. Rigoni
Monroe Comm. College

Lou Rosamillia
Hudson Valley Comm. College

Eric Rothernburg
Kingsborough Comm. College

Richard Sarkisian
Camden Comm. College

Gerald Savage
Essex Comm. College

Janice Stoudemire
Midlands Technical College

Linda H. Tarrago
Hillsborough Comm. College

Judy Toland
Buck Comm. College

Bob Urell
Irvine Valley College

Carol Welsh
Rowan Univ.

Chris Widmer
Tidewater Comm. College

Gloria Worthy
Southwest Tennessee Comm. College

Lynnette Mayne Yerbury
Salt Lake Comm. College

The following instructors participated in our Adopter Advisory Board.

Lizabeth Austen
East Carolina Univ.

Robert Adkins
Clark State Comm. College

Candace S. Blankenship
Belmont Univ.

Patrick M. Borja
Citrus College and California State Univ.—Los Angeles

Gary Bower
Comm. College of Rhode Island

Gregory Brookins
Santa Monica College

Martha Cavalaris
Miami Dade Comm. College—North Campus

Sue Cook
Tulsa Comm. College

Leonard Cronin
Rochester Comm. and Technical College

Bruce England
Massasoit Comm. College

Robert T. Fahnestock
Univ. of West Florida

Michael J. Farina
Cerritos College

Brenda S. Fowler
Alamance Comm. College

Mark Fronke
Cerritos College

Marina Grau
Houston Comm. College

Paul C. Harris Jr.
Camden County College

James L. Haydon
East Los Angeles Comm. College

Brenda Hester
Volunteer State Comm. College

Cheryl Honoré
Riverside Comm. College

Calvin Hoy
County College of Morris

Frank D. Iazzetta
Long Beach City College

Anne C. Kenner
Brevard Comm. College

Satoshi K. Kojima
East Los Angeles College

Susan Logorda
Lehigh Carbon Comm. College

Don Lucy
Indian River Comm. College

Cathy Mallory
San Antonio College

Marjorie A. Marinovic
Univ. of Texas at El Paso

Patricia Norton
Northwest Mississippi Comm. College

Ken O'Brien
Farmington State Univ.

Craig Pence
Highland Comm. College

Rachel Pernia
Essex County College

Abe Qastin
Lakeland College

Paul Rivers
Bunker Hill Comm. College

Patrick D. Rogan
Cosumnes River College

Gary M. Rupp
Farmingdale State Univ.

Richard M. Sarkisian
Camden County College

Debra L. Schmidt
Cerritos Colzlege

Larry L. Simpson
Davenport Univ., Lansing Campus

Robert K. Smolin
Citrus College

Dawn W. Stevens
Northwest Mississippi Comm. College

John F. Templeton
Houston Comm. College

Kathryn Williams
St. Johns River Comm. College

Karen Wisniewski
County College of Morris

Wayne Yesbick
Darton College

The following instructors participated in the review process and in focus groups.

Heather Albinger
Concordia Univ.

Sylvia Allen
Los Angeles Valley College

Beverley Alleyne
Belmont Univ.

Felix Amenkhienan
Radford Univ.

Sheila Ammons
Austin Comm. College

Rick Andrews
Sinclair Comm. College

Joseph Aubert
Bemidji State Univ.

Elenita Ayuyao
Los Angeles City College

Progyan Basu
The Univ. of Georgia

Diane Bechtel
Northwest State Comm. College

Terry Bechtel
Northwestern State Univ. of Louisiana

Margaret A. Berezewski
Robert Morris College

Bernard Beatty
Wake Forest Univ.

Cynthia Birk
Univ. of Nevada—Reno

Kathy Blondell
St. Johns River Comm. College

Julio C. Borges
Miami Dade College

Carolyn Bottjer
Lehigh Carbon Comm. College

Angele Brill
Castleton State College

Rada Brooks
Univeristy of California—Berkeley

Rebecca F. Brown
Des Moines Area Comm. College

Charles I. Bunn Jr.
Wake Technical Comm. College

Janet Butler
Texas State Univ.—San Marcos

Robert Carpenter
Eastfield College

Bill Carter
Univ. of Virginia

Fonda L. Carter
Columbus State Univ.

Stanley Chu
Borough of Manhattan Comm. College

Marilyn G. Ciolino
Delgado Comm. College

Gretchen Charrier
The Univ. of Texas at Austin

Alexander Clifford
Kennebec Valley Comm. College

Weldon Terry
Dancer Arkansas State Univ.

Vaun C. Day
Central Arizona College

Stan Deal
Azusa Pacific Univ.

John E. Delaney
Southwestern Univ.

Beatrix DeMott
Park Univ.

Edward Douthett
George Mason Univ.

Richard Dugger
Kilgore College

Carol Dutchover
Eastern New Mexico Univ., Roswell

Steve Easter
Mineral Area College

Ronald Edward
Camp Trinity Valley Comm. College

Rafik Z. Elias
California State Univ.—Los Angeles

Carl Essig
Montgomery County Comm. College

Jack Fatica
Terra Comm. College

Kathleen Fitzpatrick
Univ. of Toledo

Daniel Fulks
Transylvania Univ.

Thurman Gardner
Harold Washington College

Caroline C. Garrett
The Victoria College

J. Rendall Garrett
Southern Nazarene Univ.

Earl Godfrey
Gardner—Webb Univ.

Saturnino Gonzalez
El Paso Comm. College

Edward Gordon
Triton College

Thomas Grant
Kutztown Univ.

Barbara Gregorio
Nassau Comm. College

Jeri W. Griego
Laramie County Comm. College

Kenneth Haling, Jr.
Gateway Technical College

Carolyn J. Hays
Mount San Jacinto College

Mark Henry
The Victoria College

Aleecia Hibbets
Univ. of Louisiana—Monroe

Linda Hischke
Northeast Wisconsin Technical College

Patricia H. Holmes
Des Moines Area Comm. College

Anita Hope
Tarrant County College

Allison Hubley
Davenport Univ.

Dawn A. Humburg
Iowa Central Comm. College

Marianne L. James
California State Univ.—Los Angeles

Bettye Bishop Johnson
Northwest Mississippi Comm. College

Tara Laken Joliet
Junior College

Becky Knickel
Brookhaven College

Larry W. Koch
Navarro College, Ellis County Campus

Ellen L. Landgraf
Loyola Univ. Chicago

Cathy X. Larson
Middlesex Comm. College

Brenda Lauer
Davenport Univ.—Kalamazoo Campus

Greg Lauer
North Iowa Area Comm. College

James Lukawitz
Univ. of Memphis

Terri Lukshaitis
Davenport Univ.

Debbie Luna
El Paso Comm. College

Diane Marker
Univ. of Toledo

Matthew Maron
Univ. of Bridgeport

John J. Masserwick
Farmingdale State Univ.

Robert McCutcheon
East Texas Baptist Univ.

Andrew M. McKee
North Country Comm. College

Michael McKittrick
Santa Fe Comm. College

Yaw Mensah
Rutgers Univ.

Leslie Michie
Big Bend Comm. College

Nancy Milleman
Central Ohio Technical College

Brian Moore
Davenport Univ.

Carol Moore
Northwest State Comm. College

Andrew Morgret
Univ. of Memphis

Tim Mulder
Davenport Univ.

Charles Murphy
Bunker Hill Comm. College

Gary Nelson
Normandale Comm. College

Patricia Norton
Northwest Mississippi Comm. College

Blanca R. Ortega
Miami Dade College

Kathy Otero
Univ. of Texas at El Paso

Carol Pace
Grayson County College

Vanda Pauwels
Lubbock Christian Univ.

John Perricone
Harper College

Timothy Prindle
Des Moines Area Comm. College

Paulette Ratliff-MIller
Arkansas State Univ.

Ronald Reed
Univ. of Northern Colordao

John Renza, Jr.
Comm. College of Rhode Island

Jenny Resnick
Santa Monica College

John C. Roberts, Jr.
St. Johns River Comm. College

Lawrence A. Roman
Cuyahoga Comm. College

Gary W. Ross
Harding Univ.

Ann Rowell
Central Piedmont Comm. College

Charles J. Russo
Bloomsburg Univ. of Pennsylvania

Maria Sanchez
Rider Univ.

Marcia A. Sandvold
Des Moines Area Comm. College

Tony Scott
Norwalk Comm. College

Bonnie Scrogham
Sullivan Univ.

Angela Seidel
Cambria-Rowe Business College

Sara Seyedin
Foothill College

Larry L. Simpson
Davenport Univ., Lansing Campus

Alice Sineath
Forsyth Technical Comm. College

Kimberly D. Smith
County College of Morris

Roberta Spigle
DuBois Business College

Mary Stevens
Univ. of Texas at El Paso

Norman Sunderman
Angelo State Univ.

Thomas Szczurek
Delaware County Comm. College

Kathy Tam
Tulsa Comm. College

Lynette E. Teal
Western Wisconsin Technical College

Wayne Thomas
Univ. of Oklahoma

Bill Townsend
Ferris State Univ.

Robin Turner
Rowan-Cabarrus Comm. College

Nancy Tyler
Dalton State College

Allan D. Unseth
Norfolk State Univ.

Bob Urell
Irvine Valley College

Michael Van Breda
Southern Methodist Univ.

Peter Vander Weyst
Edmonds Comm. College

Patricia Walczak
Lansing Comm. College

Scott Wang
Davenport Univ.

Luke A. Waller
Lindenwood Univ.

Jeffrey Waybright
Spokane Comm. College

Kimberly Webb
Texas Wesleyan Univ.

Clifford Weeks
Southwestern Michigan College

Karen Williamson
Rochester Comm. and Technical College

Judith Zander
Grossmont College

Brief Contents

Contents

WARREN   REEVE

MANAGERIAL
ACCOUNTING

9E

Managerial Accounting Concepts and Principles

© GREG BROWN/WATERLOO COURIER/ASSOCIATED PRESS

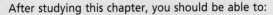
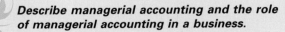
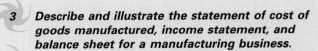

objectives

After studying this chapter, you should be able to:

1 *Describe managerial accounting and the role of managerial accounting in a business.*

2 *Describe and illustrate the following costs: direct and indirect, direct materials, direct labor, factory overhead, and product and period costs.*

3 *Describe and illustrate the statement of cost of goods manufactured, income statement, and balance sheet for a manufacturing business.*

4 *Describe the uses of managerial accounting information.*

Washburn Guitars

Dan Donnegan, guitarist for the rock band *Disturbed*, captivates millions of fans each year playing his guitar. His guitar was built by quality craftsmen at Washburn Guitars in Chicago. Washburn Guitars is no stranger to the music business. The company has been in business for over 120 years and is the guitar maker of choice for professional and amateur musicians.

Staying in business for 120 years requires a thorough understanding of how to manufacture high-quality guitars. In addition, it requires knowledge of how to account for the costs of making guitars. For example, how much should Washburn charge for its guitars? The purchase price must be greater than the cost of producing the guitar, but how is the cost of producing the guitar determined? Moreover, how many guitars does the company have to sell in a year to cover its costs? Would a new production facility be a good investment? How many employees should the company have working on each stage of the guitar manufacturing process?

All of these questions can be answered with the aid of managerial accounting information. In this chapter, we introduce cost concepts used in managerial accounting, which help answer questions like those above. We begin this chapter by describing managerial accounting and its relationship to financial accounting. Following this overview, we will describe the management process and the role of managerial accounting. We will also discuss characteristics of managerial accounting reports, various managerial accounting terms, and some of the uses of managerial accounting information.

Managerial Accounting

objective 1

Describe managerial accounting and the role of managerial accounting in a business.

Managing a business isn't easy. Managers must make numerous decisions in operating a business efficiently and in preparing for the future. Managerial accounting provides much of the information used by managers in running a business. The following sections discuss the differences between financial and managerial accounting and the role of the managerial accountant in an organization. The remaining chapters of this text are dedicated to examining the various types of managerial accounting information that managers use in operating a business.

THE DIFFERENCES BETWEEN MANAGERIAL AND FINANCIAL ACCOUNTING

Although economic information can be classified in many ways, accountants often divide information into two types: financial and managerial. The diagram in Exhibit 1 illustrates the relationship between financial accounting and managerial accounting. Understanding this relationship is useful in understanding the information needs of management.

Financial accounting information is reported in statements that are useful for stakeholders, such as creditors, who are "outside" or external to the organization. Examples of such stakeholders include:

- Shareholders,
- Creditors,
- Government agencies, and
- The general public.

The management of a company also uses the financial statements in directing current operations and planning future operations. In planning future operations, management often begins by evaluating the results of past activities as reported in the financial state-

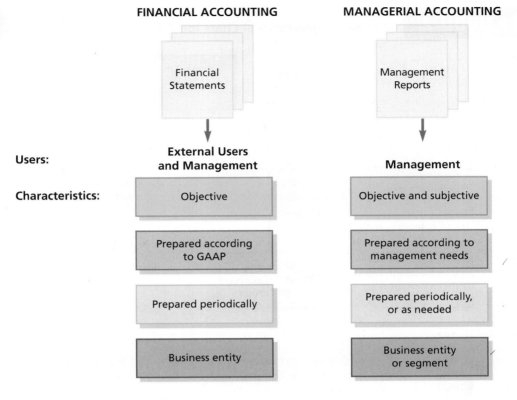

EXHIBIT 1

Financial Accounting and Managerial Accounting

FINANCIAL ACCOUNTING

Financial Statements

MANAGERIAL ACCOUNTING

Management Reports

Users:

External Users and Management

Management

Characteristics:

Objective	Objective and subjective
Prepared according to GAAP	Prepared according to management needs
Prepared periodically	Prepared periodically, or as needed
Business entity	Business entity or segment

ments. The financial statements objectively report the results of past operations at fixed periods and the financial condition of the business according to generally accepted accounting principles (GAAP).

Managerial accounting information meets the specific needs of a company's management. This information includes:

- Historical data, which provide objective measures of past operations, and
- Estimated data, which provide subjective estimates about future decisions.

Management uses both types of information in conducting daily operations, planning future operations, and developing overall business strategies. For example, subjective estimates in managerial accounting reports assist management in responding to business opportunities.

Unlike financial accounting statements, managerial accounting reports:

- Are not prepared according to generally accepted accounting principles since only management uses the information;
- Are prepared periodically, or at any time management needs information; and
- Are prepared for the business entity as a whole or a segment of the entity, such as a division, product, project, or territory.

THE MANAGEMENT ACCOUNTANT IN THE ORGANIZATION

In most large organizations, departments or similar units are assigned responsibilities for specific functions or activities. This operating structure of an organization can be shown in an organization chart. Exhibit 2 is a partial organization chart for Callaway Golf Company, the manufacturer and distributor of Big Bertha® golf clubs.

The individual reporting units in an organization can be viewed as having either (1) line responsibilities or (2) staff responsibilities. A **line department** or unit is one directly involved in the basic objectives of the organization. For Callaway Golf, the

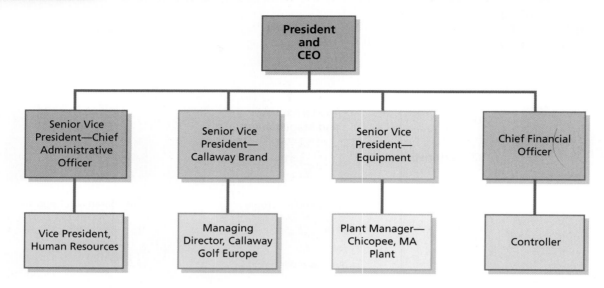

EXHIBIT 2   Partial Organizational Chart for Callaway Golf Company

The terms *line* and *staff* may be applied to service organizations. For example, the line positions in a hospital would be the nurses, doctors, and other caregivers. Staff positions would include admissions and records. The line positions for a professional basketball team, such as the Boston Celtics, would be the basketball players and coaches, since they are directly involved in the basic objectives of the organization—playing professional basketball. Staff positions would include public relations, player development and recruiting, legal staff, and accounting. These positions serve and advise the players and coaches.

senior vice president of equipment and the manager of the Chicopee, Massachusetts, plant occupy line positions because they are responsible for manufacturing Callaway's products. Likewise, the senior vice president of the Callaway Brand and other sales managers are in line positions because they are directly responsible for generating revenues.

A **staff department** or unit is one that provides services, assistance, and advice to the departments with line or other staff responsibilities. A staff department has no direct authority over a line department. For example, the senior vice president—chief administrative officer and vice president of human resources are staff positions supporting the organization. In addition, the chief financial officer (sometimes called the vice president of finance) occupies a staff position, to which the controller reports. In most business organizations, the **controller** is the chief management accountant.

The controller's staff often consists of several management accountants. Each accountant is responsible for a specialized accounting function, such as systems and procedures, general accounting, budgets and budget analysis, special reports and analysis, taxes, and cost accounting.

Experience in managerial accounting is often an excellent training ground for senior management positions. This is not surprising, since accounting and finance bring an individual into contact with all phases of operations.

MANAGERIAL ACCOUNTING IN THE MANAGEMENT PROCESS

In its role as a staff department, managerial accounting supports management and the management process. The **management process** has five basic phases:

1. Planning
2. Directing
3. Controlling
4. Improving
5. Decision making

As shown in Exhibit 3, the five phases interact with each other as the basis for a company's strategies and operations. Management's actions in the management process are, to some extent, measured by the company's operating results.

EXHIBIT 3 | The Management Process

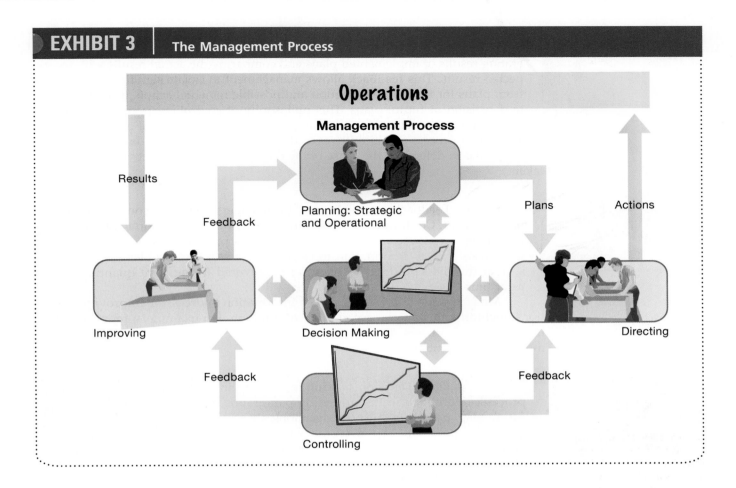

Operations

Management Process

Results • Feedback • Planning: Strategic and Operational • Plans • Actions • Improving • Decision Making • Directing • Feedback • Controlling • Feedback

Planning   **Planning** is used by management to develop the company's **objectives (goals)** and to translate these objectives into courses of actions. For example, a company, as part of the planning process, may set objectives to increase market share by 15% and introduce three new products. The courses of action, or means, for achieving these objectives must be established. In this example, the company may decide to follow three courses of action: increase the advertising budget, open a new sales territory, and increase the research and development budget.

Planning can be categorized as either strategic planning or operational planning. **Strategic planning** is developing long-range courses of action to achieve goals. Long-range courses of action, called **strategies**, can often involve periods ranging from 5 to 10 years. **Operational planning** develops short-term courses of action to manage the day-to-day operations of a business.

Directing   **Directing** is the process by which managers, given their assigned level of responsibilities, run day-to-day operations. Examples of directing include a production supervisor's efforts to keep the production line moving smoothly throughout a work shift and the credit manager's efforts to assess the credit standing of potential customers.

Managerial accounting aids managers in directing a business by providing reports that allow managers to adjust operations for changing conditions. For example, reports on the cost of defective material by vendors may aid managers in making vendor selections or improvements. In addition, managerial accounting reports are used by management to estimate the appropriate staffing and resources necessary for achieving plans.

Controlling   Once managers have planned goals and directed the action, they must monitor how well the plan is working. **Controlling** consists of monitoring the operating results of implemented plans and comparing the actual results with the expected results. This **feedback** allows management to isolate significant departures from plans for further investigation and possible remedial action. It may also lead to a revision of future plans. This philosophy of controlling is sometimes called **management by exception**. For example, if actual departmental costs incurred in maintaining a process significantly exceed expected costs, then an investigation may be conducted to determine the cause of the difference so that corrective action may be taken.

Improving   Feedback can also be used by managers to support continuous process improvement. **Continuous process improvement** is the philosophy of continually improving employees, business processes, and products. Continuous improvement uses process information to eliminate the *source* of problems in a process, so that the right products (services) are delivered in the right quantities at the right time.

    Managers use a wide variety of information sources for improving operations, including managerial accounting information. For example, a report identifying the cost of process inefficiency can be used by management to prioritize and monitor improvements.

Decision Making   **Decision making** is inherent in each of the four management processes described in the preceding paragraphs. For example, in developing a future plan, managers must decide among alternative courses of action to achieve long-range goals and objectives. Likewise, in directing operations, managers must decide on an operating structure, procedures, training, staffing, and other aspects of day-to-day operations. In controlling and improving, managers must decide how to respond to unfavorable performance.

Example Exercise 1-1

objective **1**

Three phases of the management process are planning, controlling, and improving. Match the following descriptions to the proper phase.

Phase of management process
Planning

Controlling

Continuous improvement

Description
a. Monitoring the operating results of implemented plans and comparing the actual results with expected results.
b. Rejects solving individual problems with temporary solutions that fail to address the root cause of the problem.
c. Used by management to develop the company's objectives.

Follow My Example 1-1

Phase of management process

Planning (c)
Controlling (a)
Continuous improvement (b)

For Practice: PE 1-1A, PE 1-1B

Integrity, Objectivity, and Ethics in Business

ETHICS

ENVIRONMENTAL ACCOUNTING

In recent years, the environmental impact of a business has become an increasingly important issue. Multinational agreements such as the Montreal Protocol and Kyoto Protocol have acknowledged the impact that society has on the environment and raised public awareness of the impact that businesses have on the environment. As a result, environmental issues have become an important operational issue for most businesses. Managers must now consider the environmental impact of their decisions in the same way that they would consider other operational issues.

To help managers understand the environmental impact of their business decisions, new managerial accounting measures are being developed. The emerging field of environmental management accounting focuses on developing various measures of the environmental-related costs of a business. These measures can evaluate a variety of issues, including the volume and level of emissions, the estimated costs of different levels of emissions, and the impact that environmental costs have on product cost. Thus, environmental managerial accounting can provide managers with important information to help them more clearly consider the environmental effects of their decisions.

A Tour of Manufacturing Operations: Costs and Terminology

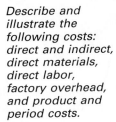

objective **2**

Describe and illustrate the following costs: direct and indirect, direct materials, direct labor, factory overhead, and product and period costs.

The operations of a business can be classified as service, merchandising, or manufacturing. Most of the managerial accounting concepts and terms described in the remaining chapters of this text apply to all three types of businesses. As an example, we focus primarily upon managerial concepts as they apply to manufacturing businesses in this textbook. We begin with a tour of a guitar manufacturer, Legend Guitars.

Like Washburn Guitars, Legend Guitars manufactures high-quality guitars that combine innovation with high-quality craftsmanship. Exhibit 4 provides an overview of Legend's guitar manufacturing operations. The process begins when a customer places an order for a custom-made guitar. Once the order is received, the production process is started by employees who cut the body and neck of the guitar out of raw lumber using a computerized saw. Once the wood is cut, the body and neck of the guitar are assembled. When the assembly is complete, the guitar is painted and finished.

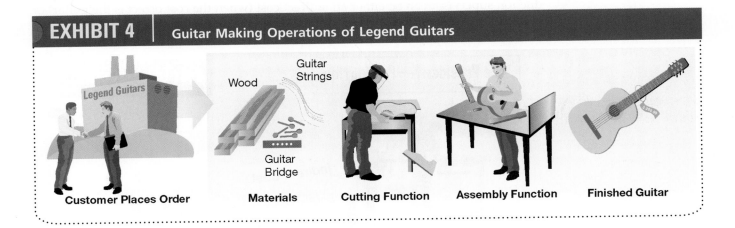

EXHIBIT 4 | **Guitar Making Operations of Legend Guitars**

Customer Places Order — Materials — Cutting Function — Assembly Function — Finished Guitar

Next, we introduce the common cost terms associated with manufacturing operations using Legend Guitars. We begin by defining *cost*. A **cost** is a payment of cash or the commitment to pay cash in the future for the purpose of generating revenues. For example, cash (or credit) used to purchase equipment is the cost of the equipment. If equipment is purchased by exchanging assets other than cash, the current market value of the assets given up is the cost of the equipment purchased.

Costs may be classified in a number of ways. Understanding these classifications provides a basis for later discussions and illustrations of managerial decision making.

DIRECT AND INDIRECT COSTS

For management's use in making decisions, costs are often classified in terms of how they relate to an object or segment of operations, often called a **cost object**. A cost object may be a product, a sales territory, a department, or some activity, such as research and development. Costs are identified with cost objects as either **direct costs** or **indirect costs**.

Direct costs are specifically attributed to the cost object. For example, if Legend Guitars is assigning costs to guitars that are produced, the cost of materials used in the guitar would be a direct cost of the guitar.

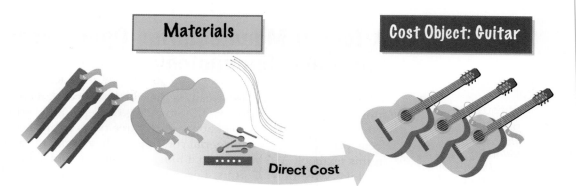

Indirect costs cannot be identified directly with a cost object. For example, the salary of the vice president of production is an indirect cost of the guitars produced by Legend Guitars. While the vice president provides an important contribution to the production of guitars produced by Legend, his salary cannot be directly identified or traced to the individual guitars produced. However, the salary of the vice president of production would be a direct cost to the overall production process. Thus, the salary of the production supervisor can be either an indirect cost (when the cost object is the guitar) or a direct cost (when the cost object is the overall production process).

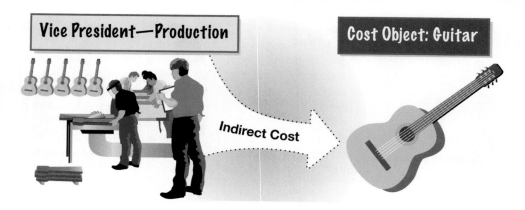

The process of classifying a cost as direct or indirect is illustrated in Exhibit 5.

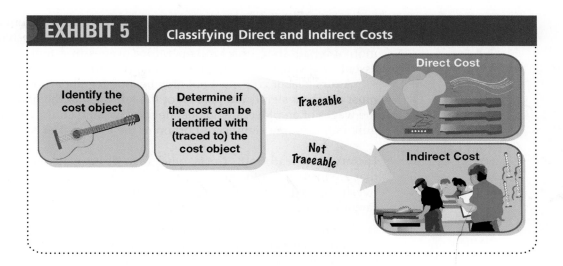

EXHIBIT 5 | **Classifying Direct and Indirect Costs**

MANUFACTURING COSTS

The cost of a manufactured product includes the cost of materials used in making the product, as well as the costs incurred in converting the materials into a finished product. For example, Legend Guitars uses employees, machines, and other inputs to convert wood and other materials into the finished product, guitars. The finished guitar is the cost object, and the cost of the finished guitars includes direct materials cost, direct labor cost, and factory overhead cost.

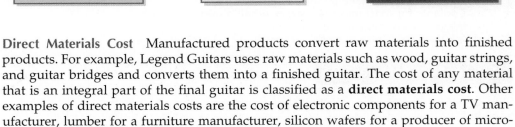

Direct Materials Cost   Manufactured products convert raw materials into finished products. For example, Legend Guitars uses raw materials such as wood, guitar strings, and guitar bridges and converts them into a finished guitar. The cost of any material that is an integral part of the final guitar is classified as a **direct materials cost**. Other examples of direct materials costs are the cost of electronic components for a TV manufacturer, lumber for a furniture manufacturer, silicon wafers for a producer of microcomputer chips, and tires for an automobile manufacturer.

As a practical matter, a direct materials cost must not only be an integral part of the finished product, but it must also be a significant portion of the total cost of the product. For Legend Guitars, the cost of wood used in the body and neck is a significant portion of the total cost of each guitar.

Direct Labor Cost   Most manufacturing processes need employees to convert materials into the final product. For example, Legend Guitars uses employees to assemble guitars by gluing together the neck and body and installing the guitar bridge and strings. The wages of each employee who is directly involved in converting materials

Direct Labor

Factory Overhead

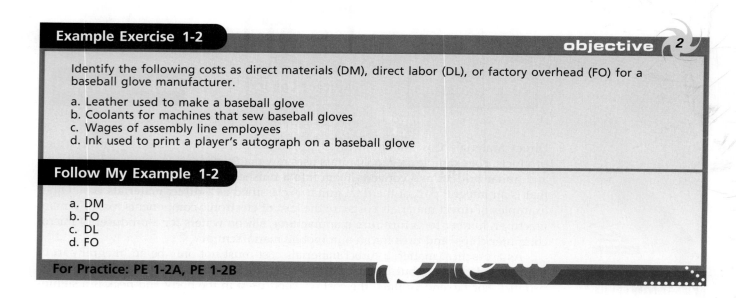

REAL WORLD

As manufacturing processes have become more automated, direct labor costs have become so small that they are often included as part of factory overhead.

into the final guitar are classified as a **direct labor cost**. Other examples of direct labor costs are carpenters' wages for a construction contractor, mechanics' wages in an automotive repair shop, machine operators' wages in a tool manufacturing plant, and assemblers' wages in a computer assembly plant.

A direct labor cost must not only be an integral part of the finished product, but it must also be a significant portion of the total cost of the product. For Legend Guitars, the wages of employees who operate the saws and cutting machines and assemble the guitars make up a significant portion of the total cost of each guitar.

Factory Overhead Cost   Costs, other than direct materials cost and direct labor cost, that are incurred in the manufacturing process are combined and classified as **factory overhead cost**. Factory overhead is sometimes called **manufacturing overhead** or **factory burden**. All factory overhead costs are indirect costs and include the costs of:

- Heating and lighting the factory,
- Repairing and maintaining factory equipment,
- Property taxes,
- Insurance, and
- Depreciation on factory plant and equipment.

Factory overhead cost also includes materials and labor costs that do not enter directly into the finished product. Examples include the cost of oil used to lubricate machinery and the wages of janitorial and supervisory employees. If the costs of direct materials or direct labor are not a significant portion of the total product cost, these costs may be classified as factory overhead.

In Legend Guitars, the costs of sandpaper, buffing compound, and glue used in the assembly of guitars enter directly into the manufacture of each guitar. However, because these costs are a small cost of each guitar, they are classified as factory overhead. Other overhead costs for Legend Guitars would include the power to run the machines, the depreciation of machines, and the salary of production supervisors (including the vice president of production).

Example Exercise 1-2   objective 2

Identify the following costs as direct materials (DM), direct labor (DL), or factory overhead (FO) for a baseball glove manufacturer.

a. Leather used to make a baseball glove
b. Coolants for machines that sew baseball gloves
c. Wages of assembly line employees
d. Ink used to print a player's autograph on a baseball glove

Follow My Example 1-2

a. DM
b. FO
c. DL
d. FO

For Practice: PE 1-2A, PE 1-2B

Prime Costs and Conversion Costs   Direct materials, direct labor, and factory overhead costs are often grouped together for analysis and reporting purposes. Two common groupings of these costs are prime costs and conversion costs. Exhibit 6 summarizes the classification of manufacturing costs into prime costs and conversion costs.

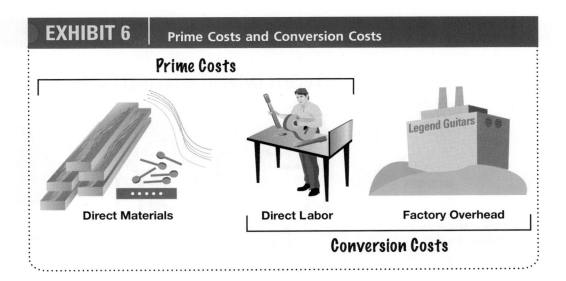

EXHIBIT 6 | **Prime Costs and Conversion Costs**

Prime Costs

Direct Materials | Direct Labor | Factory Overhead

Conversion Costs

Prime costs consist of direct materials and direct labor costs. **Conversion costs** consist of direct labor and factory overhead costs. Conversion costs are the costs of converting the materials into a finished product. As shown in Exhibit 6, direct labor is both a prime cost and a conversion cost.

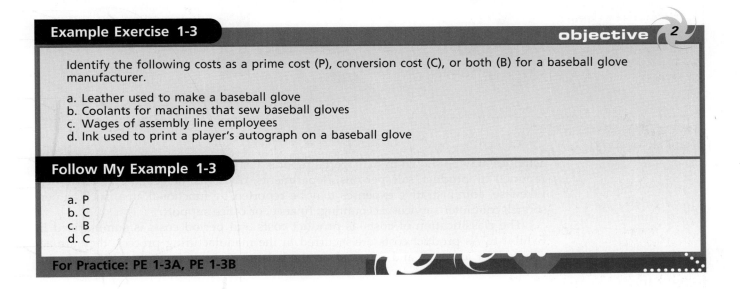

Example Exercise 1-3 objective **2**

Identify the following costs as a prime cost (P), conversion cost (C), or both (B) for a baseball glove manufacturer.

a. Leather used to make a baseball glove
b. Coolants for machines that sew baseball gloves
c. Wages of assembly line employees
d. Ink used to print a player's autograph on a baseball glove

Follow My Example 1-3

a. P
b. C
c. B
d. C

For Practice: PE 1-3A, PE 1-3B

Product Costs and Period Costs   For financial reporting purposes, costs are often classified as either product costs or period costs. **Product costs** consist of the three elements of manufacturing cost: direct materials, direct labor, and factory overhead. **Period costs** are generally classified into two categories: selling and administrative. Selling expenses are incurred in marketing the product and delivering the sold product to customers. Administrative expenses are incurred in the administration of the business and are not directly related to the manufacturing or selling functions. Examples of product costs and period costs for Legend Guitars are presented in Exhibit 7.

Classifying period costs as selling or administrative expenses assists management in controlling the costs of these two activities. Different levels of responsibility for these

| EXHIBIT 7 | Examples of Product Costs and Period Costs—Legend Guitars |

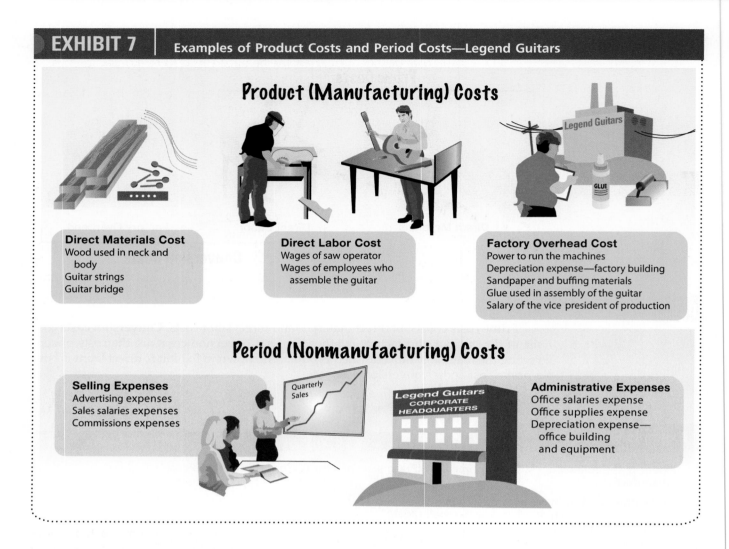

Product (Manufacturing) Costs

Direct Materials Cost
Wood used in neck and
  body
Guitar strings
Guitar bridge

Direct Labor Cost
Wages of saw operator
Wages of employees who
  assemble the guitar

Factory Overhead Cost
Power to run the machines
Depreciation expense—factory building
Sandpaper and buffing materials
Glue used in assembly of the guitar
Salary of the vice president of production

Period (Nonmanufacturing) Costs

Selling Expenses
Advertising expenses
Sales salaries expenses
Commissions expenses

Administrative Expenses
Office salaries expense
Office supplies expense
Depreciation expense—
  office building
  and equipment

activities may be shown in managerial reports. For example, selling expenses may be reported by product, salespersons, departments, divisions, or geographic territories. Likewise, administrative expenses may be reported by functional area, such as personnel, computer services, accounting, finance, or office support.

The classification of costs as product costs and period costs is summarized in Exhibit 8. As product costs are incurred in the manufacturing process, they are accounted for as assets and reported on the balance sheet as inventory. When the in-

| EXHIBIT 8 |
| **Product Costs and Period Costs** |

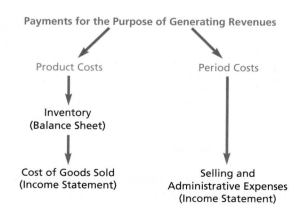

Payments for the Purpose of Generating Revenues

Product Costs

Period Costs

Inventory
(Balance Sheet)

Cost of Goods Sold
(Income Statement)

Selling and
Administrative Expenses
(Income Statement)

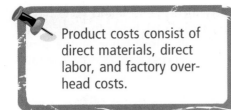

Product costs consist of direct materials, direct labor, and factory overhead costs.

ventory is sold, the direct materials, direct labor, and factory overhead costs are reported as cost of goods sold on the income statement. Period costs do not appear on the balance sheet. They are recognized as expenses in the period in which they are incurred. In the next section, we illustrate the reporting of product costs and period costs in the financial statements of manufacturing businesses.

Example Exercise 1-4

objective **2**

Identify the following costs as a product cost or a period cost for a baseball glove manufacturer.

a. Leather used to make a baseball glove
b. Cost of endorsement from a professional baseball player
c. Office supplies used at the company headquarters
d. Ink used to print a player's autograph on the baseball glove

Follow My Example 1-4

a. Product cost
b. Period cost
c. Period cost
d. Product cost

For Practice: PE 1-4A, PE 1-4B

Financial Statements for a Manufacturing Business

objective **3**

Describe and illustrate the statement of cost of goods manufactured, income statement, and balance sheet for a manufacturing business.

The financial statements for a manufacturing business are more complex than those for service and merchandising businesses. This is because a manufacturer makes the products that it sells. As a result, manufacturing costs must be properly accounted for and reported in the financial statements. These manufacturing costs primarily affect the preparation of the balance sheet and the income statement. The retained earnings and cash flow statements for merchandising and manufacturing businesses are similar to those in service and merchandising businesses. For this reason, we focus only upon the balance sheet and income statement.

BALANCE SHEET FOR A MANUFACTURING BUSINESS

A manufacturing business reports the following three types of inventory on its balance sheet:

1. **Materials inventory** (sometimes called raw materials inventory)
   • Consists of the costs of the direct and indirect materials that have not yet entered the manufacturing process.
   • For Legend Guitars, wood used to make the body and neck of the guitar is part of the materials inventory.

2. **Work in process inventory**
   • Consists of the direct materials costs, the direct labor costs, and the factory overhead costs that have entered the manufacturing process but are associated with products that have not been completed.

- For Legend Guitars, the unassembled guitars for which the neck and body have been produced are "in process" because they have not yet been put together into a finished guitar. Thus, the cost of the direct materials, direct labor, and factory overhead incurred during the period to create any in-process guitars is part of the work in process inventory.

3. **Finished goods inventory**
   - Consists of *completed* (or finished) products that have not been sold.
   - For Legend Guitars, finished goods inventory contains all of the costs incurred to manufacture the completed, but not yet sold, guitars.

Exhibit 9 compares the balance sheet presentation of inventory for a manufacturing company, Legend Guitars, to that of a merchandising company, MusicLand Stores, Inc. In both balance sheets, inventory is shown in the Current Assets section.

EXHIBIT 9

Balance Sheet Presentation of Inventory in Manufacturing and Merchandising Companies

Legend Guitars
Balance Sheet
December 31, 2008

Current assets:		
Cash		$ 21,000
Accounts receivable (net)		120,000
Inventories:		
Finished goods	$62,500	
Work in process	24,000	
Materials	35,000	121,500
Supplies		2,000
Total current assets		$264,500

MusicLand Stores, Inc.
Balance Sheet
December 31, 2008

Current assets:	
Cash	$ 25,000
Accounts receivable (net)	85,000
Merchandise inventory	142,000
Supplies	10,000
Total current assets	$262,000

INCOME STATEMENT FOR A MANUFACTURING COMPANY

The major difference in the income statements for merchandising and manufacturing businesses is in the reporting of cost of products sold during the period. A merchandising business purchases merchandise (products) in a finished state for resale to customers. The cost of products sold is called the **cost of merchandise sold**.

A manufacturer makes the products it sells, using direct materials, direct labor, and factory overhead. The cost of the product sold is generally called the cost of goods sold. For a manufacturer, the total cost of making and finishing the product is called the **cost**

of goods manufactured. This is very similar to the cost of merchandise available for sale in a merchandising business.

The income statement of manufacturing companies is supported by a **statement of cost of goods manufactured**, which provides the details of the cost of goods manufactured. To illustrate the flow of manufacturing costs to the income statement for Legend Guitars, assume the following data for 2008:

Inventories	January 1	December 31
Materials	$65,000	$35,000
Work in process	30,000	24,000
Finished goods	60,000	62,500

Materials purchased during the year		$100,000
Direct labor incurred in production		110,000
Factory overhead incurred in production:		
Indirect labor	$24,000	
Depreciation on factory equipment	10,000	
Factory supplies and utility costs	10,000	
Total		44,000
Selling expenses		20,000
Administrative expenses		15,000
Sales		366,000

The manufacturing costs for Legend Guitars would flow to the financial statements as shown in Exhibit 10.

EXHIBIT 10 Flow of Manufacturing Costs

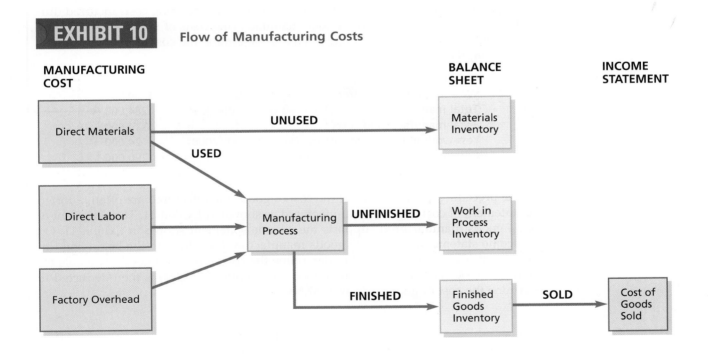

As discussed previously, three calculation steps are required to determine the cost of goods manufactured.

The cost of goods manufactured is determined by first computing the cost of direct materials used in the year as follows:

Materials inventory, January 1, 2008	$ 65,000
Add: Materials purchased during the year	100,000
Cost of materials available for use	$165,000
Less: Materials inventory, December 31, 2008	35,000
Cost of direct materials used in production	$130,000

Adding the beginning (January 1) materials inventory of $65,000 to the cost of materials purchased during the period, $100,000, yields the total cost of materials that are available for use during the period of $165,000. Deducting the ending December 31 materials inventory of $35,000 equals the cost of direct materials used in production during the year.

The total manufacturing costs incurred during the year of $284,000 is determined as follows:

Direct materials used during the year	$130,000
Direct labor	110,000
Factory overhead	44,000
Total manufacturing costs incurred during the year	$284,000

To determine the cost of goods manufactured during the year, the beginning work in process inventory of $30,000 is added to the total manufacturing costs incurred during the year of $284,000 to yield the total manufacturing costs of $314,000. The ending work in process of $24,000 is then deducted to determine the cost of goods manufactured during the year as follows:

Work in process inventory, January 1, 2008	$ 30,000
Total manufacturing costs incurred during the year	284,000
Total manufacturing costs	$314,000
Less work in process inventory, December 31, 2008	24,000
Cost of goods manufactured during the year	$290,000

The preceding computations of the cost of goods manufactured are often reported in a statement of cost of goods manufactured as shown in Exhibit 11. The statement of cost of goods manufactured supports the income statement shown in Exhibit 11. On the income statement, the cost of goods manufactured is added to the beginning finished goods inventory of $60,000 to determine the cost of finished goods available for sale of $350,000. The ending finished goods inventory of $62,500 is then deducted to determine the cost of goods sold of $287,500.

EXHIBIT 11

Manufacturing Company—Income Statement with Statement of Cost of Goods Manufactured

---

Legend Guitars
Income Statement
For the Year Ended December 31, 2008

Sales		$366,000
Cost of goods sold:		
Finished goods inventory, January 1, 2008	$ 60,000	
Cost of goods manufactured	290,000	
Cost of finished goods available for sale	$350,000	
Less finished goods inventory, December 31, 2008	62,500	
Cost of goods sold		287,500
Gross profit		$ 78,500
Operating expenses:		
Selling expenses	$ 20,000	
Administrative expenses	15,000	
Total operating expenses		35,000
Net income		$ 43,500

Legend Guitars
Statement of Cost of Goods Manufactured
For the Year Ended December 31, 2008

Work in process inventory, January 1, 2008			$ 30,000
Direct materials:			
Materials inventory, January 1, 2008	$ 65,000		
Purchases	100,000		
Cost of materials available for use	$165,000		
Less materials inventory, December 31, 2008	35,000		
Cost of direct materials used in production		$130,000	
Direct labor		110,000	
Factory overhead:			
Indirect labor	$ 24,000		
Depreciation on factory equipment	10,000		
Factory supplies and utility costs	10,000		
Total factory overhead		44,000	
Total manufacturing costs incurred during the year			284,000
Total manufacturing costs			$314,000
Less work in process inventory, December 31, 2008			24,000
Cost of goods manufactured			$290,000

Example Exercise 1-5

Gauntlet Company has the following information for January:

Cost of direct materials used in production	$25,000
Direct labor	35,000
Factory overhead	20,000
Work in process inventory, January 1	30,000
Work in process inventory, January 31	25,000
Finished goods inventory, January 1	15,000
Finished goods inventory, January 31	12,000

For January, determine (a) the cost of goods manufactured and (b) the cost of goods sold.

Follow My Example 1-5

a.	Work in process inventory, January 1		$ 30,000
	Cost of direct materials used in production	$ 25,000	
	Direct labor	35,000	
	Factory overhead	20,000	
	Total manufacturing costs incurred during January		80,000
	Total manufacturing costs		$110,000
	Less: Work in process inventory, January 31		25,000
	Cost of goods manufactured		$ 85,000
b.	Finished goods inventory, January 1		$ 15,000
	Cost of goods manufactured		85,000
	Cost of finished goods available for sale		$100,000
	Less: Finished goods inventory, January 31		12,000
	Cost of goods sold		$ 88,000

For Practice: PE 1-5A, PE 1-5B

Uses of Managerial Accounting

As discussed in the first part of this chapter, managers need information to guide their decision making. Managerial accounting provides information and reports that help managers run the day-to-day operations of their businesses. For example, Legend Guitars uses managerial information to determine the cost of manufacturing each guitar. This cost can then be used to set the selling price of guitars. In addition, comparing the costs of guitars over time can aid managers in monitoring and controlling the cost of direct materials, direct labor, and factory overhead.

Managerial reports also help managers evaluate the performance of a company's operations. Managerial accounting can be used to evaluate the efficiency in using raw materials or direct labor in the manufacturing process. For example, Legend Guitars can use performance reports to identify the cause for large amounts of unusable wood remaining after the cutting process. Managers can then use this information to make the cutting process more efficient.

Companies also use managerial accounting information to support long-term planning decisions, such as investment decisions. For example, Legend Guitars management may consider buying a new computerized saw to speed up the production process while providing higher quality cuts. Managerial accounting information can help management determine if this is a good investment.

Managerial accounting data can be used to help managers understand how many guitars need to be sold in a month in order to cover recurring monthly costs. Such information can be used to set monthly selling targets.

As these examples illustrate, managerial accounting information can be used for a variety of purposes. In the remaining chapters of this text, we examine these and other areas of managerial accounting in greater detail and discuss how this information is used to aid managerial decision making.

Business Connections

REAL WORLD

NAVIGATING THE INFORMATION HIGHWAY

Dell Inc. follows a build-to-order manufacturing process, where each computer is manufactured based on a specific customer order. In a build-to-order manufacturing process like this, customers select the features they want on their computer from the company's Web site. Once the order is submitted, the manufacturing process begins. The parts required for each feature are removed from inventory, and the computer is manufactured and shipped within days of the order. Inventory items are scanned as they are removed from inventory to keep accurate track of inventory levels and help the manufacturer determine when to reorder.

But calculating the amount of materials to reorder is not the only use of these data. Data on which parts are included in each order are placed in the company's database. This information can then be used to track manufacturing patterns such as the type of features that are frequently ordered together and seasonal changes in the features that are ordered.

In recent years, information systems have become more sophisticated, making it easier and less expensive for companies to gather large amounts of data on their manufacturing processes and customers. If used effectively, these new data sources can help a business like Dell decide what features to offer for its products, what features to discontinue, and how to combine features into a package. For example, manufacturing data might indicate that the demand for DVD drives on computers increases significantly each summer right before school starts. A

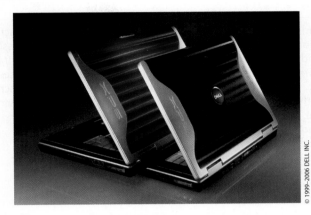

© 1999–2006 DELL INC.

build-to-order manufacturer like Dell might use this information to realign the manufacturing process during that time of year, or to offer certain packages of features in July and August.

However, the ability to generate value from this information depends on a company's ability to merge these new data with existing accounting information in a meaningful manner. The managerial accountant must now be prepared to analyze and evaluate a broader set of information and determine how it will affect a company's operational performance and profitability.

Source: "Delivering Strategic Business Value: Business Intelligence Can Help Management Accounting Reclaim Its Relevance and Rightful Role," Steve Williams, *Strategic Finance,* August 2004.

At a Glance

1. Describe managerial accounting and the role of managerial accounting in a business.			
Key Points	**Key Learning Outcomes**	**Example Exercises**	**Practice Exercises**
Managerial accounting is a staff function that supports the management process by providing reports to aid management in planning, directing, controlling, improving, and decision making. This differs from financial accounting, which provides information to stakeholders outside of the organization. Managerial accounting reports are designed to meet the specific needs of management and aid management in planning long-term strategies and running the day-to-day operations.	• Describe the differences between financial accounting and managerial accounting. • Describe the role of the management accountant in the organization. • Describe the role of managerial accounting in the management process.	1-1	1-1A, 1-1B

(continued)

2. Describe and illustrate the following costs: direct and indirect, direct materials, direct labor, factory overhead, and product and period costs.

Key Points	Key Learning Outcomes	Example Exercises	Practice Exercises
Manufacturing companies use machinery and labor to convert materials into a finished product. A direct cost can be directly traced to a finished product, while an indirect cost cannot. The cost of a finished product is made up of three components: (1) the cost of materials that are directly identifiable with the final product, (2) the wages of employees that directly convert materials to a finished product, and (3) factory overhead. Costs incurred in the manufacturing process other than direct materials and direct labor are classified as factory overhead costs. These three manufacturing costs can be categorized into prime costs (direct material and direct labor) or conversion costs (direct labor and factory overhead). Product costs consist of the elements of manufacturing cost—direct materials, direct labor, and factory overhead—while period costs consist of selling and administrative expenses.	• Describe a cost object. • Classify a cost as a direct or indirect cost for a cost object. • Describe direct materials cost. • Describe direct labor cost. • Describe factory overhead cost. • Describe prime costs and conversion costs. • Describe product costs and period costs.	1-2 1-2 1-2 1-3 1-4	1-2A, 1-2B 1-2A, 1-2B 1-2A, 1-2B 1-3A, 1-3B 1-4A, 1-4B

3. Describe and illustrate the statement of cost of goods manufactured, income statement, and balance sheet for a manufacturing business.

Key Points	Key Learning Outcomes	Example Exercises	Practice Exercises
The financial statements of manufacturing companies differ from those of merchandising companies. Manufacturing company balance sheets report three types of inventory: materials, work in process, and finished goods. The income statement of manufacturing companies reports cost of goods sold, which is the total manufacturing cost of the goods sold. The income statement is supported by the statement of cost of goods manufactured, which provides the details of the cost of goods manufactured during the period.	• Describe materials inventory. • Describe work in process inventory. • Describe finished goods inventory. • Describe the differences between merchandising and manufacturing company balance sheets. • Prepare a statement of cost of goods manufactured. • Prepare an income statement for a manufacturing company.	 1-5 1-5	 1-5A, 1-5B 1-5A, 1-5B

4. Describe the uses of managerial accounting information.

Key Points	Key Learning Outcomes	Example Exercises	Practice Exercises
Managers need information to guide their decision making. Managerial accounting provides a variety of information and reports that help managers run the operations of their businesses.	• Describe examples of how managerial accounting aids managers in decision making.		

Key Terms

continuous process improvement (6)
controller (4)
controlling (6)
conversion costs (11)
cost (7)
cost object (8)
cost of goods manufactured (14)
cost of merchandise sold (14)
decision making (6)
direct costs (8)
direct labor cost (10)
direct materials cost (9)

directing (5)
factory burden (10)
factory overhead cost (10)
feedback (6)
financial accounting (2)
finished goods inventory (14)
indirect costs (8)
line department (3)
management by exception (6)
management process (4)
managerial accounting (3)
manufacturing overhead (10)
materials inventory (13)

objectives (goals) (5)
operational planning (5)
period costs (11)
planning (5)
prime costs (11)
product costs (11)
staff department (4)
statement of cost of goods manufactured (15)
strategic planning (5)
strategies (5)
work in process inventory (13)

Illustrative Problem

The following is a list of costs that were incurred in producing this textbook:

a. Insurance on the factory building and equipment
b. Salary of the vice president of finance
c. Hourly wages of printing press operators during production
d. Straight-line depreciation on the printing presses used to manufacture the text
e. Electricity used to run the presses during the printing of the text
f. Sales commissions paid to textbook representatives for each text sold
g. Paper on which the text is printed
h. Book covers used to bind the pages
i. Straight-line depreciation on an office building
j. Salaries of staff used to develop artwork for the text
k. Glue used to bind pages to cover

Instructions

With respect to the manufacture and sale of this text, classify each cost as either a product cost or a period cost. Indicate whether each product cost is a direct materials cost, a direct labor cost, or a factory overhead cost. Indicate whether each period cost is a selling expense or an administrative expense.

Solution

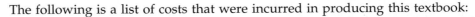

	Product Cost			Period Cost	
Cost	Direct Materials Cost	Direct Labor Cost	Factory Overhead Cost	Selling Expense	Administrative Expense
a.			X		
b.					X
c.		X			
d.			X		
e.			X		
f.				X	
g.	X				
h.	X				
i.					X
j.			X		
k.			X		

Self-Examination Questions

(Answers at End of Chapter)

1. Which of the following best describes the difference between financial and managerial accounting?
   A. Managerial accounting provides information to support decisions, while financial accounting does not.
   B. Managerial accounting is not restricted to generally accepted accounting principles (GAAP), while financial accounting is restricted to GAAP.
   C. Managerial accounting does not result in financial reports, while financial accounting does result in financial reports.
   D. Managerial accounting is concerned solely with the future and does not record events from the past, while financial accounting records only events from past transactions.

2. Which of the following is *not* one of the five basic phases of the management process?
   A. Planning   C. Decision making
   B. Controlling   D. Operating

3. Which of the following is *not* considered a cost of manufacturing a product?
   A. Direct materials cost
   B. Factory overhead cost
   C. Sales salaries
   D. Direct labor cost

4. Which of the following costs would be included as part of the factory overhead costs of a microcomputer manufacturer?
   A. The cost of memory chips
   B. Depreciation of testing equipment
   C. Wages of microcomputer assemblers
   D. The cost of disk drives

5. For the month of May, Latter Company has beginning finished goods inventory of $50,000, ending finished goods inventory of $35,000, and cost of goods manufactured of $125,000. What is the cost of goods sold for May?
   A. $90,000   C. $140,000
   B. $110,000   D. $170,000

Eye Openers

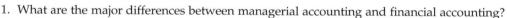

1. What are the major differences between managerial accounting and financial accounting?
2. a. Differentiate between a department with line responsibility and a department with staff responsibility.
   b. In an organization that has a Sales Department and a Personnel Department, among others, which of the two departments has (1) line responsibility and (2) staff responsibility?
3. a. What is the role of the controller in a business organization?
   b. Does the controller have a line or staff responsibility?
4. What are the five basic phases of the management process?
5. What is the term for a plan that encompasses a period ranging from five or more years and that serves as a basis for long-range actions?
6. What is the process by which management runs day-to-day operations?
7. What is the process by which management assesses how well a plan is working?
8. Describe what is meant by *management by exception*.
9. What term describes a payment in cash or the commitment to pay cash in the future for the purpose of generating revenues?
10. For a company that produces desktop computers, would memory chips be considered a direct or an indirect cost of each microcomputer produced?
11. What three costs make up the cost of manufacturing a product?
12. What manufacturing cost term is used to describe the cost of materials that are an integral part of the manufactured end product?
13. If the cost of wages paid to employees who are directly involved in converting raw materials into a manufactured end product is not a significant portion of the total product cost, how would the wages cost be classified as to type of manufacturing cost?
14. Distinguish between prime costs and conversion costs.
15. What is the difference between a product cost and a period cost?
16. Name the three inventory accounts for a manufacturing business, and describe what each balance represents at the end of an accounting period.

17. In what order should the three inventories of a manufacturing business be presented on the balance sheet?
18. What are the three categories of manufacturing costs included in the cost of finished goods and the cost of work in process?
19. For a manufacturer, what is the description of the amount that is comparable to a merchandising business's cost of merchandise sold?
20. For June, Fosina Company had beginning materials inventory of $25,000, ending materials inventory of $30,000, and materials purchases of $140,000. What is the cost of direct materials used in production?
21. How does the cost of goods sold section of the income statement differ between merchandising and manufacturing companies?
22. Describe how an automobile manufacturer might use managerial accounting information to (a) evaluate the performance of the company and (b) make strategic decisions.

Practice Exercises

PE 1-1A
Managerial accounting in the management process
obj. 1

Three phases of the management process are planning, directing, and controlling (management by exception). One type of planning is strategic planning. Match the following descriptions to the proper phase.

Phase of management process	Description
Strategic planning	a. Isolating significant departures from plans for further investigation and possible remedial action. It may lead to a revision of future plans.
Directing	b. Process by which managers, given their assigned levels of responsibilities, run day-to-day operations.
Management by exception	c. Developing long-range courses of action to achieve goals.

PE 1-1B
Managerial accounting in the management process
obj. 1

Three phases of the management process are controlling, strategies, and decision making. Match the following descriptions to the proper phase.

Phase of management process	Description
Controlling	a. Inherent in planning, directing, controlling, and improving.
Strategies	b. Monitoring the operating results of implemented plans and comparing the actual results with expected results.
Decision making	c. Long-range courses of action.

PE 1-2A
Direct materials, direct labor, and factory overhead
obj. 2

Identify the following costs as direct materials (DM), direct labor (DL), or factory overhead (FO) for a textbook publisher.

a. Maintenance on printing machines
b. Glue used to bind books
c. Wages of printing machine employees
d. Paper used to make a textbook

PE 1-2B
Direct materials, direct labor, and factory overhead
obj. 2

Identify the following costs as direct materials (DM), direct labor (DL), or factory overhead (FO) for an automobile manufacturer.

a. Wages of employees that operate painting equipment
b. Steel
c. Wages of the plant manager
d. Oil used for assembly line machinery

PE 1-3A
Prime costs vs. conversion costs

obj. 2

Identify the following costs as a prime cost (P), conversion cost (C), or both (B) for a textbook publisher.

a. Maintenance on printing machines
b. Glue used to bind books
c. Wages of printing machine employees
d. Paper used to make a textbook

PE 1-3B
Prime costs vs. conversion costs

obj. 2

Identify the following costs as a prime cost (P), conversion cost (C), or both (B) for an automobile manufacturer.

a. Wages of employees that operate painting equipment
b. Steel
c. Wages of the plant manager
d. Oil used for assembly line machinery

PE 1-4A
Product costs vs. period costs

obj. 2

Identify the following costs as a product cost or a period cost for a textbook publisher.

a. Maintenance on printing machines
b. Sales salaries
c. Depreciation expense—corporate headquarters
d. Paper used to make a textbook

PE 1-4B
Product costs vs. period costs

obj. 2

Identify the following costs as a product cost or a period cost for an automobile manufacturer.

a. Wages of employees that operate painting equipment
b. Steel
c. Accounting staff salaries
d. Rent on office building

PE 1-5A
Cost of goods sold, cost of goods manufactured

obj. 3

Nantahala Company has the following information for August:

Cost of direct materials used in production	$30,000
Direct labor	45,000
Factory overhead	22,000
Work in process inventory, August 1	10,000
Work in process inventory, August 31	8,000
Finished goods inventory, August 1	18,000
Finished goods inventory, August 31	10,000

For August, determine (a) the cost of goods manufactured and (b) the cost of goods sold.

PE 1-5B
Cost of goods sold, cost of goods manufactured

obj. 3

Tsali Company has the following information for February:

Cost of direct materials used in production	$18,000
Direct labor	54,000
Factory overhead	36,000
Work in process inventory, February 1	50,000
Work in process inventory, February 28	57,000
Finished goods inventory, February 1	22,000
Finished goods inventory, February 28	26,000

For February, determine (a) the cost of goods manufactured and (b) the cost of goods sold.

Exercises

EX 1-1
Classifying costs as materials, labor, or factory overhead
obj. 2

Indicate whether each of the following costs of an airplane manufacturer would be classified as direct materials cost, direct labor cost, or factory overhead cost:

a. Steel used in landing gear
b. Controls for flight deck
c. Welding machinery lubricants
d. Salary of test pilot
e. Wages of assembly line worker
f. Tires
g. Aircraft engines
h. Depreciation of welding equipment

EX 1-2
Classifying costs as materials, labor, or factory overhead
obj. 2

Indicate whether the following costs of Colgate-Palmolive Company would be classified as direct materials cost, direct labor cost, or factory overhead cost:

a. Packaging materials
b. Depreciation on production machinery
c. Salary of process engineers
d. Depreciation on the Clarksville, Indiana, soap plant
e. Scents and fragrances
f. Wages of Marketing Department employees
g. Resins for soap and shampoo products
h. Plant manager salary for the Morristown, Tennessee, toothpaste plant
i. Maintenance supplies
j. Wages paid to Packaging Department employees

EX 1-3
Classifying costs as factory overhead
obj. 2

Which of the following items are properly classified as part of factory overhead for Caterpillar?

a. Vice president of finance's salary
b. Interest expense on debt
c. Plant manager's salary at Aurora, Illinois, manufacturing plant
d. Consultant fees for a study of production line employee productivity
e. Factory supplies used in the Morganton, North Carolina, engine parts plant
f. Amortization of patents on new assembly process
g. Steel plate
h. Depreciation on Peoria, Illinois, headquarters building
i. Property taxes on the Danville, Kentucky, tractor tread plant
j. Sales incentive fees to dealers

EX 1-4
Classifying costs as product or period costs
obj. 2

For apparel manufacturer Ann Taylor, Inc., classify each of the following costs as either a product cost or a period cost:

a. Factory janitorial supplies
b. Depreciation on office equipment
c. Advertising expenses
d. Fabric used during production
e. Depreciation on sewing machines
f. Property taxes on factory building and equipment
g. Sales commissions
h. Wages of sewing machine operators
i. Repairs and maintenance costs for sewing machines
j. Salary of production quality control supervisor
k. Factory supervisors' salaries
l. Oil used to lubricate sewing machines

(continued)

m. Travel costs of salespersons

n. Corporate controller's salary

o. Utility costs for office building

p. Research and development costs

q. Salaries of distribution center personnel

EX 1-5
Concepts and terminology
objs. 1, 2

From the choices presented in parentheses, choose the appropriate term for completing each of the following sentences:

a. Feedback is often used to (improve, direct) operations.

b. A product, sales territory, department, or activity to which costs are traced is called a (direct cost, cost object).

c. Payments of cash or the commitment to pay cash in the future for the purpose of generating revenues are (costs, expenses).

d. The balance sheet of a manufacturer would include an account for (cost of goods sold, work in process inventory).

e. Factory overhead costs combined with direct labor costs are called (prime, conversion) costs.

f. Advertising costs are usually viewed as (period, product) costs.

g. The implementation of automatic, robotic factory equipment normally (increases, decreases) the direct labor component of product costs.

EX 1-6
Concepts and terminology
objs. 1, 2

From the choices presented in parentheses, choose the appropriate term for completing each of the following sentences:

a. Direct materials costs combined with direct labor costs are called (prime, conversion) costs.

b. The wages of an assembly worker are normally considered a (period, product) cost.

c. The phase of the management process that uses process information to eliminate the source of problems in a process so that the process delivers the correct product in the correct quantities is called (directing, improving).

d. Short-term plans are called (strategic, operational) plans.

e. The plant manager's salary would be considered (direct, indirect) to the product.

f. Materials for use in production are called (supplies, materials inventory).

g. An example of factory overhead is (sales office depreciation, plant depreciation).

EX 1-7
Classifying costs in a service company
obj. 2

A partial list of the costs for Mountain Lakes Railroad, a short hauler of freight, is provided below. Classify each cost as either indirect or direct. For purposes of classifying each cost as direct or indirect, use the train as the cost object.

a. Cost to lease (rent) train locomotives.

b. Wages of switch and classification yard personnel

c. Wages of train engineers

d. Cost to lease (rent) railroad cars

e. Maintenance costs of right of way, bridges, and buildings

f. Fuel costs

g. Payroll clerk salaries

h. Safety training costs

i. Salaries of dispatching and communications personnel

j. Costs of accident cleanup

k. Cost of track and bed (ballast) replacement

l. Depreciation of terminal facilities

EX 1-8
Classifying costs
objs. 2, 3

The following report was prepared for evaluating the performance of the plant manager of Miss-Take Inc. Evaluate and correct this report.

Miss-Take Inc.
Manufacturing Costs
For the Quarter Ended March 31, 2008

Direct labor (including $80,000 maintenance salaries)	$ 430,000
Materials used in production (including	
$40,000 of indirect materials)	680,000
Factory overhead:	
Supervisor salaries	610,000
Heat, light, and power	140,000
Sales salaries	270,000
Promotional expenses	310,000
Insurance and property taxes—plant	160,000
Insurance and property taxes—corporate offices	210,000
Depreciation—plant and equipment	80,000
Depreciation—corporate offices	100,000
Total	$2,990,000

EX 1-9
Financial statements of a manufacturing firm

obj. 3

✓a. Net income, $55,000

The following events took place for Gantt Manufacturing Company during March, the first month of its operations as a producer of digital clocks:

a. Purchased $65,000 of materials.
b. Used $50,000 of direct materials in production.
c. Incurred $75,000 of direct labor wages.
d. Incurred $105,000 of factory overhead.
e. Transferred $175,000 of work in process to finished goods.
f. Sold goods with a cost of $140,000.
g. Earned revenues of $310,000.
h. Incurred $80,000 of selling expenses.
i. Incurred $35,000 of administrative expenses.

a. Prepare the March income statement for Gantt Manufacturing Company.
b. Determine the inventory balances at the end of the first month of operations.

EX 1-10
Manufacturing company balance sheet

obj. 3

Partial balance sheet data for Ellison Company at December 31, 2008, are as follows:

Finished goods inventory	$12,500
Prepaid insurance	6,000
Accounts receivable	25,000
Work in process inventory	45,000
Supplies	15,000
Materials inventory	24,000
Cash	32,000

Prepare the Current Assets section of Ellison Company's balance sheet at December 31, 2008.

EX 1-11
Cost of direct materials used in production for a manufacturing company

obj. 3

Guzman Manufacturing Company reported the following materials data for the month ending October 31, 2008:

Materials purchased	$175,000
Materials inventory, October 1	45,000
Materials inventory, October 31	30,000

Determine the cost of direct materials used in production by Guzman during the month ended October 31, 2008.

EX 1-12
Cost of goods manufactured for a manufacturing company

obj. 3

✓ e. $4,000

Two items are omitted from each of the following three lists of cost of goods manufactured statement data. Determine the amounts of the missing items, identifying them by letter.

Work in process inventory, December 1	$ 1,000	$ 10,000	(e)
Total manufacturing costs incurred during December	12,000	(c)	60,000
Total manufacturing costs	(a)	$120,000	$64,000
Work in process inventory, December 31	2,000	20,000	(f)
Cost of goods manufactured	(b)	(d)	$58,000

EX 1-13
Cost of goods manufactured for a manufacturing company

obj. 3

The following information is available for Applebaum Manufacturing Company for the month ending January 31, 2008:

Cost of direct materials used in production	$165,000
Direct labor	145,000
Work in process inventory, January 1	70,000
Work in process inventory, January 31	125,000
Total factory overhead	65,000

Determine Applebaum's cost of goods manufactured for the month ended January 31, 2008.

EX 1-14
Income statement for a manufacturing company

obj. 3

✓ d. $190,000

Two items are omitted from each of the following three lists of cost of goods sold data from a manufacturing company income statement. Determine the amounts of the missing items, identifying them by letter.

Finished goods inventory, November 1	$ 25,000	$ 40,000	(e)
Cost of goods manufactured	160,000	(c)	350,000
Cost of finished goods available for sale	(a)	$250,000	$400,000
Finished goods inventory, November 30	30,000	60,000	(f)
Cost of goods sold	(b)	(d)	$335,000

EX 1-15
Statement of cost of goods manufactured for a manufacturing company

obj. 3

✓ a. Total manufacturing costs, $622,000

Cost data for T. Clark Manufacturing Company for the month ending April 30, 2008, are as follows:

Inventories	April 1	April 30
Materials	$125,000	$110,000
Work in process	85,000	95,000
Finished goods	65,000	75,000

Direct labor	$225,000
Materials purchased during April	240,000
Factory overhead incurred during April:	
Indirect labor	24,000
Machinery depreciation	14,000
Heat, light, and power	5,000
Supplies	4,000
Property taxes	3,500
Miscellaneous cost	6,500

a. Prepare a cost of goods manufactured statement for April 2008.
b. Determine the cost of goods sold for April 2008.

EX 1-16
Cost of goods sold, profit margin, and net income for a manufacturing company

obj. 3

✓ a. Cost of goods sold, $270,000

The following information is available for Renteria Manufacturing Company for the month ending March 31, 2008:

Cost of goods manufactured	$265,000
Selling expenses	85,000
Administrative expenses	45,000
Sales	540,000
Finished goods inventory, March 1	60,000
Finished goods inventory, March 31	55,000

For the month ended March 31, 2008, determine Renteria's (a) cost of goods sold, (b) gross profit, and (c) net income.

EX 1-17
Cost flow relationships
obj. 3

✓ a. $250,000

The following information is available for the first month of operations of Brown Company, a manufacturer of mechanical pencils:

Sales	$600,000
Gross profit	350,000
Cost of goods manufactured	300,000
Indirect labor	130,000
Factory depreciation	20,000
Materials purchased	185,000
Total manufacturing costs for the period	345,000
Materials inventory	25,000

Using the above information, determine the following missing amounts:

a. Cost of goods sold
b. Finished goods inventory
c. Direct materials cost
d. Direct labor cost
e. Work in process inventory

Problems Series A

PR 1-1A
Classifying costs
obj. 2

The following is a list of costs that were incurred in the production and sale of boats:

a. Commissions to sales representatives, based upon the number of boats sold.
b. Cost of boat for "grand prize" promotion in local bass tournament.
c. Memberships for key executives in the Bass World Association.
d. Cost of electrical wiring for boats.
e. Cost of normal scrap from defective hulls.
f. Cost of metal hardware for boats, such as ornaments and tie-down grasps.
g. Cost of paving the employee parking lot.
h. Hourly wages of assembly line workers.
i. Annual bonus paid to top executives of the company.
j. Straight-line depreciation on factory equipment.
k. Wood paneling for use in interior boat trim.
l. Steering wheels.
m. Special advertising campaign in *Bass World*.
n. Masks for use by sanders in smoothing boat hulls.
o. Power used by sanding equipment.
p. Yearly cost maintenance contract for robotic equipment.
q. Oil to lubricate factory equipment.
r. Canvas top for boats.
s. Executive end-of-year bonuses.
t. Salary of shop supervisor.
u. Decals for boat hull.
v. Annual fee to pro-fisherman Jim Bo Wilks to promote the boats.
w. Paint for boats.
x. Legal department costs for the year.
y. Fiberglass for producing the boat hull.
z. Salary of president of company.

Instructions
Classify each cost as either a product cost or a period cost. Indicate whether each product cost is a direct materials cost, a direct labor cost, or a factory overhead cost. Indicate whether

each period cost is a selling expense or an administrative expense. Use the following tabular headings for your answer, placing an "X" in the appropriate column.

	Product Costs			Period Costs	
Cost	Direct Materials Cost	Direct Labor Cost	Factory Overhead Cost	Selling Expense	Administrative Expense

---

PR 1-2A
Classifying costs
obj. 2

The following is a list of costs incurred by several businesses:

a. Cost of dyes used by a clothing manufacturer.
b. Salary of the vice president of manufacturing logistics.
c. Wages of a machine operator on the production line.
d. Travel costs of marketing executives to annual sales meeting.
e. Cost of sewing machine needles used by a shirt manufacturer.
f. Depreciation of microcomputers used in the factory to coordinate and monitor the production schedules.
g. Pens, paper, and other supplies used by the Accounting Department in preparing various managerial reports.
h. Electricity used to operate factory machinery.
i. Factory janitorial supplies.
j. Fees paid to lawn service for office grounds upkeep.
k. Wages of computer programmers for production of microcomputer software.
l. Depreciation of copying machines used by the Marketing Department.
m. Telephone charges by president's office.
n. Cost of plastic for a telephone being manufactured.
o. Oil lubricants for factory plant and equipment.
p. Cost of a 30-second television commercial.
q. Depreciation of robot used to assemble a product.
r. Wages of production quality control personnel.
s. Maintenance and repair costs for factory equipment.
t. Depreciation of tools used in production.
u. Rent for a warehouse used to store finished products.
v. Maintenance costs for factory equipment.
w. Fees charged by collection agency on past-due customer accounts.
x. Charitable contribution to United Fund.

Instructions
Classify each of the preceding costs as product costs or period costs. Indicate whether each product cost is a direct materials cost, a direct labor cost, or a factory overhead cost. Indicate whether each period cost is a selling expense or an administrative expense. Use the following tabular headings for preparing your answer, placing an "X" in the appropriate column.

	Product Costs			Period Costs	
Cost	Direct Materials Cost	Direct Labor Cost	Factory Overhead Cost	Selling Expense	Administrative Expense

---

PR 1-3A
Cost classifications—service company
obj. 2

A partial list of Highland Medical Center's costs is provided below.

a. Depreciation of X-ray equipment.
b. Cost of drugs used for patients.
c. Nurses' salaries.
d. Cost of new heart wing.
e. Overtime incurred in the Records Department due to a computer failure.

f. Cost of patient meals.
g. General maintenance of the hospital.
h. Salary of the nutritionist.
i. Cost of maintaining the staff and visitors' cafeteria.
j. Training costs for nurses.
k. Operating room supplies used on patients (catheters, sutures, etc.).
l. Utility costs of the hospital.
m. Cost of intravenous solutions.
n. Cost of blood tests.
o. Cost of improvements on the employee parking lot.
p. Cost of laundry services for operating room personnel.
q. Depreciation on patient rooms.
r. Cost of advertising hospital services on television.
s. Cost of X-ray test.
t. Salary of intensive care personnel.
u. Doctor's fee.

Instructions
1. What would be Highland's most logical definition for the final cost object?
2. Identify how each of the costs is to be classified as either direct or indirect. Define direct costs in terms of a patient as a cost object.

PR 1-4A
Manufacturing income statement, statement of cost of goods manufactured

objs. 2, 3

✓*1. c. Vinston, $301,000*

Several items are omitted from each of the following income statement and cost of goods manufactured statement data for the month of December 2008:

	Vinston Company	Turkun Company
Materials inventory, December 1	$ 25,000	$ 32,000
Materials inventory, December 31	(a)	15,000
Materials purchased	105,000	(a)
Cost of direct materials used in production	120,000	(b)
Direct labor	145,000	95,000
Factory overhead	56,000	42,000
Total manufacturing costs incurred in December	(b)	249,000
Total manufacturing costs	336,000	283,000
Work in process inventory, December 1	45,000	34,000
Work in process inventory, December 31	65,000	(c)
Cost of goods manufactured	(c)	252,000
Finished goods inventory, December 1	84,000	44,000
Finished goods inventory, December 31	74,000	(d)
Sales	425,000	320,000
Cost of goods sold	(d)	254,000
Gross profit	(e)	(e)
Operating expenses	44,000	(f)
Net income	(f)	27,000

Instructions
1. Determine the amounts of the missing items, identifying them by letter.
2. Prepare a statement of cost of goods manufactured for Vinston Company.
3. Prepare an income statement for Vinston Company.

PR 1-5A
Statement of cost of goods manufactured and income statement for a manufacturing company

objs. 2, 3

The following information is available for Sano Instrument Manufacturing Company for 2008:

Inventories	January 1	December 31
Materials	$ 85,000	$105,000
Work in process	120,000	105,000
Finished goods	125,000	110,000

Advertising expense	$ 75,000
Depreciation expense—Office equipment	25,000
Depreciation expense—Factory equipment	16,000
Direct labor	205,000
Heat, light, and power—Factory	6,500
Indirect labor	26,000
Materials purchased during 2008	135,000
Office salaries expense	85,000
Property taxes—Factory	4,500
Property taxes—Headquarters building	15,000
Rent expense—Factory	7,500
Sales	950,000
Sales salaries expense	150,000
Supplies—Factory	3,500
Miscellaneous cost—Factory	4,500

Instructions
1. Prepare the 2008 statement of cost of goods manufactured.
2. Prepare the 2008 income statement.

Problems Series B

PR 1-1B
Classifying costs

obj. 2

The following is a list of costs that were incurred in the production and sale of lawn mowers:

a. Payroll taxes on hourly assembly line employees.
b. Filter for spray gun used to paint the lawn mowers.
c. Cost of boxes used in packaging lawn mowers.
d. Premiums on insurance policy for factory buildings.
e. Gasoline engines used for lawn mowers.
f. Salary of factory supervisor.
g. Tires for lawn mowers.
h. Cost of advertising in a national magazine.
i. Plastic for outside housing of lawn mowers.
j. Salary of quality control supervisor who inspects each lawn mower before it is shipped.
k. Steering wheels for lawn mowers.
l. Cash paid to outside firm for janitorial services for factory.
m. Engine oil used in mower engines prior to shipment.
n. Attorney fees for drafting a new lease for headquarters offices.
o. Maintenance costs for new robotic factory equipment, based upon hours of usage.
p. Straight-line depreciation on the robotic machinery used to manufacture the lawn mowers.
q. License fees for use of patent for lawn mower blade, based upon the number of lawn mowers produced.
r. Telephone charges for controller's office.
s. Paint used to coat the lawn mowers.
t. Steel used in producing the lawn mowers.
u. Commissions paid to sales representatives, based upon the number of lawn mowers sold.
v. Electricity used to run the robotic machinery.
w. Factory cafeteria cashier's wages.
x. Property taxes on the factory building and equipment.
y. Salary of vice president of marketing.
z. Hourly wages of operators of robotic machinery used in production.

Instructions
Classify each cost as either a product cost or a period cost. Indicate whether each product cost is a direct materials cost, a direct labor cost, or a factory overhead cost. Indicate whether each period cost is a selling expense or an administrative expense. Use the following tabular headings for your answer, placing an "X" in the appropriate column.

	Product Costs			Period Costs	
Cost	Direct Materials Cost	Direct Labor Cost	Factory Overhead Cost	Selling Expense	Administrative Expense

PR 1-2B
Classifying costs
obj. 2

The following is a list of costs incurred by several businesses:

a. Packing supplies for products sold.
b. Tires for an automobile manufacturer.
c. Costs for television advertisement.
d. Disk drives for a microcomputer manufacturer.
e. Executive bonus for vice president of marketing.
f. Seed for grain farmer.
g. Wages of a machine operator on the production line.
h. Wages of controller's secretary.
i. Factory operating supplies.
j. First-aid supplies for factory workers.
k. Depreciation of factory equipment.
l. Salary of quality control supervisor.
m. Sales commissions.
n. Maintenance and repair costs for factory equipment.
o. Cost of hogs for meat processor.
p. Health insurance premiums paid for factory workers.
q. Lumber used by furniture manufacturer.
r. Paper used by commercial printer.
s. Hourly wages of warehouse laborers.
t. Paper used by Computer Department in processing various managerial reports.
u. Costs of operating a research laboratory.
v. Entertainment expenses for sales representatives.
w. Cost of telephone operators for a toll-free hotline to help customers operate products.
x. Protective glasses for factory machine operators.

Instructions
Classify each of the preceding costs as product costs or period costs. Indicate whether each product cost is a direct materials cost, a direct labor cost, or a factory overhead cost. Indicate whether each period cost is a selling expense or an administrative expense. Use the following tabular headings for preparing your answer. Place an "X" in the appropriate column.

	Product Costs			Period Costs	
Cost	Direct Materials Cost	Direct Labor Cost	Factory Overhead Cost	Selling Expense	Administrative Expense

PR 1-3B
Cost classifications—service company
obj. 2

A partial list of Heartland Hotel's costs is provided below.

a. Salary of the hotel president.
b. Depreciation of the hotel.
c. Cost of new carpeting.
d. Cost of soaps and shampoos for rooms.
e. Cost of food.
f. Wages of desk clerks.
g. Cost to paint lobby.
h. Cost of advertising in local newspaper.
i. Utility cost.
j. Cost of valet service.
k. General maintenance supplies.
l. Wages of maids.
m. Wages of bellhops.
n. Wages of convention setup employees.
o. Pay-for-view rental costs (in rooms).

(continued)

p. Cost of room minibar supplies.
q. Guest room telephone costs for long-distance calls.
r. Wages of kitchen employees.
s. Cost of laundering towels and bedding.
t. Cost to replace lobby furniture.
u. Training for hotel restaurant servers.
v. Cost to mail a customer survey.
w. Champagne for guests.

Instructions

1. What would be Heartland's most logical definition for the final cost object?
2. Identify how each of the costs is to be classified as either direct or indirect. Define direct costs in terms of a hotel guest as the cost object.

PR 1-4B

Manufacturing income statement, statement of cost of goods manufactured

objs. 2, 3

✓ 1. c. Washington, $515,000

Several items are omitted from each of the following income statement and cost of goods manufactured statement data for the month of December 2008:

	Washington Company	Lee Company
Materials inventory, December 1	$ 65,000	$ 85,000
Materials inventory, December 31	(a)	95,000
Materials purchased	165,000	190,000
Cost of direct materials used in production	174,000	(a)
Direct labor	245,000	(b)
Factory overhead	76,000	95,000
Total manufacturing costs incurred during December	(b)	550,000
Total manufacturing costs	620,000	755,000
Work in process inventory, December 1	125,000	205,000
Work in process inventory, December 31	105,000	(c)
Cost of goods manufactured	(c)	545,000
Finished goods inventory, December 1	110,000	95,000
Finished goods inventory, December 31	115,000	(d)
Sales	950,000	850,000
Cost of goods sold	(d)	551,000
Gross profit	(e)	(e)
Operating expenses	125,000	(f)
Net income	(f)	189,000

Instructions

1. Determine the amounts of the missing items, identifying them by letter.
2. Prepare a statement of cost of goods manufactured for Lee Company.
3. Prepare an income statement for Lee Company.

PR 1-5B

Statement of cost of goods manufactured and income statement for a manufacturing company

objs. 2, 3

The following information is available for Earp Corporation for 2008:

Inventories	January 1	December 31
Materials	$125,000	$155,000
Work in process	225,000	210,000
Finished goods	215,000	210,000

Advertising expense	$ 105,000
Depreciation expense—Office equipment	15,000
Depreciation expense—Factory equipment	20,000
Direct labor	240,000
Heat, light, and power—Factory	8,000
Indirect labor	28,000
Materials purchased during 2008	235,000
Office salaries expense	82,000
Property taxes—Factory	6,500
Property taxes—Office building	13,500
Rent expense—Factory	11,000
Sales	1,100,000
Sales salaries expense	135,000
Supplies—Factory	5,500
Miscellaneous cost—Factory	3,400

Instructions
1. Prepare the 2008 statement of cost of goods manufactured.
2. Prepare the 2008 income statement.

Special Activities

SA 1-1
Ethics and professional conduct in business

Farrar Manufacturing Company allows employees to purchase, at cost, manufacturing materials, such as metal and lumber, for personal use. To purchase materials for personal use, an employee must complete a materials requisition form, which must then be approved by the employee's immediate supervisor. Peggy Carron, an assistant cost accountant, charges the employee an amount based on Farrar's net purchase cost.

Peggy Carron is in the process of replacing a deck on her home and has requisitioned lumber for personal use, which has been approved in accordance with company policy. In computing the cost of the lumber, Peggy reviewed all the purchase invoices for the past year. She then used the lowest price to compute the amount due the company for the lumber.

Discuss whether Peggy behaved in an ethical manner.

SA 1-2
Financial vs. managerial accounting

The following statement was made by the vice president of finance of Haberman Inc.: "The managers of a company should use the same information as the shareholders of the firm. When managers use the same information in guiding their internal operations as shareholders use in evaluating their investments, the managers will be aligned with the stockholders' profit objectives."

Respond to the vice president's statement.

SA 1-3
Managerial accounting in the management process

For each of the following managers, describe how managerial accounting could be used to satisfy strategic or operational objectives:

1. The vice president of the Information Systems Division of a bank.
2. A hospital administrator.
3. The chief executive officer of a food company. The food company is divided into three divisions: Nonalcoholic Beverages, Snack Foods, and Fast-Food Restaurants.
4. The manager of the local campus copy shop.

SA 1-4
Classifying costs

On-Time Computer Repairs provides computer repair services for the community. Laurie Estes's computer was not working, and she called On-Time for a home repair visit. The On-Time technician arrived at 2:00 P.M. to begin work. By 4:00 P.M. the problem was diagnosed as a failed circuit board. Unfortunately, the technician did not have a new circuit board in the truck, since the technician's previous customer had the same problem, and a board was used on that visit. Replacement boards were available back at the On-Time shop. Therefore, the technician drove back to the shop to retrieve a replacement board. From 4:00 to 5:00 P.M., the On-Time technician drove the round trip to retrieve the replacement board from the shop.

At 5:00 P.M. the technician was back on the job at Laurie's home. The replacement procedure is somewhat complex, since a variety of tests must be performed once the board is installed. The job was completed at 6:00 P.M.

Laurie's repair bill showed the following:

Circuit board	$ 80
Labor charges	190
Total	$270

Laurie was surprised at the size of the bill and asked for some greater detail supporting the calculations. On-Time responded with the following explanations:

Cost of materials:

Purchase price of circuit board	$60
Markup on purchase price to cover storage and handling	20
Total materials charge	$80

The labor charge per hour is detailed as follows:

2:00–3:00 P.M.	$ 40
3:00–4:00 P.M.	35
4:00–5:00 P.M.	45
5:00–6:00 P.M.	70
Total labor charge	$190

Further explanations in the differences in the hourly rates are as follows:

First hour:

Base labor rate	$20
Fringe benefits	7
Overhead (other than storage and handling)	8
Total base labor rate	$35
Additional charge for first hour of any job to cover the cost of vehicle depreciation, fuel, and employee time in transit. A 30-minute transit time is assumed.	5
	$40

Third hour:

Base labor rate	$35
The trip back to the shop includes vehicle depreciation and fuel; therefore, a charge was added to the hourly rate to cover these costs. The round trip took an hour.	10
	$45

Fourth hour:

Base labor rate	$35
Overtime premium for time worked in excess of an eight-hour day (starting at 5:00 P.M.) is equal to the base rate.	35
	$70

1. ▭▭▭▭➤ If you were in Laurie's position, how would you respond to the bill? Are there parts of the bill that appear incorrect to you? If so, what argument would you employ to convince On-Time that the bill is too high?
2. Use the headings below to construct a table. Fill in the table by first listing the costs identified in the activity in the left-hand column. For each cost, place a check mark in the appropriate column identifying the correct cost classification. Assume that each service call is a job.

Cost	Direct Materials	Direct Labor	Overhead

SA 1-5
Using managerial accounting information

The following situations describe decision scenarios that could use managerial accounting information:

1. The manager of Taco Castle wishes to determine the price to charge for various lunch plates.
2. By evaluating the cost of leftover materials, the plant manager of a precision machining facility wishes to determine how effectively the plant is being run.
3. The division controller needs to determine the cost of products left in inventory.
4. The manager of the Maintenance Department wishes to plan next year's anticipated expenditures.

▭▭▭▭➤ For each situation, discuss how managerial accounting information could be used.

SA 1-6
Classifying costs

[Group Project]

With a group of students, visit a local copy and graphics shop or a pizza restaurant. As you observe the operation, consider the costs associated with running the business. As a group, identify as many costs as you can and classify them according to the following table headings:

Cost	Direct Materials	Direct Labor	Overhead	Selling Expenses

Answers to Self-Examination Questions

1. **B** Managerial accounting is not restricted to generally accepted accounting principles, as is financial accounting (answer B). Both financial and managerial accounting support decision making (answer A). Financial accounting is mostly concerned with the decision making of external users, while managerial accounting supports decision making of management. Both financial and managerial accounting can result in financial reports (answer C). Managerial accounting reports are developed for internal use by managers at various levels in the organization. Both managerial and financial accounting record events from the past (answer D); however, managerial accounting can also include information about the future in the form of budgets and cash flow projections.

2. **D** The five basic phases of the management process are planning (answer A), directing (not listed), controlling (answer B), improving (not listed), and decision making (answer C). Operating (answer D) is not one of the five basic phases, but operations are the object of managers' attention.

3. **C** Sales salaries (answer C) is a selling expense and is not considered a cost of manufacturing a product. Direct materials cost (answer A), factory overhead cost (answer B), and direct labor cost (answer D) are costs of manufacturing a product.

4. **B** Depreciation of testing equipment (answer B) is included as part of the factory overhead costs of the microcomputer manufacturer. The cost of memory chips (answer A) and the cost of disk drives (answer D) are both considered a part of direct materials cost. The wages of microcomputer assemblers (answer C) are part of direct labor costs.

5. **C** Cost of goods sold is calculated as follows:

Beginning finished goods inventory	$ 50,000
Add: Cost of goods manufactured	125,000
Less: Ending finished goods inventory	35,000
Cost of goods sold	$140,000

Job Order Cost Systems

©2005 Washburn Guitars

Disturbed | Dan Donegan plays a
Chicago | **Washburn Maya** guitar.
www.washburn.com/donegan

© WASHBURN GUITARS

objectives

After studying this chapter, you should be able to:

1 *Describe accounting systems used by manufacturing businesses.*

2 *Describe and prepare summary journal entries for a job order cost accounting system.*

3 *Use job order cost information for decision making.*

4 *Diagram the flow of costs for a service business that uses a job order cost accounting system.*

Dan Donegan's Guitar

As we discussed in the previous chapter, Dan Donegan of the rock band Disturbed uses a custom-made guitar purchased from Washburn Guitars. In fact, Dan Donegan designed his guitar in partnership with Washburn Guitars, which contributed to Washburn's Maya Series of guitars. The Maya guitar is a precision instrument for which amateurs and professionals are willing to pay between $1,400 and $7,000. In order for Washburn to stay in business, the purchase price of the guitar must be greater than the cost of producing the guitar. So, how does Washburn determine the cost of producing a guitar?

Costs associated with creating a guitar include materials such as wood and strings, the salaries of employees who build the guitar, and factory overhead. To determine the purchase price of Dan's Maya, Washburn identifies and records the costs that go into the guitar during each step of the manufacturing process. As the guitar moves through the production process, the costs of direct materials, direct labor, and factory overhead are recorded. When the guitar is complete, the costs that have been recorded are added up to determine the cost of Dan's unique Maya Series guitar. The company then prices the guitar to achieve a level of profit over the cost of the guitar. In this chapter, we will introduce you to the principles of accounting systems that accumulate costs in the same manner as they were for Dan Donegan's guitar.

Cost Accounting System Overview

objective 1

Describe accounting systems used by manufacturing businesses.

REAL WORLD

Warner Bros. and other movie studios use job order cost systems to accumulate movie production and distribution costs. Costs such as actor salaries, production costs, movie print costs, and marketing costs are accumulated in a job account for a particular movie. Cost information from the job cost report can be used to control the costs of the movie while it is being produced and to determine the profitability of the movie after it has been shown.

Managerial accounting provides useful information to managers for planning and controlling operations. For manufacturing operations, developing accurate information on product cost is a primary focus of the managerial accounting system. As described and illustrated in the previous chapter for Legend Guitars, product cost consists of direct materials, direct labor, and factory overhead. These components of product cost and their related inventories for Legend Guitars are summarized in Exhibit 1.

Cost accounting systems accumulate manufacturing costs for the goods that are produced. This product cost information is used by managers to establish product prices, control operations, and develop financial statements. In addition, the cost accounting system improves control by supplying data on the costs incurred by each manufacturing department or process.

There are two main types of cost accounting systems for manufacturing operations: job order cost systems and process cost systems. Each of the two systems is widely used, and any one manufacturer may use more than one type. In this chapter, we will illustrate the job order cost system. In the next chapter, we will illustrate the process cost system.

A **job order cost system** provides a separate record for the cost of each quantity of product that passes through the factory. A particular quantity of product is termed a *job*. A job order cost system is best suited to industries that manufacture custom goods to fill special orders from customers or that produce a wide variety of products for stock. Manufacturers that use a job order cost system are sometimes called *job shops*. An example of a job shop would be an apparel manufacturer, such as Levi Strauss & Co.

Many service firms also use job order cost systems to accumulate the costs associated with providing client services. For example, an accounting firm will accumulate all of the costs associated with a particular client engagement, such as accountant time, copying charges, and travel costs. Recording costs in this manner helps the accounting firm control costs during a client engagement and determines client billing and profitability.

EXHIBIT 1	Manufacturing Costs and Inventories for Legend Guitars

Product Costs

Direct materials cost	Includes the cost of any material that is an integral part of the final product. For Legend Guitars, this includes the cost of wood used in the neck and body.
Direct labor cost	Includes the wages of each employee who is directly involved in converting materials into the finished product. For Legend Guitars, this includes the costs of wages of employees who assemble the guitars.
Factory overhead cost	Includes costs other than direct materials and direct labor costs that are incurred in the manufacturing process. For Legend Guitars, this includes the costs of sandpaper, buffing compound, glue, and factory utilities.

Inventories

Materials inventory	Includes the materials that have not yet entered the manufacturing process. For Legend Guitars, this includes the product costs; of wood used to make the body and neck of the guitar.
Work in process inventory	Includes the product costs of units that have entered the manufacturing process but have not been completed at the end of the period. For Legend Guitars, this includes the product costs assigned to guitars for which the neck and body have been produced but have not been assembled.
Finished goods inventory	Includes the cost of completed (or finished) products that have not been sold. For Legend Guitars, this includes the product costs assigned to completed guitars that have not yet been sold.

Under a **process cost system**, costs are accumulated for each of the departments or processes within the factory. A process system is best suited for manufacturers of units of product that are not distinguishable from each other during a continuous production process. Examples would be oil refineries, paper producers, chemical processors, aluminum smelters, and food processors.

Job Order Cost Systems for Manufacturing Businesses

objective **2**

Describe and prepare summary journal entries for a job order cost accounting system.

In this section, we illustrate the job order cost system for Legend Guitars whose manufacturing process we described and illustrated in the prior chapter. The job order system accumulates manufacturing costs by jobs. At any point in time, some jobs will still be in the process of being manufactured while some jobs will have been completed. For example, although the materials for Jobs 71 and 72 have been added, they are still in the production process and are in Work in Process Inventory as shown in Exhibit 2. In contrast, Jobs 69 and 70 have been completed and are included in Finished Goods Inventory as shown in Exhibit 2. When finished guitars are sold to music stores, their costs are recorded as cost of goods sold.

In a job order cost accounting system, perpetual inventory controlling accounts and subsidiary ledgers are maintained for materials, work in process, and finished goods inventories. Each inventory account is debited for all additions and is credited for all deductions. The balance of each account thus represents the balance on hand.

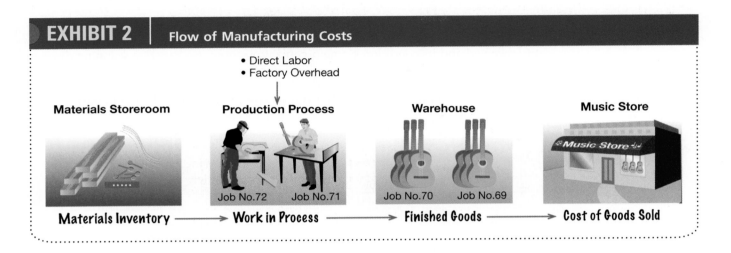

EXHIBIT 2 | **Flow of Manufacturing Costs**

MATERIALS

The procedures used to purchase, store, and issue materials to production often differ among manufacturers. Exhibit 3 shows the basic information and cost flows for the wood received and issued to production by Legend Guitars.

EXHIBIT 3

Materials Information and Cost Flows

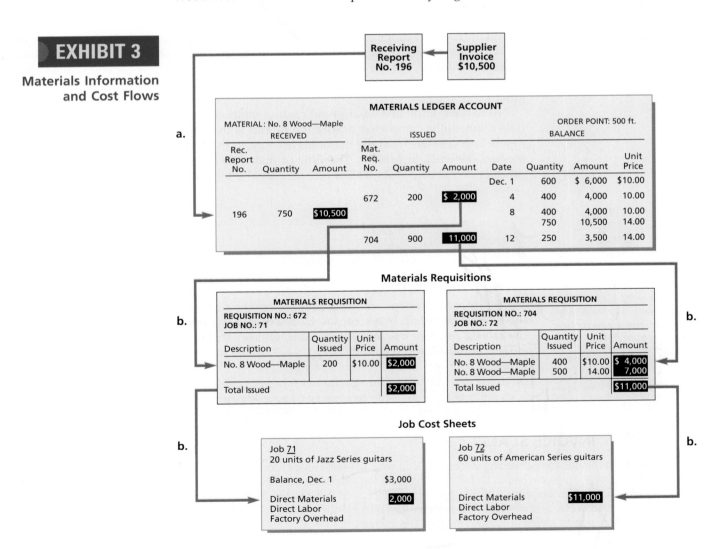

Purchased materials are first received and inspected by the Receiving Department. The Receiving Department personnel prepare a **receiving report**, showing the quantity received and its condition. Some organizations now use bar code scanning devices in place of receiving reports to record and electronically transmit incoming materials data. The receiving information and invoice are used to record the receipt and control the payment for purchased items. The journal entry to record Receiving Report No. 196 in Exhibit 3 is:

a.	Materials		10 5 0 0 00		
	Accounts Payable			10 5 0 0 00	
	Materials purchased during				
	December.				

The materials account in the general ledger is a controlling account. A separate account for each type of material is maintained in a subsidiary **materials ledger**. Details as to the quantity and cost of materials received are recorded in the materials ledger on the basis of the receiving reports. A typical form of a materials ledger account is illustrated in Exhibit 3.

Materials are released from the storeroom to the factory in response to **materials requisitions** from the Production Department. An illustration of a materials requisition is in Exhibit 3. The completed requisition for each job serves as the basis for posting quantities and dollar data to the job cost sheets in the case of direct materials or to factory overhead in the case of indirect materials. **Job cost sheets**, which are illustrated in Exhibit 3, are the work in process subsidiary ledger. For Legend Guitars, Job 71 is for 20 units of Jazz Series guitars, while Job 72 is for 60 units of American Series guitars.

In Exhibit 3, the first-in, first-out costing method is used. A summary of the materials requisitions completed during the month is the basis for transferring the cost of the direct materials from the materials account in the general ledger to the controlling account for work in process. The flow of materials from the materials storeroom into production ($2,000 + $11,000) is recorded by the following entry:

REAL WORLD

b.	Work in Process		13 0 0 0 00		
	Materials			13 0 0 0 00	
	Materials requisitioned to jobs.				

For many manufacturing firms, the direct materials cost can be greater than 50% of the total cost to manufacture a product. This is why controlling materials costs is very important.

Many organizations are using computerized information processes that account for the flow of materials. In a computerized setting, the storeroom manager would record the release of materials into a computer, which would automatically update the subsidiary materials records.

Integrity, Objectivity, and Ethics in Business

ETHICS

PHONY INVOICE SCAMS

A popular method for defrauding a company is to issue a phony invoice. The scam begins by initially contacting the target firm to discover details of key business contacts, business operations, and products. The swindler then uses this information to create a fictitious invoice. The invoice will include names, figures, and other details to give it the appearance of legitimacy. This type of scam can be avoided if invoices are matched with receiving documents prior to issuing a check.

Example Exercise 2-1 objective **2**

On March 5, Hatch Company purchased 400 units of raw materials at $14 per unit. On March 10, raw materials were requisitioned for production as follows: 200 units for Job 101 at $12 per unit and 300 units for Job 102 at $14 per unit. Journalize the entry on March 5 to record the purchase and on March 10 to record the requisition from the materials storeroom.

Follow My Example 2-1

Mar. 5	Materials	5,600	
	Accounts Payable		5,600
	$5,600 = 400 × $14.		
10	Work in Process	6,600*	
	Materials		6,600

*Job 101 $2,400 = 200 × $12
Job 102 4,200 = 300 × $14
Total $6,600

For Practice: PE 2-1A, PE 2-1B

FACTORY LABOR

There are two primary objectives in accounting for factory labor. One objective is to determine the correct amount to be paid each employee for each payroll period. A second objective is to properly allocate factory labor costs to factory overhead and individual job orders.

The amount of time spent by an employee in the factory is usually recorded on *clock cards* or *in-and-out cards*. The amount of time spent by each employee and the labor cost incurred for each individual job are recorded on **time tickets**. Exhibit 4 shows typical time ticket forms and cost flows for direct labor for Legend Guitars.

A summary of the time tickets at the end of each month is the basis for recording the direct and indirect labor costs incurred in production. Direct labor is posted to each job cost sheet, while indirect labor is debited to Factory Overhead.[1] Legend Guitars incurred 350 direct labor hours on Job 71 and 500 direct labor hours on Job 72 during December. The total direct labor costs were $11,000, divided into $3,500 for Job 71 and $7,500 for Job 72. The labor costs that flow into production are recorded by the following summary entry to the work in process controlling account:

c.	Work in Process	11 0 0 0 00	
	Wages Payable		11 0 0 0 00
	Factory labor used in production		
	of jobs.		

As with recording direct materials, many organizations are automating the labor recording process. Employees may log their time directly into computer terminals at their workstations. Alternatively, employees may be issued magnetic cards, much like credit cards, to log in and out of work assignments that are spread across a wide geographical area. For example, Shell Group uses a magnetic card system to track the work of maintenance crews in its refinery operations.

---

1 There are a variety of methods for recording direct labor costs. In the approach illustrated in this chapter, we assume that labor costs are automatically recorded to jobs or factory overhead when incurred. Alternatively, wages could first be debited to Factory Labor when incurred and then later distributed to jobs and factory overhead.

EXHIBIT 4

Labor Information and Cost Flows

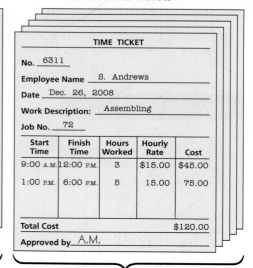

Job 71 Time Tickets

TIME TICKET

No. 4521

Employee Name D. McInnis

Date Dec. 13, 2008

Work Description: Cutting

Job No. 71

Start Time	Finish Time	Hours Worked	Hourly Rate	Cost
8:00 A.M.	12:00 P.M.	4	$10.00	$40.00
1:00 P.M.	3:00 P.M.	2	10.00	20.00
Total Cost				$60.00

Approved by T.D.

Job 72 Time Tickets

TIME TICKET

No. 6311

Employee Name S. Andrews

Date Dec. 26, 2008

Work Description: Assembling

Job No. 72

Start Time	Finish Time	Hours Worked	Hourly Rate	Cost
9:00 A.M.	12:00 P.M.	3	$15.00	$45.00
1:00 P.M.	6:00 P.M.	5	15.00	75.00
Total Cost				$120.00

Approved by A.M.

December Job 71 Hours	350
December Job 71 Labor Costs:	$3,500

December Job 72 Hours	500
December Job 72 Labor Costs:	$7,500

Job Cost Sheets

c.

Job 71
20 units of Jazz Series guitars

Balance	$3,000
Direct Materials	2,000
Direct Labor	3,500
Factory Overhead	

c.

Job 72
60 units of American Series guitars

Direct Materials	$11,000
Direct Labor	7,500
Factory Overhead	

Example Exercise 2-2

objective **2**

During March, Hatch Company accumulated 800 hours of direct labor costs on Job 101 and 600 hours on Job 102. The total direct labor was incurred at a rate of $16 per direct labor hour for Job 101, and $12 per direct labor hour for Job 102. Journalize the entry to record the flow of labor costs into production during March.

Follow My Example 2-2

Work in Process	20,000*	
Wages Payable		20,000

*Job 101	$12,800	= 800 hrs. × $16
Job 102	7,200	= 600 hrs. × $12
Total	$20,000	

For Practice: PE 2-2A, PE 2-2B

Integrity, Objectivity, and Ethics in Business

ETHICS

GHOST EMPLOYEES

Companies must guard against the fraudulent creation and cashing of payroll checks. Numerous payroll frauds involve supervisors adding fictitious employees to the payroll or failing to remove departing employees from the payroll and then cashing the checks. Requiring proper authorization and approval of employee additions, removals, or changes in pay rates can minimize this type of fraud.

FACTORY OVERHEAD COST

Factory overhead includes all manufacturing costs except direct materials and direct labor. Debits to Factory Overhead come from various sources, such as indirect materials, indirect labor, factory power, and factory depreciation. For example, the factory overhead of $4,600 incurred in December for Legend Guitars would be recorded as follows:

d.	Factory Overhead		4 6 0 0 00	
	Materials			5 0 0 00
	Wages Payable			2 0 0 0 00
	Utilities Payable			9 0 0 00
	Accumulated Depreciation			1 2 0 0 00
	Factory overhead incurred in			
	production.			

Example Exercise 2-3   objective 2

During March, Hatch Company incurred factory overhead costs as follows: indirect materials, $800; indirect labor, $3,400; utilities cost, $1,600; and depreciation, $2,500. Journalize the entry to record the factory overhead incurred during March.

Follow My Example 2-3

Factory Overhead	8,300	
Materials.		800
Wages Payable		3,400
Utilities Payable		1,600
Accumulated Depreciation		2,500

For Practice: PE 2-3A, PE 2-3B

Allocating Factory Overhead   Factory overhead is much different from direct labor and direct materials because it is indirectly related to the jobs. How, then, do the jobs get assigned a portion of overhead costs? The answer is through **cost allocation**, which is the process of assigning factory overhead costs to a cost object, such as a job. The factory overhead costs are assigned to the jobs on the basis of some known measure about each job. The measure used to allocate factory overhead is frequently called an **activity base**, *allocation base,* or *activity driver.* The estimated activity base should be a measure that reflects the consumption or use of factory overhead cost. For example, the direct labor is recorded for each job using time tickets. Thus, direct labor (hours or cost) could be used to allocate production-related factory overhead costs to each job. Likewise, direct materials costs are known about each job through the materials requisitions. Thus, materials-related factory overhead, such as Purchasing Department salaries, could logically be allocated to the job on the basis of direct materials cost.

Predetermined Factory Overhead Rate   To provide current job costs, factory overhead may be allocated or applied to production using a **predetermined factory overhead rate**. The predetermined factory overhead rate is calculated by dividing the estimated amount of factory overhead for the forthcoming year by the estimated activity base, such as machine hours, direct materials costs, direct labor costs, or direct labor hours.

To illustrate calculating a predetermined overhead rate, assume that Legend Guitars estimates the total factory overhead cost to be $50,000 for the year and the activity base to be 10,000 direct labor hours. The predetermined factory overhead rate would be calculated as $5 per direct labor hour, as follows:

$$\text{Predetermined Factory Overhead Rate} = \frac{\text{Estimated Total Factory Overhead Costs}}{\text{Estimated Activity Base}}$$

$$\text{Predetermined Factory Overhead Rate} = \frac{\$50,000}{10,000 \text{ direct labor hours}} = \$5 \text{ per direct labor hour}$$

A survey conducted by the Cost Management Group of the Institute for Management Accountants found that 20% of survey respondents had adopted activity-based costing.

Why is the predetermined overhead rate calculated from estimated numbers at the beginning of the period? The answer is to ensure timely information. If a company waited until the end of an accounting period when all overhead costs are known, the allocated factory overhead would be accurate but not timely. If the cost system is to have maximum usefulness, cost data should be available as each job is completed, even though there may be a small sacrifice in accuracy. Only through timely reporting can management make needed adjustments in pricing or in manufacturing methods and achieve the best possible combination of revenue and cost on future jobs.

A number of companies are using a new product-costing approach called activity-based costing. **Activity-based costing** is a method of accumulating and allocating factory overhead costs to products, using many overhead rates. Each rate is related to separate factory activities, such as inspecting, moving, and machining. Activity-based costing is discussed and illustrated in a later chapter of this textbook.

Applying Factory Overhead to Work in Process   As factory overhead costs are incurred, they are debited to the factory overhead account, as shown previously in transaction (d). For Legend Guitars, factory overhead costs are applied to production at the rate of $5 per direct labor hour. The amount of factory overhead applied to each job would be recorded in the job cost sheets as shown in Exhibit 5. For example, the 850 direct labor hours used in Legend's December operations would all be traced to individual jobs. Job 71 used 350 labor hours, so $1,750 (350 × $5) of factory overhead would be applied to Job 71. Similarly, $2,500 (500 × $5) of factory overhead would be applied to Job 72.

The factory overhead costs applied to production are periodically debited to the work in process account and credited to the factory overhead account. The summary entry to apply the $4,250 ($1,750 + $2,500) of factory overhead is as follows:

				Debit	Credit
e.	Work in Process			4 2 5 0 00	
	Factory Overhead				4 2 5 0 00
	Factory overhead applied to jobs				
	according to the predetermined				
	overhead rate.				

The factory overhead costs applied and the actual factory overhead costs incurred during a period will usually differ. If the amount applied exceeds the actual costs incurred, the factory overhead account will have a credit balance. This credit is described as **overapplied** or overabsorbed **factory overhead**. If the amount applied is less than the actual costs incurred, the account will have a debit balance. This debit is described as **underapplied** or underabsorbed **factory overhead**. Both cases are illustrated in the following account for Legend Guitars:

ACCOUNT *Factory Overhead*					ACCOUNT NO.		
						Balance	
Date	**Item**	**Post. Ref.**	**Debit**	**Credit**	**Debit**	**Credit**	
Dec. 1	Balance					2 0 0 00	
31	Factory overhead cost incurred		4 6 0 0 00		4 4 0 0 00		
31	Factory overhead cost applied			4 2 5 0 00	1 5 0 00		

Underapplied balance

Overapplied balance

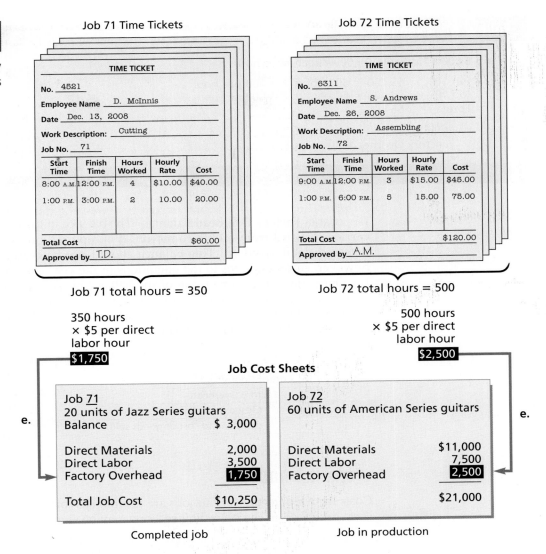

EXHIBIT 5

Assigning Factory
Overhead to Jobs

Job 71 Time Tickets

Job 71 total hours = 350

350 hours
× $5 per direct
labor hour
$1,750

Job 72 Time Tickets

Job 72 total hours = 500

500 hours
× $5 per direct
labor hour
$2,500

Job Cost Sheets

e.

Job 71
20 units of Jazz Series guitars
Balance $ 3,000

Direct Materials   2,000
Direct Labor   3,500
Factory Overhead   1,750

Total Job Cost $10,250

Completed job

Job 72
60 units of American Series guitars

Direct Materials $11,000
Direct Labor   7,500
Factory Overhead   2,500

                          $21,000

Job in production

e.

If the underapplied or overapplied balance increases in only one direction and it becomes large, the balance and the overhead rate should be investigated. For example, if a large balance is caused by changes in manufacturing methods or in production goals, the factory overhead rate should be revised. On the other hand, a large underapplied balance may indicate a serious control problem caused by inefficiencies in production methods, excessive costs, or a combination of factors.

Example Exercise 2-4   objective **2**

Hatch Company estimates that total factory overhead costs will be $100,000 for the year. Direct labor hours are estimated to be 25,000. For Hatch Company, (a) determine the predetermined factory overhead rate, (b) determine the amount of factory overhead applied to Jobs 101 and 102 in March using the data on direct labor hours from Example Exercise 2-2, and (c) prepare the journal entry to apply factory overhead to both jobs in March according to the predetermined overhead rate.

(continued)

Follow My Example 2-4

a. $4.00 = $100,000/25,000 direct labor hours

b. Job 101 $3,200 = 800 hours × $4.00 per hour
   Job 102   2,400 = 600 hours × $4.00 per hour
   Total $5,600

c. Work in Process 5,600
            Factory Overhead 5,600

For Practice: PE 2-4A, PE 2-4B

Disposal of Factory Overhead Balance The balance in the factory overhead account is carried forward from month to month. It is reported on interim balance sheets as a deferred debit or credit. This balance should not be carried over to the next year, however, since it applies to the operations of the year just ended.

One approach for disposing of the balance of factory overhead at the end of the year is to transfer the entire balance to the cost of goods sold account.[2] To illustrate, the journal entry to eliminate Legend Guitars' underapplied overhead balance of $150 at the end of the calendar year would be as follows:

f.	Cost of Goods Sold		1 5 0 00		
	Factory Overhead			1 5 0 00	
	Closed underapplied factory				
	overhead to cost of goods sold.				

WORK IN PROCESS

Costs incurred for the various jobs are debited to Work in Process. Legend Guitars' job costs described in the preceding sections may be summarized as follows:

- **Direct materials, $13,000**—Work in Process debited and Materials credited [transaction (b)]; data obtained from summary of materials requisitions.
- **Direct labor, $11,000**—Work in Process debited and Wages Payable credited [transaction (c)]; data obtained from summary of time tickets.
- **Factory overhead, $4,250**—Work in Process debited and Factory Overhead credited [transaction (e)]; data obtained from summary of time tickets.

The details concerning the costs incurred on each job order are accumulated in the job cost sheets. Exhibit 6 illustrates the relationship between the job cost sheets and the work in process controlling account.

In this example, Job 71 was started in November and completed in December. The beginning December balance for Job 71 represents the costs carried over from the end of November. Job 72 was started in December but was not yet completed at the end of the month. Thus, the balance of the incomplete Job 72, or $21,000, will be shown on the balance sheet on December 31 as work in process inventory.

When Job 71 was completed, the direct materials costs, the direct labor costs, and the factory overhead costs were totaled and divided by the number of units produced to determine the cost per unit. If we assume that 20 units of Jazz Series guitars were produced for Job 71, then the unit cost would be $512.50 ($10,250/20).

---

2 Alternatively, the balance may be allocated among the work in process, finished goods, and cost of goods sold balances. This approach brings the accounts into agreement with the costs actually incurred. Since this approach is a more complex calculation that adds little additional accuracy, it will not be used in this text.

Job Cost Sheets

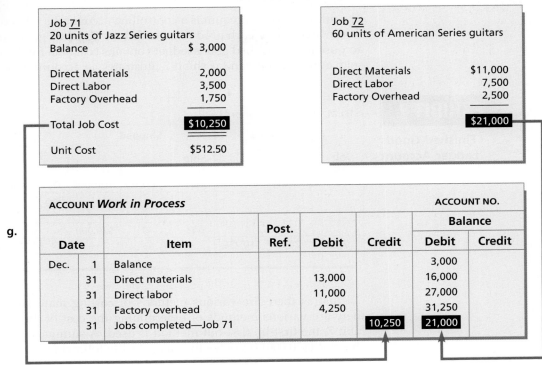

EXHIBIT 6

Job Cost Sheets and the Work in Process Controlling Account

Job 71
20 units of Jazz Series guitars

Balance	$ 3,000
Direct Materials	2,000
Direct Labor	3,500
Factory Overhead	1,750
Total Job Cost	$10,250
Unit Cost	$512.50

Job 72
60 units of American Series guitars

Direct Materials	$11,000
Direct Labor	7,500
Factory Overhead	2,500
	$21,000

g.

ACCOUNT Work in Process   **ACCOUNT NO.**

Date		Item	Post. Ref.	Debit	Credit	Balance Debit	Balance Credit
Dec.	1	Balance				3,000	
	31	Direct materials		13,000		16,000	
	31	Direct labor		11,000		27,000	
	31	Factory overhead		4,250		31,250	
	31	Jobs completed—Job 71			10,250	21,000	

Upon completing Job 71, the job cost sheet was removed from the cost ledger and filed for future reference. At the end of the accounting period (December), the total costs for all completed jobs during the period are determined, and the following entry is made:

g.	Finished Goods			10 2 5 0 00	
	Work in Process				10 2 5 0 00
	Job 71 completed in December.				

Example Exercise 2-5   objective 2

At the end of March, Hatch Company had completed Jobs 101 and 102. Job 101 is for 500 units, and Job 102 is for 1,000 units. Using the data from Example Exercises 2-1, 2-2, and 2-4, determine (a) the balance on the job cost sheets for Jobs 101 and 102 at the end of March and (b) the cost per unit for Jobs 101 and 102 at the end of March.

Follow My Example 2-5

a.
	Job 101	Job 102
Direct materials	$ 2,400	$ 4,200
Direct labor	12,800	7,200
Factory overhead	3,200	2,400
Total costs	$18,400	$13,800

b. Job 101 $36.80 = $18,400/500 units
    Job 102 $13.80 = $13,800/1,000 units

For Practice: PE 2-5A, PE 2-5B

FINISHED GOODS AND COST OF GOODS SOLD

The finished goods account is a controlling account. Its related subsidiary ledger, which has an account for each product, is called the **finished goods ledger** or *stock ledger*. Each account in the finished goods ledger contains cost data for the units manufactured, units sold, and units on hand. Exhibit 7 illustrates an account in the finished goods ledger.

EXHIBIT 7

Finished Goods Ledger Account

ITEM: *Jazz Series guitars*

Manufactured			Shipped			Balance			
Job Order No.	Quantity	Amount	Ship Order No.	Quantity	Amount	Date	Quantity	Amount	Unit Cost
						Dec. 1	40	$20,000	$500.00
			643	40	$20,000	9	—	—	—
71	20	$10,250				31	20	10,250	512.50

Just as there are various methods of costing materials entering into production, there are various methods of determining the cost of the finished goods sold. In Exhibit 7, the first-in, first-out method is used. A summary of the cost data for the units shipped ($20,000) becomes the basis for the following entry:

h.	Cost of Goods Sold			20 0 0 0 00	
	Finished Goods				20 0 0 0 00
	Cost of 40 Jazz Series guitars sold.				

Example Exercise 2-6   objective 2

Nejedly Company completed 80,000 units during the year at a cost of $680,000. The beginning finished goods inventory was 10,000 units at $80,000. Determine the cost of goods sold for 60,000 units, assuming a FIFO cost flow.

Follow My Example 2-6

$505,000 = $80,000 + (50,000 × $8.50*)

*Cost per unit of goods produced during the year = $8.50 = $680,000/80,000 units

For Practice: PE 2-6A, PE 2-6B

SALES

The selling price of the goods sold is recorded by debiting Accounts Receivable (or Cash) and crediting Sales. To illustrate, assume that Legend Guitars sold the 40 Jazz Series guitars during December for $850 per unit. The entry to the accounts receivable controlling account would be:

i.	Accounts Receivable			34 0 0 0 00	
	Sales				34 0 0 0 00
	Revenue received from guitars sold.				

PERIOD COSTS

In addition to product costs (direct materials, direct labor, and factory overhead), businesses also have period costs. Recall from the previous chapter that **period costs** are expenses that are used in generating revenue during the current period and are not involved in the manufacturing process. Period costs are generally classified into two categories: selling and administrative. *Selling expenses* are incurred in marketing the product and delivering the sold product to customers. *Administrative expenses* are incurred in the administration of the business and are not related to the manufacturing or selling functions.

For Legend Guitars, the following selling and administrative expenses were recorded for December:

j.	Sales Salaries Expense	2 0 0 0 00	
	Office Salaries Expense	1 5 0 0 00	
	Salaries Payable		3 5 0 0 00
	Recorded December period costs.		

SUMMARY OF COST FLOWS FOR LEGEND GUITARS

Exhibit 8, on page 52, shows the cost flow through the manufacturing accounts, together with summary details of the subsidiary ledgers for Legend Guitars. Entries in the accounts are identified by letters that refer to the summary journal entries introduced in the preceding section.

The balances of the general ledger controlling accounts are supported by their respective subsidiary ledgers. The balances of the three inventory accounts—Finished Goods, Work in Process, and Materials—represent the respective ending inventories of December 31 on the balance sheet. These balances are as follows:

Materials	$ 3,500
Work in process	21,000
Finished goods	10,250

The income statement for Legend Guitars would be as shown in Exhibit 9.

EXHIBIT 9

Income Statement of Legend Guitars

Legend Guitars
Income Statement
For the Month Ended December 31, 2008

Sales		$34,000
Cost of goods sold		20,150
Gross profit		$13,850
Selling and administrative expenses:		
Sales salaries expense	$2,000	
Office salaries expense	1,500	
Total selling and administrative expenses		3,500
Income from operations		$10,350

EXHIBIT 8   Flow of Manufacturing Costs for Legend Guitars

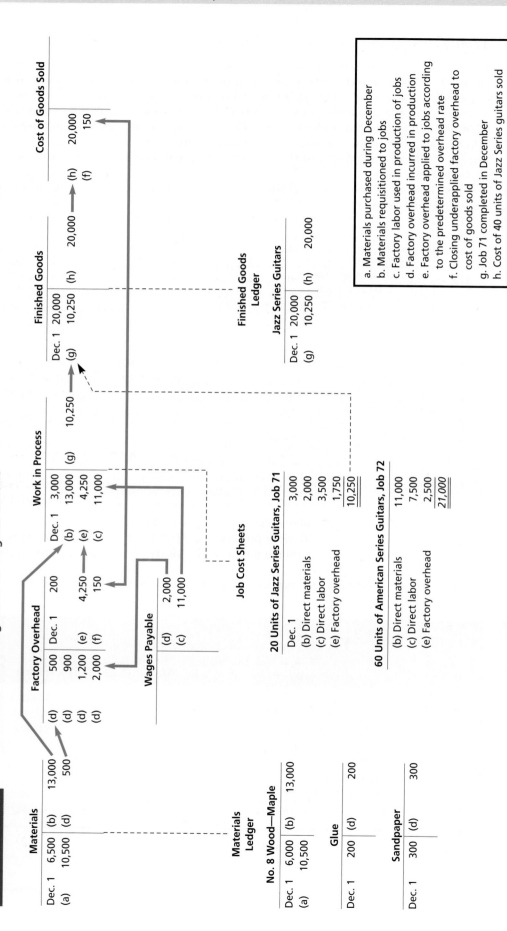

Materials

Dec. 1	6,500	(b)	13,000
(a)	10,500		

Materials Ledger

No. 8 Wood—Maple

Dec. 1	6,000	(b)	13,000
(a)	10,500		

Glue

Dec. 1	200	(d)	200

Sandpaper

Dec. 1	300	(d)	300

Factory Overhead

(d)	500	Dec. 1	200
(d)	900		
(d)	1,200	(e)	4,250
(d)	2,000	(f)	150

Wages Payable

	(d)	2,000
	(c)	11,000

Work in Process

Dec. 1	3,000	(g)	10,250
(b)	13,000		
(e)	4,250		
(c)	11,000		

Job Cost Sheets

20 Units of Jazz Series Guitars, Job 71

Dec. 1	3,000
(b) Direct materials	2,000
(c) Direct labor	3,500
(e) Factory overhead	1,750
	10,250

60 Units of American Series Guitars, Job 72

(b) Direct materials	11,000
(c) Direct labor	7,500
(e) Factory overhead	2,500
	21,000

Finished Goods

Dec. 1	20,000	(h)	20,000
(g)	10,250		

Finished Goods Ledger

Jazz Series Guitars

Dec. 1	20,000	(h)	20,000
(g)	10,250		

Cost of Goods Sold

(h)	20,000
(f)	150

a. Materials purchased during December
b. Materials requisitioned to jobs
c. Factory labor used in production of jobs
d. Factory overhead incurred in production
e. Factory overhead applied to jobs according to the predetermined overhead rate
f. Closing underapplied factory overhead to cost of goods sold
g. Job 71 completed in December
h. Cost of 40 units of Jazz Series guitars sold

Job Order Costing for Decision Making

objective **3**

Use job order cost information for decision making.

Major electric utilities such as Tennessee Valley Authority, Consolidated Edison Inc., and Pacific Gas and Electric Company use job order accounting to control the costs associated with major repairs and overhauls that occur during maintenance shutdowns.

The job order cost system that we developed in the previous sections can be used to evaluate an organization's cost performance. The unit costs for similar jobs can be compared over time to determine if costs are staying within expected ranges. If costs increase for some unexpected reason, the details in the job cost sheets can help discover the reasons.

To illustrate, Exhibit 10 shows the direct materials on the job cost sheets for Jobs 54 and 63 for Legend Guitars. The wood used in manufacturing guitars is measured in board feet. Since both job cost sheets refer to the same type and number of guitars, the direct materials cost per unit should be about the same. However, the materials cost per guitar for Job 54 is $100, while for Job 63 it is $125. The materials costs have increased since the guitars were produced for Job 54.

Job cost sheets can be used to investigate possible reasons for the increased cost. First, you should note that the price for direct materials did not change. Thus, the cost increase is not related to increasing prices. What about the wood consumption? This tells us a different story. The quantity of wood used to produce 40 guitars in Job 54 is 400 board feet. However, Job 63 required 500 board feet for the same number of guitars. How can this be explained? Any one of the following explanations is possible and could be investigated further:

1. There was a new employee that was not adequately trained for cutting the wood for guitars. As a result, the employee improperly cut and scrapped many pieces.
2. The lumber was of poor quality. As a result, the cutting operator ended up using and scrapping additional pieces of lumber.
3. The cutting tools were in need of repair. As a result, the cutting operators miscut and scrapped many pieces of wood.
4. The operator was careless. As a result of poor work, many pieces of cut wood had to be scrapped.
5. The instructions attached to the job were incorrect. The operator cut wood according to the instructions but discovered that the pieces would not fit. As a result, many pieces had to be scrapped.

You should note that many of these explanations are not necessarily related to operator error. Poor cost performance may be the result of root causes that are outside the control of the operator.

EXHIBIT 10

Comparing Data from Job Cost Sheets

Job 54
Item: 40 Jazz Series guitars

	Materials Quantity (board feet)	Materials Price	Materials Amount
Direct materials:			
No. 8 Wood—Maple	400	$10.00	$4,000
Direct materials per guitar			$100

Job 63
Item: 40 Jazz Series guitars

	Materials Quantity (board feet)	Materials Price	Materials Amount
Direct materials:			
No. 8 Wood—Maple	500	$10.00	$5,000
Direct materials per guitar			$125

Job Order Cost Systems for Professional Service Businesses

A job order cost accounting system may be useful to the management of a professional service business in planning and controlling operations. For example, an advertising agency, an attorney, and a physician all share the common characteristic of providing services to individual customers, clients, or patients. In such cases, the customer, client, or patient can be viewed as an individual job for which costs are accumulated.

Since the "product" of a service business is service, management's focus is on direct labor and overhead costs. The cost of any materials or supplies used in rendering services for a client is usually small and is normally included as part of the overhead.

The direct labor and overhead costs of rendering services to clients are accumulated in a work in process account. This account is supported by a cost ledger. A job cost sheet is used to accumulate the costs for each client's job. When a job is completed and the client is billed, the costs are transferred to a cost of services account. This account is similar to the cost of merchandise sold account for a merchandising business or the cost of goods sold account for a manufacturing business. A finished goods account and related finished goods ledger are not necessary, since the revenues associated with the services are recorded after the services have been provided. The flow of costs through a service business using a job order cost accounting system is shown in Exhibit 11.

EXHIBIT 11   Flow of Costs Through a Service Business

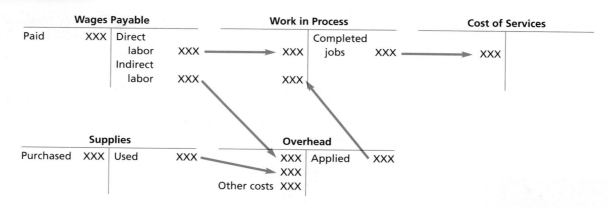

In practice, additional accounting considerations unique to service businesses may need to be considered. For example, a service business may bill clients on a weekly or monthly basis rather than waiting until a job is completed. In these situations, a portion of the costs related to each billing should be transferred from the work in process account to the cost of services account. A service business may also have advance billings that would be accounted for as deferred revenue until the services have been completed.

Business Connections

MAKING MONEY IN THE MOVIE BUSINESS

Movie making is a high risk venture. The movie must be produced and marketed before one dollar is received from the box office. If the movie is a hit, then all is well; but if the movie is a bomb, money will be lost. This is termed a "Blockbuster" business strategy and is common in businesses that have large up-front costs in the face of uncertain follow-up revenues, such as pharmaceuticals, video games, and publishing.

The profitability of a movie depends on its revenue and cost. A movie's cost is determined using job order costing; however, how costs are assigned to a movie is often complex and may be subject to disagreement. For example, in Hollywood's competitive environment, studios often negotiate payments to producers and actors based on a percentage of the film's

gross revenues. This is termed "contingent compensation." As movies become hits, compensation costs increase in proportion to the movie's revenues, which eats into a hit's profitability.

As the dollars involved get bigger, disagreements often develop between movie studios and actors or producers over the amount of contingent compensation. For example, the producer of the 2002 hit movie *Chicago* sued Miramax Film Corp. for failing to include foreign receipts and DVD sales in the revenue that was used to determine his payments. The controversial nature of contingent compensation is illustrated by the suit's claim that the accounting for contingent compensation leads to confusing and meaningless results.

© GARY BUSS/TAXI/GETTY IMAGES

At a Glance

1. Describe accounting systems used by manufacturing businesses.

Key Points	Key Learning Outcomes	Example Exercises	Practice Exercises
A cost accounting system accumulates product costs. Management uses cost accounting systems to determine product cost, establish product prices, control operations, and develop financial statements. The two primary cost accounting systems are job order and process cost systems. Job order cost systems accumulate costs for each quantity of product that passes through the factory. Process cost systems accumulate costs for each department or process within the factory.	• Describe a cost accounting system. • Describe a job order cost system. • Describe a process cost system.		

(continued)

2. Describe and prepare summary journal entries for a job order cost accounting system.

Key Points	Key Learning Outcomes	Example Exercises	Practice Exercises
A job order cost system accumulates costs for each quantity of product, or "job," that passes through the factory. Direct materials, direct labor, and factory overhead are accumulated on the job cost sheet, which is the subsidiary cost ledger for each job. Direct materials and direct labor are assigned to individual jobs based on the quantity used. Factory overhead costs are assigned to each job based on an activity base that reflects the use of factory overhead costs. As a job is finished, its costs are transferred to the finished goods ledger. When goods are sold, the cost is transferred from finished goods inventory to cost of goods sold.	• Describe the flow of materials and how materials costs are assigned in a job order cost system.		
	• Prepare the journal entry to record materials used in production.	2-1	2-1A, 2-1B
	• Describe how factory labor hours are recorded and how labor costs are assigned in a job order cost system.		
	• Prepare the journal entry to record factory labor used in production.	2-2	2-2A, 2-2B
	• Describe and illustrate how factory overhead costs are accumulated and assigned in a job order cost system.	2-3 2-4	2-3A, 2-3B 2-4A, 2-4B
	• Compute the predetermined overhead rate.	2-4	2-4A, 2-4B
	• Describe and illustrate how to dispose of the balance in the factory overhead account.		
	• Describe and illustrate how costs are accumulated for work in process and finished goods inventory and assigned to cost of goods sold in a job order cost system.	2-5 2-6	2-5A, 2-5B 2-6A, 2-6B
	• Describe and illustrate the flow of costs in a job order cost system.		

3. Use job order cost information for decision making.

Key Points	Key Learning Outcomes	Example Exercises	Practice Exercises
Job order cost systems can be used to evaluate cost performance. Unit costs can be compared over time to determine if product costs are staying within expected ranges.	• Describe and illustrate how job cost sheets can be used to investigate possible reasons for increased product costs.		

4. Diagram the flow of costs for a service business that uses a job order cost accounting system.

Key Points	Key Learning Outcomes	Example Exercises	Practice Exercises
Job order cost accounting systems can be used by service businesses to plan and control operations. Since the product is a service, the focus is on direct labor and overhead costs. The costs of providing a service are accumulated in a work in process account and transferred to a cost of services account upon completion.	• Describe how service businesses use a job order cost system.		

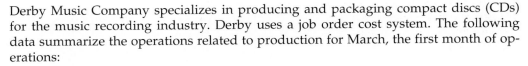

Key Terms

activity base (45)
activity-based costing (46)
cost accounting system (39)
cost allocation (45)
finished goods ledger (50)
job cost sheet (42)
job order cost system (39)

materials ledger (42)
materials requisitions (42)
overapplied factory overhead
 (46)
period costs (51)
predetermined factory overhead
 rate (45)

process cost system (40)
receiving report (42)
time tickets (43)
underapplied factory overhead
 (46)

Illustrative Problem

Derby Music Company specializes in producing and packaging compact discs (CDs) for the music recording industry. Derby uses a job order cost system. The following data summarize the operations related to production for March, the first month of operations:

a. Materials purchased on account, $15,500.
b. Materials requisitioned and labor used:

	Materials	Factory Labor
Job No. 100	$2,650	$1,770
Job No. 101	1,240	650
Job No. 102	980	420
Job No. 103	3,420	1,900
Job No. 104	1,000	500
Job No. 105	2,100	1,760
For general factory use	450	650

c. Factory overhead costs incurred on account, $2,700.
d. Depreciation of machinery, $1,750.
e. Factory overhead is applied at a rate of 70% of direct labor cost.
f. Jobs completed: Nos. 100, 101, 102, 104.
g. Jobs 100, 101, and 102 were shipped, and customers were billed for $8,100, $3,800, and $3,500, respectively.

Instructions

1. Journalize the entries to record the transactions identified above.
2. Determine the account balances for Work in Process and Finished Goods.
3. Prepare a schedule of unfinished jobs to support the balance in the work in process account.
4. Prepare a schedule of completed jobs on hand to support the balance in the finished goods account.

Solution

1. a.	Materials	15,500		
	Accounts Payable		15,500	
b.	Work in Process	11,390		
	Materials		11,390	
	Work in Process	7,000		
	Wages Payable		7,000	
	Factory Overhead	1,100		
	Materials		450	
	Wages Payable		650	*(continued)*

c.	Factory Overhead	2,700	
	Accounts Payable		2,700
d.	Factory Overhead	1,750	
	Accumulated Depreciation—Machinery		1,750
e.	Work in Process	4,900	
	Factory Overhead (70% of $7,000)		4,900
f.	Finished Goods	11,548	
	Work in Process		11,548

Computation of the cost of jobs finished:

Job	Direct Materials	Direct Labor	Factory Overhead	Total
Job No. 100	$2,650	$1,770	$1,239	$ 5,659
Job No. 101	1,240	650	455	2,345
Job No. 102	980	420	294	1,694
Job No. 104	1,000	500	350	1,850
				$11,548

g.	Accounts Receivable	15,400	
	Sales		15,400
	Cost of Goods Sold	9,698	
	Finished Goods		9,698

Cost of jobs sold computation:

Job No. 100	$5,659
Job No. 101	2,345
Job No. 102	1,694
	$9,698

2. Work in Process: $11,742 ($11,390 + $7,000 + $4,900 − $11,548)
Finished Goods: $1,850 ($11,548 − $9,698)

3.

Schedule of Unfinished Jobs

Job	Direct Materials	Direct Labor	Factory Overhead	Total
Job No. 103	$3,420	$1,900	$1,330	$ 6,650
Job No. 105	2,100	1,760	1,232	5,092
Balance of Work in Process, March 31				$11,742

4.

Schedule of Completed Jobs

Job No. 104:

Direct materials	$1,000
Direct labor	500
Factory overhead	350
Balance of Finished Goods, March 31	$1,850

Self-Examination Questions

(Answers at End of Chapter)

1. For which of the following would the job order cost system be appropriate?
   A. Antique furniture repair shop
   B. Rubber manufacturer
   C. Coal manufacturer
   D. Computer chip manufacturer

2. The journal entry to record the requisition of materials to the factory in a job order cost system is a debit to:
   A. Materials.
   B. Accounts Payable.
   C. Work in Process.
   D. Cost of Goods Sold.

3. Job order cost sheets accumulate all of the following costs *except* for:
   A. direct materials.
   B. indirect materials.
   C. direct labor.
   D. factory overhead applied.

4. A company estimated $420,000 of factory overhead cost and 16,000 direct labor hours for the period. During the period, a job was completed with $4,500 of direct materials and $3,000 of direct labor. The direct labor rate was $15 per hour. What is the factory overhead applied to this job?
   A. $2,100   C. $78,750
   B. $5,250   D. $420,000

5. If the factory overhead account has a credit balance, factory overhead is said to be:
   A. underapplied.   C. underabsorbed.
   B. overapplied.   D. in error.

Eye Openers

1. How is product cost information used by managers?
2. a. Name two principal types of cost accounting systems.
   b. Which system provides for a separate record of each particular quantity of product that passes through the factory?
   c. Which system accumulates the costs for each department or process within the factory?
3. What kind of firm would use a job order cost system?

4. Hewlett-Packard Company assembles ink jet printers in which a high volume of standardized units are assembled and tested. Is the job order cost system appropriate in this situation?
5. Which account is used in the job order cost system to accumulate direct materials, direct labor, and factory overhead applied to production costs for individual jobs?
6. How does the use of the materials requisition help control the issuance of materials from the storeroom?
7. What document is the source for (a) debiting the accounts in the materials ledger and (b) crediting the accounts in the materials ledger?
8. What is a job cost sheet?
9. a. Differentiate between the clock card and the time ticket.
   b. Why should the total time reported on an employee's time tickets for a payroll period be compared with the time reported on the employee's clock cards for the same period?
10. Describe the source of the data for debiting Work in Process for (a) direct materials, (b) direct labor, and (c) factory overhead.
11. Discuss how the predetermined factory overhead rate can be used in job order cost accounting to assist management in pricing jobs.
12. a. How is a predetermined factory overhead rate calculated?
    b. Name three common bases used in calculating the rate.
13. a. What is (1) overapplied factory overhead and (2) underapplied factory overhead?
    b. If the factory overhead account has a debit balance, was factory overhead underapplied or overapplied?
    c. If the factory overhead account has a credit balance at the end of the first month of the fiscal year, where will the amount of this balance be reported on the interim balance sheet?
14. At the end of the fiscal year, there was a relatively minor balance in the factory overhead account. What procedure can be used for disposing of the balance in the account?
15. What account is the controlling account for (a) the materials ledger, (b) the job cost sheets, and (c) the finished goods ledger?
16. How can job cost information be used to identify cost improvement opportunities?
17. Describe how a job order cost system can be used for professional service businesses.

Practice Exercises

PE 2-1A
Cost of materials issuances
obj. 2

On November 7, Taylor Company purchased 24,000 units of raw materials at $10 per unit. On November 11, raw materials were requisitioned for production as follows: 1,600 units for Job 80 at $8 per unit and 1,250 units for Job 82 at $10 per unit. Journalize the entry on November 7 to record the purchase and on November 11 to record the requisition from the materials storeroom.

PE 2-1B
Cost of materials issuances
obj. 2

On October 12, Blakely Company purchased 8,000 units of raw materials at $6 per unit. On October 21, raw materials were requisitioned for production as follows: 750 units for Job 50 at $4 per unit and 600 units for Job 51 at $6 per unit. Journalize the entry on October 12 to record the purchase and on October 21 to record the requisition from the materials storeroom.

PE 2-2A
Entry for factory labor costs
obj. 2

During November, Taylor Company accumulated 1,000 hours of direct labor costs on Job 80 and 800 hours on Job 82. The total direct labor was incurred at a rate of $14 per direct labor hour for Job 80 and $12 per direct labor hour for Job 82. Journalize the entry to record the flow of labor costs into production during November.

PE 2-2B
Entry for factory labor costs
obj. 2

During October, Blakely Company accumulated 1,500 hours of direct labor costs on Job 50 and 1,250 hours on Job 51. The total direct labor was incurred at a rate of $20 per direct labor hour for Job 50 and $16 per direct labor hour for Job 51. Journalize the entry to record the flow of labor costs into production during October.

PE 2-3A
Entry for factory overhead costs
obj. 2

During November, Taylor Company incurred factory overhead costs as follows: indirect materials, $6,500; indirect labor, $8,000; utilities cost, $3,500; and depreciation, $2,800. Journalize the entry to record the factory overhead incurred during November.

PE 2-3B
Entry for factory overhead costs
obj. 2

During October, Blakely Company incurred factory overhead costs as follows: indirect materials, $4,000; indirect labor, $4,700; utilities cost, $2,000; and depreciation $2,600. Journalize the entry to record the factory overhead incurred during October.

PE 2-4A
Predetermined factory overhead rate and applying factory overhead
obj. 2

Taylor Company estimates that total factory overhead costs will be $250,000 for the year. Direct labor hours are estimated to be 50,000. For Taylor Company, (a) determine the predetermined factory overhead rate, (b) determine the amount of factory overhead applied to Jobs 80 and 82 in November using the data on direct labor hours from Practice Exercise 2-2A, and (c) prepare the journal entry to apply factory overhead to both jobs in November according to the predetermined overhead rate.

PE 2-4B
Predetermined factory overhead rate and applying factory overhead
obj. 2

Blakely Company estimates that total factory overhead costs will be $160,000 for the year. Direct labor hours are estimated to be 20,000. For Blakely Company (a) determine the predetermined factory overhead rate, (b) determine the amount of factory overhead applied to Jobs 50 and 51 in October using the data on direct labor hours from Practice Exercise 2-2B, and (c) prepare the journal entry to apply factory overhead to both jobs in October according to the predetermined overhead rate.

PE 2-5A
Job costs
obj. 2

At the end of November, Taylor Company had completed Jobs 80 and 82. Job 80 is for 600 units, and Job 82 is for 900 units. Using the data from Practice Exercises 2-1A, 2-2A, and 2-4A, determine (a) the balance on the job cost sheets for Jobs 80 and 82 at the end of November and (b) the cost per unit for Jobs 80 and 82 at the end of November.

PE 2-5B
Job costs
obj. 2

At the end of October, Blakely Company had completed Jobs 50 and 51. Job 50 is for 1,500 units, and Job 51 is for 1,200 units. Using the data from Practice Exercises 2-1B, 2-2B, and 2-4B, determine (a) the balance on the job cost sheets for Jobs 50 and 51 at the end of October and (b) the cost per unit for Jobs 50 and 51 at the end of October.

PE 2-6A
Cost of goods sold
obj. 2

Venson Company completed 40,000 units during the year at a cost of $500,000. The beginning finished goods inventory was 5,000 units at $100,000. Determine the cost of goods sold for 30,000 units, assuming a FIFO cost flow.

PE 2-6B
Cost of goods sold
obj. 2

Berlin Company completed 90,000 units during the year at a cost of $900,000. The beginning finished goods inventory was 10,000 units at $75,000. Determine the cost of goods sold for 70,000 units, assuming a FIFO cost flow.

Exercises

EX 2-1
Transactions in a job order cost system
obj. 2

Five selected transactions for the current month are indicated by letters in the following T accounts in a job order cost accounting system:

Materials		Work in Process	
	(a)	(a)	(d)
		(b)	
		(c)	

Wages Payable		Finished Goods	
	(b)	(d)	(e)

Factory Overhead		Cost of Goods Sold	
(a)	(c)	(e)	
(b)			

Describe each of the five transactions.

EX 2-2
Cost flow relationships
obj. 2

✓ c. $271,500

The following information is available for the first month of operations of Korv Inc., a manufacturer of art and craft items:

Sales	$775,000
Gross profit	265,000
Indirect labor	63,000
Indirect materials	32,000
Other factory overhead	17,500
Materials purchased	303,000
Total manufacturing costs for the period	620,000
Materials inventory, end of period	35,000

Using the above information, determine the following missing amounts:

a. Cost of goods sold
b. Direct materials cost
c. Direct labor cost

EX 2-3
*Cost of materials
issuances under the
FIFO method*

obj. 2

✓ *b. $2,400*

An incomplete subsidiary ledger of wire cable for August is as follows:

RECEIVED			ISSUED			BALANCE			
Receiving Report Number	Quantity	Unit Price	Materials Requisition Number	Quantity	Amount	Date	Quantity	Amount	Unit Price
						Aug. 1	200	$3,200	$16.00
110	240	$18.00				Aug. 3			
			108	300		Aug. 5			
139	160	20.00				Aug. 19			
			120	180		Aug. 25			

a. Complete the materials issuances and balances for the wire cable subsidiary ledger under FIFO.
b. Determine the balance of wire cable at the end of August.
c. Journalize the summary entry to transfer materials to work in process.
d. ▭▶ Explain how the materials ledger might be used as an aid in maintaining inventory quantities on hand.

EX 2-4
*Entry for issuing
materials*

obj. 2

Materials issued for the current month are as follows:

Requisition No.	Material	Job No.	Amount
811	Aluminum	511	$10,400
812	Steel	514	18,650
813	Plastic	526	875
814	Abrasives	Indirect	325
815	Titanium alloy	533	42,300

Journalize the entry to record the issuance of materials.

EX 2-5
Entries for materials

obj. 2

✓ *c. Fabric, $31,700*

Combes Furniture Company manufactures furniture. Combes uses a job order cost system. Balances on November 1 from the materials ledger are as follows:

Fabric	$ 33,500
Polyester filling	8,100
Lumber	107,400
Glue	1,600

The materials purchased during November are summarized from the receiving reports as follows:

Fabric	$549,900
Polyester filling	104,200
Lumber	969,500
Glue	14,200

Materials were requisitioned to individual jobs as follows:

	Fabric	Polyester Filling	Lumber	Glue	Total
Job 11	$362,200	$64,500	$611,300		$1,038,000
Job 12	121,700	13,900	198,600		334,200
Job 13	67,800	10,300	182,400		260,500
Factory overhead—indirect materials				$11,700	11,700
Total	$551,700	$88,700	$992,300	$11,700	$1,644,400

The glue is not a significant cost, so it is treated as indirect materials (factory overhead).

a. Journalize the entry to record the purchase of materials in November.
b. Journalize the entry to record the requisition of materials in November.
c. Determine the November 30 balances that would be shown in the materials ledger accounts.

EX 2-6
Entry for factory labor costs
obj. 2

A summary of the time tickets for the current month follows:

Job No.	Amount	Job No.	Amount
101	$1,620	141	$ 1,780
122	1,590	Indirect labor	13,400
133	760	143	3,330
139	5,210	147	1,080

Journalize the entry to record the factory labor costs.

EX 2-7
Entry for factory labor costs
obj. 2

The weekly time tickets indicate the following distribution of labor hours for three direct labor employees:

	Hours			
	Job 111	Job 112	Job 113	Process Improvement
Johnny Daniels	18	10	5	7
Jack Walker	7	8	23	2
Jim Morgan	8	12	16	4

The direct labor rate earned by the three employees is as follows:

Daniels	$11.40
Walker	13.50
Morgan	11.75

The process improvement category includes training, quality improvement, housekeeping, and other indirect tasks.

a. Journalize the entry to record the factory labor costs for the week.
b. Assume that Jobs 111 and 112 were completed but not sold during the week and that Job 113 remained incomplete at the end of the week. How would the direct labor costs for all three jobs be reflected on the financial statements at the end of the week?

EX 2-8
Entries for direct labor and factory overhead
obj. 2

Chasse Homes Inc. manufactures mobile homes. Chasse uses a job order cost system. The time tickets from October jobs are summarized below.

Job 502	$2,352
Job 503	1,440
Job 504	960
Job 505	1,320
Factory supervision	2,760

Factory overhead is applied to jobs on the basis of a predetermined overhead rate of $20 per direct labor hour. The direct labor rate is $12 per hour.

a. Journalize the entry to record the factory labor costs.
b. Journalize the entry to apply factory overhead to production for October.

EX 2-9
Factory overhead rates, entries, and account balance
obj. 2

✓ *b. $13.00 per direct labor hour*

Staten Island Turbine operates two factories. The company applies factory overhead to jobs on the basis of machine hours in Factory 1 and on the basis of direct labor hours in Factory 2. Estimated factory overhead costs, direct labor hours, and machine hours are as follows:

	Factory 1	Factory 2
Estimated factory overhead cost for fiscal year beginning May 1	$236,800	$118,300
Estimated direct labor hours for year		9,100
Estimated machine hours for year	12,800	
Actual factory overhead costs for May	$23,200	$11,625
Actual direct labor hours for May		885
Actual machine hours for May	1,270	

a. Determine the factory overhead rate for Factory 1.
b. Determine the factory overhead rate for Factory 2.
c. Journalize the entries to apply factory overhead to production in each factory for May.
d. Determine the balances of the factory accounts for each factory as of May 31, and indicate whether the amounts represent overapplied or underapplied factory overhead.

EX 2-10
Predetermined factory overhead rate
obj. 2

The Engine Shop uses a job order cost system to determine the cost of performing engine repair work. Estimated costs and expenses for the coming period are as follows:

Engine parts	$ 650,750
Shop direct labor	520,625
Shop and repair equipment depreciation	12,800
Shop supervisor salaries	93,125
Shop property tax	22,300
Shop supplies	12,650
Advertising expense	18,100
Administrative office salaries	61,600
Administrative office depreciation expense	8,050
Total costs and expenses	$1,400,000

The average shop direct labor rate is $17 per hour.
Determine the predetermined shop overhead rate per direct labor hour.

EX 2-11
Predetermined factory overhead rate
obj. 2

✓ *a. $175 per hour*

San Jose Medical Center has a single operating room that is used by local physicians to perform surgical procedures. The cost of using the operating room is accumulated by each patient procedure and includes the direct materials costs (drugs and medical devices), physician surgical time, and operating room overhead. On August 1 of the current year, the annual operating room overhead is estimated to be:

Disposable supplies	$116,700
Depreciation expense	18,000
Utilities	11,200
Nurse salaries	164,000
Technician wages	57,600
Total operating room overhead	$367,500

The overhead costs will be assigned to procedures based on the number of surgical room hours. The Medical Center expects to use the operating room an average of seven hours per day, six days per week. In addition, the operating room will be shut down two weeks per year for general repairs.

a. Determine the predetermined operating room overhead rate for the year.
b. Allison Mann had a 5-hour procedure on August 10. How much operating room overhead would be charged to her procedure, using the rate determined in part (a)?
c. During August, the operating room was used 182 hours. The actual overhead costs incurred for August were $30,700. Determine the overhead under- or overapplied for the period.

EX 2-12
Entry for jobs completed;
cost of unfinished jobs

obj. 2

✓ b. $5,800

The following account appears in the ledger after only part of the postings have been completed for January:

Work in Process	
Balance, January 1	$15,500
Direct materials	86,200
Direct labor	64,300
Factory overhead	93,700

Jobs finished during January are summarized as follows:

Job 320	$57,600	Job 327	$26,100
Job 326	75,400	Job 350	94,800

a. Journalize the entry to record the jobs completed.
b. Determine the cost of the unfinished jobs at January 31.

EX 2-13
Entries for factory costs
and jobs completed

obj. 2

✓ d. $18,340

Tobias Printing Inc. began printing operations on July 1. Jobs 101 and 102 were completed during the month, and all costs applicable to them were recorded on the related cost sheets. Jobs 103 and 104 are still in process at the end of the month, and all applicable costs except factory overhead have been recorded on the related cost sheets. In addition to the materials and labor charged directly to the jobs, $725 of indirect materials and $6,380 of indirect labor were used during the month. The cost sheets for the four jobs entering production during the month are as follows, in summary form:

Job 101		Job 102	
Direct materials	6,800	Direct materials	3,000
Direct labor	1,560	Direct labor	880
Factory overhead	3,900	Factory overhead	2,200
Total	12,260	Total	6,080

Job 103		Job 104	
Direct materials	8,700	Direct materials	1,500
Direct labor	1,350	Direct labor	500
Factory overhead		Factory overhead	

Journalize the summary entry to record each of the following operations for July (one entry for each operation):

a. Direct and indirect materials used.
b. Direct and indirect labor used.
c. Factory overhead applied (a single overhead rate is used based on direct labor cost).
d. Completion of Jobs 101 and 102.

EX 2-14
Financial statements of a
manufacturing firm

obj. 2

✓ a. Income from
operations, $47,600

The following events took place for Wreckin Ronnie Inc. during July 2008, the first month of operations as a producer of road bikes:

- Purchased $165,800 of materials.
- Used $147,600 of direct materials in production.
- Incurred $96,250 of direct labor wages.
- Applied factory overhead at a rate of 80% of direct labor cost.
- Transferred $302,900 of work in process to finished goods.
- Sold goods with a cost of $301,300.
- Sold goods for $520,000.
- Incurred $119,000 of selling expenses.
- Incurred $52,100 of administrative expenses.

a. Prepare the July income statement for Wreckin Ronnie. Assume that Wreckin Ronnie uses the perpetual inventory method.
b. Determine the inventory balances at the end of the first month of operations.

EX 2-15

Decision making with job order costs

obj. 3

Bronx Machinery Inc. is a job shop. The management of Bronx Machinery uses the cost information from the job sheets to assess its cost performance. Information on the total cost, product type, and quantity of items produced is as follows:

Date	Job No.	Quantity	Product	Amount
Jan. 2	101	450	105X	$10,350
Jan. 24	125	1,500	205B	16,500
Feb. 18	144	750	205B	9,000
Mar. 4	162	500	105X	10,000
Mar. 28	173	1,100	120T	6,600
May 20	190	1,250	120T	11,250
June 10	201	450	105X	6,750
Aug. 9	210	1,900	120T	22,800
Sept. 16	215	500	205B	5,500
Nov. 11	227	650	105X	7,800
Dec. 9	238	1,050	120T	16,800

a. Develop a graph for *each* product (three graphs), with Job No. (in date order) on the horizontal axis and unit cost on the vertical axis. Use this information to determine Bronx Machinery's cost performance over time for the three products.

b. ▭▬▶ What additional information would you require to investigate Bronx Machinery's cost performance more precisely?

EX 2-16

Decision making with job order costs

obj. 3

Sharp Trophies Inc. uses a job order cost system for determining the cost to manufacture award products (plaques and trophies). Among the company's products is an engraved plaque that is awarded to participants who complete an executive education program at a local university. The company sells the plaque to the university for $75 each.

Each plaque has a brass plate engraved with the name of the participant. Engraving requires approximately 6 minutes per name. Improperly engraved names must be redone. The plate is screwed to a walnut backboard. This assembly takes approximately 3 minutes per unit. Improper assembly must be redone using a new walnut backboard.

During the first half of the year, the university had two separate executive education classes. The job cost sheets for the two separate jobs indicated the following information:

Job 103	March 4		
	Cost per Unit	**Units**	**Job Cost**
Direct materials:			
Wood	$20.00/unit	30 units	$ 600.00
Brass	18.00/unit	30 units	540.00
Engraving labor	40.00/hr.	3 hrs.	120.00
Assembly labor	28.00/hr.	1.5 hrs.	42.00
Factory overhead	30.00/hr.	6 hrs.	180.00
			$1,482.00
Plaques shipped		/	30
Cost per plaque		$	49.40

Job 116	April 15		
	Cost per Unit	**Units**	**Job Cost**
Direct materials:			
Wood	$20.00/unit	25 units	$ 500.00
Brass	18.00/unit	25 units	450.00
Engraving labor	40.00/hr.	4 hrs.	160.00
Assembly labor	28.00/hr.	2 hrs.	56.00
Factory overhead	30.00/hr.	4 hrs.	120.00
			$1,286.00
Plaques shipped		/	20
Cost per plaque		$	64.30

a. Why did the cost per plaque increase from $49.40 to $64.30?

b. What improvements would you recommend for Sharp Trophies Inc.?

EX 2-17
*Job order cost accounting
entries for a service
business*
obj. 4

The consulting firm of Reznick and Fedder accumulates costs associated with individual cases, using a job order cost system. The following transactions occurred during May:

May 7 Charged 440 hours of professional (lawyer) time to the Daley Co. breech of contract suit to prepare for the trial, at a rate of $175 per hour.

11 Reimbursed travel costs to employees for depositions related to the Daley case, $24,000.

22 Charged 225 hours of professional time for the Daley trial at a rate of $250 per hour.

25 Received invoice from consultants Rucker and Putnam for $47,000 for expert testimony related to the Daley trial.

30 Applied office overhead at a rate of $45 per professional hour charged to the Daley case.

31 Paid secretarial and administrative salaries of $20,000 for the month.

31 Used office supplies for the month, $6,000.

31 Paid professional salaries of $55,000 for the month.

31 Billed Daley $260,000 for successful defense of the case.

a. Provide the journal entries for each of the above transactions.
b. How much office overhead is over- or underapplied?
c. Determine the gross profit on the Daley case, assuming that over- or underapplied office overhead is closed annually to cost of services.

EX 2-18
*Job order cost accounting
entries for a service
business*
obj. 4

✓ d. Dr. Cost of Services,
$609,800

Tec Trends Inc. provides advertising services for clients across the nation. Tec Trends is presently working on four projects, each for a different client. Tec Trends accumulates costs for each account (client) on the basis of both direct costs and allocated indirect costs. The direct costs include the charged time of professional personnel and media purchases (air time and ad space). Overhead is allocated to each project as a percentage of media purchases. The predetermined overhead rate is 40% of media purchases.

On July 1, the four advertising projects had the following accumulated costs:

	July 1 Balances
Spitzer Hotel	$120,000
Gonzalez Bank	15,000
Gulliani Beverage	66,000
Koch Rentals	18,000

During July, Tec Trends Inc. incurred the following direct labor and media purchase costs related to preparing advertising for each of the four accounts:

	Direct Labor	Media Purchases
Spitzer Hotel	$ 42,000	$154,000
Gonzalez Bank	17,000	143,000
Gulliani Beverage	81,000	128,000
Koch Rentals	107,000	83,000
Total	$247,000	$508,000

At the end of July, both the Spitzer Hotel and Gonzalez Bank campaigns were completed. The costs of completed campaigns are debited to the cost of services account.
Journalize the summary entry to record each of the following for the month:

a. Direct labor costs
b. Media purchases
c. Overhead applied
d. Completion of Spitzer Hotel and Gonzalez Bank campaigns

Problems Series A

PR 2-1A
Entries for costs in a job order cost system

obj. 2

Goldberg Apparel Company uses a job order cost system. The following data summarize the operations related to production for March:

a. Materials purchased on account, $233,000.
b. Materials requisitioned, $208,300, of which $5,600 was for general factory use.
c. Factory labor used, $190,500, of which $62,500 was indirect.
d. Other costs incurred on account were for factory overhead, $89,300; selling expenses, $64,000; and administrative expenses, $37,800.
e. Prepaid expenses expired for factory overhead were $7,500; for selling expenses, $1,300; and for administrative expenses, $1,250.
f. Depreciation of factory equipment was $18,900; of office equipment, $14,700; and of store equipment, $2,600.
g. Factory overhead costs applied to jobs, $190,000.
h. Jobs completed, $583,300.
i. Cost of goods sold, $577,700.

Instructions
Journalize the entries to record the summarized operations.

PR 2-2A
Entries and schedules for unfinished jobs and completed jobs

obj. 2

✓ *3. Work in Process balance, $131,975*

Godwin Fixtures Co. uses a job order cost system. The following data summarize the operations related to production for April 2008, the first month of operations:

a. Materials purchased on account, $137,000.
b. Materials requisitioned and factory labor used:

Job	Materials	Factory Labor
No. 601	$18,100	$17,000
No. 602	20,000	25,500
No. 603	13,050	9,700
No. 604	34,500	33,550
No. 605	15,700	14,800
No. 606	17,800	18,300
For general factory use	6,600	47,000

c. Factory overhead costs incurred on account, $4,950.
d. Depreciation of machinery and equipment, $3,700.
e. The factory overhead rate is $53 per machine hour. Machine hours used:

Job	Machine Hours
No. 601	215
No. 602	230
No. 603	175
No. 604	300
No. 605	198
No. 606	225
Total	1,343

f. Jobs completed: 601, 602, 603, and 605.
g. Jobs were shipped and customers were billed as follows: Job 601, $72,750; Job 602, $88,780; Job 605, $74,500.

Instructions
1. Journalize the entries to record the summarized operations.
2. Post the appropriate entries to T accounts for Work in Process and Finished Goods, using the identifying letters as dates. Insert memorandum account balances as of the end of the month.

3. Prepare a schedule of unfinished jobs to support the balance in the work in process account.
4. Prepare a schedule of completed jobs on hand to support the balance in the finished goods account.

PR 2-3A
Job order cost sheet
objs. 2, 3

If the working papers correlating with the textbook are not used, omit Problem 2-3A.

Nu-Life Furniture Company refinishes and reupholsters furniture. Nu-Life uses a job order cost system. When a prospective customer asks for a price quote on a job, the estimated cost data are inserted on an unnumbered job cost sheet. If the offer is accepted, a number is assigned to the job, and the costs incurred are recorded in the usual manner on the job cost sheet. After the job is completed, reasons for the variances between the estimated and actual costs are noted on the sheet. The data are then available to management in evaluating the efficiency of operations and in preparing quotes on future jobs. On July 1, 2008, an estimate of $1,512.64 for reupholstering two chairs and a couch was given to Ed Douthett. The estimate was based on the following data:

Estimated direct materials:	
17 meters at $23 per meter	$ 391.00
Estimated direct labor:	
24 hours at $14 per hour	336.00
Estimated factory overhead (65% of direct labor cost)	218.40
Total estimated costs	$ 945.40
Markup (60% of production costs)	567.24
Total estimate	$1,512.64

On July 4, the chairs and couch were picked up from the residence of Ed Douthett, 411 Austin Lane, Alexandria, with a commitment to return them on September 13. The job was completed on September 10.
    The related materials requisitions and time tickets are summarized as follows:

Materials Requisition No.	Description	Amount
3480	7 meters at $23	$161
3492	11 meters at $23	253

Time Ticket No.	Description	Amount
H143	13 hours at $14	$182
H151	15 hours at $14	210

Instructions
1. Complete that portion of the job order cost sheet that would be prepared when the estimate is given to the customer.
2. Assign number 00-10-23 to the job, record the costs incurred, and complete the job order cost sheet. Comment on the reasons for the variances between actual costs and estimated costs. For this purpose, assume that two meters of materials were spoiled, the factory overhead rate has been proved to be satisfactory, and an inexperienced employee performed the work.

PR 2-4A
Analyzing manufacturing cost accounts
obj. 2

✓1. G. $245,250

Dupont Fishing Equipment Company manufactures fishing rods in a wide variety of lengths and weights. The following incomplete ledger accounts refer to transactions that are summarized for November:

Materials					
Nov. 1	Balance	10,000	Nov. 30	Requisitions	(A)
31	Purchases	120,000			

(continued)

Work in Process

Nov. 1	Balance	(B)	Nov. 30	Completed jobs	(F)
30	Materials	(C)			
30	Direct labor	(D)			
30	Factory overhead applied	(E)			

Finished Goods

Nov. 1	Balance	0	Nov. 30	Cost of goods sold	(G)
30	Completed jobs	(F)			

Wages Payable

		Nov. 30	Wages incurred	130,000

Factory Overhead

Nov. 1	Balance	2,500	Nov. 30	Factory overhead applied	(E)
30	Indirect labor	(H)			
30	Indirect materials	3,000			
30	Other overhead	60,000			

In addition, the following information is available:

a. Materials and direct labor were applied to six jobs in November:

Job No.	Style	Quantity	Direct Materials	Direct Labor
No. 111	DL-8	70	$ 15,000	$ 12,000
No. 112	DL-18	100	23,000	18,000
No. 113	DL-11	120	27,500	25,000
No. 114	SL-101	100	11,000	12,500
No. 115	SL-110	175	28,000	27,500
No. 116	DL-14	80	15,000	14,500
Total		645	$119,500	$109,500

b. Factory overhead is applied to each job at a rate of 75% of direct labor cost.
c. The November 1 Work in Process balance consisted of two jobs, as follows:

Job No.	Style	Work in Process, November 1
Job 111	DL-8	$20,000
Job 112	DL-18	30,000
Total		$50,000

d. Customer jobs completed and units sold in November were as follows:

Job No.	Style	Completed in November	Units Sold in November
Job 111	DL-8	X	60
Job 112	DL-18	X	100
Job 113	DL-11	X	80
Job 114	SL-101		0
Job 115	SL-110	X	150
Job 116	DL-14		0

Instructions

1. Determine the missing amounts associated with each letter. Provide supporting calculations by completing a table with the following headings:

Job No.	Quantity	Nov. 1 Work in Process	Direct Materials	Direct Labor	Factory Overhead	Total Cost	Unit Cost	Units Sold	Cost of Goods Sold

2. Determine the November 30 balances for each of the inventory accounts and factory overhead.

PR 2-5A
Flow of costs and income statement

obj. 2

✓ *1. Income from operations, $2,998,000*

Outdoor Software Inc. is a designer, manufacturer, and distributor of software for microcomputers. A new product, *Landscape 2008*, was released for production and distribution in early 2008. In January, $700,000 was spent to design print advertisement. For the first six months of 2008, the company spent $2,500,000 promoting *Landscape 2008* in trade magazines. The product was ready for manufacture on January 10, 2008.

Outdoor uses a job order cost system to accumulate costs associated with each software title. Direct materials unit costs are:

Blank CD	$ 4.50
Packaging	8.00
Manual	11.00
Total	$23.50

The actual production process for the software product is fairly straightforward. First, blank CDs are brought to a CD copying machine. The copying machine requires 1 hour per 1,500 CDs.

After the program is copied onto the CD, the CD is brought to assembly, where assembly personnel pack the CD and manual for shipping. The direct labor cost for this work is $0.75 per unit.

The completed packages are then sold to retail outlets through a sales force. The sales force is compensated by a 10% commission on the wholesale price for all sales.

Total completed production was 45,000 units during the year. Other information is as follows:

Number of software units sold in 2008	40,000
Wholesale price per unit	$200

Factory overhead cost is applied to jobs at the rate of $1,200 per copy machine hour. There were an additional 1,000 copied CDs, packaging, and manuals waiting to be assembled on December 31, 2008.

Instructions
1. Prepare an annual income statement for the *Landscape 2008* product, including supporting calculations, from the information above.
2. Determine the balances in the finished goods and work in process inventory for the *Landscape 2008* product on December 31, 2008.

Problems Series B

PR 2-1B
Entries for costs in a job order cost system

obj. 2

Robinson Parts Co. uses a job order cost system. The following data summarize the operations related to production for June:

a. Materials purchased on account, $705,000.
b. Materials requisitioned, $527,000, of which $45,000 was for general factory use.
c. Factory labor used, $417,800, of which $95,000 was indirect.
d. Other costs incurred on account were for factory overhead, $340,500; selling expenses, $215,000; and administrative expenses, $128,500.
e. Prepaid expenses expired for factory overhead were $23,000; for selling expenses, $15,000; and for administrative expenses, $9,000.
f. Depreciation of office building was $39,000; of office equipment, $19,700; and of warehouse equipment, $12,300.
g. Factory overhead costs applied to jobs, $579,600.
h. Jobs completed, $1,643,700.
i. Cost of goods sold, $1,650,000.

Instructions
Journalize the entries to record the summarized operations.

PR 2-2B

Entries and schedules for unfinished jobs and completed jobs

obj. 2

✓ *3. Work in Process balance, $6,800*

Hillman Tool Company uses a job order cost system. The following data summarize the operations related to production for May 2008, the first month of operations:

a. Materials purchased on account, $9,400.
b. Materials requisitioned and factory labor used:

Job	Materials	Factory Labor
No. 101	$ 875	$ 750
No. 102	1,275	985
No. 103	660	500
No. 104	2,200	1,765
No. 105	1,300	1,350
No. 106	925	790
For general factory use	270	1,000

c. Factory overhead costs incurred on account, $405.
d. Depreciation of machinery and equipment, $520.
e. The factory overhead rate is $35 per machine hour. Machine hours used:

Job	Machine Hours
No. 101	6
No. 102	10
No. 103	8
No. 104	25
No. 105	11
No. 106	7
Total	67

f. Jobs completed: 101, 102, 103, and 105.
g. Jobs were shipped and customers were billed as follows: Job 101, $4,350; Job 102, $4,800; Job 103, $2,350.

Instructions
1. Journalize the entries to record the summarized operations.
2. Post the appropriate entries to T accounts for Work in Process and Finished Goods, using the identifying letters as dates. Insert memorandum account balances as of the end of the month.
3. Prepare a schedule of unfinished jobs to support the balance in the work in process account.
4. Prepare a schedule of completed jobs on hand to support the balance in the finished goods account.

PR 2-3B

Job order cost sheet

objs. 2, 3

If the working papers correlating with the textbook are not used, omit Problem 2-3B.

Asheville Furniture Company refinishes and reupholsters furniture. Asheville uses a job order cost system. When a prospective customer asks for a price quote on a job, the estimated cost data are inserted on an unnumbered job cost sheet. If the offer is accepted, a number is assigned to the job, and the costs incurred are recorded in the usual manner on the job cost sheet. After the job is completed, reasons for the variances between the estimated and actual costs are noted on the sheet. The data are then available to management in evaluating the efficiency of operations and in preparing quotes on future jobs. On July 10, 2008, an estimate of $805.20 for reupholstering a chair and couch was given to Ed Stone. The estimate was based on the following data:

Estimated direct materials:	
12 meters at $20 per meter	$240.00
Estimated direct labor:	
15 hours at $13 per hour	195.00
Estimated factory overhead (35% of direct labor cost)	68.25
Total estimated costs	$503.25
Markup (60% of production costs)	301.95
Total estimate	$805.20

On July 16, the chair and couch were picked up from the residence of Ed Stone, 10 Publishers Lane, New York, with a commitment to return it on August 16. The job was completed on August 11.

The related materials requisitions and time tickets are summarized as follows:

Materials Requisition No.	Description	Amount
U642	6 meters at $20	$120
U651	8 meters at $20	160

Time Ticket No.	Description	Amount
1519	10 hours at $12	$120
1520	8 hours at $12	96

Instructions

1. Complete that portion of the job order cost sheet that would be prepared when the estimate is given to the customer.
2. ▬▬▶ Assign number 00-8-38 to the job, record the costs incurred, and complete the job order cost sheet. Comment on the reasons for the variances between actual costs and estimated costs. For this purpose, assume that two meters of materials were spoiled, the factory overhead rate has been proved to be satisfactory, and an inexperienced employee performed the work.

PR 2-4B
Analyzing manufacturing cost accounts

obj. 2

✓1. G. $163,272

Alpine Bliss Ski Company manufactures snow skis in a wide variety of lengths and styles. The following incomplete ledger accounts refer to transactions that are summarized for October:

Materials

Oct. 1	Balance	20,000	Oct. 31	Requisitions	(A)
31	Purchases	100,000			

Work in Process

Oct. 1	Balance	(B)	Oct. 31	Completed jobs	(F)
31	Materials	(C)			
31	Direct labor	(D)			
31	Factory overhead applied	(E)			

Finished Goods

Oct. 1	Balance	0	Oct. 31	Cost of goods sold	(G)
31	Completed jobs	(F)			

Wages Payable

			Oct. 31	Wages incurred	76,000

Factory Overhead

Oct. 1	Balance	5,000	Oct. 31	Factory overhead applied	(E)
31	Indirect labor	(H)			
31	Indirect materials	2,500			
31	Other overhead	57,500			

In addition, the following information is available:

a. Materials and direct labor were applied to six jobs in October:

Job No.	Style	Quantity	Direct Materials	Direct Labor
No. 51	V-100	175	$ 17,000	$13,000
No. 52	V-200	375	28,000	17,000
No. 53	V-500	175	10,000	4,500
No. 54	A-200	200	27,500	11,000
No. 55	V-400	150	18,000	10,500
No. 56	A-100	100	5,000	3,700
Total		1,175	$105,500	$59,700

b. Factory overhead is applied to each job at a rate of 140% of direct labor cost.

c. The October 1 Work in Process balance consisted of two jobs, as follows:

Job No.	Style	Work in Process, October 1
Job 51	V-100	$ 5,000
Job 52	V-200	11,000
Total		$16,000

d. Customer jobs completed and units sold in October were as follows:

Job No.	Style	Completed in October	Units Sold in October
Job 51	V-100	X	150
Job 52	V-200	X	215
Job 53	V-500		0
Job 54	A-200	X	160
Job 55	V-400	X	100
Job 56	A-100		0

Instructions

1. Determine the missing amounts associated with each letter. Provide supporting calculations by completing a table with the following headings:

Job No.	Quantity	Oct. 1 Work in Process	Direct Materials	Direct Labor	Factory Overhead	Total Cost	Unit Cost	Units Sold	Cost of Goods Sold

2. Determine the October 31 balances for each of the inventory accounts and factory overhead.

PR 2-5B

Flow of costs and income statement

obj. 2

✓1. Income from operations, $1,800,000

New Music Inc. is in the business of developing, promoting, and selling musical talent on compact disc (CD). The company signed a new musical act, called *The Sound*, on January 1, 2008. For the first six months of 2008, the company spent $3,500,000 on a media campaign for *The Sound* and $800,000 in legal costs. The CD production began on February 1, 2008.

New Music uses a job order cost system to accumulate costs associated with a CD title. The unit direct materials cost for the CD is:

Blank CD	$3.00
Jewel case	1.00
Song lyric insert	0.50

The production process is straightforward. First, the blank CDs are brought to a production area where the digital soundtrack is copied onto the CD. The copying machine requires one hour per 2,000 CDs.

After the CDs are copied, they are brought to an assembly area where an employee packs the CD with a jewel case and song lyric insert. The direct labor cost is $0.50 per unit.

The CDs are sold to record stores. Each record store is given promotional materials, such as posters and aisle displays. Promotional materials cost $30 per record store. In addition, shipping costs average $0.15 per CD.

Total completed production was 1,500,000 units during the year. Other information is as follows:

Number of customers (record stores)	50,000
Number of CDs sold	1,000,000
Wholesale price (to record store) per CD	$13

Factory overhead cost is applied to jobs at the rate of $500 per copy machine hour. There were an additional 20,000 copied CDs, packages, and inserts waiting to be assembled on December 31, 2008.

Instructions

1. Prepare an annual income statement for New Music Inc. for *The Sound* CD, including supporting calculations from the preceeding information.
2. Determine the balances in the work in process and finished goods inventory for the *The Sound* CD on December 31, 2008.

Special Activities

SA 2-1
Managerial analysis

The controller of the plant of Commercial Plumbing Supplies prepared a graph of the unit costs from the job cost reports for Product QQQ. The graph appeared as follows:

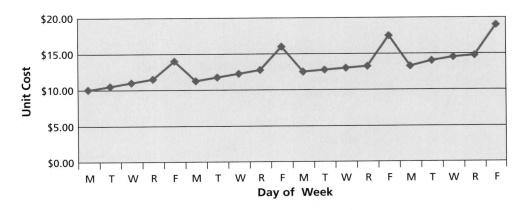

How would you interpret this information? What further information would you request?

SA 2-2
Factory overhead rate

Machine-Tech Inc., a specialized tool manufacturer, uses a job order costing system. The overhead is allocated to jobs on the basis of direct labor hours. The overhead rate is now $1,500 per direct labor hour. The design engineer thinks that this is illogical. The design engineer has stated the following:

Our accounting system doesn't make any sense to me. It tells me that every labor hour carries an additional burden of $1,500. This means that direct labor makes up only 5% of our total product cost, yet it drives all our costs. In addition, these rates give my design engineers incentives to "design out" direct labor by using machine technology. Yet, over the past years as we have had less and less direct labor, the overhead rate keeps going up and up. I won't be surprised if next year the rate is $2,000 per direct labor hour. I'm also concerned because small errors in our estimates of the direct labor content can have a large impact on our estimated costs. Just a 30-minute error in our estimate of assembly time is worth $750. Small mistakes in our direct labor time estimates really swing our bids around. I think this puts us at a disadvantage when we are going after business.

1. What is the engineer's concern about the overhead rate going "up and up"?
2. What did the engineer mean about the large overhead rate being a disadvantage when placing bids and seeking new business?
3. What do you think is a possible solution?

SA 2-3
Job order decision making and rate deficiencies

Kazaa Company makes attachments, such as backhoes and grader and bulldozer blades, for construction equipment. The company uses a job order cost system. Management is concerned about cost performance and evaluates the job cost sheets to learn more about the cost effectiveness of the operations. To facilitate a comparison, the cost sheet for Job 500 (15 Type Z bulldozer blades completed in March) was compared with Job 750, which was for 25 Type Z bulldozer blades completed in September. The two job cost sheets follow.

Job 500

Item: 15 Type Z bulldozer blades

Materials:	Direct Materials Quantity	×	Direct Materials Price	=	Amount
Steel (tons)	30		$800.00		$24,000
Steel components (pieces)	225		3.00		675
Total materials					$24,675

Direct labor	Direct Labor Hours	×	Direct Labor Rate	=	Amount
Foundry	180.0		$ 14.00		$ 2,520
Welding	120.0		16.00		1,920
Shipping	22.5		10.00		225
Total direct labor	322.5				$ 4,665

	Direct Total Labor Cost	×	Factory Overhead Rate	=	Amount
Factory overhead (400% of direct labor dollars)	$4,665	×	400%		$18,660
Total cost					$48,000
Total units					/ 15
Unit cost					$ 3,200

Job 750

Item: 25 Type Z bulldozer blades

Materials:	Direct Materials Quantity	×	Direct Materials Price	=	Amount
Steel (tons)	58		$750.00		$43,500
Steel components (pieces)	375		3.00		1,125
Total materials					$44,625

Direct labor	Direct Labor Hours	×	Direct Labor Rate	=	Amount
Foundry	325.0		$ 14.00		$ 4,550
Welding	250.0		16.00		4,000
Shipping	37.5		10.00		375
Total direct labor	612.5				$ 8,925

	Direct Total Labor Cost	×	Factory Overhead Rate	=	Amount
Factory overhead (400% of direct labor dollars)	$8,925	×	400%		$35,700
Total cost					$89,250
Total units					/ 25
Unit cost					$ 3,570

Management is concerned with the increase in unit costs over the months from March to September. To understand what has occurred, management interviewed the purchasing manager and quality manager.

Purchasing Manager: Prices have been holding steady for our raw materials during the first half of the year. I found a new supplier for our bulk steel that was willing to offer a better price than we received in the past. I saw these lower steel prices and jumped at them, knowing that a reduction in steel prices would have a very favorable impact on our costs.

Quality Manager: Something happened around midyear. All of a sudden, we were experiencing problems with respect to the quality of our steel. As a result, we've been having all sorts of problems on the shop floor in our foundry and welding operation.

1. Analyze the two job cost sheets, and identify why the unit costs have changed for the Type Z bulldozer blades. Complete the following schedule to help you in your analysis:

Item	Input Quantity per Unit—Job 500	Input Quantity per Unit—Job 750
Steel		
Foundry labor		
Welding labor		

2. ▭▭▶ How would you interpret what has happened in light of your analysis and the interviews?

SA 2-4
Recording manufacturing costs

Jake Nash just began working as a cost accountant for Marvel Industries Inc., which manufactures gift items. Jake is preparing to record summary journal entries for the month. Jake begins by recording the factory wages as follows:

Wages Expense	30,000	
Wages Payable		30,000

Then the factory depreciation:

Depreciation Expense—Factory Machinery	8,000	
Accumulated Depreciation—Factory Machinery		8,000

Jake's supervisor, Ronnie Berry, walks by and notices the entries. The following conversation takes place.

Ronnie: That's a very unusual way to record our factory wages and depreciation for the month.

Jake: What do you mean? This is exactly the way we were taught to record wages and depreciation in school. You know, debit an expense and credit Cash or payables, or in the case of depreciation, credit Accumulated Depreciation.

Ronnie: Well, it's not the credits I'm concerned about. It's the debits—I don't think you've recorded the debits correctly. I wouldn't mind if you were recording the administrative wages or office equipment depreciation this way, but I've got real questions about recording factory wages and factory machinery depreciation this way.

Jake: Now I'm really confused. You mean this is correct for administrative costs, but not for factory costs? Well, what am I supposed to do—and why?

1. ▭▭▶ Play the role of Ronnie and answer Jake's questions.
2. Why would Ronnie accept the journal entries if they were for administrative costs?

SA 2-5
Predetermined overhead rates

As an assistant cost accountant for Lovett Industries, you have been assigned to review the activity base for the predetermined factory overhead rate. The president, Calvin Adler, has expressed concern that the over- or underapplied overhead has fluctuated excessively over the years.

An analysis of the company's operations and use of the current overhead rate (direct materials usage) has narrowed the possible alternative overhead bases to direct labor cost and machine hours. For the past five years, the following data have been gathered:

	2008	2007	2006	2005	2004
Actual overhead	$ 590,000	$ 918,000	$ 450,000	$ 566,000	$ 501,000
Applied overhead	582,000	928,000	460,000	575,000	480,000
(Over-) underapplied overhead	$ 8,000	$ (10,000)	$ (10,000)	$ (9,000)	$ 21,000
Direct labor cost	$2,150,000	$3,350,000	$1,630,000	$2,040,000	$1,830,000
Machine hours	50,000	75,000	35,000	48,000	42,000

1. Calculate a predetermined factory overhead rate for each alternative base, assuming that rates would have been determined by relating the amount of factory overhead for the past five years to the base.
2. For each of the past five years, determine the over- or underapplied overhead, based on the two predetermined overhead rates developed in part (1).
3. ▭▭▶ Which predetermined overhead rate would you recommend? Discuss the basis for your recommendation.

Answers to Self-Examination Questions

1. **A**   Job order cost systems are best suited to businesses manufacturing special orders from customers, such as would be the case for a repair shop for antique furniture (answer A). A process cost system is best suited for manufacturers of similar units of products such as rubber manufacturers (answer B), coal manufacturers (answer C), and computer chip manufacturers (answer D).

2. **C**   The journal entry to record the requisition of materials to the factory in a job order cost system is a debit to Work in Process and a credit to Materials.

3. **B**   The job cost sheet accumulates the cost of materials (answer A), direct labor (answer C), and factory overhead applied (answer D). Indirect materials are *not* accumulated on the job order cost sheets, but are included as part of factory overhead applied.

4. **B**

$$\text{Predetermined Factory Overhead Rate} = \frac{\text{Estimated Total Factory Overhead Costs}}{\text{Estimated Activity Base}}$$

$$\text{Predetermined Factory Overhead Rate} = \frac{\$420,000}{16,000 \text{ dlh}} = \$26.25$$

$$\text{Hours applied to the job: } \frac{\$3,000}{\$15 \text{ per hour}} = 200 \text{ hours}$$

Factory overhead applied to the job: 200 hours $\times$ \$26.25 = \$5,250

5. **B**   If the amount of factory overhead applied during a particular period exceeds the actual overhead costs, the factory overhead account will have a credit balance and is said to be overapplied (answer B) or overabsorbed. If the amount applied is less than the actual costs, the account will have a debit balance and is said to be underapplied (answer A) or underabsorbed (answer C). Since an "estimated" predetermined overhead rate is used to apply overhead, a credit balance does not necessarily represent an error (answer D).

Process Cost Systems

© MICHAEL STRAUCH @ STREETCARMIKE.COM

objectives

After studying this chapter, you should be able to:

1 *Explain and illustrate the characteristics and cost flows for a process manufacturer.*

2 *Prepare a cost of production report, accounting for completed and partially completed units under the FIFO method.*

3 *Prepare journal entries for transactions of a process manufacturer.*

4 *Use cost of production reports for decision making.*

5 *Contrast just-in-time processing with conventional manufacturing practices.*

Dreyer's Grand Ice Cream, Inc.

To make ice cream, you would need to gather ingredients, including milk, cream, sugar, and flavoring. Next, these ingredients would be added to an electric ice cream maker to be mixed. The ingredients must be cooled during mixing so the ice cream maker would be packed with ice and salt. Finally, you would turn on the electricity to begin the mixing. After mixing for half of the required mixing time, would you have ice cream? Of course not, because you'd need to mix for a longer time before the ice cream would freeze.

Now, assume that you ask the question, "What costs have I incurred so far in making ice cream, now that it is halfway through the mixing time?" The answer requires that you begin by separating the ingredients and the electricity costs. These two costs are incurred in the process at different rates so it is convenient to identify them separately. The ingredient costs have all been incurred, since all the ingredients were introduced at the beginning of the process. The electricity costs, however, are different. Since the mixing is only 50% complete, only 50% of the electricity costs used in operating the ice cream maker have been incurred in the mixing process. Therefore, the answer to the question is that *all* the materials costs and *half* the electricity costs have been incurred in the mixing process after half of the mixing time is completed.

These same costing concepts would apply for a much larger ice cream process, like that of Dreyer's Grand Ice Cream, Inc., manufacturer of the Häagen-Dazs®, Edys®, Dreyer's®, and Nestlé® ice cream brands. Dreyer's mixes ingredients in 3,000-gallon vats in much the same way that you would mix ice cream at home. It would also account for its costs by measuring the ingredients, electricity, labor, and other factory overhead costs consumed in making ice cream.

In this chapter, we apply these concepts to manufacturers that use a process cost system. After introducing process costing, we discuss decision making with process cost system reports. We conclude the chapter with a brief discussion of just-in-time cost systems.

Overview of Process Manufacturers and Process Costing

objective *1*

Explain and illustrate the characteristics and cost flows for a process manufacturer.

As we discussed in the previous chapter, the job order cost system is best suited to industries that make special orders for customers. Industries that use job order cost systems include special-order printing, custom-made tailoring, furniture manufacturing, shipbuilding, aircraft building, custom-made musical instruments, movie studios, and construction. **Process manufacturers** typically use large machines to process a flow of raw materials into a finished state. For example, a petrochemical business processes crude oil through numerous refining steps to produce higher grades of oil until gasoline is produced. A distinguishing feature of process manufacturers is that products produced are the same. This means that one unit of product cannot be distinguished from another. Thus, in a petrochemical business one barrel of gasoline cannot be distinguished from another barrel. This is in contrast to a printing company, where one print job is not the same as another. Other examples of process manufacturers are as follows:

Industry	Example Company
Beverages	The Coca-Cola Company
Chemicals	The Dow Chemical Company
Computer chips	Intel Corporation
Food	The Hershey Foods Corporation

Industry	Example Company
Forest and paper products	Georgia-Pacific
Metals	Alcoa Inc.
Petroleum refining	ExxonMobil Corporation
Pharmaceuticals	Merck & Co., Inc.
Soap and cosmetics	Procter & Gamble

The cost accounting system used by process manufacturers is called the **process cost system**.

Integrity, Objectivity, and Ethics in Business

ETHICS

SAFETY FIRST

Chemical processors must be concerned with safety, health, and the environment. Minimizing chemical spills, unwanted emissions, and equipment hazards are concerns in this industry. E. I. du Pont de Nemours and Company (DuPont) is widely regarded as one of the strongest advocates for social responsibility and one of the safest manufacturing businesses in which to work. As a result, DuPont publicly reports that its recorded workplace-related injuries or illnesses have been less than 40% of the chemical industry average and less than 20% of all manufacturing companies. Moreover, that rate has declined every year for the last 10 years. DuPont reports its community and employee safety and health performance on its Web site at **http://www2.dupont.com/Social_Commitment/en_us/.**

Source: "Recordable Injuries per 200,000 Hours Worked," DuPont Company, 2005.

COMPARING JOB ORDER AND PROCESS COST SYSTEMS

Job order and process costing systems are similar in many ways. For example, both systems:

1. Accumulate product costs.
2. Categorize manufacturing costs into direct materials, direct labor, and factory overhead.
3. Allocate costs to products.
4. Maintain perpetual materials, work in process, and finished goods inventory records.
5. Use product cost data for decision making.

The primary differences of job order and process costing systems reflect the underlying nature of the manufacturing systems. These differences influence the methods for accumulating and allocating costs. For example, the primary differences between job order and process cost systems are listed below.

1. Manufacturing costs are accumulated to departments, rather than jobs.
2. Manufacturing costs are allocated to products based on units of production.
3. Manufacturing costs are accumulated and transferred between departments.
4. Work in process inventory consists of partially completed production within a department, rather than the sum of job cost sheets of partially completed jobs.

Exhibit 1 illustrates the main differences between the job order and process cost systems. In a job order cost system, product costs are accumulated by job and are summarized on job cost sheets. The job cost sheets provide unit cost information and can be used by management for product pricing, cost control, and inventory valuation. The process manufacturer does not manufacture according to "jobs." Rather, costs are accumulated in work in process accounts by *department.* For example, the departments that accumulate costs for an ice cream manufacturer would be the Mixing Department and the Packaging Department. These employees are assigned to departments to monitor process equipment, load and unload product, and clean process equipment

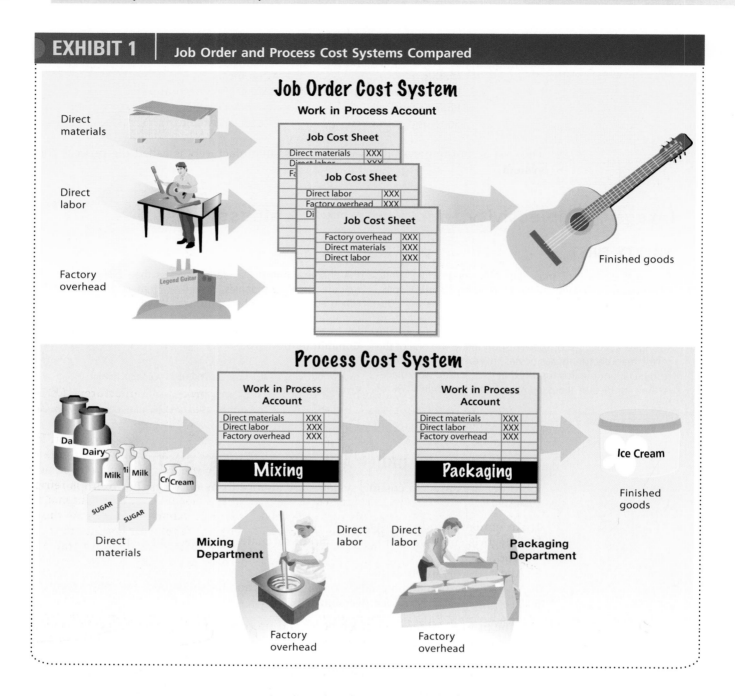

EXHIBIT 1 | **Job Order and Process Cost Systems Compared**

between product runs. Thus, the direct labor is more associated with the process department, than with the product.

Each unit of product that passes through the department is similar. Thus, the production costs reported by each department can be allocated to the product based upon the units produced within the department. The costs of one department can be transferred to a subsequent department. In this way, the cost of the product accumulates across the complete production process. For example, the costs of completed production in the Mixing Department become the costs transferred into the Packaging Department. The departmental unit cost information as well as the final unit cost information can be used by management for cost control. In a job order cost system, the work in process inventory at the end of the accounting period is the sum of the job cost sheets for partially completed jobs. In a process cost system, the amount of work in process inventory is determined by allocating costs between completed and partially completed units within a department.

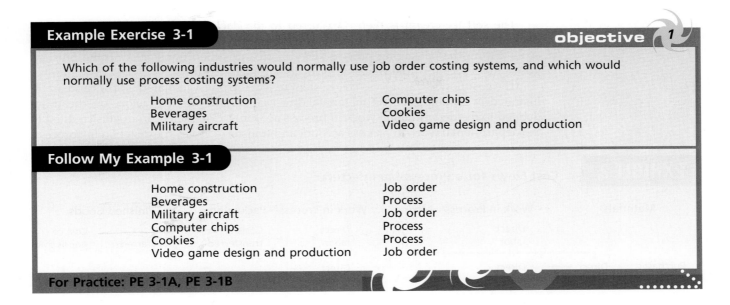

Example Exercise 3-1   objective **1**

Which of the following industries would normally use job order costing systems, and which would normally use process costing systems?

Home construction	Computer chips
Beverages	Cookies
Military aircraft	Video game design and production

Follow My Example 3-1

Home construction	Job order
Beverages	Process
Military aircraft	Job order
Computer chips	Process
Cookies	Process
Video game design and production	Job order

For Practice: PE 3-1A, PE 3-1B

COST FLOWS FOR A PROCESS MANUFACTURER

Materials costs are a large portion of the costs for most process manufacturers. Often, the materials costs can be as high as 70% of the total manufacturing costs. Thus, accounting for materials costs is very important for process operations.

Exhibit 2 illustrates the physical flow of materials for an ice cream processor. Ice cream is made in a manufacturing plant much the same way as it would be made at home, except on a much larger scale. Direct materials in the form of milk, cream, and sugar are placed into a mixing vessel in the Mixing Department. This vessel is refrigerated to a very cold temperature while the material is mixed with large automated paddles called *agitators*. The Mixing Department uses direct labor and factory overhead (conversion costs) during the mixing process. Direct labor employees prepare the vessel for material, perform vessel cleaning, and set refrigeration temperature and mix speed. Factory overhead includes power and equipment depreciation.

EXHIBIT 2	Physical Flows for a Process Manufacturer

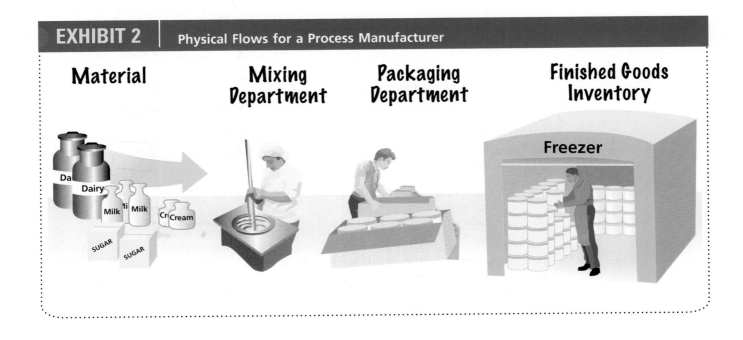

The soft ice cream is then transferred to the Packaging Department, where it is packaged into one-gallon containers. The Packaging Department also uses conversion costs during the packaging process. The ice cream is then transferred to the finished goods inventory for final freezing, prior to shipment to stores.

The cost flows in a process cost system reflect the physical material flows and are illustrated in Exhibit 3. Direct materials, direct labor, and applied factory overhead are debited to the departmental work in process accounts. Completed product is credited to the departmental work in process account and transferred to the next step in the process.

EXHIBIT 3   Cost Flows for a Process Manufacturer

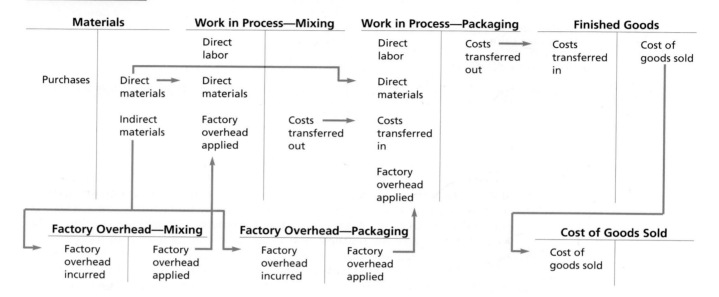

The First-In, First-Out (FIFO) Method

objective **2**

Prepare a cost of production report, accounting for completed and partially completed units under the FIFO method.

In a process cost system, the accountant determines the cost transferred out and thus the amount remaining in inventory for each department. To determine this cost, the accountant must make a cost flow assumption. Like merchandise inventory, costs can be assumed to flow through the manufacturing process using the first-in, first-out (FIFO), last in, first-out (LIFO), or average cost methods. Because the **first-in, first-out (FIFO) method** is often the same as the physical flow of units, we use the FIFO method in this chapter.[1]

Most process manufacturers have more than one department. In the illustrations that follow, Frozen Delight Ice Cream Company has two departments, Mixing and Packaging. Frozen Delight mixes milk, cream, and sugar in a refrigerated vessel, and then pumps the soft ice cream to the Packaging Department for filling one-gallon containers.

To illustrate the first-in, first-out method, we will simplify by using only the Mixing Department of Frozen Delight. The following data for the Mixing Department are for July 2008:

Inventory in process, July 1, 5,000 gallons:
Direct materials cost, for 5,000 gallons	$5,000	
Conversion costs, for 5,000 gallons, 70% completed	1,225	
Total inventory in process, July 1		$ 6,225

(continued)

---

1 The average cost method is illustrated in the appendix to this chapter.

Direct materials cost for July, 60,000 gallons	$66,000
Direct labor cost for July	10,500
Factory overhead applied for July	7,275
Total production costs to account for	$90,000
Goods transferred to Packaging in July (includes units in process on July 1), 62,000 gallons	?
Inventory in process, July 31, 3,000 gallons, 25% completed as to conversion costs	?

We assume that all materials used in the department are added at the beginning of the process, and conversion costs (direct labor and factory overhead) are incurred evenly throughout the mixing process. The objective is to determine the cost of goods completed and the ending inventory valuation, which are represented by the question marks. We determine these amounts by using the following four steps:

1. Determine the units to be assigned costs.
2. Compute equivalent units of production.
3. Determine the cost per equivalent unit.
4. Allocate costs to transferred and partially completed units.

STEP 1: DETERMINE THE UNITS TO BE ASSIGNED COSTS

The first step in our illustration is to determine the units to be assigned costs. A unit can be any measure of completed production, such as tons, gallons, pounds, barrels, or cases. We use gallons as the units for Frozen Delight.

Frozen Delight had 65,000 gallons of direct materials charged to production in the Mixing Department for July, as shown below.

Total gallons charged to production:	
In process, July 1	5,000 gallons
Received from materials storage	60,000
Total units accounted for by the Mixing Department	65,000 gallons

There are three categories of units to be assigned costs for an accounting period: **(A)** units in beginning in-process inventory, **(B)** units started and completed during the period, and **(C)** units in ending in-process inventory. Exhibit 4 illustrates these categories in the Mixing Department for July. The 5,000-gallon beginning inventory **(A)** was completed and transferred to the Packaging Department. Frozen Delight started another 60,000 gallons of material into the process during July. Of the 60,000 gallons introduced in July, 3,000 gallons were left incomplete at the end of the month **(C)**. Thus, only 57,000 of the 60,000 gallons were actually started and completed in July **(B)**.

The total units (gallons) to be assigned costs for Frozen Delight is summarized below.

(A)	Inventory in process, July 1, completed in July	5,000 gallons
(B)	Started and completed in July	57,000
	Transferred out to the Packaging Department in July	62,000 gallons
(C)	Inventory in process, July 31	3,000
	Total gallons to be assigned costs	65,000 gallons

Note that the total gallons to be assigned costs equals the total gallons accounted for by the department. The three unit categories (A, B, and C) are used in the remaining steps to determine the cost transferred to the Packaging Department and the cost remaining in the Mixing Department work in process inventory at the end of the period.

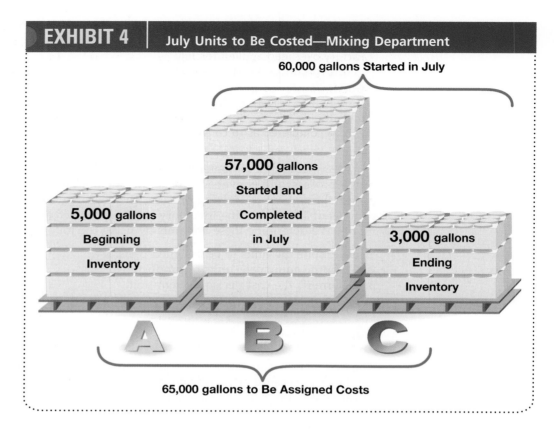

EXHIBIT 4 | **July Units to Be Costed—Mixing Department**

60,000 gallons Started in July

57,000 gallons Started and Completed in July

5,000 gallons Beginning Inventory

3,000 gallons Ending Inventory

A   B   C

65,000 gallons to Be Assigned Costs

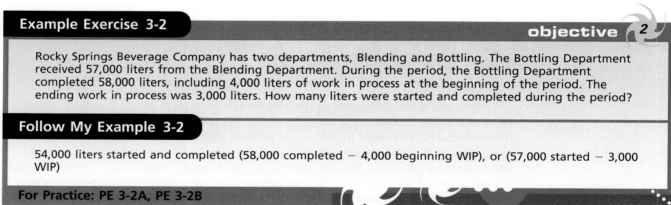

Example Exercise 3-2

objective **2**

Rocky Springs Beverage Company has two departments, Blending and Bottling. The Bottling Department received 57,000 liters from the Blending Department. During the period, the Bottling Department completed 58,000 liters, including 4,000 liters of work in process at the beginning of the period. The ending work in process was 3,000 liters. How many liters were started and completed during the period?

Follow My Example 3-2

54,000 liters started and completed (58,000 completed − 4,000 beginning WIP), or (57,000 started − 3,000 WIP)

For Practice: PE 3-2A, PE 3-2B

STEP 2: COMPUTE EQUIVALENT UNITS OF PRODUCTION

Process manufacturers often have some partially processed materials remaining in production at the end of a period. For example, Frozen Delight might end its accounting period when a batch of ice cream is still in a vessel being mixed. In this case, the costs of production must be allocated between the units that have been completed and transferred to the next process (or finished goods), and those that are only partially completed and remain within the department. This allocation is determined using whole units and equivalent units of production.

Whole units are the number of units in production during a period, whether completed or not. **Equivalent units of production** are the portion of whole units that were completed with respect to either materials or conversion costs within a given accounting period. For example, assume that a 1,000-gallon batch (vessel) of ice cream is only 40% complete in the mixing process at the end of the period. In this case, the amount of conversion effort, such as power cost, for that batch is also only 40% complete.

Equivalent units for materials and conversion costs are usually determined separately because they are often introduced at different times or at different rates in the production process. In contrast, direct labor and factory overhead are normally combined together as conversion costs because they are often incurred in production at the same time and rate.

Materials Equivalent Units To allocate materials costs between the completed and partially completed units, it is necessary to determine how materials are added during the manufacturing process. In the case of Frozen Delight, the materials are added at the beginning of the mixing process. In other words, the mixing process cannot begin without the ice cream ingredients. The equivalent unit computation for materials in July is as follows:

	Total Whole Units	Percent Materials Added in July	Equivalent Units for Direct Materials
Inventory in process, July 1	5,000	0%	0
Started and completed in July (62,000 − 5,000)	57,000	100%	57,000
Transferred out to Packaging Department in July	62,000	—	57,000
Inventory in process, July 31	3,000	100%	3,000
Total gallons to be assigned cost	65,000		60,000

The whole units from step 1 are multiplied by the percentage of materials that are added in July for the in-process inventories and units started and completed. The equivalent units for direct materials are illustrated in Exhibit 5.

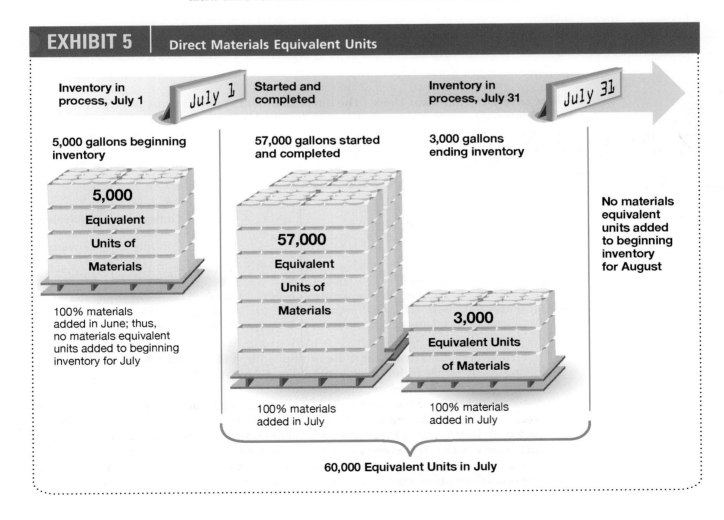

EXHIBIT 5 | **Direct Materials Equivalent Units**

Inventory in process, July 1 — July 1 — **Started and completed** — **Inventory in process, July 31** — July 31

5,000 gallons beginning inventory

5,000 Equivalent Units of Materials

100% materials added in June; thus, no materials equivalent units added to beginning inventory for July

57,000 gallons started and completed

57,000 Equivalent Units of Materials

100% materials added in July

3,000 gallons ending inventory

3,000 Equivalent Units of Materials

100% materials added in July

No materials equivalent units added to beginning inventory for August

60,000 Equivalent Units in July

The direct materials for the 5,000 gallons of July 1 in-process inventory were introduced in June. Thus, no materials units were added in July for the inventory in process on July 1. All of the 57,000 gallons started and completed in July were 100% complete with respect to materials. Thus, 57,000 equivalent units of materials were added in July. All the materials for the July 31 in-process inventory were introduced at the beginning of the process. Thus, 3,000 equivalent units of material for the July 31 in-process inventory were added in July.

Example Exercise 3-3

objective **2**

The Bottling Department of Rocky Springs Beverage Company had 4,000 liters in beginning work in process inventory (30% complete). During the period, 58,000 liters were completed. The ending work in process inventory was 3,000 liters (60% complete). What are the total equivalent units for direct materials if materials are added at the beginning of the process?

Follow My Example 3-3

	Total Whole Units	Percent Materials Added in Period	Equivalent Units for Direct Materials
Inventory in process, beginning of period	4,000	0%	0
Started and completed during the period	54,000*	100%	54,000
Transferred out of Bottling (completed)	58,000	—	54,000
Inventory in process, end of period	3,000	100%	3,000
Total units to be assigned costs	61,000		57,000

*(58,000 − 4,000)

For Practice: PE 3-3A, PE 3-3B

Conversion Equivalent Units The direct labor and applied factory overhead are often combined as conversion costs because they are both usually incurred evenly throughout a process. For example, direct labor, utilities, and machine depreciation are usually used uniformly during processing. Thus, the conversion equivalent units are added in July in direct relation to the percentage of processing completed in July. The computations for July are as follows:

	Total Whole Units	Percent Conversion Completed in July	Equivalent Units for Conversion
Inventory in process, July 1 (70% completed)	5,000	30%	1,500
Started and completed in July (62,000 − 5,000)	57,000	100%	57,000
Transferred out to Packaging Department in July	62,000	—	58,500
Inventory in process, July 31 (25% completed)	3,000	25%	750
Total gallons to be assigned cost	65,000		59,250

The whole units from step 1 are multiplied by the percentage of conversion completed in July for the in-process inventories and units started and completed. The equivalent units for conversion are illustrated in Exhibit 6.

The conversion equivalent units of the July 1 in-process inventory are 30% of the 5,000 gallons, or 1,500 equivalent units. Since 70% of the conversion had been completed on July 1, only 30% of the conversion effort for these gallons was incurred in July. All the units started and completed used converting effort in July. Thus, conversion equivalent units are 100% of these gallons. The equivalent units for the July 31 in-process inventory are 25% of the 3,000 gallons because only 25% of the converting has been completed with respect to these gallons in July.

EXHIBIT 6 | Conversion Equivalent Units

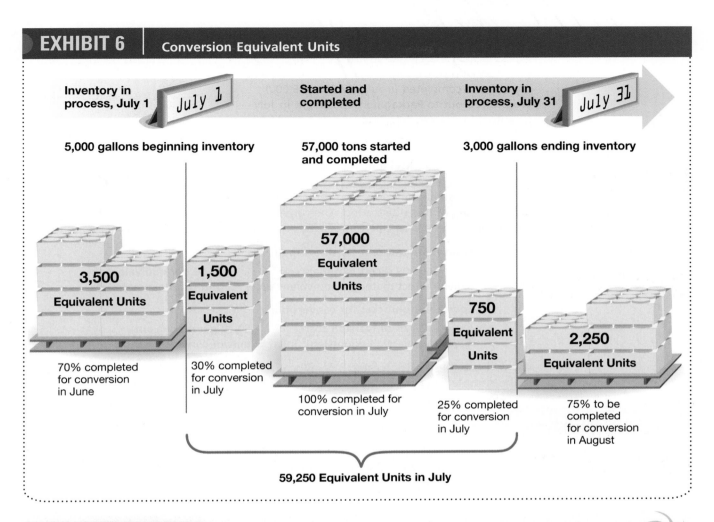

Inventory in process, July 1 — July 1 — Started and completed — Inventory in process, July 31 — July 31

5,000 gallons beginning inventory

3,500 Equivalent Units — 70% completed for conversion in June

1,500 Equivalent Units — 30% completed for conversion in July

57,000 tons started and completed

57,000 Equivalent Units — 100% completed for conversion in July

3,000 gallons ending inventory

750 Equivalent Units — 25% completed for conversion in July

2,250 Equivalent Units — 75% to be completed for conversion in August

59,250 Equivalent Units in July

Example Exercise 3-4   objective 2

The Bottling Department of Rocky Springs Beverage Company had 4,000 liters in beginning work in process inventory (30% complete). During the period, 58,000 liters were completed. The ending work in process inventory was 3,000 liters (60% complete). What are the total equivalent units for conversion costs?

Follow My Example 3-4

	Total Whole Units	Percent Conversion Completed in Period	Equivalent Units for Conversion
Inventory in process, beginning of period	4,000	70%	2,800
Started and completed during the period	54,000*	100%	54,000
Transferred out of Bottling (completed)	58,000	—	56,800
Inventory in process, end of period	3,000	60%	1,800
Total units to be assigned costs	61,000		58,600

*(58,000 − 4,000)

For Practice: PE 3-4A, PE 3-4B

STEP 3: DETERMINE THE COST PER EQUIVALENT UNIT

In step 3, we compute the cost per equivalent unit. The July direct materials and conversion cost equivalent unit totals for Frozen Delight's Mixing Department are reproduced from step 2 as follows:

	Equivalent Units	
	Direct Materials	**Conversion**
Inventory in process, July 1	0	1,500
Started and completed in July (62,000 − 5,000)	57,000	57,000
Transferred out to Packaging Department in July	57,000	58,500
Inventory in process, July 31	3,000	750
Total gallons to be assigned cost	60,000	59,250

The **cost per equivalent unit** is determined by dividing the direct materials and conversion costs incurred in July by the respective total equivalent units for direct materials and conversion costs. The direct materials and conversion costs were given at the beginning of this illustration. The conversion cost is the direct labor of $10,500 plus the factory overhead applied of $7,275, or $17,775. These calculations are as follows:

Equivalent unit cost for direct materials:

$$\frac{\$66,000 \text{ direct materials cost}}{60,000 \text{ direct materials equivalent units}} = \frac{\$1.10 \text{ per equivalent}}{\text{unit of direct materials}}$$

Equivalent unit cost for conversion:

$$\frac{\$17,775 \text{ conversion cost}}{59,250 \text{ conversion equivalent units}} = \frac{\$0.30 \text{ per equivalent}}{\text{unit of conversion}}$$

We will use these rates in step 4 to allocate the direct materials and conversion costs to the completed and partially completed units.

Example Exercise 3-5   objective **2**

The cost of direct materials transferred into the Bottling Department of Rocky Springs Beverage Company is $22,800. The conversion cost for the period in the Bottling Department is $8,790. The total equivalent units for direct materials and conversion are 57,000 liters and 58,600 liters, respectively. Determine the direct materials and conversion cost per equivalent unit.

Follow My Example 3-5

Equivalent units of direct materials: $\dfrac{\$22,800}{57,000 \text{ liters}} = \$0.40$ per liter

Equivalent units of conversion: $\dfrac{\$8,790}{58,600 \text{ liters}} = \$0.15$ per liter

For Practice: PE 3-5A, PE 3-5B

STEP 4: ALLOCATE COSTS TO TRANSFERRED AND PARTIALLY COMPLETED UNITS

In step 4, we multiply the equivalent unit rates by their respective equivalent units of production in order to determine the cost of transferred and partially completed units. The cost of the July 1 in-process inventory, completed and transferred out to the Packaging Department, is determined as follows:

	Direct Materials Costs	Conversion Costs	Total Costs
Inventory in process, July 1 balance			$6,225
Equivalent units for completing the July 1 in-process inventory	0	1,500	
Equivalent unit cost	×$1.10	×$0.30	
Cost of completed July 1 in-process inventory	0	$ 450	450
Cost of July 1 in-process inventory transferred to Packaging Department			$6,675

The July 1 in-process inventory cost of $6,225 is carried over from June and will be transferred to Packaging. The cost required to finish the July 1 in-process inventory is $450, which consists of conversion costs required to complete the remaining 30% of the processing. This total does not include direct materials costs, since these costs were added at the beginning of the process in June. The conversion costs required to complete the beginning inventory are added to the balance carried over from the previous month to yield a total cost of the completed July 1 in-process inventory of $6,675.

The 57,000 units started and completed in July receive 100% of their direct materials and conversion costs in July. The costs associated with the units started and completed are determined by multiplying the equivalent units in step 2 by the unit costs in step 3, as follows:

	Direct Materials Costs	Conversion Costs	Total Costs
Units started and completed in July	57,000	57,000	
Equivalent unit cost	× $1.10	× $0.30	
Cost to complete the units started and completed in July	$62,700	$17,100	$79,800

The total cost transferred to the Packaging Department is the sum of the beginning inventory cost from the previous period ($6,225), the additional costs incurred in July to complete the beginning inventory ($450), and the costs incurred for the units started and completed in July ($79,800). Thus, the total cost transferred to Packaging is $86,475 ($6,225 + $450 + $79,800).

The units of ending inventory have not been transferred, so they must be valued at July 31. The costs associated with the partially completed units in the ending inventory are determined by multiplying the equivalent units in step 2 by the unit costs in step 3, as follows:

	Direct Materials Costs	Conversion Costs	Total Costs
Equivalent units in ending inventory	3,000	750	
Equivalent unit cost	×$1.10	×$0.30	
Cost of ending inventory	$3,300	$225	$3,525

The units in the ending work in process inventory have received 100% of their materials in July. Thus, the materials cost incurred in July for the ending inventory is $3,300, or 3,000 equivalent units of materials multiplied by $1.10. The conversion cost incurred in July for the ending inventory is $225, which is 750 equivalent units of conversion (3,000 units, 25% complete) for the ending inventory multiplied by $0.30. Summing the conversion and materials costs, the total ending inventory cost is $3,525.

Example Exercise 3-6   objective 2

The cost per equivalent unit of direct materials and conversion in the Bottling Department of Rocky Springs Beverage Company is $0.40 and $0.15, respectively. The equivalent units to be assigned costs are as follows:

	Equivalent Units	
	Direct Materials	Conversion
Inventory in process, beginning of period	0	2,800
Started and completed during the period	54,000	54,000
Transferred out of Bottling (completed)	54,000	56,800
Inventory in process, end of period	3,000	1,800
Total units to be assigned costs	57,000	58,600

The beginning work in process inventory had a cost of $1,860. Determine the cost of completed and transferred-out production and the ending work in process inventory.

(continued)

Follow My Example 3-6

	Direct Materials Costs	Conversion Costs	Total Costs
Inventory in process, balance			$ 1,860
Inventory in process, beginning of period	0 +	2,800 × $0.15	420
Started and completed during the period	54,000 × $0.40 +	54,000 × $0.15	29,700
Transferred out of Bottling (completed)			$31,980
Inventory in process, end of period	3,000 × $0.40 +	1,800 × $0.15	1,470
Total costs assigned by the Bottling Department			$33,450

Completed and transferred out of production $31,980
Inventory in process, ending $1,470

For Practice: PE 3-6A, PE 3-6B

BRINGING IT ALL TOGETHER: THE COST OF PRODUCTION REPORT

A **cost of production report** is normally prepared for each processing department at periodic intervals. The July cost of production report for Frozen Delight's Mixing Department is shown in Exhibit 7. As can be seen on the report, the two question marks from page 85 can now be determined. The cost of goods transferred to the Packaging Department in July was $86,475, while the cost of the ending work in process in the Mixing Department on July 31 is $3,525.

The report summarizes the four previous steps by providing the following production quantity and cost data:

1. The units for which the department is accountable and the disposition of those units.
2. The production costs incurred by the department and the allocation of those costs between completed and partially completed units.

The cost of production report is also used to control costs. Each department manager is responsible for the units entering production and the costs incurred in the department. Any failure to account for all costs and any significant differences in unit product costs from one month to another should be investigated.

For example, the cost per equivalent unit for June can be compared with the cost per equivalent unit from the July cost of production report. The cost per equivalent unit for June can be determined from the beginning inventory. The Frozen Delight data on page 84 indicated that the July 1 inventory in process consisted of the following:

Direct materials cost, 5,000 gallons	$5,000
Conversion costs, 5,000 gallons, 70% completed	1,225
Total inventory in process, July 1	$6,225

Thus, the cost per equivalent unit incurred in June can be determined by dividing the direct material and conversion cost by their respective equivalent units in the beginning inventory as follows:

Direct materials cost per equivalent unit (June):

$$\frac{\$5,000}{5,000 \text{ equivalent units of materials}} = \$1.00 \text{ per equivalent unit}$$

Conversion cost per equivalent unit (June):

$$\frac{\$1,225}{(5,000 \times 70\%) \text{ equivalent units of conversion cost}} = \$0.35 \text{ per equivalent unit}$$

Thus, the cost per equivalent unit for materials increased, while the cost per equivalent unit for conversion costs decreased between June and July, as shown at the bottom of the next page.

EXHIBIT 7	Cost of Production Report for Frozen Delight's Mixing Department—FIFO

	A	B	C	D	E	
	Frozen Delight Ice Cream Company					
	Cost of Production Report—Mixing Department					
	For the Month Ended July 31, 2008					
		Step 1	**Step 2**			
		Whole Units	Equivalent Units			
	UNITS		Direct Materials	Conversion		
1	Units charged to production:					1
2	Inventory in process, July 1	5,000				2
3	Received from materials storeroom	60,000				3
4	Total units accounted for by the Mixing Department	65,000				4
5						5
6	Units to be assigned costs:					6
7	Inventory in process, July 1 (70% completed)	5,000	0	1,500		7
8	Started and completed in July	57,000	57,000	57,000		8
9	Transferred to Packaging Department in July	62,000	57,000	58,500		9
10	Inventory in process, July 31 (25% completed)	3,000	3,000	750		10
11	Total units to be assigned costs	65,000	60,000	59,250		11
12						12
13				**Costs**		13
14	**COSTS**		Direct Materials	Conversion	Total	14
15	**Step 3**					15
16	Costs per equivalent unit:					16
17	Total costs for July in Mixing Department		$ 66,000	$ 17,775		17
18	Total equivalent units (from step 2 above)		/ 60,000	/ 59,250		18
19	Cost per equivalent unit		$ 1.10	$ 0.30		19
20						20
21	Costs assigned to production:					21
22	Inventory in process, July 1				$ 6,225	22
23	Costs incurred in July				83,775[a]	23
24	Total costs accounted for by the Mixing Department				$90,000	24
25						25
26	**Step 4**					26
27	Cost allocated to completed and partially					27
28	completed units:					28
29	Inventory in process, July 1—balance				$ 6,225	29
30	To complete inventory in process, July 1		$ 0 +	$ 450[b] =	450	30
31	Started and completed in July		62,700[c] +	17,100[d] =	79,800	31
32	Transferred to Packaging Department in July				$86,475	32
33	Inventory in process, July 31		$ 3,300[e] +	$ 225[f] =	3,525	33
34	Total costs assigned by the Mixing Department				$90,000	34

[a]$66,000 + $10,500 + $7,275 = $83,775   [b]1,500 units × $0.30 = $450   [c]57,000 units × $1.10 = $62,700   [d]57,000 units × $0.30 = $17,100
[e]3,000 units × $1.10 = $3,300   [f]750 units × $0.30 = $225

	Inventory in process, July 1	July Cost of Production Report	Difference
Cost per equivalent unit— direct materials	$1.00	$1.10	$0.10 Increase
Cost per equivalent unit— conversion costs	$0.35	$0.30	$0.05 Decrease

This information would be used by Frozen Delight's management to identify cost changes requiring further investigation, such as the increase in the direct materials cost per equivalent unit.

Journal Entries for a Process Cost System

objective 3

Prepare journal entries for transactions of a process manufacturer.

To illustrate the journal entries to record the cost flows in a process costing system, we will use the July transactions for Frozen Delight. The entries in summary form for these transactions are shown here and on the following page. In practice, transactions would be recorded daily.

a. Purchased materials, including milk, cream, sugar, packaging, and indirect materials on account, $88,000.

	Materials		88 0 0 0 00	
	Accounts Payable			88 0 0 0 00

b. The Mixing Department requisitioned milk, cream, and sugar, $66,000. This is the amount originally indicated on page 85. Another $8,000 of packaging materials was requisitioned by the Packaging Department. Indirect materials for the Mixing and Packaging departments were $4,125 and $3,000, respectively.

	Work in Process—Mixing		66 0 0 0 00	
	Work in Process—Packaging		8 0 0 0 00	
	Factory Overhead—Mixing		4 1 2 5 00	
	Factory Overhead—Packaging		3 0 0 0 00	
	Materials			81 1 2 5 00

c. Incurred direct labor in the Mixing and Packaging departments of $10,500 (from page 85) and $12,000, respectively.

	Work in Process—Mixing		10 5 0 0 00	
	Work in Process—Packaging		12 0 0 0 00	
	Wages Payable			22 5 0 0 00

d. Recognized equipment depreciation for the Mixing and Packaging departments of $3,350 and $1,000, respectively.

	Factory Overhead—Mixing		3 3 5 0 00	
	Factory Overhead—Packaging		1 0 0 0 00	
	Accumulated Depreciation—Equipment			4 3 5 0 00

e. Applied factory overhead to Mixing and Packaging departments of $7,275 (from page 85) and $3,500, respectively.

	Work in Process—Mixing		7 2 7 5 00	
	Work in Process—Packaging		3 5 0 0 00	
	Factory Overhead—Mixing			7 2 7 5 00
	Factory Overhead—Packaging			3 5 0 0 00

f. Transferred costs of $86,475 from the Mixing Department to the Packaging Department per the cost of production report in Exhibit 7.

	Work in Process—Packaging		86 4 7 5 00	
	Work in Process—Mixing			86 4 7 5 00

g. Transferred goods of $106,000 out of the Packaging Department to Finished Goods according to the Packaging Department cost of production report (not illustrated).

	Finished Goods—Ice Cream		106 00 0 00		
	Work in Process—Packaging			106 00 0 00	

h. Recorded cost of goods sold out of the finished goods inventory of $107,000.

	Cost of Goods Sold		107 00 0 00		
	Finished Goods—Ice Cream			107 00 0 00	

Exhibit 8 shows the flow of costs for each transaction. Note that the highlighted amounts in Exhibit 8 were determined from assigning the costs charged to production in the Mixing Department. These amounts were computed and are shown at the bottom of the cost of production report for the Mixing Department in Exhibit 7. Likewise, the amount transferred out of the Packaging Department to Finished Goods would have also been determined from a cost of production report for the Packaging Department.

EXHIBIT 8   **Frozen Delight's Cost Flows**

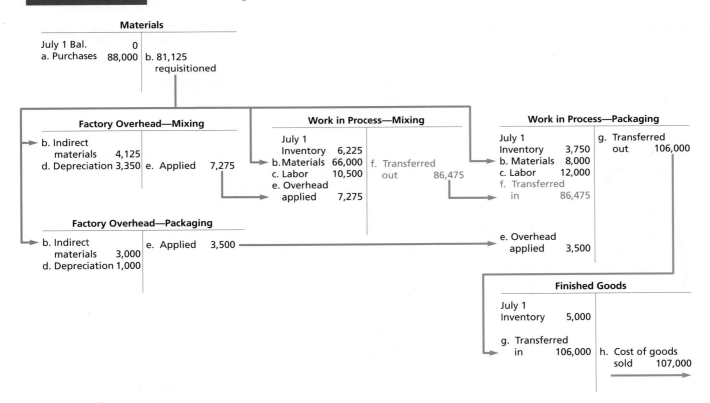

The ending inventories for Frozen Delight would be reported on the July 31 balance sheet as follows:

Materials	$ 6,875
Work in Process—Mixing Department	3,525
Work in Process—Packaging Department	7,725
Finished Goods	4,000
Total inventories	$22,125

The $3,525 of Work in Process—Mixing Department is the amount determined from the bottom of the cost of production report in Exhibit 7.

Example Exercise 3-7

objective **3**

The cost of materials transferred into the Bottling Department of Rocky Springs Beverage Company is $22,800, including $20,000 from the Blending Department and $2,800 from the materials storeroom. The conversion cost for the period in the Bottling Department is $8,790 ($3,790 factory overhead applied and $5,000 direct labor). The total cost transferred to Finished Goods for the period was $31,980. The Bottling Department had a beginning inventory of $1,860.

a.   Journalize (1) the cost of transferred-in materials, (2) conversion costs, and (3) the costs transferred out to Finished Goods.
b.   Determine the balance of Work in Process—Bottling at the end of the period.

Follow My Example 3-7

a.   1. Work in Process—Bottling 22,800
         Work in Process—Blending   20,000
         Materials   2,800

     2. Work in Process—Bottling 8,790
         Factory Overhead—Bottling   3,790
         Wages Payable   5,000

     3. Finished Goods 31,980
         Work in Process—Bottling   31,980

b. $1,470 ($1,860 + $22,800 + $8,790 − $31,980)

For Practice: PE 3-7A, PE 3-7B

Using the Cost of Production Report for Decision Making

objective **4**

Use cost of production reports for decision making.

The cost of production report is one source of information that may be used by managers to control and improve operations. A cost of production report will normally list costs in greater detail than in Exhibit 7. This greater detail helps management isolate problems and opportunities. To illustrate, assume that the Blending Department of Holland Beverage Company prepared cost of production reports for April and May. In addition, assume that the Blending Department had no beginning or ending work in process inventory either month. Thus, in this simple case, there is no need to determine equivalent units of production for allocating costs between completed and partially completed units. The cost of production reports for April and May in the Blending Department are as follows:

	A	B	C	D	
	Cost of Production Reports				
	Holland Beverage Company—Blending Department				
	For the Months Ended April 30 and May 31, 2008				
		April	**May**		
1	Direct materials	$ 20,000	$ 40,600		1
2	Direct labor	15,000	29,400		2
3	Energy	8,000	20,000		3
4	Repairs	4,000	8,000		4
5	Tank cleaning	3,000	8,000		5
6	Total	$ 50,000	$106,000		6
7	Units completed	/ 100,000	/ 200,000		7
8	Cost per unit	$ 0.50	$ 0.53		8

Note that the preceding reports provide more cost detail than simply reporting direct materials and conversion costs. The May results indicate that total unit costs have increased from $0.50 to $0.53, or 6% from the previous month. What caused this increase? To determine the possible causes for this increase, the cost of production report may be restated in per-unit terms by dividing all the cost information by the number of units completed, as shown below.

	A	B	C	D	
	Blending Department Per-Unit Expense Comparisons				
		April	May	% Change	
1	Direct materials	$0.200	$0.203	1.50%	1
2	Direct labor	0.150	0.147	−2.00%	2
3	Energy	0.080	0.100	25.00%	3
4	Repairs	0.040	0.040	0.00%	4
5	Tank cleaning	0.030	0.040	33.33%	5
6	Total	$0.500	$0.530	6.00%	6

Both energy and tank cleaning per-unit costs have increased dramatically in May. Further investigation should focus on these costs. For example, an increasing trend in energy may indicate that the machines are losing fuel efficiency, thereby requiring the company to purchase an increasing amount of fuel. This unfavorable trend could motivate management to repair the machines. The tank cleaning costs could be investigated in a similar fashion.

In addition to unit production cost trends, managers of process manufacturers are also concerned about yield trends. **Yield** is the ratio of the materials output quantity to the input quantity. A yield less than one occurs when the output quantity is less than the input quantity due to materials losses during the process. For example, if 1,000 pounds of sugar entered the packing operation, and only 980 pounds of sugar were packed, the yield would be 98%. Two percent or 20 pounds of sugar were lost or spilled during the packing process.

Example Exercise 3-8   objective 4

The cost of energy consumed in producing good units in the Bottling Department of Rocky Springs Beverage Company was $4,200 and $3,700 for March and April, respectively. The number of equivalent units produced in March and April was 70,000 liters and 74,000 liters, respectively. Evaluate the cost of energy between the two months.

Follow My Example 3-8

Energy cost per liter, March: $\dfrac{\$4,200}{70,000 \text{ liters}} = \$0.06$

Energy cost per liter, April: $\dfrac{\$3,700}{74,000 \text{ liters}} = \$0.05$

The cost of energy has appeared to improve by 1 cent per liter between March and April.

For Practice: PE 3-8A, PE 3-8B

Just-in-Time Processing

The objective of many companies is to produce products with high quality, low cost, and instant availability. One approach to achieving this objective is to implement just-in-time processing. **Just-in-time processing (JIT)** is a philosophy that focuses on reducing time and cost and eliminating poor quality. A JIT system achieves production efficiencies and flexibility by reorganizing the traditional production process.

In a traditional production process (illustrated in Exhibit 9), a product moves from process to process as each function or step is completed. Each worker is assigned a

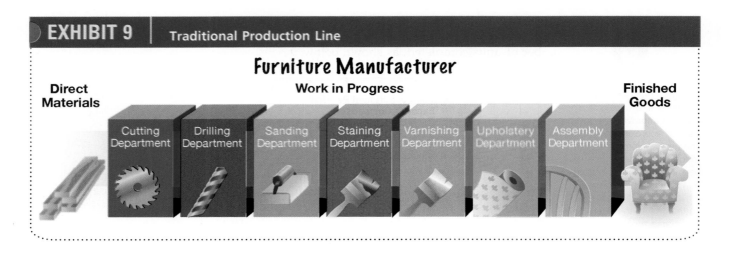

EXHIBIT 9 | Traditional Production Line

Furniture Manufacturer

Direct Materials — **Work in Progress** (Cutting Department, Drilling Department, Sanding Department, Staining Department, Varnishing Department, Upholstery Department, Assembly Department) — **Finished Goods**

The Internet complements a just-in-time processing strategy. Ford Motor Company states that the impact of the Internet is the equivalent of "the moving assembly line of the 21st Century." This is because the Internet will connect the whole supply chain—from customers to suppliers—to create a fast and efficient manufacturing system.

specific job, which is performed repeatedly as unfinished products are received from the preceding department. For example, a furniture manufacturer might use seven production departments to perform the operating functions necessary to manufacture furniture, as shown in the diagram in Exhibit 9.

For the furniture maker in the illustration, manufacturing would begin in the Cutting Department, where the wood would be cut to design specifications. Next, the Drilling Department would perform the drilling function, after which the Sanding Department would sand the wood, the Staining Department would stain the furniture, and the Varnishing Department would apply varnish and other protective coatings. Then, the Upholstery Department would add fabric and other materials. Finally, the Assembly Department would assemble the furniture to complete the process.

In the traditional production process, production supervisors attempt to enter enough materials into the process to keep all the manufacturing departments operating. Some departments, however, may process materials more rapidly than others. In addition, if one department stops production because of machine breakdowns, for example, the preceding departments usually continue production in order to avoid idle time. This may result in a build-up of work in process inventories in some departments.

In a just-in-time system, processing functions are combined into work centers, sometimes called **manufacturing cells**. For example, the seven departments illustrated above for the furniture manufacturer might be reorganized into three work centers. As shown in the diagram in Exhibit 10, Work Center One would perform the cutting, drilling, and sanding functions, Work Center Two would perform the staining and varnishing functions, and Work Center Three would perform the upholstery and assembly functions.

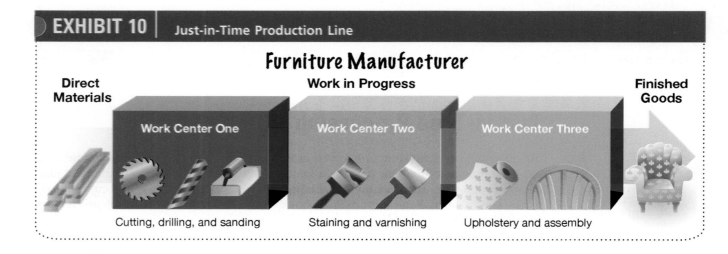

EXHIBIT 10 | Just-in-Time Production Line

Furniture Manufacturer

Direct Materials — **Work in Progress** (Work Center One, Work Center Two, Work Center Three) — **Finished Goods**

Cutting, drilling, and sanding   Staining and varnishing   Upholstery and assembly

In the traditional production line, a worker typically performs only one function. However, in a work center in which several functions take place, the workers are often cross-trained to perform more than one function. Research has indicated that workers who perform several manufacturing functions identify better with the end product. This creates pride in the product and improves quality and productivity.

Implementing JIT may also result in reorganizing service activities. Specifically, the service activities may be assigned to individual work centers, rather than to centralized service departments. For example, each work center may be assigned the responsibility for the repair and maintenance of its machinery and equipment. Accepting this responsibility creates an environment in which workers gain a better understanding of the production process and the machinery. In turn, workers tend to take better care of the machinery, which decreases repairs and maintenance costs, reduces machine downtime, and improves product quality.

In a JIT system, wasted motion from moving the product and materials is reduced. The product is often placed on a movable carrier that is centrally located in the work center. After the workers in a work center have completed their activities with the product, the entire carrier and any additional materials are moved just in time to satisfy the demand or need of the next work center. In this sense, the product is said to be "pulled through." Each work center is connected to other work centers through information contained on Kanbans, which is a Japanese term for cards.

The experience of Caterpillar illustrates the impact of JIT. Before implementing JIT, an average transmission would travel 10 miles through the factory and require 1,000 pieces of paper for materials, labor, and movement transactions. After implementing JIT, Caterpillar improved manufacturing so that an average transmission traveled only 200 feet and required only 10 pieces of paper.

In summary, the primary benefit of JIT systems is the increased efficiency of operations, which is achieved by eliminating waste and simplifying the production process. At the same time, JIT systems emphasize continuous improvement in the manufacturing process and the improvement of product quality.

Business Connections

P&G'S "PIT STOPS"

What do Procter & Gamble and Formula One racing have in common? The answer begins with P&G's Packing Department, which is where detergents and other products are filled on a "pack line." Containers move down the pack line and are filled with products from a packing machine. When it was time to change from a 36-oz. to a 54-oz. *Tide* box, for example, the changeover involved stopping the line, adjusting guide rails, retrieving items from the tool room, placing items back in the tool room, changing and cleaning the pack heads, and performing routine maintenance. Changing the pack line could be a very difficult process and typically took up to eight hours.

Management realized that it was important to reduce this time significantly in order to become more flexible and cost efficient in packing products. Where could they learn how to do changeovers faster? They turned to Formula One racing, reasoning that a pit stop was much like a changeover. As a result, P&G videotaped actual Formula One pit stops. These videos were used to form the following principles for conducting a fast changeover:

- Position the tools near their point of use on the line prior to stopping the line, to reduce time going back and forth to the tool room.
- Arrange the tools in the exact order of work, so that no time is wasted looking for a tool.
- Have each employee perform a very specific task during the changeover.
- Design the workflow so that employees don't interfere with each other.
- Have each employee in position at the moment the line is stopped.
- Train each employee, and practice, practice, practice.
- Put a stop watch on the changeover process.
- Plot improvements over time on a visible chart.

As a result of these changes, P&G was able to reduce pack-line changeover time from eight hours to 20 minutes. This allowed it to produce a much larger variety of products every day and to improve the cost performance of the Packing Department.

Appendix

Average Cost Method

A manufacturer uses a cost flow assumption in determining the costs flowing into, flowing out of, and remaining in each manufacturing department. In this chapter, we illustrated the first-in, first-out cost flow assumption for the Mixing Department of Frozen Delight Ice Cream Company. In this appendix, we illustrate the average cost flow method for S&W Ice Cream Company.

DETERMINING COSTS UNDER THE AVERAGE COST METHOD

S&W's operations are similar to those of Frozen Delight's in that S&W mixes cream and milk in refrigerated vessels and then fills containers with ice cream. Like Frozen Delight, S&W has two manufacturing departments, Mixing and Packaging. To illustrate the average cost method, we simplify by using only the Mixing Department of S&W. The manufacturing data for the Mixing Department for July 2008 are as follows:

Work in process inventory, July 1, 5,000 gallons (70% completed)	$ 6,200
Direct materials cost incurred in July, 60,000 gallons	66,000
Direct labor cost incurred in July	10,500
Factory overhead applied in July	6,405
Total production costs to account for	$89,105
Cost of goods transferred to Packaging in July (includes units in process on July 1), 62,000 gallons	?
Cost of work in process inventory, July 31, 3,000 gallons, 25% completed as to conversion costs	?

Using the average cost method, our objective is to allocate the total costs of production of $89,105 to the 62,000 gallons completed and transferred to the Packaging Department and the costs of the remaining 3,000 gallons in the ending work in process inventory. These costs are represented in the preceding table by two question marks. We determine these amounts by using the following four steps:

1. Determine the units to be assigned costs.
2. Compute equivalent units of production.
3. Determine the cost per equivalent unit.
4. Allocate costs to transferred and partially completed units.

Step 1: Determine the Units to Be Assigned Costs   The first step in our illustration is to determine the units to be assigned costs. A unit can be any measure of completed production, such as tons, gallons, pounds, barrels, or cases. We use gallons as the units for S&W.

S&W's Mixing Department had 65,000 gallons of direct materials to account for during July, as shown here:

Total gallons to account for:	
Work in process, July 1	5,000 gallons
Received from materials storeroom	60,000
Total units to account for by the Packaging Department	65,000 gallons

There are two categories of units to be assigned costs for the period: (1) units completed and transferred out and (2) units in the ending work in process inventory. During July, the Mixing Department completed and transferred 62,000 gallons to the

Packaging Department. Of the 60,000 gallons started in July, 57,000 (60,000 − 3,000) gallons were completed and transferred to the Packaging Department. Thus, the ending work in process inventory consists of 3,000 gallons.

The total units (gallons) to be assigned costs for S&W can be summarized as follows:

(1) Transferred out to the Packaging Department in July	62,000 gallons
(2) Work in process inventory, July 31	3,000
Total gallons to be assigned costs	65,000 gallons

Note that the total units (gallons) to be assigned costs (65,000 gallons) equal the total units to account for (65,000 gallons).

Step 2: Compute Equivalent Units of Production   S&W has 3,000 gallons of whole units in the work in process inventory for the Mixing Department on July 31. Since these units are 25% complete, the number of equivalent units in process in the Mixing Department on July 31 is 750 gallons (3,000 gallons × 25%). Since the units transferred to the Packaging Department have been completed, the whole units (62,000 gallons) transferred are the same as the equivalent units transferred.

The total equivalent units of production for the Mixing Department is determined by adding the equivalent units in the ending work in process inventory to the units transferred and completed during the period as shown here:

Equivalent units completed and transferred to the Packaging Department during July	62,000 gallons
Equivalent units in ending work in process, July 31	750
Total equivalent units	62,750 gallons

Step 3: Determine the Cost per Equivalent Unit   Materials and conversion costs are often combined in computing cost per equivalent unit under the average cost method. In doing so, the cost per equivalent unit is determined by dividing the total production costs by the total equivalent units of production as follows:

$$\text{Cost per Equivalent Unit} = \frac{\text{Total Production Costs}}{\text{Total Equivalent Units}} = \frac{\$89,105}{62,750 \text{ gallons}} = \$1.42$$

We use the cost per equivalent unit in step 4 to allocate the production costs to the completed and partially completed units.

Step 4: Allocate Costs to Transferred and Partially Completed Units   In step 4, we multiply the cost per equivalent unit by the equivalent units of production to determine the cost of transferred and partially completed units. For the Mixing Department, these costs are determined as follows:

(1) Transferred out to the Packaging Department (62,000 gallons × $1.42)	$88,040
(2) Work in process inventory, July 31 (3,000 gallons × 25% complete × $1.42)	1,065
Total production costs assigned	$89,105

THE COST OF PRODUCTION REPORT

The July cost of production report for S&W's Mixing Department is shown in Exhibit 11. The cost of production report in Exhibit 11 summarizes the following:

1. The units for which the department is accountable and the disposition of those units.
2. The production costs incurred by the department and the allocation of those costs between completed and partially completed units.

EXHIBIT 11

Cost of Production
Report for S&W's
Mixing Department

	A	B	C	
	S&W Ice Cream Company			
	Cost of Production Report—Mixing Department			
	For the Month Ended July 31, 2008			
	UNITS	**Step 1**	**Step 2**	
		Whole Units	Equivalent Units of Production	
1	Units to account for during production:			1
2	Work in process inventory, July 1	5,000		2
3	Received from materials storeroom	60,000		3
4	Total units accounted for by the Mixing Department	65,000		4
5				5
6	Units to be assigned costs:			6
7	Transferred to Packaging Department in July	62,000	62,000	7
8	Inventory in process, July 31 (25% completed)	3,000	750	8
9	Total units to be assigned costs	65,000	62,750	9
10				10
11	**COSTS**			11
12	**Step 3**			12
13	Cost per equivalent unit:			13
14	Total production costs for July in Mixing Department		$89,105	14
15	Total equivalent units (from step 2 above)		/62,750	15
16	Cost per equivalent unit		$ 1.42	16
17				17
18	Costs assigned to production:			18
19	Inventory in process, July 1		$ 6,200	19
20	Direct materials, direct labor, and factory overhead incurred in July		82,905	20
21	Total costs accounted for by the Mixing Department		$89,105	21
22				22
23	**Step 4**			23
24	Costs allocated to completed and partially completed units:			24
25	Transferred to Packaging Department in July (62,000 gallons × $1.42)		$88,040	25
26	Inventory in process, July 31 (3,000 gallons × 25% × $1.42)		1,065	26
27	Total costs assigned by the Mixing Department		$89,105	27

At a Glance

1. Explain and illustrate the characteristics and cost flows for a process manufacturer.

Key Points	Key Learning Outcomes	Example Exercises	Practice Exercises
The process cost system is best suited for industries that mass produce identical units of a product. Costs are charged to processing departments, rather than to jobs as with the job order cost system. These costs are transferred from one department to the next until production is completed.	• Identify the characteristics of a process manufacturer. • Compare and contrast the job order cost system with the process cost system. • Describe the physical and cost flows of a process manufacturer.	3-1	3-1A, 3-1B

2. Prepare a cost of production report, accounting for completed and partially completed units under the FIFO method.

Key Points	Key Learning Outcomes	Example Exercises	Practice Exercises
Manufacturing costs must be allocated between the units that have been completed and those that remain within the department. This allocation is accomplished by allocating costs using equivalent units of production during the period for the beginning inventory, units started and completed, and the ending inventory.	• Determine the whole units charged to production and to be assigned costs.	3-2	3-2A, 3-2B
	• Compute the equivalent units with respect to materials.	3-3	3-3A, 3-3B
	• Compute the equivalent units with respect to conversion.	3-4	3-4A, 3-4B
	• Compute the costs per equivalent unit.	3-5	3-5A, 3-5B
	• Allocate the costs to beginning inventory, units started and completed, and ending inventory.	3-6	3-6A, 3-6B
	• Prepare a cost of production report.		

3. Prepare journal entries for transactions of a process manufacturer.

Key Points	Key Learning Outcomes	Example Exercises	Practice Exercises
Prepare the summary journal entries for materials, labor, applied factory overhead, and transferred costs incurred in production.	• Prepare journal entries for process costing transactions.	3-7	3-7A, 3-7B
	• Summarize cost flows in T account form.		
	• Compute the ending inventory balances.		

4. Use cost of production reports for decision making.

Key Points	Key Learning Outcomes	Example Exercises	Practice Exercises
The cost of production report provides information for controlling and improving operations. The report(s) can provide details of a department for a single period, or over a period of time.	• Prepare and evaluate a report showing the change in costs per unit by cost element for comparative periods.	3-8	3-8A, 3-8B

5. Contrast just-in-time processing with conventional manufacturing practices.

Key Points	Key Learning Outcomes	Example Exercises	Practice Exercises
The just-in-time processing philosophy focuses on reducing time, cost, and poor quality within the process.	• Identify the characteristics of a just-in-time process.		

Key Terms

cost of production report (92)
cost per equivalent unit (90)
equivalent units of production (86)

first-in, first-out (FIFO) method (84)
just-in-time processing (JIT) (97)
manufacturing cells (98)

process cost system (81)
process manufacturers (80)
whole units (86)
yield (97)

Illustrative Problem

Southern Aggregate Company manufactures concrete by a series of four processes. All materials are introduced in Crushing. From Crushing, the materials pass through Sifting, Baking, and Mixing, emerging as finished concrete. All inventories are costed by the first-in, first-out method.

The balances in the accounts Work in Process—Mixing and Finished Goods were as follows on May 1, 2008:

Work in Process—Mixing (2,000 units, 1/4 completed)	$13,700
Finished Goods (1,800 units at $8.00 a unit)	14,400

The following costs were charged to Work in Process—Mixing during May:

Direct materials transferred from Baking:	
15,200 units at $6.50 a unit	$98,800
Direct labor	17,200
Factory overhead	11,780

During May, 16,000 units of concrete were completed, and 15,800 units were sold. Inventories on May 31 were as follows:

Work in Process—Mixing: 1,200 units, 1/2 completed
Finished Goods: 2,000 units

Instructions

1. Prepare a cost of production report for the Mixing Department.
2. Determine the cost of goods sold (indicate number of units and unit costs).
3. Determine the finished goods inventory, May 31, 2008.

Solution

1.

	A	B	C	D	E	
	Southern Aggregate Company					
	Cost of Production Report—Mixing Department					
	For the Month Ended May 31, 2008					
			Equivalent Units			
	UNITS	Whole Units	Direct Materials	Conversion		
1	Units charged to production:					1
2	Inventory in process, May 1	2,000				2
3	Received from Baking	15,200				3
4	Total units accounted for by the Mixing Department	17,200				4
5						5
6	Units to be assigned costs:					6
7	Inventory in process, May 1 (25% completed)	2,000	0	1,500		7
8	Started and completed in May	14,000	14,000	14,000		8
9	Transferred to finished goods in May	16,000	14,000	15,500		9
10	Inventory in process, May 31 (50% completed)	1,200	1,200	600		10
11	Total units to be assigned costs	17,200	15,200	16,100		11
12						12

13				Costs			13
14	**COSTS**			Direct Materials	Conversion	Total	14
15	Unit costs:						15
16	Total costs for May in Mixing			$ 98,800	$ 28,980		16
17	Total equivalent units (row 11)			/ 15,200	/ 16,100		17
18	Cost per equivalent unit			$ 6.50	$ 1.80		18
19							19
20	Costs assigned to production:						20
21	Inventory in process, May 1					$ 13,700	21
22	Costs incurred in May					127,780	22
23	Total costs accounted for by the Mixing Department					$141,480	23
24							24
25	Cost allocated to completed and partially						25
26	completed units:						26
27	Inventory in process, May 1—balance					$ 13,700	27
28	To complete inventory in process, May 1			$ 0	$ 2,700ª	2,700	28
29	Started and completed in May			91,000ᵇ	25,200ᶜ	116,200	29
30	Transferred to finished goods in May					$132,600	30
31	Inventory in process, May 31			$ 7,800ᵈ	$ 1,080ᵉ	8,880	31
32	Total costs assigned by the Mixing Department					$141,480	32

ª1,500 × $1.80 = $2,700   ᵇ14,000 × $6.50 = $91,000   ᶜ14,000 × $1.80 = $25,200   ᵈ1,200 × $6.50 = $7,800
ᵉ600 × $1.80 = $1,080

2. Cost of goods sold:

1,800 units at $8.00	$ 14,400	(from finished goods beginning inventory)
2,000 units at $8.20*	16,400	(from work in process beginning inventory)
12,000 units at $8.30**	99,600	(from May production started and completed)
15,800 units	$130,400	

*($13,700 + $2,700)/2,000
**$116,200/14,000

3. Finished goods inventory, May 31:

2,000 units at $8.30 $16,600

Self-Examination Questions

(Answers at End of Chapter)

1. For which of the following businesses would the process cost system be most appropriate?
   A. Custom furniture manufacturer
   B. Commercial building contractor
   C. Crude oil refinery
   D. Automobile repair shop

2. There were 2,000 pounds in process at the beginning of the period in the Packing Department. Packing received 24,000 pounds from the Blending Department during the month, of which 3,000 pounds were in process at the end of the month. How many pounds were completed and transferred to finished goods from the Packing Department?
   A. 23,000   C. 26,000
   B. 21,000   D. 29,000

3. Information relating to production in Department A for May is as follows:

May 1	Balance, 1,000 units, ¾ completed	$22,150
31	Direct materials, 5,000 units	75,000
31	Direct labor	32,500
31	Factory overhead	16,250

If 500 units were one-fourth completed at May 31, 5,500 units were completed during May, and inventories are costed by the first-in, first-out method, what was the number of equivalent units of production with respect to conversion costs for May?
   A. 4,500   C. 5,500
   B. 4,875   D. 6,000

4. Based on the data presented in Question 3, what is the conversion cost per equivalent unit?
   A. $10   C. $25
   B. $15   D. $32

5. Information from the accounting system revealed the following:

	Day 1	Day 2	Day 3	Day 4	Day 5
Materials	$ 20,000	$18,000	$ 22,000	$ 20,000	$ 20,000
Electricity	2,500	3,000	3,500	4,000	4,700
Maintenance	4,000	3,750	3,400	3,000	2,800
Total costs	$ 26,500	$24,750	$ 28,900	$ 27,000	$ 27,500
Pounds produced	÷10,000	÷9,000	÷11,000	÷10,000	÷10,000
Cost per unit	$ 2.65	$ 2.75	$ 2.63	$ 2.70	$ 2.75

Which of the following statements best interprets this information?
A. The total costs are out of control.
B. The product costs have steadily increased because of higher electricity costs.
C. Electricity costs have steadily increased because of lack of maintenance.
D. The unit costs reveal a significant operating problem.

Eye Openers

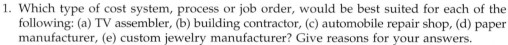

1. Which type of cost system, process or job order, would be best suited for each of the following: (a) TV assembler, (b) building contractor, (c) automobile repair shop, (d) paper manufacturer, (e) custom jewelry manufacturer? Give reasons for your answers.
2. In job order cost accounting, the three elements of manufacturing cost are charged directly to job orders. Why is it not necessary to charge manufacturing costs in process cost accounting to job orders?
3. In a job order cost system, direct labor and factory overhead applied are debited to individual jobs. How are these items treated in a process cost system and why?
4. What are transferred-out materials?
5. What are the four steps for determining the cost of goods completed and the ending inventory?
6. What is meant by the term *equivalent units*?
7. Why is the cost per equivalent unit often determined separately for direct materials and conversion costs?
8. What is the purpose for determining the cost per equivalent unit?
9. Rameriz Company is a process manufacturer with two production departments, Blending and Filling. All direct materials are introduced in Blending from the materials store area. What is included in the cost transferred to Filling?
10. How is actual factory overhead accounted for in a process manufacturer?
11. What is the most important purpose of the cost of production report?
12. How are cost of production reports used for controlling and improving operations?
13. How is "yield" determined for a process manufacturer?
14. What is just-in-time processing?
15. How does just-in-time processing differ from the conventional manufacturing process?

Practice Exercises

PE 3-1A
Job order vs. process costing
obj. 1

Which of the following industries would typically use job order costing, and which would typically use process costing?

Aluminum production	Papermaking
Gasoline refining	Print shop
Movie studio	Web designer

PE 3-1B
Job order vs. process costing
obj. 1

Which of the following industries would typically use job order costing, and which would typically use process costing?

Apparel manufacturing	Automobile repair
Business consulting	Plastic manufacturing
CD manufacture	Steel manufacturing

PE 3-2A
Determine the units to be assigned costs
obj. 2

Keystone Personal Care Company consists of two departments, Blending and Filling. The Filling Department received 532,000 ounces from the Blending Department. During the period, the Filling Department completed 545,000 ounces, including 32,000 ounces of work in process at the beginning of the period. The ending work in process inventory was 19,000 ounces. How many ounces were started and completed during the period?

PE 3-2B
Determine the units to be assigned costs
obj. 2

Mohawk Valley Steel Company has two departments, Casting and Rolling. In the Rolling Department, ingots from the Casting Department are rolled into steel sheet. The Rolling Department received 83,680 tons from the Casting Department. During the period, the Rolling Department completed 81,450 tons, including 3,450 tons of work in process at the beginning of the period. The ending work in process inventory was 5,680 tons. How many tons were started and completed during the period?

PE 3-3A
Determine the equivalent units of materials
obj. 2

The Filling Department of Keystone Personal Care Company had 32,000 ounces in beginning work in process inventory (40% complete). During the period, 545,000 ounces were completed. The ending work in process inventory was 19,000 ounces (75% complete). What are the total equivalent units for direct materials if materials are added at the beginning of the process?

PE 3-3B
Determine the equivalent units of materials
obj. 2

The Rolling Department of Mohawk Valley Steel Company had 3,450 tons in beginning work in process inventory (20% complete). During the period, 81,450 tons were completed. The ending work in process inventory was 5,680 tons (25% complete). What are the total equivalent units for direct materials if materials are added at the beginning of the process?

PE 3-4A
Determine the equivalent units of conversion cost
obj. 2

The Filling Department of Keystone Personal Care Company had 32,000 ounces in beginning work in process inventory (40% complete). During the period, 545,000 ounces were completed. The ending work in process inventory was 19,000 ounces (75% complete). What are the total equivalent units for conversion costs?

PE 3-4B
Determine the equivalent units of conversion cost
obj. 2

The Rolling Department of Mohawk Valley Steel Company had 3,450 tons in beginning work in process inventory (20% complete). During the period, 81,450 tons were completed. The ending work in process inventory was 5,680 tons (25% complete). What are the total equivalent units for conversion costs?

PE 3-5A
Determine the cost per equivalent unit
obj. 2

The cost of direct materials transferred into the Filling Department of Keystone Personal Care Company is $170,240. The conversion cost for the period in the Filling Department is $87,432. The total equivalent units for direct materials and conversion are 532,000 ounces and 546,450 ounces, respectively. Determine the direct materials and conversion cost per equivalent unit.

PE 3-5B
Determine the cost per equivalent unit
obj. 2

The cost of direct materials transferred into the Rolling Department of Mohawk Valley Steel Company is $4,895,280. The conversion cost for the period in the Rolling Department is $953,288. The total equivalent units for direct materials and conversion are 83,680 tons and 82,180 tons, respectively. Determine the direct materials and conversion cost per equivalent unit.

PE 3-6A
Determine the cost of completed production and the ending work in process balance
obj. 2

The cost per equivalent unit of direct materials and conversion in the Filling Department of Keystone Personal Care Company is $0.32 and $0.16, respectively. The equivalent units to be assigned costs are as follows:

	Equivalent Units	
	Direct Materials	**Conversion**
Inventory in process, beginning of period	0	19,200
Started and completed during the period	513,000	513,000
Transferred out of Filling (completed)	513,000	532,200
Inventory in process, end of period	19,000	14,250
Total units to be assigned costs	532,000	546,450

The beginning work in process inventory had a cost of $12,500. Determine the cost of completed and transferred-out production and the ending work in process inventory.

PE 3-6B
Determine the cost of completed production and the ending work in process balance
obj. 2

The cost per equivalent unit of direct materials and conversion in the Rolling Department of Mohawk Valley Steel Company is $58.50 and $11.60, respectively. The equivalent units to be assigned costs are as follows:

	Equivalent Units	
	Direct Materials	Conversion
Inventory in process, beginning of period	0	2,760
Started and completed during the period	78,000	78,000
Transferred out of Rolling (completed)	78,000	80,760
Inventory in process, end of period	5,680	1,420
Total units to be assigned costs	83,680	82,180

The beginning work in process inventory had a cost of $209,000. Determine the cost of completed and transferred-out production and the ending work in process inventory.

PE 3-7A
Journalize process costing transactions
obj. 3

The cost of materials transferred into the Filling Department of Keystone Personal Care Company is $170,240, including $50,100 from the Blending Department and $120,140 from the materials storeroom. The conversion cost for the period in the Filling Department is $87,432 ($35,432 factory overhead applied and $52,000 direct labor). The total cost transferred to Finished Goods for the period was $261,812. The Filling Department had a beginning inventory of $12,500.

a. Journalize (1) the cost of transferred-in materials, (2) conversion costs, and (3) the costs transferred out to Finished Goods.
b. Determine the balance of Work in Process—Filling at the end of the period.

PE 3-7B
Journalize process costing transactions
obj. 3

The cost of materials transferred into the Rolling Department of Mohawk Valley Steel Company is $4,895,280 from the Casting Department. The conversion cost for the period in the Rolling Department is $953,288 ($553,038 factory overhead applied and $400,250 direct labor). The total cost transferred to Finished Goods for the period was $5,708,816. The Rolling Department had a beginning inventory of $209,000.

a. Journalize (1) the cost of transferred-in materials, (2) conversion costs, and (3) the costs transferred out to Finished Goods.
b. Determine the balance of Work in Process—Rolling at the end of the period.

PE 3-8A
Decision making
obj. 4

The cost of materials consumed in producing good units in the Forming Department was $88,000 and $80,500 for July and August, respectively. The number of equivalent units produced in July and August was 400 tons and 350 tons, respectively. Evaluate the cost of materials between the two months.

PE 3-8B
Decision making
obj. 4

The cost of energy consumed in producing good units in the Baking Department was $150,000 and $154,000 for October and November, respectively. The number of equivalent units produced in October and November was 500,000 pounds and 550,000 pounds, respectively. Evaluate the cost of energy between the two months.

Exercises

EX 3-1
Entries for materials cost flows in a process cost system
objs. 1, 3

The Hershey Foods Company manufactures chocolate confectionery products. The three largest raw materials are cocoa beans, sugar, and dehydrated milk. These raw materials first go into the Blending Department. The blended product is then sent to the Molding Department, where the bars of candy are formed. The candy is then sent to the Packing Department, where the bars are wrapped and boxed. The boxed candy is then sent to the distribution center, where it is eventually sold to food brokers and retailers.

Show the accounts debited and credited for each of the following business events:

a. Materials used by the Blending Department.
b. Transfer of blended product to the Molding Department.
c. Transfer of chocolate to the Packing Department.
d. Transfer of boxed chocolate to the distribution center.
e. Sale of boxed chocolate.

EX 3-2
Flowchart of accounts related to service and processing departments
obj. 1

Alcoa Inc. is the world's largest producer of aluminum products. One product that Alcoa manufactures is aluminum sheet products for the aerospace industry. The entire output of the Smelting Department is transferred to the Rolling Department. Part of the fully processed goods from the Rolling Department are sold as rolled sheet, and the remainder of the goods are transferred to the Converting Department for further processing into sheared sheet.

Prepare a chart of the flow of costs from the processing department accounts into the finished goods accounts and then into the cost of goods sold account. The relevant accounts are as follows:

Cost of Goods Sold	Finished Goods—Rolled Sheet
Materials	Finished Goods—Sheared Sheet
Factory Overhead—Smelting Department	Work in Process—Smelting Department
Factory Overhead—Rolling Department	Work in Process—Rolling Department
Factory Overhead—Converting Department	Work in Process—Converting Department

EX 3-3
Entries for flow of factory costs for process cost system
objs. 1, 3

Domino Foods, Inc., manufactures a sugar product by a continuous process, involving three production departments—Refining, Sifting, and Packing. Assume that records indicate that direct materials, direct labor, and applied factory overhead for the first department, Refining, were $355,000, $132,000, and $93,600, respectively. Also, work in process in the Refining Department at the beginning of the period totaled $25,500, and work in process at the end of the period totaled $31,200.

Journalize the entries to record (a) the flow of costs into the Refining Department during the period for (1) direct materials, (2) direct labor, and (3) factory overhead, and (b) the transfer of production costs to the second department, Sifting.

EX 3-4
Factory overhead rate, entry for applying factory overhead, and factory overhead account balance
objs. 1, 3
✓ a. 140%

The chief cost accountant for Crystal Spring Beverage Co. estimated that total factory overhead cost for the Blending Department for the coming fiscal year beginning March 1 would be $455,000, and total direct labor costs would be $325,000. During March, the actual direct labor cost totaled $27,000, and factory overhead cost incurred totaled $36,000.

a. What is the predetermined factory overhead rate based on direct labor cost?
b. Journalize the entry to apply factory overhead to production for March.
c. What is the March 31 balance of the account Factory Overhead—Blending Department?
d. Does the balance in part (c) represent overapplied or underapplied factory overhead?

EX 3-5
Equivalent units of production
obj. 2
✓ Direct materials, 15,640 units

The Converting Department of Stay-Soft Napkin Company had 760 units in work in process at the beginning of the period, which were 75% complete. During the period, 15,400 units were completed and transferred to the Packing Department. There were 1,000 units in process at the end of the period, which were 30% complete. Direct materials are placed into the process at the beginning of production. Determine the number of equivalent units of production with respect to direct materials and conversion costs.

EX 3-6
Equivalent units of production

obj. 2

✓ *a. Conversion, 68,220 units*

Units of production data for the two departments of Global Cable and Wire Company for June of the current fiscal year are as follows:

	Drawing Department	Winding Department
Work in process, June 1	6,200 units, 30% completed	1,500 units, 60% completed
Completed and transferred to next processing department during June	68,000 units	67,700 units
Work in process, June 30	3,200 units, 65% completed	1,800 units, 25% completed

If all direct materials are placed in process at the beginning of production, determine the direct materials and conversion equivalent units of production for June for (a) the Drawing Department and (b) the Winding Department.

EX 3-7
Equivalent units of production

obj. 2

✓ *b. Conversion, 124,600*

The following information concerns production in the Extruding Department for August. All direct materials are placed in process at the beginning of production.

ACCOUNT *Work in Process—Extruding Department*   **ACCOUNT NO.**

Date		Item	Debit	Credit	Balance Debit	Balance Credit
Aug.	1	Bal., 12,000 units, $^2/_5$ completed			26,000	
	31	Direct materials, 125,000 units	237,500		263,500	
	31	Direct labor	68,000		331,500	
	31	Factory overhead	37,910		369,410	
	31	Goods finished, 118,000 units		323,620	45,790	
	31	Bal.—units, $^3/_5$ completed			45,790	

a. Determine the number of units in work in process inventory at the end of the month.
b. Determine the equivalent units of production for direct materials and conversion costs in August.

EX 3-8
Costs per equivalent unit

obj. 2

✓ *a. 2. Conversion cost per equivalent unit, $0.85*

a. Based upon the data in Exercise 3-7, determine the following:
   1. Direct materials cost per equivalent unit.
   2. Conversion cost per equivalent unit.
   3. Cost of the beginning work in process completed during August.
   4. Cost of units started and completed during August.
   5. Cost of the ending work in process.
b. Assuming that the direct materials cost is the same for July and August, did the conversion cost per equivalent unit increase, decrease, or remain the same in August?

EX 3-9
Equivalent units of production

obj. 2

Kellogg Company manufactures cold cereal products, such as *Frosted Flakes*. Assume that the inventory in process on October 1 for the Packing Department included 2,250 pounds of cereal in the packing machine hopper. In addition, there were 1,500 empty 24-oz. boxes held in the package carousel of the packing machine. During October, 26,500 boxes of 24-oz. cereal were packaged. Conversion costs are incurred when a box is filled with cereal. On October 31, the packing machine hopper held 900 pounds of cereal, and the package carousel held 600 empty 24-oz. ($1^1/_2$-pound) boxes. Assume that once a box is filled with cereal, it is immediately transferred to the finished goods warehouse.

Determine the equivalent units of production for cereal, boxes, and conversion costs for October. An equivalent unit is defined as "pounds" for cereal and "24-oz. boxes" for boxes and conversion costs.

EX 3-10
Costs per equivalent unit

obj. 2

✓ *c. $2.90*

Pacific Products Inc. completed and transferred 150,000 particle board units of production from the Pressing Department. There was no beginning inventory in process in the department. The ending in-process inventory was 14,000 units, which were $^3/_5$ complete as to conversion cost. All materials are added at the beginning of the process. Direct materials cost incurred was $475,600, direct labor cost incurred was $69,720, and factory overhead applied was $25,320.

Determine the following for the Pressing Department:

a. Total conversion cost
b. Conversion cost per equivalent unit
c. Direct materials cost per equivalent unit

EX 3-11
Equivalent units of production and related costs

obj. 2

✓ a. 7,500 units

The charges to Work in Process—Assembly Department for a period, together with information concerning production, are as follows. All direct materials are placed in process at the beginning of production.

Work in Process—Assembly Department			
Bal., 3,000 units, 40% completed	8,550	To Finished Goods, 62,500 units	?
Direct materials, 67,000 units @ $1.55	103,850		
Direct labor	145,300		
Factory overhead	56,860		
Bal. _?_ units, 25% completed	?		

Determine the following:

a. The number of units in work in process inventory at the end of the period.
b. Equivalent units of production for direct materials and conversion.
c. Costs per equivalent unit for direct materials and conversion.
d. Cost of the units started and completed during the period.

EX 3-12
Cost of units completed and in process

obj. 2

✓ a. 1. $14,310

a. Based upon the data in Exercise 3-11, determine the following:
   1. Cost of beginning work in process inventory completed this period.
   2. Cost of units transferred to finished goods during the period.
   3. Cost of ending work in process inventory.
   4. Cost per unit of beginning work in process completed during the period.
b. Did the production costs change from the preceding period? Explain.
c. Assuming that the direct materials cost per unit did not change from the preceding period, did the conversion costs per equivalent unit increase, decrease, or remain the same for the current period?

EX 3-13
Errors in equivalent unit computation

obj. 2

Louisiana Oil Refining Company processes gasoline. At June 1 of the current year, 4,500 units were ³/₅ completed in the Blending Department. During June, 20,000 units entered the Blending Department from the Refining Department. During June, the units in process at the beginning of the month were completed. Of the 20,000 units entering the department, all were completed except 6,200 units that were ¹/₅ completed. The equivalent units for conversion costs for June for the Blending Department were computed as follows:

Equivalent units of production in June:	
To process units in inventory on June 1:	
4,500 × ³/₅	2,700
To process units started and completed in June:	
20,000 − 4,500	15,500
To process units in inventory on June 30:	
6,200 × ¹/₅	1,240
Equivalent units of production	19,440

List the errors in the computation of equivalent units for conversion costs for the Blending Department for June.

EX 3-14
Cost per equivalent unit

obj. 2

✓ a. 54,000 units

The following information concerns production in the Forging Department for November. All direct materials are placed into the process at the beginning of production, and conversion costs are incurred evenly throughout the process. The beginning inventory consists of $105,750 of direct materials.

(continued)

ACCOUNT **Work in Process—Forging Department**   ACCOUNT NO.

Date		Item	Debit	Credit	Balance Debit	Balance Credit
Nov.	1	Bal., 9,000 units, 60% completed			127,350	
	30	Direct materials, 50,000 units	580,000		707,350	
	30	Direct labor	78,970		786,320	
	30	Factory overhead	125,415		911,735	
	30	Goods transferred, _?_ units		?	?	
	30	Bal., 5,000 units, 25% completed			?	

a. Determine the number of units transferred to the next department.
b. Determine the cost per equivalent unit of direct materials and conversion.
c. Determine the cost of units started and completed in November.

EX 3-15
Costs per equivalent unit and production costs
obj. 2

✓a. $142,110

Based upon the data in Exercise 3-14, determine the following:

a. Cost of beginning work in process inventory completed in November.
b. Cost of units transferred to the next department during November.
c. Cost of ending work in process inventory on November 30.
d. Cost per equivalent unit of direct materials and conversion included in the November 1 beginning work in process.
e. The November increase or decrease in cost per equivalent unit for direct materials and conversion.

EX 3-16
Cost of production report
obj. 2

✓d. $26,676

The debits to Work in Process—Cooking Department for Yankee Bean Company for March 2008, together with information concerning production, are as follows:

Work in process, March 1, 3,000 pounds, 30% completed		$ 14,160*
*Direct materials (3,000 × $4.00)	$12,000	
Conversion (3,000 × 30% × $2.40)	2,160	
	$14,160	

Beans added during March, 85,900 pounds	352,190
Conversion costs during March	194,242
Work in process, March 31, 5,700 pounds, 25% completed	?
Goods finished during March, 83,200 pounds	?

All direct materials are placed in process at the beginning of production. Prepare a cost of production report, presenting the following computations:

a. Direct materials and conversion equivalent units of production for March.
b. Direct materials and conversion cost per equivalent unit for March.
c. Cost of goods finished during March.
d. Cost of work in process at March 31, 2008.

EX 3-17
Cost of production report
obj. 2

✓ Conversion rate, $5.20

Prepare a cost of production report for the Cutting Department of Aladdin Carpet Company for May 2008, using the following data and assuming that all materials are added at the beginning of the process:

Work in process, May 1, 5,000 units, 75% completed		$ 49,800*
*Direct materials (5,000 × $6.00)	$30,000	
Conversion (5,000 × 75% × $5.28)	19,800	
	$49,800	

Materials added during May from Weaving Department, 186,000 units	1,134,600
Direct labor for May	405,600
Factory overhead for May	540,436
Goods finished during May (includes goods in process, May 1), 183,400 units	—
Work in process, May 31, 7,600 units, 30% completed	—

EX 3-18
Cost of production and journal entries
objs. 1, 2, 3

✓ b. $31,100

Titanium Metals Inc. casts blades for turbine engines. Within the Casting Department, alloy is first melted in a crucible, then poured into molds to produce the castings. On October 1, there were 700 pounds of alloy in process, which were 60% complete as to conversion. The Work in Process balance for these 700 pounds was $45,920, determined as follows:

Direct materials (700 × $47)	$32,900
Conversion (700 × 60% × $31)	13,020
	$45,920

During October, the Casting Department was charged $441,000 for 9,000 pounds of alloy and $108,000 for direct labor. Factory overhead is applied to the department at a rate of 150% of direct labor. The department transferred out 9,200 pounds of finished castings to the Machining Department. The October 31 inventory in process was 44% complete as to conversion.

a. Prepare the following October journal entries for the Casting Department:
   1. The materials charged to production.
   2. The conversion costs charged to production.
   3. The completed production transferred to the Machining Department.
b. Determine the Work in Process—Casting Department October 31 balance.

EX 3-19
Cost of production and journal entries
objs. 1, 2, 3

✓ b. $49,800

Papyrus Paper Company manufactures newsprint. The product is manufactured in two departments, Papermaking and Converting. Pulp is first placed into a vessel at the beginning of papermaking production. The following information concerns production in the Papermaking Department for July.

ACCOUNT Work in Process—Papermaking Department   **ACCOUNT NO.**

Date		Item	Debit	Credit	Balance Debit	Balance Credit
July	1	Bal., 5,000 units, 20% completed			24,500	
	31	Direct materials, 68,000 units	306,000		330,500	
	31	Direct labor	100,000		430,500	
	31	Factory overhead	61,000		491,500	
	31	Goods transferred, 65,000 units		?	?	
	31	Bal., 8,000 units, 75% completed			?	

a. Prepare the following July journal entries for the Papermaking Department:
   1. The materials charged to production.
   2. The conversion costs charged to production.
   3. The completed production transferred to the Converting Department.
b. Determine the Work in Process—Papermaking Department July 31 balance.

EX 3-20
Decision making
obj. 4

Oasis Bottling Company bottles popular beverages in the Bottling Department. The beverages are produced by blending concentrate with water and sugar. The concentrate is purchased from a concentrate producer. The concentrate producer sets higher prices for the more popular concentrate flavors. Below is a simplified Bottling Department cost of production report separating the cost of bottling the four flavors.

	A	B Orange	C Cola	D Lemon-Lime	E Root Beer	
1	Concentrate	$ 5,400	$110,000	$ 63,000	$1,800	1
2	Water	1,800	30,000	18,000	600	2
3	Sugar	3,000	50,000	30,000	1,000	3
4	Bottles	6,600	110,000	66,000	2,200	4
5	Flavor changeover	3,000	6,000	3,600	3,000	5
6	Conversion cost	2,400	25,000	15,000	800	6
7	Total cost transferred to finished goods	$22,200	$331,000	$195,600	$9,400	7
8	Number of cases	3,000	50,000	30,000	1,000	8

Beginning and ending work in process inventories are negligible, so are omitted from the cost of production report. The flavor changeover cost represents the cost of cleaning the bottling machines between production runs of different flavors.

➤ Prepare a memo to the production manager analyzing this comparative cost information. In your memo, provide recommendations for further action, along with supporting schedules showing the total cost per case and cost per case by cost element.

EX 3-21
Decision making
obj. 4

Instant Memories Inc. produces film products for cameras. One of the processes for this operation is a coating (solvent spreading) operation, where chemicals are coated on to film stock. There has been some concern about the cost performance of this operation. As a result, you have begun an investigation. You first discover that all input prices have not changed for the last six months. If there is a problem, it is related to the quantity of input. You have discovered three possible problems from some of the operating personnel whose quotes follow:

Operator 1: "I've been keeping an eye on my operating room instruments. I feel as though our energy consumption is becoming less efficient."

Operator 2: "Every time the coating machine goes down, we produce waste on shutdown and subsequent startup. It seems like during the last half year we have had more unscheduled machine shutdowns than in the past. Thus, I feel as though our yields must be dropping."

Operator 3: "My sense is that our coating costs are going up. It seems to me like we are spreading a thicker coating than we should. Perhaps the coating machine needs to be recalibrated."

The Coating Department had no beginning or ending inventories for any month during the study period. The following data from the cost of production report are made available:

	A	B	C	D	E	F	G	
		January	February	March	April	May	June	
1	Materials	$54,880	$68,600	$61,740	$51,450	$54,880	$68,600	1
2	Coating cost	$15,680	$21,560	$22,050	$20,580	$22,736	$31,360	2
3	Conversion cost (incl. energy)	$39,200	$49,000	$44,100	$36,750	$39,200	$49,000	3
4	Pounds input to the process	80,000	100,000	90,000	75,000	80,000	100,000	4
5	Pounds transferred out	78,400	98,000	88,200	73,500	78,400	98,000	5

a. Prepare a table showing the materials cost per output pound, coating cost per output pound, conversion cost per output pound, and yield for each month.
b. Interpret your table results.

EX 3-22
Just-in-time manufacturing
obj. 5

The following are some quotes provided by a number of managers at Mesa Machining Company regarding the company's planned move toward a just-in-time manufacturing system:

Director of Sales: I'm afraid we'll miss some sales if we don't keep a large stock of items on hand just in case demand increases. It only makes sense to me to keep large inventories in order to assure product availability for our customers.

Director of Purchasing: I'm very concerned about moving to a just-in-time system for materials. What would happen if one of our suppliers were unable to make a shipment? A supplier could fall behind in production or have a quality problem. Without some safety stock in our materials, our whole plant would shut down.

Director of Manufacturing: If we go to just-in-time, I think our factory output will drop. We need in-process inventory in order to "smooth out" the inevitable problems that occur during manufacturing. For example, if a machine that is used to process a product breaks down, I would starve the next machine if I don't have in-process inventory between the two machines. If I have in-process inventory, then I can keep the next operation busy while I fix the broken machine. Thus, the in-process inventories give me a safety valve that I can use to keep things running when things go wrong.

➤ How would you respond to these managers?

**APPENDIX
EX 3-23**
*Equivalent units of
production: average cost
method*

✓ a. 25,400

The Converting Department of Kwan Napkin Company uses the average cost method and had 1,500 units in work in process that were 60% complete at the beginning of the period. During the period, 24,500 units were completed and transferred to the Packing Department. There were 900 units in process that were 40% complete at the end of the period.

a. Determine the number of whole units to be accounted for and to be assigned costs for the period.
b. Determine the number of equivalent units of production for the period.

**APPENDIX
EX 3-24**
*Equivalent units of
production: average cost
method*

✓ a. 94,500 units to be
accounted for

Units of production data for the two departments of Frontier Cable and Wire Company for March of the current fiscal year are as follows:

	Drawing Department	Winding Department
Work in process, March 1	1,700 units, 50% completed	1,000 units, 30% completed
Completed and transferred to next processing department during March	92,000 units	90,400 units
Work in process, March 31	2,500 units, 65% completed	2,600 units, 25% completed

Each department uses the average cost method.

a. Determine the number of whole units to be accounted for and to be assigned costs and the equivalent units of production for the Drawing Department.
b. Determine the number of whole units to be accounted for and to be assigned costs and the equivalent units of production for the Winding Department.

**APPENDIX
EX 3-25**
*Equivalent units of
production: average cost
method*

✓ a. 9,000

The following information concerns production in the Finishing Department for March. The Finishing Department uses the average cost method.

ACCOUNT *Work in Process—Finishing Department*   **ACCOUNT NO.**

					Balance	
Date		Item	Debit	Credit	Debit	Credit
Mar.	1	Bal., 12,000 units, 40% completed			22,320	
	31	Direct materials, 125,000 units	325,000		347,320	
	31	Direct labor	174,500		521,820	
	31	Factory overhead	93,200		615,020	
	31	Goods transferred, 128,000 units		586,240	28,780	
	31	Bal., _?_ units, 70% completed			28,780	

a. Determine the number of units in work in process inventory at the end of the month.
b. Determine the number of whole units to be accounted for and to be assigned costs and the equivalent units of production for March.

**APPENDIX
EX 3-26**
*Equivalent units of
production and related
costs*

✓ b. 82,720 units

The charges to Work in Process—Baking Department for a period as well as information concerning production are as follows. The Baking Department uses the average cost method, and all direct materials are placed in process during production.

Work in Process—Baking Department			
Bal., 5,000 units, 70% completed	10,000	To Finished Goods, 81,100 units	?
Direct materials, 81,500 units	195,700		
Direct labor	123,036		
Factory overhead	89,000		
Bal., 5,400 units, 30% completed	?		

Determine the following:

a. The number of whole units to be accounted for and to be assigned costs.
b. The number of equivalent units of production.   *(continued)*

c. The cost per equivalent unit.
d. The cost of the units transferred to Finished Goods.
e. The cost of ending Work in Process.

**APPENDIX
EX 3-27**
*Cost per equivalent unit:
average cost method*

✓ a. $20.00

The following information concerns production in the Forging Department for April. The Forging Department uses the average cost method.

ACCOUNT *Work in Process—Forging Department*　　　　　　　　　　　　**ACCOUNT NO.**

Date		Item	Debit	Credit	Balance Debit	Balance Credit
Apr.	1	Bal., 3,000 units, 40% completed			24,000	
	30	Direct materials, 28,500 units	355,800		379,800	
	30	Direct labor	128,200		508,000	
	30	Factory overhead	100,500		608,500	
	30	Goods transferred, 27,200 units		?	?	
	30	Bal., 4,300 units, 75% completed			?	

a. Determine the cost per equivalent unit.
b. Determine the cost of the units transferred to Finished Goods.
c. Determine the cost of ending Work in Process.

**APPENDIX
EX 3-28**
*Cost of production report:
average cost method*

✓ *Cost per equivalent
unit, $2.15*

The increases to Work in Process—Cooking Department for Boston Beans Company for January 2008 as well as information concerning production are as follows:

Work in process, January 1, 1,000 pounds, 40% completed	$ 900
Beans added during January, 58,200 pounds	92,400
Conversion costs during January	33,593
Work in process, January 31, 600 pounds, 70% completed	—
Goods finished during January, 58,600 pounds	—

Prepare a cost of production report, using the average cost method.

**APPENDIX
EX 3-29**
*Cost of production report:
average cost method*

✓ *Cost per equivalent
unit, $5.98*

Prepare a cost of production report for the Cutting Department of North Georgia Carpet Company for May 2008. Use the average cost method with the following data:

Work in process, May 1, 13,000 units, 75% completed	$ 58,000
Materials added during May from Weaving Department, 205,000 units	914,780
Direct labor for May	158,600
Factory overhead for May	100,500
Goods finished during May (includes goods in process, May 1), 202,000 units	—
Work in process, May 31, 16,000 units, 25% completed	—

Problems Series A

PR 3-1A
*Entries for process cost
system*

objs. 1, 3

✓ *2. Materials October
31 balance, $47,400*

Living Decor Carpet Company manufactures carpets. Fiber is placed in process in the Spinning Department, where it is spun into yarn. The output of the Spinning Department is transferred to the Tufting Department, where carpet backing is added at the beginning of the process and the process is completed. On October 1, Living Decor Carpet Company had the following inventories:

Finished Goods	$56,900
Work in Process—Spinning Department	7,900
Work in Process—Tufting Department	21,400
Materials	36,200

Departmental accounts are maintained for factory overhead, and both have zero balances on October 1.

Manufacturing operations for October are summarized as follows:

a. Materials purchased on account	$810,900
b. Materials requisitioned for use:	
Fiber—Spinning Department	$532,400
Carpet backing—Tufting Department	201,800
Indirect materials—Spinning Department	50,700
Indirect materials—Tufting Department	14,800
c. Labor used:	
Direct labor—Spinning Department	$224,100
Direct labor—Tufting Department	178,900
Indirect labor—Spinning Department	134,200
Indirect labor—Tufting Department	115,500
d. Depreciation charged on fixed assets:	
Spinning Department	$56,200
Tufting Department	33,000
e. Expired prepaid factory insurance:	
Spinning Department	$10,000
Tufting Department	8,000
f. Applied factory overhead:	
Spinning Department	$244,600
Tufting Department	173,200
g. Production costs transferred from Spinning Department to Tufting Department	$946,700
h. Production costs transferred from Tufting Department to Finished Goods	$1,400,500
i. Cost of goods sold during the period	$1,395,800

Instructions

1. Journalize the entries to record the operations, identifying each entry by letter.
2. Compute the October 31 balances of the inventory accounts.
3. Compute the October 31 balances of the factory overhead accounts.

PR 3-2A
Entries for process cost system

objs. 1, 3

Appalachian Bakery Company manufactures cookies. Materials are placed in production in the Baking Department and after processing are transferred to the Packing Department, where packing materials are added. The finished products emerge from the Packing Department.

There were no inventories of work in process at the beginning or at the end of August 2008. Finished goods inventory at August 1 was 900 cases of cookies at a total cost of $40,500.

Transactions related to manufacturing operations for August are summarized as follows:

a. Materials purchased on account, $425,000.
b. Materials requisitioned for use: Baking Department, $345,500 ($334,500 entered directly into the product); Packing Department, $73,500 ($72,000 entered directly into the product).
c. Labor costs incurred: Baking Department, $168,000 ($154,300 entered directly into the product); Packing Department, $127,000 ($119,600 entered directly into the product).
d. Miscellaneous costs and expenses incurred on account: Baking Department, $16,300; Packing Department, $6,300.
e. Depreciation charged on fixed assets: Baking Department, $22,400; Packing Department, $11,900.
f. Expiration of various prepaid expenses: Baking Department, $4,700; Packing Department, $2,300.
g. Factory overhead applied to production, based on machine hours: $67,500 for Baking and $30,700 for Packing.
h. Output of Baking Department: 17,000 cases.
i. Output of Packing Department: 17,000 cases of cookies.
j. Sales on account: 17,600 cases of cookies at $90. Credits to the finished goods account are to be made according to the first-in, first-out method.

Instructions

Journalize the entries to record the transactions, identifying each by letter. Include as an explanation for entry (j) the number of cases and the cost per case of cookies sold.

PR 3-3A
Cost of production report
obj. 2

✓ *1. Conversion cost per equivalent unit, $3.60*

Mountain Air Coffee Company roasts and packs coffee beans. The process begins by placing coffee beans into the Roasting Department. From the Roasting Department, coffee beans are then transferred to the Packing Department. The following is a partial work in process account of the Roasting Department at October 31, 2008:

ACCOUNT *Work in Process—Roasting Department*					ACCOUNT NO.	
					Balance	
Date		**Item**	**Debit**	**Credit**	**Debit**	**Credit**
Oct.	1	Bal., 12,000 units, ²/₅ completed			84,600	
	31	Direct materials, 285,000 units	1,624,500		1,709,100	
	31	Direct labor	568,900		2,278,000	
	31	Factory overhead	428,480		2,706,480	
	31	Goods finished, 276,800 units		?		
	31	Bal. _?_ units, ¹/₄ completed			?	

Instructions

1. Prepare a cost of production report, and identify the missing amounts for Work in Process—Roasting Department.
2. Assuming that the October 1 Work in Process inventory includes $67,800 of direct materials, determine the increase or decrease in the cost per equivalent unit for direct materials and conversion between September and October.

PR 3-4A
Equivalent units and related costs; cost of production report; entries
objs. 2, 3

✓ *2. Transferred to Packaging Dept., $1,079,400*

Blanco Flour Company manufactures flour by a series of three processes, beginning with wheat grain being introduced in the Milling Department. From the Milling Department, the materials pass through the Sifting and Packaging departments, emerging as packaged refined flour.

The balance in the account Work in Process—Sifting Department was as follows on May 1, 2008:

Work in Process—Sifting Department (20,000 units, 80% completed):
Direct materials (20,000 × $1.37) $27,400
Conversion (20,000 × 80% × $0.55)   8,800
                                                                    $36,200

The following costs were charged to Work in Process—Sifting Department during May:

Direct materials transferred from Milling Department:
  560,000 units at $1.40 a unit $784,000
Direct labor   179,000
Factory overhead   101,200

During May, 568,000 units of flour were completed. Work in Process—Sifting Department on May 31 was 12,000 units, 70% completed.

Instructions

1. Prepare a cost of production report for the Sifting Department for May.
2. Journalize the entries for costs transferred from Milling to Sifting and the costs transferred from Sifting to Packaging.
3. Determine the increase or decrease in the cost per equivalent unit from April to May for direct materials and conversion costs.
4. ➤ Discuss the uses of the cost of production report and the results of part (3).

PR 3-5A
Work in process account data for two months; cost of production reports
objs. 1, 2, 3

Won-Ton Soup Co. uses a process cost system to record the costs of processing soup, which requires a series of three processes. The inventory of Work in Process—Filling on July 1 and debits to the account during July 2008 were as follows:

✓ 1. c. Transferred to
finished goods in July,
$570,895

Bal., 2,000 units, 30% completed:	
Direct materials (2,000 × $3.20)	$6,400
Conversion (2,000 × 30% × $1.25)	750
	$7,150
From Cooking Department, 126,000 units	$409,500
Direct labor	93,345
Factory overhead	71,950

During July, 2,000 units in process on July 1 were completed, and of the 126,000 units entering the department, all were completed except 2,500 units that were 90% completed. Charges to Work in Process—Filling for August were as follows:

From Cooking Department, 138,000 units	$455,400
Direct labor	101,480
Factory overhead	77,578

During August, the units in process at the beginning of the month were completed, and of the 138,000 units entering the department, all were completed except 4,000 units that were 35% completed.

Instructions
1. Enter the balance as of July 1, 2008, in a four-column account for Work in Process—Filling. Record the debits and the credits in the account for July. Construct a cost of production report, and present computations for determining (a) equivalent units of production for materials and conversion, (b) equivalent costs per unit, (c) cost of goods finished, differentiating between units started in the prior period and units started and finished in July, and (d) work in process inventory.
2. Provide the same information for August by recording the August transactions in the four-column work in process account. Construct a cost of production report, and present the August computations (a through d) listed in part (1).
3. ━━━━▶ Comment on the change in cost per equivalent unit for June through August for direct materials and conversion costs.

APPENDIX
PR 3-6A
Cost of production report: average cost method

✓ *Cost per equivalent unit, $9.30*

Arabica Coffee Company roasts and packs coffee beans. The process begins in the Roasting Department. From the Roasting Department, the coffee beans are transferred to the Packing Department. The following is a partial work in process account of the Roasting Department at March 31, 2008:

ACCOUNT *Work in Process—Roasting Department*   **ACCOUNT NO.**

Date		Item	Debit	Credit	Balance Debit	Balance Credit
Mar.	1	Bal., 12,500 units, 60% completed			92,500	
	31	Direct materials, 215,400 units	1,345,900		1,438,400	
	31	Direct labor	365,766		1,804,166	
	31	Factory overhead	284,800		2,088,966	
	31	Goods finished, 219,700 units		?	?	
	31	Bal. ? units, 60% completed			?	

Instructions
Prepare a cost of production report, using the average cost method, and identify the missing amounts for Work in Process—Roasting Department.

APPENDIX
PR 3-7A
Equivalent units and related costs; cost of production report: average cost method

Snowflake Flour Company manufactures flour by a series of three processes, beginning in the Milling Department. From the Milling Department, the materials pass through the Sifting and Packaging departments, emerging as packaged refined flour.

(continued)

✓ *Transferred to Packaging Dept., $1,976,620*

The balance in the account Work in Process—Sifting Department was as follows on July 1, 2008:

Work in Process—Sifting Department (19,600 units, 75% completed)	$66,000

The following costs were charged to Work in Process—Sifting Department during July:

Direct materials transferred from Milling Department: 426,800 units	$1,435,000
Direct labor	375,925
Factory overhead	118,900

During July, 429,700 units of flour were completed. Work in Process—Sifting Department on July 31 was 16,700 units, 25% completed.

Instructions

Prepare a cost of production report for the Sifting Department for July, using the average cost method.

Problems Series B

PR 3-1B
Entries for process cost system
objs. 1, 3

✓ *2. Materials December 31 balance, $8,720*

G&P Soap Company manufactures powdered detergent. Phosphate is placed in process in the Making Department, where it is turned into granulars. The output of Making is transferred to the Packing Department, where packaging is added at the beginning of the process. On December 1, G&P Soap Company had the following inventories:

Finished Goods	$14,500
Work in Process—Making	5,670
Work in Process—Packing	7,230
Materials	3,200

Departmental accounts are maintained for factory overhead, which both have zero balances on December 1.

Manufacturing operations for December are summarized as follows:

a. Materials purchased on account	$167,900
b. Materials requisitioned for use:	
Phosphate—Making Department	$114,200
Packaging—Packing Department	42,500
Indirect materials—Making Department	4,100
Indirect materials—Packing Department	1,580
c. Labor used:	
Direct labor—Making Department	$79,400
Direct labor—Packing Department	53,200
Indirect labor—Making Department	15,000
Indirect labor—Packing Department	26,900
d. Depreciation charged on fixed assets:	
Making Department	$14,800
Packing Department	11,300
e. Expired prepaid factory insurance:	
Making Department	$3,000
Packing Department	1,200
f. Applied factory overhead:	
Making Department	$37,500
Packing Department	40,100
g. Production costs transferred from Making Department to Packing Department	$215,800
h. Production costs transferred from Packing Department to Finished Goods	$351,200
i. Cost of goods sold during the period	$354,800

Instructions

1. Journalize the entries to record the operations, identifying each entry by letter.
2. Compute the December 31 balances of the inventory accounts.
3. Compute the December 31 balances of the factory overhead accounts.

PR 3-2B

Entries for process cost system

objs. **1, 3**

Ozark Refining Company processes gasoline. Petroleum is placed in production in the Refining Department and, after processing, is transferred to the Blending Department, where detergents are added. The finished blended gasoline emerges from the Blending Department.

There were no inventories of work in process at the beginning or at the end of December 2008. Finished goods inventory at December 1 was 8,000 barrels of gasoline at a total cost of $296,000.

Transactions related to manufacturing operations for December are summarized as follows:

a. Materials purchased on account, $682,400.
b. Materials requisitioned for use: Refining, $580,200 ($567,800 entered directly into the product); Blending, $98,400 ($92,200 entered directly into the product).
c. Labor costs incurred: Refining, $165,100 ($134,200 entered directly into the product); Blending, $80,200 ($57,800 entered directly into the product).
d. Miscellaneous costs and expenses incurred on account: Refining, $21,100; Blending, $7,000.
e. Expiration of various prepaid expenses: Refining, $5,000; Blending, $3,000.
f. Depreciation charged on plant assets: Refining, $43,500; Blending, $19,200.
g. Factory overhead applied to production, based on processing hours: $111,900 for Refining and $58,100 for Blending.
h. Output of Refining: 28,000 barrels.
i. Output of Blending: 28,000 barrels of gasoline.
j. Sales on account: 30,000 barrels of gasoline at $60 per barrel. Credits to the finished goods account are to be made according to the first-in, first-out method.

Instructions

Journalize the entries to record the transactions, identifying each by letter. Include as an explanation for entry (j) the number of barrels and the cost per barrel of gasoline sold.

PR 3-3B

Cost of production report

obj. **2**

✓ *1. Conversion cost per equivalent unit, $0.75*

Belgian Delight Chocolate Company processes chocolate into candy bars. The process begins by placing direct materials (raw chocolate, milk, and sugar) into the Blending Department. All materials are placed into production at the beginning of the blending process. After blending, the milk chocolate is then transferred to the Molding Department, where the milk chocolate is formed into candy bars. The following is a partial work in process account of the Blending Department at March 31, 2008:

ACCOUNT *Work in Process—Blending Department*					ACCOUNT NO.	
					Balance	
Date		**Item**	**Debit**	**Credit**	**Debit**	**Credit**
Mar.	1	Bal., 9,000 units, 20% completed			28,260	
	31	Direct materials, 300,000 units	870,000		898,260	
	31	Direct labor	128,450		1,026,710	
	31	Factory overhead	100,300		1,127,010	
	31	Goods finished, 305,000 units		?		
	31	Bal. _?_ units, 45% completed			?	

Instructions

1. Prepare a cost of production report, and identify the missing amounts for Work in Process—Blending Department.
2. Assuming that the March 1 Work in Process inventory includes direct materials of $27,000, determine the increase or decrease in the cost per equivalent unit for direct materials and conversion between February and March.

PR 3-4B

Equivalent units and related costs; cost of production report; entries

objs. **2, 3**

Delaware Chemical Company manufactures specialty chemicals by a series of three processes, all materials being introduced in the Distilling Department. From the Distilling Department, the materials pass through the Reaction and Filling departments, emerging as finished chemicals.

✓2. Transferred to
finished goods, $929,819

The balance in the account Work in Process—Filling was as follows on December 1, 2008:

Work in Process—Filling Department
(2,200 units, 10% completed):

Direct materials (2,200 × $12.10)	$26,620
Conversion (2,200 × 10% × $8.65)	1,903
	$28,523

The following costs were charged to Work in Process—Filling during December:

Direct materials transferred from Reaction Department: 44,400 units at $12.20 a unit	$541,680
Direct labor	105,600
Factory overhead	292,425

During December, 44,500 units of specialty chemicals were completed. Work in Process—Filling Department on December 31 was 2,100 units, 70% completed.

Instructions
1. Prepare a cost of production report for the Filling Department for December.
2. Journalize the entries for costs transferred from Reaction to Filling and the cost transferred from Filling to Finished Goods.
3. Determine the increase or decrease in the cost per equivalent unit from November to December for direct materials and conversion costs.
4. 🖊 Discuss the uses of the cost of production report and the results of part (3).

PR 3-5B
Work in process account data for two months; cost of production reports
objs. 1, 2, 3

✓1. c. Transferred to
finished goods in
September, $7,975,700

Dayton Aluminum Company uses a process cost system to record the costs of manufacturing rolled aluminum, which requires a series of four processes. The inventory of Work in Process—Rolling on September 1, 2008, and debits to the account during September were as follows:

Bal., 4,000 units, 1/4 completed:	
Direct materials (4,000 × $41.00)	$ 164,000
Conversion (4,000 × 1/4 × $12.30)	12,300
	$ 176,300
From Smelting Department, 150,000 units	$6,195,000
Direct labor	773,780
Factory overhead	1,138,900

During September, 4,000 units in process on September 1 were completed, and of the 150,000 units entering the department, all were completed except 6,000 units that were $^4/_5$ completed.

Charges to Work in Process—Rolling for October were as follows:

From Smelting Department, 165,000 units	$6,930,000
Direct labor	824,500
Factory overhead	1,242,530

During October, the units in process at the beginning of the month were completed, and of the 165,000 units entering the department, all were completed except 6,800 units that were $^2/_5$ completed.

Instructions
1. Enter the balance as of September 1, 2008, in a four-column account for Work in Process—Rolling. Record the debits and the credits in the account for September. Construct a cost of production report and present computations for determining (a) equivalent units of production for materials and conversion, (b) equivalent costs per unit, (c) cost of goods finished, differentiating between units started in the prior period and units started and finished in September, and (d) work in process inventory.
2. Provide the same information for October by recording the October transactions in the four-column work in process account. Construct a cost of production report, and present the October computations (a through d) listed in part (1).
3. 🖊 Comment on the change in cost per equivalent unit for August through October for direct materials and conversion cost.

APPENDIX PR 3-6B
Cost of production report: average cost method

✓ *Cost per equivalent unit, $4.00*

Robusta Coffee Company roasts and packs coffee beans. The process begins in the Roasting Department. From the Roasting Department, the coffee beans are transferred to the Packing Department. The following is a partial work in process account of the Roasting Department at July 31, 2008:

ACCOUNT *Work in Process—Roasting Department*					ACCOUNT NO.	
					Balance	
Date		Item	Debit	Credit	Debit	Credit
July	1	Bal., 18,000 units, 25% completed			18,450	
	31	Direct materials, 345,000 units	968,750		987,200	
	31	Direct labor	229,000		1,216,200	
	31	Factory overhead	203,600		1,419,800	
	31	Goods finished, 340,000 units		?	?	
	31	Bal. _?_ units, 65% completed			?	

Instructions

Prepare a cost of production report, using the average cost method, and identify the missing amounts for Work in Process—Roasting Department.

APPENDIX PR 3-7B
Equivalent units and related costs; cost of production report: average cost method

✓ *Transferred to Packaging Dept., $865,060*

Blue Ribbon Flour Company manufactures flour by a series of three processes, beginning in the Milling Department. From the Milling Department, the materials pass through the Sifting and Packaging departments, emerging as packaged refined flour.

The balance in the account Work in Process—Sifting Department was as follows on October 1, 2008:

Work in Process—Sifting Department (15,000 units, 75% completed) $42,000

The following costs were charged to Work in Process—Sifting Department during October:

Direct materials transferred from Milling Department: 235,800 units	$632,600
Direct labor	160,735
Factory overhead	76,900

During October, 233,800 units of flour were completed. Work in Process—Sifting Department on October 31 was 17,000 units, 75% completed.

Instructions

Prepare a cost of production report for the Sifting Department for October, using the average cost method.

Special Activities

SA 3-1
Ethics and professional conduct in business

ETHICS

Assume you are the division controller for Prairie Cookie Company. Prairie has introduced a new chocolate chip cookie called Full of Chips, and it is a success. As a result, the product manager responsible for the launch of this new cookie was promoted to division vice president and became your boss. A new product manager, Davis, has been brought in to replace the promoted manager. Davis notices that the Full of Chips cookie uses a lot of chips, which increases the cost of the cookie. As a result, Davis has ordered that the amount of chips used in the cookies be reduced by 10%. The manager believes that a 10% reduction in chips will not adversely affect sales, but will reduce costs, and hence improve margins. The increased margins would help Davis meet profit targets for the period.

You are looking over some cost of production reports segmented by cookie line. You notice that there is a drop in the materials costs for Full of Chips. On further investigation, you discover why the chip costs have declined (fewer chips). Both you and Davis report to the division vice president, who was the original product manager for Full of Chips. You are trying to decide what to do, if anything.

➤ Discuss the options you might consider.

SA 3-2
Accounting for materials costs

In papermaking operations for companies such as International Paper Company, wet pulp is fed into paper machines, which press and dry pulp into a continuous sheet of paper. The paper is formed at very high speeds (60 mph). Once the paper is formed, the paper is rolled onto a reel at the back end of the paper machine. One of the characteristics of papermaking is the creation of "broke" paper. Broke is paper that fails to satisfy quality standards and is therefore rejected for final shipment to customers. Broke is recycled back to the beginning of the process by combining the recycled paper with virgin (new) pulp material. The combination of virgin pulp and recycled broke is sent to the paper machine for papermaking. Broke is fed into this recycle process continuously from all over the facility.

In this industry, it is typical to charge the papermaking operation with the cost of direct materials, which is a mixture of virgin materials and broke. Broke has a much lower cost than does virgin pulp. Therefore, the more broke in the mixture, the lower the average cost of direct materials to the department. Papermaking managers will frequently comment on the importance of broke for keeping their direct materials costs down.

a. ▬▬▶ How do you react to this accounting procedure?
b. ▬▬▶ What "hidden costs" are not considered when accounting for broke as described above?

SA 3-3
Analyzing unit costs

Natcan Inc. manufactures cans for the canned food industry. The operations manager of a can manufacturing operation wants to conduct a cost study investigating the relationship of tin content in the material (can stock) to the energy cost for enameling the cans. The enameling was necessary to prepare the cans for labeling. A higher percentage of tin content in the can stock increases the cost of material. The operations manager believed there was a relationship between the tin content and energy costs for enameling. During the analysis period, the amount of tin content in the steel can stock was increased for every month, from April to September. The following operating reports were available from the controller:

	A	B	C	D	E	F	G	
		April	May	June	July	August	September	
1	Energy	$ 13,000	$ 28,800	$ 24,200	$ 14,000	$ 16,200	$ 15,000	1
2	Materials	12,000	30,000	28,600	18,900	25,200	29,000	2
3	Total cost	$ 25,000	$ 58,800	$ 52,800	$ 32,900	$ 41,400	$ 44,000	3
4	Units produced	/50,000	/120,000	/110,000	/70,000	/90,000	/100,000	4
5	Cost per unit	$ 0.50	$ 0.49	$ 0.48	$ 0.47	$ 0.46	$ 0.44	5

Differences in materials unit costs were entirely related to the amount of tin content. ▬▬▶ Interpret this information and report to the operations manager your recommendations with respect to tin content.

SA 3-4
Decision making

Lane Anderson, plant manager of Willow Run Paper Company's papermaking mill, was looking over the cost of production reports for July and August for the Papermaking Department. The reports revealed the following:

	July	August
Pulp and chemicals	$300,000	$307,000
Conversion cost	150,000	153,000
Total cost	$450,000	$460,000
Number of tons	/ 1,250	/ 1,150
Cost per ton	$ 360	$ 400

Lane was concerned about the increased cost per ton from the output of the department. As a result, he asked the plant controller to perform a study to help explain these results. The controller, Sarah Nold, began the analysis by performing some interviews of key plant personnel in order to understand what the problem might be. Excerpts from an interview with Jake Bennick, a paper machine operator, follow:

Jake: We have two papermaking machines in the department. I have no data, but I think paper machine 1 is applying too much pulp, and thus is wasting both conversion and materials resources. We haven't had repairs on paper machine 1 in a while. Maybe this is the problem.

Sarah: How does too much pulp result in wasted resources?

Jake: Well, you see, if too much pulp is applied, then we will waste pulp material. The customer will not pay for the extra weight. Thus, we just lose that amount of material. Also, when there is too much pulp, the machine must be slowed down in order to complete the drying process. This results in a waste of conversion costs.

Sarah: Do you have any other suspicions?

Jake: Well, as you know, we have two products—green paper and yellow paper. They are identical except for the color. The color is added to the papermaking process in the paper machine. I think that during August these two color papers have been behaving very differently. I don't have any data, but it just seems as though the amount of waste associated with the green paper has increased.

Sarah: Why is this?

Jake: I understand that there has been a change in specifications for the green paper, starting near the beginning of August. This change could be causing the machines to run poorly when making green paper. If this is the case, the cost per ton would increase for green paper.

Sarah also asked for a computer printout providing greater detail on August's operating results.

Computer run: 09085   September 9   Requested by: Sarah Nold

Papermaking Department—August detail

	A	B	C	D	E	F	
	Production Run Number	Paper Machine	Color	Material Costs	Conversion Costs	Tons	
1	1	1	Green	41,800	20,400	160	1
2	2	1	Yellow	41,700	21,200	140	2
3	3	1	Green	44,600	22,500	150	3
4	4	1	Yellow	36,100	18,100	120	4
5	5	2	Green	38,300	18,800	160	5
6	6	2	Yellow	35,300	16,900	150	6
7	7	2	Green	35,600	18,100	130	7
8	8	2	Yellow	33,600	17,000	140	8
9		Total		307,000	153,000	1,150	9

Assuming that you're Sarah Nold, write a memo to Lane Anderson with a recommendation to management. You should analyze the August data to determine whether the paper machine or the paper color explains the increase in the unit cost from July. Include any supporting schedules that are appropriate.

SA 3-5
Process costing companies

Group Project

Internet Project

The following categories represent typical process manufacturing industries:

Beverages   Metals
Chemicals   Petroleum refining
Food   Pharmaceuticals
Forest and paper products   Soap and cosmetics

In each category, identify one company (following your instructor's specific instructions) and determine the following:

1. Typical products manufactured by the selected company, including brand names.
2. Typical raw materials used by the selected company.
3. Types of processes used by the selected company.

Use annual reports, the Internet, or library resources in doing this activity.

Answers to Self-Examination Questions

1. **C** The process cost system is most appropriate for a business where manufacturing is conducted by continuous operations and involves a series of uniform production processes, such as the processing of crude oil (answer C). The job order cost system is most appropriate for a business where the product is made to customers' specifications, such as custom furniture manufacturing (answer A), commercial building construction (answer B), or automobile repair shop (answer D).

2. **A** The total pounds transferred to finished goods (23,000) are the 2,000 in-process pounds at the beginning of the period plus the number of pounds started and completed during the month, 21,000 (24,000 − 3,000). Answer B incorrectly assumes that the beginning inventory is not transferred during the month. Answer C assumes that all 24,000 pounds started during the month are transferred to finished goods, instead of only the portion started and completed. Answer D incorrectly adds all the numbers together.

3. **B** The number of units that could have been produced from start to finish during a period is termed equivalent units. The 4,875 equivalent units (answer B) is determined as follows:

To process units in inventory on May 1 (1,000 × ¼)	250
To process units started and completed in May (5,500 units − 1,000 units)	4,500
To process units in inventory on May 31 (500 units × ¼)	125
Equivalent units of production in May	4,875

4. **A** The conversion costs (direct labor and factory overhead) totaling $48,750 are divided by the number of equivalent units (4,875) to determine the unit conversion cost of $10 (answer A).

5. **C** The electricity costs have increased, and maintenance costs have decreased. Answer C would be a reasonable explanation for these results. The total costs, materials costs, and costs per unit do not reveal any type of pattern over the time period. In fact, the materials costs have stayed at exactly $2.00 per pound over the time period. This demonstrates that aggregated numbers can sometimes hide underlying information that can be used to improve the process.

Cost Behavior and Cost-Volume-Profit Analysis

© PAUL SAKUMA/ASSOCIATED PRESS

objectives

After studying this chapter, you should be able to:

1 Classify costs by their behavior as variable costs, fixed costs, or mixed costs.

2 Compute the contribution margin, the contribution margin ratio, and the unit contribution margin, and explain how they may be useful to managers.

3 Using the unit contribution margin, determine the break-even point and the volume necessary to achieve a target profit.

4 Using a cost-volume-profit chart and a profit-volume chart, determine the break-even point and the volume necessary to achieve a target profit.

5 Compute the break-even point for a business selling more than one product, the operating leverage, and the margin of safety.

Netflix

How do you decide whether you are going to buy or rent a video game? It probably depends on how much you think you are going to use the game. If you are going to play the game a lot, you are probably better off buying the game than renting. The one-time cost of buying the game would be much less expensive than the cost of multiple rentals. If, on the other hand, you are uncertain about how frequently you are going to play the game, it may be less expensive to rent. The cost of an individual rental is much less than the cost of purchase. Understanding how the costs of rental and purchase behave is an important element of your decision.

Understanding how costs behave is also important to companies like Netflix, an online DVD movie rental service. For a fixed monthly fee, Netflix customers can select DVDs from the convenience of their own computers and have the DVDs delivered to their homes along with a prepaid return envelope. Customers can keep the DVDs as long as they want but must return the DVDs before they rent additional movies. The number of DVDs that members can check out at one time varies between one and three, depending on their subscription plans.

In order to entice customers to subscribe, Netflix had to invest in a well-stocked library of DVD titles and build a warehouse to hold and distribute these titles. These costs do not change with the number of subscriptions. But how many subscriptions does Netflix need in order to make a profit? That depends on the price of each subscription, the costs incurred with each DVD rental, and the costs associated with maintaining the DVD library.

As with Netflix, understanding how costs behave, and the relationship between costs, profits, and volume is important for all businesses. In this chapter, we discuss commonly used methods for classifying costs according to how they change. We also discuss techniques that management can use to evaluate costs in order to make sound business decisions.

Cost Behavior

objective **1**

Classify costs by their behavior as variable costs, fixed costs, or mixed costs.

Knowing how costs behave is useful to management for a variety of purposes. For example, knowing how costs behave allows managers to predict profits as sales and production volumes change. Knowing how costs behave is also useful for estimating costs. Estimated costs, in turn, affect a variety of management decisions, such as whether to use excess machine capacity to produce and sell a product at a reduced price.

Cost behavior refers to the manner in which a cost changes as a related activity changes. To understand cost behavior, two factors must be considered. First, we must identify the activities that are thought to relate to the cost incurred. Such activities are called **activity bases** (or *activity drivers*). Second, we must specify the range of activity over which the changes in the cost are of interest. This range of activity is called the **relevant range**.

To illustrate, hospital administrators must plan and control hospital food costs. Why and how food costs change can be evaluated in terms of an activity base. The number of patients *treated* by the hospital would not be a good activity base, since some patients are outpatients who do not stay in the hospital. The number of patients who *stay* in the hospital, however, is a good activity base for studying food costs. Once the proper activity base is identified, food costs can then be analyzed over the range of the number of patients who normally stay in the hospital (the relevant range).

Three of the most common classifications of cost behavior are variable costs, fixed costs, and mixed costs.

VARIABLE COSTS

When the level of activity is measured in units produced, direct materials and direct labor costs are generally classified as variable costs. **Variable costs are costs that vary in proportion to changes in the level of activity.** For example, assume that Jason Inc. produces stereo sound systems under the brand name of J-Sound. The parts for the stereo systems are purchased from outside suppliers for $10 per unit and are assembled in Jason Inc.'s Waterloo plant. The direct materials costs for Model JS-12 for the relevant range of 5,000 to 30,000 units of production are shown below.

Number of Units of Model JS-12 Produced	Direct Materials Cost per Unit	Total Direct Materials Cost
5,000 units	$10	$ 50,000
10,000	10	100,000
15,000	10	150,000
20,000	10	200,000
25,000	10	250,000
30,000	10	300,000

Variable costs are the same per unit, while the total variable cost changes in proportion to changes in the activity base. For Model JS-12, for example, the direct materials cost for 10,000 units ($100,000) is twice the direct materials cost for 5,000 units ($50,000). The total direct materials cost varies in proportion to the number of units produced because the direct materials cost per unit ($10) is the same for all levels of production. Thus, producing 20,000 additional units of JS-12 will increase the direct materials cost by $200,000 (20,000 × $10), producing 25,000 additional units will increase the materials cost by $250,000, and so on.

Exhibit 1 illustrates how the variable costs for direct materials for Model JS-12 behave in total and on a per-unit basis as production changes.

EXHIBIT 1   Variable Cost Graphs

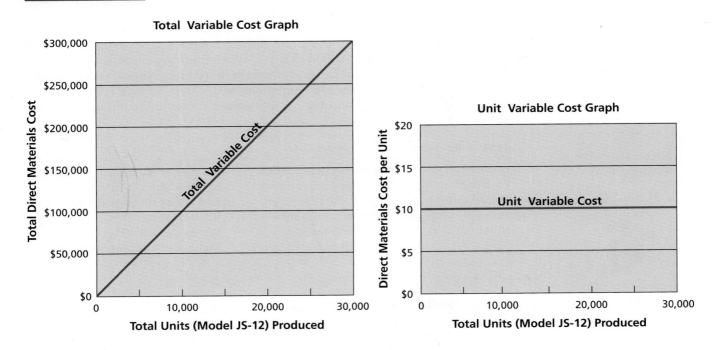

There are a variety of activity bases used by managers for evaluating cost behavior. The following list provides some examples of variable costs, along with their related activity bases for various types of businesses.

Type of Business	Cost	Activity Base
University	Instructor salaries	Number of classes
Passenger airline	Fuel	Number of miles flown
Manufacturing	Direct materials	Number of units produced
Hospital	Nurse wages	Number of patients
Hotel	Maid wages	Number of guests
Bank	Teller wages	Number of banking transactions

FIXED COSTS

Fixed costs are costs that remain the same in total dollar amount as the level of activity changes. To illustrate, assume that Minton Inc. manufactures, bottles, and distributes La Fleur Perfume at its Los Angeles plant. The production supervisor at the Los Angeles plant is Jane Sovissi, who is paid a salary of $75,000 per year. The relevant range of activity for a year is 50,000 to 300,000 bottles of perfume. Sovissi's salary is a fixed cost that does not vary with the number of units produced. Regardless of the number of bottles produced within the range of 50,000 to 300,000 bottles, Sovissi receives a salary of $75,000.

Although the total fixed cost remains the same as the number of bottles produced changes, the fixed cost per bottle changes. As more bottles are produced, the total fixed costs are spread over a larger number of bottles, and thus the fixed cost per bottle decreases. This relationship is shown below for Jane Sovissi's $75,000 salary.

Number of Bottles of Perfume Produced	Total Salary for Jane Sovissi	Salary per Bottle of Perfume Produced
50,000 bottles	$75,000	$1.500
100,000	75,000	0.750
150,000	75,000	0.500
200,000	75,000	0.375
250,000	75,000	0.300
300,000	75,000	0.250

Exhibit 2 illustrates how the fixed cost of Jane Sovissi's salary behaves in total and on a per-unit basis as production changes. When units produced is the measure of activity, examples of fixed costs include straight-line depreciation of factory equipment, insurance on factory plant and equipment, and salaries of factory supervisors. Other examples of fixed costs and their activity bases for a variety of businesses are as follows:

Type of Business	Fixed Cost	Activity Base
University	Building depreciation	Number of students
Passenger airline	Airplane depreciation	Number of miles flown
Manufacturing	Plant manager salary	Number of units produced
Hospital	Property insurance	Number of patients
Hotel	Property taxes	Number of guests
Bank	Branch manager salary	Number of customer accounts

A salesperson's compensation can be a mixed cost comprised of a salary (fixed portion) plus a commission as a percent of sales (variable portion).

MIXED COSTS

A **mixed cost** has characteristics of both a variable and a fixed cost. For example, over one range of activity, the total mixed cost may remain the same. It thus behaves as a fixed cost. Over another range of activity, the mixed cost may change in proportion to

> ▶ **EXHIBIT 2** Fixed Cost Graphs

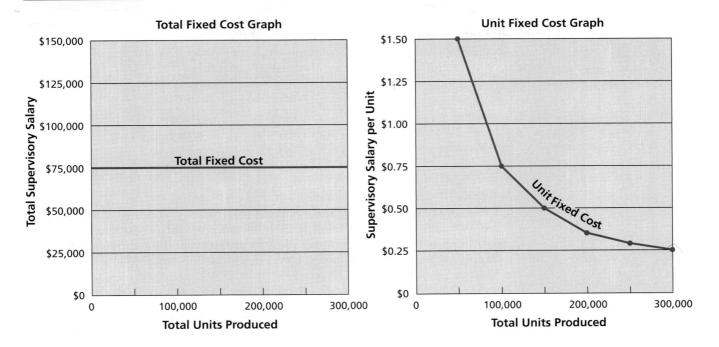

changes in the level of activity. It thus behaves as a variable cost. Mixed costs are sometimes called *semivariable* or *semifixed* costs.

To illustrate, assume that Simpson Inc. manufactures sails, using rented machinery. The rental charges are $15,000 per year, plus $1 for each machine hour used over 10,000 hours. If the machinery is used 8,000 hours, the total rental charge is $15,000. If the machinery is used 20,000 hours, the total rental charge is $25,000 [$15,000 + (10,000 hours × $1)], and so on. Thus, if the level of activity is measured in machine hours and the relevant range is 0 to 40,000 hours, the rental charges are a fixed cost up to 10,000 hours and a variable cost thereafter. This mixed cost behavior is shown graphically in Exhibit 3.

> ▶ **EXHIBIT 3**
>
> Mixed Costs

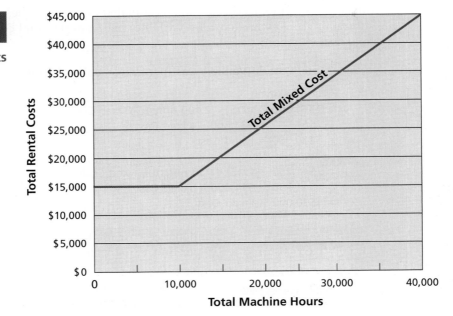

In analyses, mixed costs are usually separated into their fixed and variable components. The **high-low method** is a cost estimation technique that may be used for this purpose.[1] The high-low method uses the highest and lowest activity levels and their related costs to estimate the variable cost per unit and the fixed cost component of mixed costs.

To illustrate, assume that the Equipment Maintenance Department of Kason Inc. incurred the following costs during the past five months:

	Production	Total Cost
June	1,000 units	$45,550
July	1,500	52,000
August	2,100	61,500
September	1,800	57,500
October	750	41,250

The number of units produced is the measure of activity, and the number of units produced between June and October is the relevant range of production. For Kason Inc., the difference between the number of units produced and the difference between the total cost at the highest and lowest levels of production are as follows:

	Production	Total Cost
Highest level	2,100 units	$61,500
Lowest level	750	41,250
Difference	1,350 units	$20,250

Since the total fixed cost does not change with changes in volume of production, the $20,250 difference in the total cost is the change in the total variable cost. Hence, dividing the difference in the total cost by the difference in production provides an estimate of the variable cost per unit. For Kason Inc., this estimate is $15, as shown below.

$$\text{Variable Cost per Unit} = \frac{\text{Difference in Total Cost}}{\text{Difference in Production}}$$

$$\text{Variable Cost per Unit} = \frac{\$20,250}{1,350 \text{ units}} = \$15$$

The fixed cost will be the same at both the highest and the lowest levels of production. Thus, the fixed cost can be estimated at either of these levels. This is done by subtracting the estimated total variable cost from the total cost, using the following total cost equation:

Total Cost = (Variable Cost per Unit × Units of Production) + Fixed Cost

Highest level:
$61,500 = ($15 × 2,100 units) + Fixed Cost
$61,500 = $31,500 + Fixed Cost
$30,000 = Fixed Cost
Lowest level:
$41,250 = ($15 × 750 units) + Fixed Cost
$41,250 = $11,250 + Fixed Cost
$30,000 = Fixed Cost

The total equipment maintenance cost for Kason Inc. can thus be analyzed as a $30,000 fixed cost and a $15-per-unit variable cost. Using these amounts in the total

---

1 Other methods of estimating costs, such as the scattergraph method and the least squares method, are discussed in cost accounting textbooks.

cost equation, the total equipment maintenance cost at other levels of production can be estimated.

Example Exercise 4-1   objective   1

The manufacturing costs of Alex Industries for the first three months of the year are provided below.

	Total Cost	Production
January	$ 80,000	1,000 units
February	125,000	2,500
March	100,000	1,800

Using the high-low method, determine (a) the variable cost per unit and (b) the total fixed cost.

Follow My Example 4-1

a. $30 per unit = ($125,000 − $80,000)/(2,500 − 1,000)
b. $50,000 = $125,000 − ($30 × 2,500) or $80,000 − ($30 × 1,000)

For Practice: PE 4-1A, PE 4-1B

SUMMARY OF COST BEHAVIOR CONCEPTS

The following table summarizes the cost behavior attributes of variable costs and fixed costs:

	Effect of Changing Activity Level	
Cost	**Total Amount**	**Per-Unit Amount**
Variable	Increases and decreases proportionately with activity level.	Remains the same regardless of activity level.
Fixed	Remains the same regardless of activity level.	Increases and decreases inversely with activity level.

Examples of common variable, fixed, and mixed costs when the number of units produced is the activity base are:

Variable Cost	**Fixed Cost**	**Mixed Cost**
Direct materials	Depreciation expense	Quality Control Department salaries
Direct labor	Property taxes	Purchasing Department salaries
Electricity expense	Officer salaries	Maintenance expenses
Sales commissions	Insurance expense	Warehouse expenses

Mixed costs contain a fixed cost component that is incurred even if nothing is produced. For analyses, the fixed and variable cost components of mixed costs should be separated. Separating costs into their variable and fixed components for reporting purposes can be useful for decision making. One method of reporting variable and fixed costs is called **variable costing** or *direct costing*. Under variable costing, only the variable manufacturing costs (direct materials, direct labor, and variable factory overhead) are included in the product cost. The fixed factory overhead is an expense of the period in which it is incurred.[2]

---

2 The variable costing concept is discussed more fully in the next chapter.

Cost-Volume-Profit Relationships

After costs have been classified as fixed and variable, their effect on revenues, volume, and profits can be studied by using cost-volume-profit analysis. **Cost-volume-profit analysis** is the systematic examination of the relationships among selling prices, sales and production volume, costs, expenses, and profits.

Cost-volume-profit analysis provides management with useful information for decision making. For example, cost-volume-profit analysis may be used in setting selling prices, selecting the mix of products to sell, choosing among marketing strategies, and analyzing the effects of changes in costs on profits. In today's business environment, management must make such decisions quickly and accurately. As a result, the importance of cost-volume-profit analysis has increased in recent years.

CONTRIBUTION MARGIN CONCEPT

One relationship among cost, volume, and profit is the contribution margin. The **contribution margin** is the excess of sales revenues over variable costs. The contribution margin concept is especially useful in business planning because it gives insight into the profit potential of a firm. To illustrate, the income statement of Lambert Inc. in Exhibit 4 has been prepared in a contribution margin format.

EXHIBIT 4

Contribution Margin Income Statement

Sales	$1,000,000
Variable costs	600,000
Contribution margin	$ 400,000
Fixed costs	300,000
Income from operations	$ 100,000

Contribution Margin

Fixed Costs

Income from Operations

The contribution margin of $400,000 is available to cover the fixed costs of $300,000. Once the fixed costs are covered, any remaining amount adds directly to the income from operations of the company. Consider the graphic to the left. The fixed costs are a bucket and the contribution margin is water filling the bucket. Once the bucket is filled, the overflow represents income from operations. Up until the point of overflow, however, the contribution margin contributes to fixed costs (filling the bucket).

Contribution Margin Ratio   The contribution margin can also be expressed as a percentage. The **contribution margin ratio**, sometimes called the *profit-volume ratio*, indicates the percentage of each sales dollar available to cover the fixed costs and to provide income from operations. For Lambert Inc., the contribution margin ratio is 40%, as computed below.

$$\text{Contribution Margin Ratio} = \frac{\text{Sales} - \text{Variable Costs}}{\text{Sales}}$$

$$\text{Contribution Margin Ratio} = \frac{\$1,000,000 - \$600,000}{\$1,000,000} = 40\%$$

The contribution margin ratio measures the effect of an increase or a decrease in sales volume on income from operations. For example, assume that the management of Lambert Inc. is studying the effect of adding $80,000 in sales orders. Multiplying the contribution margin ratio (40%) by the change in sales volume ($80,000) indicates that income from operations will increase $32,000 if the additional orders are obtained. The validity of this analysis is illustrated by the following contribution margin income statement of Lambert Inc.:

Sales	$1,080,000
Variable costs ($1,080,000 × 60%)	648,000
Contribution margin ($1,080,000 × 40%)	$ 432,000
Fixed costs	300,000
Income from operations	$ 132,000

Variable costs as a percentage of sales are equal to 100% minus the contribution margin ratio. Thus, in the above income statement, the variable costs are 60% (100% − 40%) of sales, or $648,000 ($1,080,000 × 60%). The total contribution margin, $432,000, can also be computed directly by multiplying the sales by the contribution margin ratio ($1,080,000 × 40%).

In using the contribution margin ratio in analysis, factors other than sales volume, such as variable cost per unit and sales price, are assumed to remain constant. If such factors change, their effect must be considered.

The contribution margin ratio is also useful in setting business policy. For example, if the contribution margin ratio of a firm is large and production is at a level below 100% capacity, a large increase in income from operations can be expected from an increase in sales volume. A firm in such a position might decide to devote more effort to sales promotion because of the large change in income from operations that will result from changes in sales volume. In contrast, a firm with a small contribution margin ratio will probably want to give more attention to reducing costs before attempting to promote sales.

UNIT CONTRIBUTION MARGIN

The unit contribution margin is also useful for analyzing the profit potential of proposed projects. The **unit contribution margin** is the sales price less the variable cost per unit. For example, if Lambert Inc.'s unit selling price is $20 and its unit variable cost is $12, the unit contribution margin is $8 ($20 − $12).

The *contribution margin ratio* is most useful when the increase or decrease in sales volume is measured in sales *dollars*. The *unit contribution margin* is most useful when the increase or decrease in sales volume is measured in sales *units* (quantities). To illustrate, assume that Lambert Inc. sold 50,000 units. Its income from operations is $100,000, as shown in the following contribution margin income statement:

Sales (50,000 units × $20)	$1,000,000
Variable costs (50,000 units × $12)	600,000
Contribution margin (50,000 units × $8)	$ 400,000
Fixed costs	300,000
Income from operations	$ 100,000

A $350-per-night room at The Ritz-Carlton Hotel may have a variable cost, including maids' salaries, laundry, soap, and utilities, of only $40 per night and thus a high unit contribution margin per room. The high contribution margin per unit is necessary to cover the high fixed costs for the hotel.

If Lambert Inc.'s sales could be increased by 15,000 units, from 50,000 units to 65,000 units, its income from operations would increase by $120,000 (15,000 units × $8), as shown below.

Sales (65,000 units × $20)	$1,300,000
Variable costs (65,000 units × $12)	780,000
Contribution margin (65,000 units × $8)	$ 520,000
Fixed costs	300,000
Income from operations	$ 220,000

Unit contribution margin analyses can provide useful information for managers. The preceding illustration indicates, for example, that Lambert could spend up to $120,000 for special advertising or other product promotions to increase sales by 15,000 units.

Example Exercise 4-2

objective **2**

Molly Company sells 20,000 units at $12 per unit. Variable costs are $9 per unit, and fixed costs are $25,000. Determine the (a) contribution margin ratio, (b) unit contribution margin, and (c) income from operations.

Follow My Example 4-2

a. 25% = ($12 − $9)/$12 or ($240,000 − $180,000)/$240,000
b. $3 per unit = $12 − $9

c.

Sales	$240,000	(20,000 units × $12 per unit)
Variable costs	180,000	(20,000 units × $9 per unit)
Contribution margin	$ 60,000	[20,000 units × ($12 − $9)]
Fixed costs	25,000	
Income from operations	$ 35,000	

For Practice: PE 4-2A, PE 4-2B

Mathematical Approach to Cost-Volume-Profit Analysis

objective **3**

Using the unit contribution margin, determine the break-even point and the volume necessary to achieve a target profit.

Accountants use various approaches for expressing the relationship of costs, sales (volume), and income from operations (operating profit). The mathematical approach is one approach that is used often in practice.

The mathematical approach to cost-volume-profit analysis uses equations (1) to determine the units of sales necessary to achieve the break-even point in operations or (2) to determine the units of sales necessary to achieve a target or desired profit. We will next describe and illustrate these equations and their use by management in profit planning.

BREAK-EVEN POINT

The **break-even point** is the level of operations at which a business's revenues and expired costs are exactly equal. At break-even, a business will have neither an income nor a loss from operations. The break-even point is useful in business planning, especially when expanding or decreasing operations.

To illustrate the computation of the break-even point, assume that the fixed costs for Barker Corporation are estimated to be $90,000. The unit selling price, unit variable cost, and unit contribution margin for Barker Corporation are as follows:

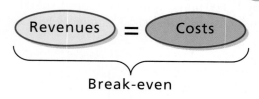

Revenues = Costs

Break-even

Unit selling price	$25
Unit variable cost	15
Unit contribution margin	$10

The break-even point is 9,000 units, which can be computed by using the following equation:

$$\text{Break-Even Sales (units)} = \frac{\text{Fixed Costs}}{\text{Unit Contribution Margin}}$$

$$\text{Break-Even Sales (units)} = \frac{\$90,000}{\$10} = 9,000 \text{ units}$$

The following income statement verifies the preceding computation:

Sales (9,000 units × $25)	$225,000
Variable costs (9,000 units × $15)	135,000
Contribution margin	$ 90,000
Fixed costs	90,000
Income from operations	$ 0

The break-even point is affected by changes in the fixed costs, unit variable costs, and the unit selling price. Next, we will briefly describe the effect of each of these factors on the break-even point.

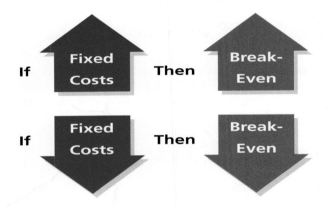

Effect of Changes in Fixed Costs   Although fixed costs do not change in total with changes in the level of activity, they may change because of other factors. For example, changes in property tax rates or factory supervisors' salaries change fixed costs. Increases in fixed costs will raise the break-even point. Likewise, decreases in fixed costs will lower the break-even point.

To illustrate, assume that Bishop Co. is evaluating a proposal to budget an additional $100,000 for advertising. Fixed costs before the additional advertising are estimated at $600,000, and the unit contribution margin is $20. The break-even point before the additional expense is 30,000 units, computed as follows:

$$\text{Break-Even Sales (units)} = \frac{\text{Fixed Costs}}{\text{Unit Contribution Margin}}$$

$$\text{Break-Even Sales (units)} = \frac{\$600,000}{\$20} = 30,000 \text{ units}$$

If the additional amount is spent, the fixed costs will increase by $100,000 and the break-even point will increase to 35,000 units, computed as follows:

$$\text{Break-Even Sales (units)} = \frac{\text{Fixed Costs}}{\text{Unit Contribution Margin}}$$

$$\text{Break-Even Sales (units)} = \frac{\$700,000}{\$20} = 35,000 \text{ units}$$

The $100,000 increase in the fixed costs requires an additional 5,000 units ($100,000/$20) of sales to break even. In other words, an increase in sales of 5,000 units is required in order to generate an additional $100,000 of total contribution margin (5,000 units × $20) to cover the increased fixed costs.

Effect of Changes in Unit Variable Costs   Although unit variable costs are not affected by changes in volume of activity, they may be affected by other factors. For example, changes in the price of direct materials and the wages for factory workers providing direct labor will change unit variable costs. Increases in unit variable costs will raise the break-even point. Likewise, decreases in unit variable costs will lower the break-even point. For example, when fuel prices rise or decline, there is a direct impact on the break-even freight load for the Union Pacific railroad.

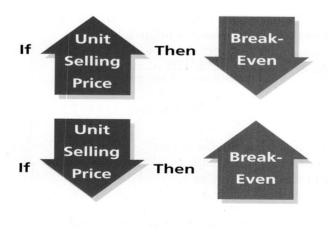

To illustrate, assume that Park Co. is evaluating a proposal to pay an additional 2% commission on sales to its salespeople as an incentive to increase sales. Fixed costs are estimated at $840,000, and the unit selling price, unit variable cost, and unit contribution margin before the additional 2% commission are as follows:

Unit selling price	$250
Unit variable cost	145
Unit contribution margin	$105

The break-even point is 8,000 units, computed as follows:

$$\text{Break-Even Sales (units)} = \frac{\text{Fixed Costs}}{\text{Unit Contribution Margin}}$$

$$\text{Break-Even Sales (units)} = \frac{\$840,000}{\$105} = 8,000 \text{ units}$$

If the sales commission proposal is adopted, variable costs will increase by $5 per unit ($250 × 2%). This increase in the variable costs will decrease the unit contribution margin by $5 (from $105 to $100). Thus, the break-even point is raised to 8,400 units, computed as follows:

$$\text{Break-Even Sales (units)} = \frac{\text{Fixed Costs}}{\text{Unit Contribution Margin}}$$

$$\text{Break-Even Sales (units)} = \frac{\$840,000}{\$100} = 8,400 \text{ units}$$

At the original break-even point of 8,000 units, the new unit contribution margin of $100 would provide only $800,000 to cover fixed costs of $840,000. Thus, an additional 400 units of sales will be required in order to provide the additional $40,000 (400 units × $100) contribution margin necessary to break even.

Effect of Changes in Unit Selling Price   Increases in the unit selling price will lower the break-even point, while decreases in the unit selling price will raise the break-even point. To illustrate, assume that Graham Co. is evaluating a proposal to increase the unit selling price of its product from $50 to $60. The following data have been gathered:

	Current	Proposed
Unit selling price	$50	$60
Unit variable cost	30	30
Unit contribution margin	$20	$30
Total fixed costs	$600,000	$600,000

The break-even point based on the current selling price is 30,000 units, computed as follows:

$$\text{Break-Even Sales (units)} = \frac{\text{Fixed Costs}}{\text{Unit Contribution Margin}}$$

$$\text{Break-Even Sales (units)} = \frac{\$600,000}{\$20} = 30,000 \text{ units}$$

If the selling price is increased by $10 per unit, the break-even point is decreased to 20,000 units, computed as follows:

$$\text{Break-Even Sales (units)} = \frac{\text{Fixed Costs}}{\text{Unit Contribution Margin}}$$

$$\text{Break-Even Sales (units)} = \frac{\$600,000}{\$30} = 20,000 \text{ units}$$

The increase of $10 per unit in the selling price increases the unit contribution margin by $10. Thus, the break-even point decreases by 10,000 units (from 30,000 units to 20,000 units).

Summary of Effects of Changes on Break-Even Point The break-even point in sales (units) moves in the same direction as changes in the variable cost per unit and fixed costs. In contrast, the break-even point in sales (units) moves in the opposite direction to changes in the sales price per unit. A summary of the impact of these changes on the break-even point in sales (units) is shown below.

Type of Change	Direction of Change	Effect of Change on Break-Even Sales (Units)
Fixed cost	Increase	Increase
	Decrease	Decrease
Variable cost per unit	Increase	Increase
	Decrease	Decrease
Unit sales price	Increase	Decrease
	Decrease	Increase

Business Connections

BREAKING EVEN ON HOWARD STERN

Satellite radio, one of the fastest growing forms of entertainment, has seen remarkable growth in recent years. Customers are able to choose from a variety of types of music and talk radio and listen from just about anywhere in the country with limited commercials. The satellite radio market is dominated by two companies, XM Satellite Radio and SIRIUS Satellite Radio. XM is the older of the two companies and has the largest market share. However, in 2005, Sirius tripled its customer base by diversifying its product line and signing high profile talk personalities. As part of this strategy, Sirius signed a five-year $500 million contract with radio "shock jock" Howard Stern. But how did Sirius determine that adding the self-proclaimed "King of All Media" to its play list was worth such a large amount of money? It used break-even analy-

sis. Prior to signing with Sirius, 12 million listeners tuned in to Stern's show on Infinity Broadcasting Corporation. At the time the contract was signed, Sirius had about 600,000 subscribers. The company estimated that it would need 1 million of Stern's fans to subscribe to Sirius in order to break even on the $500 million fixed cost of the contract. Initial projections estimated that Stern's show would attract as many as 10 million listeners. It appears that the company's strategy is beginning to work, as Sirius's subscriber base had grown to 3.3 million customers by the end of 2005.

Example Exercise 4-3

objective **3**

Nicolas Enterprises sells a product for $60 per unit. The variable cost is $35 per unit, while fixed costs are $80,000. Determine the (a) break-even point in sales units and (b) break-even point if the selling price were increased to $67 per unit.

Follow My Example 4-3

a. 3,200 units = $80,000/($60 − $35)
b. 2,500 units = $80,000/($67 − $35)

For Practice: PE 4-3A, PE 4-3B

TARGET PROFIT

At the break-even point, sales and costs are exactly equal. However, the break-even point is not the goal of most businesses. Rather, managers seek to maximize profits. By modifying the break-even equation, the sales volume required to earn a target or desired amount of profit may be estimated. For this purpose, target profit is added to the break-even equation as shown below.

$$\text{Sales (units)} = \frac{\text{Fixed Costs} + \text{Target Profit}}{\text{Unit Contribution Margin}}$$

To illustrate, assume that fixed costs are estimated at $200,000, and the desired profit is $100,000. The unit selling price, unit variable cost, and unit contribution margin are as follows:

Unit selling price	$75
Unit variable cost	45
Unit contribution margin	$30

The sales volume necessary to earn the target profit of $100,000 is 10,000 units, computed as follows:

$$\text{Sales (units)} = \frac{\text{Fixed Costs} + \text{Target Profit}}{\text{Unit Contribution Margin}}$$

$$\text{Sales (units)} = \frac{\$200,000 + \$100,000}{\$30} = 10,000 \text{ units}$$

The following income statement verifies this computation:

Sales (10,000 units × $75)	$750,000
Variable costs (10,000 units × $45)	450,000
Contribution margin (10,000 units × $30)	$300,000
Fixed costs	200,000
Income from operations	$100,000

← Target profit

Example Exercise 4-4

objective **3**

Forest Company sells a product for $140 per unit. The variable cost is $60 per unit, and fixed costs are $240,000. Determine the (a) break-even point in sales units and (b) break-even point in sales units if the company desires a target profit of $50,000.

(continued)

Follow My Example 4-4

a. 3,000 units = $240,000/($140 − $60)
b. 3,625 units = ($240,000 + $50,000)/($140 − $60)

For Practice: PE 4-4A, PE 4-4B

ETHICS

Integrity, Objectivity, and Ethics in Business

ORPHAN DRUGS

Each year, pharmaceutical companies develop new drugs that cure a variety of physical conditions. In order to be profitable, drug companies must sell enough of a product to exceed break-even for a reasonable selling price. Break-even points, however, create a problem for drugs targeted at rare diseases, called "orphan drugs." These drugs are typically expensive to develop and have low sales volumes, making it impossible to achieve break-even. To ensure that orphan drugs are not overlooked, Congress passed the Orphan Drug Act that provides incentives for pharmaceutical companies to develop drugs for rare diseases that might not generate enough sales to reach break-even. The program has been a great success. Since 1982, over 200 orphan drugs have come to market, including Jacobus Pharmaceuticals Company, Inc.'s drug for the treatment of tuberculosis and Novartis AG's drug for the treatment of Paget's disease.

Graphic Approach to Cost-Volume-Profit Analysis

objective 4

Using a cost-volume-profit chart and a profit-volume chart, determine the break-even point and the volume necessary to achieve a target profit.

Cost-volume-profit analysis can be presented graphically as well as in equation form. Many managers prefer the graphic format because the income or loss from operations (operating profit or loss) for different levels of sales can readily be determined. Next, we describe two graphic approaches that managers find useful.

COST-VOLUME-PROFIT (BREAK-EVEN) CHART

A **cost-volume-profit chart**, sometimes called a *break-even chart*, may assist management in understanding relationships among costs, sales, and operating profit or loss. To illustrate, the cost-volume-profit chart in Exhibit 5 is based on the following data:

Unit selling price	$50
Unit variable cost	30
Unit contribution margin	$20
Total fixed costs	$100,000

We constructed the cost-volume-profit chart in Exhibit 5 as follows:

A. Volume expressed in units of sales is indicated along the horizontal axis. The range of volume shown on the horizontal axis should reflect the *relevant range* in which the business expects to operate. Dollar amounts representing total sales and costs are indicated along the vertical axis.

B. A sales line is plotted by beginning at zero on the left corner of the graph. A second point is determined by multiplying any units of sales on the horizontal axis by the unit sales price of $50. For example, for 10,000 units of sales, the total sales would be $500,000 (10,000 units × $50). The sales line is drawn upward to the right from zero through the $500,000 point.

C. A cost line is plotted by beginning with total fixed costs, $100,000, on the vertical axis. A second point is determined by multiplying any units of sales on the horizontal axis by the unit variable costs and adding the fixed costs. For example, for 10,000 units of sales, the total estimated costs would be $400,000 [(10,000 units × $30) + $100,000]. The cost line is drawn upward to the right from $100,000 on the vertical axis through the $400,000 point.

EXHIBIT 5

Cost-Volume-Profit
Chart

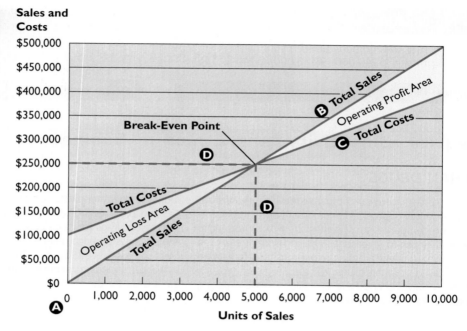

D. Horizontal and vertical lines are drawn at the intersection point of the sales and cost lines, which is the break-even point, and the areas representing operating profit and operating loss are identified.

In Exhibit 5, the dotted lines drawn from the intersection point of the total sales line and the total cost line identify the break-even point in total sales dollars and units. The break-even point is $250,000 of sales, which represents a sales volume of 5,000 units. Operating profits will be earned when sales levels are to the right of the break-even point (operating profit area). Operating losses will be incurred when sales levels are to the left of the break-even point (operating loss area).

Changes in the unit selling price, total fixed costs, and unit variable costs can be analyzed by using a cost-volume-profit chart. Using the data in Exhibit 5, assume that a proposal to reduce fixed costs by $20,000 is to be evaluated. In this case, the total fixed costs would be $80,000 ($100,000 − $20,000). As shown in Exhibit 6, the total cost

EXHIBIT 6

Revised Cost-Volume-
Profit Chart

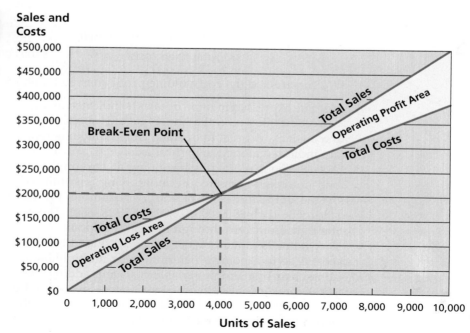

line should be redrawn, starting at the $80,000 point (total fixed costs) on the vertical axis. A second point is determined by multiplying any units of sales on the horizontal axis by the unit variable costs and adding the fixed costs. For example, for 10,000 units of sales, the total estimated costs would be $380,000 [(10,000 units × $30) + $80,000]. The cost line is drawn upward to the right from $80,000 on the vertical axis through the $380,000 point. The revised cost-volume-profit chart in Exhibit 6 indicates that the break-even point decreases to $200,000 or 4,000 units of sales.

PROFIT-VOLUME CHART

Another graphic approach to cost-volume-profit analysis, the **profit-volume chart**, focuses on profits. This is in contrast to the cost-volume-profit chart, which focuses on sales and costs. The profit-volume chart plots only the difference between total sales and total costs (or profits). In this way, the profit-volume chart allows managers to determine the operating profit (or loss) for various levels of operations.

To illustrate, assume that the profit-volume chart in Exhibit 7 is based on the same data as used in Exhibit 5. These data are as follows:

Unit selling price	$50
Unit variable cost	30
Unit contribution margin	$20
Total fixed costs	$100,000

EXHIBIT 7

Profit-Volume Chart

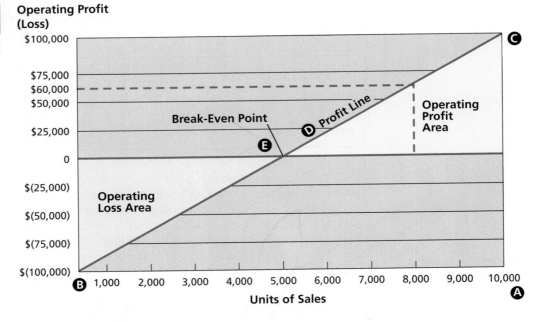

The maximum operating loss is equal to the fixed costs of $100,000. Assuming that the maximum unit sales within the relevant range is 10,000 units, the maximum operating profit is $100,000, computed as follows:

Sales (10,000 units × $50)	$500,000
Variable costs (10,000 units × $30)	300,000
Contribution margin (10,000 units × $20)	$200,000
Fixed costs	100,000
Operating profit	$100,000	← Maximum profit

We constructed the profit-volume chart in Exhibit 7 as follows:

A. Volume expressed in units of sales is indicated along the horizontal axis. The range of volume shown on the horizontal axis should reflect the *relevant range* in which the business expects to operate. In this illustration, the maximum number of sales units within the relevant range is assumed to be 10,000 units. Dollar amounts indicating operating profits and losses are shown along the vertical axis.

B. A point representing the maximum operating loss is plotted on the vertical axis at the left. This loss is equal to the total fixed costs at the zero level of sales.

C. A point representing the maximum operating profit within the relevant range is plotted on the right.

D. A diagonal profit line is drawn connecting the maximum operating loss point with the maximum operating profit point.

E. The profit line intersects the horizontal zero operating profit line at the break-even point expressed in units of sales, and the areas indicating operating profit and loss are identified.

In Exhibit 7, the break-even point is 5,000 units of sales, which is equal to total sales of $250,000 (5,000 units × $50). Operating profit will be earned when sales levels are to the right of the break-even point (operating profit area). Operating losses will be incurred when sales levels are to the left of the break-even point (operating loss area). For example, at sales of 8,000 units, an operating profit of $60,000 will be earned, as shown in Exhibit 7.

The effect of changes in the unit selling price, total fixed costs, and unit variable costs on profit can be analyzed using a profit-volume chart. To illustrate, using the data in Exhibit 7, we will evaluate the effect on profit of an increase of $20,000 in fixed costs. In this case, the total fixed costs would be $120,000 ($100,000 + $20,000), and the maximum operating loss would also be $120,000. If the maximum sales within the relevant range is 10,000 units, the maximum operating profit would be $80,000, computed as follows:

Sales (10,000 units × $50)	$500,000
Variable costs (10,000 units × $30)	300,000
Contribution margin (10,000 units × $20)	$200,000
Fixed costs	120,000
Operating profit	$ 80,000	← Revised maximum profit

A revised profit-volume chart is constructed by plotting the maximum operating loss and maximum operating profit points and drawing the revised profit line. The original and the revised profit-volume charts are shown in Exhibit 8.

The revised profit-volume chart indicates that the break-even point is 6,000 units of sales. This is equal to total sales of $300,000 (6,000 units × $50). The operating loss area of the chart has increased, while the operating profit area has decreased under the proposed change in fixed costs.

USE OF COMPUTERS IN COST-VOLUME-PROFIT ANALYSIS

With computers, the graphic approach and the mathematical approach to cost-volume-profit analysis are easy to use. Managers can vary assumptions regarding selling prices, costs, and volume and can immediately see the effects of each change on the break-even point and profit. Such an analysis is called a *"what if"* analysis or *sensitivity analysis*.

ASSUMPTIONS OF COST-VOLUME-PROFIT ANALYSIS

The reliability of cost-volume-profit analysis depends upon the validity of several assumptions. The primary assumptions are as follows:

1. Total sales and total costs can be represented by straight lines.
2. Within the relevant range of operating activity, the efficiency of operations does not change.

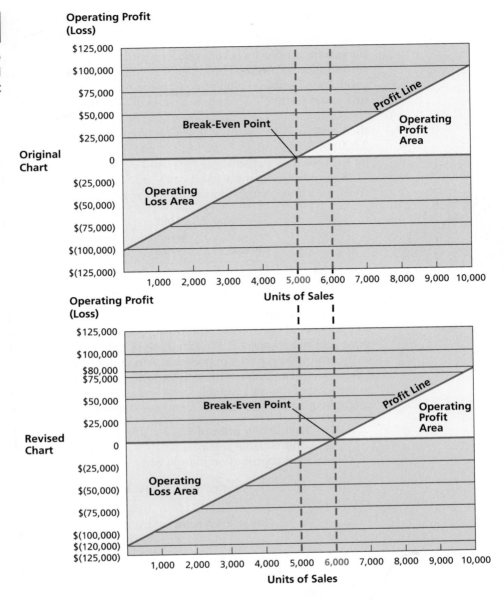

EXHIBIT 8

Original Profit-Volume Chart and Revised Profit-Volume Chart

3. Costs can be accurately divided into fixed and variable components.
4. The sales mix is constant.
5. There is no change in the inventory quantities during the period.

These assumptions simplify cost-volume-profit analysis. Since they are often valid for the relevant range of operations, cost-volume-profit analysis is useful to decision making.[3]

Special Cost-Volume-Profit Relationships

objective 5

Compute the break-even point for a business selling more than one product, the operating leverage, and the margin of safety.

Cost-volume-profit analysis can also be used in a variety of ways other than those already illustrated in this chapter. These include the use of break-even analysis when a company sells several products with different costs and prices. In addition, operating leverage and the margin of safety are useful in summarizing important cost-volume-profit relationships.

---

3 The impact of violating these assumptions is discussed in advanced accounting texts.

SALES MIX CONSIDERATIONS

In most businesses, more than one product is sold at varying selling prices. In addition, the products often have different unit variable costs, and each product makes a different contribution to profits. Thus, the sales volume necessary to break even or to earn a target profit for a business selling two or more products depends upon the sales mix. The **sales mix** is the relative distribution of sales among the various products sold by a business.

To illustrate the calculation of the break-even point for a company that sells more than one product, assume that Cascade Company sold 8,000 units of Product A and 2,000 units of Product B during the past year. The sales mix for products A and B can be expressed as percentages (80% and 20%) or as a ratio (80:20).

Cascade Company's fixed costs are $200,000. The unit selling prices, unit variable costs, and unit contribution margins for products A and B are as follows:

Sales Mix

Product	Unit Selling Price	Unit Variable Cost	Unit Contribution Margin
A	$ 90	$70	$20
B	140	95	45

In computing the break-even point, it is useful to think of the individual products as components of one overall enterprise product. For Cascade Company, this overall enterprise product is called E. We can think of the unit selling price of E as equal to the total of the unit selling prices of products A and B, multiplied by their sales mix percentages. Likewise, we can think of the unit variable cost and unit contribution margin of E as equal to the total of the unit variable costs and unit contribution margins of products A and B, multiplied by the sales mix percentages. These computations are as follows:

Unit selling price of E: ($90 × 0.8) + ($140 × 0.2) = $100
Unit variable cost of E: ($70 × 0.8) + ($ 95 × 0.2) =   75
Unit contribution margin of E: = $ 25

The break-even point of 8,000 units of E can be determined in the normal manner as follows:

$$\text{Break-Even Sales (units)} = \frac{\text{Fixed Costs}}{\text{Unit Contribution Margin}}$$

$$\text{Break-Even Sales (units)} = \frac{\$200,000}{\$25} = 8,000 \text{ units}$$

Since the sales mix for products A and B is 80% and 20%, respectively, the break-even quantity of A is 6,400 units (8,000 units × 80%) and B is 1,600 units (8,000 units × 20%). This analysis can be verified in the following income statement:

	Product A	Product B	Total
Sales:			
6,400 units × $90	$576,000		$576,000
1,600 units × $140		$224,000	224,000
Total sales	$576,000	$224,000	$800,000
Variable costs:			
6,400 units × $70	$448,000		$448,000
1,600 units × $95		$152,000	152,000
Total variable costs	$448,000	$152,000	$600,000
Contribution margin	$128,000	$ 72,000	$200,000
Fixed costs			200,000
Income from operations			$ 0	← Break-even point

The effects of changes in the sales mix on the break-even point can be determined by repeating this analysis, assuming a different sales mix.

Example Exercise 4-5   objective **5**

Megan Company has fixed costs of $180,000. The unit selling price, variable cost per unit, and contribution margin per unit for the company's two products are provided below.

Product	Selling Price	Variable Cost per Unit	Contribution Margin per Unit
Q	$160	$100	$60
Z	100	80	20

The sales mix for products Q and Z is 75% and 25%, respectively. Determine the break-even point in units of Q and Z.

Follow My Example 4-5

Unit Selling Price of E: [($160 × 0.75) + ($100 × 0.25)] = $145
Unit Variable Cost of E: [($100 × 0.75) + ($80 × 0.25)] = __95__
Unit Contribution Margin of E: $ 50

Break-Even Sales (units) = 3,600 units = $180,000/$50

For Practice: PE 4-5A, PE 4-5B

OPERATING LEVERAGE

The relative mix of a business's variable costs and fixed costs is measured by the **operating leverage**. It is computed as follows:

$$\text{Operating Leverage} = \frac{\text{Contribution Margin}}{\text{Income from Operations}}$$

REAL WORLD

One type of business that has high operating leverage is what is called a "network" business—one in which service is provided over a network that moves either goods or information. Examples of network businesses include American Airlines, Verizon Communications, Yahoo!, and Google.

Since the difference between contribution margin and income from operations is fixed costs, companies with large amounts of fixed costs will generally have a high operating leverage. Thus, companies in capital-intensive industries, such as the airline and automotive industries, will generally have a high operating leverage. A low operating leverage is normal for companies in industries that are labor-intensive, such as professional services.

Managers can use operating leverage to measure the impact of changes in sales on income from operations. A high operating leverage indicates that a small increase in sales will yield a large percentage increase in income from operations. In contrast, a low operating leverage indicates that a large increase in sales is necessary to significantly increase income from operations. To illustrate, assume the following operating data for Jones Inc. and Wilson Inc.:

	Jones Inc.	Wilson Inc.
Sales	$400,000	$400,000
Variable costs	300,000	300,000
Contribution margin	$100,000	$100,000
Fixed costs	80,000	50,000
Income from operations	$ 20,000	$ 50,000

Both companies have the same sales, the same variable costs, and the same contribution margin. Jones Inc. has larger fixed costs than Wilson Inc. and, as a result, a lower income from operations and a higher operating leverage. The operating leverage for each company is computed as follows:

Jones Inc.

$$\text{Operating Leverage} = \frac{\$100,000}{\$20,000} = 5$$

Wilson Inc.

$$\text{Operating Leverage} = \frac{\$100,000}{\$50,000} = 2$$

Jones Inc.'s operating leverage indicates that, for each percentage point change in sales, income from operations will change five times that percentage. In contrast, for each percentage point change in sales, the income from operations of Wilson Inc. will change only two times that percentage. For example, if sales increased by 10% ($40,000) for each company, income from operations will increase by 50% (10% × 5), or $10,000 (50% × $20,000), for Jones Inc. The sales increase of $40,000 will increase income from operations by only 20% (10% × 2), or $10,000 (20% × $50,000), for Wilson Inc. The validity of this analysis is shown as follows:

	Jones Inc.	Wilson Inc.
Sales	$440,000	$440,000
Variable costs	330,000	330,000
Contribution margin	$110,000	$110,000
Fixed costs	80,000	50,000
Income from operations	$ 30,000	$ 60,000

For Jones Inc., even a small increase in sales will generate a large percentage increase in income from operations. Thus, Jones's managers may be motivated to think of ways to increase sales. In contrast, Wilson's managers might attempt to increase operating leverage by reducing variable costs and thereby change the cost structure.

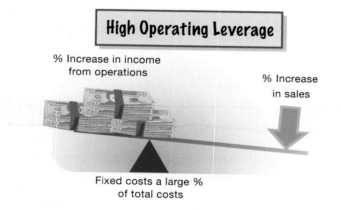

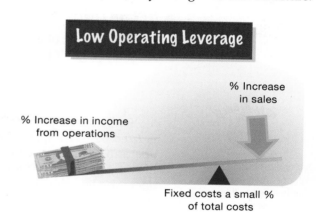

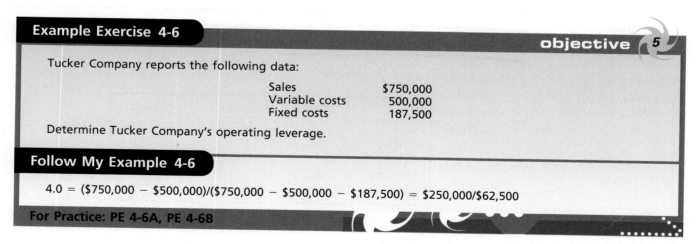

Example Exercise 4-6

objective 5

Tucker Company reports the following data:

Sales	$750,000
Variable costs	500,000
Fixed costs	187,500

Determine Tucker Company's operating leverage.

Follow My Example 4-6

4.0 = ($750,000 − $500,000)/($750,000 − $500,000 − $187,500) = $250,000/$62,500

For Practice: PE 4-6A, PE 4-6B

MARGIN OF SAFETY

The difference between the current sales revenue and the sales revenue at the break-even point is called the **margin of safety**. It indicates the possible decrease in sales that may occur before an operating loss results. For example, if the margin of safety is low, even a small decline in sales revenue may result in an operating loss.

If sales are $250,000, the unit selling price is $25, and sales at the break-even point are $200,000, the margin of safety is 20%, computed as follows:

$$\text{Margin of Safety} = \frac{\text{Sales} - \text{Sales at Break-Even Point}}{\text{Sales}}$$

$$\text{Margin of Safety} = \frac{\$250,000 - \$200,000}{\$250,000} = 20\%$$

The margin of safety may also be stated in terms of units. In this illustration, for example, the margin of safety of 20% is equivalent to $50,000 ($250,000 × 20%). In units, the margin of safety is 2,000 units ($50,000/$25). Thus, the current sales of $250,000 may decline $50,000 or 2,000 units before an operating loss occurs.

Example Exercise 4-7
objective **5**

The Rachel Company has sales of $400,000, and the break-even point in sales dollars is $300,000. Determine the company's margin of safety.

Follow My Example 4-7

25% = ($400,000 − $300,000)/$400,000

For Practice: PE 4-7A, PE 4-7B

At a Glance

1. Classify costs by their behavior as variable costs, fixed costs, or mixed costs.			
Key Points	**Key Learning Outcomes**	**Example Exercises**	**Practice Exercises**
Cost behavior refers to the manner in which costs change as a related activity changes. Variable costs vary in proportion to changes in the level of activity. Fixed costs remain the same in total dollar amount as the level of activity changes. Mixed costs are comprised of both fixed and variable costs.	• Describe variable costs. • Describe fixed costs. • Describe mixed costs. • Separate mixed costs using the high-low method.	4-1	4-1A, 4-1B

2. Compute the contribution margin, the contribution margin ratio, and the unit contribution margin, and explain how they may be useful to managers.			
Key Points	**Key Learning Outcomes**	**Example Exercises**	**Practice Exercises**
Contribution margin is the excess of sales revenue over variable costs and can be expressed as a ratio (contribution margin ratio) or a dollar amount (unit contribution margin). The contribution margin concept is useful for business planning because it provides insight into the profit potential of the firm.	• Describe contribution margin. • Compute the contribution margin ratio.	4-2	4-2A, 4-2B
	• Compute the unit contribution margin.	4-2	4-2A, 4-2B

(continued)

3. Using the unit contribution margin, determine the break-even point and the volume necessary to achieve a target profit.

Key Points	Key Learning Outcomes	Example Exercises	Practice Exercises
The break-even point is the point at which a business's revenues exactly equal expired costs. The mathematical approach to cost-volume-profit analysis uses the unit contribution margin concept and mathematical equations to determine the break-even point and the volume necessary to achieve a target profit for a business.	• Compute the break-even point in units. • Describe how changes in fixed costs affect the break-even point. • Describe how changes in unit variable costs affect the break-even point.	4-3	4-3A, 4-3B
	• Describe how a change in the unit selling price affects the break-even point.	4-3	4-3A, 4-3B
	• Compute the break-even point to earn a target profit.	4-4	4-4A, 4-4B

4. Using a cost-volume-profit chart and a profit-volume chart, determine the break-even point and the volume necessary to achieve a target profit.

Key Points	Key Learning Outcomes	Example Exercises	Practice Exercises
Graphical methods can be used to determine the break-even point and the volume necessary to achieve a target profit. A cost-volume-profit chart focuses on the relationship among costs, sales, and operating profit or loss. The profit-volume chart focuses on profits rather than on revenues and costs.	• Describe how to construct a cost-volume-profit chart. • Determine the break-even point using a cost-volume-profit chart. • Describe how to construct a profit-volume chart. • Determine the break-even point using a profit-volume chart. • Describe factors affecting the reliability of cost-volume-profit analysis.		

5. Compute the break-even point for a business selling more than one product, the operating leverage, and the margin of safety.

Key Points	Key Learning Outcomes	Example Exercises	Practice Exercises
Cost-volume-profit relationships can be used for analyzing (1) sales mix, (2) operating leverage, and (3) margin of safety. Sales mix computes the break-even point for a business selling more than one product. Operating leverage measures the impact of changes in sales on income from operations. The margin of safety measures the possible decrease in sales that may occur before an operating loss results.	• Compute the break-even point for more than one product.	4-5	4-5A, 4-5B
	• Compute operating leverage.	4-6	4-6A, 4-6B
	• Compute the margin of safety.	4-7	4-7A, 4-7B

Key Terms

activity bases (drivers) (128)
break-even point (136)
contribution margin (134)
contribution margin ratio (134)
cost behavior (128)
cost-volume-profit analysis (134)

cost-volume-profit chart (141)
fixed costs (130)
high-low method (132)
margin of safety (148)
mixed cost (130)
operating leverage (147)

profit-volume chart (143)
relevant range (128)
sales mix (146)
unit contribution margin (135)
variable costing (133)
variable costs (129)

Illustrative Problem

Wyatt Inc. expects to maintain the same inventories at the end of the year as at the beginning of the year. The estimated fixed costs for the year are $288,000, and the estimated variable costs per unit are $14. It is expected that 60,000 units will be sold at a price of $20 per unit. Maximum sales within the relevant range are 70,000 units.

Instructions
1. What is (a) the contribution margin ratio and (b) the unit contribution margin?
2. Determine the break-even point in units.
3. Construct a cost-volume-profit chart, indicating the break-even point.
4. Construct a profit-volume chart, indicating the break-even point.
5. What is the margin of safety?

Solution
1. a. $\text{Contribution Margin Ratio} = \dfrac{\text{Sales} - \text{Variable Costs}}{\text{Sales}}$

$\text{Contribution Margin Ratio} = \dfrac{(60{,}000 \text{ units} \times \$20) - (60{,}000 \text{ units} \times \$14)}{(60{,}000 \text{ units} \times \$20)}$

$\text{Contribution Margin Ratio} = \dfrac{\$1{,}200{,}000 - \$840{,}000}{\$1{,}200{,}000} = \dfrac{\$360{,}000}{\$1{,}200{,}000}$

$\text{Contribution Margin Ratio} = 30\%$

b. Unit Contribution Margin = Unit Selling Price − Unit Variable Costs
Unit Contribution Margin = $20 − $14 = $6

2. $\text{Break-Even Sales (units)} = \dfrac{\text{Fixed Costs}}{\text{Unit Contribution Margin}}$

$\text{Break-Even Sales (units)} = \dfrac{\$288{,}000}{\$6} = 48{,}000 \text{ units}$

3. Sales and Costs

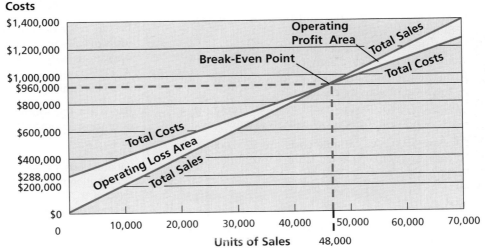

4. Operating Profit (Loss)

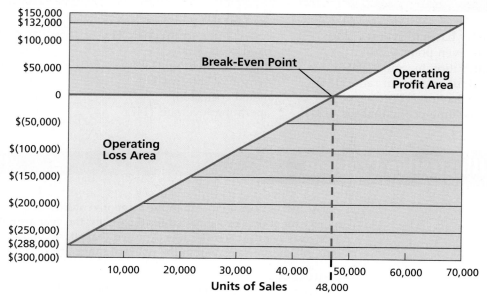

5. Margin of safety:

Expected sales (60,000 units × $20)	$1,200,000
Break-even point (48,000 units × $20)	960,000
Margin of safety	$ 240,000

or

$$\text{Margin of Safety} = \frac{\text{Sales} - \text{Sales at Break-Even Point}}{\text{Sales}}$$

$$\text{Margin of Safety} = \frac{\$240,000}{\$1,200,000} = 20\%$$

Self-Examination Questions

(Answers at End of Chapter)

1. Which of the following statements describes variable costs?
   A. Costs that vary on a per-unit basis as the level of activity changes.
   B. Costs that vary in total in direct proportion to changes in the level of activity.
   C. Costs that remain the same in total dollar amount as the level of activity changes.
   D. Costs that vary on a per-unit basis but remain the same in total as the level of activity changes.

2. If sales are $500,000, variable costs are $200,000, and fixed costs are $240,000, what is the contribution margin ratio?
   A. 40%   C. 52%
   B. 48%   D. 60%

3. If the unit selling price is $16, the unit variable cost is $12, and fixed costs are $160,000, what are the break-even sales (units)?

   A. 5,714 units   C. 13,333 units
   B. 10,000 units   D. 40,000 units

4. Based on the data presented in Question 3, how many units of sales would be required to realize income from operations of $20,000?
   A. 11,250 units   C. 40,000 units
   B. 35,000 units   D. 45,000 units

5. Based on the following operating data, what is the operating leverage?

Sales	$600,000
Variable costs	240,000
Contribution margin	$360,000
Fixed costs	160,000
Income from operations	$200,000

   A. 0.8   C. 1.8
   B. 1.2   D. 4.0

Eye Openers

1. Describe how total variable costs and unit variable costs behave with changes in the level of activity.
2. How would each of the following costs be classified if units produced is the activity base?
   a. Direct labor costs
   b. Direct materials costs
   c. Electricity costs of $0.35 per kilowatt hour
3. Describe the behavior of (a) total fixed costs and (b) unit fixed costs as the level of activity increases.
4. How would each of the following costs be classified if units produced is the activity base?
   a. Straight-line depreciation of plant and equipment
   b. Salary of factory supervisor ($70,000 per year)
   c. Property insurance premiums of $4,000 per month on plant and equipment
5. In cost analyses, how are mixed costs treated?
6. Which of the following graphs illustrates how total variable costs behave with changes in total units produced?

(a) 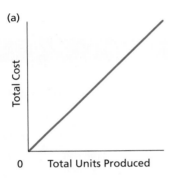   (b)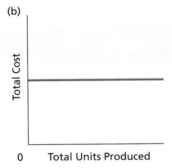

7. Which of the following graphs illustrates how unit variable costs behave with changes in total units produced?

(a) 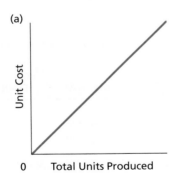   (b)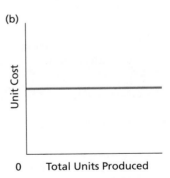

8. Which of the following graphs best illustrates fixed costs per unit as the activity base changes?

(a) 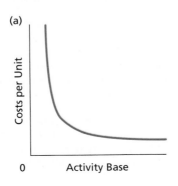   (b)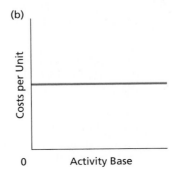

9. In applying the high-low method of cost estimation, how is the total fixed cost estimated?

10. If fixed costs increase, what would be the impact on the (a) contribution margin? (b) income from operations?

11. An examination of the accounting records of Mulgrew Company disclosed a high contribution margin ratio and production at a level below maximum capacity. Based on this information, suggest a likely means of improving income from operations. Explain.

12. If the unit cost of direct materials is decreased, what effect will this change have on the break-even point?

13. If insurance rates are increased, what effect will this change in fixed costs have on the break-even point?

14. Both Stratton Company and Callahan Company had the same sales, total costs, and income from operations for the current fiscal year; yet Stratton Company had a lower break-even point than Callahan Company. Explain the reason for this difference in break-even points.

15. The reliability of cost-volume-profit (CVP) analysis depends on several key assumptions. What are those primary assumptions?

16. How does the sales mix affect the calculation of the break-even point?

17. What does operating leverage measure, and how is it computed?

Practice Exercises

PE 4-1A
High-low method
obj. **1**

The manufacturing costs of Jake Industries for the first three months of the year are provided below.

	Total Costs	Production
January	$180,000	2,500 units
February	250,000	5,000
March	145,000	3,200

Using the high-low method, determine (a) the variable cost per unit and (b) the total fixed cost.

PE 4-1B
High-low method
obj. **1**

The manufacturing costs of Big T Enterprises for the first three months of the year are provided below.

	Total Costs	Production
January	$ 80,000	800 units
February	140,000	1,600
March	105,000	1,100

Using the high-low method, determine (a) the variable cost per unit and (b) the total fixed cost.

PE 4-2A
Contribution margin ratio
obj. **2**

Skinny Company sells 15,000 units at $20 per unit. Variable costs are $18 per unit, and fixed costs are $10,000. Determine (a) the contribution margin ratio, (b) the unit contribution margin, and (c) income from operations.

PE 4-2B
Contribution margin ratio
obj. **2**

Thorup Company sells 5,000 units at $40 per unit. Variable costs are $34 per unit, and fixed costs are $10,000. Determine (a) the contribution margin ratio, (b) the unit contribution margin, and (c) income from operations.

PE 4-3A
Break-even sales
obj. **3**

Frankel Enterprises sells a product for $25 per unit. The variable cost is $20 per unit, while fixed costs are $25,000. Determine (a) the break-even point in sales units and (b) the break-even point if the selling price were increased to $28 per unit.

PE 4-3B
Break-even sales
obj. 3

Barts Inc. sells a product for $120 per unit. The variable cost is $100 per unit, while fixed costs are $40,000. Determine (a) the break-even point in sales units and (b) the break-even point if the selling price were decreased to $110 per unit.

PE 4-4A
Break-even sales and sales to realize target profit
obj. 3

Melka Inc. sells a product for $80 per unit. The variable cost is $70 per unit, and fixed costs are $25,000. Determine (a) the break-even point in sales units and (b) the break-even point in sales units if the company desires a target profit of $25,000.

PE 4-4B
Break-even sales and sales to realize target profit
obj. 3

Averill Company sells a product for $100 per unit. The variable cost is $80 per unit, and fixed costs are $140,000. Determine (a) the break-even point in sales units and (b) the break-even point in sales units if the company desires a target profit of $30,000.

PE 4-5A
Sales mix and break-even sales
obj. 5

Simon Inc. has fixed costs of $150,000. The unit selling price, variable cost per unit, and contribution margin per unit for the company's two products are provided below.

Product	Selling Price	Variable Cost per Unit	Contribution Margin per Unit
X	$100	$ 60	$40
Y	140	125	15

The sales mix for products X and Y is 60% and 40%, respectively. Determine the break-even point in units of X and Y.

PE 4-5B
Sales mix and break-even sales
obj. 5

Brubaker Company has fixed costs of $120,000. The unit selling price, variable cost per unit, and contribution margin per unit for the company's two products are provided below.

Product	Selling Price	Variable Cost per Unit	Contribution Margin per Unit
Q	$90	$70	$20
Z	75	65	10

The sales mix for products Q and Z is 20% and 80%, respectively. Determine the break-even point in units of Q and Z.

PE 4-6A
Operating leverage
obj. 5

Ross Enterprises reports the following data:

Sales	$600,000
Variable costs	250,000
Fixed costs	100,000

Determine Ross Enterprises's operating leverage.

PE 4-6B
Operating leverage
obj. 5

EmilyCo reports the following data:

Sales	$900,000
Variable costs	400,000
Fixed costs	250,000

Determine EmilyCo's operating leverage.

PE 4-7A
Margin of safety
obj. 5

Miller Inc. has sales of $1,000,000, and the break-even point in sales dollars is $800,000. Determine the company's margin of safety.

PE 4-7B
Margin of safety
obj. 5

Ribisl Company has sales of $200,000, and the break-even point in sales dollars is $140,000. Determine the company's margin of safety.

Exercises

EX 4-1
Classify costs
obj. 1

Following is a list of various costs incurred in producing frozen pizzas. With respect to the production and sale of frozen pizzas, classify each cost as either variable, fixed, or mixed.

1. Property insurance premiums, $1,500 per month plus $0.005 for each dollar of property over $3,000,000
2. Packaging
3. Hourly wages of inspectors
4. Pension cost, $0.50 per employee hour on the job
5. Hourly wages of machine operators
6. Rent on warehouse, $5,000 per month plus $5 per square foot of storage used
7. Refrigerant used in refrigeration equipment
8. Pepperoni
9. Dough
10. Tomato paste
11. Property taxes, $50,000 per year on factory building and equipment
12. Electricity costs, $0.08 per kilowatt hour
13. Salary of plant manager
14. Straight-line depreciation on the production equipment
15. Janitorial costs, $3,000 per month

EX 4-2
Identify cost graphs
obj. 1

The following cost graphs illustrate various types of cost behavior:

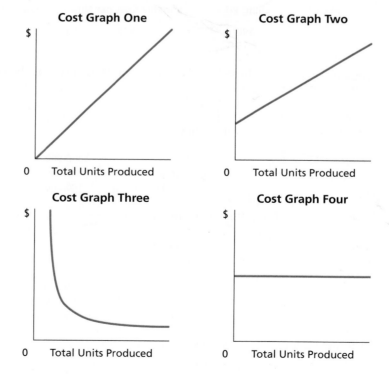

For each of the following costs, identify the cost graph that best illustrates its cost behavior as the number of units produced increases.

a. Per-unit direct labor cost

b. Salary of quality control supervisor, $5,000 per month
c. Total direct materials cost
d. Electricity costs of $3,000 per month plus $0.05 per kilowatt hour
e. Per-unit cost of straight-line depreciation on factory equipment

---

EX 4-3
Identify activity bases
obj. 1

For a major university, match each cost in the following table with the activity base most appropriate to it. An activity base may be used more than once, or not used at all.

Cost:	Activity Base:
1. Financial aid office salaries	a. Number of enrolled students and alumni
2. Instructor salaries	b. Student credit hours
3. Housing personnel wages	c. Number of student/athletes
4. Admissions office salaries	d. Number of enrollment applications
5. School supplies	e. Number of students living on campus
6. Record office salaries	f. Number of financial aid applications

---

EX 4-4
Identify activity bases
obj. 1

From the following list of activity bases for an automobile dealership, select the base that would be most appropriate for each of these costs: (1) preparation costs (cleaning, oil, and gasoline costs) for each car received, (2) salespersons' commission of 3% of the sales price for each car sold, and (3) administrative costs for ordering cars.

a. Dollar amount of cars on hand
b. Dollar amount of cars received
c. Dollar amount of cars sold
d. Dollar amount of cars ordered
e. Number of cars ordered
f. Number of cars sold
g. Number of cars on hand
h. Number of cars received

EX 4-5
Identify fixed and variable costs
obj. 1

Intuit Inc. develops and sells software products for the personal finance market, including popular titles such as Quicken® and TurboTax®. Classify each of the following costs and expenses for this company as either variable or fixed to the number of units produced and sold:

a. Straight-line depreciation of computer equipment
b. Sales commissions
c. Advertising
d. Packaging costs
e. CDs
f. Shipping expenses
g. Salaries of customer support personnel
h. Salaries of software developers
i. Wages of telephone order assistants
j. User's guides
k. President's salary
l. Property taxes on general offices

EX 4-6
Relevant range and fixed and variable costs
obj. 1
✓ a. $0.40

Laser Tex Inc. manufactures low-end computer components within a relevant range of 100,000 to 140,000 disks per year. Within this range, the following partially completed manufacturing cost schedule has been prepared:

CDs produced	100,000	120,000	140,000
Total costs:			
Total variable costs	$ 40,000	(d)	(j)
Total fixed costs	84,000	(e)	(k)
Total costs	$124,000	(f)	(l)
Cost per unit:			
Variable cost per unit	(a)	(g)	(m)
Fixed cost per unit	(b)	(h)	(n)
Total cost per unit	(c)	(i)	(o)

Complete the cost schedule, identifying each cost by the appropriate letter (a) through (o).

EX 4-7
High-low method
obj. 1

✓ *a. $10.00 per unit*

W & O Inc. has decided to use the high-low method to estimate the total cost and the fixed and variable cost components of the total cost. The data for various levels of production are as follows:

Units Produced	Total Costs
10,000	$750,000
22,500	845,000
30,000	950,000

a. Determine the variable cost per unit and the fixed cost.
b. Based on part (a), estimate the total cost for 25,000 units of production.

EX 4-8
High-low method for service company
obj. 1

✓ *Fixed cost, $250,000*

Great Plains Railroad decided to use the high-low method and operating data from the past six months to estimate the fixed and variable components of transportation costs. The activity base used by Great Plains Railroad is a measure of railroad operating activity, termed "gross-ton miles," which is the total number of tons multiplied by the miles moved.

	Transportation Costs	Gross-Ton Miles
January	$1,050,000	285,000
February	1,150,000	325,000
March	1,350,000	400,000
April	1,000,000	250,000
May	1,225,000	375,000
June	1,600,000	450,000

Determine the variable cost per gross-ton mile and the fixed cost.

EX 4-9
Contribution margin ratio
obj. 2

✓ *a. 55%*

a. Spock Company budgets sales of $840,000, fixed costs of $378,000, and variable costs of $378,000. What is the contribution margin ratio for Spock Company?
b. If the contribution margin ratio for Kirk Company is 34%, sales were $600,000, and fixed costs were $175,000, what was the income from operations?

EX 4-10
Contribution margin and contribution margin ratio
obj. 2

✓ *b. 34.00%*

For a recent year, McDonald's had the following sales and expenses (in millions):

Sales	$15,352
Food and packaging	$ 5,204
Payroll	4,040
Occupancy (rent, depreciation, etc.)	1,022
General, selling, and administrative expenses	2,220
	$12,486
Income from operations	$ 2,866

Assume that the variable costs consist of food and packaging, payroll, and 40% of the general, selling, and administrative expenses.

a. What is McDonald's contribution margin? Round to the nearest million.
b. What is McDonald's contribution margin ratio? Round to two decimal places.
c. How much would income from operations increase if same-store sales increased by $450 million for the coming year, with no change in the contribution margin ratio or fixed costs?

EX 4-11
Break-even sales and sales to realize income from operations
obj. 3

✓ *b. 20,435 units*

For the current year ending March 31, Zing Company expects fixed costs of $425,750, a unit variable cost of $40, and a unit selling price of $65.

a. Compute the anticipated break-even sales (units).
b. Compute the sales (units) required to realize income from operations of $85,125.

EX 4-12
Break-even sales
obj. 3

✓ a. 74,884,566 barrels

Anheuser-Busch Companies, Inc., reported the following operating information for a recent year (in millions):

Net sales	$14,935
Cost of goods sold	$ 8,983
Marketing and distribution	2,590
	$11,573
Income from operations	$ 3,362*

*Before special items

In addition, Anheuser-Busch sold 136 million barrels of beer during the year. Assume that variable costs were 70% of the cost of goods sold and 45% of marketing and distribution expenses. Assume that the remaining costs are fixed. For the following year, assume that Anheuser-Busch expects pricing, variable costs per barrel, and fixed costs to remain constant, except that new distribution and general office facilities are expected to increase fixed costs by $133 million.

Rounding to the nearest cent:

a. Compute the break-even sales (barrels) for the current year.
b. Compute the anticipated break-even sales (barrels) for the following year.

EX 4-13
Break-even sales
obj. 3

✓ a. 9,600 units

Currently, the unit selling price of a product is $300, the unit variable cost is $225, and the total fixed costs are $720,000. A proposal is being evaluated to increase the unit selling price to $345.

a. Compute the current break-even sales (units).
b. Compute the anticipated break-even sales (units), assuming that the unit selling price is increased and all costs remain constant.

EX 4-14
Break-even analysis
obj. 3

The Junior League of Tampa, Florida, collected recipes from members and published a cookbook entitled *Life of the Party*. The book will sell for $22 per copy. The chairwoman of the cookbook development committee estimated that the league needed to sell 16,000 books to break even on its $140,000 investment. What is the variable cost per unit assumed in the Junior League's analysis? Round to the nearest cent.

EX 4-15
Break-even analysis
obj. 3

The America Online division of Time Warner has fueled its growth by using aggressive promotion strategies. One of these strategies is to send compact disk software to potential customers, offering free AOL service for a period of time. Assume that during a given promotional campaign, AOL mailed 3,200,000 disks to potential customers, offering three months' free service. In addition, assume the following information:

Cost per disk (including mailing)	$1.50
Number of months an average new customer stays	
with the service (including the three free months)	30 months
Revenue per month per customer account	$10.00
Variable cost per month per customer account	$1.00

Determine the number of new customer accounts needed to break even on the cost of the promotional campaign. In forming your answer, (1) treat the cost of mailing the disk as a fixed cost, and (2) treat the revenue less variable cost per account for the service period as the unit contribution margin.

EX 4-16
Break-even analysis
obj. 3

Sprint Nextel is one of the largest digital wireless service providers in the United States. In a recent year, it had 39.7 million direct subscribers (accounts) that generated revenue of $14,647 million. Costs and expenses for the year were as follows (in millions):

(continued)

Cost of revenue	$6,091
Selling, general, and administrative expenses	4,411
Depreciation	2,557

Assume that 70% of the cost of revenue and 40% of the selling, general, and administrative expenses are variable to the number of direct subscribers (accounts).

a. What is Sprint Nextel's break-even number of accounts, using the data and assumptions above? Round units to the nearest million.
b. How much revenue per account would be sufficient for Sprint Nextel to break even if the number of accounts remained constant?

EX 4-17
Cost-volume-profit chart
obj. 4

✓ b. $500,000

For the coming year, Knight Inc. anticipates fixed costs of $200,000, a unit variable cost of $15, and a unit selling price of $25. The maximum sales within the relevant range are $1,000,000.

a. Construct a cost-volume-profit chart.
b. Estimate the break-even sales (dollars) by using the cost-volume-profit chart constructed in part (a).
c. ▭▭▭▶ What is the main advantage of presenting the cost-volume-profit analysis in graphic form rather than equation form?

EX 4-18
Profit-volume chart
obj. 4

✓ b. $200,000

Using the data for Knight Inc. in Exercise 4-17, (a) determine the maximum possible operating loss, (b) compute the maximum possible income from operations, (c) construct a profit-volume chart, and (d) estimate the break-even sales (units) by using the profit-volume chart constructed in part (c).

EX 4-19
Break-even chart
obj. 4

Name the following chart, and identify the items represented by the letters (a) through (f).

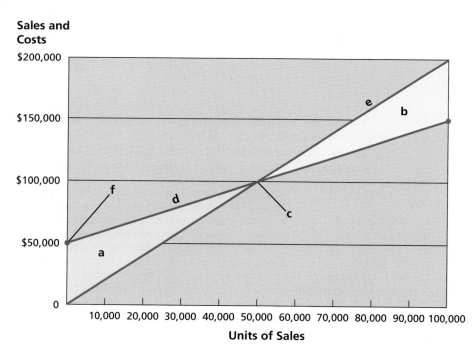

EX 4-20
Break-even chart
obj. 4

Name the following chart, and identify the items represented by the letters (a) through (f).

Operating Profit (Loss)

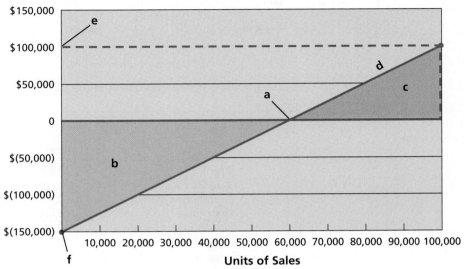

EX 4-21
Sales mix and break-even sales
obj. 5
✓a. 280,000 units

Candies Inc. manufactures and sells two products, marshmallow bunnies and jelly beans. The fixed costs are $350,000, and the sales mix is 70% marshmallow bunnies and 30% jelly beans. The unit selling price and the unit variable cost for each product are as follows:

Products	Unit Selling Price	Unit Variable Cost
Marshmallow bunnies	$2.40	$1.00
Jelly beans	1.80	0.90

a. Compute the break-even sales (units) for the overall product, E.
b. How many units of each product, marshmallow bunnies and jelly beans, would be sold at the break-even point?

EX 4-22
Break-even sales and sales mix for a service company
obj. 5
✓a. 65 seats

Fly-by-Night Airways provides air transportation services between New York and Miami. A single New York to Miami round-trip flight has the following operating statistics:

Fuel	$3,540
Flight crew salaries	7,310
Airplane depreciation	2,995
Variable cost per passenger—business class	45
Variable cost per passenger—tourist class	35
Round-trip ticket price—business class	350
Round-trip ticket price—tourist class	225

It is assumed that the fuel, crew salaries, and airplane depreciation are fixed, regardless of the number of seats sold for the round-trip flight.

a. Compute the break-even number of seats sold on a single round-trip flight for the overall product. Assume that the overall product is 20% business class and 80% tourist class tickets.
b. How many business class and tourist class seats would be sold at the break-even point?

EX 4-23
Margin of safety
obj. 5
✓a. (2) 10%

a. If Larker Company, with a break-even point at $450,000 of sales, has actual sales of $500,000, what is the margin of safety expressed (1) in dollars and (2) as a percentage of sales?
b. If the margin of safety for Porter Company was 20%, fixed costs were $600,000, and variable costs were 70% of sales, what was the amount of actual sales (dollars)? (*Hint:* Determine the break-even in sales dollars first.)

EX 4-24
Break-even and margin of safety relationships
obj. 5

At a recent staff meeting, the management of Hom Technology Products was considering discontinuing the Hercules line of laptop computers from the product line. The chief financial analyst reported the following current monthly data for the Hercules:

Units of sales	32,000
Break-even units	36,800
Margin of safety in units	4,800

✎➤ For what reason would you question the validity of these data?

EX 4-25
Operating leverage
obj. 5

✓ a. Juras, 3.00

Juras Inc. and Hinson Inc. have the following operating data:

	Juras	Hinson
Sales	$160,000	$215,000
Variable costs	130,000	115,000
Contribution margin	$ 30,000	$100,000
Fixed costs	20,000	75,000
Income from operations	$ 10,000	$ 25,000

a. Compute the operating leverage for Juras Inc. and Hinson Inc.
b. How much would income from operations increase for each company if the sales of each increased by 10%?
c. ✎➤ Why is there a difference in the increase in income from operations for the two companies? Explain.

Problems Series A ↘

PR 4-1A
Classify costs
obj. 1

New Age Furniture Company manufactures sofas for distribution to several major retail chains. The following costs are incurred in the production and sale of sofas:

a. Springs
b. Consulting fee of $25,000 paid to efficiency specialists
c. Sewing supplies
d. Electricity costs of $0.10 per kilowatt hour
e. Fabric for sofa coverings
f. Salary of production vice president
g. Salesperson's salary, $20,000 plus 5% of the selling price of each sofa sold
h. Janitorial supplies, $15 for each sofa produced
i. Employer's FICA taxes on controller's salary of $150,000
j. Rent on experimental equipment, $35 for every sofa produced
k. Wood for framing the sofas
l. Insurance premiums on property, plant, and equipment, $10,000 per year plus $15 per $10,000 of insured value over $15,000,000
m. Hourly wages of sewing machine operators
n. Salary of designers
o. Property taxes on property, plant, and equipment
p. Legal fees paid to attorneys in defense of the company in a patent infringement suit, $15,000 plus $175 per hour
q. Cartons used to ship sofas
r. Rental costs of warehouse, $15,000 per month
s. Straight-line depreciation on factory equipment
t. Foam rubber for cushion fillings

Instructions
Classify the preceding costs as either fixed, variable, or mixed. Use the following tabular headings and place an "X" in the appropriate column. Identify each cost by letter in the Cost column.

Cost	Fixed Cost	Variable Cost	Mixed Cost

PR 4-2A
Break-even sales under present and proposed conditions

objs. 2, 3

✓ 3. 13,250 units

French Broad Inc., operating at full capacity, sold 25,125 units at a price of $75 per unit during 2008. Its income statement for 2008 is as follows:

Sales		$1,884,375
Cost of goods sold		1,100,000
Gross profit		$ 784,375
Expenses:		
Selling expenses	$125,000	
Administrative expenses	125,000	
Total expenses		250,000
Income from operations		$ 534,375

The division of costs between fixed and variable is as follows:

	Fixed	Variable
Cost of sales	40%	60%
Selling expenses	50%	50%
Administrative expenses	75%	25%

Management is considering a plant expansion program that will permit an increase of $487,500 in yearly sales. The expansion will increase fixed costs by $135,000, but will not affect the relationship between sales and variable costs.

Instructions
1. Determine for 2008 the total fixed costs and the total variable costs.
2. Determine for 2008 (a) the unit variable cost and (b) the unit contribution margin.
3. Compute the break-even sales (units) for 2008.
4. Compute the break-even sales (units) under the proposed program.
5. Determine the amount of sales (units) that would be necessary under the proposed program to realize the $534,375 of income from operations that was earned in 2008.
6. Determine the maximum income from operations possible with the expanded plant.
7. If the proposal is accepted and sales remain at the 2008 level, what will the income or loss from operations be for 2009?
8. ▬▬▶ Based on the data given, would you recommend accepting the proposal? Explain.

PR 4-3A
Break-even sales and cost-volume-profit chart

objs. 3, 4

✓ 1. 17,500 units

For the coming year, Wisconsin Products Inc. anticipates a unit selling price of $72, a unit variable cost of $34, and fixed costs of $665,000.

Instructions
1. Compute the anticipated break-even sales (units).
2. Compute the sales (units) required to realize income from operations of $95,000.
3. Construct a cost-volume-profit chart, assuming maximum sales of 40,000 units within the relevant range.
4. Determine the probable income (loss) from operations if sales total 29,000 units.

PR 4-4A
Break-even sales and cost-volume-profit chart

objs. 3, 4

✓ 1. 1,500 units

Last year, Pocket PC Co. had sales of $430,000, based on a unit selling price of $215. The variable cost per unit was $155, and fixed costs were $90,000. The maximum sales within Pocket PC's relevant range are 3,000 units. Pocket PC is considering a proposal to spend an additional $24,000 on billboard advertising during the current year in an attempt to increase sales and utilize unused capacity.

Instructions
1. Construct a cost-volume-profit chart indicating the break-even sales for last year. Verify your answer, using the break-even equation.
2. Using the cost-volume-profit chart prepared in part (1), determine (a) the income from operations for last year and (b) the maximum income from operations that could have been realized during the year. Verify your answers arithmetically.
3. Construct a cost-volume-profit chart indicating the break-even sales for the current year, assuming that a noncancelable contract is signed for the additional billboard advertising. No changes are expected in the selling price or other costs. Verify your answer, using the break-even equation.

(continued)

4. Using the cost-volume-profit chart prepared in part (3), determine (a) the income from operations if sales total 2,500 units and (b) the maximum income from operations that could be realized during the year. Verify your answers arithmetically.

PR 4-5A
Sales mix and break-even sales

obj. **5**

✓ 1. 52,200 units

Data related to the expected sales of two types of decorative flower pots for Boyeva Flower Pots, Inc. for the current year, which is typical of recent years, are as follows:

Products	Unit Selling Price	Unit Variable Cost	Sales Mix
Decorative Indoor Flower Pot	$ 9.00	$3.60	25%
Rugged Outdoor Flower Pot	12.00	5.40	75%

The estimated fixed costs for the current year are $328,860.

Instructions
1. Determine the estimated units of sales of the overall product necessary to reach the break-even point for the current year.
2. Based on the break-even sales (units) in part (1), determine the unit sales of both the Decorative Indoor Flower Pot and Rugged Outdoor Flower Pot for the current year.
3. ▰▰▰▰▶ Assume that the sales mix was 50% Decorative Indoor Flower Pot and 50% Rugged Outdoor Flower Pot. Compare the break-even point with that in part (1). Why is it so different?

PR 4-6A
Contribution margin, break-even sales, cost-volume-profit chart, margin of safety, and operating leverage

objs. **2, 3, 4, 5**

✓ 2. 40.0%

Aspen Co. expects to maintain the same inventories at the end of 2008 as at the beginning of the year. The total of all production costs for the year is therefore assumed to be equal to the cost of goods sold. With this in mind, the various department heads were asked to submit estimates of the costs for their departments during 2008. A summary report of these estimates is as follows:

	Estimated Fixed Cost	Estimated Variable Cost (per unit sold)
Production costs:		
Direct materials	—	$ 8.90
Direct labor	—	3.80
Factory overhead	$ 80,200	2.10
Selling expenses:		
Sales salaries and commissions	41,200	1.70
Advertising	13,200	—
Travel	2,700	—
Miscellaneous selling expense	5,400	1.50
Administrative expenses:		
Office and officers' salaries	81,500	—
Supplies	4,700	0.70
Miscellaneous administrative expense	10,500	2.30
Total	$239,400	$21.00

It is expected that 19,000 units will be sold at a price of $35 a unit. Maximum sales within the relevant range are 30,000 units.

Instructions
1. Prepare an estimated income statement for 2008.
2. What is the expected contribution margin ratio?
3. Determine the break-even sales in units.
4. Construct a cost-volume-profit chart indicating the break-even sales.
5. What is the expected margin of safety?
6. Determine the operating leverage.

Problems Series B

PR 4-1B
Classify costs
obj. 1

Montana Jeans Inc. manufactures blue jeans for distribution to several major retail chains. The following costs are incurred in the production and sale of blue jeans:

a. Brass buttons
b. Janitorial supplies, $1,000 per month
c. Legal fees paid to attorneys in defense of the company in a patent infringement suit, $30,000 plus $150 per hour
d. Straight-line depreciation on sewing machines
e. Salary of production vice president
f. Leather for patches identifying each jean style
g. Salary of designers
h. Supplies
i. Denim fabric
j. Insurance premiums on property, plant, and equipment, $20,000 per year plus $2 per $10,000 of insured value over $7,000,000
k. Hourly wages of machine operators
l. Property taxes on property, plant, and equipment
m. Salesperson's salary, $15,000 plus 2% of the total sales
n. Rental costs of warehouse, $3,000 per month plus $2 per square foot of storage used
o. Electricity costs of $0.12 per kilowatt hour
p. Rent on experimental equipment, $30,000 per year
q. Thread
r. Blue dye
s. Shipping boxes used to ship orders
t. Consulting fee of $70,000 paid to industry specialist for marketing advice

Instructions
Classify the preceding costs as either fixed, variable, or mixed. Use the following tabular headings and place an "X" in the appropriate column. Identify each cost by letter in the cost column.

Cost	Fixed Cost	Variable Cost	Mixed Cost

PR 4-2B
Break-even sales under present and proposed conditions
objs. 2, 3

✓ 2. (a) $30.75

Castellino Company, operating at full capacity, sold 80,000 units at a price of $70.75 per unit during 2008. Its income statement for 2008 is as follows:

Sales		$5,660,000
Cost of goods sold		2,100,000
Gross profit		$3,560,000
Expenses:		
Selling expenses	$1,500,000	
Administrative expenses	900,000	
Total expenses		2,400,000
Income from operations		$1,160,000

The division of costs between fixed and variable is as follows:

	Fixed	Variable
Cost of sales	50%	50%
Selling expenses	30%	70%
Administrative expenses	60%	40%

Management is considering a plant expansion program that will permit an increase of $884,375 in yearly sales. The expansion will increase fixed costs by $265,000 but will not affect the relationship between sales and variable costs.

Instructions

1. Determine for 2008 the total fixed costs and the total variable costs.
2. Determine for 2008 (a) the unit variable cost and (b) the unit contribution margin.
3. Compute the break-even sales (units) for 2008.
4. Compute the break-even sales (units) under the proposed program.
5. Determine the amount of sales (units) that would be necessary under the proposed program to realize the $1,160,000 of income from operations that was earned in 2008.
6. Determine the maximum income from operations possible with the expanded plant.
7. If the proposal is accepted and sales remain at the 2008 level, what will the income or loss from operations be for 2009?
8. ▭▬➤ Based on the data given, would you recommend accepting the proposal? Explain.

PR 4-3B
Break-even sales and cost-volume-profit chart

objs. 3, 4

✓1. 7,600 units

For the coming year, Baker Company anticipates a unit selling price of $450, a unit variable cost of $325, and fixed costs of $950,000.

Instructions

1. Compute the anticipated break-even sales (units).
2. Compute the sales (units) required to realize income from operations of $175,000.
3. Construct a cost-volume-profit chart, assuming maximum sales of 16,000 units within the relevant range.
4. Determine the probable income (loss) from operations if sales total 8,000 units.

PR 4-4B
Break-even sales and cost-volume-profit chart

objs. 3, 4

✓1. 5,000 units

Last year, Taylor Inc. had sales of $100,000, based on a unit selling price of $20. The variable cost per unit was $10, and fixed costs were $50,000. The maximum sales within Taylor's relevant range are 10,000 units. Taylor is considering a proposal to spend an additional $20,000 on billboard advertising during the current year in an attempt to increase sales and utilize unused capacity.

Instructions

1. Construct a cost-volume-profit chart indicating the break-even sales for last year. Verify your answer, using the break-even equation.
2. Using the cost-volume-profit chart prepared in part (1), determine (a) the income from operations for last year and (b) the maximum income from operations that could have been realized during the year. Verify your answers arithmetically.
3. Construct a cost-volume-profit chart indicating the break-even sales for the current year, assuming that a noncancelable contract is signed for the additional billboard advertising. No changes are expected in the unit selling price or other costs. Verify your answer, using the break-even equation.
4. Using the cost-volume-profit chart prepared in part (3), determine (a) the income from operations if sales total 8,000 units and (b) the maximum income from operations that could be realized during the year. Verify your answers arithmetically.

PR 4-5B
Sales mix and break-even sales

obj. 5

✓1. 73,700 units

Data related to the expected sales of lacrosse sticks and hockey sticks for Athletics Inc. for the current year, which is typical of recent years, are as follows:

Products	Unit Selling Price	Unit Variable Cost	Sales Mix
Lacrosse sticks	$52.00	$28.00	70%
Hockey sticks	64.00	36.00	30%

The estimated fixed costs for the current year are $1,857,240.

Instructions

1. Determine the estimated units of sales of the overall product necessary to reach the break-even point for the current year.
2. Based on the break-even sales (units) in part (1), determine the unit sales of both lacrosse sticks and hockey sticks for the current year.
3. ▭▬➤ Assume that the sales mix was 30% lacrosse sticks and 70% hockey sticks. Compare the break-even point with that in part (1). Why is it so different?

PR 4-6B
Contribution margin, break-even sales, cost-volume-profit chart, margin of safety, and operating leverage

objs. **2, 3, 4, 5**

✓ 2. 45%

Loumis Home Care Products Inc. expects to maintain the same inventories at the end of 2008 as at the beginning of the year. The total of all production costs for the year is therefore assumed to be equal to the cost of goods sold. With this in mind, the various department heads were asked to submit estimates of the costs for their departments during 2008. A summary report of these estimates is as follows:

	Estimated Fixed Cost	Estimated Variable Cost (per unit sold)
Production costs:		
Direct materials	—	$137.70
Direct labor	—	116.40
Factory overhead	$232,000	27.20
Selling expenses:		
Sales salaries and commissions	356,225	9.15
Advertising	67,500	—
Travel	42,500	—
Miscellaneous selling expense	22,250	2.25
Administrative expenses:		
Office and officers' salaries	235,000	—
Supplies	15,525	6.30
Miscellaneous administrative expense	19,000	3.50
Total	$990,000	$302.50

It is expected that 5,000 units will be sold at a price of $550 a unit. Maximum sales within the relevant range are 10,000 units.

Instructions
1. Prepare an estimated income statement for 2008.
2. What is the expected contribution margin ratio?
3. Determine the break-even sales in units.
4. Construct a cost-volume-profit chart indicating the break-even sales.
5. What is the expected margin of safety?
6. Determine the operating leverage.

Special Activities

SA 4-1
Ethics and professional conduct in business

ETHICS

Paul Hambel is a financial consultant to Tecau Properties Inc., a real estate syndicate. Tecau Properties Inc. finances and develops commercial real estate (office buildings). The completed projects are then sold as limited partnership interests to individual investors. The syndicate makes a profit on the sale of these partnership interests. Paul provides financial information for the offering prospectus, which is a document that provides the financial and legal details of the limited partnership offerings. In one of the projects, the bank has financed the construction of a commercial office building at a rate of 7% for the first four years, after which time the rate jumps to 12% for the remaining 21 years of the mortgage. The interest costs are one of the major ongoing costs of a real estate project. Paul has reported prominently in the prospectus that the break-even occupancy for the first four years is 70%. This is the amount of office space that must be leased to cover the interest and general upkeep costs over the first four years. The 70% break-even is very low and thus communicates a low risk to potential investors. Paul uses the 70% break-even rate as a major marketing tool in selling the limited partnership interests. Buried in the fine print of the prospectus is additional information that would allow an astute investor to determine that the break-even occupancy will jump to 90% after the fourth year because of the contracted increase in the mortgage interest rate. Paul believes prospective investors are adequately informed as to the risk of the investment.

➤ Comment on the ethical considerations of this situation.

SA 4-2
*Break-even sales,
contribution margin*

"For a student, a grade of 65 percent is nothing to write home about. But for the airline . . . [industry], filling 65 percent of the seats . . . is the difference between profit and loss.

The [economy] might be just strong enough to sustain all the carriers on a cash basis, but not strong enough to bring any significant profitability to the industry. . . . For the airlines . . . , the emphasis will be on trying to consolidate routes and raise ticket prices. . . ."

▬▬▶ The airline industry is notorious for boom and bust cycles. Why is airline profitability very sensitive to these cycles? Do you think that during a down cycle the strategy to consolidate routes and raise ticket prices is reasonable? What would make this strategy succeed or fail? Why?

Source: Edwin McDowell, "Empty Seats, Empty Beds, Empty Pockets," *The New York Times*, January 6, 1992, p. C3.

SA 4-3
Break-even analysis

Southern Video Games Inc. has finished a new video game, *Olympic Competition Bobsledding*. Management is now considering its marketing strategies. The following information is available:

Anticipated sales price per unit	$30
Variable cost per unit*	$15
Anticipated volume	500,000
Production costs	$5,000,000
Anticipated advertising	$2,500,000

*The cost of the video game, packaging, and copying costs.

Two managers, Molly Smith and Alex Clarke, had the following discussion of ways to increase the profitability of this new offering.

Molly: I think we need to think of some way to increase our profitability. Do you have any ideas?

Alex: Well, I think the best strategy would be to become aggressive on price.

Molly: How aggressive?

Alex: If we drop the price to $22 per unit and maintain our advertising budget at $2,500,000, I think we will generate sales of 1,400,000 units.

Molly: I think that's the wrong way to go. You're giving too much up on price. Instead, I think we need to follow an aggressive advertising strategy.

Alex: How aggressive?

Molly: If we increase our advertising to a total of $5,000,000, we should be able to increase sales volume to 1,250,000 units without any change in price.

Alex: I don't think that's reasonable. We'll never cover the increased advertising costs.

▬▬▶ Which strategy is best: Do nothing? Follow the advice of Alex Clarke? Or follow Molly Smith's strategy?

SA 4-4
*Variable costs and
activity bases in decision
making*

The owner of Banner-Tech, a printing company, is planning direct labor needs for the upcoming year. The owner has provided you with the following information for next year's plans:

	One Color	Two Color	Three Color	Four Color	Total
Number of banners	100	150	200	400	850

Each color on the banner must be printed one at a time. Thus, for example, a four-color banner will need to be run through the printing operation four separate times. The total production volume last year was 425 banners, as shown below.

	One Color	Two Color	Three Color	Total
Number of banners	100	125	200	425

As you can see, the four-color banner is a new product offering for the upcoming year. The owner believes that the expected 425-unit increase in volume from last year means that direct labor expenses should increase by 100% (425/425). What do you think?

SA 4-5
Variable costs and activity bases in decision making

Sales volume has been dropping at Winona Publishing Company. During this time, however, the Shipping Department manager has been under severe financial constraints. The manager knows that most of the Shipping Department's effort is related to pulling inventory from the warehouse for each order and performing the paperwork. The paperwork involves preparing shipping documents for each order. Thus, the pulling and paperwork effort associated with each sales order is essentially the same, regardless of the size of the order. The Shipping Department manager has discussed the financial situation with senior management. Senior management has responded by pointing out that sales volume has been dropping, so that the amount of work in the Shipping Department should be dropping. Thus, senior management told the Shipping Department manager that costs should be decreasing in the department.

The Shipping Department manager prepared the following information:

Month	Sales Volume	Number of Customer Orders	Sales Volume per Order
January	$152,000	800	190
February	147,600	820	180
March	144,500	850	170
April	144,000	960	150
May	143,550	990	145
June	136,000	1,000	136
July	130,650	1,005	130
August	128,000	1,024	125

Given this information, how would you respond to senior management?

SA 4-6
Break-even analysis

Group Project

Break-even analysis is one of the most fundamental tools for managing any kind of business unit. Consider the management of your school. In a group, brainstorm some applications of break-even analysis at your school. Identify three areas where break-even analysis might be used. For each area, identify the revenues, variable costs, and fixed costs that would be used in the calculation.

Answers to Self-Examination Questions

1. **B**   Variable costs vary in total in direct proportion to changes in the level of activity (answer B). Costs that vary on a per-unit basis as the level of activity changes (answer A) or remain constant in total dollar amount as the level of activity changes (answer C), or both (answer D), are fixed costs.

2. **D**   The contribution margin ratio indicates the percentage of each sales dollar available to cover the fixed costs and provide income from operations and is determined as follows:

$$\text{Contribution Margin Ratio} = \frac{\text{Sales} - \text{Variable Costs}}{\text{Sales}}$$

$$\text{Contribution Margin Ratio} = \frac{\$500,000 - \$200,000}{\$500,000}$$

$$= 60\%$$

3. **D**   The break-even sales of 40,000 units (answer D) is computed as follows:

$$\text{Break-Even Sales (units)} = \frac{\text{Fixed Costs}}{\text{Unit Contribution Margin}}$$

$$\text{Break-Even Sales (units)} = \frac{\$160,000}{\$4} = 40,000 \text{ units}$$

4. **D**   Sales of 45,000 units are required to realize income from operations of $20,000, computed as follows:

$$\text{Sales (units)} = \frac{\text{Fixed Costs} + \text{Target Profit}}{\text{Unit Contribution Margin}}$$

$$\text{Sales (units)} = \frac{\$160,000 + \$20,000}{\$4} = 45,000 \text{ units}$$

5. **C**   The operating leverage is 1.8, computed as follows:

$$\text{Operating Leverage} = \frac{\text{Contribution Margin}}{\text{Income from Operations}}$$

$$\text{Operating Leverage} = \frac{\$360,000}{\$200,000} = 1.8$$

Variable Costing for Management Analysis

objectives

After studying this chapter, you should be able to:

1 Describe and illustrate income reporting under variable costing and absorption costing.

2 Describe and illustrate income analysis under variable costing and absorption costing.

3 Describe and illustrate management's use of variable costing and absorption costing for controlling costs, pricing products, planning production, analyzing contribution margins, and analyzing market segments.

4 Use variable costing for analyzing market segments, including product, territories, and salespersons segments.

5 Use variable costing for analyzing and explaining changes in contribution margin as a result of quantity and price factors.

6 Describe and illustrate the use of variable costing for service firms.

Adobe Systems, Inc.

Assume that you are interested in obtaining a temporary job during the summer and that you have three different job options. How would you evaluate these options? Naturally, there are many things to consider, including how much income each job would provide.

Determining the income from each job may not be as simple as comparing the rates of pay per hour. For example, a job as an office clerk at a local company pays $7 per hour. A job delivering pizza pays $10 per hour (including estimated tips), although you must use your own transportation. Another job working in a store located in a beach resort over 500 miles away from your home pays $8 per hour. All three jobs offer work for 40 hours per week for the whole summer. If these options were ranked according to their pay per hour, the pizza delivery job would be the most attractive. However, the costs associated with each job must also be evaluated. For example, the office job may require that you pay for downtown parking and purchase office clothes. The pizza delivery job will require you to pay for gas and maintenance for your car. The resort job will require you to move to the resort city and incur additional living costs. Only by considering the costs for each job will you be able to determine which job will provide you with the most income.

Just as you should evaluate the relative income of various choices, so must a business evaluate the income earned from its choices. Important choices include the products offered and the geographical regions to be served. Thus, a company will often evaluate the profitability of products and regions. For example, Adobe Systems Inc., one of the largest software companies in the world, determines the income earned from their various product lines, such as Acrobat®, Photoshop®, Premier®, and Dreamweaver® software. Adobe uses this information to establish product line pricing, as well as sales, support, and development effort. Likewise, Adobe evaluates the income earned in the geographic regions it serves, such as the United States, Europe, and Asia. Again, such information aids management in managing revenue and expenses within the regions.

In this chapter we will discuss how businesses measure profitability, using absorption costing and variable costing. After illustrating and comparing these concepts, we discuss how businesses use them for controlling costs, pricing products, planning production, analyzing market segments, and analyzing contribution margins.

The Income Statement Under Variable Costing and Absorption Costing

objective 1

Describe and illustrate income reporting under variable costing and absorption costing.

One of the most important items affecting a manufacturing business's net income is the cost of goods sold. In many cases, the cost of goods sold is larger than all of the other expenses combined. The cost of goods sold can be determined under either the absorption costing or variable costing concept.

Under **absorption costing**, all manufacturing costs are included in finished goods and remain there as an asset until the goods are sold. Absorption costing is necessary in determining historical costs for financial reporting to external users and for tax reporting.

Variable costing may be more useful to management in making decisions. In **variable costing**, which is also called *direct costing*, the cost of goods manufactured is composed only of *variable* manufacturing costs—costs that increase or decrease as the volume of production rises or falls. These costs are the direct materials, direct labor, and only those factory overhead costs that vary with the rate of production. The remaining factory overhead costs, which are fixed or nonvariable costs, are generally related to the productive capacity of the manufacturing plant and are not affected by changes in the quantity of product manufactured. For example, depreciation on the

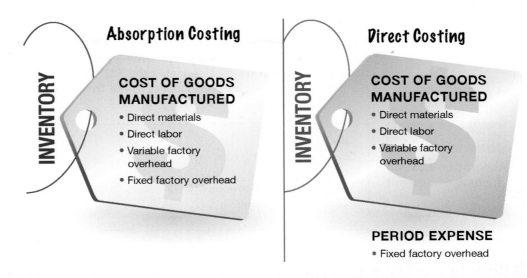

factory building is a cost that does not change with changes in the rate of production. Thus, the fixed factory overhead does not become a part of the cost of goods manufactured but is treated as an expense of the period in which it is incurred.

To illustrate the difference between the variable costing income statement and the absorption costing income statement, assume that Belling Co. manufactured 15,000 units at the following costs:

	A	B	C	D	
		Total Cost	Number of Units	Unit Cost	
1	Manufacturing costs:				1
2	Variable	$375,000	15,000	$25	2
3	Fixed	150,000	15,000	10	3
4	Total	$525,000		$35	4
5	Selling and administrative expenses:				5
6	Variable ($5 per unit sold)	$ 75,000			6
7	Fixed	50,000			7
8	Total	$125,000			8

The units sell at a price of $50, as shown in the variable costing income statement for Belling Co. in Exhibit 1. In this income statement, variable costs are separated from fixed costs. The variable cost of goods sold, which includes the variable manufacturing costs, is deducted from sales to yield the **manufacturing margin** of $375,000. The variable selling and administrative expenses of $75,000 are deducted from the manufacturing margin to yield the contribution margin of $300,000. Thus, the **contribution margin** is sales less variable costs, as we defined in the previous chapter. The income from operations of $100,000 is then determined by deducting fixed costs of $200,000 from the contribution margin.

> The variable costing income statement includes only variable manufacturing costs in the cost of goods sold.

EXHIBIT 1

Variable Costing Income Statement

Sales (15,000 × $50)		$750,000
Variable cost of goods sold (15,000 × $25)		375,000
Manufacturing margin		$375,000
Variable selling and administrative expenses		75,000
Contribution margin		$300,000
Fixed costs:		
Fixed manufacturing costs	$150,000	
Fixed selling and administrative expenses	50,000	200,000
Income from operations		$100,000

Exhibit 2 shows the absorption costing income statement prepared for Belling Co. The absorption costing income statement does not distinguish between variable and fixed costs. All manufacturing costs are included in the cost of goods sold. Deducting cost of goods sold from sales yields the $225,000 gross profit. Deducting selling and administrative expenses then yields income from operations of $100,000.

EXHIBIT 2

Absorption Costing Income Statement

Sales (15,000 × $50)	$750,000
Cost of goods sold (15,000 × $35)	525,000
Gross profit	$225,000
Selling and administrative expenses ($75,000 + $50,000)	125,000
Income from operations	$100,000

Example Exercise 5-1

objective 1

Leone Company has the following information for March:

Sales	$450,000
Variable cost of goods sold	220,000
Fixed manufacturing costs	80,000
Variable selling and administrative expenses	50,000
Fixed selling and administrative expenses	35,000

Determine (a) the manufacturing margin, (b) the contribution margin, and (c) income from operations for Leone Company for the month of March.

Follow My Example 5-1

a. $230,000 ($450,000 − $220,000)
b. $180,000 ($230,000 − $50,000)
c. $65,000 ($180,000 − $80,000 − $35,000)

For Practice: PE 5-1A, PE 5-1B

Different regions of the world emphasize different approaches to reporting income. For example, Scandinavian companies have a strong variable costing tradition, while German cost accountants have developed some of the most advanced absorption costing practices in the world.

INCOME FROM OPERATIONS WHEN UNITS MANUFACTURED EQUAL UNITS SOLD

In Exhibits 1 and 2, 15,000 units were manufactured and sold. Both the variable and the absorption costing income statements reported the same income from operations of $100,000. Thus, when the number of units manufactured equals the number of units sold, income from operations will be the same under both methods.

INCOME FROM OPERATIONS WHEN UNITS MANUFACTURED EXCEED UNITS SOLD

When the number of units manufactured exceeds the number of units sold, the variable costing income from operations will be *less* than the absorption costing income from operations. To illustrate, assume that in the preceding example only 12,000 units of the 15,000 units manufactured were sold. Exhibit 3 shows the two income statements that result.

The $30,000 difference ($70,000 − $40,000) in the amount of income from operations is due to the different treatment of the fixed manufacturing costs. The entire amount of the $150,000 of fixed manufacturing costs is included as an expense of the period in the variable costing statement. The ending inventory in the absorption costing statement includes $30,000 (3,000 units × $10) of fixed manufacturing costs.

EXHIBIT 3

Units Manufactured
Exceed Units Sold

Variable Costing Income Statement

Sales (12,000 × $50)		$600,000
Variable cost of goods sold:		
Variable cost of goods manufactured (15,000 × $25)	$375,000	
Less ending inventory (3,000 × $25)	75,000	
Variable cost of goods sold		300,000
Manufacturing margin		$300,000
Variable selling and administrative expenses (12,000 × $5)		60,000
Contribution margin		$240,000
Fixed costs:		
Fixed manufacturing costs	$150,000	
Fixed selling and administrative expenses	50,000	200,000
Income from operations		$ 40,000

Absorption Costing Income Statement

Sales (12,000 × $50)		$600,000
Cost of goods sold:		
Cost of goods manufactured (15,000 × $35)	$525,000	
Less ending inventory (3,000 × $35)	105,000	
Cost of goods sold		420,000
Gross profit		$180,000
Selling and administrative expenses ($60,000 + $50,000)		110,000
Income from operations		$ 70,000

This $30,000 is excluded from the current cost of goods sold in the absorption costing statement and is thus deferred to a future period.

Example Exercise 5-2 objective 1

Fixed manufacturing costs are $40 per unit, and variable manufacturing costs are $120 per unit. Production was 125,000 units, while sales were 120,000 units. Determine (a) whether variable costing income from operations is less than or greater than absorption costing income from operations, and (b) the difference in variable costing and absorption costing income from operations.

Follow My Example 5-2

a. Variable costing income from operations is less than absorption costing income from operations.
b. $200,000 ($40 per unit × 5,000 units)

For Practice: PE 5-2A, PE 5-2B

INCOME FROM OPERATIONS WHEN UNITS MANUFACTURED ARE LESS THAN UNITS SOLD

When the number of units manufactured is less than the number of units sold, the variable costing income from operations will be *greater* than the absorption costing income from operations. To illustrate, assume that 5,000 units of inventory were on hand at the beginning of a period, 10,000 units were manufactured during the period, and 15,000 units were sold (10,000 units manufactured during the period plus the 5,000 units on hand at the beginning of the period) at $50 per unit. The manufacturing costs and selling and administrative expenses are as follows. Exhibit 4 shows the two income statements prepared from this information.

	A	B	C	D	
			Number	Unit	
		Total Cost	of Units	Cost	
1	Beginning inventory:				1
2	Manufacturing costs:				2
3	Variable	$125,000	5,000	$25	3
4	Fixed	50,000	5,000	10	4
5	Total	$175,000		$35	5
6	Current period:				6
7	Manufacturing costs:				7
8	Variable	$250,000	10,000	$25	8
9	Fixed	150,000	10,000	15	9
10	Total	$400,000		$40	10
11	Selling and administrative expenses:				11
12	Variable ($5 per unit sold)	$ 75,000			12
13	Fixed	50,000			13
14	Total	$125,000			14

EXHIBIT 4

**Units Manufactured
Are Less than
Units Sold**

Variable Costing Income Statement

Sales (15,000 × $50)		$750,000
Variable cost of goods sold:		
Beginning inventory (5,000 × $25)	$125,000	
Variable cost of goods manufactured (10,000 × $25)	250,000	
Variable cost of goods sold		375,000
Manufacturing margin		$375,000
Variable selling and administrative expenses (15,000 × $5)		75,000
Contribution margin		$300,000
Fixed costs:		
Fixed manufacturing costs	$150,000	
Fixed selling and administrative expenses	50,000	200,000
Income from operations		$100,000

Absorption Costing Income Statement

Sales (15,000 × $50)		$750,000
Cost of goods sold:		
Beginning inventory (5,000 × $35)	$175,000	
Cost of goods manufactured (10,000 × $40)	400,000	
Cost of goods sold		575,000
Gross profit		$175,000
Selling and administrative expenses ($75,000 + $50,000)		125,000
Income from operations		$ 50,000

The $50,000 difference ($100,000 − $50,000) in the income from operations is caused by the different treatment of the fixed manufacturing costs. The beginning inventory in the absorption costing income statement includes $50,000 (5,000 units × $10) of fixed manufacturing costs incurred in the preceding period. By being included in the beginning inventory, this $50,000 is included in the cost of goods sold for the current period. Under variable costing, however, this $50,000 was included as an expense in an income statement of a prior period. Therefore, none of it is included as an expense in the current income statement.

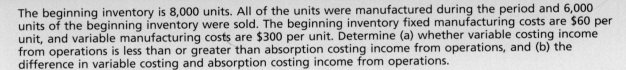

Example Exercise 5-3   **objective** 1

The beginning inventory is 8,000 units. All of the units were manufactured during the period and 6,000 units of the beginning inventory were sold. The beginning inventory fixed manufacturing costs are $60 per unit, and variable manufacturing costs are $300 per unit. Determine (a) whether variable costing income from operations is less than or greater than absorption costing income from operations, and (b) the difference in variable costing and absorption costing income from operations.

Follow My Example 5-3

a.   Variable costing income from operations is greater than absorption costing income from operations.
b. $360,000 ($60 per unit × 6,000 units)

For Practice: PE 5-3A, PE 5-3B

COMPARING INCOME FROM OPERATIONS UNDER THE TWO CONCEPTS

The two preceding examples illustrate the effects of the variable costing and absorption costing concepts on income from operations when the number of units sold do *not* equal the number of units produced. These effects are summarized below.

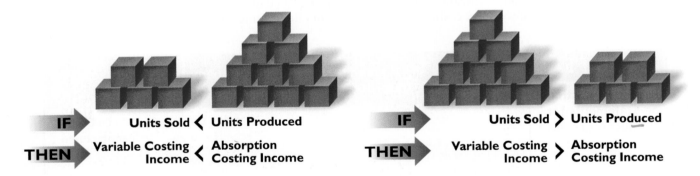

Income Analysis Under Variable Costing and Absorption Costing

objective 2

Describe and illustrate income analysis under variable costing and absorption costing.

As we have illustrated, the income from operations under variable costing can differ from the income from operations under absorption costing. This difference results from changes in the quantity of the finished goods inventory, which are caused by differences in the levels of sales and production. In analyzing and evaluating operations, management should be aware of the possible effects of changing inventory levels under the two concepts. To illustrate, assume that Frand Manufacturing Company has no beginning inventory and sales are estimated to be 20,000 units at $75 per unit, regardless of production levels. Assume further that the following two proposed production levels are being evaluated by the management of Frand Manufacturing Company:

	A	B	C	D	
	Proposal 1: 20,000 Units to Be Manufactured and Sold				
			Number	**Unit**	
		Total Cost	**of Units**	**Cost**	
1	Manufacturing costs:				1
2	Variable	$ 700,000	20,000	$35	2
3	Fixed	400,000	20,000	20	3
4	Total costs	$1,100,000		$55	4
5	Selling and administrative expenses:				5
6	Variable ($5 per unit sold)	$ 100,000			6
7	Fixed	100,000			7
8	Total expenses	$ 200,000			8

	A	B	C	D	
	Proposal 2: 25,000 Units to Be Manufactured: 20,000 Units to Be Sold				
			Number	**Unit**	
		Total Cost	**of Units**	**Cost**	
1	Manufacturing costs:				1
2	Variable	$ 875,000	25,000	$35	2
3	Fixed	400,000	25,000	16	3
4	Total costs	$1,275,000		$51	4
5	Selling and administrative expenses:				5
6	Variable ($5 per unit sold)	$ 100,000			6
7	Fixed	100,000			7
8	Total expenses	$ 200,000			8

If Frand Manufacturing Company manufactures 20,000 units, which is an amount equal to the estimated sales, income from operations under absorption costing would be $200,000. However, the income from operations could be increased by $80,000 by manufacturing 25,000 units and adding 5,000 units to the finished goods inventory. The absorption costing income statements illustrating this effect are shown in Exhibit 5.

EXHIBIT 5

Absorption Costing
Income Statements for
Two Production Levels

Frand Manufacturing Company
Absorption Costing Income Statements

	20,000 Units Manufactured	25,000 Units Manufactured
Sales (20,000 units × $75)	$1,500,000	$1,500,000
Cost of goods sold:		
Cost of goods manufactured:		
(20,000 units × $55)	$1,100,000	
(25,000 units × $51)		$1,275,000
Less ending inventory:		
(5,000 units × $51)		255,000
Cost of goods sold	$1,100,000	$1,020,000
Gross profit.	$ 400,000	$ 480,000
Selling and administrative expenses		
($100,000 + $100,000)	200,000	200,000
Income from operations	$ 200,000	$ 280,000

The $80,000 increase in income from operations would be caused by allocating the fixed manufacturing costs of $400,000 over a greater number of units of production. Specifically, an increase in production from 20,000 units to 25,000 units meant that the fixed manufacturing costs per unit decreased from $20 ($400,000/20,000 units) to $16 ($400,000/25,000 units). Thus, the cost of goods sold when 25,000 units are manufactured would be $4 per unit less, or $80,000 less in total (20,000 units sold × $4). Since the cost of goods sold is less, income from operations is $80,000 more when 25,000 units rather than 20,000 units are manufactured.

Under variable costing, income from operations would have been $200,000, regardless of the amount by which units manufactured exceeded sales, because no fixed manufacturing costs are allocated to the units manufactured. To illustrate, Exhibit 6 presents the variable costing income statements for Frand Manufacturing Company for the production of 20,000 units, 25,000 units, and 30,000 units. In each case, the income from operations is $200,000.

EXHIBIT 6			
Variable Costing Income Statements for Three Production Levels			

Frand Manufacturing Company
Variable Costing Income Statements

	Level 1 20,000 Units Manufactured	Level 2 25,000 Units Manufactured	Level 3 30,000 Units Manufactured
Sales (20,000 units × $75)........	$1,500,000	$1,500,000	$1,500,000
Variable cost of goods sold:			
Variable cost of goods manufactured:			
(20,000 units × $35).......	$ 700,000		
(25,000 units × $35).......		$ 875,000	
(30,000 units × $35).......			$1,050,000
Less ending inventory:			
(0 units × $35)	0		
(5,000 units × $35)........		175,000	
(10,000 units × $35).......			350,000
Variable cost of goods sold....	$ 700,000	$ 700,000	$ 700,000
Manufacturing margin..........	$ 800,000	$ 800,000	$ 800,000
Variable selling and administrative expenses...................	100,000	100,000	100,000
Contribution margin...........	$ 700,000	$ 700,000	$ 700,000
Fixed costs:			
Fixed manufacturing costs	$ 400,000	$ 400,000	$ 400,000
Fixed selling and administrative expenses	100,000	100,000	100,000
Total fixed costs	$ 500,000	$ 500,000	$ 500,000
Income from operations.........	$ 200,000	$ 200,000	$ 200,000

As illustrated, if absorption costing is used, management should be careful in analyzing income from operations when large changes in inventory levels occur. Managers could misinterpret increases or decreases in income from operations, due to mere changes in inventory levels, to be the result of business events, such as changes in sales volume, prices, or costs.

Many accountants believe that variable costing should be used for evaluating operating performance because absorption costing encourages management to produce inventory. This is because producing inventory absorbs fixed costs and causes the income from operations to appear higher, as we have illustrated previously. In the long run, building inventory without the promise of future sales may lead to higher handling, storage, financing, and obsolescence costs.

Example Exercise 5-4

objective 2

Variable manufacturing costs are $100 per unit, and fixed manufacturing costs are $50,000. Sales are estimated to be 4,000 units.

a. How much would absorption costing income from operations differ between a plan to produce 4,000 units and a plan to produce 5,000 units?
b. How much would variable costing income from operations differ between the two production plans?

Follow My Example 5-4

a. $10,000 greater in producing 5,000 units. 4,000 units × ($12.50 − $10.00), or [1,000 units × ($50,000/5,000 units)].
b. There would be no difference in variable costing income from operations between the two plans.

For Practice: PE 5-4A, PE 5-4B

Integrity, Objectivity, and Ethics in Business

ETHICS

TAKING AN "ABSORPTION HIT"

Aligning production to demand is a critical decision in business. Managers must not allow the temporary benefits of excess production through higher absorption of fixed costs to guide their decisions. Likewise, if demand falls, production should be dropped and inventory liquidated to match the new demand level, even though earnings will be penalized. The following interchange provides an example of an appropriate response to lowered demand for H.J. Heinz Company:

Analyst's question: *Could you talk for a moment about manufacturing costs during the quarter? You had highlighted that they were up and that gross margins at Heinz USA were down. Why was that the case?*

Heinz executive's response: *Yeah. The manufacturing costs were somewhat up . . . as we improve our inventory position, obviously you've got less inventory to spread your fixed costs over, so you'll take what accountants would call an absorption hit as we reduce costs. And that will be something that as we pull down inventory over the years, that will be an additional P&L cost hurdle that we need to overcome.*

Management operating with integrity will seek the tangible benefits of reducing inventory, even though there may be an adverse impact on published financial statements caused by absorption costing.

Management's Use of Variable Costing and Absorption Costing

objective 3

Describe and illustrate management's use of variable costing and absorption costing for controlling costs, pricing products, planning production, analyzing contribution margins, and analyzing market segments.

Managerial accountants should carefully analyze each situation in evaluating whether variable costing or absorption costing reports would be more useful to management. In many situations, preparing reports under both concepts provides useful insights. In the following paragraphs, we discuss such reports and their advantages and disadvantages to management in making decisions related to the items identified in Exhibit 7.

CONTROLLING COSTS

All costs are controllable in the long run by someone within a business, but they are not all controllable at the same level of management. For example, plant supervisors, as members of operating management, are responsible for controlling the use of direct materials in their departments. They have no control, however, of insurance costs related to the buildings housing their departments. For a specific level of management, **controllable costs** are costs that can be influenced by management at that level, and **noncontrollable costs** are costs that another level of management controls. This distinction is useful in fixing the responsibility for incurring costs and for reporting costs to those responsible for their control.

| EXHIBIT 7 | Accounting Reports and Management Decisions |

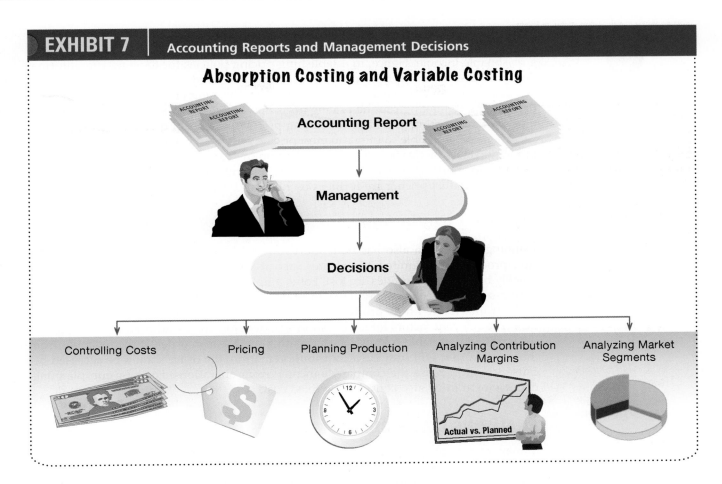

Absorption Costing and Variable Costing

REAL WORLD

Most chemical companies, such as Union Carbide or Dow Chemical, use variable costing to evaluate the profitability of their operations. These approaches prevent fixed costs outside of managers' control to be used for evaluation purposes.

Variable manufacturing costs are controlled at the operating level. If the product's cost includes only variable manufacturing costs, the cost can be controlled by operating management. The fixed factory overhead costs are normally the responsibility of a higher level of management. When the fixed factory overhead costs are reported as a separate item in the variable costing income statement, they are easier to identify and control than when they are spread among units of product, as they are under absorption costing.

As in the case with the fixed and variable manufacturing costs, the control of the variable and fixed operating expenses is usually the responsibility of different levels of management. Under variable costing, the variable selling and administrative expenses are reported separately from the fixed selling and administrative expenses. Because they are reported in this manner, both types of operating expenses are easier to identify and control than is the case under absorption costing.

PRICING PRODUCTS

Many factors enter into determining the selling price of a product. The cost of making the product is clearly significant. Microeconomic theory states that income is maximized by expanding output to the volume where the revenue realized by the sale of an additional unit (marginal revenue) equals the cost of that unit (marginal cost). Although the degree of accuracy assumed in economic theory is rarely achieved, the concepts of marginal revenue and marginal cost are useful in setting selling prices.

In the short run, a business is committed to its existing manufacturing facilities. The pricing decision should be based upon making the best use of such capacity. The fixed costs cannot be avoided, but the variable costs can be eliminated if the company does not manufacture the product. The selling price of a product, therefore, should at least be equal to the variable costs of making and selling it. Any price above this minimum selling price contributes an amount toward covering fixed costs and providing income. Variable costing procedures yield data that emphasize these relationships.

In the long run, plant capacity can be increased or decreased. If a business is to continue operating, the selling prices of its products must cover all costs and provide a reasonable income. Hence, in establishing pricing policies for the long run, information provided by absorption costing procedures is needed.

The results of a research study indicated that the companies studied used absorption costing in making routine pricing decisions. However, these companies regularly used variable costing as a basis for setting prices in many short-run situations.

There are no simple solutions to most pricing problems. Consideration must be given to many factors of varying importance. Accounting can contribute by preparing analyses of various pricing plans for both the short run and the long run. Additional analyses useful for product pricing are further described and illustrated in a later chapter.

PLANNING PRODUCTION

Planning production also has both short-run and long-run implications. In the short run, production is limited to existing capacity. Operating decisions must be made quickly before opportunities are lost. For example, a company manufacturing products with a seasonal demand may have an opportunity to obtain an off-season order that will not interfere with its production schedule nor reduce the sales of its other products. The relevant factors for such a short-run decision are the additional revenues and the additional variable costs associated with the off-season order. If the revenues from the special order will provide a contribution margin, the order should be accepted because it will increase the company's income from operations. For long-run planning, management must also consider the fixed costs.

ANALYZING CONTRIBUTION MARGINS

Managers can plan and control operations by evaluating the differences between planned and actual contribution margins. For example, an increase in the price of gasoline due to market factors would have a positive impact on the planned contribution margin of a gasoline refiner. Such analyses are discussed in a separate section to follow.

ANALYZING MARKET SEGMENTS

Market analysis is performed by the sales and marketing function in order to determine the profit contributed by market segments. A **market segment** is a portion of a business that can be analyzed using sales, costs, and expenses to determine its profitability. Often the profitability of market segments can provide insight to business direction and performance. Examples of market segments include sales territories, products, salespersons, and customers. Variable costing can aid decision making regarding such segments. We will illustrate variable cost reporting for market segments in the next section.

Variable Costing in Analyzing Market Segments

objective **4**

Use variable costing for analyzing market segments, including product, territories, and salespersons segments.

As we illustrated earlier in this chapter, businesses can use income reporting under absorption or variable costing. Operating income defined under absorption costing can be used to evaluate market segments for long-term analyses. This type of analysis is illustrated in a later chapter using activity-based costing. For a short-term analysis, management often evaluates market segment profitability using variable costing. For example, variable costing can be used by managers to support short-term price decisions, evaluate cost changes, and plan volume changes. In this section, we will illustrate segment profitability reporting using variable costing.

Most companies develop profitability reports for products, since product pricing and retention decisions are influenced by their relative profitability. In addition to product segments, managers may evaluate the profitability of geographic, customer, distribution channel, or salesperson. A distribution channel is the method for placing a product with the customer. For example, Borders Group Inc. evaluates the profitability of its Internet and retail store distribution channels. In contrast, McDonald's Corporation evaluates geographic segments. Geographic segments are more meaningful for McDonald's than are customer segments. It is difficult, and probably meaningless, to try to distinguish McDonald's customers. However, McDonald's geographic segments are unique. For example, the operating results of restaurants in the United States are different from those in Asia or Europe.

To illustrate variable costing for analyzing market segments, assume the following data for March 2008 for Camelot Fragrance Company. Camelot Fragrance Company manufactures and sells the Gwenevere perfume line for women and the Lancelot cologne line for men. For simplicity, we assume that the inventories are negligible and are thus disregarded in the reports that follow.

	Northern Territory	Southern Territory	Total
Sales:			
Gwenevere	$60,000	$30,000	$ 90,000
Lancelot	20,000	50,000	70,000
Total territory sales	$80,000	$80,000	$160,000
Variable production costs:			
Gwenevere (12% of sales)	$ 7,200	$ 3,600	$ 10,800
Lancelot (12% of sales)	2,400	6,000	8,400
Total variable production cost by territory	$ 9,600	$ 9,600	$ 19,200
Promotion costs:			
Gwenevere (variable at 30% of sales)	$18,000	$ 9,000	$ 27,000
Lancelot (variable at 20% of sales)	4,000	10,000	14,000
Total promotion cost by territory	$22,000	$19,000	$ 41,000
Sales commissions:			
Gwenevere (variable at 20% of sales)	$12,000	$ 6,000	$ 18,000
Lancelot (variable at 10% of sales)	2,000	5,000	7,000
Total sales commissions by territory	$14,000	$11,000	$ 25,000

This information can be used by Camelot Fragrance Company to prepare a sales territory, product, and salesperson profitability analysis. Each of these is discussed on the following pages.

SALES TERRITORY PROFITABILITY ANALYSIS

An income statement presenting the contribution margin by sales territories is often useful to management in evaluating past performance and in directing future sales efforts. Sales territory profitability analysis may lead management to reduce costs in lower-profit sales territories or to increase sales effort in higher-profit territories. For example, The Coca-Cola Company earns over 75% of its total corporate profits outside of the United States. This information motivates the Coca-Cola management to continue expanding operations and sales efforts around the world.

There are many possible explanations for profit differences between territories, including differences in pricing, sales unit volumes, media rates, selling costs, and the types of products sold. To illustrate the analysis of profit differences by sales territory,

Exhibit 8 shows the contribution margin by sales territory for Camelot Fragrance Company.

EXHIBIT 8

Contribution Margin by Sales Territory Report

Camelot Fragrance Company
Contribution Margin by Sales Territory
For the Month Ended March 31, 2008

	Northern Territory		Southern Territory	
Sales		$80,000		$80,000
Variable cost of goods sold		9,600		9,600
Manufacturing margin		$70,400		$70,400
Variable selling expenses:				
Promotion costs	$22,000		$19,000	
Sales commissions	14,000	36,000	11,000	30,000
Contribution margin		$34,400		$40,400
Contribution margin ratio		43%		50.5%

Rite-Aid Corporation recently reported that its gross margins increased as a result of a shift in sales mix from prescription toward generic drug sales.

The contribution margin for each territory consists of the sales less the variable costs associated with producing and selling products in each territory. In addition to the contribution margin, the contribution margin ratio (contribution margin divided by sales) for each territory is useful in evaluating sales territories and directing operations toward more profitable activities. For the Northern Territory, the contribution margin ratio is 43% ($34,400/$80,000), and for the Southern Territory, the ratio is 50.5% ($40,400/$80,000). Although each territory had the same sales, the contribution margin ratios are different. Why is this?

In this case, the difference in territory profit performance can be explained by the difference in sales mix between the two territories. **Sales mix**, sometimes referred to as *product mix*, is defined as the relative distribution of sales among the various products sold. From the assumed information, the Southern Territory had a higher relative proportion of Lancelot sales than did the Northern Territory. If the Lancelot line is more profitable than the Gwenevere line, then we would expect the Southern Territory's overall profitability to be higher than the Northern Territory's, as shown in Exhibit 8. To verify the difference between the profitabilities of the two products, product profitability analysis may be performed.

PRODUCT PROFITABILITY ANALYSIS

Customer, territory, product, and salesperson profit analysis is done by using a "data warehouse." A data warehouse is a database of revenue and cost information that can be divided into many different profit views. For example, Johnson and Johnson's data warehouse enables managers from 50 countries around the world to see various profit views at the click of a mouse.

Management should focus its sales efforts on those products that will provide the maximum total contribution margin. An income statement presenting the contribution margin by products is often used by management to guide product-related sales and promotional efforts. For example, Ford's F Series pickups are one of its most profitable product lines. Ford uses this information to motivate higher production levels and promotion effort for this brand.

Some products are more profitable than others due to differences with respect to pricing, manufacturing costs, advertising support, or salesperson support. To illustrate the analysis of these differences, Exhibit 9 shows the contribution margin by product for Camelot Fragrance Company.

As you can see, Lancelot's contribution margin ratio is greater than Gwenevere's, even though both product lines have the same manufacturing margin as a percent of sales (88%). The higher contribution margin ratio is the result of Lancelot's lower promotion costs and sales commissions as a percent of sales. The sales territory profitability analysis and the product profitability analysis both indicate the superior profit performance of the Lancelot line. Thus, management should emphasize the Lancelot product line in its marketing plans, try to reduce the promotion and sales commission expenses associated with Gwenevere sales, or increase the price of Gwenevere.

EXHIBIT 9

Contribution Margin
by Product Line Report

Camelot Fragrance Company
Contribution Margin by Product Line
For the Month Ended March 31, 2008

		Gwenevere		Lancelot
Sales		$90,000		$70,000
Variable cost of goods sold . . .		10,800		8,400
Manufacturing margin		$79,200		$61,600
Variable selling expenses:				
Promotion costs	$27,000		$14,000	
Sales commissions	18,000	45,000	7,000	21,000
Contribution margin		$34,200		$40,600
Contribution margin ratio		38%		58%

SALESPERSON PROFITABILITY ANALYSIS

In addition to the sales territory and product profitability analyses, sales managers may wish to evaluate the performance of salespersons. This may be done with a salesperson profitability analysis.

A report to management for use in evaluating the sales performance of each salesperson could include total sales, variable cost of goods sold, variable selling expenses, contribution margin, and contribution margin ratio. Exhibit 10 illustrates such a report for three salespersons in the Northern Territory of Camelot Fragrance Company.

EXHIBIT 10

Contribution Margin
by Salesperson Report

Camelot Fragrance Company
Contribution Margin by Salesperson—Northern Territory
For the Month Ended March 31, 2008

	Inez Rodriguez	Tom Ginger	Beth Williams	Northern Territory— Total
Sales	$20,000	$20,000	$40,000	$80,000
Variable cost of goods sold . . .	2,400	2,400	4,800	9,600
Manufacturing margin	$17,600	$17,600	$35,200	$70,400
Variable selling expenses:				
Promotion costs	$ 5,000	$ 5,000	$12,000	$22,000
Sales commissions	3,000	3,000	8,000	14,000
	$ 8,000	$ 8,000	$20,000	$36,000
Contribution margin	$ 9,600	$ 9,600	$15,200	$34,400
Contribution margin ratio	48%	48%	38%	43%
Sales mix (% Lancelot sales) . .	50%	50%	0	25%

The additional information provided on the total sales and costs of all three salespersons agrees with the total sales and costs for the Northern Territory in Exhibit 8. Thus, this report provides the Northern Territory manager with a more detailed analysis of the territory's performance. The report indicates that Beth Williams produced the greatest contribution margin for the company but had the lowest contribution margin ratio. Beth Williams sold $40,000 of product, which is twice as much product as the other two salespersons. However, Beth Williams sold only the Gwenevere product line, which has the lowest contribution margin ratio (from Exhibit 9). The other two salespersons sold equal amounts of Gwenevere and Lancelot. These two salespersons had higher contribution margin ratios because of the sales of the higher-margin Lancelot line. The territory manager could use this report to encourage Rodriguez and Ginger to sell more total product, while encouraging Williams to place more selling effort on the Lancelot line.

Business Connections

MCDONALD'S CORPORATION
CONTRIBUTION MARGIN BY STORE

McDonald's Corporation is the largest restaurant company, representing 2.5% of the restaurants and 7.3% of the sales of all restaurants in the United States. McDonald's annual report identifies revenues and costs for its company-owned restaurants separately from its franchised restaurants. Assume that the food, paper, payroll, and benefit costs are variable and that occupancy and other operating expenses are fixed. A contribution margin and income from operations can be constructed for the company-owned restaurants as follows:

McDonald's Corporation
Company-Owned Restaurant Contribution Margin
and Income from Operations (estimated)
For the Year Ended December 31, 2005 (in millions)

Sales		$15,352
Variable restaurant expenses:		
Food and paper	$5,207	
Payroll and employee benefits	4,039	
Total variable restaurant operating costs		9,246
Contribution margin		$ 6,106
Occupancy and other operating expenses		3,868
Income from operations		$ 2,238

The annual report also indicates that McDonald's has 9,238 company-owned restaurants. Dividing the numbers above by 9,283 yields the contribution margin and income from operations *per restaurant* as follows:

Sales	$1,653,776
Variable restaurant expenses	996,014
Contribution margin	$ 657,762
Occupancy and other operating expenses	416,676
Income from operations	$ 241,086

In addition, McDonald's segments this information by its major operating regions, such as the United States, Europe, Latin America, Canada, and Asia. McDonald's can use this information for pricing products; evaluating the sensitivity of store profitability to changes in sales volume, prices, and costs; analyzing profitability by geographic segments; and evaluating the contribution of the company-owned stores to overall corporate profitability.

Other factors should also be considered in evaluating salespersons' performance. For example, sales growth rates, years of experience, customer service, territory size, and actual performance compared to budgeted performance may also be important.

Example Exercise 5-5
objective 4

The following data are for Moss Creek Apparel:

	East	West
Sales volume (units):		
Shirts	6,000	5,000
Shorts	4,000	8,000
Sales price:		
Shirts	$12	$13
Shorts	$16	$18
Variable cost per unit:		
Shirts	$7	$7
Shorts	$10	$10

Determine the contribution margin for (a) Shorts and (b) the West Region.

(continued)

Contribution Margin Analysis

objective 5

Use variable costing for analyzing and explaining changes in contribution margin as a result of quantity and price factors.

The contribution margin concept can be used to assist managers in planning and controlling operations by focusing on the differences between planned and actual contribution margins. These differences, as well as the causes of the differences, can be systematically explained using **contribution margin analysis**.

Since contribution margin is the excess of sales over variable costs, a difference between the planned and actual contribution margin can be caused by (1) an increase or decrease in the amount of sales or (2) an increase or decrease in the amount of variable costs. An increase or decrease in either element may in turn be due to (1) an increase or decrease in the number of units sold or (2) an increase or decrease in the unit sales price or unit cost, as shown in Exhibit 11. The effect of these two factors on either sales or variable costs may be stated as follows:

1. **Quantity factor**—the effect of a difference in the number of units sold, assuming no change in unit sales price or unit cost. The quantity factor is the difference between the actual quantity sold and the planned quantity sold, multiplied by the planned unit sales price or unit cost.
2. Unit **price factor** or *unit cost factor*—the effect of a difference in unit sales price or unit cost on the number of units sold. The unit price or unit cost factor is the difference between the actual unit price or unit cost and the planned unit price or unit cost, multiplied by the actual quantity sold.

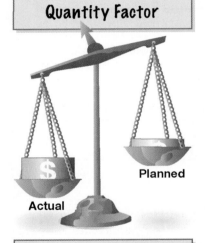

Quantity Factor

Planned

Actual

Price / Unit Cost Factor

$ Actual $ Planned

We will use the following data for Noble Inc. for the year ended December 31, 2008, as a basis for illustrating contribution margin analysis. For the sake of simplicity, we will assume a single commodity. The analysis would be more complex if several different commodities were sold, but the basic principles would not be affected.

	A	B	C	D	
		Actual	Planned	Increase or (Decrease)	
1	Sales	$937,500	$800,000	$137,500	1
2	Less: Variable cost of goods sold	$425,000	$350,000	$ 75,000	2
3	Variable selling and administrative expenses	162,500	125,000	37,500	3
4	Total	$587,500	$475,000	$112,500	4
5	Contribution margin	$350,000	$325,000	$ 25,000	5
6	Number of units sold	125,000	100,000		6
7					7
8	Per unit:				8
9	Sales price	$7.50	$8.00		9
10	Variable cost of goods sold	3.40	3.50		10
11	Variable selling and administrative expenses	1.30	1.25		11

The analysis of these data in Exhibit 12 shows that the favorable increase of $25,000 in the contribution margin was due in large part to an increase in the number of units sold. This increase was partially offset by a decrease in the unit sales price and an increase in the unit cost for variable selling and administrative expenses. The decrease in the unit cost for the variable cost of goods sold was an additional favorable result of 2008 operations.

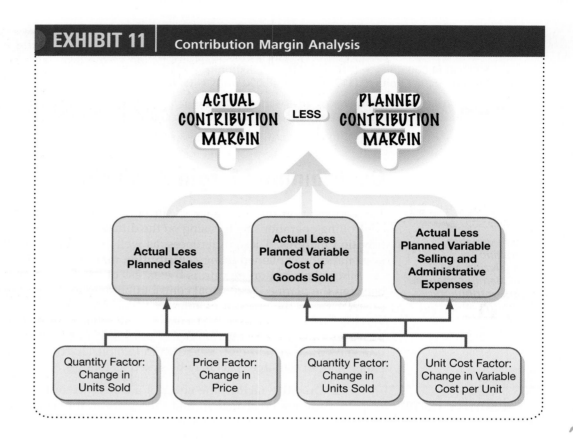

EXHIBIT 11 | Contribution Margin Analysis

EXHIBIT 12   Contribution Margin Analysis Report

	A	B	C	D	
	Noble Inc.				
	Contribution Margin Analysis				
	For the Year Ended December 31, 2008				
1	Increase in amount of sales attributed to:				1
2	Quantity factor:				2
3	Increase in number of units sold in 2008		25,000		3
4	Planned sales price in 2008		× $8.00	$200,000	4
5	Price factor:				5
6	Decrease in unit sales price in 2008		$(0.50)		6
7	Number of units sold in 2008		× 125,000	(62,500)	7
8	Net increase in amount of sales			$137,500	8
9	Increase in amount of variable cost of goods sold attributed to:				9
10	Quantity factor:				10
11	Increase in number of units sold in 2008	25,000			11
12	Planned unit cost in 2008	× $3.50	$ 87,500		12
13	Unit cost factor:				13
14	Decrease in unit cost in 2008	$(0.10)			14
15	Number of units sold in 2008	× 125,000	(12,500)		15
16	Net increase in amount of variable cost of goods sold		$ 75,000		16
17	Increase in amount of variable selling and administrative expenses attributed to:				17
18	Quantity factor:				18
19	Increase in number of units sold in 2008	25,000			19
20	Planned unit cost in 2008	× $1.25	$ 31,250		20
21	Unit cost factor:				21
22	Increase in unit cost in 2008	$0.05			22
23	Number of units sold in 2008	× 125,000	6,250		23
24	Net increase in the amount of variable selling and administrative expenses		$ 37,500		24
25	Net increase in amount of variable costs			112,500	25
26	Increase in contribution margin			$ 25,000	26

The information presented in the contribution margin analysis report is useful to management in evaluating past performance and in planning future operations. For example, the impact of the $0.50 reduction in the unit sales price on the number of units sold and on the total sales for the year is useful information that management can use in determining whether further price reductions might be desirable. The contribution margin analysis report also highlights the impact of changes in unit variable costs and expenses. For example, the $0.05 increase in the unit variable selling and administrative expenses might be a result of increased advertising expenditures. If so, the increase in the number of units sold in 2008 could be attributed to both the $0.50 price reduction and the increased advertising.

Example Exercise 5-6   objective **5**

The actual price for a product was $48 per unit, while the planned price was $40 per unit. The volume increased by 5,000 units to 60,000 actual total units. Determine (a) the quantity factor and (b) the price factor for sales.

Follow My Example 5-6

a. $200,000 increase in sales (5,000 units × $40 per unit)
b. $480,000 increase in sales [($48 − $40) × 60,000 units]

For Practice: PE 5-6A, PE 5-6B

Variable Costing for Service Firms

objective **6**

Describe and illustrate the use of variable costing for service firms.

The previous section illustrated the use of variable costing concepts for manufacturing firms. Service firms also use variable costing reports for contribution margin and segment analyses.

VARIABLE COSTING INCOME STATEMENT—SERVICE FIRM

Unlike a manufacturing firm, a service firm does not make a product for sale. As a result, service firms do not have inventory and thus do not allocate fixed costs to inventory using absorption costing concepts. In addition, most service firms do not have cost of goods sold. Thus, the variable costing reports of service firms will not report a manufacturing margin. Service firms can, however, report and analyze contribution margin as the difference between revenues and variable costs.

To illustrate, Blue Skies Airlines Inc. operates a small commercial airline. The fixed and variable costs associated with operating Blue Skies are shown in Exhibit 13.

EXHIBIT 13

Costs of Blue Skies Airlines

Cost	Amount	Cost Behavior	Activity Base
Depreciation expense	$3,600,000	Fixed	
Food and beverage service expense	444,000	Variable	Number of passengers
Fuel expense	4,080,000	Variable	Number of miles flown
Rental expense	800,000	Fixed	
Selling expense	3,256,000	Variable	Number of passengers
Wages expense	6,120,000	Variable	Number of miles flown

As discussed in the prior chapter, a cost is fixed or variable by defining its behavior relative to changes in an activity base. The activity base in a ~~manufacturing firm is often the number of units produced and sold~~. A service firm, however, may have multiple activity bases. For example, some airline costs, such as food and beverage costs, vary with the number of passengers. An airline also has costs that vary with the number of miles flown, such as fuel and wage costs. As a result, it is important to identify the proper activity base. For example, if an airline increases the average number of passengers flown per flight, called the *load factor*, but not the number of flights, then only the selling and food and beverage costs will increase. However, the fuel and wage costs will not change because the number of miles flown is unchanged.[1]

The variable costing income statement for Blue Skies, assuming revenue of $19,238,000, is shown in Exhibit 14. In comparing this report to the variable costing income statement for a manufacturing firm (Exhibit 6), you will notice that there are no cost of goods sold, inventory, or manufacturing margin. However, as shown in Exhibit 14, contribution margin is reported separately from income from operations.

EXHIBIT 14

Variable Costing Income Statement

Blue Skies Airlines Inc. Variable Costing Income Statement For the Month Ended April 30, 2008		
Revenue		$19,238,000
Variable costs:		
Fuel expense	$4,080,000	
Wages expense	6,120,000	
Food and beverage service expense	444,000	
Selling expenses	3,256,000	
Total variable costs		13,900,000
Contribution margin		$ 5,338,000
Fixed costs:		
Depreciation expense	$3,600,000	
Rental expense	800,000	
Total fixed costs		4,400,000
Income from operations		$ 938,000

MARKET SEGMENT ANALYSIS—SERVICE FIRM

As is the case with a manufacturing firm, the contribution margin report for service firms can be prepared to evaluate the contribution margin of market segments. The following table illustrates typical segments used in various service industries:

Service Industry	Market Segments
Electric power	Regions, customer types (industrial, consumer)
Banking	Customer types (commercial, retail), products (loans, savings accounts)
Airlines	Products (passengers, cargo), routes
Railroads	Products (commodity type), routes
Hotels	Hotel properties
Telecommunications	Customer type (commercial, retail), service type (voice, data)
Health care	Procedure, payment type (Medicare, insured)

---

1 Fuel costs may increase somewhat due to added passenger weight, traffic volume, or weather. Our examples are simplified to focus only on the dominant cost behavior patterns.

The contribution margin report for Blue Skies Airlines can be segmented by the various routes (city pairs) flown by the airline. Management would use such a report to evaluate the relative contribution to profitability of the various city pairs served by the airline. To illustrate, assume that Blue Skies serves three city pairs: Chicago/Atlanta, Atlanta/Los Angeles, and Los Angeles/Chicago. The contribution margin report is constructed by identifying the revenues and variable costs for each of the segments. The following information was determined from corporate records for the month of April for each route:

	Chicago/Atlanta	Atlanta/LA	LA/Chicago
Average ticket price per passenger	$400	$1,075	$805
Total passengers served	16,000	7,000	6,600
Total miles flown	56,000	88,000	60,000

The variable costs per unit are as follows:

Fuel	$ 20 per mile
Wages	30 per mile
Food and beverage service	15 per passenger
Selling	110 per passenger

A contribution margin report by segment is illustrated in Exhibit 15. You should note that the sum of the segment contribution margins in Exhibit 15 is equal to the total contribution margin shown in Exhibit 14.

As can be seen from the report, the Chicago/Atlanta route has the lowest contribution margin ratio, while the Atlanta/Los Angeles route has the highest contribution margin ratio. We discuss the implications of Exhibit 15 for management decision making next.

EXHIBIT 15   **Contribution Margin by Segment Report—Service Firm**

Blue Skies Airlines Inc.
Contribution Margin by Route
For the Month Ended April 30, 2008

	Chicago/ Atlanta	Atlanta/ Los Angeles	Los Angeles/ Chicago	Total
Revenue				
(Ticket price × No. of passengers)	$ 6,400,000	$ 7,525,000	$ 5,313,000	$19,238,000
Aircraft fuel				
($20 × No. of miles flown)	(1,120,000)	(1,760,000)	(1,200,000)	(4,080,000)
Wages and benefits				
($30 × No. of miles flown)	(1,680,000)	(2,640,000)	(1,800,000)	(6,120,000)
Food and beverage service				
($15 × No. of passengers)	(240,000)	(105,000)	(99,000)	(444,000)
Selling expenses				
($110 × No. of passengers)	(1,760,000)	(770,000)	(726,000)	(3,256,000)
Contribution margin	$ 1,600,000	$ 2,250,000	$ 1,488,000	$ 5,338,000
Contribution margin ratio*	25%	30%	28%	28%

*Contribution margin/revenue

CONTRIBUTION MARGIN ANALYSIS

The management of Blue Skies is concerned about the low contribution margin ratio on the Chicago/Atlanta route. To improve the contribution margin of this route, management decreased the ticket price from $400 to $380 in May. The price reduction increased the number of tickets sold (passengers) on the existing flights from 16,000 to 20,000. That is, the load factor increased. In addition, the price for fuel increased, causing the cost per mile to increase from $20 to $22. The following data were used for the contribution margin analysis for the month of May, assuming planned results in May were as in April:

	A	B	C	D	
			Chicago/Atlanta Route		
				Increase	
		Actual, May	Planned, May	(Decrease)	
1	Revenue	$7,600,000	$6,400,000	$1,200,000	1
2	Less variable expenses:				2
3	Aircraft fuel	$1,232,000	$1,120,000	$ 112,000	3
4	Wages and benefits	1,680,000	1,680,000	—	4
5	Food and beverage service	300,000	240,000	60,000	5
6	Selling expenses and commissions	2,200,000	1,760,000	440,000	6
7	Total	$5,412,000	$4,800,000	$ 612,000	7
8	Contribution margin	$2,188,000	$1,600,000	$ 588,000	8
9	Contribution margin ratio	29%	25%		9
10					10
11	Number of miles flown	56,000	56,000		11
12	Number of passengers flown	20,000	16,000		12
13	Per unit:				13
14	Ticket price	$380	$400		14
15	Fuel expense	22	20		15
16	Wages expense	30	30		16
17	Food and beverage service expense	15	15		17
18	Selling expenses	110	110		18

The highlighted numbers indicate the actual changes from the planned May results. The data can be used to develop a contribution margin analysis report similar to our previous example for a manufacturing firm in Exhibit 12. The analysis in Exhibit 16 provides the various quantity and price factors that are impacted by the changes.

EXHIBIT 16

Contribution Margin Analysis Report— Service Firm

	A	B	C	D	
		Blue Skies Airlines Inc.			
		Contribution Margin Analysis			
		For the Month Ended May 31, 2008			
1	Increase in revenue attributed to:				1
2	Quantity factor:				2
3	Increase in the number of passengers in May	4,000			3
4	Planned price	× $400	$1,600,000		4
5	Price factor:				5
6	Decrease in the ticket price in May	$(20)			6
7	Number of passengers in May	× 20,000	(400,000)		7
8	Net increase in revenue			$1,200,000	8
9	Increase in fuel costs attributed to:				9
10	Unit cost factor:				10
11	Increase in per mile cost in May	$2.00			11
12	Number of miles flown	× 56,000			12
13	Net increase in fuel costs		112,000		13
14	Increase in food and beverage service attributed to:				14
15	Quantity factor:				15
16	Increase in the number of passengers in May	4,000			16
17	Planned per passenger cost in May	× $15.00			17
18	Net increase in food and beverage service costs		60,000		18
19	Increase in selling costs and commissions attributed to:				19
20	Quantity factor:				20
21	Increase in the number of passengers in May	4,000			21
22	Planned per passenger cost in May	× $110			22
23	Increase in variable cost		612,000		23
24	Net increase in selling costs			440,000	24
25	Increase in contribution margin			$ 588,000	25

The contribution margin analysis indicates that the decrease in price generated an additional $1,200,000 in revenue. This amount consists of $1,520,000 from an increased number of passengers and a $320,000 revenue reduction from the reduced ticket price. The increased fuel costs (by $2 per mile) reduced the contribution margin by $112,000. The increased number of passengers also increased the food and beverage service costs by $60,000 and the selling costs by $440,000. The net increase in contribution margin from management's actions is $588,000, indicating that their actions were successful.

At a Glance

1. Describe and illustrate income reporting under variable costing and absorption costing.

Key Points	Key Learning Outcomes	Example Exercises	Practice Exercises
Under absorption costing, direct materials, direct labor, and factory overhead become part of the cost of goods manufactured. Under variable costing, the cost of goods manufactured is composed of only variable costs—the direct materials, direct labor, and only those factory overhead costs that vary with the rate of production. The fixed factory overhead costs do not become a part of the cost of goods manufactured but are considered an expense of the period.	• Describe the difference between absorption and variable costing.		
Deducting the variable cost of goods sold from sales in the variable costing income statement yields the manufacturing margin. Deducting the variable selling and administrative expenses from the manufacturing margin yields the contribution margin. Deducting the fixed costs from the contribution margin yields the income from operations.	• Prepare a variable costing income statement for a manufacturer.	5-1	5-1A, 5-1B
	• Evaluate the difference between the variable and absorption costing income statements when production exceeds sales.	5-2	5-2A, 5-2B
	• Evaluate the difference between the variable and absorption costing income statements when sales exceed production.	5-3	5-3A, 5-3B

2. Describe and illustrate income analysis under variable costing and absorption costing.

Key Points	Key Learning Outcomes	Example Exercises	Practice Exercises
Management should be aware of the effects of changes in inventory levels on income from operations reported under variable costing and absorption costing. If absorption costing is used, managers could misinterpret increases or decreases in income from operations due to changes in inventory levels to be the result of operating efficiencies or inefficiencies.	• Determine absorption costing and variable costing income under different planned levels of production for a given sales level.	5-4	5-4A, 5-4B

(continued)

3. Describe and illustrate management's use of variable costing and absorption costing for controlling costs, pricing products, planning production, analyzing contribution margins, and analyzing market segments.

Key Points	Key Learning Outcomes	Example Exercises	Practice Exercises
Variable costing is especially useful at the operating level of management because the amount of variable manufacturing costs are controllable at this level. The fixed factory overhead costs are ordinarily controllable by a higher level of management. In the short run, variable costing may be useful in establishing the selling price of a product. This price should be at least equal to the variable costs of making and selling the product. In the long run, however, absorption costing is useful in establishing selling prices because all costs must be covered and a reasonable amount of operating income must be earned.	• Describe the management's use of variable and absorption costing for controlling costs, pricing products, planning production, analyzing contribution margins, and analyzing market segments.		

4. Use variable costing for analyzing market segments, including product, territories, and salespersons segments.

Key Points	Key Learning Outcomes	Example Exercises	Practice Exercises
Variable costing can support management decision making in analyzing and evaluating market segments, such as territories, products, salespersons, and customers. Contribution margin reports by segment can be used by managers to support price decisions, evaluate cost changes, and plan volume changes.	• Describe management's uses of contribution margin reports by segment. • Prepare a contribution margin report by sales territory. • Prepare a contribution margin report by product. • Prepare a contribution margin report by salesperson.	5-5	5-5A, 5-5B

5. Use variable costing for analyzing and explaining changes in contribution margin as a result of quantity and price factors.

Key Points	Key Learning Outcomes	Example Exercises	Practice Exercises
Contribution margin analysis is the systematic examination of differences between planned and actual contribution margins. These differences can be caused by an increase/decrease in the amount of sales or variable costs, which can be caused by changes in the amount of units sold, unit sales price, or unit cost.	• Prepare a contribution margin analysis identifying changes between actual and planned contribution margin by price/cost and quantity factors.	5-6	5-6A, 5-6B

6. Describe and illustrate the use of variable costing for service firms.

Key Points	Key Learning Outcomes	Example Exercises	Practice Exercises
Service firms will not have inventories, manufacturing margin, or cost of goods sold. Service firms can prepare variable costing income statements and contribution margin reports for market segments. In addition, service firms can use contribution margin analysis to plan and control operations.	• Prepare a variable costing income statement for a service firm. • Prepare contribution margin reports by market segments for a service firm. • Prepare a contribution margin analysis for a service firm.		

Key Terms

absorption costing (172)
contribution margin (173)
contribution margin analysis (187)
controllable cost (180)

manufacturing margin (173)
market segment (182)
noncontrollable cost (180)
price factor (187)

quantity factor (187)
sales mix (184)
variable costing (172)

Illustrative Problem

During the current period, McLaughlin Company sold 60,000 units of product at $30 per unit. At the beginning of the period, there were 10,000 units in inventory and McLaughlin Company manufactured 50,000 units during the period. The manufacturing costs and selling and administrative expenses were as follows:

	Total Cost	Number of Units	Unit Cost
Beginning inventory:			
Direct materials	$ 67,000	10,000	$ 6.70
Direct labor	155,000	10,000	15.50
Variable factory overhead	18,000	10,000	1.80
Fixed factory overhead	20,000	10,000	2.00
Total	$ 260,000		$26.00
Current period costs:			
Direct materials	$ 350,000	50,000	$ 7.00
Direct labor	810,000	50,000	16.20
Variable factory overhead	90,000	50,000	1.80
Fixed factory overhead	100,000	50,000	2.00
Total	$1,350,000		$27.00
Selling and administrative expenses:			
Variable	$ 65,000		
Fixed	45,000		
Total	$ 110,000		

Instructions

1. Prepare an income statement based on the variable costing concept.
2. Prepare an income statement based on the absorption costing concept.
3. Give the reason for the difference in the amount of income from operations in 1 and 2.

Solution

1.

Variable Costing Income Statement		
Sales (60,000 × $30)		$1,800,000
Variable cost of goods sold:		
Beginning inventory (10,000 × $24)	$ 240,000	
Variable cost of goods manufactured (50,000 × $25)	1,250,000	
Variable cost of goods sold		1,490,000
Manufacturing margin		$ 310,000
Variable selling and administrative expenses		65,000
Contribution margin		$ 245,000
Fixed costs:		
Fixed manufacturing costs	$ 100,000	
Fixed selling and administrative expenses	45,000	145,000
Income from operations		$ 100,000

(continued)

2.

Absorption Costing Income Statement			
Sales (60,000 × $30)			$1,800,000
Cost of goods sold:			
Beginning inventory (10,000 × $26)		$ 260,000	
Cost of goods manufactured (50,000 × $27)		1,350,000	
Cost of goods sold			1,610,000
Gross profit			$ 190,000
Selling and administrative expenses ($65,000 + $45,000)			110,000
Income from operations			$ 80,000

3. The difference of $20,000 ($100,000 − $80,000) in the amount of income from operations is attributable to the different treatment of the fixed manufacturing costs. The beginning inventory in the absorption costing income statement includes $20,000 (10,000 units × $2) of fixed manufacturing costs incurred in the preceding period. This $20,000 was included as an expense in a variable costing income statement of a prior period. Therefore, none of it is included as an expense in the current period variable costing income statement.

Self-Examination Questions
(Answers at End of Chapter)

1. Sales were $750,000, the variable cost of goods sold was $400,000, the variable selling and administrative expenses were $90,000, and fixed costs were $200,000. The contribution margin was:
   A. $60,000   C. $350,000
   B. $260,000   D. none of the above

2. During a year in which the number of units manufactured exceeded the number of units sold, the income from operations reported under the absorption costing concept would be:
   A. larger than the income from operations reported under the variable costing concept.
   B. smaller than the income from operations reported under the variable costing concept.
   C. the same as the income from operations reported under the variable costing concept.
   D. none of the above.

3. The beginning inventory consists of 6,000 units, all of which are sold during the period. The beginning inventory fixed costs are $20 per unit, and variable costs are $90 per unit. What is the difference in income from operations between variable and absorption costing?
   A. Variable costing income from operations is $540,000 less than under absorption costing.

   B. Variable costing income from operations is $660,000 greater than under absorption costing.
   C. Variable costing income from operations is $120,000 less than under absorption costing.
   D. Variable costing income from operations is $120,000 greater than under absorption costing.

4. Variable costs are $70 per unit and fixed costs are $150,000. Sales are estimated to be 10,000 units. How much would absorption costing income from operations differ between a plan to produce 10,000 units and 12,000 units?
   A. $150,000 greater for 12,000 units
   B. $150,000 less for 12,000 units
   C. $25,000 greater for 12,000 units
   D. $25,000 less for 12,000 units

5. If actual sales totaled $800,000 for the current year (80,000 units at $10 each) and planned sales were $765,000 (85,000 units at $9 each), the difference between actual and planned sales due to the quantity factor is:
   A. a $50,000 increase   C. a $45,000 decrease
   B. a $35,000 increase   D. none of the above

Eye Openers

1. What types of costs are customarily included in the cost of manufactured products under (a) the absorption costing concept and (b) the variable costing concept?

2. Which type of manufacturing cost (direct materials, direct labor, variable factory overhead, fixed factory overhead) is included in the cost of goods manufactured under the absorption costing concept but is excluded from the cost of goods manufactured under the variable costing concept?

3. Which of the following costs would be included in the cost of a manufactured product according to the variable costing concept: (a) rent on factory building, (b) direct materials, (c) property taxes on factory building, (d) electricity purchased to operate factory equipment, (e) salary of factory supervisor, (f) depreciation on factory building, (g) direct labor?

4. In the following equations, based on the variable costing income statement, identify the items designated by X:
   a. Net sales − X = manufacturing margin
   b. Manufacturing margin − X = contribution margin
   c. Contribution margin − X = income from operations

5. In the variable costing income statement, how are the fixed manufacturing costs reported and how are the fixed selling and administrative expenses reported?

6. If the quantity of the ending inventory is larger than that of the beginning inventory, will the amount of income from operations determined by absorption costing be more than or less than the amount determined by variable costing? Explain.

7. Since all costs of operating a business are controllable, what is the significance of the term *noncontrollable cost*?

8. Discuss how financial data prepared on the basis of variable costing can assist management in the development of short-run pricing policies.

9. How might management analyze sales territory profitability?

10. Why might management analyze product profitability?

11. Explain why rewarding sales personnel on the basis of total sales might not be in the best interests of a business whose goal is to maximize profits.

12. Discuss the two factors affecting both sales and variable costs to which a change in contribution margin can be attributed.

13. How is the quantity factor for an increase or decrease in the amount of sales computed in using contribution margin analysis?

14. How is the unit cost factor for an increase or decrease in the amount of variable cost of goods sold computed in using contribution margin analysis?

15. Provide examples of market segments for an entertainment company, such as The Walt Disney Co.

Practice Exercises

PE 5-1A
Variable costing income statement
obj. 1

Banner Company has the following information for October:

Sales	$150,000
Variable cost of goods sold	55,000
Fixed manufacturing costs	35,000
Variable selling and administrative expenses	12,000
Fixed selling and administrative expenses	10,000

Determine (a) the manufacturing margin, (b) the contribution margin, and (c) income from operations for Banner Company for the month of October.

PE 5-1B
Variable costing income statement
obj. 1

Mendoza Company has the following information for June:

Sales	$780,000
Variable cost of goods sold	400,000
Fixed manufacturing costs	70,000
Variable selling and administrative expenses	200,000
Fixed selling and administrative expenses	45,000

Determine (a) the manufacturing margin, (b) the contribution margin, and (c) income from operations for Mendoza Company for the month of June.

PE 5-2A
Variable costing difference—production exceeds sales
obj. 1

Fixed manufacturing costs are $90 per unit, and variable manufacturing costs are $175 per unit. Production was 200,000 units, while sales were 180,000 units. Determine (a) whether variable costing income from operations is less than or greater than absorption costing income from operations, and (b) the difference in variable costing and absorption costing income from operations.

PE 5-2B
Variable costing difference—production exceeds sales
obj. 1

Fixed manufacturing costs are $12 per unit, and variable manufacturing costs are $28 per unit. Production was 12,000 units, while sales were 9,000 units. Determine (a) whether variable costing income from operations is less than or greater than absorption costing income from operations, and (b) the difference in variable costing and absorption costing income from operations.

PE 5-3A
Variable costing difference—sales exceed production
obj. 1

The beginning inventory is 6,000 units. All of the units were manufactured during the period and 2,000 units of the beginning inventory were sold. The beginning inventory fixed manufacturing costs are $19 per unit, and variable manufacturing costs are $54 per unit. Determine (a) whether variable costing income from operations is less than or greater than absorption costing income from operations, and (b) the difference in variable costing and absorption costing income from operations.

PE 5-3B
Variable costing difference—sales exceed production
obj. 1

The beginning inventory is 54,000 units. All of the units were manufactured during the period and 31,000 units of the beginning inventory were sold. The beginning inventory fixed manufacturing costs are $4.20 per unit, and variable manufacturing costs are $8.50 per unit. Determine (a) whether variable costing income from operations is less than or greater than absorption costing income from operations, and (b) the difference in variable costing and absorption costing income from operations.

PE 5-4A
Income analysis under absorption and variable costing
obj. 2

Variable manufacturing costs are $14 per unit, and fixed manufacturing costs are $60,000. Sales are estimated to be 12,000 units.

a. How much would absorption costing income from operations differ between a plan to produce 12,000 units and a plan to produce 12,500 units?
b. How much would variable costing income from operations differ between the two production plans?

PE 5-4B
Income analysis under absorption and variable costing
obj. 2

Variable manufacturing costs are $26 per unit, and fixed manufacturing costs are $120,000. Sales are estimated to be 6,000 units.

a. How much would absorption costing income from operations differ between a plan to produce 6,000 units and a plan to produce 8,000 units?
b. How much would variable costing income from operations differ between the two production plans?

PE 5-5A
Contribution margin by segment
obj. 4

The following information is for Green Jacket Golf, Inc.:

	North	South
Sales volume (units):		
Ballistic	10,000	24,000
Pro Ballistic	9,500	28,000
Sales price:		
Ballistic	$20	$22
Pro Ballistic	$28	$32
Variable cost per unit:		
Ballistic	$9	$9
Pro Ballistic	$10	$10

Determine the contribution margin for (a) Ballistic golf balls and (b) North Region.

PE 5-5B
Contribution margin by segment
obj. **4**

The following information is for RAM Technologies, Inc.:

	Northern California	Southern California
Sales volume (units):		
Palm Pod Basic	2,500	4,000
Palm Pod Executive	6,500	15,000
Sales price:		
Palm Pod Basic	$125	$110
Palm Pod Executive	$180	$175
Variable cost per unit:		
Palm Pod Basic	$45	$45
Palm Pod Executive	$55	$55

Determine the contribution margin for (a) Palm Pod Executive hand-held data organizer and (b) Southern California Region.

PE 5-6A
Contribution margin analysis of sales
obj. **5**

The actual price for a product was $12 per unit, while the planned price was $10.50 per unit. The volume decreased by 15,000 units to 340,000 actual total units. Determine (a) the quantity factor and (b) the price factor for sales.

PE 5-6B
Contribution margin analysis of variable cost of goods sold
obj. **5**

The actual variable cost of goods sold for a product was $245 per unit, while the planned variable cost of goods sold was $236 per unit. The volume increased by 900 units to 6,800 actual total units. Determine (a) the quantity factor and (b) the price factor for variable cost of goods sold.

Exercises

EX 5-1
Inventory valuation under absorption costing and variable costing
obj. **1**
✓ b. Inventory, $104,625

At the end of the first year of operations, 2,700 units remained in the finished goods inventory. The unit manufacturing costs during the year were as follows:

Direct materials	$24.00
Direct labor	11.60
Fixed factory overhead cost	3.90
Variable factory overhead cost	3.15

Determine the cost of the finished goods inventory reported on the balance sheet under (a) the absorption costing concept and (b) the variable costing concept.

EX 5-2
Income statements under absorption costing and variable costing
obj. **1**
✓ a. Income from operations, $281,600

Dillon Sounds Inc. assembles and sells CD players. The company began operations on May 1, 2008, and operated at 100% of capacity during the first month. The following data summarize the results for May:

Sales (12,000 units)		$2,160,000
Production costs (14,000 units):		
Direct materials	$896,000	
Direct labor	448,000	
Variable factory overhead	235,200	
Fixed factory overhead	145,600	1,724,800
Selling and administrative expenses:		
Variable selling and administrative expenses	$300,000	
Fixed selling and administrative expenses	100,000	400,000

(continued)

a. Prepare an income statement according to the absorption costing concept.
b. Prepare an income statement according to the variable costing concept.
c. What is the reason for the difference in the amount of income from operations reported in (a) and (b)?

EX 5-3
Income statements under absorption costing and variable costing

obj. 1

✓ *b. Income from operations, $974,000*

Runway Fashions Inc. manufactures and sells women's clothes. The company began operations on August 1, 2009, and operated at 100% of capacity (35,000 units) during the first month, creating an ending inventory of 2,500 units. During September, the company produced 32,500 garments during the month but sold 35,000 units at $115 per unit. The September manufacturing costs and selling and administrative expenses were as follows:

	Total Cost	Number of Units Produced	Unit Cost
Manufacturing costs in Sept. beginning inventory:			
Variable	$ 115,000	2,500	$46.00
Fixed	32,500	2,500	13.00
Total	$ 147,500		$59.00
September manufacturing costs:			
Variable	$1,495,000	32,500	$46.00
Fixed	455,000	32,500	14.00
Total	$1,950,000		$60.00
Selling and administrative expenses:			
Variable ($21.60 per unit sold)	$ 756,000		
Fixed	230,000		
Total	$ 986,000		

a. Prepare an income statement according to the absorption costing concept for September.
b. Prepare an income statement according to the variable costing concept for September.
c. What is the reason for the difference in the amount of income from operations reported in (a) and (b)?

EX 5-4
Cost of goods manufactured, using variable costing and absorption costing

obj. 1

✓ *b. Unit cost of goods manufactured, $36,625*

On July 31, the end of the first year of operations, Myatt Equipment Company manufactured 800 units and sold 700 units. The following income statement was prepared, based on the variable costing concept:

Myatt Equipment Company
Variable Costing Income Statement
For the Year Ended July 31, 2009

Sales		$36,400,000
Variable cost of goods sold:		
Variable cost of goods manufactured	$20,000,000	
Less inventory, August 31	2,500,000	
Variable cost of goods sold		17,500,000
Manufacturing margin		$18,900,000
Variable selling and administrative expenses		4,300,000
Contribution margin		$14,600,000
Fixed costs:		
Fixed manufacturing costs	$ 9,300,000	
Fixed selling and administrative expenses	2,800,000	12,100,000
Income from operations		$ 2,500,000

Determine the unit cost of goods manufactured, based on (a) the variable costing concept and (b) the absorption costing concept.

EX 5-5
Variable costing income statement

obj. 1

On June 30, the end of the first month of operations, Lone Star Petroleum Company prepared the following income statement, based on the absorption costing concept:

✓ Income from operations, $7,450

Lone Star Petroleum Company
Absorption Costing Income Statement
For the Month Ended June 30, 2009

Sales (3,600 units)		$90,000
Cost of goods sold:		
Cost of goods manufactured (4,200 units)	$67,200	
Less inventory, June 30 (600 units)	9,600	
Cost of goods sold		57,600
Gross profit		$32,400
Selling and administrative expenses		22,550
Income from operations		$ 9,850

If the fixed manufacturing costs were $16,800 and the variable selling and administrative expenses were $7,600, prepare an income statement according to the variable costing concept.

EX 5-6
Absorption costing income statement

obj. 1

✓ Income from operations, $251,870

On April 30, the end of the first month of operations, Country Manor Furniture Company prepared the following income statement, based on the variable costing concept:

Country Manor Furniture Company
Variable Costing Income Statement
For the Month Ended April 30, 2008

Sales (9,000 units)		$1,080,000
Variable cost of goods sold:		
Variable cost of goods manufactured	$540,000	
Less inventory, April 30 (1,800 units)	90,000	
Variable cost of goods sold		450,000
Manufacturing margin		$ 630,000
Variable selling and administrative expenses		245,000
Contribution margin		$ 385,000
Fixed costs:		
Fixed manufacturing costs	$108,000	
Fixed selling and administrative expenses	43,130	151,130
Income from operations		$ 233,870

Prepare an income statement under absorption costing.

EX 5-7
Variable costing income statement

obj. 1

✓ a. Income from operations, $10,469

The following data were adapted from a recent income statement of Procter & Gamble Company:

	(in millions)
Net sales	$56,741
Operating costs:	
Cost of products sold	$27,872
Marketing, administrative, and other expenses	18,400
Total operating costs	$46,272
Income from operations	$10,469

Assume that the variable amount of each category of operating costs is as follows:

	(in millions)
Cost of products sold	$16,000
Marketing, administrative, and other expenses	7,300

a. Based on the above data, prepare a variable costing income statement for Procter & Gamble Company, assuming that the company maintained constant inventory levels during the period.
b. If Procter & Gamble reduced its inventories during the period, what impact would that have on the income from operations determined under absorption costing?

EX 5-8

*Estimated income
statements, using
absorption and variable
costing*

objs. 1, 2

✓ a. 1. Income from
operations, $17,950
(9,000 units)

Prior to the first month of operations ending March 31, 2009, Power Storage Inc. estimated the following operating results:

Sales (9,000 × $86)	$774,000
Manufacturing costs (9,000 units):	
Direct materials	486,000
Direct labor	121,500
Variable factory overhead	58,050
Fixed factory overhead	54,000
Fixed selling and administrative expenses	11,900
Variable selling and administrative expenses	24,600

The company is evaluating a proposal to manufacture 10,000 units instead of 9,000 units, thus creating an ending inventory of 1,000 units. Manufacturing the additional units will not change sales, unit variable factory overhead costs, total fixed factory overhead cost, or total selling and administrative expenses.

a. Prepare an estimated income statement, comparing operating results if 9,000 and 10,000 units are manufactured in (1) the absorption costing format and (2) the variable costing format.
b. What is the reason for the difference in income from operations reported for the two levels of production by the absorption costing income statement?

EX 5-9

*Variable and absorption
costing*

obj. 1

REAL WORLD

✓ a. Contribution margin,
$4,525

Whirlpool Corporation had the following abbreviated income statement for a recent year:

	(in millions)
Net sales	$14,317
Cost of goods sold	$11,269
Selling, administrative, and other expenses	2,256
Total expenses	$13,525
Income from operations	$ 792

Assume that there were $2,900 million fixed manufacturing costs and $800 million fixed selling, administrative, and other costs for the year.

The finished goods inventories at the beginning and end of the year from the balance sheet were as follows:

January 1	$1,701 million
December 31	$1,591 million

Assume that 30% of the beginning and ending inventory consists of fixed costs. Assume work in process and materials inventory were unchanged during the period.

a. Prepare an income statement according to the variable costing concept for Whirlpool Corporation for the recent year.
b. Explain the difference between the amount of income from operations reported under the absorption costing and variable costing concepts.

EX 5-10

*Variable and absorption
costing—three products*

objs. 2, 3

Tahoe Boot Company manufactures and sells three types of boots. The income statements prepared under the absorption costing method for the three boots are as follows:

Tahoe Boot Company
Product Income Statements—Absorption Costing
For the Year Ended December 31, 2008

	Hiking Boots	Fishing Boots	Ski Boots
Revenues	$580,000	$490,000	$420,000
Cost of goods sold	300,000	240,000	280,000
Gross profit	$280,000	$250,000	$140,000
Selling and administrative expenses	240,000	180,000	235,000
Income from operations	$ 40,000	$ 70,000	$ (95,000)

In addition, you have determined the following information with respect to allocated fixed costs:

	Hiking Boots	Fishing Boots	Ski Boots
Fixed costs:			
Cost of goods sold	$90,000	$65,000	$80,000
Selling and administrative expenses	70,000	60,000	80,000

These fixed costs are used to support all three product lines. In addition, you have determined that the inventory is negligible.

The management of the company has deemed the profit performance of the ski boot line as unacceptable. As a result, it has decided to eliminate the ski boot line. Management does not expect to be able to increase sales in the other two lines. However, as a result of eliminating the ski boot line, management expects the profits of the company to increase by $95,000.

a. Do you agree with management's decision and conclusions?
b. Prepare a variable costing income statement for the three products.
c. Use the report in (b) to determine the profit impact of eliminating the ski boot line, assuming no other changes.

EX 5-11
Change in sales mix and contribution margin
obj. 4

Signature Pen Company manufactures ballpoint and fountain pens and is operating at less than full capacity. Market research indicates that 6,000 additional ballpoint pens and 8,500 additional fountain pens could be sold. The income from operations by unit of product is as follows:

	Ballpoint Pen	Fountain Pen
Sales price	$5.50	$15.00
Variable cost of goods sold	2.80	8.30
Manufacturing margin	$2.70	$ 6.70
Variable selling and administrative expenses	1.10	2.80
Contribution margin	$1.60	$ 3.90
Fixed manufacturing costs	0.50	1.00
Income from operations	$1.10	$ 2.90

Prepare an analysis indicating the increase or decrease in total profitability if 6,000 additional ballpoint pens and 8,500 additional fountain pens are produced and sold, assuming that there is sufficient capacity for the additional production.

EX 5-12
Product profitability analysis
obj. 4

✓ *a. Plasma contribution margin, $131,200*

ViewPoint Video Inc. manufactures and sells two styles of televisions, LCD panel and plasma, from a single manufacturing facility. The manufacturing facility operates at 100% of capacity. The following per unit information is available for the two products:

	LCD Panel	Plasma
Sales price	$640	$500
Variable cost of goods sold	405	350
Manufacturing margin	$235	$150
Variable selling expenses	115	68
Contribution margin	$120	$ 82
Fixed expenses	70	32
Income from operations	$ 50	$ 50

In addition, the following unit volume information for the period is as follows:

	LCD Panel	Plasma
Sales unit volume	2,500	1,600

a. Prepare a contribution margin by product report. Calculate the contribution margin ratio for each product as a whole percent, rounded to two decimal places.

(continued)

b. What advice would you give to the management of ViewPoint Video Inc. regarding the relative profitability of the two products?

EX 5-13
Territory and product profitability analysis
obj. **4**

✓ *a. France contribution margin, $1,060,000*

PedalSport Inc. manufactures and sells two styles of bicycles, touring and mountain. These bicycles are sold in two countries, the Netherlands and France. Information about the two bicycles is as follows:

	Touring Bike	Mountain Bike
Sales price	$625	$415
Variable cost of goods sold per unit	230	205
Manufacturing margin per unit	$395	$210
Variable selling expense per unit	260	80
Contribution margin per unit	$135	$130

The sales unit volume for the territories and products for the period is as follows:

	Netherlands	France
Touring Bike	8,000	4,000
Mountain Bike	0	4,000

a. Prepare a contribution margin by sales territory report. Calculate the contribution margin ratio for each territory as a whole percent, rounded to one decimal place.
b. What advice would you give to the management of PedalSport Inc. regarding the relative profitability of the two territories?

EX 5-14
Sales territory and salesperson profitability analysis
obj. **4**

✓ *a. Raul A. contribution margin, $173,880*

Handy Hardware Company manufactures and sells a wide variety of hardware products to retailers in the Northern and Southern regions. There are two salespersons assigned to each territory. Higher commission rates go to the most experienced salespersons. The following sales statistics are available for each salesperson:

	Northern		Southern	
	Sarah M.	Raul A.	Benson L.	Tamara T.
Average per unit:				
Sales price	$80.00	$70.00	$90.00	$65.00
Variable cost of goods sold	$48.00	$28.00	$54.00	$26.00
Commission rate	10%	14%	14%	10%
Units sold	6,200	5,400	5,000	8,000
Manufacturing margin ratio	40%	60%	40%	60%

a. 1. Prepare a contribution margin by salesperson report. Calculate the contribution margin ratio for each salesperson.
  2. Interpret the report.
b. 1. Prepare a contribution margin by territory report. Calculate the contribution margin for each territory as a whole percent, rounded to one decimal place.
  2. Interpret the report.

EX 5-15
Segment profitability analysis
obj. **4**

✓ *a. North America contribution margin, $3,495.20*

Provided below are the marketing segment sales for Caterpillar, Inc., for a recent year.

Caterpillar, Inc.
Machinery and Engines Marketing Segment Sales
(in millions)

	Asia/Pacific	Europe/Africa/ Middle East (EAME)	Latin America	Power Products	North America
Sales	$2,462	$4,441	$2,275	$4,669	$10,998

The Power Products segment designs, manufactures, and markets engines. The geographic segments sell Caterpillar equipment to their respective regions.
Assume the following information:

	Asia/Pacific	Europe/Africa/ Middle East (EAME)	Latin America	Power Products	North America
Variable cost of goods sold as a percent of sales	50%	60%	45%	60%	52%
Dealer commissions as a percent of sales	8%	12%	8%	5%	8%
Variable promotion expenses (in millions)	$400	$450	$300	$750	$900

a. Use the sales information and the additional assumed information to prepare a contribution margin by segment report. Calculate the contribution margin ratio for each segment as a whole percent, rounded to one decimal place.
b. Prepare a table showing the manufacturing margin, dealer commissions, and variable promotion expenses as a percent of sales for each segment. Round whole percents to one decimal place.
c. [pencil icon] Use the information in (a) and (b) to interpret the segment performance.

EX 5-16
Segment contribution margin analysis
objs. **4, 6**

✓ *a. Film, $8,889.75, 75%*

The operating revenues of the four largest business segments for Time Warner, Inc., for a recent year are shown below. Each segment includes a number of businesses, examples of which are indicated in parentheses.

Time Warner, Inc.
Segment Revenues
(in millions)

AOL	$ 8,692
Cable (TWC, Inc.)	8,484
Filmed Entertainment (Warner Bros.)	11,853
Networks (CNN, HBO, WB)	9,054
Publishing (*Time*, *People*, *Sports Illustrated*)	5,565

Assume that the variable costs as a percent of sales for each segment are as follows:

AOL	15%
Cable	15%
Filmed Entertainment	25%
Networks	20%
Publishing	75%

a. Determine the contribution margin and contribution margin ratio for each segment from the above information.
b. Why is the contribution margin ratio for the publishing segment smaller than for the other segments?
c. Does your answer to (b) mean that the other segments are more profitable businesses than the publishing segment?

EX 5-17
Contribution margin analysis—sales
obj. **4**

Back Beat Music Company sells recorded CD music. Management decided early in the year to reduce the price of the CD in order to increase sales volume. As a result, for the year ended December 31, 2009, the sales increased by $27,000 from the planned level of $171,000. The following information is available from the accounting records for the year ended December 31, 2009:

	Actual	Planned	Difference— Increase (Decrease)
Sales	$198,000	$171,000	$27,000
Number of units sold	12,000	9,500	2,500
Sales price	$16.50	$18.00	$(1.50)
Variable cost per unit	$8.00	$8.00	0

(continued)

a. Prepare an analysis of the sales quantity and price factors.
b. Did the price decrease generate sufficient volume to result in a net increase in contribution margin if the actual variable cost per unit was $8, as planned?

EX 5-18
Contribution margin analysis—sales

obj. 4

✓ *Sales quantity factor, $(82,500)*

The following data for Aesthetic Products Inc. are available:

For the Year Ended December 31, 2008	Actual	Planned	Difference—Increase or (Decrease)
Sales	$2,537,500	$2,475,000	$ 62,500
Less:			
Variable cost of goods sold	$1,334,000	$1,305,000	$ 29,000
Variable selling and administrative expenses	261,000	292,500	(31,500)
Total variable costs	$1,595,000	$1,597,500	$ (2,500)
Contribution margin	$ 942,500	$ 877,500	$ 65,000
Number of units sold	14,500	15,000	
Per unit:			
Sales price	$175.00	$165.00	
Variable cost of goods sold	92.00	87.00	
Variable selling and administrative expenses	18.00	19.50	

Prepare an analysis of the sales quantity and price factors.

EX 5-19
Contribution margin analysis—variable costs

obj. 4

✓ *Variable cost of goods sold unit cost factor, $72,500*

Based upon the data in Exercise 5-18, prepare a contribution analysis of the variable costs for Aesthetic Products Inc. for the year ended December 31, 2008.

EX 5-20
Variable costing income statement—service company

objs. 4, 6

Atlantic Railroad Company transports commodities among three routes (city-pairs): Atlanta/Baltimore, Baltimore/Pittsburgh, and Pittsburgh/Atlanta. Significant costs, their cost behavior, and activity rates for August 2008 are as follows:

Cost	Amount	Cost Behavior	Activity Rate
Labor costs for loading and unloading railcars	$275,600	Variable	$53 per railcar
Fuel costs	602,000	Variable	14 per train-mile
Train crew labor costs	344,000	Variable	8 per train-mile
Switchyard labor costs	187,200	Variable	36 per railcar
Track and equipment depreciation	225,000	Fixed	
Maintenance	150,000	Fixed	

Operating statistics from the management information system reveal the following for August:

	Atlanta/Baltimore	Baltimore/Pittsburgh	Pittsburgh/Atlanta	Total
Number of train-miles	15,100	11,900	16,000	43,000
Number of railcars	600	2,975	1,625	5,200
Revenue per railcar	$640	$320	$510	

a. Prepare a contribution margin by route report for Atlantic Railroad Company for the month of August. Calculate the contribution margin ratio in whole percents, rounded to one decimal place.
b. Evaluate the route performance of the railroad using the report in (a).

EX 5-21
Contribution margin reporting and analysis—service company
objs. 5, 6

The management of Atlantic Railroad Company introduced in Exercise 20-20 improved the profitability of the Atlanta/Baltimore route in September by reducing the price of a railcar from $640 to $580. This price reduction increased the demand for rail services. Thus, the number of railcars increased by 200 railcars to a total of 800 railcars. This was accomplished by increasing the size of each train but not the number of trains. Thus, the number of train-miles was unchanged. All the activity rates remained unchanged.

a. Prepare a contribution margin report for the Atlanta/Baltimore route for September. Calculate the contribution margin ratio in percentage terms to one decimal place.
b. Prepare a contribution margin analysis to evaluate management's actions in September. Assume that the September planned quantity, price, and unit cost was the same as August.

EX 5-22
Variable costing income statement and contribution margin analysis—service company
objs. 5, 6

The actual and planned data for Sage University for the Fall term 2008 were as follows:

	Actual	Planned
Enrollment	4,700	4,300
Tuition per credit hour	$125	$140
Credit hours	63,000	45,000
Registration, records, and marketing cost per enrolled student	$290	$290
Instructional costs per credit hour	$66	$62
Depreciation on classrooms and equipment	$860,000	$860,000

Registration, records, and marketing costs vary by the number of enrolled students, while instructional costs vary by the number of credit hours. Depreciation is a fixed cost.

a. Prepare a variable costing income statement showing the contribution margin and income from operations for the Fall 2008 term.
b. Prepare a contribution margin analysis report comparing planned with actual performance for the Fall 2008 term.

Problems Series A

PR 5-1A
Absorption and variable costing income statements
objs. 1, 2
✓ 2. Contribution margin, $170,275

During the first month of operations ended September 30, 2008, Zap Electronics Inc. manufactured 7,400 modems, of which 6,950 were sold. Operating data for the month are summarized as follows:

Sales		$764,500
Manufacturing costs:		
Direct materials	$362,600	
Direct labor	111,000	
Variable manufacturing cost	96,200	
Fixed manufacturing cost	48,100	617,900
Selling and administrative expenses:		
Variable	$ 59,075	
Fixed	27,800	86,875

Instructions
1. Prepare an income statement based on the absorption costing concept.
2. Prepare an income statement based on the variable costing concept.
3. Explain the reason for the difference in the amount of income from operations reported in (1) and (2).

PR 5-2A
Income statements under absorption costing and variable costing
objs. 1, 2

The demand for shampoo, one of numerous products manufactured by Venus Beauty Products Inc., has dropped sharply because of recent competition from a similar product. The company's chemists are currently completing tests of various new formulas, and it is anticipated that the manufacture of a superior product can be started on March 1, one month hence. No changes will be needed in the present production facilities to manufacture the new product because only the mixture of the various materials will be changed.

✓2. Contribution
margin, $193,375

The controller has been asked by the president of the company for advice on whether to continue production during February or to suspend the manufacture of shampoo until March 1. The controller has assembled the following pertinent data:

Venus Beauty Products Inc.
Income Statement—Shampoo
For the Month Ended January 31, 2008

Sales (70,000 units)	$868,000
Cost of goods sold	708,500
Gross profit	$159,500
Selling and administrative expenses	155,000
Income from operations	$ 4,500

The production costs and selling and administrative expenses, based on production of 70,000 units in January, are as follows:

Direct materials	$ 2.30 per unit
Direct labor	2.85 per unit
Variable manufacturing cost	1.40 per unit
Variable selling and administrative expenses	1.60 per unit
Fixed manufacturing costs	250,000 for January
Fixed selling and administrative expenses	43,000 for January

Sales for February are expected to drop about 35% below those of the preceding month. No significant changes are anticipated in the fixed costs or variable costs per unit. No extra costs will be incurred in discontinuing operations in the portion of the plant associated with shampoo. The inventory of shampoo at the beginning and end of February is expected to be inconsequential.

Instructions

1. Prepare an estimated income statement in absorption costing form for February for shampoo, assuming that production continues during the month.
2. Prepare an estimated income statement in variable costing form for February for shampoo, assuming that production continues during the month.
3. What would be the estimated loss in income from operations if the shampoo production were temporarily suspended for February?
4. ▭▭▭▶ What advice should the controller give to management?

PR 5-3A
Absorption and variable costing income statements for two months and analysis

objs. 1, 2

✓2. a. Manufacturing
margin, $18,560

During the first month of operations ended October 31, 2008, Sweet Occasions Inc. baked 3,200 cakes, of which 2,900 were sold. Operating data for the month are summarized as follows:

Sales		$36,250
Baking costs:		
Direct materials	$11,200	
Direct labor	5,440	
Variable manufacturing cost	2,880	
Fixed manufacturing cost	3,840	23,360
Selling and administrative expenses:		
Variable	$ 2,900	
Fixed	1,305	4,205

During November, Sweet Occasions Inc. baked 2,600 cakes and sold 2,900 cakes. Operating data for November are summarized as follows:

Sales		$36,250
Baking costs:		
Direct materials	$9,100	
Direct labor	4,420	
Variable manufacturing cost	2,340	
Fixed manufacturing cost	3,840	19,700
Selling and administrative expenses:		
Variable	$2,900	
Fixed	1,305	4,205

Instructions

1. Using the absorption costing concept, prepare income statements for (a) October and (b) November.
2. Using the variable costing concept, prepare income statements for (a) October and (b) November.
3. a. [▭▭▶] Explain the reason for the differences in the amount of income from operations in (1) and (2) for October.
   b. [▭▭▶] Explain the reason for the differences in the amount of income from operations in (1) and (2) for November.
4. Based upon your answers to (1) and (2), did Sweet Occasions Inc. operate more profitably in October or in November? Explain.

PR 5-4A
Salespersons' report and analysis
obj. **4**

✓ *1. Michel contribution margin ratio, 29.5%*

Tumbleweed Western Wear Inc. employs seven salespersons to sell and distribute its product throughout the state. Data taken from reports received from the salespersons during the year ended June 30, 2008, are as follows:

Salesperson	Total Sales	Variable Cost of Goods Sold	Variable Selling Expenses
Corso	$360,000	$180,000	$ 74,880
Eastwood	470,000	211,500	82,250
Lassiter	510,000	260,100	122,400
Michel	490,000	230,300	115,150
Ng	430,000	202,100	116,100
Ramon	490,000	235,200	88,200
Wayne	480,000	232,800	105,600

Instructions

1. Prepare a table indicating contribution margin, variable cost of goods sold as a percent of sales, variable selling expenses as a percent of sales, and contribution margin ratio by salesperson (round whole percent to one digit after decimal point).
2. Which salesperson generated the highest contribution margin ratio for the year and why?
3. Briefly list factors other than contribution margin that should be considered in evaluating the performance of salespersons.

PR 5-5A
Variable costing income statement and effect on income of change in operations
obj. **4**

✓ *3. Income from operations, $99,750*

Portable Seating Company manufactures three sizes of folding chairs—small (S), medium (M), and large (L). The income statement has consistently indicated a net loss for the M size, and management is considering three proposals: (1) continue Size M, (2) discontinue Size M and reduce total output accordingly, or (3) discontinue Size M and conduct an advertising campaign to expand the sales of Size S so that the entire plant capacity can continue to be used.

If Proposal 2 is selected and Size M is discontinued and production curtailed, the annual fixed production costs and fixed operating expenses could be reduced by $150,000 and $30,000, respectively. If Proposal 3 is selected, it is anticipated that an additional annual expenditure of $90,000 for the salary of an assistant brand manager (classified as a fixed operating expense) would yield an increase of 125% in Size S sales volume. It is also assumed that the increased production of Size S would utilize the plant facilities released by the discontinuance of Size M.

The sales and costs have been relatively stable over the past few years, and they are expected to remain so for the foreseeable future. The income statement for the past year ended January 31, 2009, is as follows:

| | Size | | | |
	S	M	L	Total
Sales	$1,050,000	$1,150,000	$1,000,000	$3,200,000
Cost of goods sold:				
Variable costs	$ 570,000	$ 760,000	$ 600,000	$1,930,000
Fixed costs	255,000	305,000	265,000	825,000
Total cost of goods sold	$ 825,000	$1,065,000	$ 865,000	$2,755,000
Gross profit	$ 225,000	$ 85,000	$ 135,000	$ 445,000

(continued)

	Size			
	S	M	L	Total
Less operating expenses:				
Variable expenses	$ 125,000	$ 115,000	$ 90,000	$ 330,000
Fixed expenses	34,000	45,000	15,000	94,000
Total operating expenses	$ 159,000	$ 160,000	$ 105,000	$ 424,000
Income from operations	$ 66,000	$ (75,000)	$ 30,000	$ 21,000

Instructions

1. Prepare an income statement for the past year in the variable costing format. Use the following headings:

Size			
S	M	L	Total

Data for each style should be reported through contribution margin. The fixed costs should be deducted from the total contribution margin, as reported in the "Total" column, to determine income from operations.

2. Based on the income statement prepared in (1) and the other data presented above, determine the amount by which total annual income from operations would be reduced below its present level if Proposal 2 is accepted.

3. Prepare an income statement in the variable costing format, indicating the projected annual income from operations if Proposal 3 is accepted. Use the following headings:

Size		
S	L	Total

Data for each style should be reported through contribution margin. The fixed costs should be deducted from the total contribution margin as reported in the "Total" column. For purposes of this problem, the additional expenditure of $90,000 for the assistant brand manager's salary can be added to the fixed operating expenses.

4. By how much would total annual income increase above its present level if Proposal 3 is accepted? Explain.

PR 5-6A
Contribution margin analysis
obj. 5

✓1. Sales price factor, $(26,000)

Bay Company manufactures only one product. For the year ended December 31, 2008, the contribution margin increased by $2,000 from the planned level of $258,000. The president of Bay Company has expressed serious concern about such a small increase and has requested a follow-up report.

The following data have been gathered from the accounting records for the year ended December 31, 2008:

	Actual	Planned	Difference— Increase or (Decrease)
Sales	$773,500	$738,000	$35,500
Less:			
Variable cost of goods sold	$396,500	$384,000	$12,500
Variable selling and administrative expenses	117,000	96,000	21,000
Total	$513,500	$480,000	$33,500
Contribution margin	$260,000	$258,000	$ 2,000
Number of units sold	6,500	6,000	
Per unit:			
Sales price	$119.00	$123.00	
Variable cost of goods sold	61.00	64.00	
Variable selling and administrative expenses	18.00	16.00	

Instructions

1. Prepare a contribution margin analysis report for the year ended December 31, 2008.

2. ▭▭▭▭▭ At a meeting of the board of directors on January 30, 2009, the president, after reviewing the contribution margin analysis report, made the following comment:

"It looks as if the price decrease of $4.00 had the effect of increasing sales. However, we lost control over the variable cost of goods sold and variable selling and administrative expenses. Let's look into these expenses and get them under control! Also, let's consider decreasing the sales price to $110 to increase sales further."

Do you agree with the president's comment? Explain.

Problems Series B

PR 5-1B
Absorption and variable costing income statements

objs. 1, 2

✓ 2. Income from operations, $156,200

During the first month of operations ended May 31, 2008, Frost Zone Appliance Company manufactured 1,540 refrigerators, of which 1,430 were sold. Operating data for the month are summarized as follows:

Sales		$972,400
Manufacturing costs:		
Direct materials	$385,000	
Direct labor	161,700	
Variable manufacturing cost	61,600	
Fixed manufacturing cost	115,500	723,800
Selling and administrative expenses:		
Variable	$ 92,950	
Fixed	42,900	135,850

Instructions
1. Prepare an income statement based on the absorption costing concept.
2. Prepare an income statement based on the variable costing concept.
3. ▭▭▭▭▭ Explain the reason for the difference in the amount of income from operations reported in (1) and (2).

PR 5-2B
Income statements under absorption costing and variable costing

objs. 1, 2

✓ 2. Contribution margin, $79,776

The demand for solvent, one of numerous products manufactured by Erie Products Inc., has dropped sharply because of recent competition from a similar product. The company's chemists are currently completing tests of various new formulas, and it is anticipated that the manufacture of a superior product can be started on May 1, one month hence. No changes will be needed in the present production facilities to manufacture the new product because only the mixture of the various materials will be changed.

The controller has been asked by the president of the company for advice on whether to continue production during April or to suspend the manufacture of solvent until May 1. The controller has assembled the following pertinent data:

Erie Products Inc.
Income Statement—Solvent
For the Month Ended March 31, 2009

Sales (3,600 units)	$360,000
Cost of goods sold	295,080
Gross profit	$ 64,920
Selling and administrative expenses	59,700
Income from operations	$ 5,220

The production costs and selling and administrative expenses, based on production of 3,600 units in March, are as follows:

Direct materials	$ 39.00 per unit
Direct labor	13.50 per unit
Variable manufacturing cost	12.80 per unit
Variable selling and administrative expenses	7.00 per unit
Fixed manufacturing costs	60,000 for March
Fixed selling and administrative expenses	34,500 for March

Sales for April are expected to drop about 20% below those of the preceding month. No significant changes are anticipated in the fixed costs or variable costs per unit. No extra costs will be incurred in discontinuing operations in the portion of the plant associated with solvent. The inventory of solvent at the beginning and end of April is expected to be inconsequential.

Instructions

1. Prepare an estimated income statement in absorption costing form for April for solvent, assuming that production continues during the month.
2. Prepare an estimated income statement in variable costing form for April for solvent, assuming that production continues during the month.
3. What would be the estimated loss in income from operations if the solvent production were temporarily suspended for April?
4. ▭▭▭▶ What advice should the controller give to management?

PR 5-3B

Absorption and variable costing income statements for two months and analysis

objs. 1, 2

✓ *1. b. Income from operations, $30,600*

During the first month of operations ended July 31, 2009, Buzz T-Shirt Company produced 42,000 T-shirts, of which 39,000 were sold. Operating data for the month are summarized as follows:

Sales		$448,500
Manufacturing costs:		
Direct materials	$268,800	
Direct labor	71,400	
Variable manufacturing cost	33,600	
Fixed manufacturing cost	31,500	405,300
Selling and administrative expenses:		
Variable	$ 21,450	
Fixed	15,600	37,050

During August, Buzz T-Shirt Company produced 36,000 T-shirts and sold 39,000 shirts. Operating data for August are summarized as follows:

Sales		$448,500
Manufacturing costs:		
Direct materials	$230,400	
Direct labor	61,200	
Variable manufacturing cost	28,800	
Fixed manufacturing cost	31,500	351,900
Selling and administrative expenses:		
Variable	$ 21,450	
Fixed	15,600	37,050

Instructions

1. Using the absorption costing concept, prepare income statements for (a) July and (b) August.
2. Using the variable costing concept, prepare income statements for (a) July and (b) August.
3. a. ▭▭▭▶ Explain the reason for the differences in the amount of income from operations in (1) and (2) for July.
   b. ▭▭▭▶ Explain the reason for the differences in the amount of income from operations in (1) and (2) for August.
4. Based upon your answers to (1) and (2), did Buzz T-Shirt Company operate more profitably in July or in August? Explain.

PR 5-4B

Salespersons' report and analysis

obj. 4

Gabriel Horn Company employs seven salespersons to sell and distribute its product throughout the state. Data taken from reports received from the salespersons during the year ended December 31, 2008, are as follows:

✓1. Severinsen
contribution margin
ratio, 25%

Salesperson	Total Sales	Variable Cost of Goods Sold	Variable Selling Expenses
Armstrong	$550,000	$330,000	$110,000
Brown	550,000	330,000	119,900
Davis	450,000	271,000	80,000
Driscoll	500,000	200,000	100,000
Marsalis	525,000	300,300	99,750
Morrison	680,000	265,000	109,000
Severinsen	490,000	277,500	90,000

Instructions

1. Prepare a table indicating contribution margin, variable cost of goods sold as a percent of sales, variable selling expenses as a percent of sales, and contribution margin ratio by salesperson. Round whole percents to a single digit.
2. Which salesperson generated the highest contribution margin ratio for the year and why?
3. Briefly list factors other than contribution margin that should be considered in evaluating the performance of salespersons.

PR 5-5B
Segment variable costing income statement and effect on income of change in operations

obj. 4

✓1. Income from
operations, $75,000

Canadian Coat Company manufactures three sizes of winter coats—small (S), medium (M), and large (L). The income statement has consistently indicated a net loss for the M size, and management is considering three proposals: (1) continue Size M, (2) discontinue Size M and reduce total output accordingly, or (3) discontinue Size M and conduct an advertising campaign to expand the sales of Size S so that the entire plant capacity can continue to be used.

If Proposal 2 is selected and Size M is discontinued and production curtailed, the annual fixed production costs and fixed operating expenses could be reduced by $40,000 and $28,000, respectively. If Proposal 3 is selected, it is anticipated that an additional annual expenditure of $30,000 for the rental of additional warehouse space would yield an increase of 125% in Size S sales volume. It is also assumed that the increased production of Size S would utilize the plant facilities released by the discontinuance of Size M.

The sales and costs have been relatively stable over the past few years, and they are expected to remain so for the foreseeable future. The income statement for the past year ended June 30, 2008, is as follows:

	Size S	Size M	Size L	Total
Sales	$580,000	$640,000	$830,000	$2,050,000
Cost of goods sold:				
Variable costs	$260,000	$310,000	$380,000	$ 950,000
Fixed costs	65,000	120,000	150,000	335,000
Total cost of goods sold	$325,000	$430,000	$530,000	$1,285,000
Gross profit	$255,000	$210,000	$300,000	$ 765,000
Less operating expenses:				
Variable expenses	$115,000	$135,000	$170,000	$ 420,000
Fixed expenses	80,000	90,000	100,000	270,000
Total operating expenses	$195,000	$225,000	$270,000	$ 690,000
Income from operations	$ 60,000	$ (15,000)	$ 30,000	$ 75,000

Instructions

1. Prepare an income statement for the past year in the variable costing format. Use the following headings:

Size			
S	M	L	Total

Data for each style should be reported through contribution margin. The fixed costs should be deducted from the total contribution margin, as reported in the "Total" column, to determine income from operations.

(continued)

2. Based on the income statement prepared in (1) and the other data presented, determine the amount by which total annual income from operations would be reduced below its present level if Proposal 2 is accepted.

3. Prepare an income statement in the variable costing format, indicating the projected annual income from operations if Proposal 3 is accepted. Use the following headings:

	Size	
S	L	Total

Data for each style should be reported through contribution margin. The fixed costs should be deducted from the total contribution margin as reported in the "Total" column. For purposes of this problem, the expenditure of $30,000 for the rental of additional warehouse space can be added to the fixed operating expenses.

4. By how much would total annual income increase above its present level if Proposal 3 is accepted? Explain.

PR 5-6B
Contribution margin analysis
obj. 5

1. Sales quantity factor,
$(38,000)

Lyon Industries Inc. manufactures only one product. For the year ended December 31, 2008, the contribution margin decreased by $10,000 from the planned level of $110,000. The president of Lyon Industries Inc. has expressed some concern about this decrease and has requested a follow-up report.

The following data have been gathered from the accounting records for the year ended December 31, 2008:

	Actual	Planned	Difference—Increase (Decrease)
Sales	$430,000	$418,000	$ 12,000
Less:			
Variable cost of goods sold	190,000	198,000	(8,000)
Variable selling and administrative expense	140,000	110,000	30,000
Total	$330,000	$308,000	$ 22,000
Contribution margin	$100,000	$110,000	$(10,000)
Number of units sold	10,000	11,000	
Per unit:			
Sales price	$43.00	$38.00	
Variable cost of goods sold	19.00	18.00	
Variable selling and administrative expenses	14.00	10.00	

Instructions

1. Prepare a contribution margin analysis report for the year ended December 31, 2008.

2. At a meeting of the board of directors on January 30, 2009, the president, after reviewing the contribution margin analysis report, made the following comment:

It looks as if the price increase of $5.00 had the effect of decreasing sales volume. However, this was a favorable tradeoff. The variable cost of goods sold was less than planned. Apparently, we are efficiently managing our variable cost of goods sold. However, the variable selling and administrative expenses appear out of control. Let's look into these expenses and get them under control! Also, let's consider increasing the sales price to $50 and continue this favorable tradeoff between higher price and lower volume.

Do you agree with the president's comment? Explain.

Special Activities

SA 5-1
Ethics and professional conduct in business

The Sporting Goods Division of Star Brands Inc. uses absorption costing for profit reporting. The general manager of the Sporting Goods Division is concerned about meeting the income objectives of the division. At the beginning of the reporting period, the division had an adequate supply of inventory. The general manager has decided to increase production of goods in the plant in order to allocate fixed manufacturing cost over a greater number of units. Unfortunately, the increased production cannot be sold and will increase the inventory. However, the impact on earnings will be positive because the lower cost per unit will be matched against sales. The general manager has come to Blaine Thompson, the controller, to determine exactly how much additional production is required in order to increase net income enough to meet the division's profit objectives. Thompson analyzes the data and determines that the inventory will need to be increased by 30% in order to absorb enough fixed costs and meet the income objective. Thompson reports this information to the division manager.

Discuss whether Thompson is acting in an ethical manner.

SA 5-2
Inventories under absorption costing

Circle-D manufactures control panels for the electronics industry and has just completed its first year of operations. The following discussion took place between the controller, Nelson Driver, and the company president, Emily Prince:

Emily: I've been looking over our first year's performance by quarters. Our earnings have been increasing each quarter, even though our sales have been flat and our prices and costs have not changed. Why is this?

Nelson: Our actual sales have stayed even throughout the year, but we've been increasing the utilization of our factory every quarter. By keeping our factory utilization high, we will keep our costs down by allocating the fixed plant costs over a greater number of units. Naturally, this causes our cost per unit to be lower than it would be otherwise.

Emily: Yes, but what good is this if we have been unable to sell everything that we make? Our inventory is also increasing.

Nelson: This is true. However, our unit costs are lower because of the additional production. When these lower costs are matched against sales, it has a positive impact on our earnings.

Emily: Are you saying that we are able to create additional earnings merely by building inventory? Can this be true?

Nelson: Well, I've never thought about it quite that way . . . but I guess so.

Emily: And another thing. What will happen if we begin to reduce our production in order to liquidate the inventory? Don't tell me our earnings will go down even though our production effort drops!

Nelson: Well . . .

Emily: There must be a better way. I'd like our quarterly income statements to reflect what's really going on. I don't want our income reports to reward building inventory and penalize reducing inventory.

Nelson: I'm not sure what I can do—we have to follow generally accepted accounting principles.

1. Why does reporting income under generally accepted accounting principles "reward" building inventory and "penalize" reducing inventory?
2. ⬤▭▭▭▸ What advice would you give to Nelson in responding to Emily's concern about the present method of profit reporting?

SA 5-3
Segmented contribution margin analysis

ACD Inc. manufactures and sells devices used in cardiovascular surgery. The company has two salespersons, Harken and King.

A contribution margin by salesperson report was prepared as follows:

ACD Inc.
Contribution Margin by Salesperson

	Harken	King
Sales	$180,000	$200,000
Variable cost of goods sold	81,000	130,000
Manufacturing margin	$ 99,000	$ 70,000
Variable promotion expenses	$ 52,200	$ 18,0
Variable sales commission expenses	19,800	2
	$ 72,000	$
Contribution margin	$ 27,000	
Manufacturing margin as a percent of sales		
(manufacturing margin ratio)	55.00%	
Contribution margin ratio	15.0	

Interpret the report, and provide recommendations to the two salespersons for improving profitability.

SA 5-4
Margin analysis

Empire Equipment Inc. manufactures and sells kitchen cooking products throughout the state. The company employs four salespersons. The following contribution margin by salesperson analysis was prepared:

Empire Equipment Inc.
Contribution Margin Analysis by Salesperson

	Borland	Chow	Juarez	Mann
Sales	$130,000	$150,000	$140,000	$100,000
Variable cost of goods sold	52,000	90,000	84,000	60,000
Manufacturing margin	$ 78,000	$ 60,000	$ 56,000	$ 40,000
Variable selling expenses:				
Commissions	$ 6,000	$ 7,500	$ 7,000	$ 5,000
Promotion expenses	39,500	37,500	35,000	25,000
Total variable selling expenses	$ 45,500	$ 45,000	$ 42,000	$ 30,000
Contribution margin	$ 32,500	$ 15,000	$ 14,000	$ 10,000

1. Calculate the manufacturing margin as a percent of sales and the contribution margin ratio for each salesperson.
2. Explain the results of the analysis.

SA 5-5
Contribution margin analysis

Picasso Art Supply Company sells artistic supplies to retailers in three different states—North Carolina, Tennessee, and Virginia. The following profit analysis by state was prepared by the company:

	North Carolina	Tennessee	Virginia
Revenue	$400,000	$350,000	$420,000
Cost of goods sold	200,000	190,000	200,000
Gross profit	$200,000	$160,000	$220,000
Selling expenses	130,000	120,000	150,000
Income from operations	$ 70,000	$ 40,000	$ 70,000

The following fixed costs have also been provided:

	North Carolina	Tennessee	Virginia
Fixed manufacturing costs	$40,000	$80,000	$45,000
Fixed selling expenses	30,000	48,000	40,400

In addition, assume that inventories have been negligible.

Management believes it could increase state sales by 20%, without increasing any of the fixed costs, by spending an additional $15,000 per state on advertising.

1. Prepare a contribution margin by state report for Picasso Art Supply Company.
2. Determine how much state operating profit will be generated for an additional $15,000 per state on advertising.
3. Which state will provide the greatest profit return for a $15,000 increase in advertising? Why?

Goll Company is a family-owned business in which you own 20% of the common stock and your brothers and sisters own the remaining shares. The employment contract of Goll's new president, Glen Nash, stipulates a base salary of $150,000 per year plus 7% of income from operations in excess of $800,000. Nash uses the absorption costing method of reporting income from operations, which has averaged approximately $1,000,000 for the past several years.

Sales for 2008, Nash's first year as president of Goll Company, are estimated at 100,000 units at a selling price of $60 per unit. To maximize the use of Goll's productive capacity,

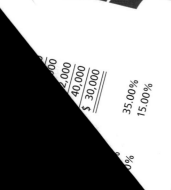

Nash has decided to manufacture 150,000 units, rather than the 100,000 units of estimated sales. The beginning inventory at January 1, 2008, is insignificant in amount, and the manufacturing costs and selling and administrative expenses for the production of 100,000 and 150,000 units are as follows:

100,000 Units to Be Manufactured

	Total Cost	Number of Units	Unit Cost
Manufacturing costs:			
Variable	$3,200,000	100,000	$32
Fixed	900,000	100,000	9
Total	$4,100,000		$41
Selling and administrative expenses:			
Variable	$ 900,000		
Fixed	300,000		
Total	$1,200,000		

150,000 Units to Be Manufactured

	Total Cost	Number of Units	Unit Cost
Manufacturing costs:			
Variable	$4,800,000	150,000	$32
Fixed	900,000	150,000	6
Total	$5,700,000		$38
Selling and administrative expenses:			
Variable	$ 900,000		
Fixed	300,000		
Total	$1,200,000		

1. In one group, prepare an absorption costing income statement for the year ending December 31, 2008, based upon sales of 100,000 units and the manufacture of 100,000 units. In the other group, conduct the same analysis, assuming production of 150,000 units.
2. ▭▭▭ Explain the difference in the income from operations reported in (1).
3. Compute Nash's total salary for the year 2008, based on sales of 100,000 units and the manufacture of 100,000 units (Group 1) and 150,000 units (Group 2). Compare your answers.
4. ▭▭▭ In addition to maximizing the use of Goll Company's productive capacity, why might Nash wish to manufacture 150,000 units rather than 100,000 units?
5. ▭▭▭ Can you suggest an alternative way in which Nash's salary could be determined, using a base salary of $150,000 and 7% of income from operations in excess of $800,000, so that the salary could not be increased by simply manufacturing more units?

Answers to Self-Examination Questions

1. **B** The contribution margin of $260,000 (answer B) is determined by deducting all of the variable costs ($400,000 + $90,000) from sales ($750,000).

2. **A** In a period in which the number of units manufactured exceeds the number of units sold, the income from operations reported under the absorption costing concept is larger than the income from operations reported under the variable costing concept (answer A). This is because a portion of the fixed manufacturing costs are deferred when the absorption costing concept is used. This deferment has the effect of excluding a portion of the fixed manufacturing costs from the current cost of goods sold.

3. **D** (6,000 units × $20 per unit). Answer A incorrectly calculates the difference in income from operations using the variable cost per unit, while Answer B incorrectly calculates the difference in income from operations using the total cost per unit. Answer C is incorrect because variable costing income from operations will be greater than absorption costing income from operations when units manufactured is less than units sold.

4. **C** [2,000 units × ($150,000/12,000 units)]. Answers A and B incorrectly calculate the difference in income from operations using variable cost per unit. When production exceeds sales, absorption costing will include fixed costs in the ending inventory, which causes cost of goods sold to decline and income from operations to increase. Thus, income from operations would not decline (answer D) for a production level of 12,000 units.

5. **C**   A difference between planned and actual sales can be attributed to a unit price factor. The $45,000 decrease (answer C) attributed to the quantity factor is determined as follows:

Decrease in number of units sold	5,000
Planned unit sales price	× $9
Quantity factor—decrease	$45,000

The unit price factor can be determined as follows:

Increase in unit sales price	$1
Actual number of units sold	× 80,000
Price factor—increase	$80,000

The increase of $80,000 attributed to the price factor less the decrease of $45,000 attributed to the quantity factor accounts for the $35,000 increase in total sales.

Budgeting

objectives

After studying this chapter, you should be able to:

1 *Describe budgeting, its objectives, and its impact on human behavior.*

2 *Describe the basic elements of the budget process, the two major types of budgeting, and the use of computers in budgeting.*

3 *Describe the master budget for a manufacturing business.*

4 *Prepare the basic income statement budgets for a manufacturing business.*

5 *Prepare balance sheet budgets for a manufacturing business.*

The North Face

You may have financial goals for your life. To achieve these goals, it is necessary to plan for future expenses. For example, you may consider taking a part-time job to save money for school expenses for the coming school year. How much money would you need to earn and save in order to pay these expenses? One way to find an answer to this question would be to prepare a budget. For example, a budget would show an estimate of your expenses associated with school, such as tuition, fees, and books. In addition, you would have expenses for day-to-day living, such as rent, food, and clothing. You might also have expenses for travel and entertainment. Once the school year begins, you can use the budget as a tool for guiding your spending priorities during the year.

The budget is used in businesses in much the same way as it can be used in personal life. For example, The North Face sponsors mountain climbing expeditions throughout the year for professional and amateur climbers. These events require budgeting to plan for the trip expenses, much like you might use a budget to plan a vacation.

Budgeting is also used by The North Face to plan the manufacturing costs associated with its outdoor clothing and equipment production. For example, budgets would be used to determine the number of coats to be produced, number of people to be employed, and amount of material to be purchased. The budget provides the company a "game plan" for the year. In this chapter, you will see how budgets can be used for financial planning and control.

Nature and Objectives of Budgeting

If you were driving across the country, you might plan your trip with the aid of a road map. The road map would lay out your route across the country, identify stopovers, and reduce your chances of getting lost. In the same way, a **budget** charts a course for a business by outlining the plans of the business in financial terms. Like the road map, the budget can help a company navigate through the year and reach the destination, while minimizing bad results.

Although budgets are normally associated with profit-making businesses, they also play an important role in operating most units of government. For example, budgets are important in managing rural school districts and small villages as well as agencies of the federal government. Budgets are also important for managing the operations of churches, hospitals, and other nonprofit institutions. Individuals and families also use budgeting techniques in managing their financial affairs. In this chapter, we emphasize the principles of budgeting in the context of a business organized for profit.

OBJECTIVES OF BUDGETING

Budgeting involves (1) establishing specific goals, (2) executing plans to achieve the goals, and (3) periodically comparing actual results with the goals. These goals include both the overall business goals as well as the specific goals for the individual units within the business. Establishing specific goals for future operations is part of the *planning* function of management, while executing

The chart below shows the estimated portion of your total monthly income that should be budgeted for various living expenses.

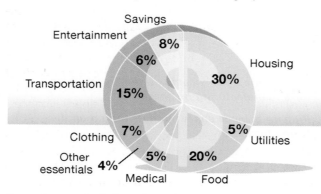

Source: Consumer Credit Counseling Service.

actions to meet the goals is the *directing* function of management. Periodically comparing actual results with these goals and taking appropriate action is the *controlling* function of management. The relationships of these functions are illustrated in Exhibit 1.

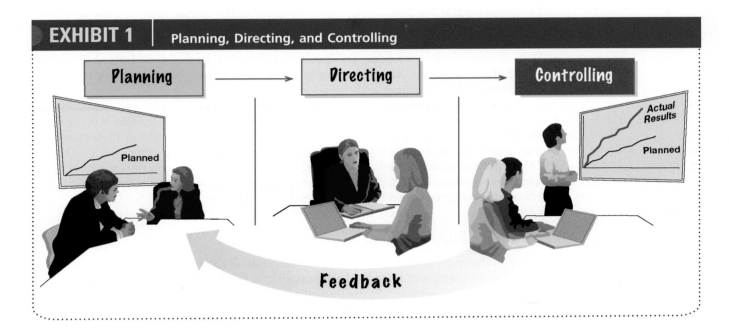

EXHIBIT 1 | Planning, Directing, and Controlling

Planning is also an important part of personal finances. Visa offers an online budget calculator and other helpful personal financial information at **http://www.practical moneyskills.com**.

Planning   A set of goals is often necessary to guide and focus individual and group actions. For example, students set academic goals, athletes set athletic goals, employees set career goals, and businesses set financial goals. In the same way, budgeting supports the planning process by requiring all organizational units to establish their goals for the upcoming period. These goals, in turn, motivate individuals and groups to perform at high levels. For example, General Motors Corporation is using its budget process to plan and execute a reduction of 25,000 manufacturing jobs through 2008 in order to better align its manufacturing capacity with the demand for vehicles.

Planning not only motivates employees to attain goals but also improves overall decision making. During the planning phase of the budget process, all viewpoints are considered, options identified, and cost reduction opportunities assessed. This effort leads to better decision making for the organization. As a result, the budget process may reveal opportunities or threats that were not known prior to the budget planning process. For example, the financial planning process helped Microsoft Corporation plan its expansion into the home and entertainment market with Xbox 360®.

Directing   Once the budget plans are in place, they can be used to direct and coordinate operations in order to achieve the stated goals. For example, your goal to receive an "A" in a course would result in certain activities, such as reading the book, completing assignments, participating in class, and studying for exams. Such actions are fairly easy to direct and coordinate. A business, however, is much more complex and requires more formal direction and coordination. The budget is one way to direct and coordinate business activities and units to achieve stated goals. The budgetary units of an organization are called **responsibility centers**. Each responsibility center is led by a manager who has the authority over and responsibility for the unit's performance.

If there is a change in the external environment, the budget process can also be used by unit managers to readjust the operations. For example, S-K-I Limited uses weather information to plan expenditures at its Killington and Mt. Snow ski resorts in Vermont. When the weather is forecasted to turn cold and dry, the company increases expenditures in snow-making activities and adds to the staff in order to serve a greater number of skiers.

Controlling   As time passes, the actual performance of an operation can be compared against the planned goals. This provides prompt feedback to employees about their performance. If necessary, employees can use such *feedback* to adjust their activities in the future. For example, a salesperson may be given a quota to achieve $100,000 in sales for the period. If the actual sales are only $75,000, the salesperson can use this feedback about underperformance to change sales tactics and improve future sales. Feedback is not only helpful to individuals, but it can also redirect a complete organization. For example, Eastman Kodak Company is responding to recent declines in the traditional chemical-based photo imaging business with an ambitious strategy to expand on-demand photo printing and digital image solutions.

Comparing actual results to the plan also helps prevent unplanned expenditures. The budget encourages employees to establish their spending priorities. For example, departments in universities have budgets to support faculty travel to conferences and meetings. The travel budget communicates to the faculty the upper limit on travel. Often, desired travel exceeds the budget. Thus, the budget requires the faculty to prioritize travel-related opportunities. In the next chapter, we will discuss comparing actual costs with budgeted costs in greater detail.

HUMAN BEHAVIOR AND BUDGETING

In the budgeting process, business, team, and individual goals are established. Human behavior problems can arise if (1) the budget goal is too tight and thus is very hard for the employees to achieve, (2) the budget goal is too loose and thus is very easy for the employees to achieve, or (3) the budget goals of the business conflict with the objectives of the employees. This is illustrated in Exhibit 2.

EXHIBIT 2 | **Human Behavior Problems in Budgeting**

Budget Goals Too Tight   Budget Goals Too Loose   Conflicting Budget Goals

Setting Budget Goals Too Tightly   People can become discouraged if performance expectations are set too high. For example, would you be inspired or discouraged by a guitar instructor expecting you to play like Eric Clapton after only a few lessons? You'd probably be discouraged. This same kind of problem can occur in businesses if employees view budget goals as unrealistic or unachievable. In such a case, the budget discourages employees from achieving the goals. On the other hand, aggressive but attainable goals are likely to inspire employees to achieve the goals. Therefore, it is important that employees (managers and nonmanagers) be involved in establishing reasonable budget estimates.

Involving all employees encourages cooperation both within and among departments. It also increases awareness of each department's importance to the overall objectives of the company. Employees view budgeting more positively when they have an opportunity to participate in the budget-setting process. This is because employees with a greater sense of control over the budget process will have a greater commitment to achieving its goals. In such cases, budgets are valuable planning tools that increase the possibility of achieving business goals.

Loose budgets may be appropriate in settings involving high uncertainty, such as research and development. The loose budget acts as a "shock absorber," giving managers maneuvering room to minimize work disruptions.

The state of Illinois' budget process requires unspent budget monies to be returned to the state when the fiscal year ends. According to the state comptroller, this encourages "an orgy of spending" at the end of a fiscal year.

Setting Budget Goals Too Loosely   Although it is desirable to establish attainable goals, it is undesirable to plan lower goals than may be possible. Such budget "padding" is termed **budgetary slack**. An example of budgetary slack is including spare employees in the plan. Managers may plan slack in the budget in order to provide a "cushion" for unexpected events or improve the appearance of operations. Budgetary slack can be avoided if lower- and mid-level managers are required to support their spending requirements with operational plans.

Slack budgets can cause employees to develop a "spend it or lose it" mentality. This often occurs at the end of the budget period when actual spending is less than the budget. Employees may attempt to spend the remaining budget (purchase equipment, hire consultants, purchase supplies) in order to avoid having the budget cut next period.

Setting Conflicting Budget Goals   **Goal conflict** occurs when individual self-interest differs from business objectives or when different departments are given conflicting objectives. Often, such conflicts are subtle. For example, the Sales Department manager may be given a sales goal, while the Manufacturing Department manager may be given a cost reduction goal. It is possible for both goals to conflict. The Sales Department may increase sales by promising customers small product deviations that are difficult and unprofitable to make. This would increase sales at the expense of Manufacturing's expense reduction goal and impact the overall profitability objectives of the firm. Likewise, Manufacturing may schedule the plant for maximum manufacturing efficiency with little regard for actual customer product demand. This would reduce manufacturing costs at the expense of the sales goal and reduce the overall profitability of the firm. Goal conflict can be avoided if budget goals are carefully designed for consistency across all areas of the organization.

Integrity, Objectivity, and Ethics in Business

ETHICS

BUDGET GAMES

The budgeting system is designed to plan and control a business. However, it is common for the budget to be "gamed" by its participants. For example, managers may pad their budgets with excess resources. In this way, the managers have additional resources for unexpected events during the period. If the budget is being used to establish the incentive plan, then sales managers have incentives to understate the sales potential of a territory in order to ensure hitting their quotas. Other times, managers engage in "land grabbing," which occurs when they overstate the sales potential of a territory in order to guarantee access to resources. If managers believe that unspent resources will not roll over to future periods, then they may be encouraged to "spend it or lose it," causing wasteful expenditures. These types of problems can be partially overcome by separating the budget into planning and incentive components. This is why many organizations have two budget processes, one for resource planning and another, more challenging budget, for motivating managers.

Budgeting Systems

Budgeting systems vary among businesses because of such factors as organizational structure, complexity of operations, and management philosophy. Differences in budget systems are even more significant among different types of businesses, such as manufacturers and service businesses. The details of a budgeting system used by an automobile manufacturer such as Ford Motor Company would obviously differ from a service company such as American Airlines. However, the basic budgeting concepts illustrated in the following paragraphs apply to all types of businesses and organizations.

The budgetary period for operating activities normally includes the fiscal year of a business. A year is short enough that future operations can be estimated fairly accurately, yet long enough that the future can be viewed in a broad context. However, to achieve effective control, the annual budgets are usually subdivided into shorter time periods, such as quarters of the year, months, or weeks.

A variation of fiscal-year budgeting, called **continuous budgeting**, maintains a 12-month projection into the future. The 12-month budget is continually revised by removing the data for the period just ended and adding estimated budget data for the same period next year, as shown in Exhibit 3.

Developing budgets for the next fiscal year usually begins several months prior to the end of the current year. This responsibility is normally assigned to a budget committee. Such a committee often consists of the budget director and such high-level executives as the controller, the treasurer, the production manager, and the sales manager. Once the budget has been approved, the budget process is monitored and summarized by the Accounting Department, which reports to the committee.

There are several methods of developing budget estimates. One method, termed **zero-based budgeting**, requires managers to estimate sales, production, and other operating data as though operations are being started for the first time. This approach has the benefit of taking a fresh view of operations each year. A more common approach is to start with last year's budget and revise it for actual results and expected changes for the coming year. Two major budgets using this approach are the static budget and the flexible budget.

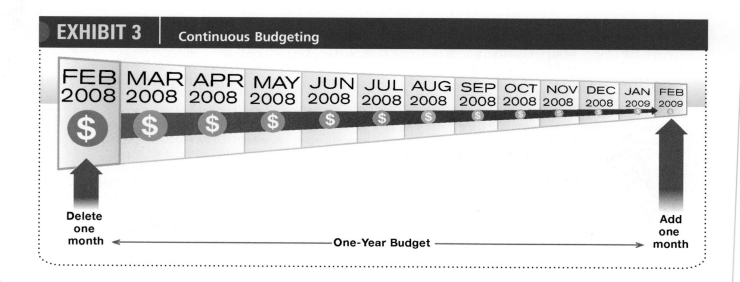

EXHIBIT 3 | **Continuous Budgeting**

FEB 2008 · MAR 2008 · APR 2008 · MAY 2008 · JUN 2008 · JUL 2008 · AUG 2008 · SEP 2008 · OCT 2008 · NOV 2008 · DEC 2008 · JAN 2009 · FEB 2009

Delete one month ←——————— One-Year Budget ———————→ Add one month

STATIC BUDGET

A **static budget** shows the expected results of a responsibility center for only one activity level. Once the budget has been determined, it is not changed, even if the activity changes. Static budgeting is used by many service companies and for some administrative functions of manufacturing companies, such as purchasing, engineering, and accounting. For example, the Assembly Department manager for Colter Manufacturing Company prepared the static budget for the upcoming year, shown in Exhibit 4.

EXHIBIT 4

Static Budget

	A	B	
	Colter Manufacturing Company		
	Assembly Department Budget		
	For the Year Ending July 31, 2008		
1	Direct labor	$40,000	1
2	Electric power	5,000	2
3	Supervisor salaries	15,000	3
4	Total department costs	$60,000	4

A disadvantage of static budgets is that they do not adjust for changes in activity levels. For example, assume that the actual amounts spent by the Assembly Department of Colter Manufacturing totaled $72,000, which is $12,000 or 20% ($12,000/$60,000) more than budgeted. Is this good news or bad news? At first you might think that this is a bad result. However, this conclusion may not be valid, since static budget results may be difficult to interpret. To illustrate, assume that the assembly manager developed the budget based on plans to assemble *8,000* units during the year. However, if *10,000* units were actually produced, should the additional $12,000 in spending in excess of the budget be considered "bad news"? Maybe not. The Assembly Department provided 25% (2,000 units/8,000 units) more output for only 20% more cost.

Business Connections

REAL WORLD

BUILD VERSUS HARVEST

Budgeting systems are not "one size fits all" solutions but must adapt to the underlying business conditions. For example, a business can adopt either a build strategy or a harvest strategy. A *build* strategy is one where the business is designing, launching, and growing new products and markets. Build strategies often require short-term profit sacrifice in order to grow market share. Apple Computer, Inc.'s iPod® is an example of a product managed under a build strategy. A *harvest* strategy is often employed for business units with mature products enjoying high market share in low-growth industries. Harvest strategies maximize short-term earnings and cash flow, sometimes at the expense of market share. Often the term "cash cow" is used to describe a product managed under a harvest strategy. H.J. Heinz Company's Ketchup® and Ivory soap are examples of such products. Compared to the harvest strategy, a build strategy often has greater uncertainty, unpredictability, and change. The differences between build and harvest strategies imply different budgeting approaches.

The build strategy should employ a budget approach that is flexible to the uncertainty of the business. Thus,

budgets should adapt to changing conditions by allowing periodic revisions and flexible targets. Often the managers controlled by the budget will participate in setting budget targets, so that all uncertainties are considered. In addition, the budget will complement other, more subjective, evaluation criteria. Overall, the budget serves as a short-term planning tool to guide management in executing an uncertain and evolving product market strategy.

Under the harvest strategy, the business is often much more stable and is managed to maximize profitability and cash flow. Cost control is much more important in a harvest strategy; thus, the budget is used to restrict the actions of managers. In addition, the managers controlled by the budget often do not participate in its development. Rather, the budget is imposed. In a harvest business, the budget is the major control tool and is often not supplemented with other more subjective performance measures.

FLEXIBLE BUDGET

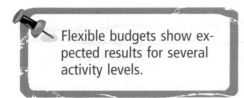

Flexible budgets show expected results for several activity levels.

Unlike static budgets, **flexible budgets** show the expected results of a responsibility center for several activity levels. You can think of a flexible budget as a series of static budgets for different levels of activity. Such budgets are especially useful in estimating and controlling factory costs and operating expenses. Exhibit 5 is a flexible budget for the annual manufacturing expense in the Assembly Department of Colter Manufacturing Company.

EXHIBIT 5

Flexible Budget

	A	B	C	D	
	Colter Manufacturing Company				
	Assembly Department Budget				
	For the Year Ending July 31, 2008				
		Level 1	Level 2	Level 3	
1	Units of production	8,000	9,000	10,000	1
2	Variable cost:				2
3	Direct labor ($5 per unit)	$40,000	$45,000	$50,000	3
4	Electric power ($0.50 per unit)	4,000	4,500	5,000	4
5	Total variable cost	$44,000	$49,500	$55,000	5
6	Fixed cost:				6
7	Electric power	$ 1,000	$ 1,000	$ 1,000	7
8	Supervisor salaries	15,000	15,000	15,000	8
9	Total fixed cost	$16,000	$16,000	$16,000	9
10	Total department costs	$60,000	$65,500	$71,000	10

Many hospitals use flexible budgeting to plan the number of nurses for patient floors. These budgets use a measure termed "relative value units," which is a measure of nursing effort. The more patients and the more severe their illnesses, the higher the total relative value units, and thus the higher the staffing budget.

When constructing a flexible budget, we first identify the relevant activity levels. In Exhibit 5, these are 8,000, 9,000, and 10,000 units of production. Alternative activity bases, such as machine hours or direct labor hours, may be used in measuring the volume of activity. Second, we identify the fixed and variable cost components of the costs being budgeted. For example, in Exhibit 5, the electric power cost is separated into its fixed cost ($1,000 per year) and variable cost ($0.50 per unit). Lastly, we prepare the budget for each activity level by multiplying the variable cost per unit by the activity level and then adding the monthly fixed cost.

With a flexible budget, the department manager can be evaluated by comparing actual expenses to the budgeted amount for actual activity. For example, if Colter Manufacturing Company's Assembly Department actually spent $72,000 to produce 10,000 units, the manager would be considered over budget by $1,000 ($72,000 − $71,000). Under the static budget in Exhibit 4, the department was $12,000 over budget. Exhibit 6

Example Exercise 6-1

objective 2

At the beginning of the period, the Assembly Department budgeted direct labor of $45,000 and supervisor salaries of $30,000 for 5,000 hours of production. The department actually completed 6,000 hours of production. Determine the budget for the department, assuming that it uses flexible budgeting.

Follow My Example 6-1

Variable cost:
Direct labor (6,000 hours × $9* per hour) $54,000

Fixed cost:
Supervisor salaries 30,000
Total department costs $84,000

*$45,000/5,000 hours

For Practice: PE 6-1A, PE 6-1B

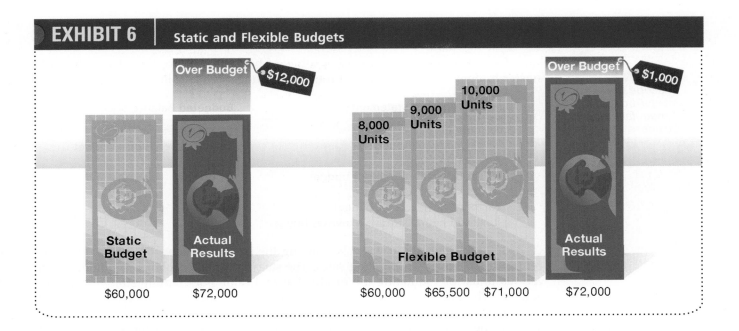

| | EXHIBIT 6 | Static and Flexible Budgets |

Over Budget $12,000

8,000 Units   9,000 Units   10,000 Units

Over Budget $1,000

| Static Budget | Actual Results | | Flexible Budget | | | Actual Results |
| $60,000 | $72,000 | | $60,000 | $65,500 | $71,000 | $72,000 |

illustrates this comparison. The flexible budget for the Assembly Department is much more accurate than the static budget, because budget amounts adjust for changes in activity.

COMPUTERIZED BUDGETING SYSTEMS

In developing budgets, firms use a variety of computerized approaches. A recent survey reported that 67% of the respondents relied on spreadsheets for budgeting and planning.[1] The remaining firms use integrated computerized budget and planning (B&P) systems. Such systems speed up and reduce the cost of preparing the budget. This is especially true when large quantities of data need to be processed. The same survey reported that companies relying on spreadsheets required 30 more days to prepare the budget than those relying on integrated B&P systems. For example, Fujitsu, a major Japanese technology company, used B&P software to streamline its budgeting process from 6 to 8 weeks down to 10 to 15 days.

Integrated B&P software is also useful in continuous budgeting. The newest B&P systems are accomplishing this by using Web-based applications to link thousands of employees together. With these systems, employees can input budget information onto the Web pages that are automatically aggregated and summarized throughout the organization. In this way, an organization can link the top-level strategy to the lower-level operational goals—and do so quickly and consistently across the organization. The use of Web-based B&P systems is moving companies closer to the real-time budget, wherein the budget is being "rolled" every day and represents the best assumptions at any moment in time.[2]

Managers often use computer spreadsheets or simulation models to represent the operating and budget relationships. By using computer simulation models, the impact of various operating alternatives on the budget can be assessed. For example, the budget can be revised to show the impact of a proposed change in indirect labor wage rates. Likewise, the budgetary effect of a proposed product line can be determined. In the next section, we illustrate how a company ties its budgets together, using a master budget.

---

1 Tim Reason, "Budgeting in the Real World," *CFO Magazine,* July 1, 2005.
2 Janet Kersnar, "Rolling Along," *CFO Europe,* September 14, 2004.

Master Budget

Manufacturing operations require a series of budgets that are linked together in a **master budget**. The major parts of the master budget are as follows:

Budgeted Income Statement	Budgeted Balance Sheet
Sales budget	Cash budget
Cost of goods sold budget:	Capital expenditures budget
Production budget	
Direct materials purchases budget	
Direct labor cost budget	
Factory overhead cost budget	
Selling and administrative expenses budget	

Exhibit 7 shows the relationship among the income statement budgets. The budget process begins by estimating sales. The sales information is then provided to the various units for estimating the production and selling and administrative expenses budgets. The production budgets are used to prepare the direct materials purchases, direct labor cost, and factory overhead cost budgets. These three budgets are used to develop the cost of goods sold budget. Once these budgets and the selling and administrative expenses budget have been completed, the budgeted income statement can be prepared, as we illustrate in the following section.

EXHIBIT 7

Income Statement Budgets

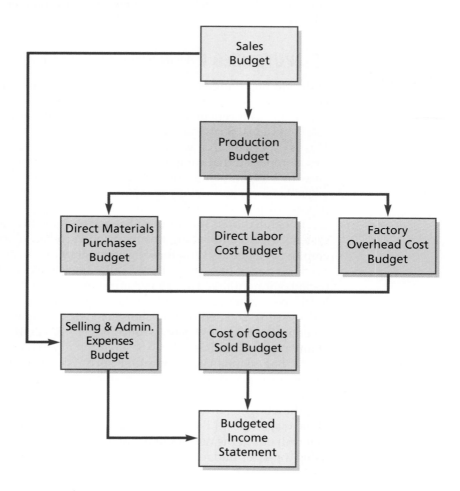

After the budgeted income statement has been developed, the budgeted balance sheet can be prepared. Two major budgets comprising the budgeted balance sheet are the cash budget and the capital expenditures budget, which we illustrate later.

Income Statement Budgets

objective 4

Prepare the basic income statement budgets for a manufacturing business.

In the following sections, we will illustrate the major elements of the income statement budget. We will use a small manufacturing business, Elite Accessories Inc., as the basis for our illustration.

SALES BUDGET

The **sales budget** normally indicates for each product (1) the quantity of estimated sales and (2) the expected unit selling price. These data are often reported by regions or by sales representatives.

In estimating the quantity of sales for each product, past sales volumes are often used as a starting point. These amounts are revised for factors that are expected to affect future sales, such as the factors listed below.

- backlog of unfilled sales orders
- planned advertising and promotion
- expected industry and general economic conditions
- productive capacity
- projected pricing policy
- findings of market research studies

Once an estimate of the sales volume is obtained, the expected sales revenue can be determined by multiplying the volume by the expected unit sales price. Exhibit 8 is the sales budget for Elite Accessories Inc.

EXHIBIT 8

Sales Budget

	A	B	C	D	
	Elite Accessories Inc.				
	Sales Budget				
	For the Year Ending December 31, 2008				
		Unit Sales	Unit Selling		
	Product and Region	Volume	Price	Total Sales	
1	Wallet:	287,000	$12.00	$ 3,444,000	1
2	East	241,000	12.00	2,892,000	2
3	West	528,000		$ 6,336,000	3
4	Total				4
5					5
6	Handbag:				6
7	East	156,400	$25.00	$ 3,910,000	7
8	West	123,600	25.00	3,090,000	8
9	Total	280,000		$ 7,000,000	9
10					10
11	Total revenue from sales			$13,336,000	11

For control purposes, management can compare actual sales and budgeted sales by product, region, or sales representative. Management would investigate any significant differences and take possible corrective actions.

PRODUCTION BUDGET

Production should be carefully coordinated with the sales budget to ensure that production and sales are kept in balance during the period. The number of units to be manufactured to meet budgeted sales and inventory needs for each product is set forth in the **production budget**. The budgeted volume of production is determined as follows:

Expected units to be sold
+ Desired units in ending inventory
− Estimated units in beginning inventory
Total units to be produced

Exhibit 9 is the production budget for Elite Accessories Inc.

EXHIBIT 9

Production Budget

	A	B	C	
	Elite Accessories Inc.			
	Production Budget			
	For the Year Ending December 31, 2008			
		Units		
		Wallet	Handbag	
1	Expected units to be sold (from Exhibit 8)	528,000	280,000	1
2	Plus desired ending inventory, December 31, 2008	80,000	60,000	2
3	Total	608,000	340,000	3
4	Less estimated beginning inventory, January 1, 2008	88,000	48,000	4
5	Total units to be produced	520,000	292,000	5

Example Exercise 6-2   objective **4**

Landon Awards Co. projected sales of 45,000 brass plaques for 2008. The estimated January 1, 2008, inventory is 3,000 units, and the desired December 31, 2008, inventory is 5,000 units. What is the budgeted production (in units) for 2008?

Follow My Example 6-2

Expected units to be sold	45,000
Plus desired ending inventory, December 31, 2008	5,000
Total	50,000
Less estimated beginning inventory, January 1, 2008	3,000
Total units to be produced	47,000

For Practice: PE 6-2A, PE 6-2B

DIRECT MATERIALS PURCHASES BUDGET

The production budget is the starting point for determining the estimated quantities of direct materials to be purchased. Multiplying these quantities by the expected unit purchase price determines the total cost of direct materials to be purchased.

> Materials required for production
> + Desired ending materials inventory
> − Estimated beginning materials inventory
> _____
> Direct materials to be purchased

In Elite Accessories Inc.'s production operations, leather and lining are required for wallets and handbags. The quantity of direct materials expected to be used for each unit of product is as follows:

Wallet:
  Leather: 0.30 square yard per unit
  Lining: 0.10 square yard per unit

Handbag:
  Leather: 1.25 square yards per unit
  Lining: 0.50 square yard per unit

Based on these data and the production budget, the **direct materials purchases budget** is prepared. As shown in the budget in Exhibit 10, for Elite Accessories Inc. to produce 520,000 wallets, 156,000 square yards (520,000 units × 0.30 square yard per unit) of leather are needed. Likewise, to produce 292,000 handbags, 365,000 square yards (292,000 units × 1.25 square yards per unit) of leather are needed. We can compute the needs for lining in a similar manner. Then adding the desired ending inventory for each material and deducting the estimated beginning inventory determines the

EXHIBIT 10

Direct Materials
Purchases Budget

	A	B	C	D	E	
			Elite Accessories Inc.			
			Direct Materials Purchases Budget			
			For the Year Ending December 31, 2008			
			Direct Materials			
			Leather	Lining	Total	
1	Square yards required for production:					1
2	Wallet (Note A)		156,000	52,000		2
3	Handbag (Note B)		365,000	146,000		3
4	Plus desired inventory, December 31, 2008		20,000	12,000		4
5	Total		541,000	210,000		5
6	Less estimated inventory, January 1, 2008		18,000	15,000		6
7	Total square yards to be purchased		523,000	195,000		7
8	Unit price (per square yard)		× $4.50	× $1.20		8
9	Total direct materials to be purchased		$2,353,500	$234,000	$2,587,500	9
10						10
11	Note A: Leather: 520,000 units × 0.30 sq. yd. per unit = 156,000 sq. yds.					11
12	Lining: 520,000 units × 0.10 sq. yd. per unit = 52,000 sq. yds.					12
13						13
14	Note B: Leather: 292,000 units × 1.25 sq. yds. per unit = 365,000 sq. yds.					14
15	Lining: 292,000 units × 0.50 sq. yd. per unit = 146,000 sq. yds.					15

amount of each material to be purchased. Multiplying these amounts by the estimated cost per square yard yields the total materials purchase cost.

The direct materials purchases budget helps management maintain inventory levels within reasonable limits. For this purpose, the timing of the direct materials purchases should be coordinated between the purchasing and production departments.

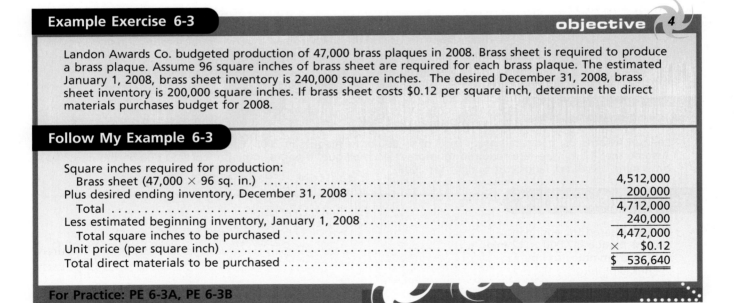

Example Exercise 6-3 objective 4

Landon Awards Co. budgeted production of 47,000 brass plaques in 2008. Brass sheet is required to produce a brass plaque. Assume 96 square inches of brass sheet are required for each brass plaque. The estimated January 1, 2008, brass sheet inventory is 240,000 square inches. The desired December 31, 2008, brass sheet inventory is 200,000 square inches. If brass sheet costs $0.12 per square inch, determine the direct materials purchases budget for 2008.

Follow My Example 6-3

Square inches required for production:	
Brass sheet (47,000 × 96 sq. in.)	4,512,000
Plus desired ending inventory, December 31, 2008	200,000
Total	4,712,000
Less estimated beginning inventory, January 1, 2008	240,000
Total square inches to be purchased	4,472,000
Unit price (per square inch)	× $0.12
Total direct materials to be purchased	$ 536,640

For Practice: PE 6-3A, PE 6-3B

DIRECT LABOR COST BUDGET

The production budget also provides the starting point for preparing the direct labor cost budget. For Elite Accessories Inc., the labor requirements for each unit of product are estimated as follows:

Wallet:
  Cutting Department: 0.10 hour per unit
  Sewing Department: 0.25 hour per unit

Handbag:
  Cutting Department: 0.15 hour per unit
  Sewing Department: 0.40 hour per unit

Based on these data and the production budget, Elite Accessories Inc. prepares the direct labor budget. As shown in the budget in Exhibit 11, for Elite Accessories Inc. to produce 520,000 wallets, 52,000 hours (520,000 units × 0.10 hour per unit) of labor in the Cutting Department are required. Likewise, to produce 292,000 handbags, 43,800 hours (292,000 units × 0.15 hour per unit) of labor in the Cutting Department are required. In a similar manner, we can determine the direct labor hours needed in the Sewing Department to meet the budgeted production. Multiplying the direct labor hours for each department by the estimated department hourly rate yields the total direct labor cost for each department.

EXHIBIT 11

Direct Labor Cost Budget

	A	B	C	D	E	
		Elite Accessories Inc.				
		Direct Labor Cost Budget				
		For the Year Ending December 31, 2008				
			Cutting	Sewing	Total	
1	Hours required for production:					1
2	Wallet (Note A)		52,000	130,000		2
3	Handbag (Note B)		43,800	116,800		3
4	Total		95,800	246,800		4
5	Hourly rate		× $12.00	× $15.00		5
6	Total direct labor cost		$1,149,600	$3,702,000	$4,851,600	6
7						7
8	Note A:	Cutting Department: 520,000 units × 0.10 hour per unit = 52,000 hours				8
9		Sewing Department: 520,000 units × 0.25 hour per unit = 130,000 hours				9
10						10
11	Note B:	Cutting Department: 292,000 units × 0.15 hour per unit = 43,800 hours				11
12		Sewing Department: 292,000 units × 0.40 hour per unit = 116,800 hours				12

The direct labor needs should be coordinated between the production and personnel departments. This ensures that there will be enough labor available for production.

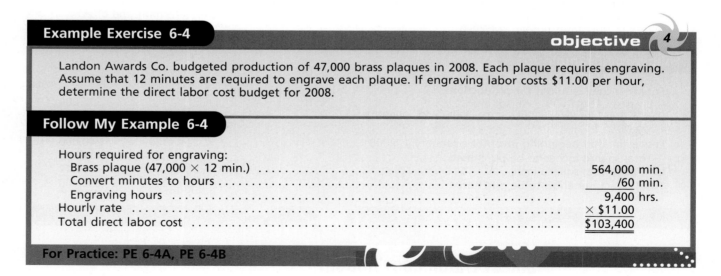

Example Exercise 6-4   objective 4

Landon Awards Co. budgeted production of 47,000 brass plaques in 2008. Each plaque requires engraving. Assume that 12 minutes are required to engrave each plaque. If engraving labor costs $11.00 per hour, determine the direct labor cost budget for 2008.

Follow My Example 6-4

Hours required for engraving:
Brass plaque (47,000 × 12 min.) .... 564,000 min.
Convert minutes to hours .... /60 min.
Engraving hours .... 9,400 hrs.
Hourly rate .... × $11.00
Total direct labor cost $103,400

For Practice: PE 6-4A, PE 6-4B

FACTORY OVERHEAD COST BUDGET

The estimated factory overhead costs necessary for production make up the factory overhead cost budget. This budget usually includes the total estimated cost for each item of factory overhead, as shown in Exhibit 12.

A business may prepare supporting departmental schedules, in which the factory overhead costs are separated into their fixed and variable cost elements. Such schedules

EXHIBIT 12

Factory Overhead
Cost Budget

	A	B	
	Elite Accessories Inc.		
	Factory Overhead Cost Budget		
	For the Year Ending December 31, 2008		
1	Indirect factory wages	$ 732,800	1
2	Supervisor salaries	360,000	2
3	Power and light	306,000	3
4	Depreciation of plant and equipment	288,000	4
5	Indirect materials	182,800	5
6	Maintenance	140,280	6
7	Insurance and property taxes	79,200	7
8	Total factory overhead cost	$2,089,080	8

enable department managers to direct their attention to those costs for which they are responsible and to evaluate performance.

COST OF GOODS SOLD BUDGET

The direct materials purchases budget, direct labor cost budget, and factory overhead cost budget are the starting point for preparing the **cost of goods sold budget**. To illustrate, these data are combined with the desired ending inventory and the estimated beginning inventory data below to determine the budgeted cost of goods sold shown in Exhibit 13.

Estimated inventories on January 1, 2008:
    Finished goods $1,095,600
    Work in process 214,400

Desired inventories on December 31, 2008:
    Finished goods $1,565,000
    Work in process 220,000

EXHIBIT 13

Cost of Goods
Sold Budget

	A	B	C	D	E	F	
		Elite Accessories Inc.					
		Cost of Goods Sold Budget					
		For the Year Ending December 31, 2008					
1	Finished goods inventory, January 1, 2008					$ 1,095,600	1
2	Work in process inventory, January 1, 2008			$ 214,400			2
3	Direct materials:						3
4	Direct materials inventory,						4
5	January 1, 2008 (Note A)		$ 99,000				5
6	Direct materials purchases (from Exhibit 10)		2,587,500				6
7	Cost of direct materials available for use		$2,686,500				7
8	Less direct materials inventory,						8
9	December 31, 2008 (Note B)		104,400				9
10	Cost of direct materials placed in production		$2,582,100				10
11	Direct labor (from Exhibit 11)		4,851,600				11
12	Factory overhead (from Exhibit 12)		2,089,080				12
13	Total manufacturing costs			9,522,780			13
14	Total work in process during period			$9,737,180			14
15	Less work in process inventory,						15
16	December 31, 2008			220,000			16
17	Cost of goods manufactured				9,517,180		17
18	Cost of finished goods available for sale				$10,612,780		18
19	Less finished goods inventory,						19
20	December 31, 2008				1,565,000		20
21	Cost of goods sold				$ 9,047,780		21
22							22
23	Note A: Leather:	18,000 sq. yds. × $4.50 per sq. yd.		$ 81,000			23
24	Lining:	15,000 sq. yds. × $1.20 per sq. yd.		18,000			24
25	Direct materials inventory, January 1, 2008			$ 99,000			25
26	Note B: Leather:	20,000 sq. yds. × $4.50 per sq. yd.		$ 90,000			26
27	Lining:	12,000 sq. yds. × $1.20 per sq. yd.		14,400			27
28	Direct materials inventory, December 31, 2008			$104,400			28

Direct materials purchases budget

Direct labor cost budget

Factory overhead cost budget

Example Exercise 6-5

objective **4**

Prepare a cost of goods sold budget for Landon Awards Co. using the information in Example Exercises 6-3 and 6-4. Assume the estimated inventories on January 1, 2008, for finished goods and work in process were $54,000 and $47,000, respectively. Also assume the desired inventories on December 31, 2008, for finished goods and work in process were $50,000 and $49,000, respectively. Factory overhead was budgeted for $126,000.

Follow My Example 6-5

Finished goods inventory, January 1, 2008			$ 54,000
Work in process inventory, January 1, 2008		$ 47,000	
Direct materials:			
Direct materials inventory, January 1, 2008 (240,000 × $0.12, from EE 6-3)	$ 28,800		
Direct materials purchases (from EE 6-3)	536,640		
Cost of direct materials available for use	$565,440		
Less direct materials inventory, December 31, 2008 (200,000 × $0.12, from EE 6-3)	24,000		
Cost of direct materials placed in production	$541,440		
Direct labor (from EE 6-4)	103,400		
Factory overhead	126,000		
Total manufacturing costs		770,840	
Total work in process during period		$817,840	
Less work in process inventory, December 31, 2008		49,000	
Cost of goods manufactured			768,840
Cost of finished goods available for sale			$822,840
Less finished goods inventory, December 31, 2008			50,000
Cost of goods sold			$772,840

For Practice: PE 6-5A, PE 6-5B

SELLING AND ADMINISTRATIVE EXPENSES BUDGET

The sales budget is often used as the starting point for estimating the selling and administrative expenses. For example, a budgeted increase in sales may require more advertising. Exhibit 14 is a selling and administrative expenses budget for Elite Accessories Inc.

Detailed supporting schedules are often prepared for major items in the selling and administrative expenses budget. For example, an advertising expense schedule for the Marketing Department should include the advertising media to be used (newspaper, direct mail, television), quantities (column inches, number of pieces, minutes), and the cost per unit. Attention to such details results in realistic budgets. Effective control results from assigning responsibility for achieving the budget to department supervisors.

EXHIBIT 14

Selling and Administrative Expenses Budget

	A	B	C	
	Elite Accessories Inc.			
	Selling and Administrative Expenses Budget			
	For the Year Ending December 31, 2008			
1	Selling expenses:			1
2	Sales salaries expense	$715,000		2
3	Advertising expense	360,000		3
4	Travel expense	115,000		4
5	Total selling expenses		$1,190,000	5
6	Administrative expenses:			6
7	Officers' salaries expense	$360,000		7
8	Office salaries expense	258,000		8
9	Office rent expense	34,500		9
10	Office supplies expense	17,500		10
11	Miscellaneous administrative expenses	25,000		11
12	Total administrative expenses		695,000	12
13	Total selling and administrative expenses		$1,885,000	13

BUDGETED INCOME STATEMENT

The budgets for sales, cost of goods sold, and selling and administrative expenses, combined with the data on other income, other expense, and income tax, are used to prepare the budgeted income statement. Exhibit 15 is a budgeted income statement for Elite Accessories Inc.

EXHIBIT 15

Budgeted Income Statement

	A	B	C	
	Elite Accessories Inc.			
	Budgeted Income Statement			
	For the Year Ending December 31, 2008			
1	Revenue from sales (from Exhibit 8)		$13,336,000	1
2	Cost of goods sold (from Exhibit 13)		9,047,780	2
3				3
4	Gross profit		$ 4,288,220	4
5	Selling and administrative expenses:			5
6	Selling expenses (from Exhibit 14)	$1,190,000		6
7				7
8	Administrative expenses (from Exhibit 14)	695,000		8
9	Total selling and administrative expenses		1,885,000	9
10	Income from operations		$ 2,403,220	10
11	Other income:			11
12	Interest revenue	$ 98,000		12
13	Other expenses:			13
14	Interest expense	90,000	8,000	14
15	Income before income tax		$ 2,411,220	15
16	Income tax		600,000	16
17	Net income		$ 1,811,220	17

— Sales budget
— Cost of goods sold budget
— Selling and administrative expenses budget

The budgeted income statement summarizes the estimates of all phases of operations. This allows management to assess the effects of the individual budgets on profits for the year. If the budgeted net income is too low, management could review and revise operating plans in an attempt to improve income.

Balance Sheet Budgets

objective 5

Prepare balance sheet budgets for a manufacturing business.

Balance sheet budgets are used by managers to plan financing, investing, and cash objectives for the firm. The balance sheet budgets illustrated for Elite Accessories Inc. in the following sections are the cash budget and the capital expenditures budget.

CASH BUDGET

The **cash budget** is one of the most important elements of the budgeted balance sheet. The cash budget presents the expected receipts (inflows) and payments (outflows) of cash for a period of time.

Information from the various operating budgets, such as the sales budget, the direct materials purchases budget, and the selling and administrative expenses budget, affects the cash budget. In addition, the capital expenditures budget, dividend policies, and plans for equity or long-term debt financing also affect the cash budget.

We illustrate the monthly cash budget for January, February, and March 2008, for Elite Accessories Inc. We begin by developing the estimated cash receipts and estimated cash payments portion of the cash budget.

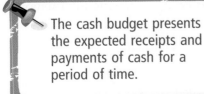

The cash budget presents the expected receipts and payments of cash for a period of time.

Estimated Cash Receipts Estimated cash receipts are planned additions to cash from sales and other sources, such as issuing securities or collecting interest. A supporting schedule can be used in determining the collections from sales. To illustrate this schedule, assume the following information for Elite Accessories Inc.:

Accounts receivable, January 1, 2008 . . . . $370,000

	January	February	March
Budgeted sales	$1,080,000	$1,240,000	$970,000

Elite Accessories Inc. expects to sell 10% of its merchandise for cash. Of the remaining 90% of the sales on account, 60% are expected to be collected in the month of the sale and the remainder in the next month. Thus, all of the accounts receivable are expected to be collectible.

Using this information, we prepare the schedule of collections from sales, shown in Exhibit 16. The cash receipts from sales on account are determined by adding the amounts collected from credit sales earned in the current period (60%) and the amounts accrued from sales in the previous period as accounts receivable (40%).

EXHIBIT 16

Schedule of Collections from Sales

	A	B	C	D	E	
		Elite Accessories Inc.				
		Schedule of Collections from Sales				
		For the Three Months Ending March 31, 2008				
			January	February	March	
1	Receipts from cash sales:					1
2		Cash sales (10% × current month's sales—				2
3		Note A)	$108,000	$ 124,000	$ 97,000	3
4						4
5	Receipts from sales on account:					5
6		Collections from prior month's sales (40% of				6
7		previous month's credit sales—Note B)	$370,000	$ 388,800	$446,400	7
8		Collections from current month's sales (60%				8
9		of current month's credit sales—Note C)	583,200	669,600	523,800	9
10	Total receipts from sales on account		$953,200	$1,058,400	$970,200	10
11						11
12	Note A:	$108,000 = $1,080,000 × 10%				12
13		$124,000 = $1,240,000 × 10%				13
14		$ 97,000 = $ 970,000 × 10%				14
15						15
16	Note B:	$370,000, given as January 1, 2008, Accounts Receivable balance				16
17		$388,800 = $1,080,000 × 90% × 40%				17
18		$446,400 = $1,240,000 × 90% × 40%				18
19						19
20	Note C:	$583,200 = $1,080,000 × 90% × 60%				20
21		$669,600 = $1,240,000 × 90% × 60%				21
22		$523,800 = $ 970,000 × 90% × 60%				22

Estimated Cash Payments Estimated cash payments are planned reductions in cash from manufacturing costs, selling and administrative expenses, capital expenditures, and other sources, such as buying securities or paying interest or dividends. A supporting schedule can be used in estimating the cash payments for manufacturing costs. To illustrate, the schedule shown in Exhibit 17 is based on the following information for Elite Accessories:

Accounts payable, January 1, 2008 . . . . $190,000

	January	February	March
Manufacturing costs	$840,000	$780,000	$812,000

EXHIBIT 17

Schedule of Payments
for Manufacturing
Costs

	A	B	C	D	E	
		Elite Accessories Inc.				
		Schedule of Payments for Manufacturing Costs				
		For the Three Months Ending March 31, 2008				
			January	February	March	
1	Payments of prior month's manufacturing costs					1
2	{[25% × previous month's manufacturing costs					2
3	(less depreciation)]—Note A}		$190,000	$204,000	$189,000	3
4	Payments of current month's manufacturing costs					4
5	{[75% × current month's manufacturing costs					5
6	(less depreciation)]—Note B}		612,000	567,000	591,000	6
7	Total payments		$802,000	$771,000	$780,000	7
8						8
9	Note A:	$190,000, given as January 1, 2008, Accounts Payable balance				9
10		$204,000 = ($840,000 − $24,000) × 25%				10
11		$189,000 = ($780,000 − $24,000) × 25%				11
12						12
13	Note B:	$612,000 = ($840,000 − $24,000) × 75%				13
14		$567,000 = ($780,000 − $24,000) × 75%				14
15		$591,000 = ($812,000 − $24,000) × 75%				15

Depreciation expense on machines is estimated to be $24,000 per month and is included in the manufacturing costs. The accounts payable were incurred for manufacturing costs. Elite Accessories Inc. expects to pay 75% of the manufacturing costs in the month in which they are incurred and the balance in the next month.

In Exhibit 17, the cash payments are determined by adding the amounts paid from costs incurred in the current period (75%) and the amounts accrued as a liability from costs in the previous period (25%). The $24,000 of depreciation must be excluded from all calculations, since depreciation is a noncash expense that should not be included in the cash budget.

Completing the Cash Budget To complete the cash budget for Elite Accessories Inc., as shown in Exhibit 18, assume that Elite Accessories Inc. is expecting the following:

Cash balance on January 1	$280,000
Quarterly taxes paid on March 31	150,000
Quarterly interest expense paid on January 10	22,500
Quarterly interest revenue received on March 21	24,500
Sewing equipment purchased in February	274,000

In addition, monthly selling and administrative expenses, which are paid in the month incurred, are estimated as follows:

	January	February	March
Selling and administrative expenses	$160,000	$165,000	$145,000

We can compare the estimated cash balance at the end of the period with the minimum balance required by operations. Assuming that the minimum cash balance for Elite Accessories Inc. is $340,000, we can determine any expected excess or deficiency.

The minimum cash balance protects against variations in estimates and for unexpected cash emergencies. For effective cash management, much of the minimum cash balance should be deposited in income-producing securities that can be readily converted to cash. U.S. Treasury Bills or Notes are examples of such securities.

EXHIBIT 18   Cash Budget

A	C	D	E	
Elite Accessories Inc.				
Cash Budget				
For the Three Months Ending March 31, 2008				
	January	February	March	
1 Estimated cash receipts from:				1
2 Cash sales (from Exhibit 16)	$ 108,000	$ 124,000	$ 97,000	2
3 Collections of accounts receivable				3
4 (from Exhibit 16)	953,200	1,058,400	970,200	4
5 Interest revenue			24,500	5
6 Total cash receipts	$1,061,200	$1,182,400	$1,091,700	6
7 Estimated cash payments for:				7
8 Manufacturing costs (from Exhibit 17)	$ 802,000	$ 771,000	$ 780,000	8
9 Selling and administrative expenses	160,000	165,000	145,000	9
10 Capital additions		274,000		10
11 Interest expense	22,500			11
12 Income taxes			150,000	12
13 Total cash payments	$ 984,500	$1,210,000	$1,075,000	13
14 Cash increase (decrease)	$ 76,700	$ (27,600)	$ 16,700	14
15 Cash balance at beginning of month	280,000	356,700	329,100	15
16 Cash balance at end of month	$ 356,700	$ 329,100	$ 345,800	16
17 Minimum cash balance	340,000	340,000	340,000	17
18 Excess (deficiency)	$ 16,700	$ (10,900)	$ 5,800	18

Schedule of collections from sales

Schedule of cash payments for manufacturing costs

Example Exercise 6-6

objective 5

Landon Awards Co. collects 25% of its sales on account in the month of the sale and 75% in the month following the sale. If sales on account are budgeted to be $100,000 for March and $126,000 for April, what are the budgeted cash receipts from sales on account for April?

Follow My Example 6-6

	April
Collections from March sales (75% × $100,000)	$ 75,000
Collections from April sales (25% × $126,000)	31,500
Total receipts from sales on account	$106,500

For Practice: PE 6-6A, PE 6-6B

CAPITAL EXPENDITURES BUDGET

The **capital expenditures budget** summarizes plans for acquiring fixed assets. Such expenditures are necessary as machinery and other fixed assets wear out, become obsolete, or for other reasons need to be replaced. In addition, expanding plant facilities may be necessary to meet increasing demand for a company's product.

The useful life of many fixed assets extends over long periods of time. In addition, the amount of the expenditures for such assets may vary from year to year. It is normal to project the plans for a number of periods into the future in preparing the capital expenditures budget. Exhibit 19 is a five-year capital expenditures budget for Elite Accessories Inc.

The capital expenditures budget should be considered in preparing the other operating budgets. For example, the estimated depreciation of new equipment affects the factory overhead cost budget and the selling and administrative expenses budget. The plans for financing the capital expenditures may also affect the cash budget.

EXHIBIT 19

Capital Expenditures Budget

	A	B	C	D	E	F	
	Elite Accessories Inc.						
	Capital Expenditures Budget						
	For the Five Years Ending December 31, 2012						
	Item	2008	2009	2010	2011	2012	
1	Machinery—Cutting Department	$400,000			$280,000	$360,000	1
2	Machinery—Sewing Department	274,000	$260,000	$560,000	200,000		2
3	Office equipment		90,000			60,000	3
4	Total	$674,000	$350,000	$560,000	$480,000	$420,000	4

BUDGETED BALANCE SHEET

The budgeted balance sheet estimates the financial condition at the end of a budget period. The budgeted balance sheet assumes that all operating budgets and financing plans are met. It is similar to a balance sheet based on actual data in the accounts. For this reason, we do not illustrate a budgeted balance sheet for Elite Accessories Inc. If the budgeted balance sheet indicates a weakness in financial position, revising the financing plans or other plans may be necessary. For example, a large amount of long-term debt in relation to stockholders' equity might require revising financing plans for capital expenditures. Such revisions might include issuing equity rather than debt.

At a Glance

1. Describe budgeting, its objectives, and its impact on human behavior.

Key Points	Key Learning Outcomes	Example Exercises	Practice Exercises
Budgeting involves (1) establishing plans (planning), (2) directing operations (directing), and (3) evaluating performance (controlling). In addition, budgets should be established to avoid human behavior problems.	• Describe the planning, directing, controlling, and feedback elements of the budget process. • Describe the behavioral issues associated with tight goals, loose goals, and goal conflict.		

2. Describe the basic elements of the budget process, the two major types of budgeting, and the use of computers in budgeting.

Key Points	Key Learning Outcomes	Example Exercises	Practice Exercises
The budget process is often initiated by the budget committee. The budget estimates received by the committee should be carefully studied, analyzed, revised, and integrated. The static and continuous budgets are two major budgeting approaches. Computers can be used to make the budget process more efficient and organizationally integrated.	• Describe a static budget and explain when it might be used. • Describe and prepare a flexible budget and explain when it might be used. • Describe the role of computers in the budget process.	6-1	6-1A, 6-1B

(continued)

3. Describe the master budget for a manufacturing business.

Key Points	Key Learning Outcomes	Example Exercises	Practice Exercises
The master budget consists of the budgeted income statement and budgeted balance sheet.	• Illustrate the connection between the major income statement and balance sheet budgets.		

4. Prepare the basic income statement budgets for a manufacturing business.

Key Points	Key Learning Outcomes	Example Exercises	Practice Exercises
The basic income statement budgets are the sales budget, production budget, direct materials purchases budget, direct labor cost budget, factory overhead cost budget, cost of goods sold budget, and selling and administrative expenses budget.	• Prepare a sales budget. • Prepare a production budget. • Prepare a direct materials purchases budget. • Prepare a direct labor cost budget. • Prepare a factory overhead cost budget. • Prepare a cost of goods sold budget. • Prepare a selling and administrative expenses budget.	6-2 6-3 6-4 6-5	6-2A, 6-2B 6-3A, 6-3B 6-4A, 6-4B 6-5A, 6-5B

5. Prepare balance sheet budgets for a manufacturing business.

Key Points	Key Learning Outcomes	Example Exercises	Practice Exercises
The cash budget and capital expenditures budget can be used in preparing the budgeted balance sheet.	• Prepare cash receipts and cash payments budgets. • Prepare a capital expenditures budget.	6-6	6-6A, 6-6B

Key Terms

budget (220)
budgetary slack (223)
capital expenditures budget (238)
cash budget (235)
continuous budgeting (224)
cost of goods sold budget (233)

direct materials purchases budget (230)
flexible budget (226)
goal conflict (223)
master budget (228)
production budget (229)

responsibility center (221)
sales budget (229)
static budget (225)
zero-based budgeting (224)

Illustrative Problem

Selected information concerning sales and production for Cabot Co. for July 2008 are summarized as follows:

a. Estimated sales:

Product K: 40,000 units at $30.00 per unit
Product L: 20,000 units at $65.00 per unit

b. Estimated inventories, July 1, 2008:

Material A: 4,000 lbs.	Product K: 3,000 units at $17 per unit	$ 51,000
Material B: 3,500 lbs.	Product L: 2,700 units at $35 per unit	94,500
	Total	$145,500

There were no work in process inventories estimated for July 1, 2008.

c. Desired inventories at July 31, 2008:

Material A: 3,000 lbs.	Product K: 2,500 units at $17 per unit	$ 42,500
Material B: 2,500 lbs.	Product L: 2,000 units at $35 per unit	70,000
	Total	$112,500

There were no work in process inventories desired for July 31, 2008.

d. Direct materials used in production:

	Product K	Product L
Material A:	0.7 lb. per unit	3.5 lbs. per unit
Material B:	1.2 lbs. per unit	1.8 lbs. per unit

e. Unit costs for direct materials:

Material A: $4.00 per lb.
Material B: $2.00 per lb.

f. Direct labor requirements:

	Department 1	Department 2
Product K	0.4 hour per unit	0.15 hour per unit
Product L	0.6 hour per unit	0.25 hour per unit

g.

	Department 1	Department 2
Direct labor rate	$12.00 per hour	$16.00 per hour

h. Estimated factory overhead costs for July:

Indirect factory wages	$200,000
Depreciation of plant and equipment	40,000
Power and light	25,000
Indirect materials	34,000
Total	$299,000

Instructions

1. Prepare a sales budget for July.
2. Prepare a production budget for July.
3. Prepare a direct materials purchases budget for July.
4. Prepare a direct labor cost budget for July.
5. Prepare a cost of goods sold budget for July.

Solution

1.

	A	B	C	D	
		Cabot Co.			
		Sales Budget			
		For the Month Ending July 31, 2008			
	Product	**Unit Sales Volume**	**Unit Selling Price**	**Total Sales**	
1	Product K	40,000	$30.00	$1,200,000	1
2	Product L	20,000	65.00	1,300,000	2
3	Total revenue from sales			$2,500,000	3

2.

	A	C	D	
		Cabot Co.		
		Production Budget		
		For the Month Ending July 31, 2008		
		Units		
		Product K	**Product L**	
1	Sales	40,000	20,000	1
2	Plus desired inventories at July 31, 2008	2,500	2,000	2
3	Total	42,500	22,000	3
4	Less estimated inventories, July 1, 2008	3,000	2,700	4
5	Total production	39,500	19,300	5

3.

	A	B	C	D	E	F	G	
			Cabot Co.					
			Direct Materials Purchases Budget					
			For the Month Ending July 31, 2008					
			Direct Materials					
			Material A		**Material B**		**Total**	
1	Units required for production:							1
2	Product K (39,500 × lbs. per unit)		27,650	lbs.*	47,400	lbs.*		2
3	Product L (19,300 × lbs. per unit)		67,550	**	34,740	**		3
4	Plus desired units of inventory,							4
5	July 31, 2008		3,000		2,500			5
6	Total		98,200	lbs.	84,640	lbs.		6
7	Less estimated units of inventory,							7
8	July 1, 2008		4,000		3,500			8
9	Total units to be purchased		94,200	lbs.	81,140	lbs.		9
10	Unit price		× $4.00		× $2.00			10
11	Total direct materials purchases		$376,800		$162,280		$539,080	11
12								12
13	*27,650 = 39,500 × 0.7 47,400 = 39,500 × 1.2							13
14	**67,550 = 19,300 × 3.5 34,740 = 19,300 × 1.8							14

4.

	A	B	C	D	E	F	G	
			Cabot Co.					
			Direct Labor Cost Budget					
			For the Month Ending July 31, 2008					
			Department 1		**Department 2**		**Total**	
1	Hours required for production:							1
2	Product K (39,500 × hours per unit)		15,800	*	5,925	*		2
3	Product L (19,300 × hours per unit)		11,580	**	4,825	**		3
4	Total		27,380		10,750			4
5	Hourly rate		× $12.00		× $16.00			5
6	Total direct labor cost		$328,560		$172,000		$500,560	6
7								7
8	*15,800 = 39,500 × 0.4 5,925 = 39,500 × 0.15							8
9	**11,580 = 19,300 × 0.6 4,825 = 19,300 × 0.25							9

5.

	A	B	C	D	
	Cabot Co.				
	Cost of Goods Sold Budget				
	For the Month Ending July 31, 2008				
1	Finished goods inventory, July 1, 2008			$ 145,500	1
2	Direct materials:				2
3	Direct materials inventory, July 1, 2008—(Note A)		$ 23,000		3
4	Direct materials purchases		539,080		4
5	Cost of direct materials available for use		$562,080		5
6	Less direct materials inventory, July 31, 2008—(Note B)		17,000		6
7	Cost of direct materials placed in production		$545,080		7
8	Direct labor		500,560		8
9	Factory overhead		299,000		9
10	Cost of goods manufactured			1,344,640	10
11	Cost of finished goods available for sale			$1,490,140	11
12	Less finished goods inventory, July 31, 2008			112,500	12
13	Cost of goods sold			$1,377,640	13
14					14
15	Note A:				15
16	Material A 4,000 lbs. at $4.00 per lb.	$16,000			16
17	Material B 3,500 lbs. at $2.00 per lb.	7,000			17
18	Direct materials inventory, July 1, 2008	$23,000			18
19					19
20	Note B:				20
21	Material A 3,000 lbs. at $4.00 per lb.	$12,000			21
22	Material B 2,500 lbs. at $2.00 per lb.	5,000			22
23	Direct materials inventory, July 31, 2008	$17,000			23

Self-Examination Questions

(Answers at End of Chapter)

1. A tight budget may create:
   A. budgetary slack.
   B. discouragement.
   C. a flexible budget.
   D. a "spend it or lose it" mentality.

2. The first step of the budget process is:
   A. plan.   C. control.
   B. direct.   D. feedback.

3. Static budgets are often used by:
   A. production departments.
   B. administrative departments.
   C. responsibility centers.
   D. capital projects.

4. The total estimated sales for the coming year is 250,000 units. The estimated inventory at the beginning of the year is 22,500 units, and the desired inventory at the end of the year is 30,000 units. The total production indicated in the production budget is:
   A. 242,500 units.   C. 280,000 units.
   B. 257,500 units.   D. 302,500 units.

5. Dixon Company expects $650,000 of credit sales in March and $800,000 of credit sales in April. Dixon historically collects 70% of its sales in the month of sale and 30% in the following month. How much cash does Dixon expect to collect in April?
   A. $800,000   C. $755,000
   B. $560,000   D. $1,015,000

Eye Openers

1. What are the three major objectives of budgeting?
2. What is the manager's role in a responsibility center?
3. Briefly describe the type of human behavior problems that might arise if budget goals are set too tightly.
4. Why should all levels of management and all departments participate in preparing and submitting budget estimates?

5. Give an example of budgetary slack.
6. What behavioral problems are associated with setting a budget too loosely?
7. What behavioral problems are associated with establishing conflicting goals within the budget?
8. When would a company use zero-based budgeting?
9. Under what circumstances would a static budget be appropriate?
10. How do computerized budgeting systems aid firms in the budgeting process?
11. What is the first step in preparing a master budget?
12. Why should the production requirements set forth in the production budget be carefully coordinated with the sales budget?
13. Why should the timing of direct materials purchases be closely coordinated with the production budget?
14. In preparing the budget for the cost of goods sold, what are the three budgets from which data on relevant estimates of quantities and costs are combined with data on estimated inventories?
15. a. Discuss the purpose of the cash budget.
    b. If the cash for the first quarter of the fiscal year indicates excess cash at the end of each of the first two months, how might the excess cash be used?
16. How does a schedule of collections from sales assist in preparing the cash budget?
17. Give an example of how the capital expenditures budget affects other operating budgets.

Practice Exercises

PE 6-1A
Flexible budgeting
obj. 2

At the beginning of the period, the Assembly Department budgeted direct labor of $110,500 and property taxes of $50,000 for 8,500 hours of production. The department actually completed 10,000 hours of production. Determine the budget for the department, assuming that it uses flexible budgeting.

PE 6-1B
Flexible budgeting
obj. 2

At the beginning of the period, the Fabricating Department budgeted direct labor of $18,400 and equipment depreciation of $14,000 for 800 hours of production. The department actually completed 700 hours of production. Determine the budget for the department, assuming that it uses flexible budgeting.

PE 6-2A
Production budget
obj. 4

OnTime Publishers Inc. projected sales of 220,000 schedule planners for 2008. The estimated January 1, 2008, inventory is 15,000 units, and the desired December 31, 2008, inventory is 11,000 units. What is the budgeted production (in units) for 2008?

PE 6-2B
Production budget
obj. 4

New England Candle Co. projected sales of 95,000 candles for 2008. The estimated January 1, 2008, inventory is 2,400 units, and the desired December 31, 2008, inventory is 3,000 units. What is the budgeted production (in units) for 2008?

PE 6-3A
Direct materials purchases budget
obj. 4

OnTime Publishers Inc. budgeted production of 216,000 schedule planners in 2008. Paper is required to produce a planner. Assume 90 square feet of paper are required for each planner. The estimated January 1, 2008, paper inventory is 100,000 square feet. The desired December 31, 2008, paper inventory is 160,000 square feet. If paper costs $0.08 per square foot, determine the direct materials purchases budget for 2008.

PE 6-3B
Direct materials purchases budget
obj. 4

New England Candle Co. budgeted production of 95,600 candles in 2008. Wax is required to produce a candle. Assume 8 ounces (one half of a pound) of wax is required for each candle. The estimated January 1, 2008, wax inventory is 1,400 pounds. The desired December 31, 2008, wax inventory is 1,100 pounds. If candle wax costs $3.60 per pound, determine the direct materials purchases budget for 2008.

PE 6-4A
Direct labor cost budget
obj. **4**

OnTime Publishers Inc. budgeted production of 216,000 schedule planners in 2008. Each planner requires assembly. Assume that 15 minutes are required to assemble each planner. If assembly labor costs $12.50 per hour, determine the direct labor cost budget for 2008.

PE 6-4B
Direct labor cost budget
obj. **4**

New England Candle Co. budgeted production of 95,600 candles in 2008. Each candle requires molding. Assume that 12 minutes are required to mold each candle. If molding labor costs $14.00 per hour, determine the direct labor cost budget for 2008.

PE 6-5A
Cost of goods sold budget
obj. **4**

Prepare a cost of goods sold budget for OnTime Publishers Inc. using the information in Practice Exercises 6-3A and 6-4A. Assume the estimated inventories on January 1, 2008, for finished goods and work in process were $43,000 and $22,000, respectively. Also assume the desired inventories on December 31, 2008, for finished goods and work in process were $40,000 and $25,000, respectively. Factory overhead was budgeted at $245,000.

PE 6-5B
Cost of goods sold budget
obj. **4**

Prepare a cost of goods sold budget for New England Candle Co. using the information in Practice Exercises 6-3B and 6-4B. Assume the estimated inventories on January 1, 2008, for finished goods and work in process were $14,000 and $6,300, respectively. Also assume the desired inventories on December 31, 2008, for finished goods and work in process were $12,000 and $7,000, respectively. Factory overhead was budgeted at $95,000.

PE 6-6A
Cash budget
obj. **5**

OnTime Publishers Inc. collects 30% of its sales on account in the month of the sale and 70% in the month following the sale. If sales on account are budgeted to be $400,000 for June and $360,000 for July, what are the budgeted cash receipts from sales on account for July?

PE 6-6B
Cash budget
obj. **5**

New England Candle Co. pays 10% of its purchases on account in the month of the purchase and 90% in the month following the purchase. If purchases are budgeted to be $14,000 for August and $16,000 for September, what are the budgeted cash payments for purchases on account for September?

Exercises

EX 6-1
Personal cash budget
objs. **2, 5**

✓ *a. December 31 cash balance, $2,900*

At the beginning of the 2008 school year, Monroe Baker decided to prepare a cash budget for the months of September, October, November, and December. The budget must plan for enough cash on December 31 to pay the spring semester tuition, which is the same as the fall tuition. The following information relates to the budget:

Cash balance, September 1 (from a summer job)	$6,500
Purchase season football tickets in September	140
Additional entertainment for each month	225
Pay fall semester tuition on September 3	3,500
Pay rent at the beginning of each month	350
Pay for food each month	215
Pay apartment deposit on September 2 (to be returned Dec. 15)	600
Part-time job earnings each month (net of taxes)	800

a. Prepare a cash budget for September, October, November, and December.
b. Are the budgets prepared as static budgets or flexible budgets?
c.  What are the budget implications for Monroe Baker?

EX 6-2
Flexible budget for selling and administrative expenses

objs. 2, 4

✓ *Total selling and administrative expenses at $140,000 sales, $65,550*

Master Electronics Company uses flexible budgets that are based on the following data:

Sales commissions	7% of sales
Advertising expense	18% of sales
Miscellaneous selling expense	$1,750 plus 4% of sales
Office salaries expense	$12,000 per month
Office supplies expense	5% of sales
Miscellaneous administrative expense	$1,400 per month plus 2% of sales

Prepare a flexible selling and administrative expenses budget for January 2008 for sales volumes of $100,000, $120,000, and $140,000. (Use Exhibit 5 as a model.)

EX 6-3
Static budget vs. flexible budget

objs. 2, 4

✓ *b. Excess of actual over budget for March, $100,000*

The production supervisor of the Machining Department for Landers Company agreed to the following monthly static budget for the upcoming year:

Landers Company
Machining Department
Monthly Production Budget

Wages	$ 960,000
Utilities	300,000
Depreciation	60,000
Total	$1,320,000

The actual amount spent and the actual units produced in the first three months of 2008 in the Machining Department were as follows:

	Amount Spent	Units Produced
January	$1,090,000	60,000
February	1,050,000	55,000
March	1,000,000	50,000

The Machining Department supervisor has been very pleased with this performance, since actual expenditures have been less than the monthly budget. However, the plant manager believes that the budget should not remain fixed for every month but should "flex" or adjust to the volume of work that is produced in the Machining Department. Additional budget information for the Machining Department is as follows:

Wages per hour	$16.00
Utility cost per direct labor hour	$5.00
Direct labor hours per unit	0.80
Planned unit production	75,000

a. Prepare a flexible budget for the actual units produced for January, February, and March in the Machining Department.
b. ➤ Compare the flexible budget with the actual expenditures for the first three months. What does this comparison suggest?

EX 6-4
Flexible budget for Fabrication Department

obj. 2

✓ *Total department cost at 12,000 units, $957,600*

Steelcase Inc. is one of the largest manufacturers of office furniture in the United States. In Grand Rapids, Michigan, it produces filing cabinets in two departments: Fabrication and Trim Assembly. Assume the following information for the Fabrication Department:

Steel per filing cabinet	50 pounds
Direct labor per filing cabinet	18 minutes
Supervisor salaries	$130,000 per month
Depreciation	$20,000 per month
Direct labor rate	$16 per hour
Steel cost	$1.25 per pound

Prepare a flexible budget for 12,000, 15,000, and 18,000 filing cabinets for the month of October 2008, similar to Exhibit 5, assuming that inventories are not significant.

EX 6-5
Sales and production budgets
obj. 4

✔ *b. Model DL total production, 7,420 units*

Melody Audio Company manufactures two models of speakers, DL and XL. Based on the following production and sales data for September 2007, prepare (a) a sales budget and (b) a production budget.

	DL	XL
Estimated inventory (units), September 1	380	140
Desired inventory (units), September 30	450	110
Expected sales volume (units):		
East Region	4,400	3,200
West Region	2,950	2,100
Unit sales price	$120.00	$170.00

EX 6-6
Professional fees earned budget
obj. 4

✔ *Total professional fees earned, $13,956,000*

Kimble and Sanchez, CPAs, offer three types of services to clients: auditing, tax, and small business accounting. Based on experience and projected growth, the following billable hours have been estimated for the year ending December 31, 2008:

	Billable Hours
Audit Department:	
Staff	34,500
Partners	5,200
Tax Department:	
Staff	27,700
Partners	4,150
Small Business Accounting Department:	
Staff	22,800
Partners	6,300

The average billing rate for staff is $120 per hour, and the average billing rate for partners is $240 per hour. Prepare a professional fees earned budget for Kimble and Sanchez, CPAs, for the year ending December 31, 2008, using the following column headings and showing the estimated professional fees by type of service rendered:

Billable Hours   **Hourly Rate**   **Total Revenue**

EX 6-7
Professional labor cost budget
obj. 4

✔ *Staff total labor cost, $6,375,000*

Based on the data in Exercise 6-6 and assuming that the average compensation per hour for staff is $75 and for partners is $140, prepare a professional labor cost budget for Kimble and Sanchez, CPAs, for the year ending December 31, 2008. Use the following column headings:

Staff   **Partners**

EX 6-8
Direct materials purchases budget
obj. 4

✔ *Total cheese purchases, $131,813*

Roma Frozen Pizza Inc. has determined from its production budget the following estimated production volumes for 12" and 16" frozen pizzas for November 2008:

	Units	
	12" Pizza	16" Pizza
Budgeted production volume	16,400	25,600

There are three direct materials used in producing the two types of pizza. The quantities of direct materials expected to be used for each pizza are as follows:

	12" Pizza	16" Pizza
Direct materials:		
Dough	1.00 lb. per unit	1.50 lbs. per unit
Tomato	0.60	0.90
Cheese	0.80	1.30

In addition, Roma has determined the following information about each material:

	Dough	Tomato	Cheese
Estimated inventory, November 1, 2008	675 lbs.	190 lbs.	525 lbs.
Desired inventory, November 30, 2008	480 lbs.	250 lbs.	375 lbs.
Price per pound	$1.20	$2.40	$2.85

Prepare November's direct materials purchases budget for Roma Frozen Pizza Inc.

EX 6-9
Direct materials purchases budget
obj. 4

✓ *Concentrate budgeted purchases, $90,900*

Coca-Cola Enterprises is the largest bottler of Coca-Cola® in North America. The company purchases Coke® and Sprite® concentrate from The Coca-Cola Company, dilutes and mixes the concentrate with carbonated water, and then fills the blended beverage into cans or plastic two-liter bottles. Assume that the estimated production for Coke and Sprite two-liter bottles at the Chattanooga, Tennessee, bottling plant are as follows for the month of June:

Coke	192,000 two-liter bottles
Sprite	148,000 two-liter bottles

In addition, assume that the concentrate costs $75 per pound for both Coke and Sprite and is used at a rate of 0.2 pound per 100 liters of carbonated water in blending Coke and 0.15 pound per 100 liters of carbonated water in blending Sprite. Assume that two-liter bottles cost $0.07 per bottle and carbonated water costs $0.05 per liter.
  Prepare a direct materials purchases budget for June 2008, assuming no changes between beginning and ending inventories for all three materials.

EX 6-10
Direct materials purchases budget
obj. 4

✓ *Total steel belt purchases, $1,108,625*

Anticipated sales for Goodstone Tire Company were 38,000 passenger car tires and 14,000 truck tires. There were no anticipated beginning finished goods inventories for either product. The planned ending finished goods inventories were 2,750 units for each product. Rubber and steel belts are used in producing passenger car and truck tires according to the following table:

	Passenger Car	Truck
Rubber	30 lbs. per unit	65 lbs. per unit
Steel belts	4 lbs. per unit	9 lbs. per unit

The purchase prices of rubber and steel are $2.90 and $3.50 per pound, respectively. The desired ending inventories of rubber and steel belts are 45,000 and 9,000 pounds, respectively. The estimated beginning inventories for rubber and steel belts are 72,000 and 6,000 pounds, respectively.
  The following direct materials purchases budget was prepared for Goodstone Tire Company:

Goodstone Tire Company
Direct Materials Purchases Budget
For the Year Ending December 31, 2008

	Rubber	Steel Belts	Total
Units required for production:			
Passenger tires	1,140,000[1] lbs.	152,000[3] lbs.	
Truck tires	910,000[2]	126,000[4]	
Total	2,050,000 lbs.	278,000 lbs.	
Unit price	× $2.90	× $3.50	
Total direct materials purchases	$5,945,000	$973,000	$6,918,000

1. 38,000 tires × 30 lbs. = 1,140,000 lbs.
2. 14,000 tires × 65 lbs. = 910,000 lbs.
3. 38,000 tires × 4 lbs. = 152,000 lbs.
4. 14,000 tires × 9 lbs. = 126,000 lbs.

Correct the direct materials purchases budget for Goodstone Tire Company.

EX 6-11
Direct labor cost budget
obj. **4**

✓*Total direct labor cost, Assembly, $186,225*

Match Point Racket Company manufactures two types of tennis rackets, the Junior and Pro Striker models. The production budget for March for the two rackets is as follows:

	Junior	Pro Striker
Production budget	7,300 units	18,400 units

Both rackets are produced in two departments, Forming and Assembly. The direct labor hours required for each racket are estimated as follows:

	Forming Department	Assembly Department
Junior	0.25 hour per unit	0.45 hour per unit
Pro Striker	0.40 hour per unit	0.60 hour per unit

The direct labor rate for each department is as follows:

Forming Department	$18.00 per hour
Assembly Department	$13.00 per hour

Prepare the direct labor cost budget for March 2008.

EX 6-12
Direct labor budget— service business
obj. **4**

✓*Average weekday total, $1,696*

Night Rest Inn Inc. operates a downtown hotel property that has 240 rooms. On average, 75% of Night Rest's rooms are occupied on weekdays, and 50% are occupied during the weekend. The manager has asked you to develop a direct labor budget for the housekeeping and restaurant staff for weekdays and weekends. You have determined that the housekeeping staff requires 45 minutes to clean each occupied room. The housekeeping staff is paid $8 per hour. The restaurant has five full-time staff (eight-hour day) on duty, regardless of occupancy. However, for every 30 occupied rooms, an additional person is brought in to work in the restaurant for the eight-hour day. The restaurant staff is paid $7 per hour.

Determine the estimated housekeeping and restaurant direct labor cost for an average weekday and weekend day. Format the budget in two columns, labeled as weekday and weekend day.

EX 6-13
Production and direct labor cost budgets
obj. **4**

✓*a. Total production of 501 Jeans, 47,000*

Levi Strauss & Co. manufactures slacks and jeans under a variety of brand names, such as Dockers® and 501 Jeans®. Slacks and jeans are assembled by a variety of different sewing operations. Assume that the sales budget for Dockers and 501 Jeans shows estimated sales of 23,800 and 46,200 pairs, respectively, for March 2008. The finished goods inventory is assumed as follows:

	Dockers	501 Jeans
March 1 estimated inventory	320	1,230
March 31 desired inventory	520	2,030

Assume the following direct labor data per 10 pairs of Dockers and 501 Jeans for four different sewing operations:

	Direct Labor per 10 Pairs	
	Dockers	501 Jeans
Inseam	18 minutes	12 minutes
Outerseam	22	15
Pockets	7	9
Zipper	10	6
Total	57 minutes	42 minutes

a. Prepare a production budget for March. Prepare the budget in two columns: Dockers® and 501 Jeans®.
b. Prepare the March direct labor cost budget for the four sewing operations, assuming a $12 wage per hour for the inseam and outerseam sewing operations and a $14 wage per hour for the pocket and zipper sewing operations. Prepare the direct labor cost budget in four columns: inseam, outerseam, pockets, and zipper.

EX 6-14
Factory overhead cost budget
obj. **4**

✓ *Total variable factory overhead costs, $243,000*

Fresh Mint Candy Company budgeted the following costs for anticipated production for July 2008:

Advertising expenses	$275,000	Production supervisor wages	$125,000
Manufacturing supplies	14,000	Production control salaries	33,000
Power and light	42,000	Executive officer salaries	205,000
Sales commissions	290,000	Materials management salaries	29,000
Factory insurance	23,000	Factory depreciation	17,000

Prepare a factory overhead cost budget, separating variable and fixed costs. Assume that factory insurance and depreciation are the only factory fixed costs.

EX 6-15
Cost of goods sold budget
obj. **4**

✓ *Cost of goods sold, $1,269,300*

Dover Chemical Company uses oil to produce two types of plastic products, P1 and P2. Dover budgeted 30,000 barrels of oil for purchase in June for $28 per barrel. Direct labor budgeted in the chemical process was $150,000 for June. Factory overhead was budgeted $275,000 during June. The inventories on June 1 were estimated to be:

Oil	$15,300
P1	8,700
P2	9,200
Work in process	11,800

The desired inventories on June 30 were:

Oil	$12,200
P1	8,300
P2	9,500
Work in process	10,700

Use the preceding information to prepare a cost of goods sold budget for June.

EX 6-16
Cost of goods sold budget
obj. **4**

✓ *Cost of goods sold, $397,320*

The controller of Moravian Ceramics Inc. wishes to prepare a cost of goods sold budget for April. The controller assembled the following information for constructing the cost of goods sold budget:

Direct materials:	Enamel	Paint	Porcelain	Total
Total direct materials purchases budgeted for April	$32,450	$4,730	$114,240	$151,420
Estimated inventory, April 1, 2008	1,150	2,800	4,330	8,280
Desired inventory, April 30, 2008	2,500	2,050	6,000	10,550

Direct labor cost:	Kiln Department	Decorating Department	Total
Total direct labor cost budgeted for April	$37,500	$134,400	$171,900

Finished goods inventories:	Dish	Bowl	Figurine	Total
Estimated inventory, April 1, 2008	$4,280	$2,970	$2,470	$ 9,720
Desired inventory, April 30, 2008	3,350	4,150	3,700	11,200

Work in process inventories:

Estimated inventory, April 1, 2008	$2,800
Desired inventory, April 30, 2008	1,750

Budgeted factory overhead costs for April:

Indirect factory wages	$55,500
Depreciation of plant and equipment	12,600
Power and light	4,900
Indirect materials	3,700
Total	$76,700

Use the preceding information to prepare a cost of goods sold budget for April 2008.

EX 6-17

Schedule of cash collections of accounts receivable

obj. 5

✓ *Total cash collected in May, $535,700*

Happy Tails Wholesale Inc., a pet wholesale supplier, was organized on March 1, 2008. Projected sales for each of the first three months of operations are as follows:

March	$450,000
April	520,000
May	560,000

The company expects to sell 10% of its merchandise for cash. Of sales on account, 50% are expected to be collected in the month of the sale, 40% in the month following the sale, and the remainder in the second month following the sale.

Prepare a schedule indicating cash collections from sales for March, April, and May.

EX 6-18

Schedule of cash collections of accounts receivable

obj. 5

✓ *Total cash collected in January, $307,600*

Office Warehouse Supplies Inc. has "cash and carry" customers and credit customers. Office Warehouse estimates that 40% of monthly sales are to cash customers, while the remaining sales are to credit customers. Of the credit customers, 30% pay their accounts in the month of sale, while the remaining 70% pay their accounts in the month following the month of sale. Projected sales for the first three months of 2008 are as follows:

January	$220,000
February	275,000
March	260,000

The Accounts Receivable balance on December 31, 2007, was $180,000.

Prepare a schedule of cash collections from sales for January, February, and March.

EX 6-19

Schedule of cash payments

obj. 5

✓ *Total cash payments in August, $107,875*

A+ Learning Systems Inc. was organized on May 31, 2009. Projected selling and administrative expenses for each of the first three months of operations are as follows:

June	$114,800
July	124,500
August	129,000

Depreciation, insurance, and property taxes represent $20,000 of the estimated monthly expenses. The annual insurance premium was paid on May 31, and property taxes for the year will be paid in December. Three-fourths of the remainder of the expenses are expected to be paid in the month in which they are incurred, with the balance to be paid in the following month.

Prepare a schedule indicating cash payments for selling and administrative expenses for June, July, and August.

EX 6-20

Schedule of cash payments

obj. 5

✓ *Total cash payments in December, $128,720*

Total Flex Physical Therapy Inc. is planning its cash payments for operations for the fourth quarter (October–December), 2009. The Accrued Expenses Payable balance on October 1 is $22,600. The budgeted expenses for the next three months are as follows:

	October	November	December
Salaries	$ 58,200	$ 63,500	$ 74,500
Utilities	5,300	5,600	7,100
Other operating expenses	44,700	52,800	62,700
Total	$108,200	$121,900	$144,300

Other operating expenses include $10,500 of monthly depreciation expense and $600 of monthly insurance expense that was prepaid for the year on March 1 of the current year. Of the remaining expenses, 80% are paid in the month in which they are incurred, with the remainder paid in the following month. The Accrued Expenses Payable balance on October 1 relates to the expenses incurred in September.

Prepare a schedule of cash payments for operations for October, November, and December.

EX 6-21
*Capital expenditures
budget*

obj. 5

✓*Total capital
expenditures in 2008,
$7,000,000*

On January 1, 2008, the controller of Garden Master Tools Inc. is planning capital expenditures for the years 2008–2011. The following interviews helped the controller collect the necessary information for the capital expenditures budget.

Director of Facilities: A construction contract was signed in late 2007 for the construction of a new factory building at a contract cost of $12,000,000. The construction is scheduled to begin in 2008 and be completed in 2009.

Vice President of Manufacturing: Once the new factory building is finished, we plan to purchase $1.5 million in equipment in late 2009. I expect that an additional $300,000 will be needed early in the following year (2010) to test and install the equipment before we can begin production. If sales continue to grow, I expect we'll need to invest another million in equipment in 2011.

Vice President of Marketing: We have really been growing lately. I wouldn't be surprised if we need to expand the size of our new factory building in 2011 by at least 40%. Fortunately, we expect inflation to have minimal impact on construction costs over the next four years.

Director of Information Systems: We need to upgrade our information systems to wireless network technology. It doesn't make sense to do this until after the new factory building is completed and producing product. During 2010, once the factory is up and running, we should equip the whole facility with wireless technology. I think it would cost us $1,600,000 today to install the technology. However, prices have been dropping by 25% per year, so it should be less expensive at a later date.

President: I am excited about our long-term prospects. My only short-term concern is financing the $7,000,000 of construction costs on the portion of the new factory building scheduled to be completed in 2008.

Use the interview information above to prepare a capital expenditures budget for Garden Master Tools Inc. for the years 2008–2011.

Problems Series A

PR 6-1A
*Forecast sales volume
and sales budget*

obj. 4

✓*3. Total revenue from
sales, $1,869,918*

Rembrandt Frame Company prepared the following sales budget for the current year:

Rembrandt Frame Company
Sales Budget
For the Year Ending December 31, 2008

Product and Area	Unit Sales Volume	Unit Selling Price	Total Sales
8" × 10" Frame:			
East	29,000	$14.00	$ 406,000
Central	22,000	14.00	308,000
West	31,500	14.00	441,000
Total	82,500		$1,155,000
12" × 16" Frame:			
East	16,000	$24.00	$ 384,000
Central	10,500	24.00	252,000
West	15,000	24.00	360,000
Total	41,500		$ 996,000
Total revenue from sales			$2,151,000

At the end of December 2008, the following unit sales data were reported for the year:

	Unit Sales	
	8" × 10" Frame	12" × 16" Frame
East	29,725	16,480
Central	22,770	10,710
West	30,240	14,325

For the year ending December 31, 2009, unit sales are expected to follow the patterns established during the year ending December 31, 2008. The unit selling price for the 8" × 10" frame is expected to change to $12, and the unit selling price for the 12" × 16" frame is expected to change to $21, effective January 1, 2009.

Instructions

1. Compute the increase or decrease of actual unit sales for the year ended December 31, 2008, over budget. Place your answers in a columnar table with the following format:

	Unit Sales, Year Ended 2008		Increase (Decrease) Actual Over Budget	
	Budget	Actual Sales	Amount	Percent
8" × 10" Frame:				
East				
Central				
West				
12" × 16" Frame:				
East				
Central				
West				

2. Assuming that the trend of sales indicated in part (1) is to continue in 2009, compute the unit sales volume to be used for preparing the sales budget for the year ending December 31, 2009. Place your answers in a columnar table similar to that in part (1) above but with the following column heads. Round budgeted units to the nearest unit.

2008 Actual Units	Percentage Increase (Decrease)	2009 Budgeted Units (rounded)

3. Prepare a sales budget for the year ending December 31, 2009.

PR 6-2A
Sales, production, direct materials purchases, and direct labor cost budgets

obj. 4

✓ *3. Total direct materials purchases, $9,806,650*

The budget director of Outdoor Chef Grill Company requests estimates of sales, production, and other operating data from the various administrative units every month. Selected information concerning sales and production for October 2008 is summarized as follows:

a. Estimated sales for October by sales territory:

Maine:
    Backyard Chef ....   4,500 units at $800 per unit
    Master Chef ....   1,600 units at $1,600 per unit
Vermont:
    Backyard Chef ....   3,800 units at $900 per unit
    Master Chef ....   1,700 units at $1,450 per unit
New Hampshire:
    Backyard Chef ....   4,200 units at $850 per unit
    Master Chef ....   1,800 units at $1,700 per unit

b. Estimated inventories at October 1:

Direct materials:
    Grates ....   1,200 units
    Stainless steel ....   2,300 lbs.
    Burner subassemblies ......   650 units
    Shelves ....   500 units

Finished products:
    Backyard Chef ....   1,600 units
    Master Chef ....   500 units

c. Desired inventories at October 31:

Direct materials:		Finished products:	
Grates	900 units	Backyard Chef	1,300 units
Stainless steel	2,000 lbs.	Master Chef	600 units
Burner subassemblies	800 units		
Shelves	450 units		

d. Direct materials used in production:

In manufacture of Backyard Chef:
Grates	3 units per unit of product
Stainless steel	25 lbs. per unit of product
Burner subassemblies	2 units per unit of product
Shelves	5 units per unit of product

In manufacture of Master Chef:
Grates	6 units per unit of product
Stainless steel	50 lbs. per unit of product
Burner subassemblies	4 units per unit of product
Shelves	6 units per unit of product

e. Anticipated purchase price for direct materials:

Grates	$18 per unit	Burner subassemblies	$115 per unit
Stainless steel	$5 per lb.	Shelves	$6 per unit

f. Direct labor requirements:

Backyard Chef:
Stamping Department	0.60 hour at $15 per hour
Forming Department	0.80 hour at $12 per hour
Assembly Department	1.50 hours at $9 per hour

Master Chef:
Stamping Department	0.80 hour at $15 per hour
Forming Department	1.60 hours at $12 per hour
Assembly Department	2.50 hours at $9 per hour

Instructions
1. Prepare a sales budget for October.
2. Prepare a production budget for October.
3. Prepare a direct materials purchases budget for October.
4. Prepare a direct labor cost budget for October.

PR 6-3A
Budgeted income statement and supporting budgets

obj. 4

✓ *4. Total direct labor cost in Fabrication Dept., $282,170*

The budget director of Backyard Habitat Inc., with the assistance of the controller, treasurer, production manager, and sales manager, has gathered the following data for use in developing the budgeted income statement for December 2008:

a. Estimated sales for December:

Bird House	34,500 units at $40 per unit
Bird Feeder	25,800 units at $70 per unit

b. Estimated inventories at December 1:

Direct materials:		Finished products:	
Wood	2,600 ft.	Bird House	4,900 units at $25 per unit
Plastic	3,200 lbs.	Bird Feeder	2,500 units at $35 per unit

c. Desired inventories at December 31:

Direct materials:		Finished products:	
Wood	3,500 ft.	Bird House	5,300 units at $24 per unit
Plastic	2,800 lbs.	Bird Feeder	2,100 units at $36 per unit

d. Direct materials used in production:

In manufacture of Bird House:

    Wood . . . . .   0.80 ft. per unit of product

    Plastic . . . . .   0.50 lb. per unit of product

In manufacture of Bird Feeder:

    Wood . . . .   1.20 ft. per unit of product

    Plastic . . . .   0.75 lb. per unit of product

e. Anticipated cost of purchases and beginning and ending inventory of direct materials:

    Wood . . . . $6.50 per ft.   Plastic . . . . . . $0.90 per lb.

f. Direct labor requirements:

Bird House:

Fabrication Department	0.25 hour at $14 per hour
Assembly Department	0.30 hour at $10 per hour

Bird Feeder:

Fabrication Department	0.45 hour at $14 per hour
Assembly Department	0.35 hour at $10 per hour

g. Estimated factory overhead costs for December:

Indirect factory wages	$650,000	Power and light	$42,000
Depreciation of plant and equipment	165,000	Insurance and property tax	15,400

h. Estimated operating expenses for December:

Sales salaries expense	$675,000
Advertising expense	148,600
Office salaries expense	214,800
Depreciation expense—office equipment	4,900
Telephone expense—selling	5,200
Telephone expense—administrative	1,700
Travel expense—selling	39,200
Office supplies expense	3,500
Miscellaneous administrative expense	5,000

i. Estimated other income and expense for December:

Interest revenue	$16,900
Interest expense	10,600

j. Estimated tax rate: 35%

Instructions

1. Prepare a sales budget for December.
2. Prepare a production budget for December.
3. Prepare a direct materials purchases budget for December.
4. Prepare a direct labor cost budget for December.
5. Prepare a factory overhead cost budget for December.
6. Prepare a cost of goods sold budget for December. Work in process at the beginning of December is estimated to be $27,000, and work in process at the end of December is estimated to be $32,400.
7. Prepare a selling and administrative expenses budget for December.
8. Prepare a budgeted income statement for December.

PR 6-4A
Cash budget
obj. 5

✓ *1. October deficiency,*
$64,500

The controller of Santa Fe Housewares Inc. instructs you to prepare a monthly cash budget for the next three months. You are presented with the following budget information:

	August	September	October
Sales	$630,000	$715,000	$845,000
Manufacturing costs	350,000	360,000	410,000
Selling and administrative expenses	170,000	205,000	235,000
Capital expenditures			150,000

    The company expects to sell about 10% of its merchandise for cash. Of sales on account, 70% are expected to be collected in full in the month following the sale and the remainder the following month. Depreciation, insurance, and property tax expense represent $25,000 of the estimated monthly manufacturing costs. The annual insurance premium is paid in July, and the annual property taxes are paid in November. Of the remainder of the manufacturing costs, 80% are expected to be paid in the month in which they are incurred and the balance in the following month.

Current assets as of August 1 include cash of $50,000, marketable securities of $85,000, and accounts receivable of $635,000 ($500,000 from July sales and $135,000 from June sales). Sales on account for June and July were $450,000 and $500,000, respectively. Current liabilities as of August 1 include a $100,000, 15%, 90-day note payable due October 20 and $65,000 of accounts payable incurred in July for manufacturing costs. All selling and administrative expenses are paid in cash in the period they are incurred. It is expected that $1,800 in dividends will be received in August. An estimated income tax payment of $39,000 will be made in September. Santa Fe's regular quarterly dividend of $12,000 is expected to be declared in September and paid in October. Management desires to maintain a minimum cash balance of $40,000.

Instructions

1. Prepare a monthly cash budget and supporting schedules for August, September, and October.
2. On the basis of the cash budget prepared in part (1), what recommendation should be made to the controller?

PR 6-5A
Budgeted income statement and balance sheet

objs. 4, 5

✓ *1. Budgeted net income, $175,850*

As a preliminary to requesting budget estimates of sales, costs, and expenses for the fiscal year beginning January 1, 2009, the following tentative trial balance as of December 31, 2008, is prepared by the Accounting Department of Coconut Grove Soap Co.:

Cash	$ 90,000	
Accounts Receivable	108,600	
Finished Goods	72,400	
Work in Process	27,500	
Materials	49,700	
Prepaid Expenses	3,400	
Plant and Equipment	350,000	
Accumulated Depreciation—Plant and Equipment		$130,400
Accounts Payable		57,000
Common Stock, $10 par		185,000
Retained Earnings		329,200
	$701,600	$701,600

Factory output and sales for 2009 are expected to total 215,000 units of product, which are to be sold at $4.60 per unit. The quantities and costs of the inventories at December 31, 2009, are expected to remain unchanged from the balances at the beginning of the year.

Budget estimates of manufacturing costs and operating expenses for the year are summarized as follows:

	Estimated Costs and Expenses	
	Fixed **(Total for Year)**	**Variable** **(Per Unit Sold)**
Cost of goods manufactured and sold:		
Direct materials	—	$0.80
Direct labor	—	0.45
Factory overhead:		
Depreciation of plant and equipment	$45,000	—
Other factory overhead	7,000	0.30
Selling expenses:		
Sales salaries and commissions	40,000	0.35
Advertising	55,000	—
Miscellaneous selling expense	4,500	0.15
Administrative expenses:		
Office and officers salaries	67,100	0.17
Supplies	3,000	0.06
Miscellaneous administrative expense	2,000	0.09

Balances of accounts receivable, prepaid expenses, and accounts payable at the end of the year are not expected to differ significantly from the beginning balances. Federal income tax of $80,000 on 2009 taxable income will be paid during 2009. Regular quarterly cash dividends of $0.80 a share are expected to be declared and paid in March, June, September, and December. It is anticipated that fixed assets will be purchased for $60,000 cash in May.

Instructions

1. Prepare a budgeted income statement for 2009.
2. Prepare a budgeted balance sheet as of December 31, 2009, with supporting calculations.

Problems Series B

PR 6-1B
Forecast sales volume and sales budget

obj. **4**

✓ 3. Total revenue from sales, $33,161,100

Detect and Secure Devices Inc. prepared the following sales budget for the current year:

Detect and Secure Devices Inc.
Sales Budget
For the Year Ending December 31, 2008

Product and Area	Unit Sales Volume	Unit Selling Price	Total Sales
Home Alert System:			
United States	26,400	$240	$ 6,336,000
Europe	7,100	240	1,704,000
Asia	5,200	240	1,248,000
Total	38,700		$ 9,288,000
Business Alert System:			
United States	13,500	$850	$11,475,000
Europe	5,800	850	4,930,000
Asia	3,700	850	3,145,000
Total	23,000		$19,550,000
Total revenue from sales			$28,838,000

At the end of December 2008, the following unit sales data were reported for the year:

	Unit Sales	
	Home Alert System	Business Alert System
United States	27,720	14,040
Europe	6,816	5,916
Asia	5,356	3,589

For the year ending December 31, 2009, unit sales are expected to follow the patterns established during the year ending December 31, 2008. The unit selling price for the Home Alert System is expected to increase to $290, and the unit selling price for the Business Alert System is expected to be increased to $880, effective January 1, 2009.

Instructions

1. Compute the increase or decrease of actual unit sales for the year ended December 31, 2008, over budget. Place your answers in a columnar table with the following format:

	Unit Sales, Year Ended 2008		Increase (Decrease) Actual Over Budget	
	Budget	Actual Sales	Amount	Percent
Home Alert System:				
United States				
Europe				
Asia				

(continued)

	Unit Sales, Year Ended 2008		Increase (Decrease) Actual Over Budget	
	Budget	Actual Sales	Amount	Percent
Business Alert System:				
United States				
Europe				
Asia				

2. Assuming that the trend of sales indicated in part (1) is to continue in 2009, compute the unit sales volume to be used for preparing the sales budget for the year ending December 31, 2009. Place your answers in a columnar table similar to that in part (1) above but with the following column heads. Round budgeted units to the nearest unit.

2008 Actual Units	Percentage Increase (Decrease)	2009 Budgeted Units (rounded)

3. Prepare a sales budget for the year ending December 31, 2009.

PR 6-2B

Sales, production, direct materials purchases, and direct labor cost budgets

obj. 4

✓ *3. Total direct materials purchases, $6,679,381*

The budget director of Kingdom Furniture Company requests estimates of sales, production, and other operating data from the various administrative units every month. Selected information concerning sales and production for May 2008 is summarized as follows:

a. Estimated sales of King and Prince chairs for May by sales territory:

  Northern Domestic:
    King . . . .   5,800 units at $650 per unit
    Prince . . . .   6,700 units at $420 per unit
  Southern Domestic:
    King . . . .   3,500 units at $590 per unit
    Prince . . . .   3,800 units at $480 per unit
  International:
    King . . . .   1,200 units at $700 per unit
    Prince . . . .   1,000 units at $530 per unit

b. Estimated inventories at May 1:

  Direct materials: Finished products:
    Fabric . . . .   5,000 sq. yds.   King . . . .   920 units
    Wood . . . .   6,500 lineal ft.   Prince . . . .   260 units
    Filler . . . .   3,000 cu. ft.
    Springs . . . .   7,250 units

c. Desired inventories at May 31:

  Direct materials: Finished products:
    Fabric . . . .   4,400 sq. yds.   King . . . .   800 units
    Wood . . . .   5,800 lineal ft.   Prince . . . .   400 units
    Filler . . . .   3,100 cu. ft.
    Springs . . . .   7,500 units

d. Direct materials used in production:

  In manufacture of King:
    Fabric . . . .   4.6 sq. yds. per unit of product
    Wood . . . .   35 lineal ft. per unit of product
    Filler . . . .   3.8 cu. ft. per unit of product
    Springs . . . .   14 units per unit of product
  In manufacture of Prince:
    Fabric . . . .   3 sq. yds. per unit of product
    Wood . . . .   25 lineal ft. per unit of product
    Filler . . . .   3.2 cu. ft. per unit of product
    Springs . . . .   10 units per unit of product

e. Anticipated purchase price for direct materials:

Fabric	$8.00 per square yard	Filler	$3.50 per cubic foot
Wood	7.00 per lineal foot	Springs	4.50 per unit

f. Direct labor requirements:

King:
Framing Department ...... 2.5 hours at $12 per hour
Cutting Department .... 1.5 hours at $9 per hour
Upholstery Department .... 2.0 hours at $15 per hour
Prince:
Framing Department ...... 1.8 hours at $12 per hour
Cutting Department .... 0.5 hour at $9 per hour
Upholstery Department .... 2.3 hours at $15 per hour

Instructions
1. Prepare a sales budget for May.
2. Prepare a production budget for May.
3. Prepare a direct materials purchases budget for May.
4. Prepare a direct labor cost budget for May.

PR 6-3B
Budgeted income statement and supporting budgets

obj. **4**

✓ *4. Total direct labor cost in Assembly Dept., $73,548*

The budget director of Safety Athletic Inc., with the assistance of the controller, treasurer, production manager, and sales manager, has gathered the following data for use in developing the budgeted income statement for January 2008:

a. Estimated sales for January:

Batting helmet .... 3,500 units at $65 per unit
Football helmet .... 6,800 units at $130 per unit

b. Estimated inventories at January 1:

Direct materials:		Finished products:	
Plastic	900 lbs.	Batting helmet	270 units at $32 per unit
Foam lining	490 lbs.	Football helmet	400 units at $52 per unit

c. Desired inventories at January 31:

Direct materials:		Finished products:	
Plastic	1,240 lbs.	Batting helmet	240 units at $34 per unit
Foam lining	470 lbs.	Football helmet	360 units at $55 per unit

d. Direct materials used in production:

In manufacture of batting helmet:
Plastic .... 1.20 lbs. per unit of product
Foam lining .... 0.50 lb. per unit of product
In manufacture of football helmet:
Plastic .... 2.80 lbs. per unit of product
Foam lining .... 1.40 lbs. per unit of product

e. Anticipated cost of purchases and beginning and ending inventory of direct materials:

Plastic .... $7.00 per lb.
Foam lining .... $4.00 per lb.

f. Direct labor requirements:

Batting helmet:
Molding Department .... 0.20 hour at $14 per hour
Assembly Department .... 0.50 hour at $12 per hour
Football helmet:
Molding Department .... 0.30 hour at $14 per hour
Assembly Department .... 0.65 hour at $12 per hour

g. Estimated factory overhead costs for January:

Indirect factory wages	$105,000	Power and light	$16,000
Depreciation of plant and equipment	30,000	Insurance and property tax	8,700

h. Estimated operating expenses for January:

Sales salaries expense	$265,800
Advertising expense	135,600
Office salaries expense	84,300
Depreciation expense—office equipment	5,200
Telephone expense—selling	3,500
Telephone expense—administrative	700
Travel expense—selling	43,100
Office supplies expense	4,900
Miscellaneous administrative expense	5,200

i. Estimated other income and expense for January:

Interest revenue	$14,500
Interest expense	18,700

j. Estimated tax rate: 30%

Instructions
1. Prepare a sales budget for January.
2. Prepare a production budget for January.
3. Prepare a direct materials purchases budget for January.
4. Prepare a direct labor cost budget for January.
5. Prepare a factory overhead cost budget for January.
6. Prepare a cost of goods sold budget for January. Work in process at the beginning of January is estimated to be $12,500, and work in process at the end of January is desired to be $13,500.
7. Prepare a selling and administrative expenses budget for January.
8. Prepare a budgeted income statement for January.

PR 6-4B
Cash budget
obj. 5

✓ 1. June deficiency, $10,000

The controller of Swift Shoes Inc. instructs you to prepare a monthly cash budget for the next three months. You are presented with the following budget information:

	April	May	June
Sales	$100,000	$150,000	$180,000
Manufacturing costs	40,000	50,000	54,000
Selling and administrative expenses	32,000	38,000	45,000
Capital expenditures	—	—	30,000

The company expects to sell about 10% of its merchandise for cash. Of sales on account, 60% are expected to be collected in full in the month following the sale and the remainder the following month. Depreciation, insurance, and property tax expense represent $18,000 of the estimated monthly manufacturing costs. The annual insurance premium is paid in July, and the annual property taxes are paid in November. Of the remainder of the manufacturing costs, 80% are expected to be paid in the month in which they are incurred and the balance in the following month.

Current assets as of April 1 include cash of $40,000, marketable securities of $65,000, and accounts receivable of $117,800 ($85,000 from March sales and $32,800 from February sales). Sales on account in February and March were $82,000 and $85,000, respectively. Current liabilities as of April 1 include a $50,000, 12%, 90-day note payable due June 20 and $29,000 of accounts payable incurred in March for manufacturing costs. All selling and administrative expenses are paid in cash in the period they are incurred. It is expected that $3,500 in dividends will be received in April. An estimated income tax payment of $34,000 will be made in May. Swift Shoes' regular quarterly dividend of $8,000 is expected to be declared in May and paid in June. Management desires to maintain a minimum cash balance of $35,000.

Instructions

1. Prepare a monthly cash budget and supporting schedules for April, May, and June 2008.
2. On the basis of the cash budget prepared in part (1), what recommendation should be made to the controller?

PR 6-5B
Budgeted income statement and balance sheet

objs. **4, 5**

✓ 1. Budgeted net income, $619,800

As a preliminary to requesting budget estimates of sales, costs, and expenses for the fiscal year beginning January 1, 2009, the following tentative trial balance as of December 31, 2008, is prepared by the Accounting Department of Cornerstone Publishing Co.:

Cash	$ 122,500	
Accounts Receivable	246,700	
Finished Goods	157,800	
Work in Process	37,800	
Materials	57,800	
Prepaid Expenses	4,500	
Plant and Equipment	620,000	
Accumulated Depreciation—Plant and Equipment		$ 267,000
Accounts Payable		184,500
Common Stock, $15 par		450,000
Retained Earnings		345,600
	$1,247,100	$1,247,100

Factory output and sales for 2009 are expected to total 30,000 units of product, which are to be sold at $110 per unit. The quantities and costs of the inventories at December 31, 2009, are expected to remain unchanged from the balances at the beginning of the year.

Budget estimates of manufacturing costs and operating expenses for the year are summarized as follows:

	Estimated Costs and Expenses	
	Fixed (Total for Year)	**Variable** (Per Unit Sold)
Cost of goods manufactured and sold:		
Direct materials	—	$26.00
Direct labor	—	8.50
Factory overhead:		
Depreciation of plant and equipment	$ 40,000	—
Other factory overhead	12,000	5.00
Selling expenses:		
Sales salaries and commissions	118,000	14.00
Advertising	114,200	—
Miscellaneous selling expense	10,500	2.15
Administrative expenses:		
Office and officers salaries	83,600	6.50
Supplies	4,400	1.25
Miscellaneous administrative expense	2,000	1.45

Balances of accounts receivable, prepaid expenses, and accounts payable at the end of the year are not expected to differ significantly from the beginning balances. Federal income tax of $350,000 on 2009 taxable income will be paid during 2009. Regular quarterly cash dividends of $1.75 a share are expected to be declared and paid in March, June, September, and December. It is anticipated that fixed assets will be purchased for $180,000 cash in May.

Instructions

1. Prepare a budgeted income statement for 2009.
2. Prepare a budgeted balance sheet as of December 31, 2009, with supporting calculations.

Special Activities

SA 6-1
Ethics and professional conduct in business

ETHICS

The director of marketing for Mobile Computer Co., Sheri Keller, had the following discussion with the company controller, Isaiah Johnson, on July 26 of the current year:

Sheri: Isaiah, it looks like I'm going to spend much less than indicated on my July budget.
Isaiah: I'm glad to hear it.
Sheri: Well, I'm not so sure it's good news. I'm concerned that the president will see that I'm under budget and reduce my budget in the future. The only reason that I look good is that we've delayed an advertising campaign. Once the campaign hits in September, I'm sure my actual expenditures will go up. You see, we are also having our sales convention in September. Having the advertising campaign and the convention at the same time is going to kill my September numbers.
Isaiah: I don't think that's anything to worry about. We all expect some variation in actual spending month to month. What's really important is staying within the budgeted targets for the year. Does that look as if it's going to be a problem?
Sheri: I don't think so, but just the same, I'd like to be on the safe side.
Isaiah: What do you mean?
Sheri: Well, this is what I'd like to do. I want to pay the convention-related costs in advance this month. I'll pay the hotel for room and convention space and purchase the airline tickets in advance. In this way, I can charge all these expenditures to July's budget. This would cause my actual expenses to come close to budget for July. Moreover, when the big advertising campaign hits in September, I won't have to worry about expenditures for the convention on my September budget as well. The convention costs will already be paid. Thus, my September expenses should be pretty close to budget.
Isaiah: I can't tell you when to make your convention purchases, but I'm not too sure that it should be expensed on July's budget.
Sheri: What's the problem? It looks like "no harm, no foul" to me. I can't see that there's anything wrong with this—it's just smart management.

▭▭▭▷ How should Isaiah Johnson respond to Sheri Keller's request to expense the advanced payments for convention-related costs against July's budget?

SA 6-2
Evaluating budgeting systems

REAL WORLD

Children's Hospital of the King's Daughters Health System in Norfolk, Virginia, introduced a new budgeting method that allowed the hospital's annual plan to be updated for changes in operating plans. For example, if the budget was based on 400 patient-days (number of patients × number of days in the hospital) and the actual count rose to 450 patient-days, the variable costs of staffing, lab work, and medication costs could be adjusted to reflect this change. The budget manager stated, "I work with hospital directors to turn data into meaningful information and effect change before the month ends."

a. What budgeting methods are being used under the new approach?
b. ▭▭▭▷ Why are these methods superior to the former approaches?

SA 6-3
Service company static decision making

A bank manager of Citizens Bank Inc. uses the managerial accounting system to track the costs of operating the various departments within the bank. The departments include Cash Management, Trust Commercial Loans, Mortgage Loans, Operations, Credit Card, and Branch Services. The budget and actual results for the Operations Department are as follows:

Resources	Budget	Actual
Salaries	$150,000	$150,000
Benefits	30,000	30,000
Supplies	45,000	42,000
Travel	20,000	30,000
Training	25,000	35,000
Overtime	25,000	20,000
Total	$295,000	$307,000
Excess of actual over budget	$ 12,000	

a. 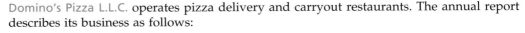 What information is provided by the budget? Specifically, what questions can the bank manager ask of the Operations Department manager?

b. What information does the budget fail to provide? Specifically, could the budget information be presented differently to provide even more insight for the bank manager?

SA 6-4
Objectives of the master budget

Domino's Pizza L.L.C. operates pizza delivery and carryout restaurants. The annual report describes its business as follows:

> We offer a focused menu of high-quality, value priced pizza with three types of crust (Hand-Tossed, Thin Crust, and Deep Dish), along with buffalo wings, bread sticks, cheesy bread, CinnaStix®, and Coca-Cola® products. Our hand-tossed pizza is made from fresh dough produced in our regional distribution centers. We prepare every pizza using real cheese, pizza sauce made from fresh tomatoes, and a choice of high-quality meat and vegetable toppings in generous portions. Our focused menu and use of premium ingredients enable us to consistently and efficiently produce the highest-quality pizza.
>
> Over the 41 years since our founding, we have developed a simple, cost-efficient model. We offer a limited menu, our stores are designed for delivery and carry-out, and we do not generally offer dine-in service. As a result, our stores require relatively small, lower-rent locations and limited capital expenditures.

How would a master budget support planning, directing, and control for Domino's?

SA 6-5
Integrity and evaluating budgeting systems

The city of Westwood has an annual budget cycle that begins on July 1 and ends on June 30. At the beginning of each budget year, an annual budget is established for each department. The annual budget is divided by 12 months to provide a constant monthly static budget. On June 30, all unspent budgeted monies for the budget year from the various city departments must be "returned" to the General Fund. Thus, if department heads fail to use their budget by year-end, they will lose it. A budget analyst prepared a chart of the difference between the monthly actual and budgeted amounts for the recent fiscal year. The chart was as follows:

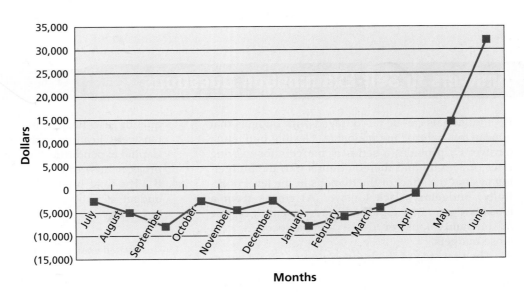

a. Interpret the chart.
b. Suggest an improvement in the budget system.

SA 6-6
Objectives of budgeting

At the beginning of the year, Kevin Frey decided to prepare a cash budget for the year, based upon anticipated cash receipts and payments. The estimates in the budget represent a "best guess." The budget is as follows:

Expected annual cash receipts:

Salary from part-time job	$10,500	
Salary from summer job	5,000	
Total receipts		$15,500
Expected annual cash payments:		
Tuition	$ 5,000	
Books	400	
Rent	4,200	
Food	2,500	
Utilities	900	
Entertainment	4,000	
Total payments		17,000
Net change in cash		$ (1,500)

1. ▭▬► What does this budget suggest? In what ways is this information useful to Kevin?
2. a. ▭▬► Some items in the budget are more certain than are others. Which items are the most certain? Which items are the most uncertain? What are the implications of these different levels of certainty to Kevin's planning?
   b. ▭▬► Some payment items are more controllable than others. Assuming that Kevin plans to go to school, classify the items as controllable, partially controllable, or not controllable. What are the implications of controllable items to planning?
3. ▭▬► What actions could Kevin take in order to avoid having the anticipated shortfall of $1,500 at the end of the year?
4. ▭▬► What does this budget fail to consider, and what are the implications of these omissions to Kevin's planning?

SA 6-7
Budget for a state government

> Group Project

> Internet Project

In a group, find the home page of the state in which you presently live. The home page will be of the form *statename.gov*. At the home page site, search for annual budget information.

1. What are the budgeted sources of revenue and their percentage breakdown?
2. What are the major categories of budgeted expenditures (or appropriations) and their percentage breakdown?
3. Is the projected budget in balance?

Answers to Self-Examination Questions

1. **B** Individuals can be discouraged with budgets that appear too tight or unobtainable. Flexible budgeting (answer C) provides a series of budgets for varying rates of activity and thereby builds into the budgeting system the effect of fluctuations in the level of activity. Budgetary slack (answer A) comes from a loose budget, not a tight budget. A "spend it or lose it" mentality (answer D) is often associated with loose budgets.
2. **A** The first step of the budget process is to develop a plan. Once plans are established, management may direct actions (answer B). The results of actions can be controlled (answer C) by comparing them to the plan. This feedback (answer D) can be used by management to change plans or redirect actions.
3. **B** Administrative departments (answer B), such as Purchasing or Human Resources, will often use static budgeting. Production departments (answer A) fre-

quently use flexible budgets. Responsibility centers (answer C) can use either static or flexible budgeting. Capital expenditures budgets are used to plan capital projects (answer D).
4. **B** The total production indicated in the production budget is 257,500 units (answer B), which is computed as follows:

Sales	250,000 units
Plus desired ending inventory	30,000 units
Total	280,000 units
Less estimated beginning inventory	22,500 units
Total production	257,500 units

5. **C** Dixon expects to collect 70% of April sales ($560,000) plus 30% of the March sales ($195,000) in April, for a total of $755,000 (answer C). Answer A is 100% of April sales. Answer B is 70% of April sales. Answer D adds 70% of both March and April sales.

chapter 7

Performance Evaluation Using Variances from Standard Costs

© ALASTAIR GRANT/ASSOCIATED PRESS

1959-2000

After studying this chapter, you should be able to:

1 *Describe the types of standards and how they are established for businesses.*

2 *Explain and illustrate how standards are used in budgeting.*

3 *Compute and interpret direct materials and direct labor variances.*

4 *Compute and interpret factory overhead controllable and volume variances.*

5 *Journalize the entries for recording standards in the accounts and prepare an income statement that includes variances from standard.*

6 *Explain and provide examples of nonfinancial performance measures.*

BMW Group—Mini Cooper

When you play a sport, you are evaluated with respect to how well you perform compared to a standard or to a competitor. In bowling, for example, your score is compared to a perfect score of 300 or to the scores of your competitors. In this class, you are compared to performance standards. These standards are often described in terms of letter grades, which provide a measure of how well you achieved the class objectives. On your job, you are also evaluated according to performance standards.

Just as your class performance is evaluated, managers are evaluated according to goals and plans. For example, BMW Group uses manufacturing standards at its automobile assembly plants to guide performance. The Mini Cooper, a BMW Group car, is manufactured in a modern facility in Oxford, England. There are a number of performance targets applied in this plant. For example, the combined energy use in manufacturing a car has declined throughout this decade. The bodyshell is welded by over 250 robots so as to be two to three times stiffer than rival cars. In addition, the bodyshell dimensions are tested to the accuracy of the width of a human hair. Such performance standards are not surprising given the automotive racing background of John W. Cooper, the designer of the original Mini Cooper.

Performance is often measured as the difference between actual results and planned results. In this chapter, we will discuss and illustrate the ways in which business performance is evaluated.

If you want to take an online tour of the Oxford plant to see how a Mini Cooper is manufactured, go to **http://www.mini.com/com/en/manufacturing/index.jsp**.

Standards

objective **1**

Describe the types of standards and how they are established for businesses.

What are standards? *Standards* are performance goals. Service, merchandising, and manufacturing businesses may all use standards to evaluate and control operations. For example, drivers for United Parcel Service, Inc., are expected to drive a standard distance per day. Salespersons for The Limited, Inc., are expected to meet sales standards.

Manufacturers normally use standard costs for each of the three manufacturing costs: direct materials, direct labor, and factory overhead. Accounting systems that use standards for these costs are called **standard cost systems**. These systems enable management to determine how much a product should cost (**standard cost**), how much it does cost (actual cost), and the causes of any difference (**cost variances**). When actual costs are compared with standard costs, only the exceptions or variances are reported for cost control. This reporting by the *principle of exceptions* allows management to focus on correcting the variances. Thus, using standard costs assists management in controlling costs and in motivating employees to focus on costs.

Standard cost systems are commonly used with job order and process systems. Automated manufacturing operations may also integrate standard cost data with the computerized system that directs operations. Such systems detect and report variances automatically and make adjustments to operations in progress.

SETTING STANDARDS

Setting standards is both an art and a science. The standard-setting process normally requires the joint efforts of accountants, engineers, and other management personnel. The accountant plays an essential role by expressing in dollars and cents the results of judgments and studies. Engineers contribute to the standard-setting process by identifying the materials, labor, and machine requirements needed to produce the product. For example, engineers determine the direct materials requirements by studying the materials specifications for products and estimating normal spoilage in production. Time and motion studies may be used to determine the time and direct labor required for each manufacturing operation. Engineering studies may also be used to determine standards for factory overhead, such as the amount of power needed to operate machinery.

Setting standards often begins with analyzing past operations. However, standards are not just an extension of past costs, and caution must be used in relying on past cost data. For example, inefficiencies may be contained within past costs. In addition, changes in technology, machinery, or production methods may make past costs irrelevant for future operations.

TYPES OF STANDARDS

Standards imply an acceptable level of production efficiency. One of the major objectives in setting standards is to motivate workers to achieve efficient operations.

Like the budgets we discussed earlier, tight, unrealistic standards may have a negative impact on performance. This is because workers may become frustrated with an inability to meet the standards and may give up trying to do their best. Such standards can be achieved only under perfect operating conditions, such as no idle time, no machine breakdowns, and no materials spoilage. These standards are called **ideal standards** or *theoretical standards*. Although ideal standards are not widely used, a few firms use ideal standards to motivate changes and improvement. Such an approach is termed "Kaizen costing." Kaizen is a Japanese term meaning "continuous improvement."

Standards that are too loose might not motivate employees to perform at their best. This is because the standard level of performance can be reached too easily. As a result, operating performance may be lower than what could be achieved.

Most companies use **currently attainable standards** (sometimes called *normal standards*). These standards can be attained with reasonable effort. Such standards allow for normal production difficulties and mistakes, such as materials spoilage and machine breakdowns. When reasonable standards are used, employees become more focused on cost and are more likely to put forth their best efforts.

An example from the game of golf illustrates the distinction between ideal and normal standards. In golf, "par" is an *ideal* standard for most players. Each player's USGA (United States Golf Association) handicap is the player's *normal* standard. The motivation of average players is to beat their handicaps because they may view beating par as unrealistic. Normal and ideal standards are illustrated as follows:

Mohawk Forest Products had a normal standard cost for a premium grade paper of $2,900 per ton, while the ideal cost was $1,342 per ton. The company used the ideal standard to motivate cost improvement. The resulting improvements allowed the company to reduce the normal standard cost to $1,738 per ton.

Currently attainable
(personal best)

Ideal
(world record)

REVIEWING AND REVISING STANDARDS

Standard costs should be continuously reviewed and should be revised when they no longer reflect operating conditions. Inaccurate standards may distort management decision making and may weaken management's ability to plan and control operations.

Business Connections

MAKING THE GRADE IN THE REAL WORLD—THE 360-DEGREE REVIEW

When you leave school and take your first job, you will likely be subject to an employee evaluation and feedback. These reviews provide feedback on performance that is often very detailed, providing insights to strengths and weaknesses that often go beyond mere grades.

One feedback trend is the 360-degree review. As stated by the human resources consulting firm Towers Perrin, the 360-degree review "is a huge wave that's just hitting—not only here, but all over the world." In a 360-

degree review, six to twelve evaluators who encircle an employee's sphere of influence, such as superiors, peers, and subordinates, are selected to fill out anonymous questionnaires. These questionnaires rate the employee on various criteria including the ability to work in groups, form a consensus, make timely decisions, motivate employees, and achieve objectives. The results are summarized and used to identify and strengthen weaknesses.

For example, one individual at Intel Corporation was very vocal during team meetings. In the 360-degree review, the manager thought this behavior was "refreshing." However, the employee's peers thought the vocal behavior monopolized conversations. Thus, what the manager viewed as a positive, the peer group viewed as a negative. The 360-degree review provided valuable information to both the manager and the employee to adjust behavior. Without the 360-degree feedback, the manager might have been blind to the group's reaction to the vocal behavior and reinforced behavior that was actually harmful to the group.

Sources: Llana DeBare, "360-Degrees of Evaluation: More Companies Turning to Full-Circle Job Reviews," *San Francisco Chronicle,* May 5, 1997; Francie Dalton, "Using 360 Degree Feedback Mechanisms," *Occupational Health and Safety,* Vol. 74, Issue 7, 2005.

Standards should not be revised, however, just because they differ from actual costs. They should be revised only when they no longer reflect the operating conditions that they were intended to measure. For example, the direct labor standard would not be revised simply because workers were unable to meet properly determined standards. On the other hand, standards should be revised when prices, product designs, labor rates, or manufacturing methods change. For example, when aluminum beverage cans were redesigned to taper slightly at the top of the can, manufacturers reduced the standard amount of aluminum per can because less aluminum was required for the top piece of the tapered can.

Using standards for performance evaluation has been criticized by some. Critics believe the following:

- Standards limit operating improvements by discouraging improvement beyond the standard.
- Standards are too difficult to maintain in a dynamic manufacturing environment, resulting in "stale standards."
- Standards can cause workers to lose sight of the larger objectives of the organization by focusing only on efficiency improvement.
- Standards can cause workers to unduly focus on their own operations to the possible harm of other operations that rely on them.

These critics believe that operating performance is more complex than just improving a single performance target. Advocates of standards would respond that standards are only part of the performance measurement system and that standards combined with other nonperformance measures, as discussed later in this chapter, can overcome these objections. Regardless of these criticisms, standards are widely used. Most managers strongly support standard cost systems and regard standards as critical for running large businesses efficiently.

Integrity, Objectivity, and Ethics in Business

ETHICS

COMPANY REPUTATION: THE BEST AND THE WORST

Harris Interactive annually ranks American corporations in terms of reputation. The ranking is based upon how respondents rate corporations on 20 attributes in six major areas. The six areas are emotional appeal, products and services, financial performance, workplace environment, social responsibility, and vision and leadership. What are the five highest and lowest ranked companies in its 2005 survey? The five highest (best) ranked companies were

Johnson & Johnson, The Coca-Cola Company, Google, United Parcel Service of America, Inc. (UPS), and 3M. The five lowest (worst) companies were United Airlines, Haliburton Company, Adelphia Communications, MCI, and Enron. Not surprisingly, these latter companies are involved in either corporate scandal, financial distress, or bankruptcy.

Source: Harris Interactive, November 2005.

Budgetary Performance Evaluation

objective 2

Explain and illustrate how standards are used in budgeting.

As we discussed in the previous chapter, the master budget assists a company in planning, directing, and controlling performance. In the remainder of this chapter, we will discuss using the master budget for control purposes. The control function, or budgetary performance evaluation, compares the actual performance against the budget.

We illustrate budget performance evaluation using Western Rider Inc., a manufacturer of blue jeans. Western Rider Inc. uses standard manufacturing costs in its budgets. The standards for direct materials, direct labor, and factory overhead are separated into two components: (1) a price standard and (2) a quantity standard. Multiplying these two elements together yields the standard cost per unit for a given manufacturing cost category, as shown for style XL jeans in Exhibit 1.

> **EXHIBIT 1**
>
> **Standard Cost for XL Jeans**

Manufacturing Costs	Standard Price	×	Standard Quantity per Pair	=	Standard Cost per Pair of XL Jeans
Direct materials	$5.00 per square yard		1.5 square yards		$ 7.50
Direct labor	$9.00 per hour		0.80 hour per pair		7.20
Factory overhead	$6.00 per hour		0.80 hour per pair		4.80
Total standard cost per pair					$19.50

The standard price and quantity are separated because the means of controlling them are normally different. For example, the direct materials price per square yard is controlled by the Purchasing Department, and the direct materials quantity per pair is controlled by the Production Department.

As we illustrated in the previous chapter, the budgeted costs at planned volumes are included in the master budget at the beginning of the period. The standard amounts budgeted for materials purchases, direct labor, and factory overhead are determined by multiplying the standard costs per unit by the *planned* level of production. At the end of the month, the standard costs per unit are multiplied by the *actual* production and compared to the actual costs.

To illustrate, assume that Western Rider produced and sold 5,000 pairs of XL jeans. It incurred direct materials costs of $40,150, direct labor costs of $38,500, and factory overhead costs of $22,400. The **budget performance report** shown in Exhibit 2 summarizes the actual costs, the standard amounts for the actual level of production achieved, and the differences between the two amounts. These differences are called

EXHIBIT 2

Budget Performance
Report

Western Rider Inc.
Budget Performance Report
For the Month Ended June 30, 2008

Manufacturing Costs	Actual Costs	Standard Cost at Actual Volume (5,000 pairs of XL Jeans)*	Cost Variance— (Favorable) Unfavorable
Direct materials	$ 40,150	$37,500	$ 2,650
Direct labor	38,500	36,000	2,500
Factory overhead	22,400	24,000	(1,600)
Total manufacturing costs	$101,050	$97,500	$ 3,550

*5,000 pairs × $7.50 per pair = $37,500
5,000 pairs × $7.20 per pair = $36,000
5,000 pairs × $4.80 per pair = $24,000

cost variances. A *favorable* cost variance occurs when the actual cost is less than the standard cost (at actual volumes). An *unfavorable* variance occurs when the actual cost exceeds the standard cost (at actual volumes).

Based on the information in the budget performance report, management can investigate major differences and take corrective action. In Exhibit 2, for example, the direct materials cost variance is an unfavorable $2,650. There are two possible explanations for this variance: (1) the amount of blue denim used per pair of blue jeans was different than expected, and/or (2) the purchase price of blue denim was different than expected. In the next sections, we will illustrate how to separate the price and quantity variances for direct materials, the rate and time variances for direct labor, and the controllable and volume variances for factory overhead.

The relationship of these variances to the total manufacturing cost variance is shown below.

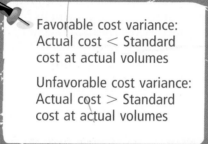

Favorable cost variance:
Actual cost < Standard
cost at actual volumes

Unfavorable cost variance:
Actual cost > Standard
cost at actual volumes

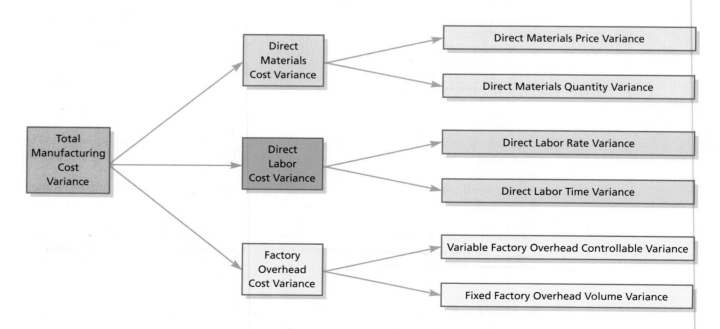

Direct Materials and Direct Labor Variances

objective **3**

Compute and interpret direct materials and direct labor variances.

The total cost of most goods or services is based on price multiplied by quantity. For example, your power bill is determined by multiplying the price per kilowatt hour by the number of kilowatt hours used during the month. Direct materials are determined by multiplying price by quantity, while direct labor is determined by multiplying the direct labor rate by time. Thus, the total cost variance for direct materials and direct labor can be separated into the portion of a cost variance that is caused by price (rate) differences and the portion that is caused by quantity (time) differences. These are illustrated next.

DIRECT MATERIALS VARIANCES

What caused Western Rider Inc.'s unfavorable materials variance of $2,650? Recall that the direct materials standards from Exhibit 1 are as follows:

> Price standard: $5.00 per square yard
> Quantity standard: 1.5 square yards per pair of XL jeans

To determine the number of standard square yards of denim budgeted, multiply the actual production for June 2008 (5,000 pairs) by the quantity standard (1.5 square yards per pair). Then multiply the standard square yards by the standard price per square yard ($5.00) to determine the *standard* budgeted cost at the actual volume. The calculation is shown as follows:

Standard square yards per pair of jeans	1.5 sq. yards
Actual units produced	× 5,000 pairs of XL jeans
Standard square yards of denim budgeted for	
actual production	7,500 sq. yards
Standard price per square yard	× $5.00
Standard direct materials cost at actual production	
(same as Exhibit 2)	$37,500

This calculation assumes that there is no change in the beginning and ending materials inventories. Thus, the amount of materials budgeted for production equals the amount purchased.

Assume that the *actual* total cost for denim used during June 2008 was as follows:

Actual quantity of denim used in production	7,300 sq. yards
Actual price per square yard	× $5.50
Total actual direct materials cost	
(same as Exhibit 2)	$40,150

The total unfavorable cost variance of $2,650 ($40,150 − $37,500) results from an excess price per square yard of $0.50 ($5.50 − $5.00) and using 200 (7,300 sq. yards − 7,500 sq. yards) fewer square yards of denim. These two reasons can be reported as two separate variances, as shown in the next sections.

Direct Materials Price Variance   The **direct materials price variance** is the difference between the actual price per unit ($5.50) and the standard price per unit ($5.00), multiplied by the actual quantity used (7,300 square yards). If the actual price per unit exceeds the standard price per unit, the variance is unfavorable, as shown for Western Rider Inc. If the actual price per unit is less than the standard price per unit, the variance is favorable. The calculation for Western Rider Inc. is as follows:

Price variance:	
Actual price per unit	$5.50 per square yard
Standard price per unit	5.00 per square yard
Price variance—unfavorable	$0.50 per square yard × actual qty., 7,300 sq. yds. = $3,650 U

Most restaurants use standards to control the amount of food served to customers. For example, Darden Restaurants, Inc., the operator of the Red Lobster chain, establishes standards for the number of shrimp, scallops, or clams on a seafood plate. In the same way, Keystone Foods LLC, a major food supplier to Mc-Donald's, uses standards to carefully control the size and weight of chicken nuggets.

Direct Materials Quantity Variance   The **direct materials quantity variance** is the difference between the actual quantity used (7,300 square yards) and the standard quantity at actual production (7,500 square yards), multiplied by the standard price per unit ($5.00). If the actual quantity of materials used exceeds the standard quantity budgeted, the variance is unfavorable. If the actual quantity of materials used is less than the standard quantity, the variance is favorable, as shown for Western Rider Inc.:

Quantity variance:
Actual quantity	7,300 square yards
Standard quantity at	
actual production	7,500
Quantity variance—favorable	(200) square yards × standard price, $5.00 = ($1,000) F

Direct Materials Variance Relationships   The direct materials variances can be illustrated by making the three calculations shown in Exhibit 3.

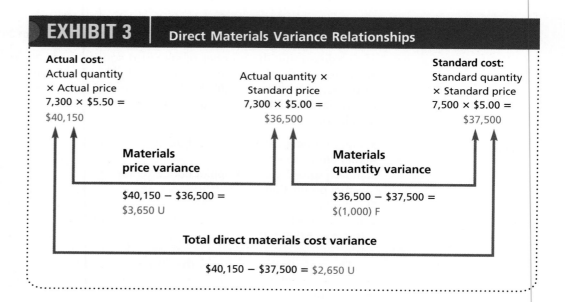

EXHIBIT 3 | **Direct Materials Variance Relationships**

Actual cost:
Actual quantity
× Actual price
7,300 × $5.50 =
$40,150

Actual quantity ×
Standard price
7,300 × $5.00 =
$36,500

Standard cost:
Standard quantity
× Standard price
7,500 × $5.00 =
$37,500

Materials price variance

Materials quantity variance

$40,150 − $36,500 =
$3,650 U

$36,500 − $37,500 =
$(1,000) F

Total direct materials cost variance

$40,150 − $37,500 = $2,650 U

Reporting Direct Materials Variances   The direct materials quantity variance should be reported to the proper operating management level for corrective action. For example, an unfavorable quantity variance might have been caused by malfunctioning equipment that has not been properly maintained or operated. However, unfavorable materials quantity variances are not always caused by operating departments. For example, the excess materials usage may be caused by purchasing inferior raw materials. In this case, the Purchasing Department should be held responsible for the variance.

The materials price variance should normally be reported to the Purchasing Department, which may or may not be able to control this variance. If materials of the same quality could have been purchased from another supplier at the standard price, the variance was controllable. On the other hand, if the variance resulted from a marketwide price increase, the variance may not be controllable.

Example Exercise 7-1

objective **3**

Tip Top Corp. produces a product that requires six standard pounds per unit. The standard price is $4.50 per pound. If 3,000 units required 18,500 pounds, which were purchased at $4.35 per pound, what is the direct materials (a) price variance, (b) quantity variance, and (c) cost variance?

(continued)

Follow My Example 7-1

a.	Direct materials price variance (favorable)	($2,775) [($4.35 − $4.50) × 18,500 pounds]
b.	Direct materials quantity variance (unfavorable)	$2,250 [(18,500 pounds − 18,000 pounds*) × $4.50]
c.	Direct materials cost variance (favorable)	($525) [($2,775) + $2,250] or [($4.35 × 18,500 pounds) − ($4.50 × 18,000 pounds)] = $80,475 − $81,000

*3,000 units × 6 pounds

For Practice: PE 7-1A, PE 7-1B

DIRECT LABOR VARIANCES

Western Rider Inc.'s direct labor cost variance can also be separated into two parts. Recall that the direct labor standards from Exhibit 1 are as follows:

Rate standard: $9.00 per hour
Time standard: 0.80 hour per pair of XL jeans

The actual production (5,000 pairs) is multiplied by the time standard (0.80 hour per pair) to determine the number of standard direct labor hours budgeted. The standard direct labor hours are then multiplied by the standard rate per hour ($9.00) to determine the *standard* direct labor cost at actual volumes. These calculations are shown below.

Standard direct labor hours per pair of XL jeans	0.80 direct labor hours
Actual units produced	× 5,000 pairs of jeans
Standard direct labor hours budgeted for actual production	4,000 direct labor hours
Standard rate per direct labor hour	× $9.00
Standard direct labor cost at actual production (same as Exhibit 2)	$36,000

Assume that the *actual* total cost for direct labor during June 2008 was as follows:

Actual direct labor hours used in production	3,850 direct labor hours
Actual rate per direct labor hour	× $10.00
Total actual direct labor cost (same as Exhibit 2)	$ 38,500

The total unfavorable cost variance $2,500 ($38,500 − $36,000) results from an excess rate of $1.00 ($10.00 − $9.00) per direct labor hour and using 150 (3,850 hours − 4,000 hours) fewer direct labor hours. These two reasons can be reported as two separate variances, as we discuss next.

Direct Labor Rate Variance   The **direct labor rate variance** is the difference between the actual rate per hour ($10.00) and the standard rate per hour ($9.00), multiplied by the actual hours worked (3,850 hours). If the actual rate per hour is less than the standard rate per hour, the variance is favorable. If the actual rate per hour exceeds the standard rate per hour, the variance is unfavorable, as shown below for Western Rider Inc.

Rate variance:	
Actual rate	$10.00 per hour
Standard rate	9.00
Rate variance—unfavorable	$ 1.00 per hour × actual time, 3,850 hours = $3,850 U

Direct Labor Time Variance   The **direct labor time variance** is the difference between the actual hours worked (3,850 hours) and the standard hours at actual production (4,000 hours), multiplied by the standard rate per hour ($9.00). If the actual hours worked exceed the standard hours, the variance is unfavorable. If the actual hours worked are less than the standard hours, the variance is favorable, as shown at the top of the next page for Western Rider Inc.

Time variance:

Actual hours	3,850 direct labor hours
Standard hours at actual production	4,000
Time variance—favorable	(150) direct labor hours × standard rate, $9.00 = ($1,350) F

Direct Labor Variance Relationships   The direct labor variances can be illustrated by making the three calculations shown in Exhibit 4.

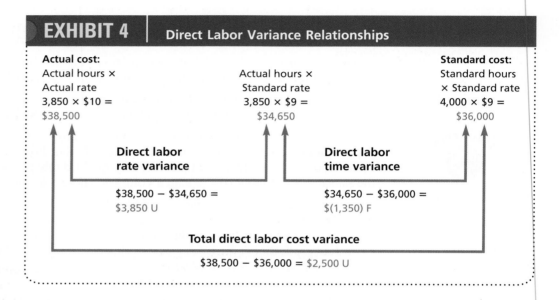

EXHIBIT 4 | **Direct Labor Variance Relationships**

Actual cost:
Actual hours ×
Actual rate
3,850 × $10 =
$38,500

Actual hours ×
Standard rate
3,850 × $9 =
$34,650

Standard cost:
Standard hours
× Standard rate
4,000 × $9 =
$36,000

Direct labor
rate variance

Direct labor
time variance

$38,500 − $34,650 =
$3,850 U

$34,650 − $36,000 =
$(1,350) F

Total direct labor cost variance

$38,500 − $36,000 = $2,500 U

Reporting Direct Labor Variances   Controlling direct labor cost is normally the responsibility of the production supervisors. To aid them, reports analyzing the cause of any direct labor variance may be prepared. Differences between standard direct labor hours and actual direct labor hours can be investigated. For example, a time variance may be incurred because of the shortage of skilled workers. Such variances may be uncontrollable unless they are related to high turnover rates among employees, in which case the cause of the high turnover should be investigated.

Likewise, differences between the rates paid for direct labor and the standard rates can be investigated. For example, unfavorable rate variances may be caused by the improper scheduling and use of workers. In such cases, skilled, highly paid workers may be used in jobs that are normally performed by unskilled, lower-paid workers. In this case, the unfavorable rate variance should be reported for corrective action to the managers who schedule work assignments.

Hospitals use time standards, termed *standard treatment protocols*, to evaluate the efficiency of performing hospital procedures.

Direct Labor Standards for Nonmanufacturing Activities   Direct labor time standards can also be applied to nonmanufacturing administrative, selling, and service activities, which are repetitive and produce a common output. In these cases, the use of standards is similar to that described in this section for a manufactured product. For example, standards can be applied to the work of customer service personnel who process sales orders. A standard time for processing a sales order (the output) could be developed. The variance between the actual time of processing a volume of sales orders and the standard time could then be used to control sales order processing costs. Other nonmanufacturing activities that have been used in conjunction with standards are help desk operations, warehouse operations, nursing care, and insurance application processing.

However, when nonmanufacturing activities are not repetitive, direct labor time standards are less commonly used. This occurs when the time to perform nonmanufacturing activities is not directly related to a unit of output. For example, the time associated with the work of a senior executive or the work of a research and development scientist is not easily related to a measurable output. In these cases, nonmanufacturing expenses are normally controlled by using static budgets.

Example Exercise 7-2 | objective **3**

Tip Top Corp. produces a product that requires 2.5 standard hours per unit at a standard hourly rate of $12 per hour. If 3,000 units required 7,420 hours at an hourly rate of $12.30 per hour, what is the direct labor (a) rate variance, (b) time variance, and (c) cost variance?

Follow My Example 7-2

a. Direct labor rate variance (unfavorable) $2,226 [($12.30 − $12.00) × 7,420 hours]
b. Direct labor time variance (favorable)   ($960) [(7,420 hours − 7,500 hours*) × $12.00]
c. Direct labor cost variance (unfavorable) $1,266 [$2,226 + ($960)] or [($12.30 × 7,420 hours) − ($12.00 × 7,500 hours)] = $91,266 − $90,000

*3,000 units × 2.5 hours

For Practice: PE 7-2A, PE 7-2B

Factory Overhead Variances

objective **4**

Compute and interpret factory overhead controllable and volume variances.

Factory overhead costs are more difficult to manage than are direct labor and materials costs. This is because the relationship between production volume and indirect costs is not easy to determine. For example, when production is increased, the direct materials will increase. But what about the Engineering Department overhead? The relationship between production volume and cost is less clear for the Engineering Department. Companies normally respond to this difficulty by separating factory overhead into variable and fixed costs. For example, manufacturing supplies are considered variable to production volume, whereas straight-line plant depreciation is considered fixed. In the following sections, we discuss the approaches used to budget and control factory overhead by separating overhead into fixed and variable components.

THE FACTORY OVERHEAD FLEXIBLE BUDGET

A flexible budget may be used to determine the impact of changing production on fixed and variable factory overhead costs. The standard overhead rate is determined by dividing the budgeted factory overhead costs by the standard amount of productive activity, such as direct labor hours. Exhibit 5 is a flexible factory overhead budget for Western Rider Inc.

In Exhibit 5, the standard factory overhead cost rate is $6.00. It is determined by dividing the total budgeted cost of 100% of normal capacity (6,250 units produced) by the standard hours required at 100% of normal capacity, or $30,000/5,000 hours = $6.00 per hour. This rate can be subdivided into $3.60 per hour for variable factory overhead ($18,000/5,000 hours) and $2.40 per hour for fixed factory overhead ($12,000/5,000 hours).

Variances from standard for factory overhead cost result from:

1. Actual variable factory overhead cost greater or less than budgeted variable factory overhead for actual production.
2. Actual production at a level above or below 100% of normal capacity.

The first factor results in the controllable variance for variable overhead costs. The second factor results in a volume variance for fixed overhead costs. We will discuss each of these variances next.

EXHIBIT 5

Factory Overhead Cost Budget Indicating Standard Factory Overhead Rate

	A	B	C	D	E	
	Western Rider Inc.					
	Factory Overhead Cost Budget					
	For the Month Ending June 30, 2008					
1	Percent of normal capacity	80%	90%	100%	110%	1
2	Units produced	5,000	5,625	6,250	6,875	2
3	Direct labor hours (0.80 hour per unit)	4,000	4,500	5,000	5,500	3
4	Budgeted factory overhead:					4
5	Variable costs:					5
6	Indirect factory wages	$ 8,000	$ 9,000	$10,000	$11,000	6
7	Power and light	4,000	4,500	5,000	5,500	7
8	Indirect materials	2,400	2,700	3,000	3,300	8
9	Total variable cost	$14,400	$16,200	$18,000	$19,800	9
10	Fixed costs:					10
11	Supervisory salaries	$ 5,500	$ 5,500	$ 5,500	$ 5,500	11
12	Depreciation of plant					12
13	and equipment	4,500	4,500	4,500	4,500	13
14	Insurance and property taxes	2,000	2,000	2,000	2,000	14
15	Total fixed cost	$12,000	$12,000	$12,000	$12,000	15
16	Total factory overhead cost	$26,400	$28,200	$30,000	$31,800	16
17						17
18	Factory overhead rate per direct labor hour, $30,000/5,000 hours = $6.00					18

VARIABLE FACTORY OVERHEAD CONTROLLABLE VARIANCE

The variable factory overhead **controllable variance** is the difference between the actual variable overhead incurred and the budgeted variable overhead for actual production. The controllable variance measures the *efficiency* of using variable overhead resources. Thus, if the actual variable overhead is less than the budgeted variable overhead, the variance is favorable. If the actual variable overhead exceeds the budgeted variable overhead, the variance is unfavorable.

To illustrate, recall that Western Rider Inc. produced 5,000 pairs of XL jeans in June. Each pair requires 0.80 standard labor hour for production. As a result, Western Rider Inc. had 4,000 standard hours at actual production (5,000 jeans × 0.80 hour). This represents 80% of normal productive capacity (4,000 hours/5,000 hours). The standard variable overhead at 4,000 hours worked, according to the budget in Exhibit 5, was $14,400 (4,000 direct labor hours × $3.60). The following actual factory overhead costs were incurred in June:

Actual costs:	
Variable factory overhead	$10,400
Fixed factory overhead	12,000
Total actual factory overhead	$22,400

The controllable variance can be calculated as follows:

Controllable variance:	
Actual variable factory overhead	$10,400
Budgeted variable factory overhead for actual amount produced (4,000 hrs. × $3.60)	14,400
Variance—favorable	$ (4,000) F

The variable factory overhead controllable variance indicates management's ability to keep the factory overhead costs within the budget limits. Since variable factory overhead costs are normally controllable at the department level, responsibility for controlling this variance usually rests with department supervisors.

Example Exercise 7-3   objective   4

Tip Top Corp. produced 3,000 units of product that required 2.5 standard hours per unit. The standard variable overhead cost per unit is $2.20 per hour. The actual variable factory overhead was $16,850. Determine the variable factory overhead controllable variance.

Follow My Example 7-3

$350 unfavorable
$16,850 − [$2.20 × (3,000 units × 2.5 hours)]

For Practice: PE 7-3A, PE 7-3B

FIXED FACTORY OVERHEAD VOLUME VARIANCE

Using currently attainable standards, Western Rider Inc. set its budgeted normal capacity at 5,000 direct labor hours. This is the amount of expected capacity that management believes will be used under normal business conditions. You should note that this amount may be much less than the total available capacity if management believes demand will be low.

The fixed factory overhead **volume variance** is the difference between the budgeted fixed overhead at 100% of normal capacity and the standard fixed overhead for the actual production achieved during the period. The volume variance measures the use of fixed overhead resources. If the standard fixed overhead exceeds the budgeted overhead at 100% of normal capacity, the variance is favorable. Thus, the firm used its plant and equipment more than would be expected under normal operating conditions. If the standard fixed overhead is less than the budgeted overhead at 100% of normal capacity, the variance is unfavorable. Thus, the company used its plant and equipment less than would be expected under normal operating conditions.

The volume variance for Western Rider Inc. is shown in the following calculation:

100% of normal capacity (6,250 units produced)	5,000 direct labor hours
Standard hours at actual production	4,000
Capacity not used	1,000 direct labor hours
Standard fixed overhead rate	× $2.40
Volume variance—unfavorable	$ 2,400 U

Exhibit 6 illustrates the volume variance graphically. For Western Rider Inc., the budgeted fixed overhead is $12,000 at all levels. The standard fixed overhead at 5,000 hours is also $12,000. This is the point at which the standard fixed overhead line intersects the budgeted fixed cost line. For actual volume greater than 100% of normal capacity, the volume variance is favorable. For volume at less than 100% of normal volume, the volume variance is unfavorable. For Western Rider Inc., the volume variance is unfavorable because the actual production is 4,000 standard hours, or 80% of normal volume. The amount of the volume variance, $2,400, can be viewed as the cost of the unused capacity (1,000 hours).

An unfavorable volume variance may be due to such factors as failure to maintain an even flow of work, machine breakdowns, repairs causing work stoppages, and failure to obtain enough sales orders to keep the factory operating at normal capacity. Management should determine the causes of the unfavorable variance and consider taking corrective action. A volume variance caused by an uneven flow of work, for example, can be remedied by changing operating procedures. Volume variances caused by lack of sales orders may be corrected through increased advertising or other sales effort.

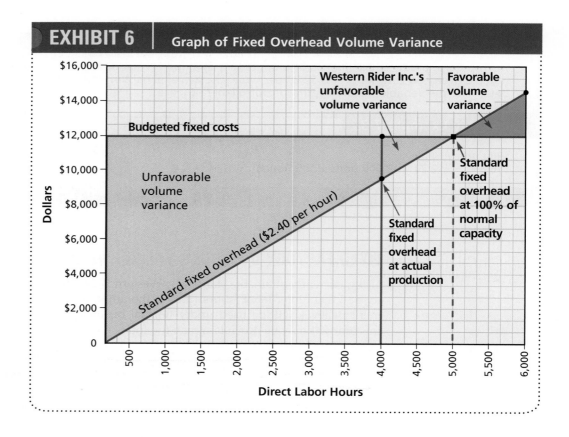

EXHIBIT 6 | Graph of Fixed Overhead Volume Variance

Many companies develop customized variances to fit their business. For example, Parker Hannifin Corp. reports a "standard run quantity variance" (which measures the difference between actual lot size and ideal lot size), "material substitution variance" (which measures the financial impact of substituted material), and "method variance" (which measures the financial impact of a change in processing methods).

Volume variances tend to encourage manufacturing managers to run the factory above the normal capacity. This is favorable when the additional production can be sold. However, if the additional production cannot be sold and must be stored as inventory, favorable volume variances may actually be harmful. For example, one paper company ran paper machines above normal volume in order to create favorable volume variances. Unfortunately, this created a six months' supply of finished goods inventory that had to be stored in public warehouses. The "savings" from the favorable volume variances were exceeded by the additional inventory carrying costs. By creating incentives for manufacturing managers to overproduce, the volume variances produced *goal conflicts*, as we described in the preceding chapter.

Example Exercise 7-4   objective 4

Tip Top Corp. produced 3,000 units of product that required 2.5 standard hours per unit. The standard fixed overhead cost per unit is $0.90 per hour at 8,000 hours, which is 100% of normal capacity. Determine the fixed factory overhead volume variance.

Follow My Example 7-4

$450 unfavorable
$0.90 × [8,000 hours − (3,000 units × 2.5 hours)]

For Practice: PE 7-4A, PE 7-4B

REPORTING FACTORY OVERHEAD VARIANCES

The total factory overhead cost variance is the difference between the actual factory overhead and the total overhead applied to production. This calculation is as follows:

Total actual factory overhead	$22,400
Factory overhead applied (4,000 hours × $6.00 per hour)	24,000
Total factory overhead cost variance—favorable	$ (1,600) F

The factory overhead cost variance may be broken down by each variable factory overhead cost and fixed factory overhead cost element in a *factory overhead cost variance report*. Such a report, which is useful to management in controlling costs, is shown in Exhibit 7. The report indicates both the controllable variance and the volume variance.

EXHIBIT 7

Factory Overhead Cost Variance Report

	A	B	C	D	E	
	Western Rider Inc.					
	Factory Overhead Cost Variance Report					
	For the Month Ending June 30, 2008					
1	Productive capacity for the month (100% of normal)	5,000 hours				1
2	Actual production for the month	4,000 hours				2
3						3
4		**Budget**				4
5		**(at Actual**		**Variances**		5
6		**Production)**	**Actual**	**Favorable**	**Unfavorable**	6
7	Variable factory overhead costs:					7
8	Indirect factory wages	$ 8,000	$ 5,100	$2,900		8
9	Power and light	4,000	4,200		$ 200	9
10	Indirect materials	2,400	1,100	1,300		10
11	Total variable factory					11
12	overhead cost	$14,400	$10,400			12
13	Fixed factory overhead costs:					13
14	Supervisory salaries	$ 5,500	$ 5,500			14
15	Depreciation of plant and					15
16	equipment	4,500	4,500			16
17	Insurance and property taxes	2,000	2,000			17
18	Total fixed factory					18
19	overhead cost	$12,000	$12,000			19
20	Total factory overhead cost	$26,400	$22,400			20
21	Total controllable variances			$4,200	$ 200	21
22						22
23						23
24	Net controllable variance—favorable				$4,000	24
25	Volume variance—unfavorable:					25
26	Capacity not used at the standard rate for fixed					26
27	factory overhead—1,000 × $2.40				2,400	27
28	Total factory overhead cost variance—favorable				$1,600	28

FACTORY OVERHEAD VARIANCES AND THE FACTORY OVERHEAD ACCOUNT

At the end of the period, the factory overhead account normally has a balance. As we discussed in an earlier chapter, a debit balance in Factory Overhead is underapplied overhead, while a credit balance is overapplied overhead. This end-of-period balance, which represents the difference between actual overhead incurred and applied overhead, is also the total factory overhead variance for the period. A debit balance, underapplied overhead, represents an unfavorable total factory overhead variance, while a credit balance, overapplied overhead, is a favorable variance.

To illustrate, the factory overhead account for Western Rider Inc. for the month ending June 30, 2008, is shown below.

Factory Overhead

Actual factory overhead ($10,400 + $12,000)	22,400		24,000	Applied factory overhead (4,000 hrs. × $6.00 per hr.)
		Bal., June 30	1,600	Overapplied factory overhead

The $1,600 overapplied factory overhead is the favorable total factory cost variance shown in Exhibit 7. The variable factory overhead controllable variance and the volume variance can be computed using the factory overhead account and comparing it with the budgeted total overhead for the actual amount produced. As shown below, the difference between the actual overhead incurred and the budgeted overhead is the controllable variance. The difference between the applied overhead and the budgeted overhead is the volume variance.

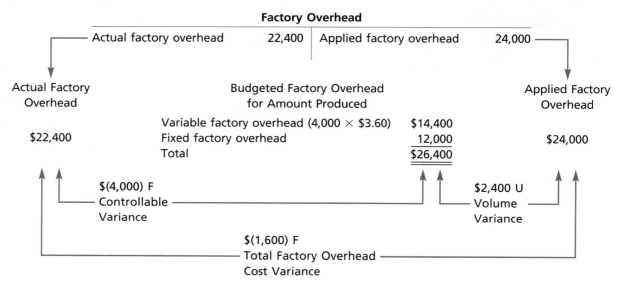

If the actual factory overhead exceeds (is less than) the budgeted factory overhead, the controllable variance is unfavorable (favorable). In contrast, if the applied factory overhead is less than (exceeds) the budgeted factory overhead, the volume variance is unfavorable (favorable). This is because, when the applied overhead is less than the budgeted overhead, the company has operated at less than normal capacity, and thus the volume variance is unfavorable.

It is also possible to break down many of the individual factory overhead cost variances into quantity and price variances, similar to direct materials and direct labor. For example, the indirect factory wages variance may include both time and rate variances. Likewise, the indirect materials variance may include both a quantity variance and a price variance. Such variances are illustrated in advanced textbooks.

objective 5

Journalize the entries for recording standards in the accounts and prepare an income statement that includes variances from standard.

Recording and Reporting Variances from Standards

Standard costs can be used solely as a management tool separate from the accounts in the general ledger. However, many companies include both standard costs and variances, in addition to actual costs, in their accounts. In doing so, one approach is to record the standard costs and variances at the same time the actual manufacturing costs are recorded in the accounts. To illustrate, assume that Western Rider Inc. purchased, on account, the 7,300 square yards of blue denim used at $5.50 per square yard. The standard price for direct materials is $5.00 per square yard. The entry to record the purchase and the unfavorable direct materials price variance is as follows:

Materials (7,300 sq. yds. × $5.00)		36 5 0 0 00		
Direct Materials Price Variance		3 6 5 0 00		
Accounts Payable (7,300 sq. yds. × $5.50)				40 1 5 0 00

The materials account is debited for the actual quantity purchased at the standard price, $36,500 (7,300 square yards × $5.00). Accounts Payable is credited for the $40,150 actual cost. The unfavorable direct materials price variance is $3,650 [($5.50 actual price per square yard − $5.00 standard price per square yard) × 7,300 square yards purchased]. It is recorded by debiting Direct Materials Price Variance. If the variance had been favorable, Direct Materials Price Variance would have been credited for the amount of the variance.

The direct materials quantity variance is recorded in a similar manner. For example, Western Rider Inc. used 7,300 square yards of blue denim to produce 5,000 pairs of XL jeans, compared to a standard of 7,500 square yards. The entry to record the materials used is as follows:

Work in Process (7,500 sq. yds. × $5.00)		37 5 0 0 00		
Direct Materials Quantity Variance				1 0 0 0 00
Materials (7,300 sq. yds. × $5.00)				36 5 0 0 00

The work in process account is debited for the standard price of the standard amount of direct materials required, $37,500 (7,500 square yards × $5.00). Materials is credited for the actual amount of materials used at the standard price, $36,500 (7,300 square yards × $5.00). The favorable direct materials quantity variance of $1,000 [(7,500 standard square yards − 7,300 actual square yards) × $5.00 standard price per square yard] is credited to Direct Materials Quantity Variance. If the variance had been unfavorable, Direct Materials Quantity Variance would have been debited for the amount of the variance.

Example Exercise 7-5   objective 5

Tip Top Corp. produced 3,000 units that require six standard pounds per unit at $4.50 standard price per pound. The company actually used 18,500 pounds in production. Journalize the entry to record the standard direct materials used in production.

Follow My Example 7-5

Work in Process (18,000* pounds × $4.50)   81,000
Direct Materials Quantity Variance [(18,500 pounds − 18,000 pounds) × $4.50]   2,250
    Materials (18,500 pounds × $4.50)   83,250

*3,000 units × 6 pounds per unit = 18,000 standard pounds for units produced

For Practice: PE 7-5A, PE 7-5B

The entries for direct labor are recorded in a manner similar to direct materials. Thus, the work in process account is debited for the standard cost of direct labor and the wages payable account credited for the actual direct labor cost. Direct labor rate and time variances would be either debited (unfavorable) or credited (favorable) as appropriate. Factory overhead would be treated in a similar manner as illustrated with the factory overhead T account in the previous section. As goods are completed, the work in process account is credited for the standard cost of the product transferred, and the finished goods account is debited.

In a given period, it is possible to have both favorable and unfavorable variances. At the end of the period, the balances of the variance accounts will indicate the net favorable or unfavorable variance for the period.

Variances from standard costs are usually not reported to stockholders and others outside the business. If standards are recorded in the accounts, however, the variances may be reported in income statements prepared for management's use. Exhibit 8 is an example of such an income statement prepared for Western Rider Inc.'s internal use. In this exhibit, we assume a sales price of $28 per pair of jeans, selling expenses of $14,500, and administrative expenses of $11,225.

At the end of the fiscal year, the variances from standard are usually transferred to the cost of goods sold account. However, if the variances are significant or if many of the products manufactured are still in inventory, the variances should be allocated to the work in process, finished goods, and cost of goods sold accounts. Such an allocation converts these account balances from standard cost to actual cost.

EXHIBIT 8

Variances from Standards in Income Statement

Western Rider Inc.
Income Statement
For the Month Ended June 30, 2008

	Favorable	Unfavorable	
Sales			$140,000[1]
Cost of goods sold—at standard			97,500[2]
Gross profit—at standard			$ 42,500
Less variances from standard cost:			
Direct materials price		$ 3,650	
Direct materials quantity	$1,000		
Direct labor rate		3,850	
Direct labor time	1,350		
Factory overhead controllable	4,000		
Factory overhead volume	_____	2,400	3,550
Gross profit			$ 38,950
Operating expenses:			
Selling expenses		$14,500	
Administrative expenses		11,225	25,725
Income before income tax			$ 13,225

[1]5,000 × $28
[2]$37,500 + $36,000 + $24,000 (from Exhibit 2),
  or 5,000 × $19.50 (from Exhibit 1)

Example Exercise 7-6   objective **5**

Prepare an income statement for the year ended December 31, 2008, through gross profit for Tip Top Corp. using the variance data in Example Exercises 7-1 through 7-4. Assume Tip Top sold 3,000 units at $100 per unit.

(continued)

Follow My Example 7-6

TIP TOP CORP.
INCOME STATEMENT THROUGH GROSS PROFIT
For the Year Ended December 31, 2008

		Favorable	Unfavorable	
Sales (3,000 units × $100)				$300,000
Cost of goods sold—at standard				194,250*
Gross profit—at standard				$105,750
Less variances from standard cost:				
Direct materials price (EE7-1)		$2,775		
Direct materials quantity (EE7-1)			$2,250	
Direct labor rate (EE7-2)			2,226	
Direct labor time (EE7-2)		960		
Factory overhead controllable (EE7-3)			350	
Factory overhead volume (EE7-4)			450	1,541
Gross profit—actual				$104,209

*Direct materials (3,000 units × 6 pounds × $4.50)	$ 81,000	
Direct labor (3,000 units × 2.5 hours × $12.00)	90,000	
Factory overhead [3,000 units × 2.5 hours × ($2.20 + $0.90)]	23,250	
Cost of goods sold at standard	$194,250	

For Practice: PE 7-6A, PE 7-6B

Nonfinancial Performance Measures

objective 6

Explain and provide examples of nonfinancial performance measures.

Many managers believe that financial performance measures, such as variances from standard, should be supplemented with nonfinancial performance measures. A **nonfinancial performance measure** is a performance measure expressed in units other than dollars. Nonfinancial performance measures are often used to evaluate the time, quality, or quantity of a business activity. Examples of nonfinancial performance measures from the airline industry are on-time performance, percent of bags lost, and number of customer complaints.

Measuring both financial and nonfinancial performance helps employees consider multiple, and sometimes conflicting, performance objectives. For example, one company had a machining operation that was measured according to a direct labor time standard. Employees did their work quickly in order to create favorable direct labor time variances. Unfortunately, the fast work resulted in poor quality that, in turn, created difficulty in the assembly operation. The company decided to use both a labor time standard and a quality standard in order to encourage employees to consider both the speed and quality of their work.

In the preceding example, nonfinancial performance measures brought additional perspectives, such as quality of work, to evaluating performance. Some additional examples of nonfinancial performance measures are as follows:

Nonfinancial Performance Measures

Inventory turnover
Percent on-time delivery
Elapsed time between a customer order and product delivery
Customer preference rankings compared to competitors
Response time to a service call
Time to develop new products
Employee satisfaction
Number of customer complaints

Nonfinancial measures can be linked to either the inputs or outputs of an activity or process. A **process** is a sequence of activities linked together for performing a particular task. For example, the fast food service process consists of the "food preparation" and "counter service" activities that are performed in providing fast food. The relationship between a process or activity and its inputs and outputs is shown as follows:

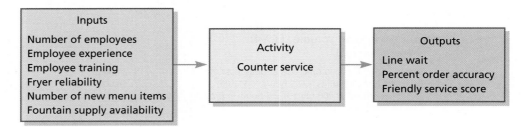

To illustrate nonfinancial measures for a single activity, consider the counter service activity of a fast food restaurant. The following input/output relationship could be identified:

The outputs of the counter service activity include the customer line wait, order accuracy, and service experience. The inputs that impact these outputs include the number of employees, level of employee experience and training, reliability of the french fryer, menu complexity, fountain drink supply, and the like. Also, note that the inputs for one activity could be the outputs of another.

To illustrate, fryer reliability is an input to the counter service activity, but is an output of the french frying activity. Moving back, fryer maintenance would be an input to the french frying activity. Thus, a chain of inputs and outputs can be developed between a set of connected activities or processes. The fast food restaurant can develop a set of linked nonfinancial performance measures across the chain of inputs and outputs. The output measures tell management how the activity is performing, such as keeping the line wait to a minimum. The input measures are the *levers* that impact the activity's performance. Thus, if the fast food restaurant line wait is too long, then the input measures might indicate a need for more training, more employees, or better fryer reliability.

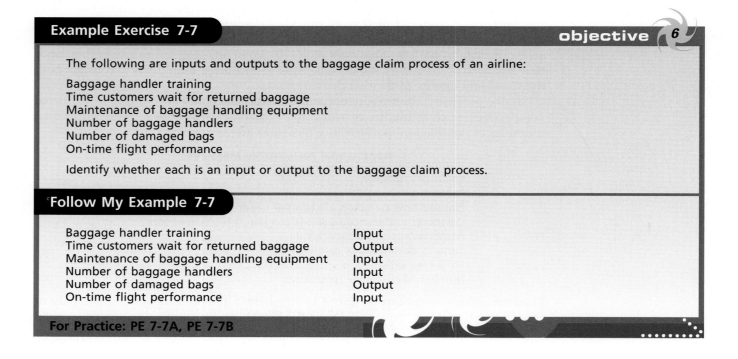

Example Exercise 7-7   objective 6

The following are inputs and outputs to the baggage claim process of an airline:

Baggage handler training
Time customers wait for returned baggage
Maintenance of baggage handling equipment
Number of baggage handlers
Number of damaged bags
On-time flight performance

Identify whether each is an input or output to the baggage claim process.

Follow My Example 7-7

Baggage handler training	Input
Time customers wait for returned baggage	Output
Maintenance of baggage handling equipment	Input
Number of baggage handlers	Input
Number of damaged bags	Output
On-time flight performance	Input

For Practice: PE 7-7A, PE 7-7B

At a Glance ↘

1. Describe the types of standards and how they are established for businesses.

Key Points	Key Learning Outcomes	Example Exercises	Practice Exercises
Standards represent performance benchmarks that can be compared to actual results in evaluating performance. Standards are established so that they are neither too high nor too low, but are attainable.	• Define *ideal* and *normal standards* and explain how they are used in setting standards. • Describe some of the criticisms of the use of standards.		

2. Explain and illustrate how standards are used in budgeting.

Key Points	Key Learning Outcomes	Example Exercises	Practice Exercises
Budgets are prepared by multiplying the standard cost per unit by the planned production. To measure performance, the standard cost per unit is multiplied by the actual number of units produced, and the actual results are compared with the standard cost at actual volumes (cost variance).	• Compute the standard cost per unit of production for materials, labor, and factory overhead. • Compute the direct labor, direct materials, and factory overhead cost variances. • Prepare a budget performance report.		

3. Compute and interpret direct materials and direct labor variances.

Key Points	Key Learning Outcomes	Example Exercises	Practice Exercises
The direct materials cost variance can be separated into direct materials price and quantity variances. The direct labor cost variance can be separated into direct labor rate and time variances.	• Compute and interpret direct materials price and quantity variances. • Compute and interpret direct labor rate and time variances. • Describe and illustrate how time standards are used in nonmanufacturing settings.	7-1 7-2	7-1A, 7-1B 7-2A, 7-2B

4. Compute and interpret factory overhead controllable and volume variances.

Key Points	Key Learning Outcomes	Example Exercises	Practice Exercises
The factory overhead cost variance can be separated into a variable factory overhead controllable variance and a fixed factory overhead volume variance.	• Prepare a factory overhead flexible budget. • Compute and interpret the variable factory overhead controllable variance. • Compute and interpret the fixed factory overhead volume variance. • Prepare a factory overhead cost variance report. • Evaluate factory overhead variances using a T account.	7-3 7-4	7-3A, 7-3B 7-4A, 7-4B

(continued)

5. Journalize the entries for recording standards in the accounts and prepare an income statement that includes variances from standard.

Key Points	Key Learning Outcomes	Example Exercises	Practice Exercises
Standard costs and variances can be recorded in the accounts at the same time the manufacturing costs are recorded in the accounts. Work in Process is debited at standard. Under a standard cost system, the cost of goods sold will be reported at standard cost. Manufacturing variances can be disclosed on the income statement to adjust the gross profit at standard to the actual gross profit.	• Journalize the entries to record the purchase and use of direct materials at standard, recording favorable or unfavorable variances.	7-5	7-5A, 7-5B
	• Prepare an income statement, disclosing favorable and unfavorable direct materials, direct labor, and factory overhead variances.	7-6	7-6A, 7-6B

6. Explain and provide examples of nonfinancial performance measures.

Key Points	Key Learning Outcomes	Example Exercises	Practice Exercises
Many companies use a combination of financial and nonfinancial measures in order for multiple perspectives to be incorporated in evaluating performance. Nonfinancial measures are often used in conjunction with the inputs or outputs of a process or an activity.	• Define, provide the rationale for, and provide examples of nonfinancial performance measures.		
	• Identify nonfinancial inputs and outputs to an activity.	7-7	7-7A, 7-7B

Key Terms

budget performance report (269)
controllable variance (276)
cost variance (266)
currently attainable standards (267)
direct labor rate variance (273)
direct labor time variance (273)

direct materials price variance (271)
direct materials quantity variance (272)
ideal standards (267)
nonfinancial performance measure (283)

process (283)
standard cost (266)
standard cost systems (266)
volume variance (277)

Illustrative Problem

Hawley Inc. manufactures woven baskets for national distribution. The standard costs for the manufacture of Folk Art style baskets were as follows:

	Standard Costs	Actual Costs
Direct materials	1,500 pounds at $35	1,600 pounds at $32
Direct labor	4,800 hours at $11	4,500 hours at $11.80
Factory overhead	Rates per labor hour, based on 100% of normal capacity of 5,500 labor hours:	
	Variable cost, $2.40	$12,300 variable cost
	Fixed cost, $3.50	$19,250 fixed cost

Instructions

1. Determine the quantity variance, price variance, and total direct materials cost variance for the Folk Art style baskets.
2. Determine the time variance, rate variance, and total direct labor cost variance for the Folk Art style baskets.
3. Determine the controllable variance, volume variance, and total factory overhead cost variance for the Folk Art style baskets.

Solution

1.

Direct Materials Cost Variance

Quantity variance:		
Actual quantity	1,600 pounds	
Standard quantity	1,500	
Variance—unfavorable	100 pounds × standard price, $35	$ 3,500
Price variance:		
Actual price	$32.00 per pound	
Standard price	35.00	
Variance—favorable	$ (3.00) per pound × actual quantity, 1,600	(4,800)
Total direct materials cost variance—favorable		$(1,300)

2.

Direct Labor Cost Variance

Time variance:		
Actual time	4,500 hours	
Standard time	4,800 hours	
Variance—favorable	(300) hours × standard rate, $11	$(3,300)
Rate variance:		
Actual rate	$11.80	
Standard rate	11.00	
Variance—unfavorable	$ 0.80 per hour × actual time, 4,500 hrs.	3,600
Total direct labor cost variance—unfavorable		$ 300

3.

Factory Overhead Cost Variance

Variable factory overhead—controllable variance:		
Actual variable factory overhead cost incurred	$12,300	
Budgeted variable factory overhead for 4,800 hours	11,520*	
Variance—unfavorable		$ 780
Fixed factory overhead—volume variance:		
Budgeted hours at 100% of normal capacity	5,500 hours	
Standard hours for actual production	4,800	
Productive capacity not used	700 hours	
Standard fixed factory overhead cost rate	× $3.50 per hour	
Variance—unfavorable		2,450
Total factory overhead cost variance—unfavorable		$3,230

*4,800 hrs. × $2.40 = $11,520

Self-Examination Questions

(Answers at End of Chapter)

1. The actual and standard direct materials costs for producing a specified quantity of product are as follows:

   Actual: 51,000 pounds at $5.05 $257,550
   Standard: 50,000 pounds at $5.00 $250,000

   The direct materials price variance is:
   A. $50 unfavorable.
   B. $2,500 unfavorable.
   C. $2,550 unfavorable.
   D. $7,550 unfavorable.

2. Bower Company produced 4,000 units of product. Each unit requires 0.5 standard hour. The standard labor rate is $12 per hour. Actual direct labor for the period was $22,000 (2,200 hours × $10 per hour). The direct labor time variance is:
   A. 200 hours unfavorable.
   B. $2,000 unfavorable.
   C. $4,000 favorable.
   D. $2,400 unfavorable.

(continued)

3. The actual and standard factory overhead costs for producing a specified quantity of product are as follows:

Actual: Variable factory overhead $72,500
           Fixed factory overhead   40,000 $112,500
Standard: 19,000 hours at $6
           ($4 variable and $2 fixed)   114,000

If 1,000 hours were unused, the fixed factory overhead volume variance would be:
A. $1,500 favorable.   C. $4,000 unfavorable.
B. $2,000 unfavorable.   D. $6,000 unfavorable.

4. Ramathan Company produced 6,000 units of Product Y, which is 80% of capacity. Each unit required 0.25 standard machine hour for production. The standard variable factory overhead rate is $5.00 per machine hour. The actual variable factory overhead incurred during the period was $8,000. The variable factory overhead controllable variance is:
A. $500 favorable.   C. $1,875 favorable.
B. $500 unfavorable.   D. $1,875 unfavorable.

5. Applegate Company has a normal budgeted capacity of 200 machine hours. Applegate produced 600 units. Each unit requires a standard 0.2 machine hour to complete. The standard fixed factory overhead is $12.00 per hour, determined at normal capacity. The fixed factory overhead volume variance is:
A. $4,800 unfavorable.   C. $960 favorable.
B. $4,800 favorable.   D. $960 unfavorable.

Eye Openers

1. What are the basic objectives in the use of standard costs?
2. How can standards be used by management to help control costs?
3. What is meant by reporting by the "principle of exceptions," as the term is used in reference to cost control?
4. How often should standards be revised?
5. How are standards used in budgetary performance evaluation?
6. a. What are the two variances between the actual cost and the standard cost for direct materials?
   b. Discuss some possible causes of these variances.
7. The materials cost variance report for Nickols Inc. indicates a large favorable materials price variance and a significant unfavorable materials quantity variance. What might have caused these offsetting variances?
8. a. What are the two variances between the actual cost and the standard cost for direct labor?
   b. Who generally has control over the direct labor cost?
9. A new assistant controller recently was heard to remark: "All the assembly workers in this plant are covered by union contracts, so there should be no labor variances." Was the controller's remark correct? Discuss.
10. Would the use of standards be appropriate in a nonmanufacturing setting, such as a fast food restaurant?
11. a. Describe the two variances between the actual costs and the standard costs for factory overhead.
    b. What is a factory overhead cost variance report?
12. What are budgeted fixed costs at normal volume?
13. If variances are recorded in the accounts at the time the manufacturing costs are incurred, what does a debit balance in Direct Materials Price Variance represent?
14. If variances are recorded in the accounts at the time the manufacturing costs are incurred, what does a credit balance in Direct Materials Quantity Variance represent?
15. Briefly explain why firms might use nonfinancial performance measures.

Practice Exercises

PE 7-1A
Direct materials variances

obj. **3**

Brewster Company produces a product that requires four standard pounds per unit. The standard price is $6.80 per pound. If 1,500 units required 6,400 pounds, which were purchased at $6.50 per pound, what is the direct materials (a) price variance, (b) quantity variance, and (c) cost variance?

PE 7-1B
Direct materials variances
obj. 3

Tipton Company produces a product that requires eight standard gallons per unit. The standard price is $12.40 per gallon. If 800 units required 6,200 gallons, which were purchased at $12.75 per gallon, what is the direct materials (a) price variance, (b) quantity variance, and (c) cost variance?

PE 7-2A
Direct labor variances
obj. 3

Brewster Company produces a product that requires 1.5 standard hours per unit at a standard hourly rate of $15 per hour. If 1,500 units required 2,100 hours at an hourly rate of $15.50 per hour, what is the direct labor (a) rate variance, (b) time variance, and (c) cost variance?

PE 7-2B
Direct labor variances
obj. 3

Tipton Company produces a product that requires four standard hours per unit at a standard hourly rate of $10 per hour. If 800 units required 3,380 hours at an hourly rate of $9.60 per hour, what is the direct labor (a) rate variance, (b) time variance, and (c) cost variance?

PE 7-3A
Factory overhead controllable variance
obj. 4

Brewster Company produced 1,500 units of product that required 1.5 standard hours per unit. The standard variable overhead cost per unit is $1.70 per hour. The actual variable factory overhead was $3,900. Determine the variable factory overhead controllable variance.

PE 7-3B
Factory overhead controllable variance
obj. 4

Tipton Company produced 800 units of product that required four standard hours per unit. The standard variable overhead cost per unit is $4.50 per hour. The actual variable factory overhead was $14,100. Determine the variable factory overhead controllable variance.

PE 7-4A
Factory overhead volume variance
obj. 4

Brewster Company produced 1,500 units of product that required 1.5 standard hours per unit. The standard fixed overhead cost per unit is $0.50 per hour at 2,500 hours, which is 100% of normal capacity. Determine the fixed factory overhead volume variance.

PE 7-4B
Factory overhead volume variance
obj. 4

Tipton Company produced 800 units of product that required four standard hours per unit. The standard fixed overhead cost per unit is $1.20 per hour at 3,000 hours, which is 100% of normal capacity. Determine the fixed factory overhead volume variance.

PE 7-5A
Standard cost journal entries
obj. 5

Brewster Company produced 1,500 units that require four standard pounds per unit at $6.80 standard price per pound. The company actually used 6,400 pounds in production. Journalize the entry to record the standard direct materials used in production.

PE 7-5B
Standard cost journal entries
obj. 5

Tipton Company produced 800 units that require eight standard gallons per unit at $12.40 standard price per gallon. The company actually used 6,200 gallons in production. Journalize the entry to record the standard direct materials used in production.

PE 7-6A
Standard cost income statement with variances from standard
obj. 5

Prepare an income statement through gross profit for Brewster Company using the variance data in Practice Exercises 7-1A, 7-2A, 7-3A, and 7-4A. Assume Brewster sold 1,500 units at $80 per unit.

PE 7-6B
Standard cost income statement with variances from standard
obj. 5

Prepare an income statement through gross profit for Tipton Company using the variance data in Practice Exercises 7-1B, 7-2B, 7-3B, and 7-4B. Assume Tipton sold 800 units at $200 per unit.

PE 7-7A
Identify activity inputs and outputs
obj. 6

The following are inputs and outputs to the copying process of a copy shop:

Copy machine downtime (broken)
Number of customer complaints
Number of employee errors
Number of pages copied per hour
Number of times paper supply runs out
Percent jobs done on time

Identify whether each is an input or output to the copying process.

PE 7-7B
Identify activity inputs and outputs
obj. 6

The following are inputs and outputs to the cooking process of a restaurant:

Number of customer complaints
Number of hours kitchen equipment is down for repairs
Number of server order mistakes
Number of times ingredients are missing
Number of unexpected cook absences
Percent of meals prepared on time

Identify whether each is an input or output to the cooking process.

Exercises

EX 7-1
Standard direct materials cost per unit
obj. 2

Sweet Swiss Chocolate Company produces chocolate bars. The primary materials used in producing chocolate bars are cocoa, sugar, and milk. The standard costs for a batch of chocolate (1,000 bars) are as follows:

Ingredient	Quantity	Price
Cocoa	465 pounds	$0.30 per pound
Sugar	168 pounds	$0.50 per pound
Milk	110 gallons	$1.15 per gallon

Determine the standard direct materials cost per bar of chocolate.

EX 7-2
Standard product cost
obj. 2

Carolina Furniture Company manufactures unfinished oak furniture. Carolina uses a standard cost system. The direct labor, direct materials, and factory overhead standards for an unfinished dining room table are as follows:

Direct labor:	standard rate	$17.00 per hour
	standard time per unit	3 hours
Direct materials (oak):	standard price	$8.60 per board foot
	standard quantity	16 board feet
Variable factory overhead:	standard rate	$2.60 per direct labor hour
Fixed factory overhead:	standard rate	$1.20 per direct labor hour

Determine the standard cost per dining room table.

EX 7-3
Budget performance report
obj. 2

✓ b. Direct labor cost variance, $120 F

Vernon Bottle Company (VBC) manufactures plastic two-liter bottles for the beverage industry. The cost standards per 100 two-liter bottles are as follows:

Cost Category	Standard Cost per 100 Two-Liter Bottles
Direct labor	$1.28
Direct materials	5.21
Factory overhead	0.42
Total	$6.91

At the beginning of August, VBC management planned to produce 620,000 bottles. The actual number of bottles produced for August was 650,000 bottles. The actual costs for August of the current year were as follows:

Cost Category	Actual Cost for the Month Ended August 31, 2008
Direct labor	$ 8,200
Direct materials	34,500
Factory overhead	2,800
Total	$45,500

a. Prepare the August manufacturing standard cost budget (direct labor, direct materials, and factory overhead) for VBC, assuming planned production.
b. Prepare a budget performance report for manufacturing costs, showing the total cost variances for direct materials, direct labor, and factory overhead for August.
c. Interpret the budget performance report.

EX 7-4
Direct materials variances
obj. 3

✓ *a. Price variance,*
$26,048 F

The following data relate to the direct materials cost for the production of 4,000 automobile tires:

Actual:	130,240 pounds at $1.65	$214,896
Standard:	128,760 pounds at $1.85	$238,206

a. Determine the price variance, quantity variance, and total direct materials cost variance.
b. To whom should the variances be reported for analysis and control?

EX 7-5
Standard direct materials cost per unit from variance data
objs. 2, 3

The following data relating to direct materials cost for March of the current year are taken from the records of Top Toys Inc., a manufacturer of plastic toys:

Quantity of direct materials used	40,000 pounds
Actual unit price of direct materials	$1.48 per pound
Units of finished product manufactured	7,600 units
Standard direct materials per unit of finished product	5 pounds
Direct materials quantity variance—unfavorable	$2,700
Direct materials price variance—unfavorable	$5,200

Determine the standard direct materials cost per unit of finished product, assuming that there was no inventory of work in process at either the beginning or the end of the month.

EX 7-6
Standard product cost, direct materials variance
objs. 2, 3

H.J. Heinz Company uses standards to control its materials costs. Assume that a batch of ketchup (1,500 pounds) has the following standards:

	Standard Quantity	Standard Price
Whole tomatoes	2,400 pounds	$0.40 per pound
Vinegar	130 gallons	2.50 per gallon
Corn syrup	10 gallons	8.00 per gallon
Salt	54 pounds	2.50 per pound

The actual materials in a batch may vary from the standard due to tomato characteristics. Assume that the actual quantities of materials for batch W196 were as follows:

2,500 pounds of tomatoes
115 gallons of vinegar
13 gallons of corn syrup
53 pounds of salt

a. Determine the standard unit materials cost per pound for a standard batch.
b. Determine the direct materials quantity variance for batch W196.

EX 7-7
Direct labor variances
obj. 3

The following data relate to labor cost for production of 12,500 cellular telephones:

✓ *a. Rate variance,*
$2,040 U

Actual:	13,600 hours at $16.15	$219,640
Standard:	13,725 hours at $16.00	$219,600

a. Determine the rate variance, time variance, and total direct labor cost variance.

b. ▭▭▭▭▭ Discuss what might have caused these variances.

EX 7-8
Direct labor variances
obj. 3

✓ *a. Time variance,*
$1,281 F

Blue Ridge Bicycle Company manufactures mountain bikes. The following data for May of the current year are available:

Quantity of direct labor used	1,400 hours
Actual rate for direct labor	$16.15 per hour
Bicycles completed in May	280
Standard direct labor per bicycle	5.30 hours
Standard rate for direct labor	$15.25 per hour
Planned bicycles for May	210

a. Determine the direct labor rate and time variances.

b. How much direct labor should be debited to Work in Process?

EX 7-9
Direct labor variances
obj. 3

✓ *a. Cutting Department time variance, $4,400 unfavorable*

The Lifestyle Clothes Company produced 24,000 units during April of the current year. The Cutting Department used 4,000 direct labor hours at an actual rate of $11.20 per hour. The Sewing Department used 8,000 direct labor hours at an actual rate of $10.50 per hour. Assume there were no work in process inventories in either department at the beginning or end of the month. The standard labor rate is $11.00. The standard labor time for the Cutting and Sewing departments is 0.15 hour and 0.35 hour per unit, respectively.

a. Determine the direct labor rate and time variance for the (1) Cutting Department and (2) Sewing Department.

b. ▭▭▭▭▭ Interpret your results.

EX 7-10
Direct labor standards for nonmanufacturing expenses
obj. 3

✓ *a. $2,520*

Midlands Hospital began using standards to evaluate its Admissions Department. The standard was broken into two types of admissions as follows:

Type of Admission	Standard Time to Complete Admission Record
Unscheduled admission	60 minutes
Scheduled admission	40 minutes

The unscheduled admission took longer, since name, address, and insurance information needed to be determined at the time of admission. Information was collected on scheduled admissions prior to the admissions, which was less time consuming.

The Admissions Department employs three full-time people (40 productive hours per week, with no overtime) at $21 per hour. For the most recent week, the department handled 48 unscheduled and 150 scheduled admissions.

a. How much was actually spent on labor for the week?

b. What are the standard hours for the actual volume for the week? Round to one decimal place.

c. Calculate a time variance, and report how well the department performed for the week.

EX 7-11
Direct labor standards for nonmanufacturing operations
objs. 2, 3

REAL WORLD

One of the operations in the U.S. Post Office is a mechanical mail sorting operation. In this operation, letter mail is sorted at a rate of one letter per second. The letter is mechanically sorted from a three-digit code input by an operator sitting at a keyboard. The manager of the mechanical sorting operation wishes to determine the number of temporary employees to hire for December. The manager estimates that there will be an additional 32,400,000 pieces of mail in December, due to the upcoming holiday season.

Assume that the sorting operators are temporary employees. The union contract requires that temporary employees be hired for one month at a time. Each temporary employee is hired to work 150 hours in the month.

a. How many temporary employees should the manager hire for December?

b. If each employee earns a standard $16 per hour, what would be the labor time variance if the actual number of letters sorted in December was 32,814,000?

EX 7-12

Direct materials and direct labor variances

objs. 2, 3

✓ *Direct materials quantity variance, $400 F*

At the beginning of July, Commercial Printers Company budgeted 14,000 books to be printed in July at standard direct materials and direct labor costs as follows:

Direct materials	$28,000
Direct labor	24,500
Total	$52,500

The standard materials price is $0.80 per pound. The standard direct labor rate is $14 per hour. At the end of July, the actual direct materials and direct labor costs were as follows:

Actual direct materials	$31,200
Actual direct labor	28,400
Total	$59,600

There were no direct materials price or direct labor rate variances for July. In addition, assume no changes in the direct materials inventory balances in July. Commercial Printers Company actually produced 15,800 units during July.

Determine the direct materials quantity and direct labor time variances.

EX 7-13

Flexible overhead budget

obj. 4

✓ *Total factory overhead, 12,000 hrs.: $139,400*

Pine Knoll Wood Products Company prepared the following factory overhead cost budget for the Press Department for February 2008, during which it expected to require 10,000 hours of productive capacity in the department:

Variable overhead cost:		
Indirect factory labor	$28,000	
Power and light	4,500	
Indirect materials	22,000	
Total variable cost		$ 54,500
Fixed overhead cost:		
Supervisory salaries	$36,000	
Depreciation of plant and equipment	30,000	
Insurance and property taxes	8,000	
Total fixed cost		74,000
Total factory overhead cost		$128,500

Assuming that the estimated costs for March are the same as for February, prepare a flexible factory overhead cost budget for the Press Department for March for 8,000, 10,000, and 12,000 hours of production.

EX 7-14

Flexible overhead budget

obj. 4

Kompton Company has determined that the variable overhead rate is $2.10 per direct labor hour in the Fabrication Department. The normal production capacity for the Fabrication Department is 14,000 hours for the month. Fixed costs are budgeted at $54,600 for the month.

a. Prepare a monthly factory overhead flexible budget for 13,000, 14,000, and 15,000 hours of production.

b. How much overhead would be applied to production if 15,000 hours were used in the department during the month?

EX 7-15

Factory overhead cost variances

obj. 4

✓ *Volume variance, $28,080 U*

The following data relate to factory overhead cost for the production of 25,000 computers:

Actual:	Variable factory overhead	$650,000
	Fixed factory overhead	78,000
Standard:	32,000 hours at $21	672,000

If productive capacity of 100% was 50,000 hours and the factory overhead cost budgeted at the level of 32,000 standard hours was $700,080, determine the variable factory overhead controllable variance, fixed factory overhead volume variance, and total factory overhead cost variance. The fixed factory overhead rate was $1.56 per hour.

EX 7-16
Factory overhead cost variances
obj. **4**

✓ a. $4,850 F

Banner Textiles Corporation began January with a budget for 28,000 hours of production in the Weaving Department. The department has a full capacity of 36,000 hours under normal business conditions. The budgeted overhead at the planned volumes at the beginning of January was as follows:

Variable overhead	$ 78,400
Fixed overhead	54,000
Total	$132,400

The actual factory overhead was $135,250 for January. The actual fixed factory overhead was as budgeted. During January, the Weaving Department had standard hours at actual production volume of 30,750 hours.

a. Determine the variable factory overhead controllable variance.
b. Determine the fixed factory overhead volume variance.

EX 7-17
Factory overhead variance corrections
obj. **4**

The data related to Osage Sporting Goods Company's factory overhead cost for the production of 60,000 units of product are as follows:

Actual:	Variable factory overhead	$274,500
	Fixed factory overhead	224,000
Standard:	76,000 hours at $6.30 ($3.50 for variable factory overhead)	478,800

Productive capacity at 100% of normal was 80,000 hours, and the factory overhead cost budgeted at the level of 76,000 standard hours was $490,000. Based upon these data, the chief cost accountant prepared the following variance analysis:

Variable factory overhead controllable variance:		
Actual variable factory overhead cost incurred	$274,500	
Budgeted variable factory overhead for 76,000 hours	266,000	
Variance—unfavorable		$ 8,500
Fixed factory overhead volume variance:		
Normal productive capacity at 100%	80,000 hours	
Standard for amount produced	76,000	
Productive capacity not used	4,000 hours	
Standard variable factory overhead rate	× $6.30	
Variance—unfavorable		25,200
Total factory overhead cost variance—unfavorable		$33,700

Identify the errors in the factory overhead cost variance analysis.

EX 7-18
Factory overhead cost variance report
obj. **4**

✓ Net controllable variance, $450 U

Form Fit Molded Products Inc. prepared the following factory overhead cost budget for the Trim Department for October 2008, during which it expected to use 20,000 hours for production:

Variable overhead cost:		
Indirect factory labor	$49,000	
Power and light	12,000	
Indirect materials	32,000	
Total variable cost		$ 93,000
Fixed overhead cost:		
Supervisory salaries	$35,000	
Depreciation of plant and equipment	28,400	
Insurance and property taxes	21,600	
Total fixed cost		85,000
Total factory overhead cost		$178,000

Form Fit Molded Products has available 34,000 hours of monthly productive capacity in the Trim Department under normal business conditions. During October, the Trim Department actually used 24,000 hours for production. The actual fixed costs were as budgeted. The actual variable overhead for October was as follows:

Actual variable factory overhead cost:	
Indirect factory labor	$ 58,300
Power and light	15,000
Indirect materials	38,750
Total variable cost	$112,050

Construct a factory overhead cost variance report for the Trim Department for October.

EX 7-19
Recording standards in accounts
obj. 5

Thexton Manufacturing Company incorporates standards in its accounts and identifies variances at the time the manufacturing costs are incurred. Journalize the entries to record the following transactions:

a. Purchased 1,400 units of copper tubing on account at $49.50 per unit. The standard price is $45.00 per unit.
b. Used 870 units of copper tubing in the process of manufacturing 110 air conditioners. Eight units of copper tubing are required, at standard, to produce one air conditioner.

EX 7-20
Recording standards in accounts
obj. 5

The Assembly Department produced 1,600 units of product during June. Each unit required 1.4 standard direct labor hours. There were 2,200 actual hours used in the Assembly Department during June at an actual rate of $12.00 per hour. The standard direct labor rate is $12.50 per hour. Assuming direct labor for a month is paid on the fifth day of the following month, journalize the direct labor in the Assembly Department on June 30.

EX 7-21
Income statement indicating standard cost variance
obj. 5
✓ Income before income tax, $75,500

The following data were taken from the records of Nomad Company for March 2008:

Administrative expenses	$ 58,000
Cost of goods sold (at standard)	885,500
Direct materials price variance—favorable	1,800
Direct materials quantity variance—unfavorable	2,250
Direct labor rate variance—favorable	900
Direct labor time variance—unfavorable	3,950
Variable factory overhead controllable variance—favorable	4,625
Fixed factory overhead volume variance—unfavorable	11,000
Interest expense	1,800
Sales	1,150,000
Selling expenses	119,325

Prepare an income statement for presentation to management.

EX 7-22
Nonfinancial performance measures
obj. 6

Windytrail.com is an Internet retailer of sporting good products. Customers order sporting goods from the company, using an online catalog. The company processes these orders and delivers the requested product from its warehouse. The company wants to provide customers with an excellent purchase experience in order to expand the business through favorable word-of-mouth advertising and to drive repeat business. To help monitor performance, the company developed a set of performance measures for its order placement and delivery process.

Average computer response time to customer "clicks"
Dollar amount of returned goods
Elapsed time between customer order and product delivery
Maintenance dollars divided by hardware investment
Number of customer complaints divided by the number of orders
Number of misfilled orders
Number of orders per warehouse employee
Number of page faults or errors due to software programming errors
Server (computer) downtime
System capacity divided by customer demands
Training dollars per programmer

Identify the input and output measures related to the "order placement and delivery" process.

EX 7-23
Nonfinancial performance measures
obj. 6

Metro College wishes to monitor the efficiency and quality of its course registration process.

a. Identify three input and three output measures for this process.
b. Why would Metro College use nonfinancial measures for monitoring this process?

Problems Series A

PR 7-1A
Direct materials and direct labor variance analysis

objs. 2, 3

✓ c. Rate variance, $48 U

Dresses by Melissa Inc. manufactures dresses in a small manufacturing facility. Manufacturing has 15 employees. Each employee presently provides 32 hours of productive labor per week. Information about a production week is as follows:

Standard wage per hour	$10.40
Standard labor time per dress	15 minutes
Standard number of yards of fabric per dress	4.2 yards
Standard price per yard of fabric	$2.65
Actual price per yard of fabric	$2.70
Actual yards of fabric used during the week	7,200 yards
Number of dresses produced during the week	1,900
Actual wage per hour	$10.50
Actual hours per week	480 hours

Instructions
Determine (a) the standard cost per dress for direct materials and direct labor; (b) the price variance, quantity variance, and total direct materials cost variance; and (c) the rate variance, time variance, and total direct labor cost variance.

PR 7-2A
Flexible budgeting and variance analysis

objs. 2, 3

✓ 1. a. Direct materials quantity variance, $4,540 U

Koko Chocolate Company makes dark chocolate and light chocolate. Both products require cocoa and sugar. The following planning information has been made available:

	Standard Quantity		
	Dark Chocolate	Light Chocolate	Standard Price per Pound
Cocoa	14 lbs.	9 lbs.	$8.80
Sugar	12 lbs.	15 lbs.	1.40
Standard labor time	0.30 hr.	0.45 hr.	
Planned production	3,200 cases	4,600 cases	
Standard labor rate	$16.40 per hour	$16.20 per hour	

Koko Chocolate does not expect there to be any beginning or ending inventories of cocoa or sugar. At the end of the budget year, Koko Chocolate had the following actual results:

	Dark Chocolate	Light Chocolate
Actual production (cases)	2,500	4,500

	Actual Price per Pound	Actual Pounds Purchased and Used
Cocoa	$8.50	74,250
Sugar	1.65	108,600

	Actual Labor Rate	Actual Labor Hours Used
Dark chocolate	$16.50	760
Light chocolate	16.50	2,000

Instructions

1. Prepare the following variance analyses, based on the actual results and production levels at the end of the budget year:
   a. Direct materials price, quantity, and total variance.
   b. Direct labor rate, time, and total variance.
2. ▶ Why are the standard amounts in part (1) based on the actual production for the year instead of the planned production for the year?

PR 7-3A
Direct materials, direct labor, and factory overhead cost variance analysis

objs. 3, 4

✓ c. Controllable variance, $155 F

Gulf Coast Resins Company processes a base chemical into plastic. Standard costs and actual costs for direct materials, direct labor, and factory overhead incurred for the manufacture of 2,600 units of product were as follows:

	Standard Costs	Actual Costs
Direct materials	6,850 pounds at $6.40	7,000 pounds at $6.35
Direct labor	2,050 hours at $19.80	2,100 hours at $20.20
Factory overhead	Rates per direct labor hour, based on 100% of normal capacity of 1,950 direct labor hours:	
	Variable cost, $2.50	$4,970 variable cost
	Fixed cost, $4.50	$8,775 fixed cost

Each unit requires 0.6 hour of direct labor.

Instructions

Determine (a) the price variance, quantity variance, and total direct materials cost variance; (b) the rate variance, time variance, and total direct labor cost variance; and (c) variable factory overhead controllable variance, the fixed factory overhead volume variance, and total factory overhead cost variance.

PR 7-4A
Standard factory overhead variance report

objs. 4, 6

✓ Controllable variance, $300 F

Power Equipment Inc., a manufacturer of construction equipment, prepared the following factory overhead cost budget for the Welding Department for July 2008. The company expected to operate the department at 100% of normal capacity of 4,800 hours.

Variable costs:		
Indirect factory wages	$14,160	
Power and light	7,680	
Indirect materials	8,880	
Total variable cost		$30,720
Fixed costs:		
Supervisory salaries	$16,000	
Depreciation of plant and equipment	43,500	
Insurance and property taxes	6,740	
Total fixed cost		66,240
Total factory overhead cost		$96,960

During July, the department operated at 5,000 standard hours, and the factory overhead costs incurred were indirect factory wages, $14,000; power and light, $9,250; indirect materials, $8,450; supervisory salaries, $16,000; depreciation of plant and equipment, $43,500; and insurance and property taxes, $6,740.

Instructions

Prepare a factory overhead cost variance report for July. To be useful for cost control, the budgeted amounts should be based on 5,000 hours.

PR 7-5A
Standards for nonmanufacturing expenses

objs. 3, 6

✓ 3. $640 U

Elite Technologies Inc. does software development. One important activity in software development is writing software code. The manager of the WritePro Development Team determined that the average software programmer could write 45 lines of code in an hour. The plan for the first week in May called for 6,840 lines of code to be written on the WritePro product. The WritePro Team has four programmers. Each programmer is hired from an employment firm that requires temporary employees to be hired for a minimum of a 40-hour week. Programmers are paid $32.00 per hour. The manager offered a bonus if the team could generate more than 7,200 lines for the week, without overtime. Due to a project emergency, the programmers wrote more code in the first week of May than planned. The actual amount of code written in the first week of May was 7,650 lines, without overtime. As a result, the bonus caused the average programmer's hourly rate to increase to $36.00 per hour during the first week in May.

Instructions

1. If the team generated 6,840 lines of code according to the original plan, what would have been the labor time variance?
2. What was the actual labor time variance as a result of generating 7,650 lines of code?
3. What was the labor rate variance as a result of the bonus?
4. The manager is trying to determine if a better decision would have been to hire a temporary programmer to meet the higher programming demand in the first week of May, rather than paying out the bonus. If another employee was hired from the employment firm, what would have been the labor time variance in the first week?
5. ▭▶ Which decision is better, paying the bonus or hiring another programmer?
6. ▭▶ Are there any performance-related issues that the labor time and rate variances fail to consider? Explain.

Problems Series B

PR 7-1B
Direct materials and direct labor variance analysis

objs. 2, 3

✓ c. Direct labor time variance, $1,680 F

AtHome Fixtures Company manufactures faucets in a small manufacturing facility. The faucets are made from zinc. Manufacturing has 80 employees. Each employee presently provides 36 hours of labor per week. Information about a production week is as follows:

Standard wage per hour	$14.00
Standard labor time per faucet	15 minutes
Standard number of pounds of zinc	1.8 lbs.
Standard price per pound of zinc	$9.50
Actual price per pound of zinc	$9.20
Actual pounds of zinc used during the week	21,900 lbs.
Number of faucets produced during the week	12,000
Actual wage per hour	$14.50
Actual hours per week	2,880 hours

Instructions

Determine (a) the standard cost per unit for direct materials and direct labor; (b) the price variance, quantity variance, and total direct materials cost variance; and (c) the rate variance, time variance, and total direct labor cost variance.

PR 7-2B
Flexible budgeting and variance analysis

objs. 2, 3

✓ 1. a. Price variance, $9,000 F

Arctic Coat Company makes women's and men's coats. Both products require filler and lining material. The following planning information has been made available:

	Standard Quantity		
	Women's Coats	Men's Coats	Standard Price per Unit
Filler	2.5 lbs.	4.0 lbs.	$29.00
Liner	6.0 yds.	8.5 yds.	5.00
Standard labor time	0.40 hr.	0.60 hr.	
Planned production	2,500 units	4,000 units	
Standard labor rate	$12.80 per hour	$15.50 per hour	

Arctic Coat does not expect there to be any beginning or ending inventories of filler and lining material. At the end of the budget year, Arctic Coat experienced the following actual results:

	Women's Coats	Men's Coats
Actual production	2,300	3,500

	Actual Price per Unit	Actual Quantity Purchased and Used
Filler	$27.50	20,400
Liner	5.50	43,200

	Actual Labor Rate	Actual Labor Hours Used
Women's Coats	$12.00	1,050
Men's Coats	15.80	1,980

The expected beginning inventory and desired ending inventory were realized.

Instructions
1. Prepare the following variance analyses, based on the actual results and production levels at the end of the budget year:
   a. Direct materials price, quantity, and total variance.
   b. Direct labor rate, time, and total variance.
2. ▬▬▬► Why are the standard amounts in part (1) based on the actual production at the end of the year instead of the planned production at the beginning of the year?

PR 7-3B
Direct materials, direct labor, and factory overhead cost variance analysis

objs. 3, 4

✓ a. Price variance,
$28,840 U

SureGrip Tire Co. manufactures automobile tires. Standard costs and actual costs for direct materials, direct labor, and factory overhead incurred for the manufacture of 39,000 tires were as follows:

	Standard Costs	Actual Costs
Direct materials	68,000 pounds at $4.80	72,100 pounds at $5.20
Direct labor	15,600 hours at $16.00	15,400 hours at $15.70
Factory overhead	Rates per direct labor hour, based on 100% of normal capacity of 21,000 direct labor hours:	
	Variable cost, $2.70	$41,650 variable cost
	Fixed cost, $3.65	$76,650 fixed cost

Each tire requires 0.40 hour of direct labor.

Instructions
Determine (a) the price variance, quantity variance, and total direct materials cost variance; (b) the rate variance, time variance, and total direct labor cost variance; and (c) variable factory overhead controllable variance, the fixed factory overhead volume variance, and total factory overhead cost variance.

PR 7-4B
Standard factory overhead variance report

objs. 4, 6

✓ Controllable variance,
$6,900 F

Med-Tech Company, a manufacturer of disposable medical supplies, prepared the following factory overhead cost budget for the Assembly Department for August 2008. The company expected to operate the department at 100% of normal capacity of 28,000 hours.

Variable costs:		
Indirect factory wages	$246,400	
Power and light	179,200	
Indirect materials	44,800	
Total variable cost		$470,400
Fixed costs:		
Supervisory salaries	$130,000	
Depreciation of plant and equipment	105,000	
Insurance and property taxes	22,600	
Total fixed cost		257,600
Total factory overhead cost		$728,000

During August, the department operated at 25,250 hours, and the factory overhead costs incurred were indirect factory wages, $216,500; power and light, $162,600; indirect materials, $38,200; supervisory salaries, $130,000; depreciation of plant and equipment, $105,000; and insurance and property taxes, $22,600.

Instructions
Prepare a factory overhead cost variance report for August. To be useful for cost control, the budgeted amounts should be based on 25,250 hours.

PR 7-5B
Standards for nonmanufacturing expenses

objs. 3, 6

✓2. $150 F

The Radiology Department provides imaging services for Memorial Medical Center. One important activity in the Radiology Department is transcribing tape-recorded analyses of images into a written report. The manager of the Radiology Department determined that the average transcriptionist could type 800 lines of a report in an hour. The plan for the first week in July called for 60,000 typed lines to be written. The Radiology Department has two transcriptionists. Each transcriptionist is hired from an employment firm that requires temporary employees to be hired for a minimum of a 40-hour week. Transcriptionists are paid $15.00 per hour. The manager offered a bonus if the department could type more than 70,000 lines for the week, without overtime. Due to high service demands, the transcriptionists typed more lines in the first week of July than planned. The actual amount of lines typed in the first week of July was 72,000 lines, without overtime. As a result, the bonus caused the average transcriptionist hourly rate to increase to $18.00 per hour during the first week in July.

Instructions
1. If the department typed 60,000 lines according to the original plan, what would have been the labor time variance?
2. What was the labor time variance as a result of typing 72,000 lines?
3. What was the labor rate variance as a result of the bonus?
4. The manager is trying to determine if a better decision would have been to hire a temporary transcriptionist to meet the higher typing demands in the first week of July, rather than paying out the bonus. If another employee was hired from the employment firm, what would have been the labor time variance in the first week?
5. ▭▭▭▭▸ Which decision is better, paying the bonus or hiring another transcriptionist?
6. ▭▭▭▭▸ Are there any performance-related issues that the labor time and rate variances fail to consider? Explain.

Comprehensive Problem ↘

Royal Essentials, Inc. began operations on January 1, 2008. The company produces a hand and body lotion in an eight-ounce bottle called *Eternal Beauty*. The lotion is sold wholesale in 12-bottle cases for $80 per case. There is a selling commission of $16 per case. The January direct materials, direct labor, and factory overhead costs are as follows:

DIRECT MATERIALS

	Cost Behavior	Units per Case	Cost per Unit	Direct Materials Cost per Case
Cream base	Variable	72 ozs.	$0.015	$ 1.08
Natural oils	Variable	24 ozs.	0.250	6.00
Bottle (8-oz.)	Variable	12 bottles	0.400	4.80
				$11.88

DIRECT LABOR

Department	Cost Behavior	Time per Case	Labor Rate per Hour	Direct Labor Cost per Case
Mixing	Variable	16.80 min.	$15.00	$4.20
Filling	Variable	4.20 min.	12.00	0.84
		21.00 min.		$5.04

FACTORY OVERHEAD

	Cost Behavior	Total Cost
Utilities	Mixed	$ 230
Facility lease	Fixed	9,694
Equipment depreciation	Fixed	3,600
Supplies	Fixed	600
		$14,124

Part A—Break-Even Analysis

The management of Royal Essentials, Inc., wishes to determine the number of cases required to break even per month. The utilities cost, which is part of factory overhead, is a mixed cost. The following information was gathered from the first six months of operation regarding this cost:

2008	Case Production	Utility Total Cost
January	300	$230
February	600	265
March	1,000	300
April	900	292
May	750	275
June	825	280

Instructions

1. Determine the fixed and variable portion of the utility cost using the high-low method.
2. Determine the contribution margin per case.
3. Determine the fixed costs per month, including the utility fixed cost from part (1).
4. Determine the break-even number of cases per month.

Part B—Variable versus Absorption Costing Income Statements

There was no finished goods inventory on July 1, 2008, for Royal Essentials. The company operated the manufacturing facility at 100% of capacity during July. The following data summarize the results for Royal Essentials Inc. for July:

Sales (1,350 cases × $80 per case)		$108,000
Production costs (1,500 cases):		
Direct materials	$18,000	
Direct labor	7,500	
Variable factory overhead	150	
Fixed factory overhead	14,100	39,750
Variable selling expenses (1,350 cases × $16 per case)		21,600

Instructions

5. Prepare an income statement according to the absorption costing concept.
6. Prepare an income statement according to the variable costing concept.
7. What is the reason for the difference in the amount of income from operations reported in (5) and (6)?

Part C—August Budgets

During July of the current year, the management of Royal Essentials, Inc., asked the controller to prepare August manufacturing and income statement budgets. Demand was expected to be 1,200 cases at $80 per case for August. Inventory planning information is provided as follows:

Finished Goods Inventory:

	Cases	Cost
Estimated finished goods inventory, August 1, 2008	150	$3,160
Desired finished goods inventory, August 31, 2008	100	2,100

Materials Inventory:

	Cream Base (ozs.)	Oils (ozs.)	Bottles (bottles)
Estimated materials inventory, August 1, 2008	500	260	500
Desired materials inventory, August 31, 2008	700	300	400

There was negligible work in process inventory assumed for either the beginning or end of the month; thus, none was assumed. In addition, there was no change in the cost per unit or estimated units per case operating data from January.

Instructions

8. Prepare the August production budget.
9. Prepare the August direct materials purchases budget.
10. Prepare the August direct labor budget.
11. Prepare the August factory overhead budget.
12. Prepare the August budgeted income statement, including selling expenses.

Part D—August Variance Analysis

During September of the current year, the controller was asked to perform variance analyses for August. The January operating data provided the standard prices, rates, times, and quantities per case. There were 1,200 actual cases produced during August, which was 50 more cases than planned at the beginning of the month. Actual data for August were as follows:

	Actual Direct Materials Price per Case	Actual Direct Materials Quantity per Case
Cream base	$1.00 (for 72 ozs.)	75 ozs.
Natural oils	6.20 (for 24 ozs.)	25 ozs.
Bottle (8-oz.)	4.50 (for 12 bottles)	12.2 bottles

	Actual Direct Labor Rate	Actual Direct Labor Time per Case
Mixing	$15.25	16.50 min.
Filling	11.50	4.50 min.

Actual variable overhead	$125.00
Normal volume	1,500 cases

The prices of the materials were different than standard due to fluctuations in market prices. Specifically, the prices of the cream base and bottles were below the standard price, while the price of natural oils was above the standard price. The standard quantity of materials used per case was an ideal standard. The Mixing Department used a higher grade labor classification during the month, thus causing the actual labor rate to exceed standard. The Filling Department used a lower grade labor classification during the month, thus causing the actual labor rate to be less than standard.

Instructions

13. Determine and interpret the direct materials price and quantity variances for the three materials.
14. Determine and interpret the direct labor rate and time variances for the two departments.
15. Determine and interpret the factory overhead controllable variance.
16. Determine and interpret the factory overhead volume variance.
17. Why are the standard direct labor and direct materials costs in the calculations for parts (13) and (14) based on the actual 1,200-case production volume rather than the planned 1,150 cases of production used in the budgets for parts (9) and (10)?

Special Activities

SA 7-1
Ethics and professional conduct in business using nonmanufacturing standards

ETHICS

Trey McIntyre is a cost analyst with Global Insurance Company. Global is applying standards to its claims payment operation. Claims payment is a repetitive operation that could be evaluated with standards. Trey used time and motion studies to identify an ideal standard of 36 claims processed per hour. The Claims Processing Department manager, Carol Mann, has rejected this standard and has argued that the standard should be 30 claims processed per hour. Carol and Trey were unable to agree, so they decided to discuss this matter openly at a joint meeting with the vice president of operations, who would arbitrate a final decision. Prior to the meeting, Trey wrote the following memo to the VP.

> To: T. J. Logan, Vice President of Operations
> From: Trey McIntyre
> Re: Standards in the Claims Processing Department
>
> As you know, Carol and I are scheduled to meet with you to discuss our disagreement with respect to the appropriate standards for the Claims Processing Department. I have conducted time and motion studies and have determined that the ideal standard is 36 claims processed per hour. Carol argues that 30 claims processed per hour would be more appropriate. I believe she is trying to "pad" the budget with some slack. I'm not sure what she is trying to get away with, but I believe a tight standard will drive efficiency up in her area. I hope you will agree when we meet with you next week.

▭▬▶ Discuss the ethical and professional issues in this situation.

SA 7-2
Nonfinancial performance measures

The senior management of Lannigan Company has proposed the following three performance measures for the company:

1. Net income as a percent of stockholders' equity
2. Revenue growth
3. Employee satisfaction

   Management believes these three measures combine both financial and nonfinancial measures and are thus superior to using just financial measures.
▭▬▶ What advice would you give Lannigan Company for improving its performance measurement system?

SA 7-3
Nonfinancial performance measures

REAL WORLD

At the Soladyne Division of Rogers Corporation, a manufacturer of specialty materials for the electronics industry, the controller used a number of measures to provide managers information about the performance of a just-in-time (JIT) manufacturing operation. Three measures used by the company are:

- Scrap Index: The sales dollar value of scrap for the period.
- Orders Past Due: Sales dollar value of orders that were scheduled for shipment, but were not shipped during the period.
- Buyer's Misery Index: Number of different customers that have orders that are late (scheduled for shipment, but not shipped).

1. ▭▬▶ Why do you think the scrap index is measured at sales dollar value, rather than at cost?
2. ▭▬▶ How is the "orders past due" measure different from the "buyer's misery index," or are the two measures just measuring the same thing?

SA 7-4
Variance interpretation

You have been asked to investigate some cost problems in the Assembly Department of Digital Life Electronics Co., a consumer electronics company. To begin your investigation, you have obtained the following budget performance report for the department for the last quarter:

Digital Life Electronics Co.—Assembly Department
Quarterly Budget Performance Report

	Standard Quantity at Standard Rates	Actual Quantity at Standard Rates	Quantity Variances
Direct labor	$ 78,750	$113,750	$35,000 U
Direct materials	148,750	192,500	43,750 U
Total	$227,500	$306,250	$78,750 U

The following reports were also obtained:

Digital Life Electronics Co.—Purchasing Department
Quarterly Budget Performance Report

	Actual Quantity at Standard Rates	Actual Quantity at Actual Rates	Price Variance
Direct materials	$218,750	$192,500	$26,250 F

Digital Life Electronics Co.—Fabrication Department
Quarterly Budget Performance Report

	Standard Quantity at Standard Rates	Actual Quantity at Standard Rates	Quantity Variances
Direct labor	$122,500	$101,500	$21,000 F
Direct materials	70,000	70,000	0
Total	$192,500	$171,500	$21,000 F

You also interviewed the Assembly Department supervisor. Excerpts from the interview follow.

Q: *What explains the poor performance in your department?*
A: *Listen, you've got to understand what it's been like in this department recently. Lately, it seems no matter how hard we try, we can't seem to make the standards. I'm not sure what is going on, but we've been having a lot of problems lately.*
Q: *What kind of problems?*
A: *Well, for instance, all this quarter we've been requisitioning purchased parts from the material storeroom, and the parts just didn't fit together very well. I'm not sure what is going on, but during most of this quarter we've had to scrap and sort purchased parts—just to get our assemblies put together. Naturally, all this takes time and material. And that's not all.*
Q: *Go on.*
A: *All this quarter, the work that we've been receiving from the Fabrication Department has been shoddy. I mean, maybe around 20% of the stuff that comes in from Fabrication just can't be assembled. The fabrication is all wrong. As a result, we've had to scrap and rework a lot of the stuff. Naturally, this has just shot our quantity variances.*

➤ Interpret the variance reports in light of the comments by the Assembly Department supervisor.

SA 7-5
Variance interpretation

Sound Sensation Inc. is a small manufacturer of electronic musical instruments. The plant manager received the following variable factory overhead report for the period:

	Actual	Budgeted Variable Factory Overhead at Actual Production
Supplies	$28,000	$26,520
Power and light	35,000	33,990
Indirect factory wages	26,112	20,400
Total	$89,112	$80,910

Actual units produced: 10,200 (85% of practical capacity)

The plant manager is not pleased with the $8,202 unfavorable variable factory overhead controllable variance and has come to discuss the matter with the controller. The following discussion occurred:

Plant Manager: I just received this factory report for the latest month of operation. I'm not very pleased with these figures. Before these numbers go to headquarters, you and I will need to reach an understanding.
Controller: Go ahead, what's the problem?
Plant Manager: What's the problem? Well, everything. Look at the variance. It's too large. If I understand the accounting approach being used here, you are assuming that my costs are variable to the units produced. Thus, as the production volume declines, so should these costs. Well, I don't believe that these costs are variable at all. I think they are fixed costs. As a result, when we operate below capacity, the costs really don't go down at all. I'm being penalized for costs I have no control over at all. I need this report to be redone to reflect this fact. If anything, the difference between actual and budget is essentially a volume variance. Listen, I know that you're a team player. You really need to reconsider your assumptions on this one.

➤ If you were in the controller's position, how would you respond to the plant manager?

SA 7-6
Nonmanufacturing performance measures— government

Group Project

Internet Project

Municipal governments are discovering that you can control only what you measure. As a result, many municipal governments are introducing nonfinancial performance measures to help improve municipal services. In a group, use the Google search engine to perform a search for "municipal government performance measurement." Google will provide a list of Internet sites that outline various city efforts in using nonfinancial performance measures. As a group, report on the types of measures used by one of the cities from the search.

Answers to Self-Examination Questions

1. **C** The unfavorable direct materials price variance of $2,550 is determined as follows:

Actual price	$5.05 per pound
Standard price	5.00
Price variance—unfavorable	$0.05 per pound

$0.05 × 51,000 actual pounds = $2,550

2. **D** The unfavorable direct labor time variance of $2,400 is determined as follows:

Actual direct labor time	2,200
Standard direct labor time	2,000
Direct labor time variance—unfavorable	200 × $12 standard rate = $2,400

3. **B** The unfavorable factory overhead volume variance of $2,000 is determined as follows:

Productive capacity not used	1,000 hours
Standard fixed factory overhead cost rate	× $2
Factory overhead volume variance—unfavorable	$2,000

4. **B** The controllable variable factory overhead variance is determined as follows:

6,000 units × 0.25 hour = 1,500 hours
1,500 hours × $5.00 per hour = $7,500

Actual variable overhead	$8,000
Less: Budgeted variable overhead at actual volume	7,500
Unfavorable controllable variance	$ 500

5. **D** The fixed factory overhead volume variance can be determined as follows:

Actual production in standard hours:
  600 units × 0.2 machine hour = 120 machine hours

Practical capacity	200 machine hours
Standard hours at actual production	120
Idle capacity	80 machine hours

80 hours × $12.00 = $960 unfavorable volume variance

Performance Evaluation for Decentralized Operations

© INDIANHEAD MOUNTAIN SKI RESORT/PRNEWSFOTO (AP TOPIC GALLERY)

objectives

After studying this chapter, you should be able to:

1 List and explain the advantages and disadvantages of decentralized operations.

2 Prepare a responsibility accounting report for a cost center.

3 Prepare responsibility accounting reports for a profit center.

4 Compute and interpret the rate of return on investment, the residual income, and the balanced scorecard for an investment center.

5 Explain how the market price, negotiated price, and cost price approaches to transfer pricing may be used by decentralized segments of a business.

K2 Sports

Have you ever wondered why large retail stores like Wal-Mart, The Home Depot, and Sports Authority are divided into departments? Dividing into departments allows these retailers to provide products and expertise in specialized areas, while still offering a broad line of products. Departments allow companies to assign and follow financial performance. This information can be used to make product decisions, evaluate operations, and guide company strategy. Strong performance in a department might be attributed to a good department manager, who might be rewarded with a promotion. Poor departmental performance might lead to a change in the mix of products that the department sells.

Like retailers, most large businesses organize into operational units, such as divisions and depart-

ments. For example, K2 Sports, a leading maker of athletic and outdoor equipment, manages its business across four primary business segments: Marine and Outdoor, Action Sports, Team Sports, and Footwear and Apparel. These segments are further broken down into individual product lines, such as K2 skis, Rawlings athletic equipment, Marmot outdoor products, and WGP Paintball. Managers are responsible for running the operations of their respective segment of the business. Each segment is evaluated based on operating profit, and this information is used to plan and control K2's operations. In this chapter, we will discuss the role of accounting in assisting managers in planning and controlling organizational units, such as departments, divisions, and stores.

Centralized and Decentralized Operations

objective **1**

List and explain the advantages and disadvantages of decentralized operations.

REAL WORLD

In 2006, Wachovia Corporation, a national bank, decentralized decisions about how the bank does business over the Internet. Each business unit independently decides how it will conduct business over the Internet. For example, the Mortgage Loan Division allows customers to check current mortgage rates and apply for mortgages online.

A *centralized* business is one in which all major planning and operating decisions are made by top management. For example, a one-person, owner/manager-operated business is centralized because all plans and decisions are made by one person. In a small owner/manager-operated business, centralization may be desirable. This is because the owner/manager's close supervision ensures that the business will be operated in the way the owner/manager wishes.

Separating a business into **divisions** or operating units and delegating responsibility to unit managers is called **decentralization**. In a decentralized business, the unit managers are responsible for planning and controlling the operations of their units.

Divisions are often structured around common functions, products, customers, or regions. For example, Delta Air Lines is organized around *functions*, such as the Flight Operations Division. Procter & Gamble is organized around common *products*, such as the Soap Division, which sells a wide array of cleaning products. Norfolk Southern Corporation decentralizes its railroad operations into Eastern, Western, and Northern regional divisions.

There is no one best amount of decentralization for all businesses. In some companies, division managers have authority over all operations, including fixed asset acquisitions and retirements. In other companies, division managers have authority over profits but not fixed asset acquisitions and retirements. The proper amount of decentralization for a company depends on its advantages and disadvantages for the company's unique circumstances.

ADVANTAGES OF DECENTRALIZATION

As a business grows, it becomes more difficult for top management to maintain close daily contact with all operations. In such cases, delegating authority to managers closest to the operations usually results in better decisions. These managers often anticipate and react to operating data more quickly than could top management. In addition, as a company expands into a wide range of products and services, it becomes more difficult for top management to maintain operating expertise in all product lines and services. Decentralization allows managers to focus on acquiring expertise in their areas of responsibility. For example, in a company that maintains operations in insurance, banking, and health care, managers could become "experts" in their area of operation and responsibility.

Decentralized decision making also provides excellent training for managers. This may be a factor in helping a company retain quality managers. Since the art of management is best acquired through experience, delegating responsibility allows managers to acquire and develop managerial expertise early in their careers.

Businesses that work closely with customers, such as hotels, are often decentralized. This helps managers create good customer relations by responding quickly to customers' needs. In addition, because managers of decentralized operations tend to identify with customers and with operations, they are often more creative in suggesting operating and product improvements.

DISADVANTAGES OF DECENTRALIZATION

A primary disadvantage of decentralized operations is that decisions made by one manager may negatively affect the profitability of the entire company. For example, the Pizza Hut chain added chicken to its menu and ended up taking business away from KFC. Then KFC retaliated with a blistering ad campaign against Pizza Hut. This happened even though both chains are part of the same company, Yum! Brands, Inc.

Another potential disadvantage of decentralized operations is duplicating assets and costs in operating divisions. For example, each manager of a product line might have a separate sales force and administrative office staff. Centralizing these personnel could save money. For example, in 2003, Hewlett-Packard Company announced that it would merge its consulting division with the division that sells business equipment in order to simplify its operations following the acquisition of Compaq. Advantages and disadvantages of decentralization are summarized in Exhibit 1.

EXHIBIT 1

Advantages and Disadvantages of Decentralized Operations

Advantages of Decentralization

- Lets managers closest to the operations make decisions.
- Allows managers to acquire expertise in their areas of responsibility.
- Provides excellent training opportunity for managers.
- Helps retain quality managers.
- Improves customer relations in businesses that work closely with customers, such as hotels.

Disadvantages of Decentralization

- Decisions made by one manager may negatively affect the profitability of the entire company.
- Assets and costs may be duplicated.

RESPONSIBILITY ACCOUNTING

In a decentralized business, an important function of accounting is to assist unit managers in evaluating and controlling their areas of responsibility, called *responsibility centers*. **Responsibility accounting** is the process of measuring and reporting operating data by responsibility center. Three common types of responsibility centers are cost centers, profit centers, and investment centers. These three responsibility centers differ in their scope of responsibility, as shown at the top of the following page.

Cost Center	Profit Center	Investment Center
	Revenue	Revenue
Cost	− Cost	− Cost
	Profit	Profit
		Investment in assets

Responsibility Accounting for Cost Centers

objective   *2*

*Prepare a
responsibility
accounting report
for a cost center.*

In a **cost center**, the unit manager has responsibility and authority for controlling the costs incurred. For example, the supervisor of the Power Department has responsibility for the costs incurred in providing power. A cost center manager does not make decisions concerning sales or the amount of fixed assets invested in the center.

Cost centers may vary in size from a small department to an entire manufacturing plant. In addition, cost centers may exist within other cost centers. For example, we could view an entire university as a cost center, and each college and department within the university could also be a cost center, as shown in Exhibit 2.

EXHIBIT 2 | Cost Centers in a University

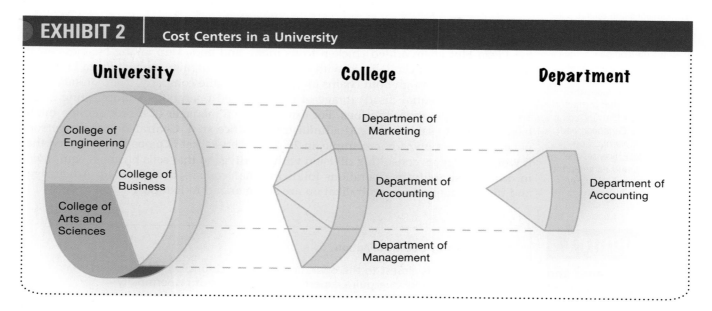

University

College of Engineering

College of Business

College of Arts and Sciences

College

Department of Marketing

Department of Accounting

Department of Management

Department

Department of Accounting

Since managers of cost centers have responsibility and authority over costs, responsibility accounting for cost centers focuses on costs. To illustrate, the budget performance reports in Exhibit 3 are part of a responsibility accounting system. These reports aid the managers in controlling costs.

In Exhibit 3, the reports prepared for the department supervisors show the budgeted and actual manufacturing costs for their departments. The supervisors can use these reports to focus on areas of significant difference, such as the difference between the budgeted and actual materials cost. The supervisor of Department 1 in Plant A may use additional information from a scrap report to determine why materials are over budget. Such a report might show that materials were scrapped as a result of machine malfunctions, improper use of machines by employees, or low quality materials.

For higher levels of management, responsibility accounting reports are usually more summarized than for lower levels of management. In Exhibit 3, for example, the budget performance report for the plant manager summarizes budget and actual cost data for the departments under the manager's supervision. This report enables the plant manager to identify the department supervisors responsible for major differences. Likewise, the report for the vice president of production summarizes the cost data for each plant. The plant managers can thus be held responsible for major differences in budgeted and actual costs in their plants.

EXHIBIT 3

Responsibility
Accounting Reports
for Cost Centers

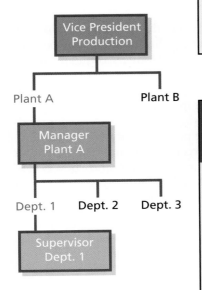

Budget Performance Report
Vice President, Production
For the Month Ended October 31, 2008

	Budget	Actual	Over Budget	Under Budget
Administration	$ 19,500	$ 19,700	$ 200	
Plant A	467,475	470,330	2,855 ←	
Plant B	395,225	394,300		$925
	$882,200	$884,330	$3,055	$925

Budget Performance Report
Manager, Plant A
For the Month Ended October 31, 2008

	Budget	Actual	Over Budget	Under Budget
Administration	$ 17,500	$ 17,350		$150
Department 1	→ 109,725	→ 111,280	→ $1,555	
Department 2	190,500	192,600	2,100	
Department 3	149,750	149,100		650
	$467,475	$470,330	$3,655 ←	$800

Budget Performance Report
Supervisor, Department 1—Plant A
For the Month Ended October 31, 2008

	Budget	Actual	Over Budget	Under Budget
Factory wages	$ 58,100	$ 58,000		$100
Materials	32,500	34,225	$1,725	
Supervisory salaries	6,400	6,400		
Power and light	5,750	5,690		60
Depreciation of plant and equipment	4,000	4,000		
Maintenance	2,000	1,990		10
Insurance and property taxes	975	975		
	$109,725	$111,280	$1,725	$170

Example Exercise 8-1

objective **2**

Nuclear Power Company's costs were over budget by $24,000. The company is divided into North and South regions. The North Region's costs were under budget by $2,000. Determine the amount that the South Region's costs were over or under budget.

(continued)

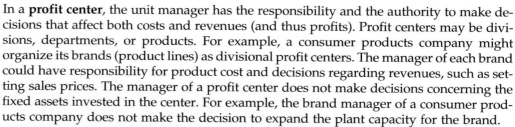

Follow My Example 8-1

$26,000 over budget ($24,000 + $2,000)

For Practice: PE 8-1A, PE 8-1B

Responsibility Accounting for Profit Centers

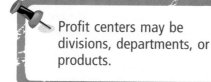

objective **3**

Prepare responsibility accounting reports for a profit center.

In a **profit center**, the unit manager has the responsibility and the authority to make decisions that affect both costs and revenues (and thus profits). Profit centers may be divisions, departments, or products. For example, a consumer products company might organize its brands (product lines) as divisional profit centers. The manager of each brand could have responsibility for product cost and decisions regarding revenues, such as setting sales prices. The manager of a profit center does not make decisions concerning the fixed assets invested in the center. For example, the brand manager of a consumer products company does not make the decision to expand the plant capacity for the brand.

> Profit centers are often viewed as an excellent training assignment for new managers. For example, Lester B. Korn, chairman and chief executive officer of Korn/Ferry International, offered the following strategy for young executives en route to top management positions:
>
> *Get Profit-Center Responsibility—Obtain a position where you can prove yourself as both a specialist with particular expertise and a generalist who can exercise leadership, authority, and inspire enthusiasm among colleagues and subordinates.*

> Profit centers may be divisions, departments, or products.

Responsibility accounting reports usually show the revenues, expenses, and income from operations for the profit center. The profit center income statement should include only revenues and expenses that are controlled by the manager. *Controllable revenues* are revenues earned by the profit center. **Controllable expenses** are costs that can be influenced (controlled) by the decisions of profit center managers. For example, the manager of the Men's Department at Nordstrom Inc. most likely controls the salaries of department personnel, but does not control the property taxes of the store.

SERVICE DEPARTMENT CHARGES

We will illustrate profit center income reporting for the Nova Entertainment Group (NEG). Assume that NEG is a diversified entertainment company with two operating divisions organized as profit centers: the Theme Park Division and the Movie Production Division. The revenues and operating expenses for the two divisions are shown below. The operating expenses consist of the direct expenses, such as the wages and salaries of a division's employees.

	Theme Park Division	Movie Production Division
Revenues	$6,000,000	$2,500,000
Operating expenses	2,495,000	405,000

In addition to direct expenses, divisions may also have expenses for services provided by internal centralized *service departments*. These service departments are often more efficient at providing service than are outside service providers. Examples of such service departments include the following:

- Research and Development
- Government Relations
- Telecommunications
- Publications and Graphics
- Facilities Management

- Purchasing
- Information Systems
- Payroll Accounting
- Transportation
- Personnel Administration

A profit center's income from operations should reflect the cost of any internal services used by the center. To illustrate, assume that NEG established a Payroll Accounting Department. The costs of the payroll services, called **service department charges**, are charged to NEG's profit centers, as shown in Exhibit 4.

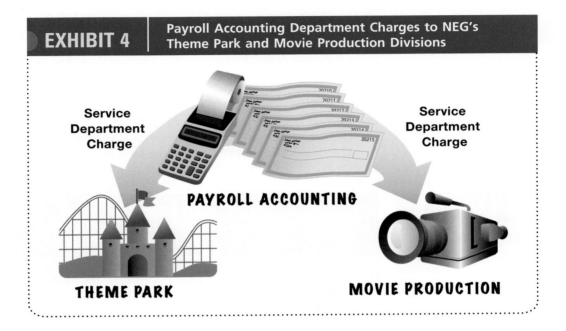

EXHIBIT 4	**Payroll Accounting Department Charges to NEG's Theme Park and Movie Production Divisions**

Service department charges are *indirect expenses* to a profit center. They are similar to the expenses that would be incurred if the profit center had purchased the services from a source outside the company. A profit center manager has control over such expenses if the manager is free to choose *how much* service is used from the service department.

To illustrate service department charges, assume that NEG has two other service departments—Purchasing and Legal, in addition to Payroll Accounting. The expenses for the year ended December 31, 2008, for each service department are as follows:

Purchasing	$400,000
Payroll Accounting	255,000
Legal	250,000
Total	$905,000

An *activity base* for each service department is used to charge service department expenses to the Theme Park and Movie Production divisions. The activity base for each service department is a measure of the services performed. For NEG, the service department activity bases are as follows:

Department	Activity Base
Purchasing	Number of purchase requisitions
Payroll Accounting	Number of payroll checks
Legal	Number of billed hours

The use of services by the Theme Park and Movie Production divisions is as follows:

Employees of IBM speak of "green money" and "blue money." Green money comes from customers. Blue money comes from providing services to other IBM departments via service department charges. IBM employees note that blue money is easier to earn than green money; yet from the stockholders' perspective, green money is the only money that counts.

	Service Usage		
	Purchasing	**Payroll Accounting**	**Legal**
Theme Park Division	25,000 purchase requisitions	12,000 payroll checks	100 billed hrs.
Movie Production Division	15,000	3,000	900
Total	40,000 purchase requisitions	15,000 payroll checks	1,000 billed hrs.

The rates at which services are charged to each division are called *service department charge rates.* These rates are determined by dividing each service department's expenses by the total service usage as follows:

$$\text{Purchasing: } \frac{\$400,000}{40,000 \text{ purchase requisitions}} = \$10 \text{ per purchase requisition}$$

$$\text{Payroll Accounting: } \frac{\$255,000}{15,000 \text{ payroll checks}} = \$17 \text{ per payroll check}$$

$$\text{Legal: } \frac{\$250,000}{1,000 \text{ hours}} = \$250 \text{ per hour}$$

The use of services by the Theme Park and Movie Production divisions is multiplied by the service department charge rates to determine the charges to each division, as shown in Exhibit 5.

EXHIBIT 5

Service Department Charges to NEG Divisions

Nova Entertainment Group
Service Department Charges to NEG Divisions
For the Year Ended December 31, 2008

Service Department	Theme Park Division	Movie Production Division
Purchasing (Note A)	$250,000	$150,000
Payroll Accounting (Note B)	204,000	51,000
Legal (Note C)	25,000	225,000
Total service department charges	$479,000	$426,000

Note A:
25,000 purchase requisitions × $10 per purchase requisition = $250,000
15,000 purchase requisitions × $10 per purchase requisition = $150,000
Note B:
12,000 payroll checks × $17 per check = $204,000
3,000 payroll checks × $17 per check = $51,000
Note C:
100 hours × $250 per hour = $25,000
900 hours × $250 per hour = $225,000

The Theme Park Division employs many temporary and part-time employees who are paid weekly. This is in contrast to the Movie Production Division, which has a more permanent payroll that is paid on a monthly basis. As a result, the Theme Park Division requires 12,000 payroll checks. This results in a large service charge from Payroll Accounting to the Theme Park Division. In contrast, the Movie Production Division uses many legal services for contract negotiations. Thus, there is a large service charge from Legal to the Movie Production Division.

PROFIT CENTER REPORTING

The divisional income statements for NEG are presented in Exhibit 6. These statements show the service department charges to the divisions.

Example Exercise 8-2

objective **3**

The centralized legal department of Johnson Company has expenses of $60,000. The department has provided a total of 2,000 hours of service for the period. The East Division has used 500 hours of legal service during the period, and the West Division has used 1,500 hours. How much should it be charged for legal services?

Follow My Example 8-2

East Division Service Charge for Legal Department:
$15,000 = 500 billed hours × ($60,000/2,000 hours)

West Division Service Charge for Legal Department:
$45,000 = 1,500 billed hours × ($60,000/2,000 hours)

For Practice: PE 8-2A, PE 8-2B

EXHIBIT 6

Divisional Income
Statements—NEG

Nova Entertainment Group
Divisional Income Statements
For the Year Ended December 31, 2008

	Theme Park Division	Movie Production Division
Revenues*	$6,000,000	$2,500,000
Operating expenses	2,495,000	405,000
Income from operations before service department charges	$3,505,000	$2,095,000
Less service department charges:		
Purchasing	$ 250,000	$ 150,000
Payroll Accounting	204,000	51,000
Legal	25,000	225,000
Total service department charges	$ 479,000	$ 426,000
Income from operations	$3,026,000	$1,669,000

*For a profit center that sells products, the income statement would show: Net sales − Cost of goods sold = Gross profit. The operating expenses would be deducted from the gross profit to get the income from operations before service department charges.

The **income from operations** is a measure of a manager's performance. In evaluating the profit center manager, the income from operations should be compared over time to a budget. It should not be compared across profit centers, since the profit centers are usually different in terms of size, products, and customers.

Example Exercise 8-3

objective **3**

Using the data for Johnson Company from Example Exercise 8-2 along with the data given below, determine the divisional income from operations for the East and West divisions.

	East Division	West Division
Sales	$300,000	$800,000
Cost of goods sold	165,000	420,000
Selling expenses	85,000	185,000

(continued)

Follow My Example 8-3

	East Division	West Division
Revenues	$300,000	$800,000
Operating expenses	250,000*	605,000**
Income from operations before		
service department charges	$ 50,000	$195,000
Service department charges	15,000	45,000
Income from operations	$ 35,000	$150,000

*$165,000 + $85,000
**$420,000 + $185,000

For Practice: PE 8-3A, PE 8-3B

Responsibility Accounting for Investment Centers

objective **4**

Compute and interpret the rate of return on investment, the residual income, and the balanced scorecard for an investment center.

In an **investment center**, the unit manager has the responsibility and the authority to make decisions that affect not only costs and revenues but also the assets invested in the center. Investment centers are widely used in highly diversified companies organized by divisions.

The manager of an investment center has more authority and responsibility than the manager of a cost center or a profit center. The manager of an investment center occupies a position similar to that of a chief operating officer or president of a company and is evaluated in much the same way.

Since investment center managers have responsibility for revenues and expenses, income from operations is an important part of investment center reporting. In addition, because the manager has responsibility for the assets invested in the center, two additional measures of performance are often used. These measures are the rate of return on investment and residual income. Top management often compares these measures across investment centers to reward performance and assess investment in the centers.

To illustrate, assume that DataLink Inc. is a cellular phone company that has three regional divisions, Northern, Central, and Southern. Condensed divisional income statements for the investment centers are shown in Exhibit 7.

EXHIBIT 7

Divisional Income Statements— DataLink Inc.

DataLink Inc.
Divisional Income Statements
For the Year Ended December 31, 2008

	Northern Division	Central Division	Southern Division
Revenues	$560,000	$672,000	$750,000
Operating expenses	336,000	470,400	562,500
Income from operations			
before service			
department charges	$224,000	$201,600	$187,500
Service department			
charges	154,000	117,600	112,500
Income from operations	$ 70,000	$ 84,000	$ 75,000

Using only income from operations, the Central Division is the most profitable division. However, income from operations does not reflect the amount of assets invested in each center. For example, a manager responsible for more assets should earn more income from operations than a manager responsible for fewer assets.

RATE OF RETURN ON INVESTMENT

Since investment center managers also control the amount of assets invested in their centers, they should be held accountable for the use of these assets. One measure that considers the amount of assets invested is the **rate of return on investment (ROI)** or *rate of return on assets*. It is one of the most widely used measures for investment centers and is computed as follows:

$$\text{Rate of Return on Investment (ROI)} = \frac{\text{Income from Operations}}{\text{Invested Assets}}$$

The rate of return on investment is useful because the three factors subject to control by divisional managers (revenues, expenses, and invested assets) are used in its computation. By measuring profitability relative to the amount of assets invested in each division, the rate of return on investment can be used to compare divisions. The higher the rate of return on investment, the better the division utilizes its assets to generate income. To illustrate, the rate of return on investment for each division of DataLink Inc., based on the book value of invested assets, is as follows:

	Northern Division	Central Division	Southern Division
Income from operations	$70,000	$84,000	$75,000
Invested assets	$350,000	$700,000	$500,000
Rate of return on investment	20%	12%	15%

Although the Central Division generated the largest income from operations, its rate of return on investment (12%) is the lowest. Hence, relative to the assets invested, the Central Division is the least profitable division. In comparison, the rate of return on investment of the Northern Division is 20% and the Southern Division is 15%. One way to analyze these differences is by using an expanded formula, called the DuPont formula, for the rate of return on investment.

The **DuPont formula**, created by a financial executive of E.I. du Pont de Nemours and Company in 1919, states that the rate earned on total assets is the product of two factors. The first factor is the ratio of income from operations to sales, often called the **profit margin**. The second factor is the ratio of sales to invested assets, often called the **investment turnover**. In the illustration at the left, profits can be earned by either increasing the investment turnover (turning the crank faster), by increasing the profit margin (increasing the size of the opening), or both.

Using the DuPont formula yields the same rate of return on investment for the Northern Division, 20%, as computed previously.

$$\text{Rate of Return on Investment (ROI)} = \text{Profit Margin} \times \text{Investment Turnover}$$

$$\text{Rate of Return on Investment (ROI)} = \frac{\text{Income from Operations}}{\text{Sales}} \times \frac{\text{Sales}}{\text{Invested Assets}}$$

$$\text{ROI} = \frac{\$70,000}{\$560,000} \times \frac{\$560,000}{\$350,000}$$

$$\text{ROI} = 12.5\% \times 1.6$$
$$\text{ROI} = 20\%$$

The DuPont formula for the rate of return on investment is useful in evaluating and controlling divisions. This is because the profit margin and the investment turnover focus on the underlying operating relationships of each division.

The profit margin component focuses on profitability by indicating the rate of profit earned on each sales dollar. If a division's profit margin increases, and all other factors

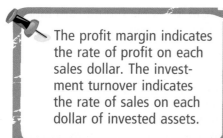

The profit margin indicates the rate of profit on each sales dollar. The investment turnover indicates the rate of sales on each dollar of invested assets.

remain the same, the division's rate of return on investment will increase. For example, a division might add more profitable products to its sales mix and thereby increase its overall profit margin and rate of return on investment.

The investment turnover component focuses on efficiency in using assets and indicates the rate at which sales are generated for each dollar of invested assets. The more sales per dollar invested, the greater the efficiency in using the assets. If a division's investment turnover increases, and all other factors remain the same, the division's rate of return on investment will increase. For example, a division might attempt to increase sales through special sales promotions or reduce inventory assets by using just-in-time principles, either of which would increase investment turnover.

The rate of return on investment, using the DuPont formula for each division of DataLink Inc., is summarized as follows:

$$\text{Rate of Return on Investment (ROI)} = \frac{\text{Income from Operations}}{\text{Sales}} \times \frac{\text{Sales}}{\text{Invested Assets}}$$

$$\text{Northern Division (ROI)} = \frac{\$70,000}{\$560,000} \times \frac{\$560,000}{\$350,000}$$

$$\text{ROI} = 12.5\% \times 1.6$$
$$\text{ROI} = 20\%$$

$$\text{Central Division (ROI)} = \frac{\$84,000}{\$672,000} \times \frac{\$672,000}{\$700,000}$$

$$\text{ROI} = 12.5\% \times 0.96$$
$$\text{ROI} = 12\%$$

$$\text{Southern Division (ROI)} = \frac{\$75,000}{\$750,000} \times \frac{\$750,000}{\$500,000}$$

$$\text{ROI} = 10\% \times 1.5$$
$$\text{ROI} = 15\%$$

Although the Northern and Central divisions have the same profit margins, the Northern Division investment turnover (1.6) is larger than that of the Central Division (0.96). Thus, by using its invested assets more efficiently, the Northern Division's rate of return on investment is higher than the Central Division's. The Southern Division's profit margin of 10% and investment turnover of 1.5 are lower than those of the Northern Division. The product of these factors results in a return on investment of 15% for the Southern Division, compared to 20% for the Northern Division.

To determine possible ways of increasing the rate of return on investment, the profit margin and investment turnover for a division may be analyzed. For example, if the Northern Division is in a highly competitive industry in which the profit margin cannot be easily increased, the division manager might focus on increasing the investment turnover. To illustrate, assume that the revenues of the Northern Division could be increased by $56,000 through increasing operating expenses, such as advertising, to $385,000. The Northern Division's income from operations will increase from $70,000 to $77,000, as shown below.

Revenues ($560,000 + $56,000)	$616,000
Operating expenses	385,000
Income from operations before service department charges	$231,000
Service department charges	154,000
Income from operations	$ 77,000

The rate of return on investment for the Northern Division, using the DuPont formula, is recomputed as follows:

$$\text{Rate of Return on Investment (ROI)} = \frac{\text{Income from Operations}}{\text{Sales}} \times \frac{\text{Sales}}{\text{Invested Assets}}$$

$$\text{Northern Division Revised ROI} = \frac{\$77,000}{\$616,000} \times \frac{\$616,000}{\$350,000}$$

$$\text{ROI} = 12.5\% \times 1.76$$
$$\text{ROI} = 22\%$$

Although the Northern Division's profit margin remains the same (12.5%), the investment turnover has increased from 1.6 to 1.76, an increase of 10% (0.16 ÷ 1.6). The 10% increase in investment turnover also increases the rate of return on investment by 10% (from 20% to 22%).

In addition to using it as a performance measure, the rate of return on investment may assist management in other ways. For example, in considering a decision to expand the operations of DataLink Inc., management might consider giving priority to the Northern Division because it earns the highest rate of return on investment. If the current rates of return on investment are maintained in the future, an investment in the Northern Division will return 20 cents (20%) on each dollar invested. In contrast, investments in the Central Division will earn only 12 cents per dollar invested, and investments in the Southern Division will return only 15 cents per dollar.

A disadvantage of the rate of return on investment as a performance measure is that it may lead divisional managers to reject new investments that could be profitable for the company as a whole. For example, the Northern Division of DataLink Inc. has an overall rate of return on investment of 20%. Assume the top management establishes

Business Connections

REAL WORLD

RETURN ON INVESTMENT

The annual reports of public companies must provide segment disclosure information identifying revenues, income from operations, and total assets. This information can be used to compute the return on investment for the segments of a company. For example, The E.W. Scripps Company, a media company, operates four major segments:

1. Newspapers: Owns and operates daily and community newspapers in 19 markets in the United States.
2. Scripps Networks: Owns and operates five national television networks: Home and Garden Television, Food

Network, DIY Network, Fine Living, and Great American Country.
3. Broadcast Television: Owns and operates several local televisions in various markets.
4. Shop at Home: Markets a range of consumer goods to television viewers and visitors to its Internet site.

The DuPont formulas for these segments, as derived from a recent annual report, are as follows:

	Segment Profit Margin	×	Investment Turnover	=	Return on Investment
Newspapers	34.9%		0.55		19.2%
Scripps Networks	42.0%		0.67		28.1%
Broadcast Television	31.6%		0.69		21.8%
Shop at Home	−7.5%		0.80		−6.0%

As can be seen from the data, E.W. Scripps' three business segments (Newspapers, Scripps Networks, and Broadcast Television) have relatively low investment turnover, with all three being slightly above 0.50. Each of these segments also had very strong profit margins, ranging from 31.6% to 42.0%. Multiplying the profit margin by the investment turnover yields the ROI. The ROI is strong for the three primary business segments. The Shop at Home segment,

however, is not performing as well. While this segment has a stronger investment turnover than the other three segments, it operates at a negative profit. This is the newest segment of the company and represents a relatively small portion of the company's total revenues. As the segment grows, the company should be careful to control costs to ensure that this segment attains a level of profitability consistent with the company's other segments.

a minimal acceptable rate of return of 10%. Assume further the manager of the Northern Division has the opportunity to invest in a new project that is estimated to earn a 14% rate of return. If the manager of the Northern Division invests in the project, however, the Northern Division's overall rate of return will decrease from 20% due to averaging. Thus, the division manager might decide to reject the project, even though the investment would exceed DataLink's minimum acceptable rate of return on investment. The CFO of Millennium Chemicals referred to a similar situation by stating: "We had too many divisional executives who failed to spend money on capital projects with more than satisfactory returns because those projects would have lowered the average return on assets of their particular business."

Example Exercise 8-4   objective 4

Campbell Company has income from operations of $35,000, invested assets of $140,000, and sales of $437,500. Use the DuPont formula to compute the rate of return on investment and show (a) the profit margin, (b) the investment turnover, and (c) the rate of return on investment.

Follow My Example 8-4

a. Profit margin = $35,000/$437,500 = 8%
b. Investment turnover = $437,500/$140,000 = 3.125
c. Rate of return on investment = 8% × 3.125 = 25%

For Practice: PE 8-4A, PE 8-4B

RESIDUAL INCOME

An additional measure of evaluating divisional performance—residual income—is useful in overcoming some of the disadvantages associated with the rate of return on investment. **Residual income**[1] is the excess of income from operations over a minimum acceptable income from operations, as illustrated below.

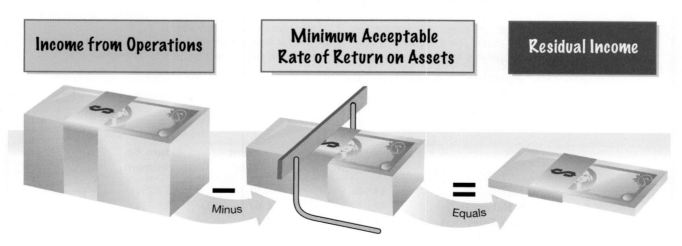

The minimum acceptable income from operations is normally computed by multiplying a minimum rate of return by the amount of divisional assets. The minimum rate is set by top management, based on such factors as the cost of financing the business operations. To illustrate, assume that DataLink Inc. has established 10% as the mini-

---

1 Another popular term for residual income is economic value added (EVA), which has been trademarked by the consulting firm Stern Stewart & Co.

mum acceptable rate of return on divisional assets. The residual incomes for the three divisions are as follows:

	Northern Division	Central Division	Southern Division
Income from operations	$70,000	$84,000	$75,000
Minimum acceptable income from operations as a percent of assets:			
$350,000 × 10%	35,000		
$700,000 × 10%		70,000	
$500,000 × 10%			50,000
Residual income	$35,000	$14,000	$25,000

The Northern Division has more residual income than the other divisions, even though it has the least amount of income from operations. This is because the assets on which to earn a minimum acceptable rate of return are less for the Northern Division than for the other divisions.

The major advantage of residual income as a performance measure is that it considers both the minimum acceptable rate of return and the total amount of the income from operations earned by each division. Residual income encourages division managers to maximize income from operations in excess of the minimum. This provides an incentive to accept any project that is expected to have a rate of return in excess of the minimum. Thus, the residual income number supports both divisional and overall company objectives.

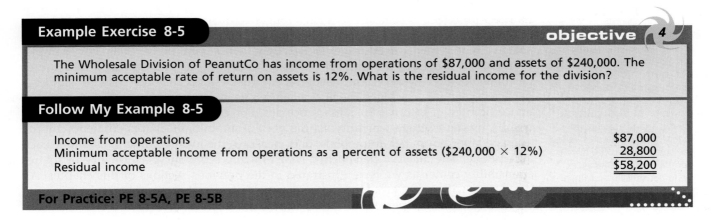

Example Exercise 8-5   objective 4

The Wholesale Division of PeanutCo has income from operations of $87,000 and assets of $240,000. The minimum acceptable rate of return on assets is 12%. What is the residual income for the division?

Follow My Example 8-5

Income from operations	$87,000
Minimum acceptable income from operations as a percent of assets ($240,000 × 12%)	28,800
Residual income	$58,200

For Practice: PE 8-5A, PE 8-5B

THE BALANCED SCORECARD[2]

In addition to financial divisional performance measures, many companies are also relying on nonfinancial divisional measures. One popular evaluation approach is the **balanced scorecard**. The balanced scorecard is a set of financial and nonfinancial measures that reflect multiple performance dimensions of a business. A common balanced scorecard design measures performance in the innovation and learning, customer, internal, and financial dimensions of a business. These four areas can be diagrammed as shown in Exhibit 8.

The *innovation and learning* perspective measures the amount of innovation in an organization. For example, a drug company, such as Merck & Co., Inc., would measure the number of drugs in its FDA (Food and Drug Administration) approval pipeline,

---

2 The balanced scorecard was developed by R. S. Kaplan and D. P. Norton and explained in *The Balanced Scorecard: Translating Strategy into Action* (Cambridge: Harvard Business School Press, 1996).

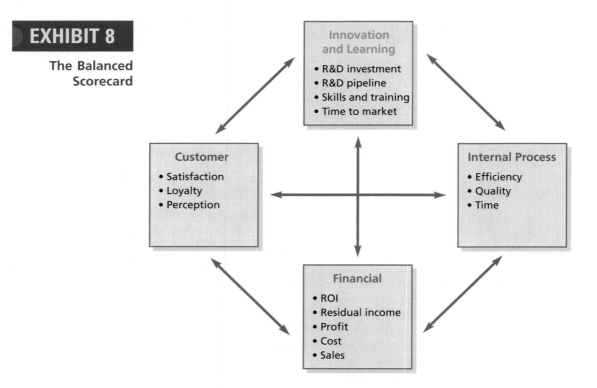

the amount of research and development (R&D) spending per period, and the length of time it takes to turn ideas into marketable products. Managing the performance of its R&D processes is critical to Merck's longer-term prospects and thus would be an additional performance perspective beyond the financial numbers. The *customer* perspective would measure customer satisfaction, loyalty, and perceptions. For example, Amazon.com measures the number of repeat visitors to its Web site as a measure of customer loyalty. Amazon.com needs repeat business because the costs to acquire a new customer are very high. The *internal process* perspective measures the effectiveness and efficiency of internal business processes. For example, DaimlerChrysler measures quality by the average warranty claims per automobile, measures efficiency by the average labor hours per automobile, and measures the average time to assemble each automobile. The *financial* perspective measures the economic performance of the responsibility center as we have illustrated in the previous sections of this chapter. All companies will use financial measures. The measures most commonly used are income from operations as a percent of sales and rate of return on investment.

The balanced scorecard is designed to reveal the underlying nonfinancial drivers, or causes, of financial performance. For example, if a business improves customer satisfaction, this will likely lead to improved financial performance. In addition, the balanced scorecard helps managers consider trade-offs between short- and long-term performance. For example, additional investment in research and development (R&D) would penalize the short-term financial perspective, because R&D is an expense that reduces income from operations. However, the innovation perspective would measure additional R&D expenditures favorably, because current R&D expenditures will lead to future profits from new products. The balanced scorecard will motivate the manager to invest in new R&D, even though it is recognized as a current period expense. A survey by Bain & Co., a consulting firm, indicated that 57% of large companies use the balanced scorecard.[3] Thus, the balanced scorecard is gaining acceptance because of its ability to reveal the underlying causes of financial performance, while helping managers consider the short- and long-term implications of their decisions.

---

3 Bain & Co., "Management Tools 2005."

Transfer Pricing

When divisions transfer products or render services to each other, a **transfer price** is used to charge for the products or services. Since transfer prices affect the goals for both divisions, setting these prices is a sensitive matter for division managers.

Transfer prices should be set so that overall company income is increased when goods are transferred between divisions. As we will illustrate, however, transfer prices may be misused in such a way that overall company income suffers.

In the following paragraphs, we discuss various approaches to setting transfer prices. Exhibit 9 shows the range of prices that results from common approaches to setting transfer prices.[4] Transfer prices can be set as low as the variable cost per unit or as high as the market price. Often, transfer prices are negotiated at some point between variable cost per unit and market price.

EXHIBIT 9	Commonly Used Transfer Prices

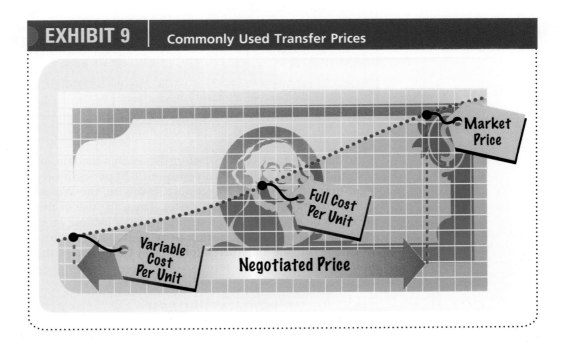

Transfer prices may be used when decentralized units are organized as cost, profit, or investment centers. To illustrate, we will use a packaged snack food company (Wilson Company) with no service departments and two operating divisions (Eastern and Western) organized as investment centers. Condensed divisional income statements for Wilson Company, assuming no transfers between divisions, are shown in Exhibit 10.

MARKET PRICE APPROACH

Using the **market price approach**, the transfer price is the price at which the product or service transferred could be sold to outside buyers. If an outside market exists for the product or service transferred, the current market price may be a proper transfer price.

To illustrate, assume that materials used by Wilson Company in producing snack food in the Western Division are currently purchased from an outside supplier at $20 per unit. The same materials are produced by the Eastern Division. The Eastern Division is operating at full capacity of 50,000 units and can sell all it produces to either the Western Division or to outside buyers. A transfer price of $20 per unit (the market

---

4 The discussion in this chapter highlights the essential concepts of transfer pricing. In-depth discussion of transfer pricing can be found in advanced texts.

EXHIBIT 10

Income Statements—
No Transfers Between
Divisions

Wilson Company			
Divisional Income Statements			
For the Year Ended December 31, 2008			
	Eastern Division	Western Division	Total
Sales:			
50,000 units × $20 per unit	$1,000,000		$1,000,000
20,000 units × $40 per unit		$800,000	800,000
			$1,800,000
Expenses:			
Variable:			
50,000 units × $10 per unit . . .	$ 500,000		$ 500,000
20,000 units × $30* per unit . .		$600,000	600,000
Fixed	300,000	100,000	400,000
Total expenses	$ 800,000	$700,000	$1,500,000
Income from operations	$ 200,000	$100,000	$ 300,000

*$20 of the $30 per unit represents materials costs, and the remaining $10 per unit represents other variable conversion expenses incurred within the Western Division.

price) has no effect on the Eastern Division's income or total company income. The Eastern Division will earn revenues of $20 per unit on all its production and sales, regardless of who buys its product. Likewise, the Western Division will pay $20 per unit for materials (the market price). Thus, the use of the market price as the transfer price has no effect on the Eastern Division's income or total company income. In this situation, the use of the market price as the transfer price is proper. The condensed divisional income statements for Wilson Company in this case are also shown in Exhibit 10.

NEGOTIATED PRICE APPROACH

If unused or excess capacity exists in the supplying division (the Eastern Division), and the transfer price is equal to the market price, total company profit may not be maximized. This is because the manager of the Western Division will be indifferent toward purchasing materials from the Eastern Division or from outside suppliers. Thus, the Western Division may purchase the materials from outside suppliers. If, however, the Western Division purchases the materials from the Eastern Division, the difference between the market price of $20 and the variable costs of the Eastern Division can cover fixed costs and contribute to company profits. When the negotiated price approach is used in this situation, the manager of the Western Division is encouraged to purchase the materials from the Eastern Division.

The **negotiated price approach** allows the managers of decentralized units to agree (negotiate) among themselves as to the transfer price. The only constraint on the negotiations is that the transfer price be less than the market price but greater than the supplying division's variable costs per unit.

To illustrate the use of the negotiated price approach, assume that instead of a capacity of 50,000 units, the Eastern Division's capacity is 70,000 units. In addition, assume that the Eastern Division can continue to sell only 50,000 units to outside buyers. A transfer price less than $20 would encourage the manager of the Western Division to purchase from the Eastern Division. This is because the Western Division's materials cost per unit would decrease, and its income from operations would increase. At the same time, a transfer price above the Eastern Division's variable costs per unit of $10 (from Exhibit 10) would encourage the manager of the Eastern Division to use the excess capacity to supply materials to the Western Division. In doing so, the Eastern Division's income from operations would increase.

We continue the illustration with the aid of Exhibit 11, assuming that Wilson Company's division managers agree to a transfer price of $15 for the Eastern Division's product. By purchasing from the Eastern Division, the Western Division's materials cost would be $5 per unit less. At the same time, the Eastern Division would increase its sales by $300,000 (20,000 units × $15 per unit) and increase its income by $100,000 ($300,000 sales − $200,000 variable costs). The effect of reducing the Western Division's materials cost by $100,000 (20,000 units × $5 per unit) is to increase its income by $100,000. Therefore, Wilson Company's income is increased by $200,000 ($100,000 reported by the Eastern Division and $100,000 reported by the Western Division), as shown in the condensed income statements in Exhibit 11.

EXHIBIT 11

Income Statements—
Negotiated Transfer
Price

Wilson Company
Divisional Income Statements
For the Year Ended December 31, 2008

	Eastern Division	Western Division	Total
Sales:			
50,000 units × $20 per unit	$1,000,000		$1,000,000
20,000 units × $15 per unit	300,000		300,000
20,000 units × $40 per unit		$800,000	800,000
	$1,300,000	$800,000	$2,100,000
Expenses:			
Variable:			
70,000 units × $10 per unit . . .	$ 700,000		$ 700,000
20,000 units × $25* per unit . .		$500,000	500,000
Fixed	300,000	100,000	400,000
Total expenses	$1,000,000	$600,000	$1,600,000
Income from operations	$ 300,000	$200,000	$ 500,000

*$10 of the $25 represents variable conversion expenses incurred solely within the Western Division, and $15 per unit represents the transfer price per unit from the Eastern Division.

In this illustration, any transfer price less than the market price of $20 but greater than the Eastern Division's unit variable costs of $10 would increase each division's income. In addition, overall company profit would increase by $200,000. By establishing a range of $20 to $10 for the transfer price, each division manager has an incentive to negotiate the transfer of the materials.

Example Exercise 8-6   objective   5

The materials used by the Winston-Salem Division of Fox Company are currently purchased from outside suppliers at $30 per unit. These same materials are produced by Fox's Flagstaff Division. The Flagstaff Division can produce the materials needed by the Winston-Salem Division at a variable cost of $15 per unit. The division is currently producing 70,000 units and has capacity of 100,000 units. The two divisions have recently negotiated a transfer price of $22 per unit for 30,000 units. By how much will each division's income increase as a result of this transfer?

(continued)

Follow My Example 8-6

Winston-Salem Division

Change in sales	$ 0
Decrease in variable costs [30,000 units × ($30 − $22)]	(240,000)
Increase in income	$240,000

Flagstaff Division

Increase in sales (30,000 units × $22)	$660,000
Increase in variable costs (30,000 units × $15)	450,000
Increase in income	$210,000

For Practice: PE 8-6A, PE 8-6B

COST PRICE APPROACH

Under the **cost price approach**, cost is used to set transfer prices. With this approach, a variety of cost concepts may be used. For example, cost may refer to either total product cost per unit or variable product cost per unit. If total product cost per unit is used, direct materials, direct labor, and factory overhead are included in the transfer price. If variable product cost per unit is used, the fixed factory overhead component of total product cost is excluded from the transfer price.

Either actual costs or standard (budgeted) costs may be used in applying the cost price approach. If actual costs are used, inefficiencies of the producing division are transferred to the purchasing division. Thus, there is little incentive for the producing division to control costs carefully. For this reason, most companies use standard costs in the cost price approach. In this way, differences between actual and standard costs remain with the producing division for cost control purposes.

When division managers have responsibility for cost centers, the cost price approach to transfer pricing is proper and is often used. The cost price approach may not be proper, however, for decentralized operations organized as profit or investment centers. In profit and investment centers, division managers have responsibility for both revenues and expenses. The use of cost as a transfer price ignores the supplying division manager's responsibility for revenues. When a supplying division's sales are all intracompany transfers, for example, using the cost price approach prevents the supplying division from reporting any income from operations. A cost-based transfer price may therefore not motivate the division manager to make intracompany transfers, even though they are in the best interests of the company.

Integrity, Objectivity, and Ethics in Business

ETHICS

SHIFTING INCOME THROUGH TRANSFER PRICES

Transfer prices allow companies to minimize taxes by shifting taxable income from countries with high tax rates to countries with low taxes. For example, GlaxoSmithKline, a British company, and the second biggest drug maker in the world, has been in a dispute with the U.S. Internal Revenue Service (IRS) over international transfer prices since the early 1990s. The company pays U.S. taxes on income from its U.S. Division and British taxes on income from the British Division. The IRS claims that the transfer prices on sales from the British Division to the U.S. Division were too high, which reduced profits and taxes in the U.S. Division. In January 2005, the company received a new tax bill from the IRS for almost $1.9 billion related to the transfer pricing issue, raising the total bill to almost $5 billion. The company has filed suit in the U.S. Tax Court to dispute the IRS assessment.

Source: J. Whalen, "Glaxo Gets New IRS Bill Seeking Another $1.9 Billion in Back Tax," *The Wall Street Journal,* January 27, 2005.

At a Glance

1. List and explain the advantages and disadvantages of decentralized operations.

Key Points	Key Learning Outcomes	Example Exercises	Practice Exercises
In a centralized business, all major planning and operating decisions are made by top management. In a decentralized business, these responsibilities are delegated to unit managers. Decentralization may allow a company to be more effective because operational decisions are made by the managers closest to the operations, allowing top management to focus on strategic issues.	• Describe the advantages of decentralization. • Describe the disadvantages of decentralization. • Describe the common types of responsibility centers and the role of responsibility accounting.		

2. Prepare a responsibility accounting report for a cost center.

Key Points	Key Learning Outcomes	Example Exercises	Practice Exercises
Cost centers limit the responsibility and authority of managers to decisions related to the costs of their unit. The primary accounting tool for planning and controlling costs for a cost center are budgets and budget performance reports.	• Describe cost centers. • Describe the responsibility reporting for a cost center. • Compute the over (under) budgeted costs for a cost center.	8-1	8-1A, 8-1B

3. Prepare responsibility accounting reports for a profit center.

Key Points	Key Learning Outcomes	Example Exercises	Practice Exercises
In a profit center, managers have the responsibility and authority to make decisions that affect both revenues and costs. Responsibility reports for a profit center usually show income from operations for the unit.	• Describe profit centers. • Determine how service department charges are allocated to profit centers. • Describe the responsibility reporting for a profit center. • Compute income from operations for a profit center.	8-2 8-3	8-2A, 8-2B 8-3A, 8-3B

4. Compute and interpret the rate of return on investment, the residual income, and the balanced scorecard for an investment center.

Key Points	Key Learning Outcomes	Example Exercises	Practice Exercises
In an investment center, the unit manager has the responsibility and authority to make decisions that affect the unit's revenues, expenses, and assets invested in the center. Three measures are commonly used to assess investment center performance: return on investment (ROI), residual income, and the balanced scorecard. These measures are often used to compare and assess investment center performance.	• Describe investment centers. • Describe the responsibility reporting for an investment center. • Compute the rate of return on investment (ROI). • Compute residual income. • Describe the balanced scorecard approach.	8-4 8-5	8-4A, 8-4B 8-5A, 8-5B

5. **Explain how the market price, negotiated price, and cost price approaches to transfer pricing may be used by decentralized segments of a business.**

Key Points	Key Learning Outcomes	Example Exercises	Practice Exercises
When divisions within a company transfer products or provide services to each other, a transfer price is used to charge for the products or services. Transfer prices should be set so that the overall company income is increased when goods are transferred between divisions. One of three common approaches is typically used to establish transfer prices: market price, negotiated price, or cost price.	• Describe how companies determine the price used to transfer products or services between divisions. • Determine transfer prices using the market price approach. • Determine transfer prices using the negotiated price approach. • Describe the cost price approach to determining transfer price.	8-6	8-6A, 8-6B

Key Terms

balanced scorecard (321)
controllable expenses (312)
cost center (310)
cost price approach (326)
decentralization (308)
division (308)
DuPont formula (317)

income from operations (315)
investment center (316)
investment turnover (317)
market price approach (323)
negotiated price approach (324)
profit center (312)
profit margin (317)

rate of return on investment (ROI) (317)
residual income (320)
responsibility accounting (309)
service department charges (313)
transfer price (323)

Illustrative Problem

Quinn Company has two divisions, Domestic and International. Invested assets and condensed income statement data for each division for the past year ended December 31 are as follows:

	Domestic Division	International Division
Revenues	$675,000	$480,000
Operating expenses	450,000	372,400
Service department charges	90,000	50,000
Invested assets	600,000	384,000

Instructions
1. Prepare condensed income statements for the past year for each division.
2. Using the DuPont formula, determine the profit margin, investment turnover, and rate of return on investment for each division.
3. If management's minimum acceptable rate of return is 10%, determine the residual income for each division.

Solution

1.

Quinn Company
Divisional Income Statements
For the Year Ended December 31, 2008

	Domestic Division	International Division
Revenues	$675,000	$480,000
Operating expenses	450,000	372,400
Income from operations before		
service department charges	$225,000	$107,600
Service department charges	90,000	50,000
Income from operations	$135,000	$ 57,600

2.

$$\text{Rate of Return on Investment (ROI)} = \text{Profit Margin} \times \text{Investment Turnover}$$

$$\text{Rate of Return on Investment (ROI)} = \frac{\text{Income from Operations}}{\text{Sales}} \times \frac{\text{Sales}}{\text{Invested Assets}}$$

$$\text{Domestic Division: ROI} = \frac{\$135,000}{\$675,000} \times \frac{\$675,000}{\$600,000}$$

$$\text{ROI} = 20\% \times 1.125$$
$$\text{ROI} = 22.5\%$$

$$\text{International Division: ROI} = \frac{\$57,600}{\$480,000} \times \frac{\$480,000}{\$384,000}$$

$$\text{ROI} = 12\% \times 1.25$$
$$\text{ROI} = 15\%$$

3. Domestic Division: $75,000 [$135,000 − (10% × $600,000)]
   International Division: $19,200 [$57,600 − (10% × $384,000)]

Self-Examination Questions

(Answers at End of Chapter)

1. When the manager has the responsibility and authority to make decisions that affect costs and revenues but no responsibility for or authority over assets invested in the department, the department is called a(n):
   A. cost center.   C. investment center.
   B. profit center.   D. service department.

2. The Accounts Payable Department has expenses of $600,000 and makes 150,000 payments to the various vendors who provide products and services to the divisions. Division A has income from operations of $900,000, before service department charges, and requires 60,000 payments to vendors. If the Accounts Payable Department is treated as a service department, what is Division A's income from operations?
   A. $300,000   C. $660,000
   B. $900,000   D. $540,000

3. Division A of Kern Co. has sales of $350,000, cost of goods sold of $200,000, operating expenses of $30,000,

   and invested assets of $600,000. What is the rate of return on investment for Division A?
   A. 20%   C. 33%
   B. 25%   D. 40%

4. Division L of Liddy Co. has a rate of return on investment of 24% and an investment turnover of 1.6. What is the profit margin?
   A. 6%   C. 24%
   B. 15%   D. 38%

5. Which approach to transfer pricing uses the price at which the product or service transferred could be sold to outside buyers?
   A. Cost price approach
   B. Negotiated price approach
   C. Market price approach
   D. Standard cost approach

Eye Openers

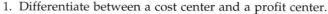

1. Differentiate between a cost center and a profit center.
2. Differentiate between a profit center and an investment center.
3. In what major respect would budget performance reports prepared for the use of plant managers of a manufacturing business with cost centers differ from those prepared for the use of the various department supervisors who report to the plant managers?
4. For what decisions is the manager of a cost center *not* responsible?
5. Weyerhaeuser developed a system that assigns service department expenses to user divisions on the basis of actual services consumed by the division. Here are a number of Weyerhaeuser's activities in its central Financial Services Department:

    • Payroll
    • Accounts payable
    • Accounts receivable
    • Database administration—report preparation

    For each activity, identify an output measure that could be used to charge user divisions for service.
6. What is the major shortcoming of using income from operations as a performance measure for investment centers?
7. Why should the factors under the control of the investment center manager (revenues, expenses, and invested assets) be considered in computing the rate of return on investment?
8. In a decentralized company in which the divisions are organized as investment centers, how could a division be considered the least profitable even though it earned the largest amount of income from operations?
9. How does using the rate of return on investment facilitate comparability between divisions of decentralized companies?
10. The rates of return on investment for Kardin Co.'s three divisions, East, Central, and West, are 22%, 18%, and 16%, respectively. In expanding operations, which of Kardin Co.'s divisions should be given priority? Explain.
11. Why would a firm use a balanced scorecard in evaluating divisional performance?
12. What is the objective of transfer pricing?
13. When is the negotiated price approach preferred over the market price approach in setting transfer prices?
14. Why would standard cost be a more appropriate transfer cost between cost centers than actual cost?
15. When using the negotiated price approach to transfer pricing, within what range should the transfer price be established?

Practice Exercises

PE 8-1A
Budgetary performance
obj. 2

Wizard Company's costs were under budget by $100,000. The company is divided into North and South regions. The North Region's costs were over budget by $20,000. Determine the amount that the South Region's costs were over or under budget.

PE 8-1B
Budgetary performance
obj. 2

Quick Start Company's costs were over budget by $42,000. The company is divided into Southwest and Northeast regions. The Southwest Region's costs were under budget by $8,000. Determine the amount that the Northeast Region's costs were over or under budget.

PE 8-2A
Service department charges
obj. 3

The centralized employee Travel Department of Wilson Company has expenses of $150,000. The department has serviced a total of 2,500 travel reservations for the period. The Midwest Division has made 1,000 reservations during the period, and the Southeast Division has made 1,500 reservations. How much should each division be charged for travel services?

PE 8-2B
Service department charges
obj. 3

The centralized Help Desk of Exton Company has expenses of $120,000. The department has provided a total of 12,000 hours of service for the period. The Fabrication Division has used 5,000 hours of Help Desk service during the period, and the Assembly Division has used 7,000 hours of Help Desk service. How much should each division be charged for travel services?

PE 8-3A
Income from operations
obj. 3

Using the data for the Wilson Company from Practice Exercise 8-2A along with the data provided below, determine the divisional income from operations for the Midwest and Southeast divisions.

	Midwest Division	Southeast Division
Sales	$600,000	$750,000
Cost of goods sold	315,000	450,000
Selling expenses	138,750	165,000

PE 8-3B
Income from operations
obj. 3

Using the data for the Exton Company from Practice Exercise 8-2B along with the data provided below, determine the divisional income from operations for the Fabrication and Assembly divisions.

	Fabrication Division	Assembly Division
Sales	$1,080,000	$1,200,000
Cost of goods sold	567,000	740,000
Selling expenses	249,750	230,000

PE 8-4A
Profit margin, investment turnover, and rate of return on investment
obj. 4

Fain Company has income from operations of $31,500, invested assets of $84,000, and sales of $262,500. Use the DuPont formula to compute the rate of return on investment and show (a) the profit margin, (b) the investment turnover, and (c) the rate of return on investment.

PE 8-4B
Profit margin, investment turnover, and rate of return on investment
obj. 4

Felton Company has income from operations of $51,250, invested assets of $280,000, and sales of $644,000. Use the DuPont formula to compute the rate of return on investment and show (a) the profit margin, (b) the investment turnover, and (c) the rate of return on investment.

PE 8-5A
Residual income
obj. 4

The Distribution Division has income from operations of $75,000 and assets of $500,000. The minimum acceptable rate of return on assets is 10%. What is the residual income for the division?

PE 8-5B
Residual income
obj. 4

The Consumer Division has income from operations of $45,000 and assets of $425,000. The minimum acceptable rate of return on assets is 9%. What is the residual income for the division?

PE 8-6A
Transfer pricing
obj. 5

The materials used by the Toms River Division of Jadelis Company are currently purchased from outside suppliers at $35 per unit. These same materials are produced by Jadelis's Racine Division. The Racine Division can produce the materials needed by the Toms River Division at a variable cost of $22 per unit. The division is currently producing 60,000 units and has capacity of 80,000 units. The two divisions have recently negotiated a transfer price of $28 per unit for 20,000 units. By how much will each division's income increase as a result of this transfer?

PE 8-6B
Transfer pricing
obj. 5

The materials used by the Colorado Division of the Soprano Company are currently purchased from outside suppliers at $40 per unit. These same materials are produced by the Florida Division. The Florida Division can produce the materials needed by the Colorado Division at a variable cost of $25 per unit. The division is currently producing 160,000 units and has capacity of 200,000 units. The two divisions have recently negotiated a transfer price of $33 per unit for 40,000 units. By how much will each division's income increase as a result of this transfer?

Exercises

EX 8-1
Budget performance reports for cost centers
obj. 2

✓ a. (c) $2,310

Partially completed budget performance reports for Qual-Tech Company, a manufacturer of air conditioners, are provided below.

Qual-Tech Company
Budget Performance Report—Vice President, Production
For the Month Ended April 30, 2008

Plant	Budget	Actual	Over Budget	Under Budget
North Region	$362,460	$360,920		$1,540
Central Region	259,980	258,580		1,400
South Region	(g)	(h)	$ (i)	
	$ (j)	$ (k)	$ (l)	$2,940

Qual-Tech Company
Budget Performance Report—Manager, South Region Plant
For the Month Ended April 30, 2008

Department	Budget	Actual	Over Budget	Under Budget
Chip Fabrication	$ (a)	$ (b)	$ (c)	
Electronic Assembly	74,480	75,460	980	
Final Assembly	119,980	119,560		$420
	$ (d)	$ (e)	$ (f)	$420

Qual-Tech Company
Budget Performance Report—Supervisor, Chip Fabrication
For the Month Ended April 30, 2008

Costs	Budget	Actual	Over Budget	Under Budget
Factory wages	$ 21,560	$ 23,100	$1,540	
Materials	60,900	60,480		$420
Power and light	3,360	3,990	630	
Maintenance	5,880	6,440	560	
	$ 91,700	$ 94,010	$2,730	$420

a. Complete the budget performance reports by determining the correct amounts for the lettered spaces.
b. ▬▬▶ Compose a memo to Dana Johnson, vice president of production for Qual-Tech Company, explaining the performance of the production division for April.

EX 8-2
Divisional income statements
obj. 3

The following data were summarized from the accounting records for Huggins Construction Company for the year ended June 30, 2008:

Cost of goods sold:		Service department charges:	
Residential Division	$300,800	Residential Division	$ 54,240
Industrial Division	167,840	Industrial Division	24,960

✓ *Residential Division income from operations, $80,640*

Administrative expenses:		Net sales:	
Residential Division	$80,320	Residential Division	$516,000
Industrial Division	66,560	Industrial Division	321,920

Prepare divisional income statements for Huggins Construction Company.

EX 8-3
Service department charges and activity bases
obj. 3

For each of the following service departments, identify an activity base that could be used for charging the expense to the profit center.

a. Accounts receivable
b. Electronic data processing
c. Central purchasing

d. Legal
e. Telecommunications
f. Duplication services

EX 8-4
Activity bases for service department charges
obj. 3

For each of the following service departments, select the activity base listed that is most appropriate for charging service expenses to responsible units.

Service Department	Activity Base
a. Training	1. Number of conference attendees
b. Employee Travel	2. Number of computers
c. Payroll Accounting	3. Number of employees trained
d. Accounts Receivable	4. Number of telephone lines
e. Conferences	5. Number of purchase requisitions
f. Telecommunications	6. Number of sales invoices
g. Computer Support	7. Number of payroll checks
h. Central Purchasing	8. Number of travel claims

EX 8-5
Service department charges
obj. 3

✓ *b. Commercial payroll, $9,960*

In divisional income statements prepared for Franklin Electrical Company, the Payroll Department costs are charged back to user divisions on the basis of the number of payroll checks, and the Purchasing Department costs are charged back on the basis of the number of purchase requisitions. The Payroll Department had expenses of $44,010, and the Purchasing Department had expenses of $18,720 for the year. The following annual data for Residential, Commercial, and Government Contract divisions were obtained from corporate records:

	Residential	Commercial	Government Contract
Sales	$420,000	$500,000	$1,800,000
Number of employees:			
Weekly payroll (52 weeks per year)	144	72	108
Monthly payroll	25	20	18
Number of purchase requisitions per year	1,800	1,530	1,350

a. Determine the total amount of payroll checks and purchase requisitions processed per year by each division.
b. Using the activity base information in (a), determine the annual amount of payroll and purchasing costs charged back to the Residential, Commercial, and Government Contract divisions from payroll and purchasing services.
c. ▭▭▬► Why does the Residential Division have a larger service department charge than the other two divisions, even though its sales are lower?

EX 8-6
Service department charges and activity bases
obj. 3

✓ *b. Help desk, $28,800*

Harris Corporation, a manufacturer of electronics and communications systems, uses a service department charge system to charge profit centers with Computing and Communications Services (CCS) service department costs. The following table identifies an abbreviated list of service categories and activity bases used by the CCS department. The table also includes some assumed cost and activity base quantity information for each service for October.

CCS Service Category	Activity Base	Assumed Cost	Assumed Activity Base Quantity
Help desk	Number of calls	$ 73,600	2,300
Network center	Number of devices monitored	614,250	9,450
Electronic mail	Number of user accounts	53,550	6,300
Local voice support	Number of phone extensions	127,238	8,775

One of the profit centers for Harris Corporation is the Communication Systems (COMM) sector. Assume the following information for the COMM sector:

- The sector has 4,000 employees, of whom 50% are office employees.
- All the office employees have a phone, and 90% of them have a computer on the network.
- Ninety percent of the employees with a computer also have an e-mail account.
- The average number of help desk calls for October was 0.50 call per individual with a computer.
- There are 300 additional printers, servers, and peripherals on the network beyond the personal computers.

a. Determine the service charge rate for the four CCS service categories for October.
b. Determine the charges to the COMM sector for the four CCS service categories for October.

EX 8-7
Divisional income statements with service department charges

obj. 3

✓ *Consumer income from operations, $1,154,650*

Waverunner Watersports Company has two divisions, Commercial and Consumer, and two corporate service departments, Tech Support and Accounts Payable. The corporate expenses for the year ended December 31, 2008, are as follows:

Tech Support Department	$ 588,000
Accounts Payable Department	231,000
Other corporate administrative expenses	343,000
Total corporate expense	$1,162,000

The other corporate administrative expenses include officers' salaries and other expenses required by the corporation. The Tech Support Department charges the divisions for services rendered, based on the number of computers in the department, and the Accounts Payable Department charges divisions for services, based on the number of checks issued. The usage of service by the two divisions is as follows:

	Tech Support	Accounts Payable
Commercial Division	252 computers	5,880 checks
Consumer Division	168	10,920
Total	420 computers	16,800 checks

The service department charges of the Tech Support Department and the Accounts Payable Department are considered controllable by the divisions. Corporate administrative expenses are not considered controllable by the divisions. The revenues, cost of goods sold, and operating expenses for the two divisions are as follows:

	Commerical	Consumer
Revenues	$5,600,000	$4,760,000
Cost of goods sold	2,940,000	2,240,000
Operating expenses	1,050,000	980,000

Prepare the divisional income statements for the two divisions.

EX 8-8
Corrections to service department charges

obj. 3

Worldwide Air, Inc., has two divisions organized as profit centers, the Passenger Division and the Cargo Division. The following divisional income statements were prepared:

✓b. Income from
operations, Cargo
Division, $255,000

Worldwide Air, Inc.
Divisional Income Statements
For the Year Ended July 31, 2008

	Passenger Division		Cargo Division	
Revenues		$600,000		$600,000
Operating expenses		300,000		250,000
Income from operations before				
service department charges		$300,000		$350,000
Less service department charges:				
Training	$50,000		$50,000	
Trip scheduling	60,000		60,000	
Reservations	80,000	190,000	80,000	190,000
Income from operations		$110,000		$160,000

The service department charge rate for the service department costs was based on revenues. Since the revenues of the two divisions were the same, the service department charges to each division were also the same.

The following additional information is available:

	Passenger Division	Cargo Division	Total
Number of personnel trained	40	10	50
Number of trips	30	50	80
Number of reservations requested	4,000	—	4,000

a. Does the income from operations for the two divisions accurately measure performance?
b. Correct the divisional income statements, using the activity bases provided above in revising the service department charges.

EX 8-9
Profit center responsibility reporting
objs. 3, 5

✓ Income from operations,
Winter Sports Division,
$11,700

Outdoor Athletic Equipment Co. operates two divisions—the Winter Sports Division and the Summer Sports Division. The following income and expense accounts were provided from the trial balance as of June 30, 2008, the end of the current fiscal year, after all adjustments, including those for inventories, were recorded and posted:

Sales—Winter Sports (WS) Division	$ 950,000
Sales—Summer Sports (SS) Division	1,437,500
Cost of Goods Sold—Winter Sports (WS) Division	512,500
Cost of Goods Sold—Summer Sports (SS) Division	687,500
Sales Expense—Winter Sports (WS) Division	150,000
Sales Expense—Summer Sports (SS) Division	205,000
Administrative Expense—Winter Sports (WS) Division	97,000
Administrative Expense—Summer Sports (SS) Division	128,000
Advertising Expense	64,500
Transportation Expense	100,700
Accounts Receivable Collection Expense	58,100
Warehouse Expense	120,000

The bases to be used in allocating expenses, together with other essential information, are as follows:

a. Advertising expense—incurred at headquarters, charged back to divisions on the basis of usage: Winter Sports Division, $28,000; Summer Sports Division, $36,500.
b. Transportation expense—charged back to divisions at a transfer price of $7.60 per bill of lading: Winter Sports Division, 6,000 bills of lading; Summer Sports Division, 7,250 bills of lading.
c. Accounts receivable collection expense—incurred at headquarters, charged back to divisions at a transfer price of $5.60 per invoice: Winter Sports Division, 4,500 sales invoices; Summer Sports Division, 5,875 sales invoices.
d. Warehouse expense—charged back to divisions on the basis of floor space used in storing division products: Winter Sports Division, 25,000 square feet; Summer Sports Division, 12,500 square feet.

Prepare a divisional income statement with two column headings: Winter Sports Division and Summer Sports Division. Provide supporting schedules for determining service department charges.

EX 8-10
Rate of return on investment

obj. 4

✓ *a. Textbook Division, 26%*

The income from operations and the amount of invested assets in each division of Deacon Publishing Company are as follows:

	Income from Operations	Invested Assets
Magazine Division	$ 96,000	$ 800,000
Textbook Division	166,400	640,000
Business Publishing Division	260,400	1,240,000

a. Compute the rate of return on investment for each division.
b. Which division is the most profitable per dollar invested?

EX 8-11
Residual income

obj. 4

✓ *a. Magazine Division, $0*

Based on the data in Exercise 8-10, assume that management has established a 12% minimum acceptable rate of return for invested assets.

a. Determine the residual income for each division.
b. Which division has the most residual income?

EX 8-12
Determining missing items in rate of return computation

obj. 4

✓ *d. 2.0*

One item is omitted from each of the following computations of the rate of return on investment:

Rate of Return on Investment	=	Profit Margin	×	Investment Turnover
24%	=	15%	×	(a)
(b)	=	8%	×	2.50
12%	=	(c)	×	0.80
24%	=	12%	×	(d)
(e)	=	10%	×	1.60

Determine the missing items, identifying each by the appropriate letter.

EX 8-13
Profit margin, investment turnover, and rate of return on investment

obj. 4

✓ *a. ROI, 11%*

The condensed income statement for the European Division of Cougar Motors Inc. is as follows (assuming no service department charges):

Sales	$875,000
Cost of goods sold	400,000
Gross profit	$475,000
Administrative expenses	282,500
Income from operations	$192,500

The manager of the European Division is considering ways to increase the rate of return on investment.

a. Using the DuPont formula for rate of return on investment, determine the profit margin, investment turnover, and rate of return on investment of the European Division, assuming that $1,750,000 of assets have been invested in the European Division.
b. If expenses could be reduced by $52,500 without decreasing sales, what would be the impact on the profit margin, investment turnover, and rate of return on investment for the European Division?

EX 8-14
Rate of return on investment

obj. 4

✓ *a. Media Networks ROI, 10.1%*

The Walt Disney Company has four major sectors, described as follows:

• **Media Networks:** The ABC television and radio network, Disney channel, ESPN, A&E, E!, and Disney.com.
• **Parks and Resorts:** Walt Disney World Resort, Disneyland, Disney Cruise Line, and other resort properties.
• **Studio Entertainment:** Walt Disney Pictures, Touchstone Pictures, Hollywood Pictures, Miramax Films, and Buena Vista Theatrical Productions.
• **Consumer Products:** Character merchandising, Disney stores, books, and magazines.

Disney recently reported sector income from operations, revenue, and invested assets (in millions) as follows:

	Income from Operations	Revenue	Invested Assets
Media Networks	$2,749	$13,027	$26,926
Parks and Resorts	1,178	9,023	15,807
Studio Entertainment	207	7,587	5,965
Consumer Products	520	2,157	877

a. Use the DuPont formula to determine the rate of return on investment for the four Disney sectors. Round whole percents to one decimal place and investment turnover to one decimal place.

b. How do the four sectors differ in their profit margin, investment turnover, and return on investment?

EX 8-15
Determining missing items in rate of return and residual income computations

obj. 4

✓c. $38,625

Data for Grobe Products Company is presented in the following table of rates of return on investment and residual incomes:

Invested Assets	Income from Operations	Rate of Return on Investment	Minimum Rate of Return	Minimum Acceptable Income from Operations	Residual Income
$643,750	$115,875	(a)	12%	(b)	(c)
$418,750	(d)	(e)	(f)	$62,813	$16,750
$275,000	(g)	12%	(h)	$44,000	(i)
$600,000	$84,000	(j)	10%	(k)	(l)

Determine the missing items, identifying each item by the appropriate letter.

EX 8-16
Determining missing items from computations

obj. 4

✓a. (e) $500,000

Data for the North, East, South, and West divisions of Tor Max Semiconductor Communication Company are as follows:

	Sales	Income from Operations	Invested Assets	Rate of Return on Investment	Profit Margin	Investment Turnover
North	$425,000	(a)	(b)	20%	10%	(c)
East	(d)	$50,000	(e)	(f)	8%	1.25
South	$400,000	(g)	$125,000	12%	(h)	(i)
West	$750,000	$180,000	$1,250,000	(j)	(k)	(l)

a. Determine the missing items, identifying each by the letters (a) through (l).

b. Determine the residual income for each division, assuming that the minimum acceptable rate of return established by management is 9%.

c. Which division is the most profitable in terms of (1) return on investment and (2) residual income?

EX 8-17
Rate of return on investment, residual income

obj. 4

REAL WORLD

Hilton Hotels Corporation provides lodging services around the world. The company is separated into three major divisions:

- **Hotel Ownership:** Hotels owned and operated by Hilton.
- **Managing and Franchising:** Hotels franchised to others or managed for others.
- **Timeshare:** Resort properties managed for timeshare vacation owners.

Financial information for each division, from a recent annual report, is as follows (in millions):

	Hotel Ownership	Managing and Franchising	Timeshare
Revenues	$2,215	$1,510	$421
Income from operations	394	343	99
Total assets	4,825	2,112	507

a. Use the DuPont formula to determine the return on investment for each of the Hilton business divisions. Round whole percents to one decimal place and investment turnover to one decimal place.

b. Determine the residual income for each division, assuming a minimum acceptable income of 14% of total assets. Round minimal acceptable return to the nearest million dollars.

c. ▭▬▶ Interpret your results.

EX 8-18
Balanced scorecard
obj. 4

American Express Company is a major financial services company, noted for its American Express® card. Below are some of the performance measures used by the company in its balanced scorecard.

Average cardmember spending	Number of merchant signings
Cards in force	Number of card choices
Earnings growth	Number of new card launches
Hours of credit consultant training	Return on equity
Investment in information technology	Revenue growth
Number of Internet features	

For each measure, identify whether the measure best fits the innovation, customer, internal process, or financial dimension of the balanced scorecard.

EX 8-19
Balanced scorecard
obj. 4

Several years ago, United Parcel Service (UPS) believed that the Internet was going to change the parcel delivery market and would require UPS to become a more nimble and customer-focused organization. As a result, UPS replaced its old measurement system, which was 90% oriented toward financial performance, with a balanced scorecard. The scorecard emphasized four "point of arrival" measures, which were:

1. Customer satisfaction index—a measure of customer satisfaction.
2. Employee relations index—a measure of employee sentiment and morale.
3. Competitive position—delivery performance relative to competition.
4. Time in transit—the time from order entry to delivery.

a. ▭▬▶ Why did UPS introduce a balanced scorecard and nonfinancial measures in its new performance measurement system?

b. ▭▬▶ Why do you think UPS included a factor measuring employee sentiment?

EX 8-20
Decision on transfer pricing
obj. 5

✓ a. $1,000,000

Materials used by the Industrial Division of Crow Manufacturing are currently purchased from outside suppliers at a cost of $120 per unit. However, the same materials are available from the Materials Division. The Materials Division has unused capacity and can produce the materials needed by the Industrial Division at a variable cost of $95 per unit.

a. If a transfer price of $105 per unit is established and 40,000 units of materials are transferred, with no reduction in the Materials Division's current sales, how much would Crow Manufacturing's total income from operations increase?

b. How much would the Industrial Division's income from operations increase?

c. How much would the Materials Division's income from operations increase?

EX 8-21
Decision on transfer pricing
obj. 5

✓ b. $400,000

Based on Crow Manufacturing's data in Exercise 8–20, assume that a transfer price of $110 has been established and that 40,000 units of materials are transferred, with no reduction in the Materials Division's current sales.

a. How much would Crow Manufacturing's total income from operations increase?

b. How much would the Industrial Division's income from operations increase?

c. How much would the Materials Division's income from operations increase?

d. ▭▬▶ If the negotiated price approach is used, what would be the range of acceptable transfer prices and why?

Problems Series A

PR 8-1A
Budget performance report for a cost center

obj. 2

The Southwest District of Pop Soft Drinks, Inc., is organized as a cost center. The budget for the Southwest District of Pop Soft Drinks, Inc., for the month ended May 31, 2008, is as follows:

Sales salaries	$406,725
System support salaries	222,300
Customer relations salaries	75,975
Accounting salaries	48,975
Repair and service	134,625
Depreciation of plant and equipment	45,750
Insurance and property taxes	20,475
Total	$954,825

During May, the costs incurred in the Southwest District were as follows:

Sales salaries	$406,200
System support salaries	222,075
Customer relations salaries	89,025
Accounting salaries	48,675
Repair and service	135,375
Depreciation of plant and equipment	45,750
Insurance and property taxes	20,550
Total	$967,650

Instructions

1. Prepare a budget performance report for the manager of the Southwest District of Pop Soft Drinks for the month of May.
2. ➤ For which costs might the supervisor be expected to request supplemental reports?

PR 8-2A
Profit center responsibility reporting

obj. 3

✓1. Income from operations, South Region, $280,800

Cross-Country Transport Company organizes its three divisions, the Southeast, East, and South regions, as profit centers. The chief executive officer (CEO) evaluates divisional performance, using income from operations as a percent of revenues. The following quarterly income and expense accounts were provided from the trial balance as of December 31, 2008:

Revenues—SE Region	$1,740,000
Revenues—E Region	2,820,000
Revenues—S Region	2,340,000
Operating Expenses—SE Region	1,134,400
Operating Expenses—E Region	2,097,300
Operating Expenses—S Region	1,721,700
Corporate Expenses—Dispatching	500,000
Corporate Expenses—Equipment	525,000
Corporate Expenses—Treasurer's	375,000
General Corporate Officers' Salaries	710,000

The company operates three service departments: the Dispatching Department, the Equipment Management Department, and the Treasurer's Department. The Dispatching Department manages the scheduling and releasing of completed trains. The Equipment Management Department manages the railroad cars inventories. It makes sure the right freight cars are at the right place at the right time. The Treasurer's Department conducts a variety of services for the company as a whole. The following additional information has been gathered:

	Southeast	East	South
Number of scheduled trains	400	680	520
Number of railroad cars in inventory	4,800	6,400	5,600

Instructions

1. Prepare quarterly income statements showing income from operations for the three regions. Use three column headings: Southeast, East, and South.
2. Identify the most successful region according to the profit margin.
3. ━━━► Provide a recommendation to the CEO for a better method for evaluating the performance of the regions. In your recommendation, identify the major weakness of the present method.

PR 8-3A
Divisional income statements and rate of return on investment analysis
obj. **4**

✓ *2. Retail Division ROI, 16%*

Hi-Growth Investments Inc. is a diversified investment company with three operating divisions organized as investment centers. Condensed data taken from the records of the three divisions for the year ended June 30, 2008, are as follows:

	Retail Division	Electronic Brokerage Division	Investment Banking Division
Fee revenue	$1,250,000	$750,000	$1,500,000
Operating expenses	750,000	682,500	1,170,000
Invested assets	3,125,000	250,000	2,000,000

The management of Hi-Growth Investments Inc. is evaluating each division as a basis for planning a future expansion of operations.

Instructions

1. Prepare condensed divisional income statements for the three divisions, assuming that there were no service department charges.
2. Using the DuPont formula for rate of return on investment, compute the profit margin, investment turnover, and rate of return on investment for each division.
3. ━━━► If available funds permit the expansion of operations of only one division, which of the divisions would you recommend for expansion, based on parts (1) and (2)? Explain.

PR 8-4A
Effect of proposals on divisional performance
obj. **4**

✓ *3. Proposal 3 ROI, 13.6%*

A condensed income statement for the Paintball Division of Outdoor Games Inc. for the year ended January 31, 2008, is as follows:

Sales	$900,000
Cost of goods sold	500,000
Gross profit	$400,000
Operating expenses	274,000
Income from operations	$126,000

Assume that the Paintball Division received no charges from service departments.

The president of Outdoor Games Inc. has indicated that the division's rate of return on a $720,000 investment must be increased to at least 20% by the end of the next year if operations are to continue. The division manager is considering the following three proposals:

Proposal 1: Transfer equipment with a book value of $120,000 to other divisions at no gain or loss and lease similar equipment. The annual lease payments would be less than the amount of depreciation expense on the old equipment by $18,000. This decrease in expense would be included as part of the cost of goods sold. Sales would remain unchanged.

Proposal 2: Reduce invested assets by discontinuing a product line. This action would eliminate sales of $75,000, cost of goods sold of $35,000, and operating expenses of $37,750. Assets of $32,500 would be transferred to other divisions at no gain or loss.

Proposal 3: Purchase new and more efficient machinery and thereby reduce the cost of goods sold by $27,000. Sales would remain unchanged, and the old machinery, which has no remaining book value, would be scrapped at no gain or loss. The new machinery would increase invested assets by $405,000 for the year.

Instructions

1. Using the DuPont formula for rate of return on investment, determine the profit margin, investment turnover, and rate of return on investment for the Paintball Division for the past year.

2. Prepare condensed estimated income statements and compute the invested assets for each proposal.
3. Using the DuPont formula for rate of return on investment, determine the profit margin, investment turnover, and rate of return on investment for each proposal.
4. Which of the three proposals would meet the required 20% rate of return on investment?
5. If the Paintball Division were in an industry where the profit margin could not be increased, how much would the investment turnover have to increase to meet the president's required 20% rate of return on investment? Round to two decimal places.

PR 8-5A
Divisional performance analysis and evaluation

obj. 4

✓ 2. *Personal Computing Division ROI, 32%*

The vice president of operations of I4 Computers Inc. is evaluating the performance of two divisions organized as investment centers. Invested assets and condensed income statement data for the past year for each division are as follows:

	Personal Computing Division	Business Computing Division
Sales	$800,000	$1,200,000
Cost of goods sold	460,000	780,000
Operating expenses	180,000	156,000
Invested assets	500,000	2,000,000

Instructions
1. Prepare condensed divisional income statements for the year ended December 31, 2008, assuming that there were no service department charges.
2. Using the DuPont formula for rate of return on investment, determine the profit margin, investment turnover, and rate of return on investment for each division.
3. If management's minimum acceptable rate of return is 15%, determine the residual income for each division.
4. ▭▬▶ Discuss the evaluation of the two divisions, using the performance measures determined in parts (1), (2), and (3).

PR 8-6A
Transfer pricing

obj. 5

✓ 3. *Navigational Systems Division, $195,200*

Goho Manufacturing Company is a diversified aerospace company, including two operating divisions, Specialized Semiconductors and Navigational Systems Divisions. Condensed divisional income statements, which involve no intracompany transfers and which include a breakdown of expenses into variable and fixed components, are as follows:

Goho Manufacturing Company
Divisional Income Statements
For the Year Ended December 31, 2008

	Specialized Semiconductors Division	Navigational Systems Division	Total
Sales:			
640 units × $1,320 per unit	$844,800		$ 844,800
1,000 units × $1,984 per unit		$1,984,000	1,984,000
			$2,828,800
Expenses:			
Variable:			
640 units × $776 per unit	$496,640		$ 496,640
1,000 units × $1,560* per unit		$1,560,000	1,560,000
Fixed	195,200	254,400	449,600
Total expenses	$691,840	$1,814,400	$2,506,240
Income from operations	$152,960	$ 169,600	$ 322,560

*$1,320 of the $1,560 per unit represents materials costs, and the remaining $240 per unit represents other variable conversion expenses incurred within the Navigational Systems Division.

The Specialized Semiconductors Division is presently producing 640 units out of a total capacity of 800 units. Materials used in producing the Navigational Systems Division's product are currently purchased from outside suppliers at a price of $1,320 per unit. The Specialized Semiconductors Division is able to produce the components used by the

Navigational Systems Division. Except for the possible transfer of materials between divisions, no changes are expected in sales and expenses.

Instructions

1. ▭▭▶ Would the market price of $1,320 per unit be an appropriate transfer price for Goho Manufacturing Company? Explain.

2. ▭▭▶ If the Navigational Systems Division purchases 160 units from the Specialized Semiconductors Division, rather than externally, at a negotiated transfer price of $1,160 per unit, how much would the income from operations of each division and total company income from operations increase?

3. Prepare condensed divisional income statements for Goho Manufacturing Company, based on the data in part (2).

4. ▭▭▶ If a transfer price of $880 per unit is negotiated, how much would the income from operations of each division and total company income from operations increase?

5. a. ▭▭▶ What is the range of possible negotiated transfer prices that would be acceptable for Goho Manufacturing Company?

   b. Assuming that the managers of the two divisions cannot agree on a transfer price, what price would you suggest as the transfer price?

Problems Series B

PR 8-1B
Budget performance report for a cost center
obj. 2

The Furnishings Company sells furnishings and fixtures over the Internet. The International Division is organized as a cost center. The budget for the International Division for the month ended October 31, 2008, is as follows (in millions):

Customer service salaries	$ 119
Insurance and property taxes	32
Distribution salaries	238
Marketing salaries	336
Engineer salaries	217
Warehouse wages	147
Equipment depreciation	45
Total	$1,134

During October, the costs incurred in the International Division were as follows:

Customer service salaries	$ 153
Insurance and property taxes	31
Distribution salaries	235
Marketing salaries	377
Engineer salaries	213
Warehouse wages	141
Equipment depreciation	45
Total	$1,195

Instructions

1. Prepare a budget performance report for the director of the International Division for the month of October.

2. For which costs might the director be expected to request supplemental reports?

PR 8-2B
Profit center responsibility reporting
obj. 3

Diversified Railroad has three regional divisions organized as profit centers. The chief executive officer (CEO) evaluates divisional performance, using income from operations as a percent of revenues. The following quarterly income and expense accounts were provided from the trial balance as of December 31, 2008:

Revenues—East Division	$500,000
Revenues—West Division	690,000
Revenues—Metro Division	944,000
Operating Expenses—East Division	303,000
Operating Expenses—West Division	399,600
Operating Expenses—Metro Division	536,000
Corporate Expenses—Shareholder Relations	75,000
Corporate Expenses—Customer Support	192,000
Corporate Expenses—Legal	102,000
General Corporate Officers' Salaries	180,000

The company operates three service departments: Shareholder Relations, Customer Support, and Legal. The Shareholder Relations Department conducts a variety of services for shareholders of the company. The Customer Support Department is the company's point of contact for new service, complaints, and requests for repair. The department believes that the number of customer contacts is an activity base for this work. The Legal Department provides reports for division management. The department believes that the number of hours billed is an activity base for this work. The following additional information has been gathered:

	East	West	Metro
Number of customer contacts	3,200	3,680	5,920
Number of hours billed	640	1,120	960

Instructions
1. Prepare quarterly income statements showing income from operations for the three divisions. Use three column headings: East, West, and Metro.
2. Identify the most successful division according to the profit margin.
3. ▭▭▭▭▶ Provide a recommendation to the CEO for a better method for evaluating the performance of the divisions. In your recommendation, identify the major weakness of the present method.

PR 8-3B
Divisional income statements and rate of return on investment analysis

obj. **4**

✓2. Bread Division, ROI, 12.8%

Fresh Tracks Baking Company is a diversified food products company with three operating divisions organized as investment centers. Condensed data taken from the records of the three divisions for the year ended June 30, 2008, are as follows:

	Bread Division	Snack Cake Division	Retail Bakeries Division
Sales	$1,450,000	$1,750,000	$1,000,000
Cost of goods sold	950,000	1,125,000	650,000
Operating expenses	268,000	380,000	170,000
Invested assets	1,812,500	2,187,500	800,000

The management of Fresh Tracks Baking Company is evaluating each division as a basis for planning a future expansion of operations.

Instructions
1. Prepare condensed divisional income statements for the three divisions, assuming that there were no service department charges.
2. Using the DuPont formula for rate of return on investment, compute the profit margin, investment turnover, and rate of return on investment for each division.
3. ▭▭▭▭▶ If available funds permit the expansion of operations of only one division, which of the divisions would you recommend for expansion, based on parts (1) and (2)? Explain.

PR 8-4B
Effect of proposals on divisional performance

obj. **4**

A condensed income statement for the Turbine Division of Mega Engines Inc. for the year ended December 31, 2008, is as follows:

Sales	$600,000
Cost of goods sold	338,000
Gross profit	$262,000
Operating expenses	190,000
Income from operations	$ 72,000

✓1. ROI, 12%

Assume that the Turbine Division received no charges from service departments. The president of Mega Engines has indicated that the division's rate of return on a $600,000 investment must be increased to at least 20% by the end of the next year if operations are to continue. The division manager is considering the following three proposals:

Proposal 1: Transfer equipment with a book value of $120,000 to other divisions at no gain or loss and lease similar equipment. The annual lease payments would exceed the amount of depreciation expense on the old equipment by $18,000. This increase in expense would be included as part of the cost of goods sold. Sales would remain unchanged.

Proposal 2: Purchase new and more efficient machining equipment and thereby reduce the cost of goods sold by $48,000. Sales would remain unchanged, and the old equipment, which has no remaining book value, would be scrapped at no gain or loss. The new equipment would increase invested assets by an additional $150,000 for the year.

Proposal 3: Reduce invested assets by discontinuing an engine line. This action would eliminate sales of $180,000, cost of goods sold of $133,200, and operating expenses of $42,000. Assets of $300,000 would be transferred to other divisions at no gain or loss.

Instructions

1. Using the DuPont formula for rate of return on investment, determine the profit margin, investment turnover, and rate of return on investment for the Turbine Division for the past year.
2. Prepare condensed estimated income statements and compute the invested assets for each proposal.
3. Using the DuPont formula for rate of return on investment, determine the profit margin, investment turnover, and rate of return on investment for each proposal.
4. Which of the three proposals would meet the required 20% rate of return on investment?
5. If the Turbine Division were in an industry where the profit margin could not be increased, how much would the investment turnover have to increase to meet the president's required 20% rate of return on investment?

PR 8-5B
Divisional performance analysis and evaluation
obj. 4

✓2. Road Bike Division ROI, 25%

The vice president of operations of Cantor-Simmons Cycle Company is evaluating the performance of two divisions organized as investment centers. Invested assets and condensed income statement data for the past year for each division are as follows:

	Road Bike Division	Mountain Bike Division
Sales	$750,000	$ 950,000
Cost of goods sold	412,500	560,000
Operating expenses	187,500	181,000
Invested assets	600,000	1,187,500

Instructions

1. Prepare condensed divisional income statements for the year ended December 31, 2008, assuming that there were no service department charges.
2. Using the DuPont formula for rate of return on investment, determine the profit margin, investment turnover, and rate of return on investment for each division.
3. If management desires a minimum acceptable rate of return of 18%, determine the residual income for each division.
4. ▬▬▶ Discuss the evaluation of the two divisions, using the performance measures determined in parts (1), (2), and (3).

PR 8-6B
Transfer pricing
obj. 5

Hi-Tech Electronics, Inc. manufactures electronic products, with two operating divisions, the Specialized Electronic Component and MP3 Player divisions. Condensed divisional income statements, which involve no intracompany transfers and which include a breakdown of expenses into variable and fixed components, are as follows:

Hi-Tech Electronics, Inc.
Divisional Income Statements
For the Year Ended December 31, 2008

	Specialized Electronic Component Division	MP3 Player Division	Total
Sales:			
12,000 units × $126 per unit	$1,512,000		$1,512,000
18,000 units × $228 per unit		$4,104,000	4,104,000
			$5,616,000
Expenses:			
Variable:			
12,000 units × $86 per unit	$1,032,000		$1,032,000
18,000 units × $162* per unit		$2,916,000	2,916,000
Fixed	186,000	432,000	618,000
Total expenses	$1,218,000	$3,348,000	$4,566,000
Income from operations	$ 294,000	$ 756,000	$1,050,000

*$126 of the $162 per case represents materials costs, and the remaining $36 per case represents other variable conversion expenses incurred within the MP3 Player Division.

The Specialized Electronic Component Division is presently producing 12,000 units out of a total capacity of 14,400 units. Materials used in producing the MP3 Player Division's product are currently purchased from outside suppliers at a price of $126 per unit. The Specialized Electronic Component Division is able to produce the materials used by the MP3 Player Division. Except for the possible transfer of materials between divisions, no changes are expected in sales and expenses.

Instructions
1. ▭▭▭▸ Would the market price of $126 per unit be an appropriate transfer price for Hi-Tech Electronics, Inc.? Explain.
2. ▭▭▭▸ If the MP3 Player Division purchases 2,400 units from the Specialized Electronic Component Division, rather than externally, at a negotiated transfer price of $96 per unit, how much would the income from operations of each division and the total company income from operations increase?
3. Prepare condensed divisional income statements for Hi-Tech Electronics, Inc., based on the data in part (2).
4. ▭▭▭▸ If a transfer price of $120 per unit is negotiated, how much would the income from operations of each division and the total company income from operations increase?
5. a. ▭▭▭▸ What is the range of possible negotiated transfer prices that would be acceptable for Hi-Tech Electronics, Inc.?
   b. Assuming that the managers of the two divisions cannot agree on a transfer price, what price would you suggest as the transfer price?

Special Activities

SA 8-1
Ethics and professional conduct in business

ETHICS

Micro Tech Company has two divisions, the Semiconductor Division and the PC Division. The PC Division may purchase semiconductors from the Semiconductor Division or from outside suppliers. The Semiconductor Division sells semiconductor products both internally and externally. The market price for semiconductors is $250 per 100 semiconductors. Michael Blount is the controller of the PC Division, and Lynn Williams is the controller of the Semiconductor Division. The following conversation took place between Michael and Lynn:

Michael: I hear you are having problems selling semiconductors out of your division. Maybe I can help.

Lynn: You've got that right. We're producing and selling at about 80% of our capacity to outsiders. Last year we were selling 100% of capacity. Would it be possible for your division to pick up some of our excess capacity? After all, we are part of the same company.

Michael: What kind of price could you give me?

Lynn: Well, you know as well as I that we are under strict profit responsibility in our divisions, so I would expect to get market price, $250 for 100 semiconductors.

Michael: I'm not so sure we can swing that. I was expecting a price break from a "sister" division.

Lynn: Hey, I can only take this "sister" stuff so far. If I give you a price break, our profits will fall from last year's levels. I don't think I could explain that. I'm sorry, but I must remain firm—market price. After all, it's only fair—that's what you would have to pay from an external supplier.

Michael: Fair or not, I think we'll pass. Sorry we couldn't have helped.

➤ Was Michael behaving ethically by trying to force the Semiconductor Division into a price break? Comment on Lynn's reactions.

SA 8-2
Service department charges

The Customer Service Department of Grand Lakes Technologies asked the Publications Department to prepare a brochure for its training program. The Publications Department delivered the brochures and charged the Customer Service Department a rate that was 25% higher than could be obtained from an outside printing company. The policy of the company required the Customer Service Department to use the internal publications group for brochures. The Publications Department claimed that it had a drop in demand for its services during the fiscal year, so it had to charge higher prices in order to recover its payroll and fixed costs.

➤ Should the cost of the brochure be transferred to the Customer Service Department in order to hold the department head accountable for the cost of the brochure? What changes in policy would you recommend?

SA 8-3
Evaluating divisional performance

The three divisions of Monster Foods are Snack Goods, Cereal, and Frozen Foods. The divisions are structured as investment centers. The following responsibility reports were prepared for the three divisions for the prior year:

	Snack Goods	Cereal	Frozen Foods
Revenues	$1,050,000	$2,450,000	$ 875,000
Operating expenses	420,000	1,400,000	175,000
Income from operations before service department charges	$ 630,000	$1,050,000	$ 700,000
Service department charges:			
Promotion	$ 175,000	$ 350,000	$ 308,000
Legal	87,500	70,000	140,000
	$ 262,500	$ 420,000	$ 448,000
Income from operations	$ 367,500	$ 630,000	$ 252,000
Invested assets	$2,100,000	$4,200,000	$1,260,000

1. Which division is making the best use of invested assets and thus should be given priority for future capital investments?
2. ➤ Assuming that the minimum acceptable rate of return on new projects is 12%, would all investments that produce a return in excess of 12% be accepted by the divisions?
3. ➤ Can you identify opportunities for improving the company's financial performance?

SA 8-4
Evaluating division performance over time

The Truck Division of Yang Motors Inc. has been experiencing revenue and profit growth during the years 2006–2008. The divisional income statements are provided below.

Yang Motors Inc.
Divisional Income Statements, Truck Division
For the Years Ended December 31, 2006–2008

	2006	2007	2008
Sales	$756,000	$972,000	$1,170,000
Cost of goods sold	475,200	558,000	616,500
Gross profit	$280,800	$414,000	$ 553,500
Operating expenses	167,400	209,880	261,000
Income from operations	$113,400	$204,120	$ 292,500

Assume that there are no charges from service departments. The vice president of the division, Terry Clark, is proud of his division's performance over the last three years. The president of Yang Motors Inc., Billy Clark, is discussing the division's performance with Terry, as follows:

Terry: As you can see, we've had a successful three years in the Truck Division.
Billy: I'm not too sure.
Terry: What do you mean? Look at our results. Our income from operations has nearly tripled, while our profit margins are improving.
Billy: I am looking at your results. However, your income statements fail to include one very important piece of information; namely, the invested assets. You have been investing a great deal of assets into the division. You had $315,000 in invested assets in 2006, $810,000 in 2007, and $1,950,000 in 2008.
Terry: You are right. I've needed the assets in order to upgrade our technologies and expand our operations. The additional assets are one reason we have been able to grow and improve our profit margins. I don't see that this is a problem.
Billy: The problem is that we must maintain a 20% rate of return on invested assets.

1. Determine the profit margins for the Truck Division for 2006–2008.
2. Compute the investment turnover for the Truck Division for 2006–2008.
3. Compute the rate of return on investment for the Truck Division for 2006–2008.
4. ▬▬▶ Evaluate the division's performance over the 2006–2008 time period. Why was Billy concerned about the performance?

SA 8-5
Evaluating division performance

Casual Living Furniture Inc. is a privately held diversified company with five separate divisions organized as investment centers. A condensed income statement for the Outdoor Division for the past year, assuming no service department charges, is as follows:

Casual Living Furniture Inc.—Outdoor Division
Income Statement
For the Year Ended December 31, 2007

Sales	$12,800,000
Cost of goods sold	8,080,000
Gross profit	$ 4,720,000
Operating expenses	1,520,000
Income from operations	$ 3,200,000

The manager of the Outdoor Division was recently presented with the opportunity to add an additional product line, which would require invested assets of $11,000,000. A projected income statement for the new product line is as follows:

New Product Line
Projected Income Statement
For the Year Ended December 31, 2008

Sales	$6,000,000
Cost of goods sold	3,360,000
Gross profit	$2,640,000
Operating expenses	1,680,000
Income from operations	$ 960,000

The Outdoor Division currently has $20,000,000 in invested assets, and Casual Living Furniture Inc.'s overall rate of return on investment, including all divisions, is 8%. Each division manager is evaluated on the basis of divisional rate of return on investment, and a bonus equal to $12,000 for each percentage point by which the division's rate of return on investment exceeds the company average is awarded each year.

The president is concerned that the manager of the Outdoor Division rejected the addition of the new product line, when all estimates indicated that the product line would be profitable and would increase overall company income. You have been asked to analyze the possible reasons why the Outdoor Division manager rejected the new product line.

1. Determine the rate of return on investment for the Outdoor Division for the past year.
(continued)

2. Determine the Outdoor Division manager's bonus for the past year.
3. Determine the estimated rate of return on investment for the new product line. Round whole percents to one decimal place.
4. ▭▭▷ Why might the manager of the Outdoor Division decide to reject the new product line? Support your answer by determining the projected rate of return on investment for 2008, assuming that the new product line was launched in the Outdoor Division, and 2008 actual operating results were similar to those of 2007.
5. ▭▭▷ Can you suggest an alternative performance measure for motivating division managers to accept new investment opportunities that would increase the overall company income and rate of return on investment?

SA 8-6
The balanced scorecard and EVA

Internet Project

Group Project

Divide responsibilities between two groups, with one group going to the home page of Balanced Scorecard Collaborative at **http://www.bscol.com**, and the second group going to the home page of Stern Stewart & Co. at **http://www.eva.com**. Balanced Scorecard Collaborative is a consulting firm that helped develop the balanced scorecard concept. Stern Stewart & Co. is a consulting firm that developed the concept of economic value added (EVA), another method of measuring corporate and divisional performance, similar to residual income.

After reading about the balanced scorecard at the bscol.com site, prepare a brief report describing the balanced scorecard and its claimed advantages. In the Stern group, use links in the home page of Stern Stewart & Co. to learn about EVA. After reading about EVA, prepare a brief report describing EVA and its claimed advantages. After preparing these reports, both groups should discuss their research and prepare a brief analysis comparing and contrasting these two approaches to corporate and divisional performance measurement.

Answers to Self-Examination Questions

1. **B**　The manager of a profit center (answer B) has responsibility for and authority over costs and revenues. If the manager has responsibility for only costs, the department is called a cost center (answer A). If the responsibility and authority extend to the investment in assets as well as costs and revenues, it is called an investment center (answer C). A service department (answer D) provides services to other departments. A service department could be a cost center, a profit center, or an investment center.

2. **C**　$600,000/150,000 = $4 per payment. Division A anticipates 60,000 payments or $240,000 (60,000 × $4) in service department charges from the Accounts Payable Department. Income from operations is thus $900,000 − $240,000, or $660,000. Answer A assumes that all of the service department overhead is assigned to Division A, which would be incorrect, since Division A does not use all of the accounts payable service. Answer B incorrectly assumes that there are no service department charges from Accounts Payable. Answer D incorrectly determines the accounts payable transfer rate from Division A's income from operations.

3. **A**　The rate of return on investment for Division A is 20% (answer A), computed as follows:

$$\text{Rate of Return on Investment (ROI)} = \frac{\text{Income from Operations}}{\text{Invested Assets}}$$

$$\text{ROI} = \frac{\$350,000 - \$200,000 - \$30,000}{\$600,000} = 20\%$$

4. **B**　The profit margin for Division L of Liddy Co. is 15% (answer B), computed as follows:

$$\text{Rate of Return on Investment (ROI)} = \text{Profit Margin} \times \text{Investment Turnover}$$

$$24\% = \text{Profit Margin} \times 1.6$$
$$15\% = \text{Profit Margin}$$

5. **C**　The market price approach (answer C) to transfer pricing uses the price at which the product or service transferred could be sold to outside buyers. The cost price approach (answer A) uses cost as the basis for setting transfer prices. The negotiated price approach (answer B) allows managers of decentralized units to agree (negotiate) among themselves as to the proper transfer price. The standard cost approach (answer D) is a version of the cost price approach that uses standard costs in setting transfer prices.

Differential Analysis and Product Pricing

© KEVIN P. CASEY/ASSOCIATED PRESS

objectives

After studying this chapter, you should be able to:

1 *Prepare a differential analysis report for decisions involving leasing or selling equipment, discontinuing an unprofitable segment, manufacturing or purchasing a needed part, replacing usable fixed assets, processing further or selling an intermediate product, or accepting additional business at a special price.*

2 *Determine the selling price of a product, using the total cost, product cost, and variable cost concepts.*

3 *Compute the relative profitability of products in bottleneck production environments.*

RealNetworks, Inc.

Many of the decisions that you make depend on comparing the estimated costs of alternatives. The payoff from such comparisons is described in the following report from a University of Michigan study.

Richard Nisbett and two colleagues quizzed Michigan faculty members and university seniors on such questions as how often they walk out on a bad movie, refuse to finish a bad meal, start over on a weak term paper, or abandon a research project that no longer looks promising. They believe that people who cut their losses this way are following sound economic rules: calculating the net benefits of alternative courses of action, writing off past costs that can't be recovered, and weighing the opportunity to use future time and effort more profitably elsewhere.

Among students, those who have learned to use cost-benefit analysis frequently are apt to have far better grades than their Scholastic Aptitude Test scores would have predicted. Again, the more economics courses the students have, the more likely they are to apply cost-benefit analysis outside the classroom.

Dr. Nisbett concedes that for many Americans, cost-benefit rules often appear to conflict with such traditional principles as "never give up" and "waste not, want not."

Managers must also apply cost-benefit rules in making decisions affecting their business. RealNetworks, Inc., the Internet-based music and game company, like most companies must choose between alternatives. Examples of decisions faced by this company include whether it should expand or discontinue services, such as its recent decision to Mac-enable its digital music service, Rhapsody®. Another decision is whether to accept business at special prices, such as special pricing on its Helix Media Delivery System®. Other decisions include whether to replace network equipment, develop its own software, or buy software from others.

In this chapter, we discuss differential analysis, which reports the effects of decisions on total revenues and costs. We also describe and illustrate practical approaches to setting product prices. Finally, we discuss how production bottlenecks influence product mix and pricing decisions.

Source: Alan L. Otten, "Economic Perspective Produces Steady Yields," from People Patterns, *The Wall Street Journal,* March 31, 1992, p. B1.

Differential Analysis

objective **1**

Prepare a differential analysis report for decisions involving leasing or selling equipment, discontinuing an unprofitable segment, manufacturing or purchasing a needed part, replacing usable fixed assets, processing further or selling an intermediate product, or accepting additional business at a special price.

Planning for future operations involves decision making. For some decisions, revenue and cost data from the accounting records may be useful. However, the revenue and cost data for use in evaluating courses of future operations or choosing among competing alternatives are often not available in the accounting records and must be estimated.

Consider:

- The decision by General Motors Corporation to purchase on-board communications products from Delphi Corporation instead of making them internally.
- The decision by Marriott International, Inc., to accept a special price for a bid placed on Priceline.com Inc. for a room.
- The decision by Delta Air Lines to discontinue its low-fare Song Airline subsidiary.

In each of these decisions, the estimated revenues and costs were *relevant*. The relevant revenues and costs focus on the differences between each alternative. Costs that have been incurred in the past are not relevant to the decision. These costs are called **sunk costs**. For example, a couple who decides to walk out on a bad movie ignores the original cost of the tickets. In this case, the ticket cost is sunk and thus irrelevant to the decision to walk out early. We all make decisions everyday using relevant costs and benefits. Businesses make similar decisions by considering the differential revenues and costs.

Differential revenue is the amount of increase or decrease in revenue that is expected from a course of action as compared with an alternative. To illustrate, assume

The irrelevancy of a sunk cost is sometimes difficult to apply in practice. Psychologists believe this is because acknowledging a sunk cost is the same as admitting to a past mistake. For example, one study compared the playing time of players selected in the first round of the NBA draft with other players. The study found that poor-performing first-round draftees received more court time than players with better performance but smaller contracts. Apparently, the owners felt that they had to prove that the big contract wasn't wasted, even though it meant having the wrong players on the court.

that certain equipment is being used to manufacture calculators, which are expected to generate revenue of $150,000. If the equipment could be used to make digital clocks, which would generate revenue of $175,000, the differential revenue from making and selling digital clocks is $25,000.

Differential cost is the amount of increase or decrease in cost that is expected from a course of action as compared with an alternative. For example, if an increase in advertising expenditures from $100,000 to $150,000 is being considered, the differential cost of the action is $50,000.

Differential income or loss is the difference between the differential revenue and the differential costs. Differential income indicates that a particular decision is expected to be profitable, while a differential loss indicates the opposite.

Differential analysis focuses on the effect of alternative courses of action on the relevant revenues and costs, as illustrated in Exhibit 1. For example, if a manager must decide between two alternatives, differential analysis would involve comparing the differential revenues of the two alternatives with the differential costs.

EXHIBIT 1   Differential Analysis

Differential revenue from alternatives:		
Revenue from alternative A	$XXX	
Revenue from alternative B	XXX	
Differential revenue		$ XXX
Differential cost of alternatives:		
Cost of alternative A	$XXX	
Cost of alternative B	XXX	
Differential cost		XXX
Net differential income or loss from alternatives		**$XXX**

In this chapter, we will discuss the use of differential analysis in analyzing the following alternatives:

1. Leasing or selling equipment.
2. Discontinuing an unprofitable segment.
3. Manufacturing or purchasing a needed part.
4. Replacing usable fixed assets.
5. Processing further or selling an intermediate product.
6. Accepting additional business at a special price.

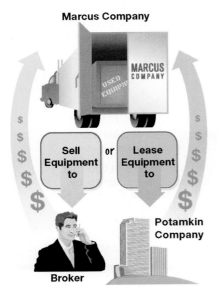

LEASE OR SELL

Management may have a choice between leasing or selling a piece of equipment that is no longer needed in the business. In deciding which option is best, management may use differential analysis. To illustrate, assume that Marcus Company is considering disposing of equipment that cost $200,000 and has $120,000 of accumulated depreciation to date. Marcus Company can sell the equipment through a broker for $100,000 less a 6% commission. Alternatively, Potamkin Company (the lessee) has offered to lease the equipment for five years for a total of $160,000. At the end of the fifth year of the lease, the equipment is expected to have no residual value. During the period of the lease, Marcus Company (the lessor) will incur repair, insurance, and property tax expenses estimated at $35,000. Exhibit 2 shows Marcus Company's analysis of whether to lease or sell the equipment.

Note that in Exhibit 2, the $80,000 book value ($200,000 − $120,000) of the equipment is a sunk cost and is not considered in the analysis. The $80,000 is a cost that resulted from a previous decision. It is not affected by the alternatives now being considered in leasing or selling the equipment. The relevant

EXHIBIT 2

Differential Analysis
Report—Lease or Sell

Proposal to Lease or Sell Equipment June 22, 2008		
Differential revenue from alternatives:		
Revenue from lease	$160,000	
Revenue from sale	100,000	
Differential revenue from lease		$60,000
Differential cost of alternatives:		
Repair, insurance, and property tax expenses	$ 35,000	
Commission expense on sale	6,000	
Differential cost of lease		29,000
Net differential income from the lease alternative		**$31,000**

factors to be considered are the differential revenues and differential costs associated with the lease or sell decision. This analysis is verified by the traditional analysis in Exhibit 3.

EXHIBIT 3

Traditional Analysis

Lease or Sell		
Lease alternative:		
Revenue from lease		$160,000
Depreciation expense for remaining five years	$80,000	
Repair, insurance, and property tax expenses	35,000	115,000
Net gain		$45,000
Sell alternative:		
Sales price		$100,000
Book value of equipment	$80,000	
Commission expense	6,000	86,000
Net gain		14,000
Net differential income from the lease alternative		**$31,000**

Many companies that manufacture expensive equipment give customers the choice of leasing the equipment. For example, construction equipment from Caterpillar can either be purchased outright or leased through Caterpillar's financial services subsidiary.

The alternatives presented in Exhibits 2 and 3 were relatively simple. However, regardless of the complexity, the approach to differential analysis is basically the same. Two additional factors that often need to be considered are (1) differential revenue from investing the funds generated by the alternatives and (2) any income tax differential. In Exhibit 2, there could be differential interest revenue related to investing the cash flows from the two alternatives. Any income tax differential would be related to the differences in the timing of the income from the alternatives and the differences in the amount of investment income. In the next chapter, we will consider these factors on management decisions.

Example Exercise 9-1

objective **1**

Casper Company owns office space with a cost of $100,000 and accumulated depreciation of $30,000 that can be sold for $150,000, less a 6% broker commission. Alternatively, the office space can be leased by Casper Company for 10 years for a total of $170,000 at the end of which there is no salvage value. In addition, repair, insurance, and property tax that would be incurred by Casper Company on the rented office space would total $24,000 over the 10 years. Determine the differential income or loss from the lease alternative for Casper Company.

(continued)

Follow My Example 9-1

Differential revenue from alternatives:		
Revenue from lease	$170,000	
Revenue from sale	150,000	
Differential revenue from lease		$20,000
Differential cost of alternatives:		
Repair, insurance, and property tax expenses	$ 24,000	
Commission expense on sale	9,000	
Differential cost of lease		15,000
Net differential income from the lease alternative		$ 5,000

For Practice: PE 9-1A, PE 9-1B

DISCONTINUE A SEGMENT OR PRODUCT

When a product or a department, branch, territory, or other segment of a business is generating losses, management may consider eliminating the product or segment. It is often assumed, sometimes in error, that the total income from operations of a business would be increased if the operating loss could be eliminated. Discontinuing the product or segment usually eliminates all of the product or segment's variable costs (direct materials, direct labor, sales commissions, and so on). However, if the product or segment is a relatively small part of the business, the fixed costs (depreciation, insurance, property taxes, and so on) may not be decreased by discontinuing it. It is possible in this case for the total operating income of a company to decrease rather than increase by eliminating the product or segment. To illustrate, the income statement for Battle Creek Cereal Co. presented in Exhibit 4 is for a normal year ending August 31, 2008.

Because Bran Flakes incurs annual losses, management is considering discontinuing it. Total annual operating income of $80,000 ($40,000 Toasted Oats + $40,000 Corn Flakes) might seem to be indicated by the income statement in Exhibit 4 if Bran Flakes is discontinued.

Discontinuing Bran Flakes, however, would actually decrease operating income by $15,000, to $54,000 ($69,000 − $15,000). This is shown by the differential analysis report in Exhibit 5, in which we assume that discontinuing Bran Flakes would have

EXHIBIT 4

Income (Loss) by Product

Battle Creek Cereal Co.
Condensed Income Statement
For the Year Ended August 31, 2008

	Corn Flakes	Toasted Oats	Bran Flakes	Total
Sales	$500,000	$400,000	$100,000	$1,000,000
Cost of goods sold:				
Variable costs	$220,000	$200,000	$ 60,000	$ 480,000
Fixed costs	120,000	80,000	20,000	220,000
Total cost of goods sold	$340,000	$280,000	$ 80,000	$ 700,000
Gross profit	$160,000	$120,000	$ 20,000	$ 300,000
Operating expenses:				
Variable expenses	$ 95,000	$ 60,000	$ 25,000	$ 180,000
Fixed expenses	25,000	20,000	6,000	51,000
Total operating expenses	$120,000	$ 80,000	$ 31,000	$ 231,000
Income (loss) from operations	$ 40,000	$ 40,000	$ (11,000)	$ 69,000

EXHIBIT 5

Differential Analysis
Report—Discontinue
an Unprofitable
Segment

Proposal to Discontinue Bran Flakes September 29, 2008		
Differential revenue from annual sales of Bran Flakes:		
Revenue from sales		$100,000
Differential cost of annual sales of Bran Flakes:		
Variable cost of goods sold	$60,000	
Variable operating expenses	25,000	85,000
Annual differential income from sales of Bran Flakes . . .		**$ 15,000**

no effect on fixed costs and expenses. The traditional analysis in Exhibit 6 verifies the differential analysis in Exhibit 5.

In Exhibit 6, only the short-term (one year) effects of discontinuing Bran Flakes are considered. When eliminating a product or segment, management may also consider the long-term effects. For example, the plant capacity made available by discontinuing Bran Flakes might be eliminated. This could reduce fixed costs. Some employees may have to be laid off, and others may have to be relocated and retrained. Further, there may be a related decrease in sales of more profitable products to those customers who were attracted by the discontinued product.

EXHIBIT 6   Traditional Analysis

Proposal to Discontinue Bran Flakes September 29, 2008			
	Bran Flakes, Toasted Oats, and Corn Flakes	Discontinue Bran Flakes*	Toasted Oats and Corn Flakes
Sales	$1,000,000	$100,000	$900,000
Cost of goods sold:			
Variable costs	$ 480,000	$ 60,000	$420,000
Fixed costs	220,000	—	220,000
Total cost of goods sold	$ 700,000	$ 60,000	$640,000
Gross profit	$ 300,000	$ 40,000	$260,000
Operating expenses:			
Variable expenses	$ 180,000	$ 25,000	$155,000
Fixed expenses	51,000	—	51,000
Total operating expenses	$ 231,000	$ 25,000	$206,000
Income (loss) from operations	**$ 69,000**	**$ 15,000**	**$ 54,000**

*Fixed costs are assumed to remain unchanged with the discontinuance of Bran Flakes.

Example Exercise 9-2   objective 1

Product A has revenue of $65,000, variable cost of goods sold of $50,000, variable selling expenses of $12,000, and fixed costs of $25,000, creating a loss from operations of $22,000.

a.   Determine the differential income or loss from sales of Product A.
b.   Should Product A be discontinued?

(continued)

Follow My Example 9-2

a. Differential revenue from annual sales of Product A:
   Revenue from sales $65,000
   Differential cost of annual sales of Product A:
   Variable cost of goods sold $50,000
   Variable selling expenses 12,000   62,000
   Annual differential income from sales of Product A .... $ 3,000

b. Product A should not be discontinued.

For Practice: PE 9-2A, PE 9-2B

NIKE does not make shoes but buys 100% of its shoe manufacturing from outside suppliers. NIKE believes that its strengths are in designing, marketing, distributing, and selling athletic shoes, not in manufacturing shoes.

MAKE OR BUY

The assembly of many parts is often a major element in manufacturing some products, such as automobiles. These parts may be made by the product's manufacturer, or they may be purchased. For example, some of the parts for an automobile, such as the motor, may be produced by the automobile manufacturer. Other parts, such as tires, may be purchased from other manufacturers. In addition, in manufacturing motors, such items as spark plugs and nuts and bolts may be acquired from suppliers.

Management uses differential costs to decide whether to make or buy a part. For example, if a part is purchased, management has concluded that it is less costly to buy the part than to manufacture it. Make or buy options often arise when a manufacturer has excess productive capacity in the form of unused equipment, space, and labor.

The differential analysis is similar, whether management is considering making a part that is currently being purchased or purchasing a part that is currently being made. To illustrate, assume that an automobile manufacturer has been purchasing instrument panels for $240 a unit. The factory is currently operating at 80% of capacity, and no major increase in production is expected in the near future. The cost per unit of manufacturing an instrument panel internally, including fixed costs, is estimated as follows:

Direct materials	$ 80
Direct labor	80
Variable factory overhead	52
Fixed factory overhead	68
Total cost per unit	$280

If the *make* price of $280 is simply compared with the *buy* price of $240, the decision is to buy the instrument panel. However, if unused capacity could be used in manufacturing the part, there would be no increase in the total amount of fixed factory overhead costs. Thus, only the variable factory overhead costs need to be considered. The relevant costs are summarized in the differential report in Exhibit 7.

Other possible effects of a decision to manufacture the instrument panel should also be considered. For example, capacity committed to the instrument panel may not be available for more production opportunities in the future. This decision may affect employees. It may also affect future business relations with the instrument panel supplier, who may provide other essential parts. The company's decision to manufacture instrument panels might jeopardize the timely delivery of these other parts.

EXHIBIT 7

Differential Analysis Report—Make or Buy

Proposal to Manufacture Instrument Panels February 15, 2008		
Purchase price of an instrument panel		$240.00
Differential cost to manufacture:		
Direct materials	$80.00	
Direct labor	80.00	
Variable factory overhead	52.00	212.00
Cost savings from manufacturing an instrument panel ...		**$ 28.00**

Example Exercise 9-3   **objective** *1*

A company manufactures a subcomponent of an assembly for $80 per unit, including fixed costs of $25 per unit. A proposal is offered to purchase the subcomponent from an outside source for $60 per unit, plus $5 per unit freight. Provide a differential analysis of the outside purchase proposal.

Follow My Example 9-3

Differential cost to purchase:		
Purchase price of the subcomponent	$60	
Freight for subcomponent	5	$65
Differential cost to manufacture:		
Variable manufacturing costs ($80 − $25 fixed costs)		55
Cost savings from manufacturing subcomponent		$10

For Practice: PE 9-3A, PE 9-3B

REPLACE EQUIPMENT

The usefulness of fixed assets may be reduced long before they are considered to be worn out. For example, equipment may no longer be efficient for the purpose for which it is used. On the other hand, the equipment may not have reached the point of complete inadequacy. Decisions to replace usable fixed assets should be based on relevant costs. The relevant costs are the future costs of continuing to use the equipment versus replacement. The book values of the fixed assets being replaced are sunk costs and are irrelevant.

Integrity, Objectivity, and Ethics in Business

 ETHICS

RELATED-PARTY DEALS

The make-or-buy decision can be complicated if the purchase (buy) is being made by a related party. A related party is one in which there is direct or indirect control of one party over another or the presence of a family member in a transaction. Such dependence or familiarity may interfere with the appropriateness of the business transaction. One investor has said, "Related parties are akin to steroids used by athletes. If you're an athlete and you can cut the mustard, you don't need steroids to make your-

self stronger or faster. By the same token, if you're a good company, you don't need related parties or deals that don't make sense." While related-party transactions are legal, GAAP (FASB Statement No. 56) and the Sarbanes-Oxley Act require that they must be disclosed under the presumption that such transactions are less than arm's length.

Source: Herb Greenberg, "Poor Relations: The Problem with Related-Party Transactions," *Fortune Advisor* (February 5, 2001), p. 198.

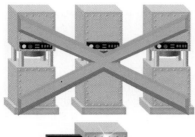

Estimated annual reduction
of costs of $75,000

To illustrate, assume that a business is considering the disposal of several identical machines having a total book value of $100,000 and an estimated remaining life of five years. The old machines can be sold for $25,000. They can be replaced by a single high-speed machine at a cost of $250,000. The new machine has an estimated useful life of five years and no residual value. Analyses indicate an estimated annual reduction in variable manufacturing costs from $225,000 with the old machine to $150,000 with the new machine. No other changes in the manufacturing costs or the operating expenses are expected. The relevant costs are summarized in the differential report in Exhibit 8.

EXHIBIT 8	Differential Analysis Report—Replace Equipment

Proposal to Replace Equipment
November 28, 2008

Annual variable costs—present equipment	$225,000	
Annual variable costs—new equipment	150,000	
Annual differential decrease in cost	$ 75,000	
Number of years applicable	× 5	
Total differential decrease in cost	$375,000	
Proceeds from sale of present equipment	25,000	$400,000
Cost of new equipment		250,000
Net differential decrease in cost, 5-year total		$150,000
Annual net differential decrease in cost—new equipment		**$ 30,000**

Other factors are often important in equipment replacement decisions. For example, differences between the remaining useful life of the old equipment and the estimated life of the new equipment could exist. In addition, the new equipment might improve the overall quality of the product, resulting in an increase in sales volume. Additional factors could include the time value of money and other uses for the cash needed to purchase the new equipment.[1]

The amount of income that is forgone from an alternative use of an asset, such as cash, is called an **opportunity cost**. For example, your opportunity cost of attending school is the income forgone from lost work hours. Although the opportunity cost does not appear as a part of historical accounting data, it is useful in analyzing alternative courses of action. To illustrate, assume that the cash outlay of $250,000 for the new equipment, less the $25,000 proceeds from the sale of the present equipment, could be invested to yield a 10% return. Thus, the annual opportunity cost related to the purchase of the new equipment is $22,500 (10% × $225,000).

Example Exercise 9-4   objective 1

A machine with a book value of $32,000 has an estimated four-year life. A proposal is offered to sell the old machine for $10,000 and replace it with a new machine at a cost of $45,000. The new machine has a four-year life with no salvage value. The new machine would reduce annual direct labor costs by $11,000. Provide a differential analysis on the proposal to replace the machine.

(continued)

---

1 The importance of the time value of money in equipment replacement decisions is discussed in the next chapter.

Follow My Example 9-4

Annual direct labor cost reduction	$11,000	
Number of years applicable	× 4	
Total differential decrease in cost	$44,000	
Proceeds from sale of old equipment	10,000	$54,000
Cost of new equipment		45,000
Net differential decrease in cost from replacing equipment, 4-year total		$ 9,000

For Practice: PE 9-4A, PE 9-4B

PROCESS OR SELL

When a product is manufactured, it progresses through various stages of production. Often a product can be sold at an intermediate stage of production, or it can be processed further and then sold. In deciding whether to sell a product at an intermediate stage or to process it further, differential analysis is useful. The differential revenues from further processing are compared to the differential costs of further processing. The costs of producing the intermediate product do not change, regardless of whether the intermediate product is sold or processed further. Thus, these costs are not differential costs and are irrelevant to the decision to process further.

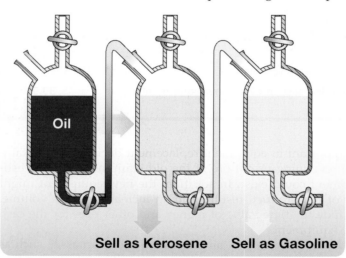

Sell as Kerosene   Sell as Gasoline

To illustrate, assume that a business produces kerosene in batches of 4,000 gallons. Standard quantities of 4,000 gallons of direct materials are processed, which cost $0.60 per gallon. Kerosene can be sold without further processing for $0.80 per gallon. It can be processed further to yield gasoline, which can be sold for $1.25 per gallon. Gasoline requires additional processing costs of $650 per batch, and 20% of the gallons of kerosene will evaporate during production. Exhibit 9 summarizes the differential revenues and costs in deciding whether to process kerosene to produce gasoline.

EXHIBIT 9

Differential Analysis Report—Process or Sell

Proposal to Process Kerosene Further October 1, 2008		
Differential revenue from further processing per batch:		
Revenue from sale of gasoline [(4,000 gallons − 800 gallons evaporation) × $1.25]	$4,000	
Revenue from sale of kerosene (4,000 gallons × $0.80)	3,200	
Differential revenue		$800
Differential cost per batch:		
Additional cost of producing gasoline		650
Differential income from further processing gasoline per batch		**$150**

The differential income from further processing kerosene into gasoline is $150 per batch. The initial cost of producing the intermediate kerosene, $2,400 (4,000 gallons × $0.60), is not considered in deciding whether to process kerosene further. This initial cost will be incurred, regardless of whether gasoline is produced.

Example Exercise 9-5

objective 1

Product T is produced for $2.50 per gallon including a $1.00 per gallon fixed cost. Product T can be sold without additional processing for $3.50 per gallon, or processed further into Product V at an additional cost of $1.60 per gallon, including a $0.90 per gallon fixed cost. Product V can be sold for $4.00 per gallon. Provide a differential analysis for further processing into Product V.

Follow My Example 9-5

Differential revenue from further processing per gallon:
Revenue per gallon from sale of Product V		$4.00
Revenue per gallon from sale of Product T		3.50
Differential revenue		$0.50
Differential cost per gallon:		
Additional cost for producing Product V ($1.60 − $0.90)		0.70
Differential loss from further processing into Product V		$0.20

For Practice: PE 9-5A, PE 9-5B

The Internet is forcing many companies to respond to "dynamic" pricing. For example, in Priceline.com Inc.'s "name your price" format, customers tell the company what they are willing to pay and then the company must decide if it is willing to sell at that price.

Order for 5,000 basketballs at $18 each

ACCEPT BUSINESS AT A SPECIAL PRICE

Differential analysis is also useful in deciding whether to accept additional business at a special price. The differential revenue that would be provided from the additional business is compared to the differential costs of producing and delivering the product to the customer. If the company is operating at full capacity, any additional production will increase both fixed and variable production costs. If, however, the normal production of the company is below full capacity, additional business may be undertaken without increasing fixed production costs. In this case, the differential costs of the additional production are the variable manufacturing costs. If operating expenses increase because of the additional business, these expenses should also be considered.

To illustrate, assume that the monthly capacity of a sporting goods business is 12,500 basketballs. Current sales and production are averaging 10,000 basketballs per month. The current manufacturing cost of $20 per unit consists of variable costs of $12.50 and fixed costs of $7.50. The normal selling price of the product in the domestic market is $30. The manufacturer receives from an exporter an offer for 5,000 basketballs at $18 each. Production can be spread over a three-month period without interfering with normal production or incurring overtime costs. Pricing policies in the domestic market will not be affected. Simply comparing the sales price of $18 with the present unit manufacturing cost of $20 indicates that the offer should be rejected. However, by focusing only on the differential cost, which in this case is the variable cost, the decision is different. Exhibit 10 shows the differential analysis report for this decision.

Proposals to sell a product in the domestic market at prices lower than the normal price may require additional considerations. For example, it may be unwise to increase sales volume in one territory by price reductions if

EXHIBIT 10

Differential Analysis Report—Sell at Special Price

Proposal to Sell Basketballs to Exporter
March 10, 2008

Differential revenue from accepting offer:	
Revenue from sale of 5,000 additional units at $18	$90,000
Differential cost of accepting offer:	
Variable costs of 5,000 additional units at $12.50	62,500
Differential income from accepting offer	**$27,500**

sales volume is lost in other areas. Manufacturers must also conform to the Robinson-Patman Act, which prohibits price discrimination within the United States unless differences in prices can be justified by different costs of serving different customers.

Example Exercise 9-6

objective **1**

Product D is normally sold for $4.40 per unit. A special price of $3.60 is offered for the export market. The variable production cost is $3.00 per unit. An additional export tariff of 10% of revenue must be paid for all export products. Determine the differential income or loss per unit from selling Product D for export.

Follow My Example 9-6

Differential revenue from export:		
Revenue per unit from export sale		$3.60
Differential cost from export:		
Variable manufacturing costs	$3.00	
Export tariff (10% × $3.60)	0.36	3.36
Differential income from accepting export sale		$0.24

For Practice: PE 9-6A, PE 9-6B

Setting Normal Product Selling Prices

objective **2**

Determine the selling price of a product, using the total cost, product cost, and variable cost concepts.

Differential analysis may be useful in deciding to lower selling prices for special short-run decisions, such as whether to accept business at a price lower than the normal price. In such cases, the minimum short-run price is set high enough to cover all variable costs. Any price above this minimum price will improve profits in the short run. In the long run, however, the normal selling price must be set high enough to cover all costs and expenses (both fixed and variable) and provide a reasonable profit. Otherwise, the business may not survive.

The normal selling price can be viewed as the target selling price to be achieved in the long run. The basic approaches to setting this price are as follows:

Market Methods	Cost-Plus Methods
1. Demand-based methods	1. Total cost concept
2. Competition-based methods	2. Product cost concept
	3. Variable cost concept

Managers using the market methods refer to the external market to determine the price. Demand-based methods set the price according to the demand for the product. If there is high demand for the product, then the price may be set high, while lower demand may require the price to be set low. An example of setting different prices according to the demand for the product is found in the lodging industry, where rates are set low for weekends and high during business days according to the demand by business travelers.

Competition-based methods set the price according to the price offered by competitors. For example, if a competitor reduces the price, then management may be required to adjust the price to meet the competition. The market-based pricing approaches are discussed in greater detail in marketing courses, so we will not expand upon them here.

Managers using the cost-plus methods price the product in order to achieve a target profit. Managers add to the cost an amount called a **markup**, so that all costs plus a profit are included in the selling price. In the following paragraphs, we describe and illustrate the three cost concepts often used in applying the cost-plus approach: (1) total cost, (2) product cost, and (3) variable cost. A cost reduction method that uses market-method pricing, called target costing, is discussed later in this section.

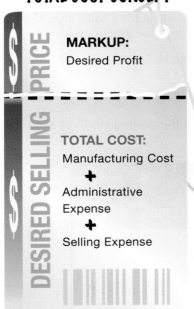

TOTAL COST CONCEPT

MARKUP:
Desired Profit

TOTAL COST:
Manufacturing Cost
+
Administrative Expense
+
Selling Expense

DESIRED SELLING PRICE

TOTAL COST CONCEPT

Using the **total cost concept**, all costs of manufacturing a product plus the selling and administrative expenses are included in the cost amount to which the markup is added. Since all costs and expenses are included in the cost amount, the dollar amount of the markup equals the desired profit.

The first step in applying the total cost concept is to determine the total cost of manufacturing the product. This cost includes the costs of direct materials, direct labor, and factory overhead and should be available from the accounting records. The next step is to add the estimated selling and administrative expenses to the total cost of manufacturing the product. The cost amount per unit is then computed by dividing the total costs by the total units expected to be produced and sold.

After the cost amount per unit has been determined, the dollar amount of the markup is determined. For this purpose, the markup is expressed as a percentage of cost. This percentage is then multiplied by the cost amount per unit. The dollar amount of the markup is then added to the cost amount per unit to arrive at the selling price.

The markup percentage for the total cost concept is determined by applying the following formula:

$$\text{Markup Percentage} = \frac{\text{Desired Profit}}{\text{Total Costs}}$$

The numerator of the formula is only the desired profit. This is because all costs and expenses are included in the cost amount to which the markup is added. The denominator of the formula is the total costs.

To illustrate, assume that the costs for calculators of Digital Solutions Inc. are as follows:

Variable costs:	
Direct materials	$ 3.00 per unit
Direct labor	10.00
Factory overhead	1.50
Selling and administrative expenses	1.50
Total	$ 16.00 per unit
Fixed costs:	
Factory overhead	$50,000
Selling and administrative expenses	20,000

Digital Solutions Inc. desires a profit equal to a 20% rate of return on assets, $800,000 of assets are devoted to producing calculators, and 100,000 units are expected to be produced and sold. The calculators' total cost is $1,670,000, or $16.70 per unit, computed as follows:

Variable costs ($16.00 × 100,000 units)		$1,600,000
Fixed costs:		
Factory overhead	$50,000	
Selling and administrative expenses	20,000	70,000
Total costs		$1,670,000
Total cost per calculator ($1,670,000/100,000 units)		$16.70

The desired profit is $160,000 (20% × $800,000), and the markup percentage for a calculator is 9.6%, computed as follows:

$$\text{Markup Percentage} = \frac{\text{Desired Profit}}{\text{Total Costs}}$$

$$\text{Markup Percentage} = \frac{\$160,000}{\$1,670,000} = 9.6\% \text{ (rounded)}$$

Based on the total cost per unit and the markup percentage for a calculator, Digital Solutions Inc. would price each calculator at $18.30 per unit, as shown below.

Total cost per calculator	$16.70
Markup ($16.70 × 9.6%)	1.60
Selling price	$18.30

The ability of the selling price of $18.30 to generate the desired profit of $160,000 is shown by the following income statement:

Digital Solutions Inc.
Income Statement
For the Year Ended December 31, 2008

Sales (100,000 units × $18.30)		$1,830,000
Expenses:		
Variable (100,000 units × $16.00)	$1,600,000	
Fixed ($50,000 + $20,000)	70,000	1,670,000
Income from operations		$ 160,000

The total cost concept of applying the cost-plus approach to product pricing is often used by contractors who sell products to government agencies. In many cases, government contractors are required by law to be reimbursed for their products on a total-cost-plus-profit basis.

Example Exercise 9-7

 objective 2

Apex Corporation produces and sells Product Z at a total cost of $30 per unit of which $20 is product cost and $10 is selling and administrative expenses. In addition, the total cost of $30 is made up of $18 variable cost and $12 is fixed cost. The desired profit is $3 per unit. Determine the markup percentage on total cost.

Follow My Example 9-7

Markup percentage on total cost: $\frac{\$3}{\$30}$ = 10.0%

For Practice: PE 9-7A, PE 9-7B

Integrity, Objectivity, and Ethics in Business

ETHICS

PRICE FIXING

Federal law prevents companies competing in similar markets from sharing cost and price information, or what is commonly termed "price fixing." For example, the Federal Trade Commission brought a suit against the major record labels and music retailers for conspiring to set CD prices at a minimum level, or MAP (minimum advertised price). In settling the suit, the major labels ceased their MAP policies and provided $143 million in cash and CDs for consumers.

PRODUCT COST CONCEPT

PRODUCT COST CONCEPT

MARKUP:

Administrative Expense

+

Selling Expense

+

Desired Profit

PRODUCTION COST:

Manufacturing Cost

PRODUCT COST CONCEPT

Using the **product cost concept**, only the costs of manufacturing the product, termed the product cost, are included in the cost amount to which the markup is added. Estimated selling expenses, administrative expenses, and profit are included in the markup. The markup percentage is determined by applying the following formula:

$$\text{Markup Percentage} = \frac{\text{Desired Profit} + \text{Total Selling and Administrative Expenses}}{\text{Total Manufacturing Costs}}$$

The numerator of the markup percentage formula is the desired profit plus the total selling and administrative expenses. These expenses must be included in the markup, since they are not included in the cost amount to which the markup is added. The denominator of the formula includes the costs of direct materials, direct labor, and factory overhead.

To illustrate, assume the same data used in the preceding illustration. The manufacturing cost for Digital Solutions Inc.'s calculator is $1,500,000, or $15 per unit, computed as follows:

Direct materials ($3 × 100,000 units)		$ 300,000
Direct labor ($10 × 100,000 units)		1,000,000
Factory overhead:		
Variable ($1.50 × 100,000 units)	$150,000	
Fixed	50,000	200,000
Total manufacturing costs		$1,500,000
Manufacturing cost per calculator ($1,500,000/100,000 units)		$15

The desired profit is $160,000 (20% × $800,000), and the total selling and administrative expenses are $170,000 [(100,000 units × $1.50 per unit) + $20,000]. The markup percentage for a calculator is 22%, computed as follows:

$$\text{Markup Percentage} = \frac{\text{Desired Profit} + \text{Total Selling and Administrative Expenses}}{\text{Total Manufacturing Costs}}$$

$$\text{Markup Percentage} = \frac{\$160,000 + \$170,000}{\$1,500,000}$$

$$\text{Markup Percentage} = \frac{\$330,000}{\$1,500,000} = 22\%$$

Based on the manufacturing cost per calculator and the markup percentage, Digital Solutions Inc. would price each calculator at $18.30 per unit, as shown below.

Manufacturing cost per calculator	$15.00
Markup ($15 × 22%)	3.30
Selling price	$18.30

Example Exercise 9-8   objective

Apex Corporation produces and sells Product Z at a total cost of $30 per unit of which $20 is product cost and $10 is selling and administrative expenses. In addition, the total cost of $30 is made up of $18 variable cost and $12 is fixed cost. The desired profit is $3 per unit. Determine the markup percentage on product cost.

(continued)

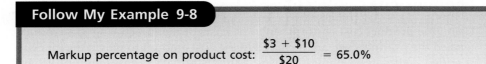

VARIABLE COST CONCEPT

VARIABLE COST CONCEPT

The **variable cost concept** emphasizes the distinction between variable and fixed costs in product pricing. Using the variable cost concept, only variable costs are included in the cost amount to which the markup is added. All variable manufacturing costs, as well as variable selling and administrative expenses, are included in the cost amount. Fixed manufacturing costs, fixed selling and administrative expenses, and profit are included in the markup.

The markup percentage is determined by applying the following formula:

$$\text{Markup Percentage} = \frac{\text{Desired Profit} + \text{Total Fixed Costs}}{\text{Total Variable Costs}}$$

The numerator of the markup percentage formula is the desired profit plus the total fixed manufacturing costs and the total fixed selling and administrative expenses. These costs and expenses must be included in the markup, since they are not included in the cost amount to which the markup is added. The denominator of the formula includes the total variable costs.

To illustrate, assume the same data used in the two preceding illustrations. The calculator variable cost is $1,600,000, or $16.00 per unit, computed as follows:

Variable costs:	
Direct materials ($3 × 100,000 units)	$ 300,000
Direct labor ($10 × 100,000 units)	1,000,000
Factory overhead ($1.50 × 100,000 units)	150,000
Selling and administrative expenses ($1.50 × 100,000 units)	150,000
Total variable costs	$1,600,000
Variable cost per calculator ($1,600,000/100,000 units)	$16.00

The desired profit is $160,000 (20% × $800,000), the total fixed manufacturing costs are $50,000, and the total fixed selling and administrative expenses are $20,000. The markup percentage for a calculator is 14.4%, computed as follows:

$$\text{Markup Percentage} = \frac{\text{Desired Profit} + \text{Total Fixed Costs}}{\text{Total Variable Costs}}$$

$$\text{Markup Percentage} = \frac{\$160,000 + \$50,000 + \$20,000}{\$1,600,000}$$

$$\text{Markup Percentage} = \frac{\$230,000}{\$1,600,000} = 14.4\%$$

Based on the variable cost per calculator and the markup percentage, Digital Solutions Inc. would price each calculator at $18.30 per unit, as shown below.

Variable cost per calculator	$16.00
Markup ($16.00 × 14.4%)	2.30
Selling price	$18.30

Example Exercise 9-9

objective **2**

Apex Corporation produces and sells Product Z at a total cost of $30 per unit of which $20 is product cost and $10 is selling and administrative expenses. In addition, the total cost of $30 is made up of $18 variable cost and $12 is fixed cost. The desired profit is $3 per unit. Determine the markup percentage on variable cost, rounding to one decimal place.

Follow My Example 9-9

Markup percentage on variable cost: $\dfrac{\$3 + \$12}{\$18}$ = 83.3%, rounded to one decimal place

For Practice: PE 9-9A, PE 9-9B

CHOOSING A COST-PLUS APPROACH COST CONCEPT

All three cost concepts produced the same selling price ($18.30) for Digital Solutions Inc. In practice, however, the three cost concepts are usually not viewed as alternatives. Each cost concept requires different estimates of costs and expenses. This difficulty and the complexity of the manufacturing operations should be considered in choosing a cost concept.

To reduce the costs of gathering data, estimated (standard) costs rather than actual costs may be used with any of the three cost concepts. However, management should exercise caution when using estimated costs in applying the cost-plus approach. The estimates should be based on normal (attainable) operating levels and not theoretical (ideal) levels of performance. In product pricing, the use of estimates based on ideal- or maximum-capacity operating levels might lead to setting product prices too low. In this case, the costs of such factors as normal spoilage or normal periods of idle time might not be considered.

The decision-making needs of management are also an important factor in selecting a cost concept for product pricing. For example, managers who often make special pricing decisions are more likely to use the variable cost concept. In contrast, a government defense contractor would be more likely to use the total cost concept.

ACTIVITY-BASED COSTING

As illustrated in the preceding paragraphs, costs are an important consideration in setting product prices. To more accurately measure the costs of producing and selling products, some companies use activity-based costing. **Activity-based costing (ABC)** identifies and traces activities to specific products.

Activity-based costing may be useful in making product pricing decisions where manufacturing operations involve large amounts of factory overhead. In such cases, traditional overhead allocation using activity bases such as units produced or machine hours may yield inaccurate cost allocations. This, in turn, may result in distorted product costs and product prices. By providing more accurate product cost allocations, activity-based costing aids in setting product prices that will cover costs and expenses.[2]

TARGET COSTING

A method that combines market-based pricing with a cost reduction emphasis is **target costing**. Under target costing, a future selling price is anticipated, using the demand-based methods or the competition-based methods discussed previously. The targeted cost is determined by *subtracting* a desired profit from the expected selling price. In contrast, the three cost-plus concepts discussed previously begin with a given cost and *add* a markup to determine the selling price.

2 Activity-based costing is further discussed and illustrated in a later chapter.

Target costing is used to motivate cost reduction as shown in Exhibit 11. The bar at the left in Exhibit 11 shows the actual cost and profit that can be earned during the present time period for a particular product. The bar at the right shows that the market price is expected to decline in the future. Thus, to earn a profit, a target cost is estimated as the difference between the expected market price and the desired profit. This target cost establishes a product cost objective that will maintain competitiveness and profitability.

Target Cost Concept

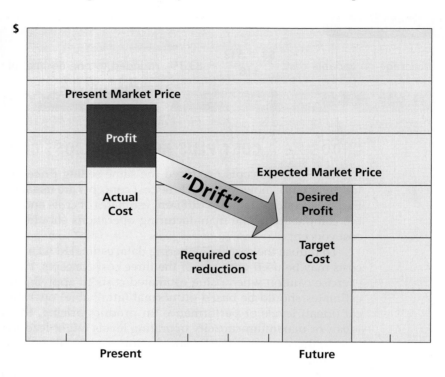

Since the target cost is less than the current cost, managers must plan and remove cost from the design and manufacture of the product. The planned cost reduction is sometimes referred to as the cost "drift." Cost can be removed from a product in a variety of ways, such as by simplifying the design, reducing the cost of direct materials, reducing the direct labor content, or eliminating waste from manufacturing operations. Using the target cost concept in this way provides managers with an improvement goal for gauging the success of their efforts over time. Target costing is especially useful in highly competitive markets that require continual product cost reductions to remain competitive, such as personal computers.

Product Profitability and Pricing Under Production Bottlenecks

objective **3**

Compute the relative profitability of products in bottleneck production environments.

An important consideration influencing production volumes and prices is production bottlenecks. A production **bottleneck** (or *constraint*) occurs at the point in the process where the demand for the company's product exceeds the ability to produce the product. The **theory of constraints (TOC)** is a manufacturing strategy that focuses on reducing the influence of bottlenecks on a process.

PRODUCT PROFITABILITY UNDER PRODUCTION BOTTLENECKS

When a company has a bottleneck in its production process, it should attempt to maximize its profitability, subject to the influence of the bottleneck. To illustrate, assume

Business Connections

REAL WORLD

WHAT IS A PRODUCT?

A product is often thought of in terms beyond just its physical attributes. For example, why a customer buys a product usually impacts how a business markets the product. Other considerations, such as warranty needs, servicing needs, and perceived quality, also affect business strategies.

Consider the four different types of products listed below. For these products, the frequency of purchase, the profit per unit, and the number of retailers differ. As a result, the sales and marketing approach for each product differs.

Product	Type of Product	Frequency of Purchase	Profit per Unit	Number of Retailers	Sales/Marketing Approach
Snickers®	Convenience	Often	Low	Many	Mass advertising
Sony® TV	Shopping	Occasional	Moderate	Many	Mass advertising; personal selling
Diamond ring	Specialty	Seldom	High	Few	Personal selling
Prearranged funeral	Unsought	Rare	High	Few	Aggressive selling

The sand in the hourglass can pass only as fast as the narrowest point in the glass will allow.

Bottleneck

that PrideCraft Tool Company makes three types of wrenches: small, medium, and large. All three products are processed through a heat treatment operation, which hardens the steel tools. PrideCraft Tool's heat treatment process is operating at full capacity and is a production bottleneck. The product unit contribution margin and the number of hours of heat treatment used by each type of wrench are as follows:

	Small Wrench	Medium Wrench	Large Wrench
Unit selling price	$130	$140	$160
Unit variable cost	40	40	40
Unit contribution margin	$ 90	$100	$120
Heat treatment hours per unit	1	4	8

The large wrench appears to be the most profitable product because its unit contribution margin is the greatest. However, the unit contribution margin can be a misleading indicator of profitability in a bottleneck operation. The correct measure of performance is the value of each bottleneck hour, or the unit contribution margin per bottleneck hour. Using this measure, each product has a much different profitability when compared to the unit contribution margin information, as shown in Exhibit 12.

EXHIBIT 12

Unit Contribution Margin per Bottleneck Hour

	Small Wrench	Medium Wrench	Large Wrench
Unit selling price	$130	$140	$160
Unit variable cost	40	40	40
Unit contribution margin	$ 90	$100	$120
Bottleneck (heat treatment) hours per unit	/ 1	/ 4	/ 8
Unit contribution margin per bottleneck hour	$ 90	$ 25	$ 15

The small wrench produces the most unit contribution margin per bottleneck hour (heat treatment) used, while the large wrench produces the smallest unit contribution margin per bottleneck hour. Thus, the small wrench is the most profitable product. This information is the opposite of that implied by the unit contribution margin.

Example Exercise 9-10   objective **3**

Product A has a unit contribution margin of $15. Product B has a unit contribution margin of $20. Product A requires three furnace hours, while Product B requires five furnace hours. Determine the most profitable product assuming the furnace is a constraint.

Follow My Example 9-10

	Product A	Product B
Unit contribution margin	$15	$20
Furnace hours per unit	/ 3	/ 5
Unit contribution margin per bottleneck hour	$ 5	$ 4

Product A is the most profitable in using bottleneck resources.

For Practice: PE 9-10A, PE 9-10B

Latrobe Steel Division of The Timken Company originally used total cost plus a markup to price its steel products. However, Latrobe recalculated the profitability of its products, based on the unit contribution margin per hour of bottleneck. This analysis caused Latrobe management to change the product mix in favor of products with high unit contribution margin per hour of bottleneck. Management estimated that these changes improved income from operations by 20%.

PRODUCT PRICING UNDER PRODUCTION BOTTLENECKS

Each hour of a bottleneck delivers profit to the company. When a company has a production bottleneck, the unit contribution margin per bottleneck hour provides a measure of the product's relative profitability. This information can also be used to adjust the product price to better reflect the value of the product's use of a bottleneck. Products that use a large number of bottleneck hours per unit require more unit contribution margin than products that use few bottleneck hours per unit. For example, PrideCraft Tool Company should increase the price of the large wrench in order to deliver more unit contribution margin per bottleneck hour.

To determine the price of the large wrench that would equate its profitability to the small wrench, we need to solve the following equation:

$$\text{Unit Contribution Margin per Bottleneck Hour for Small Wrench} = \frac{\text{Revised Price of Large Wrench} - \text{Unit Variable Cost for Large Wrench}}{\text{Bottleneck Hours per Unit for Large Wrench}}$$

$$\$90 = \frac{\text{Revised Price of Large Wrench} - \$40}{8}$$

$$\$720 = \text{Revised Price of Large Wrench} - \$40$$
$$\$760 = \text{Revised Price of Large Wrench}$$

The large wrench's price would need to be increased to $760 in order to deliver the same unit contribution margin per bottleneck hour as does the small wrench, as verified below.

Revised price of large wrench	$760
Less: Unit variable cost of large wrench	40
Unit contribution margin of large wrench	$720
Bottleneck hours per unit of large wrench	/ 8
Revised unit contribution margin per bottleneck hour	$ 90

At a price of $760, the company would be indifferent between producing and selling the small wrench or the large wrench, all else being equal. This analysis assumes that there is unlimited demand for the products. If the market were unwilling to purchase the large wrench at this price, then the company should produce the small wrench.

At a Glance

1. Prepare a differential analysis report for decisions involving leasing or selling equipment, discontinuing an unprofitable segment, manufacturing or purchasing a needed part, replacing usable fixed assets, processing further or selling an intermediate product, or accepting additional business at a special price.

Key Points	Key Learning Outcomes	Example Exercises	Practice Exercises
Differential analysis reports for leasing or selling, discontinuing a segment or product, making or buying, replacing equipment, processing or selling, and accepting business at a special price are illustrated in the text. Each analysis focuses on the differential revenues and/or costs of the alternative courses of action.	• Prepare a lease or sell differential analysis.	9-1	9-1A, 9-1B
	• Prepare a discontinued segment differential analysis.	9-2	9-2A, 9-2B
	• Prepare a make or buy differential analysis.	9-3	9-3A, 9-3B
	• Prepare an equipment replacement differential analysis.	9-4	9-4A, 9-4B
	• Prepare a process or sell differential analysis.	9-5	9-5A, 9-5B
	• Prepare an accept business at a special price differential analysis.	9-6	9-6A, 9-6B

2. Determine the selling price of a product, using the total cost, product cost, and variable cost concepts.

Key Points	Key Learning Outcomes	Example Exercises	Practice Exercises
The three cost concepts commonly used in applying the cost-plus approach to product pricing are the total cost, product cost, and variable cost concepts.	• Compute the markup percentage using the total cost concept.	9-7	9-7A, 9-7B
	• Compute the markup percentage using the product cost concept.	9-8	9-8A, 9-8B
	• Compute the markup percentage using the variable cost concept.	9-9	9-9A, 9-9B
Activity-based costing can be used to provide more accurate cost information in applying cost-plus concepts when indirect costs are significant. Target costing combines market-based methods with a cost-reduction emphasis.	• Describe activity-based costing.		
	• Define and describe target costing.		

3. Compute the relative profitability of products in bottleneck production environments.

Key Points	Key Learning Outcomes	Example Exercises	Practice Exercises
The profitability of a product in a bottleneck production environment is determined by dividing the unit contribution margin by the bottleneck hours per unit. The resulting measure indicates the product's profitability per hour of bottleneck use. This information can be used to support product pricing decisions.	• Compute the unit contribution margin per bottleneck hour.	9-10	9-10A, 9-10B
	• Compute the indifference price between products using the unit contribution margin per bottleneck hour.		

Key Terms

activity-based costing (ABC) (365)
bottleneck (366)
differential analysis (351)
differential cost (351)
differential revenue (350)

markup (360)
opportunity cost (357)
product cost concept (363)
sunk cost (350)
target costing (365)

theory of constraints (TOC) (366)
total cost concept (361)
variable cost concept (364)

Illustrative Problem

Inez Company recently began production of a new product, M, which required the investment of $1,600,000 in assets. The costs of producing and selling 80,000 units of Product M are estimated as follows:

Variable costs:		
Direct materials	$	10.00 per unit
Direct labor		6.00
Factory overhead		4.00
Selling and administrative expenses		5.00
Total	$	25.00 per unit
Fixed costs:		
Factory overhead	$800,000	
Selling and administrative expenses	400,000	

Inez Company is currently considering establishing a selling price for Product M. The president of Inez Company has decided to use the cost-plus approach to product pricing and has indicated that Product M must earn a 10% rate of return on invested assets.

Instructions

1. Determine the amount of desired profit from the production and sale of Product M.
2. Assuming that the total cost concept is used, determine (a) the cost amount per unit, (b) the markup percentage, and (c) the selling price of Product M.
3. Assuming that the product cost concept is used, determine (a) the cost amount per unit, (b) the markup percentage, and (c) the selling price of Product M.
4. Assuming that the variable cost concept is used, determine (a) the cost amount per unit, (b) the markup percentage, and (c) the selling price of Product M.
5. Assume that for the current year, the selling price of Product M was $42 per unit. To date, 60,000 units have been produced and sold, and analysis of the domestic market indicates that 15,000 additional units are expected to be sold during the remainder of the year. Recently, Inez Company received an offer from Wong Inc. for 4,000 units of Product M at $28 each. Wong Inc. will market the units in Korea under its own brand name, and no selling and administrative expenses associated with the sale will be incurred by Inez Company. The additional business is not expected to affect the domestic sales of Product M, and the additional units could be produced during the current year, using existing capacity. (a) Prepare a differential analysis report of the proposed sale to Wong Inc. (b) Based upon the differential analysis report in part (a), should the proposal be accepted?

Solution

1. $160,000 ($1,600,000 × 10%)

2. a. Total costs:

Variable ($25 × 80,000 units)	$2,000,000
Fixed ($800,000 + $400,000)	1,200,000
Total	$3,200,000

Cost amount per unit: $3,200,000/80,000 units = $40.00

b. Markup Percentage = $\dfrac{\text{Desired Profit}}{\text{Total Costs}}$

Markup Percentage = $\dfrac{\$160,000}{\$3,200,000}$ = 5%

c.
Cost amount per unit	$40.00
Markup ($40 × 5%)	2.00
Selling price	$42.00

3. a. Total manufacturing costs:

Variable ($20 × 80,000 units)	$1,600,000
Fixed factory overhead	800,000
Total	$2,400,000

Cost amount per unit: $2,400,000/80,000 units = $30.00

b. Markup Percentage = $\dfrac{\text{Desired Profit} + \text{Total Selling and Administrative Expenses}}{\text{Total Manufacturing Costs}}$

Markup Percentage = $\dfrac{\$160,000 + \$400,000 + (\$5 \times 80,000\ \text{units})}{\$2,400,000}$

Markup Percentage = $\dfrac{\$160,000 + \$400,000 + \$400,000}{\$2,400,000}$

Markup Percentage = $\dfrac{\$960,000}{\$2,400,000}$ = 40%

c.
Cost amount per unit	$30.00
Markup ($30 × 40%)	12.00
Selling price	$42.00

4. a. Variable cost amount per unit: $25
Total variable costs: $25 × 80,000 units = $2,000,000

b. Markup Percentage = $\dfrac{\text{Desired Profit} + \text{Total Fixed Costs}}{\text{Total Variable Costs}}$

Markup Percentage = $\dfrac{\$160,000 + \$800,000 + \$400,000}{\$2,000,000}$

Markup Percentage = $\dfrac{\$1,360,000}{\$2,000,000}$ = 68%

c.
Cost amount per unit	$25.00
Markup ($25 × 68%)	17.00
Selling price	$42.00

5. a.

Proposal to Sell to Wong Inc.	
Differential revenue from accepting offer:	
Revenue from sale of 4,000 additional units at $28	$112,000
Differential cost from accepting offer:	
Variable production costs of 4,000 additional units at $20	80,000
Differential income from accepting offer	$ 32,000

b. The proposal should be accepted.

Self-Examination Questions

(Answers at End of Chapter)

1. Marlo Company is considering discontinuing a product. The costs of the product consist of $20,000 fixed costs and $15,000 variable costs. The variable operating expenses related to the product total $4,000. What is the differential cost?
   A. $19,000
   B. $15,000
   C. $35,000
   D. $39,000

2. Victor Company is considering disposing of equipment that was originally purchased for $200,000 and has $150,000 of accumulated depreciation to date. The same equipment would cost $310,000 to replace. What is the sunk cost?
   A. $50,000
   B. $150,000
   C. $200,000
   D. $310,000

3. Henry Company is considering spending $100,000 for a new grinding machine. This amount could be invested to yield a 12% return. What is the opportunity cost?
   A. $112,000
   B. $88,000
   C. $12,000
   D. $100,000

4. For which cost concept used in applying the cost-plus approach to product pricing are fixed manufacturing costs, fixed selling and administrative expenses, and desired profit allowed for in determining the markup?
   A. Total cost
   B. Product cost
   C. Variable cost
   D. Standard cost

5. Mendosa Company produces three products. All the products use a furnace operation, which is a production bottleneck. The following information is available:

	Product 1	Product 2	Product 3
Unit volume—March	1,000	1,500	1,000
Per-unit information:			
Sales price	$35	$33	$29
Variable cost	15	15	15
Unit contribution margin	$20	$18	$14
Furnace hours	4	3	2

From a profitability perspective, which product should be emphasized in April's advertising campaign?
   A. Product 1
   B. Product 2
   C. Product 3
   D. All three

Eye Openers

1. Explain the meaning of (a) differential revenue, (b) differential cost, and (c) differential income.

2. It was reported that Exabyte Corporation, a fast growing Colorado marketer of backup tape drives, has decided to purchase key components of its product from others. For example, Sony Corporation of America provides Exabyte with mechanical decks, and Solectron Corporation provides circuit boards. A former chief executive officer of Exabyte stated, "If we'd tried to build our own plants, we could never have grown that fast or maybe survived." The decision to purchase key product components is an example of what type of decision illustrated in this chapter?

3. In the long run, the normal selling price must be set high enough to cover what factors?

4. A company could sell a building for $250,000 or lease it for $2,500 per month. What would need to be considered in determining if the lease option would be preferred?

5. A chemical company has a commodity-grade and premium-grade product. Why might the company elect to process the commodity-grade product further to the premium-grade product?

6. A company accepts incremental business at a special price that exceeds the variable cost. What other issues must the company consider in deciding whether to accept the business?

7. A company fabricates a component at a cost of $6.00. A supplier offers to supply the same component for $5.50. Under what circumstances is it reasonable to purchase from the supplier?

8. Many fast food restaurant chains, such as McDonald's, will occasionally discontinue restaurants in their system. What are some financial considerations in deciding to eliminate a store?

9. Why might the use of ideal standards in applying the cost-plus approach to product pricing lead to setting product prices that are too low?

10. Although the cost-plus approach to product pricing may be used by management as a general guideline, what are some examples of other factors that managers should also consider in setting product prices?
11. What method of determining product cost may be appropriate in settings where the manufacturing process is complex?
12. How does the target cost concept differ from cost-plus approaches?
13. Under what circumstances is it appropriate to use the target cost concept?
14. What is a production bottleneck?
15. What is the appropriate measure of a product's value when a firm is operating under production bottlenecks?

Practice Exercises

PE 9-1A
Lease or sell decision
obj. 1

Monroe Company owns equipment with a cost of $235,000 and accumulated depreciation of $185,000 that can be sold for $120,000, less a 4% sales commission. Alternatively, the equipment can be leased by Monroe Company for five years for a total of $135,000 at the end of which there is no salvage value. In addition, repair, insurance, and property tax that would be incurred by Monroe Company on the equipment would total $16,000 over the five years. Determine the differential income or loss from the lease alternative for Monroe Company.

PE 9-1B
Lease or sell decision
obj. 1

Stein Company owns a truck with a cost of $80,000 and accumulated depreciation of $50,000 that can be sold for $25,000, less a 5% sales commission. Alternatively, the truck can be leased by Stein Company for three years for a total of $30,000 at the end of which there is no salvage value. In addition, repair, insurance, and property tax that would be incurred by Stein Company on the truck would total $9,000 over the three years. Determine the differential income or loss from the lease alternative for Stein Company.

PE 9-2A
Discontinue a segment decision
obj. 1

Product J has revenue of $340,000, variable cost of goods sold of $290,000, variable selling expenses of $64,000, and fixed costs of $100,000, creating a loss from operations of $114,000.

a. Determine the differential income or loss from sales of Product J.
b. Should Product J be discontinued?

PE 9-2B
Discontinue a segment decision
obj. 1

Product T has revenue of $56,000, variable cost of goods sold of $40,000, variable selling expenses of $6,000, and fixed costs of $15,000, creating a loss from operations of $5,000.

a. Determine the differential income or loss from sales of Product T.
b. Should Product T be discontinued?

PE 9-3A
Make-or-buy decision
obj. 1

A company manufactures various sized plastic bottles for its medicinal product. The manufacturing cost for small bottles is $45 per unit (1,000 bottles), including fixed costs of $12 per unit. A proposal is offered to purchase small bottles from an outside source for $36 per unit, plus $4 per unit for freight. Provide a differential analysis of the outside purchase proposal.

PE 9-3B
Make-or-buy decision
obj. 1

A restaurant bakes its own bread for $150 per unit (100 loaves), including fixed costs of $25 per unit. A proposal is offered to purchase bread from an outside source for $110 per unit, plus $10 per unit for delivery. Provide a differential analysis of the outside purchase proposal.

PE 9-4A
Replace equipment decision
obj. 1

A machine with a book value of $186,000 has an estimated six-year life. A proposal is offered to sell the old machine for $165,000 and replace it with a new machine at a cost of $320,000. The new machine has a six-year life with no salvage value. The new machine would reduce annual direct labor costs by $24,000. Provide a differential analysis on the proposal to replace the machine.

PE 9-4B
Replace equipment decision
obj. 1

A machine with a book value of $49,000 has an estimated five-year life. A proposal is offered to sell the old machine for $30,000 and replace it with a new machine at a cost of $64,000. The new machine has a five-year life with no salvage value. The new machine would reduce annual direct labor costs by $8,000. Provide a differential analysis on the proposal to replace the machine.

PE 9-5A
Process or sell decision
obj. 1

Product L is produced for $1.85 per gallon including a $0.90 per gallon fixed cost. Product L can be sold without additional processing for $2.20 per gallon, or processed further into Product P at an additional cost of $0.80 per gallon, including a $0.30 per gallon fixed cost. Product P can be sold for $2.80 per gallon. Provide a differential analysis for further processing into Product P.

PE 9-5B
Process or sell decision
obj. 1

Product X is produced for $24 per pound including a $9 per pound fixed cost. Product X can be sold without additional processing for $30 per pound, or processed further into Product Y at an additional cost of $5 per pound, including a $1.50 per pound fixed cost. Product Y can be sold for $33 per pound. Provide a differential analysis for further processing into Product Y.

PE 9-6A
Accept business at a special price
obj. 1

Product N is normally sold for $58 per unit. A special price of $45 is offered for the export market. The variable production cost is $31 per unit. An additional export tariff of 20% of revenue must be paid for all export products. Determine the differential income or loss per unit from selling Product N for export.

PE 9-6B
Accept business at a special price
obj. 1

Product S is normally sold for $13 per unit. A special price of $9 is offered for the export market. The variable production cost is $7 per unit. An additional export tariff of 30% of revenue must be paid for all export products. Determine the differential income or loss per unit from selling Product S for export.

PE 9-7A
Markup percentage on total cost
obj. 2

Green Thumb Inc. produces and sells home and garden tools and equipment. A lawn mower has a total cost of $140 per unit of which $110 is product cost and $30 is selling and administrative expenses. In addition, the total cost of $140 is made up of $125 variable cost and $15 fixed cost. The desired profit is $14 per unit. Determine the markup percentage on total cost.

PE 9-7B
Markup percentage on total cost
obj. 2

Nova Corp. produces and sells lighting fixtures. An entry light has a total cost of $50 per unit of which $36 is product cost and $14 is selling and administrative expenses. In addition, the total cost of $50 is made up of $30 variable cost and $20 fixed cost. The desired profit is $10 per unit. Determine the markup percentage on total cost.

PE 9-8A
Markup percentage on product cost
obj. 2

Green Thumb Inc. produces and sells home and garden tools and equipment. A lawn mower has a total cost of $140 per unit of which $110 is product cost and $30 is selling and administrative expenses. In addition, the total cost of $140 is made up of $125 variable cost and $15 fixed cost. The desired profit is $14 per unit. Determine the markup percentage on product cost.

PE 9-8B
Markup percentage on product cost
obj. 2

Nova Corp. produces and sells lighting fixtures. An entry light has a total cost of $50 per unit of which $36 is product cost and $14 is selling and administrative expenses. In addition, the total cost of $50 is made up of $30 variable cost and $20 fixed cost. The desired profit is $10 per unit. Determine the markup percentage on product cost. Round to one decimal place.

PE 9-9A
Markup percentage on variable cost
obj. 2

Green Thumb Inc. produces and sells home and garden tools and equipment. A lawn mower has a total cost of $140 per unit of which $110 is product cost and $30 is selling and administrative expenses. In addition, the total cost of $140 is made up of $125 variable cost and $15 fixed cost. The desired profit is $14 per unit. Determine the markup percentage on variable cost.

PE 9-9B
Markup percentage on variable cost
obj. 2

Nova Corp. produces and sells lighting fixtures. An entry light has a total cost of $50 per unit of which $36 is product cost and $14 is selling and administrative expenses. In addition, the total cost of $50 is made up of $30 variable cost and $20 fixed cost. The desired profit is $10 per unit. Determine the markup percentage on variable cost.

PE 9-10A
Bottleneck profitability
obj. 3

Product E has a unit contribution margin of $24. Product F has a unit contribution margin of $30. Product E requires three furnace hours, while Product F requires six furnace hours. Determine the most profitable product assuming the furnace is a constraint.

PE 9-10B
Bottleneck profitability
obj. 3

Product S has a unit contribution margin of $100. Product T has a unit contribution margin of $80. Product S requires 10 testing hours, while Product T requires four testing hours. Determine the most profitable product assuming the testing is a constraint.

Exercises

EX 9-1
Lease or sell decision
obj. 1

✓ a. Differential revenue from lease, $30,000

Vanderhoff Construction Company is considering selling excess machinery with a book value of $260,000 (original cost of $380,000 less accumulated depreciation of $120,000) for $210,000, less a 4% brokerage commission. Alternatively, the machinery can be leased for a total of $240,000 for five years, after which it is expected to have no residual value. During the period of the lease, Vanderhoff Construction Company's costs of repairs, insurance, and property tax expenses are expected to be $28,000.

a. Prepare a differential analysis report, dated January 3, 2008, for the lease or sell decision.
b. ▭▬➤ On the basis of the data presented, would it be advisable to lease or sell the machinery? Explain.

EX 9-2
Differential analysis report for a discontinued product
obj. 1

✓ a. Differential cost of annual sales, $299,400

A condensed income statement by product line for Canadian Beverage Inc. indicated the following for Lemon Mist for the past year:

Sales	$362,000
Cost of goods sold	185,000
Gross profit	$177,000
Operating expenses	215,000
Loss from operations	$ (38,000)

It is estimated that 23% of the cost of goods sold represents fixed factory overhead costs and that 27% of the operating expenses are fixed. Since Lemon Mist is only one of many products, the fixed costs will not be materially affected if the product is discontinued.

a. Prepare a differential analysis report, dated January 3, 2008, for the proposed discontinuance of Lemon Mist.
b. ▭▬➤ Should Lemon Mist be retained? Explain.

EX 9-3
Differential analysis report for a discontinued product
obj. 1

✓ a. Differential income: bowls, $46,450

The condensed product-line income statement for Country Ceramics Company for the current year is as follows:

Country Ceramics Company
Product-Line Income Statement
For the Year Ended December 31, 2008

	Bowls	Plates	Cups
Sales	$132,000	$108,000	$83,000
Cost of goods sold	71,000	55,000	49,000
Gross profit	$ 61,000	$ 53,000	$34,000
Selling and administrative expenses	35,000	24,000	38,000
Income from operations	$ 26,000	$ 29,000	$ (4,000)

(continued)

Fixed costs are 15% of the cost of goods sold and 28% of the selling and administrative expenses. Country Ceramics assumes that fixed costs would not be materially affected if the Cups line were discontinued.

a. Prepare a differential analysis report for all three products for 2008.
b. ▭▭▶ Should the Cups line be retained? Explain.

EX 9-4
Segment analysis, Charles Schwab Corporation
obj. 1

The Charles Schwab Corporation is one of the more innovative brokerage and financial service companies in the United States. The company recently provided information about its major business segments as follows (in millions):

	Individual Investor	Institutional Investor	U.S. Trust
Revenues	$2,742	$803	$832
Income from operations	758	317	103
Depreciation	145	29	33

a. ▭▭▶ How do you believe Schwab defines the difference between the "Individual Investor" and "Institutional Investor" segments?
b. Provide a specific example of a variable and fixed cost in the "Individual Investor" segment.
c. Estimate the contribution margin for each segment.
d. If Schwab decided to sell its "Institutional Investor" accounts to another company, estimate how much operating income would decline.

EX 9-5
Decision to discontinue a product
obj. 1

On the basis of the following data, the general manager of Feet to Go Inc. decided to discontinue Children's Shoes because it reduced income from operations by $26,000. What is the flaw in this decision?

Feet to Go Inc.
Product-Line Income Statement
For the Year Ended August 31, 2008

	Children's Shoes	Men's Shoes	Women's Shoes	Total
Sales	$150,000	$300,000	$500,000	$950,000
Costs of goods sold:				
Variable costs	$ 90,000	$150,000	$220,000	$460,000
Fixed costs	40,000	60,000	120,000	220,000
Total cost of goods sold	$130,000	$210,000	$340,000	$680,000
Gross profit	$ 20,000	$ 90,000	$160,000	$270,000
Selling and adminstrative expenses:				
Variable selling and admin. expenses	$ 30,000	$ 45,000	$ 95,000	$170,000
Fixed selling and admin. expenses	16,000	20,000	25,000	61,000
Total selling and admin. expenses	$ 46,000	$ 65,000	$120,000	$231,000
Income (loss) from operations	$ (26,000)	$ 25,000	$ 40,000	$ 39,000

EX 9-6
Make-or-buy decision
obj. 1

✓a. Cost savings from making, $3.00 per case

Hart Computer Company has been purchasing carrying cases for its portable computers at a delivered cost of $68 per unit. The company, which is currently operating below full capacity, charges factory overhead to production at the rate of 35% of direct labor cost. The fully absorbed unit costs to produce comparable carrying cases are expected to be:

Direct materials	$25.00
Direct labor	32.00
Factory overhead (35% of direct labor)	11.20
Total cost per unit	$68.20

If Hart Computer Company manufactures the carrying cases, fixed factory overhead costs will not increase and variable factory overhead costs associated with the cases are expected to be 25% of the direct labor costs.

a. Prepare a differential analysis report, dated June 5, 2008, for the make-or-buy decision.
b. ▭▭▶ On the basis of the data presented, would it be advisable to make the carrying cases or to continue buying them? Explain.

EX 9-7
Make-or-buy decision

obj. 1

The Association of Retired Educators (ARE) employs five people in its Publication Department. These people lay out pages for pamphlets, brochures, and other publications for the ARE membership. The pages are delivered to an outside company for printing. The company is considering an outside publication service for the layout work. The outside service is quoting a price of $18 per layout page. The budget for the Publication Department for 2008 is as follows:

Salaries	$225,000
Benefits	38,000
Supplies	32,000
Office expenses	25,000
Office depreciation	22,000
Computer depreciation	30,000
Total	$372,000

The department expects to lay out 17,500 pages for 2008. The computers used by the department have an estimated salvage value of $5,000. The Publication Department office space would be used for future administrative needs, if the department's function were purchased from the outside.

a. Prepare a differential analysis report, dated December 15, 2007, for the make-or-buy decision, considering the 2008 differential revenues and costs.
b. ▷ On the basis of your analysis in part (a), should the page layout work be purchased from an outside company?
c. ▷ What additional considerations might factor into the decision making?

EX 9-8
Machine replacement decision

obj. 1

✓ *a. Annual differential income, $12,250*

A company is considering replacing an old piece of machinery, which cost $560,000 and has $320,000 of accumulated depreciation to date, with a new machine that costs $460,000. The old equipment could be sold for $78,000. The variable production costs associated with the old machine are estimated to be $170,000 for eight years. The variable production costs for the new machine are estimated to be $110,000 for eight years.

a. Determine the total and annualized differential income or loss anticipated from replacing the old machine.
b. What is the sunk cost in this situation?

EX 9-9
Differential analysis report for machine replacement

obj. 1

✓ *a. Annual differential increase in costs, $2,500*

Bay Area Electronics Company assembles circuit boards by using a manually operated machine to insert electronic components. The original cost of the machine is $140,000, the accumulated depreciation is $110,000, its remaining useful life is 15 years, and its salvage value is negligible. On January 20, 2008, a proposal was made to replace the present manufacturing procedure with a fully automatic machine that will cost $270,000. The automatic machine has an estimated useful life of 15 years and no significant salvage value. For use in evaluating the proposal, the accountant accumulated the following annual data on present and proposed operations:

	Present Operations	Proposed Operations
Sales	$275,000	$275,000
Direct materials	$ 80,000	$ 80,000
Direct labor	45,000	—
Power and maintenance	7,500	32,000
Taxes, insurance, etc.	3,500	8,500
Selling and administrative expenses	80,000	80,000
Total expenses	$216,000	$200,500

a. Prepare a differential analysis report for the proposal to replace the machine. Include in the analysis both the net differential change in costs anticipated over the 15 years and the net annual differential change in costs anticipated.
b. Based only on the data presented, should the proposal be accepted?
c. ▷ What are some of the other factors that should be considered before a final decision is made?

EX 9-10

Sell or process further

obj. 1

✓ a. $225

Oregon Lumber Company incurs a cost of $465 per hundred board feet in processing certain "rough-cut" lumber, which it sells for $625 per hundred board feet. An alternative is to produce a "finished cut" at a total processing cost of $545 per hundred board feet, which can be sold for $850 per hundred board feet. What is the amount of (a) the differential revenue, (b) differential cost, and (c) differential income for processing rough-cut lumber into finished cut?

EX 9-11

Sell or process further

obj. 1

Golden Roast Coffee Company produces Columbian coffee in batches of 7,700 pounds. The standard quantity of materials required in the process is 7,700 pounds, which cost $5.00 per pound. Columbian coffee can be sold without further processing for $8.90 per pound. Columbian coffee can also be processed further to yield Decaf Columbian, which can be sold for $11.60 per pound. The processing into Decaf Columbian requires additional processing costs of $18,326 per batch. The additional processing will also cause a 6% loss of product due to evaporation.

a. Prepare a differential analysis report for the decision to sell or process further.
b. Should Golden Roast sell Columbian coffee or process further and sell Decaf Columbian?
c. Determine the price of Decaf Columbian that would cause neither an advantage or disadvantage for processing further and selling Decaf Columbian.

EX 9-12

Decision on accepting additional business

obj. 1

✓ a. Differential income, $112,000

Workman's Denim Co. has an annual plant capacity of 65,000 units, and current production is 45,000 units. Monthly fixed costs are $40,000, and variable costs are $24 per unit. The present selling price is $36 per unit. On January 18, 2008, the company received an offer from Marshall Company for 16,000 units of the product at $31 each. Marshall Company will market the units in a foreign country under its own brand name. The additional business is not expected to affect the domestic selling price or quantity of sales of Workman's Denim Co.

a. Prepare a differential analysis report for the proposed sale to Marshall Company.
b. ▇▇▇▶ Briefly explain the reason why accepting this additional business will increase operating income.
c. What is the minimum price per unit that would produce a contribution margin?

EX 9-13

Accepting business at a special price

obj. 1

Jupiter Company expects to operate at 90% of productive capacity during May. The total manufacturing costs for May for the production of 25,000 batteries are budgeted as follows:

Direct materials	$272,000
Direct labor	96,000
Variable factory overhead	32,000
Fixed factory overhead	54,000
Total manufacturing costs	$454,000

The company has an opportunity to submit a bid for 1,000 batteries to be delivered by May 31 to a government agency. If the contract is obtained, it is anticipated that the additional activity will not interfere with normal production during May or increase the selling or administrative expenses. What is the unit cost below which Jupiter Company should not go in bidding on the government contract?

EX 9-14

Decision on accepting additional business

obj. 1

✓ a. Differential revenue, $1,500,000

Sure-Grip Tire and Rubber Company has capacity to produce 170,000 tires. Sure-Grip presently produces and sells 130,000 tires for the North American market at a price of $90 per tire. Sure-Grip is evaluating a special order from a European automobile company, Continental Motors. Continental is offering to buy 25,000 tires for $60 per tire. Sure-Grip's accounting system indicates that the total cost per tire is as follows:

Direct materials	$26
Direct labor	9
Factory overhead (35% variable)	22
Selling and administrative expenses (40% variable)	18
Total	$75

Sure-Grip pays a selling commission equal to 5% of the selling price on North American orders, which is included in the variable portion of the selling and administrative expenses. However, this special order would not have a sales commission. If the order was accepted, the tires would be shipped overseas for an additional shipping cost of $6.00 per tire. In addition, Continental has made the order conditional on receiving European safety certification. Sure-Grip estimates that this certification would cost $110,000.

a. Prepare a differential analysis report dated August 4, 2008, for the proposed sale to Continental Motors.
b. What is the minimum price per unit that would be financially acceptable to Sure-Grip?

EX 9-15
Total cost concept of product costing

obj. 2

✓ d. $340

Sirrus Phone Company uses the total cost concept of applying the cost-plus approach to product pricing. The costs of producing and selling 3,500 units of mobile phones are as follows:

Variable costs:		Fixed costs:	
Direct materials	$130.00 per unit	Factory overhead	$175,000
Direct labor	50.00	Selling and adm. exp.	70,000
Factory overhead	35.00		
Selling and adm. exp.	25.00		
Total	$240.00 per unit		

Sirrus desires a profit equal to a 30% rate of return on invested assets of $350,000.

a. Determine the amount of desired profit from the production and sale of mobile phones.
b. Determine the total costs and the cost amount per unit for the production and sale of 3,500 units of mobile phones.
c. Determine the markup percentage (rounded to two decimal places) for mobile phones.
d. Determine the selling price of mobile phones. Round to the nearest dollar.

EX 9-16
Product cost concept of product pricing

obj. 2

✓ b. 28.30%

Based on the data presented in Exercise 9-15, assume that Sirrus Phone Company uses the product cost concept of applying the cost-plus approach to product pricing.

a. Determine the total manufacturing costs and the cost amount per unit for the production and sale of 3,500 units of mobile phones.
b. Determine the markup percentage (rounded to two decimal places) for mobile phones.
c. Determine the selling price of mobile phones. Round to the nearest dollar.

EX 9-17
Variable cost concept of product pricing

obj. 2

✓ b. 41.67%

Based on the data presented in Exercise 9-15, assume that Sirrus Phone Company uses the variable cost concept of applying the cost-plus approach to product pricing.

a. Determine the variable costs and the cost amount per unit for the production and sale of 3,500 units of mobile phones.
b. Determine the markup percentage (rounded to two decimal places) for mobile phones.
c. Determine the selling price of mobile phones. Round to the nearest dollar.

EX 9-18
Target costing

obj. 2

Toyota Motor Corporation uses target costing. Assume that Toyota marketing personnel estimate that the competitive selling price for the Camry in the upcoming model year will need to be $34,000. Assume further that the Camry's total manufacturing cost for the upcoming model year is estimated to be $28,500 and that Toyota requires a 20% profit margin on selling price (which is equivalent to a 25% markup on product cost).

a. What price will Toyota establish for the Camry for the upcoming model year?
b. ➤ What impact will target costing have on Toyota, given the assumed information?

EX 9-19
Target costing

obj. 2

✓ b. $25

Spectrum Imaging Company manufactures color laser printers. Model A200 presently sells for $300 and has a total product cost of $250, as follows:

(continued)

Direct materials	$170
Direct labor	50
Factory overhead	30
Total	$250

It is estimated that the competitive selling price for color laser printers of this type will drop to $270 next year. Spectrum Imaging has established a target cost to maintain its historical markup percentage on product cost. Engineers have provided the following cost reduction ideas:

1. Purchase a plastic printer cover with snap-on assembly. This will reduce the amount of direct labor by six minutes per unit.
2. Add an inspection step that will add three minutes per unit of direct labor but reduce the materials cost by $6 per unit.
3. Decrease the cycle time of the injection molding machine from four minutes to three minutes per part. Thirty percent of the direct labor and 42% of the factory overhead is related to running injection molding machines.

The direct labor rate is $32 per hour.

a. Determine the target cost for Model A200 assuming that the historical markup on product cost is maintained.
b. Determine the required cost reduction.
c. Evaluate the three engineering improvements to determine if the required cost reduction (drift) can be achieved.

EX 9-20
Product decisions under bottlenecked operations
obj. 3

Samson Metals Inc. has three grades of metal product, Type 5, Type 10, and Type 20. Financial data for the three grades are as follows:

	Type 5	Type 10	Type 20
Revenues	$16,000	$20,800	$12,000
Variable cost	$ 6,000	$ 8,000	$ 5,000
Fixed cost	4,000	4,000	4,000
Total cost	$10,000	$12,000	$ 9,000
Income from operations	$ 6,000	$ 8,800	$ 3,000
Number of units	/ 4,000	/ 4,000	/ 4,000
Income from operations per unit	$ 1.50	$ 2.20	$ 0.75

Samson's operations require all three grades to be melted in a furnace before being formed. The furnace runs 24 hours a day, 7 days a week, and is a production bottleneck. The furnace hours required per unit of each product are as follows:

Type 5:   5 hours
Type 10: 10 hours
Type 20:   5 hours

The Marketing Department is considering a new marketing and sales campaign.
Which product should be emphasized in the marketing and sales campaign in order to maximize profitability?

EX 9-21
Product decisions under bottlenecked operations
obj. 3

✓ a. Total income from operations, $115,000

Gannett Glass Company manufactures three types of safety plate glass: large, medium, and small. All three products have high demand. Thus, Gannett Glass is able to sell all the safety glass that it can make. The production process includes an autoclave operation, which is a pressurized heat treatment. The autoclave is a production bottleneck. Total fixed costs are $550,000. In addition, the following information is available about the three products:

	Large	Medium	Small
Unit selling price	$240	$180	$120
Unit variable cost	126	80	68
Unit contribution margin	$114	$100	$ 52

	Large	Medium	Small
Autoclave hours per unit	6	10	4
Total process hours per unit	20	16	12
Budgeted units of production	2,500	2,500	2,500

a. Determine the contribution margin by glass type and the total company income from operations for the budgeted units of production.

b. Prepare an analysis showing which product is the most profitable per bottleneck hour.

EX 9-22
Product pricing under bottlenecked operations
obj. **3**

✓ *Medium, $270*

Based on the data presented in Exercise 9-21, assume that Gannett Glass wanted to price all products so that they produced the same profit potential as the highest profit product. Thus, determine the prices for each of the products so that they would produce a profit equal to the highest profit product.

Problems Series A

PR 9-1A
Differential analysis report involving opportunity costs

obj. **1**

On July 1, Daybreak Stores Inc. is considering leasing a building and purchasing the necessary equipment to operate a retail store. Alternatively, the company could use the funds to invest in $280,000 of 5% U.S. Treasury bonds that mature in 20 years. The bonds could be purchased at face value. The following data have been assembled:

Cost of store equipment	$280,000
Life of store equipment	20 years
Estimated residual value of store equipment	$20,000
Yearly costs to operate the store, excluding depreciation of store equipment	$70,000
Yearly expected revenues—years 1–10	$88,000
Yearly expected revenues—years 11–20	$96,000

Instructions
1. Prepare a report as of July 1, 2008, presenting a differential analysis of the proposed operation of the store for the 20 years as compared with present conditions.
2. Based on the results disclosed by the differential analysis, should the proposal be accepted?
3. If the proposal is accepted, what would be the total estimated income from operations of the store for the 20 years?

PR 9-2A
Differential analysis report for machine replacement proposal

obj. **1**

Quebec Printing Company is considering replacing a machine that has been used in its factory for four years. Relevant data associated with the operations of the old machine and the new machine, neither of which has any estimated residual value, are as follows:

Old Machine

Cost of machine, 10-year life	$360,000
Annual depreciation (straight-line)	36,000
Annual manufacturing costs, excluding depreciation	325,000
Annual nonmanufacturing operating expenses	215,000
Annual revenue	740,000
Current estimated selling price of machine	210,000

New Machine

Cost of machine, 6-year life	$410,000
Annual depreciation (straight-line)	68,333
Estimated annual manufacturing costs, exclusive of depreciation	284,000

Annual nonmanufacturing operating expenses and revenue are not expected to be affected by purchase of the new machine.

Instructions

1. Prepare a differential analysis report as of October 13, 2008, comparing operations utilizing the new machine with operations using the present equipment. The analysis should indicate the total differential income that would result over the 6-year period if the new machine is acquired.
2. ◄▬▬► List other factors that should be considered before a final decision is reached.

PR 9-3A

Differential analysis report for sales promotion proposal

obj. **1**

✓ *1. Moisturizer differential income, $163,000*

Cleopatra Cosmetics Company is planning a one-month campaign for May to promote sales of one of its two cosmetics products. A total of $110,000 has been budgeted for advertising, contests, redeemable coupons, and other promotional activities. The following data have been assembled for their possible usefulness in deciding which of the products to select for the campaign:

	Moisturizer	Perfume
Unit selling price	$56	$75
Unit production costs:		
Direct materials	$10	$14
Direct labor	5	8
Variable factory overhead	3	5
Fixed factory overhead	8	8
Total unit production costs	$26	$35
Unit variable selling expenses	12	18
Unit fixed selling expenses	4	2
Total unit costs	$42	$55
Operating income per unit	$14	$20

No increase in facilities would be necessary to produce and sell the increased output. It is anticipated that 10,500 additional units of moisturizer or 8,000 additional units of perfume could be sold without changing the unit selling price of either product.

Instructions

1. Prepare a differential analysis report as of April 15, 2008, presenting the additional revenue and additional costs anticipated from the promotion of moisturizer and perfume.
2. ◄▬▬► The sales manager had tentatively decided to promote perfume, estimating that operating income would be increased by $50,000 ($20 operating income per unit for 8,000 units, less promotion expenses of $110,000). The manager also believed that the selection of moisturizer would have less of an impact on operating income, $37,000 ($14 operating income per unit for 10,500 units, less promotion expenses of $110,000). State briefly your reasons for supporting or opposing the tentative decision.

PR 9-4A

Differential analysis report for further processing

obj. **1**

✓ *1. Differential revenue, $9,800*

The management of Delta Sugar Company is considering whether to process further raw sugar into refined sugar. Refined sugar can be sold for $1.75 per pound, and raw sugar can be sold without further processing for $1.05 per pound. Raw sugar is produced in batches of 24,000 pounds by processing 90,000 pounds of sugar cane, which costs $0.25 per pound. Refined sugar will require additional processing costs of $0.36 per pound of raw sugar, and 1.2 pounds of raw sugar will produce 1 pound of refined sugar.

Instructions

1. Prepare a report as of August 30, 2008, presenting a differential analysis of the further processing of raw sugar to produce refined sugar.
2. ◄▬▬► Briefly report your recommendations.

PR 9-5A

Product pricing using the cost-plus approach concepts; differential analysis report for accepting additional business

objs. **1, 2**

Plasma Labs Inc. recently began production of a new product, flat panel displays, which required the investment of $3,000,000 in assets. The costs of producing and selling 20,000 units of flat panel displays are estimated as follows:

✓2. b. Markup
percentage, 6%

Variable costs per unit:		Fixed costs:	
Direct materials	$150	Factory overhead	$2,000,000
Direct labor	30	Selling and administrative expenses	1,000,000
Factory overhead	50		
Selling and administrative expenses	20		
Total	$250		

Plasma Labs Inc. is currently considering establishing a selling price for flat panel displays. The president of Plasma Labs has decided to use the cost-plus approach to product pricing and has indicated that the displays must earn a 16% rate of return on invested assets.

Instructions

1. Determine the amount of desired profit from the production and sale of flat panel displays.
2. Assuming that the total cost concept is used, determine (a) the cost amount per unit, (b) the markup percentage, and (c) the selling price of flat panel displays.
3. Assuming that the product cost concept is used, determine (a) the cost amount per unit, (b) the markup percentage (rounded to two decimal places), and (c) the selling price of flat panel displays (rounded to nearest whole dollar).
4. Assuming that the variable cost concept is used, determine (a) the cost amount per unit, (b) the markup percentage, and (c) the selling price of flat panel displays.
5. ━━━▶ Comment on any additional considerations that could influence establishing the selling price for flat panel displays.
6. Assume that as of September 1, 2008, 13,000 units of flat panel displays have been produced and sold during the current year. Analysis of the domestic market indicates that 4,400 additional units are expected to be sold during the remainder of the year at the normal product price determined under the total cost concept. On September 3, Plasma Labs Inc. received an offer from Vision Systems Inc. for 2,600 units of flat panel displays at $255 each. Vision Systems Inc. will market the units in Canada under its own brand name, and no selling and administrative expenses associated with the sale will be incurred by Plasma Labs Inc. The additional business is not expected to affect the domestic sales of flat panel displays, and the additional units could be produced using existing capacity.
   a. Prepare a differential analysis report of the proposed sale to Vision Systems Inc.
   b. Based upon the differential analysis report in part (a), should the proposal be accepted?

PR 9-6A
Product pricing and profit analysis with bottleneck operations

objs. **1, 3**

✓1. High Grade, $125

Atlas Steel Company produces three grades of steel: high, good, and regular grade. Each of these products (grades) has high demand in the market, and Atlas is able to sell as much as it can produce of all three. The furnace operation is a bottleneck in the process and is running at 100% of capacity. Atlas wants to improve steel operation profitability. The variable conversion cost is $6 per process hour. The fixed cost is $1,530,000. In addition, the cost analyst was able to determine the following information about the three products:

	High Grade	Good Grade	Regular Grade
Budgeted units produced	6,000	6,000	6,000
Total process hours per unit	15	15	12
Furnace hours per unit	5	3	2
Unit selling price	$375	$350	$320
Direct materials cost per unit	$160	$140	$130

The furnace operation is part of the total process for each of these three products. Thus, for example, 5 of the 15 hours required to process High Grade steel are associated with the furnace.

Instructions

1. Determine the unit contribution margin for each product.
2. Provide an analysis to determine the relative product profitabilities, assuming that the furnace is a bottleneck.
3. Assume that management wishes to improve profitability by increasing prices on selected products. At what price would High and Good grades need to be offered in order to produce the same relative profitability as Regular Grade steel?

Problems Series B

PR 9-1B
Differential analysis report involving opportunity costs

obj. 1

On December 1, Open Gate Distribution Company is considering leasing a building and buying the necessary equipment to operate a public warehouse. Alternatively, the company could use the funds to invest in $800,000 of 7% U.S. Treasury bonds that mature in 14 years. The bonds could be purchased at face value. The following data have been assembled:

Cost of equipment	$800,000
Life of equipment	14 years
Estimated residual value of equipment	$170,000
Yearly costs to operate the warehouse, excluding depreciation of equipment	$105,000
Yearly expected revenues—years 1–7	$250,000
Yearly expected revenues—years 8–14	$190,000

Instructions

1. Prepare a report as of December 1, 2008, presenting a differential analysis of the proposed operation of the warehouse for the 14 years as compared with present conditions.
2. Based on the results disclosed by the differential analysis, should the proposal be accepted?
3. If the proposal is accepted, what is the total estimated income from operations of the warehouse for the 14 years?

PR 9-2B
Differential analysis report for machine replacement proposal

obj. 1

Saginaw Tooling Company is considering replacing a machine that has been used in its factory for two years. Relevant data associated with the operations of the old machine and the new machine, neither of which has any estimated residual value, are as follows:

Old Machine	
Cost of machine, 8-year life	$ 96,000
Annual depreciation (straight-line)	12,000
Annual manufacturing costs, excluding depreciation	26,000
Annual nonmanufacturing operating expenses	9,500
Annual revenue	45,000
Current estimated selling price of the machine	58,000

New Machine	
Cost of machine, 6-year life	$126,000
Annual depreciation (straight-line)	21,000
Estimated annual manufacturing costs, exclusive of depreciation	9,000

Annual nonmanufacturing operating expenses and revenue are not expected to be affected by purchase of the new machine.

Instructions

1. Prepare a differential analysis report as of March 22, 2008, comparing operations utilizing the new machine with operations using the present equipment. The analysis should indicate the differential income that would result over the 6-year period if the new machine is acquired.
2. ▭▭▭▶ List other factors that should be considered before a final decision is reached.

PR 9-3B
Differential analysis report for sales promotion proposal

obj. 1

Mercury Athletic Shoe Company is planning a one-month campaign for April to promote sales of one of its two shoe products. A total of $125,000 has been budgeted for advertising, contests, redeemable coupons, and other promotional activities. The following data have been assembled for their possible usefulness in deciding which of the products to select for the campaign.

✔ 1. Differential income,
tennis shoe, $195,000

	Tennis Shoe	Walking Shoe
Unit selling price	$112	$98
Unit production costs:		
Direct materials	$ 22	$17
Direct labor	12	10
Variable factory overhead	5	7
Fixed factory overhead	9	12
Total unit production costs	$ 48	$46
Unit variable selling expenses	9	12
Unit fixed selling expenses	12	16
Total unit costs	$ 69	$74
Operating income per unit	$ 43	$24

No increase in facilities would be necessary to produce and sell the increased output. It is anticipated that 5,000 additional units of tennis shoes or 7,500 additional units of walking shoes could be sold without changing the unit selling price of either product.

Instructions
1. Prepare a differential analysis report as of March 13, 2008, presenting the additional revenue and additional costs anticipated from the promotion of tennis shoes and walking shoes.
2. ▭▭▭➤ The sales manager had tentatively decided to promote tennis shoes, estimating that operating income would be increased by $90,000 ($43 operating income per unit for 5,000 units, less promotion expenses of $125,000). The manager also believed that the selection of walking shoes would increase operating income by $55,000 ($24 operating income per unit for 7,500 units, less promotion expenses of $125,000). State briefly your reasons for supporting or opposing the tentative decision.

PR 9-4B
Differential analysis report for further processing
obj. 1

✔ 1. Differential revenue, $23,700

The management of Pittsburgh Aluminum Co. is considering whether to process aluminum ingot further into rolled aluminum. Rolled aluminum can be sold for $1,650 per ton, and ingot can be sold without further processing for $980 per ton. Ingot is produced in batches of 60 tons by smelting 400 tons of bauxite, which costs $450 per ton. Rolled aluminum will require additional processing costs of $415 per ton of ingot, and 1.2 tons of ingot will produce 1 ton of rolled aluminum.

Instructions
1. Prepare a report as of December 20, 2008, presenting a differential analysis associated with the further processing of aluminum ingot to produce rolled aluminum.
2. ▭▭▭➤ Briefly report your recommendations.

PR 9-5B
Product pricing using the cost-plus approach concepts; differential analysis report for accepting additional business
objs. 1, 2

✔ 3. b. Markup percentage, 25%

Stay Glow Company recently began production of a new product, the halogen light, which required the investment of $1,000,000 in assets. The costs of producing and selling 18,000 halogen lights are estimated as follows:

Variable costs per unit:		Fixed costs:	
Direct materials	$23.00	Factory overhead	$216,000
Direct labor	12.00	Selling and administrative expenses	54,000
Factory overhead	5.00		
Selling and administrative expenses	5.00		
Total	$45.00		

Stay Glow Company is currently considering establishing a selling price for the halogen light. The president of Stay Glow Company has decided to use the cost-plus approach to product pricing and has indicated that the halogen light must earn a 9% rate of return on invested assets.

Instructions
1. Determine the amount of desired profit from the production and sale of the halogen light.

(continued)

2. Assuming that the total cost concept is used, determine (a) the cost amount per unit, (b) the markup percentage (rounded to two decimal places), and (c) the selling price of the halogen light (rounded to nearest whole dollar).
3. Assuming that the product cost concept is used, determine (a) the cost amount per unit, (b) the markup percentage, and (c) the selling price of the halogen light.
4. Assuming that the variable cost concept is used, determine (a) the cost amount per unit, (b) the markup percentage (rounded to two decimal places), and (c) the selling price of the halogen light (rounded to nearest whole dollar).
5. ▭▬▶ Comment on any additional considerations that could influence establishing the selling price for the halogen light.
6. Assume that as of June 1, 2008, 7,000 units of halogen light have been produced and sold during the current year. Analysis of the domestic market indicates that 9,000 additional units of the halogen light are expected to be sold during the remainder of the year at the normal product price determined under the total cost concept. On June 5, Stay Glow Company received an offer from Night Light Inc. for 2,000 units of the halogen light at $46 each. Night Light Inc. will market the units in Japan under its own brand name, and no selling and administrative expenses associated with the sale will be incurred by Stay Glow Company. The additional business is not expected to affect the domestic sales of the halogen light, and the additional units could be produced using existing capacity.
    a. Prepare a differential analysis report of the proposed sale to Night Light Inc.
    b. Based upon the differential analysis report in part (a), should the proposal be accepted?

PR 9-6B
Product pricing and profit analysis with bottleneck operations

objs. 1, 3

✓1. Ethylene, $34

Gulf Coast Chemical Company produces three products: ethylene, butane, and ester. Each of these products has high demand in the market, and Gulf Coast Chemical is able to sell as much as it can produce of all three. The reaction operation is a bottleneck in the process and is running at 100% of capacity. Gulf Coast wants to improve chemical operation profitability. The variable conversion cost is $8 per process hour. The fixed cost is $990,000. In addition, the cost analyst was able to determine the following information about the three products:

	Ethylene	Butane	Ester
Budgeted units produced	18,000	18,000	18,000
Total process hours per unit	3	3	2
Reactor hours per unit	0.8	0.5	0.4
Unit selling price	$168	$128	$115
Direct materials cost per unit	$110	$75	$85

The reaction operation is part of the total process for each of these three products. Thus, for example, 0.8 of the 3 hours required to process Ethylene are associated with the reactor.

Instructions
1. Determine the unit contribution margin for each product.
2. Provide an analysis to determine the relative product profitabilities, assuming that the reactor is a bottleneck.
3. Assume that management wishes to improve profitability by increasing prices on selected products. At what price would Ethylene and Ester need to be offered in order to produce the same relative profitability as Butane?

Special Activities

SA 9-1
Product pricing

ETHICS

Marcia Martinez is a cost accountant for Ascend Inc. Marcus Todd, vice president of marketing, has asked Marcia to meet with representatives of Ascend's major competitor to discuss product cost data. Marcus indicates that the sharing of these data will enable Ascend to determine a fair and equitable price for its products.
▭▬▶ Would it be ethical for Marcia to attend the meeting and share the relevant cost data?

SA 9-2
Decision on accepting additional business

A manager of Back Tee Sporting Goods Company is considering accepting an order from an overseas customer. This customer has requested an order for 20,000 dozen golf balls at a price of $20.00 per dozen. The variable cost to manufacture a dozen golf balls is $17.00 per dozen. The full cost is $23.00 per dozen. Back Tee has a normal selling price of $28.00 per dozen. Back Tee's plant has just enough excess capacity on the second shift to make the overseas order.

➤ What are some considerations in accepting or rejecting this order?

SA 9-3
Accept business at a special price

Internet Project

If you are not familiar with Priceline.com Inc., go to its Web site. Assume that an individual bids $60 on Priceline.com for a room in Dallas, Texas, on August 24. Assume that August 24 is a Saturday, with low expected room demand in Dallas at a Marriott International, Inc., hotel, so there is excess room capacity. The fully allocated cost per room per day is assumed from hotel records as follows:

Housekeeping labor cost*	$30
Hotel depreciation expense	42
Cost of room supplies (soap, paper, etc.)	5
Laundry labor and material cost*	10
Cost of desk staff	5
Utility cost (mostly air conditioning)	3
Total cost per room per day	$95

*Both housekeeping and laundry staff include many part-time workers, so that the workload is variable to demand.

➤ Should Marriott accept the customer bid for a night in Dallas on August 24 at a price of $60?

SA 9-4
Make-or-buy decision

The president of Monarch Materials Inc., Todd Bentley, asked the controller, Megan Mayfield, to provide an analysis of a make vs. buy decision for material TS-101. The material is presently processed in Monarch's Roanoke facility. TS-101 is used in processing of final products in the facility. Megan determined the following unit production costs for the material as of March 15, 2008:

Direct materials	$ 7.50
Direct labor	2.70
Variable factory overhead	1.20
Fixed factory overhead	2.00
Total production costs per unit	$13.40

In addition, material TS-101 requires special hazardous material handling. This special handling adds an additional cost of $1.60 for each unit produced.

Material TS-101 can be purchased from an overseas supplier. The supplier does not presently do business with Monarch Materials. This supplier promises monthly delivery of the material at a price of $10.10 per unit, plus transportation cost of $0.40 per unit. In addition, Monarch would need to incur additional administrative costs to satisfy import regulations for hazardous material. These additional administrative costs are estimated to be $0.80 per purchased unit. Each purchased unit would also require special hazardous material handling of $1.60 per unit.

a. Prepare a differential analysis report to support Megan's recommendation on whether to continue making material TS-101 or whether to purchase the material from the overseas supplier.
b. What additional considerations should Megan address in the recommendation?

SA 9-5
Cost-plus and target costing concepts

The following conversation took place between Theo James, vice president of marketing, and Lee Corso, controller of Astor Computer Company:

Theo: I am really excited about our new computer coming out. I think it will be a real market success.
Lee: I'm really glad you think so. I know that our price is one variable that will determine if it's a success. If our price is too high, our competitors will be the ones with the market success.

Theo: Don't worry about it. We'll just mark our product cost up by 25% and it will all work out. I know we'll make money at those markups. By the way, what does the estimated product cost look like?

Lee: Well, there's the rub. The product cost looks as if it's going to come in at around $2,400. With a 25% markup, that will give us a selling price of $3,000.

Theo: I see your concern. That's a little high. Our research indicates that computer prices are dropping by about 20% per year and that this type of computer should be selling for around $2,500 when we release it to the market.

Lee: I'm not sure what to do.

Theo: Let me see if I can help. How much of the $2,400 is fixed cost?

Lee: About $400.

Theo: There you go. The fixed cost is sunk. We don't need to consider it in our pricing decision. If we reduce the product cost by $400, the new price with a 25% markup would be right at $2,500. Boy, I was really worried for a minute there. I knew something wasn't right.

a. If you were Lee, how would you respond to Theo's solution to the pricing problem?
b. How might target costing be used to help solve this pricing dilemma?

SA 9-6
Pricing decisions and markup on variable costs

REAL WORLD

Internet Project

Group Project

Many businesses are offering their products and services over the Internet. Some of these companies and their Internet addresses are listed below.

Company Name	Internet Address (URL)	Product
Delta Air Lines	http://www.delta.com	airline tickets
Amazon.com	http://www.amazon.com	books
Dell Inc.	http://www.dell.com	personal computers

a. In groups of three, assign each person in your group to one of the Internet sites listed above. For each site, determine the following:
1. A product (or service) description.
2. A product price.
3. A list of costs that are required to produce and sell the product selected in part (1) as listed in the annual report on SEC form 10-K.
4. Whether the costs identified in part (3) are fixed costs or variable costs.
b. Which of the three products do you believe has the largest markup on variable cost?

Answers to Self-Examination Questions

1. **A** Differential cost is the amount of increase or decrease in cost that is expected from a particular course of action compared with an alternative. For Marlo Company, the differential cost is $19,000 (answer A). This is the total of the variable product costs ($15,000) and the variable operating expenses ($4,000), which would not be incurred if the product is discontinued.

2. **A** A sunk cost is not affected by later decisions. For Victor Company, the sunk cost is the $50,000 (answer A) book value of the equipment, which is equal to the original cost of $200,000 (answer C) less the accumulated depreciation of $150,000 (answer B).

3. **C** The amount of income that could have been earned from the best available alternative to a proposed use of cash is the opportunity cost. For Henry Company, the opportunity cost is 12% of $100,000, or $12,000 (answer C).

4. **C** Under the variable cost concept of product pricing (answer C), fixed manufacturing costs, fixed administrative and selling expenses, and desired profit are allowed for in determining the markup. Only desired profit is allowed for in the markup under the total cost concept (answer A). Under the product cost concept (answer B), total selling and administrative expenses and desired profit are allowed for in determining the markup. Standard cost (answer D) can be used under any of the cost-plus approaches to product pricing.

5. **C** Product 3 has the highest unit contribution margin per bottleneck hour ($14/2 = $7). Product 1 (answer A) has the largest unit contribution margin, but the lowest unit contribution per bottleneck hour ($20/4 = $5), so it is the least profitable product in the constrained environment. Product 2 (answer B) has the highest total profitability in March (1,500 units × $18), but this does not suggest that it has the highest profit potential. Product 2's unit contribution per bottleneck hour ($18/3 = $6) is between Products 1 and 3. Answer D is not true, since the products all have different profit potential in terms of unit contribution margin per bottleneck hour.

chapter 10

Capital Investment Analysis

© XM SATELLITE RADIO/PRNEWSFOTO (AP TOPIC GALLERY)

objectives

After studying this chapter, you should be able to:

1 *Explain the nature and importance of capital investment analysis.*

2 *Evaluate capital investment proposals, using the following methods: average rate of return, cash payback, net present value, and internal rate of return.*

3 *List and describe factors that complicate capital investment analysis.*

4 *Diagram the capital rationing process.*

XM Satellite Radio

Why are you paying tuition, studying this text, and spending time and money on a higher education? Most people believe that the money and time spent now will return them more earnings in the future. In other words, the cost of higher education is an investment in your future earning ability. How would you know if this investment is worth it?

One method would be for you to compare the cost of a higher education against the estimated increase in your future earning power. The more your future increased earnings exceed the investment, the more attractive the investment. As you will see in this chapter, the same is true for business investments in fixed assets. Business organizations analyze potential capital investments by using various methods that compare investment costs to future earnings and cash flows.

For example, XM Satellite Radio provides access to music, sports, and special feature radio programming from anywhere in the United States using satel-lite technology. XM's spacecraft system required an investment of over $600 million. XM Satellite Radio used capital investment analysis to compare this investment with the future earnings ability of this system over its 17-year expected life. XM must be satisfied with its investments, because it will be launching several more satellites during the end of this decade.

In this chapter, we will describe analyses useful for making investment decisions, which may involve thousands, millions, or even billions of dollars. We will emphasize the similarities and differences among the most commonly used methods of evaluating investment proposals, as well as the uses of each method. We will also discuss qualitative considerations affecting investment analyses. Finally, we will discuss considerations complicating investment analyses and the process of allocating available investment funds among competing proposals.

Nature of Capital Investment Analysis

objective **1**

Explain the nature and importance of capital investment analysis.

How do companies decide to make significant investments such as the following?

■ Yum! Brands, Inc., adds 375 new international Taco Bell, Pizza Hut, and KFC units.

■ The Walt Disney Company commits to investing $315 million to build a new theme park in Hong Kong.

■ XM Satellite Radio commits to launching its fourth and fifth satellites at a cost of over $300 million by the end of 2007.

Companies use capital investment analysis to help evaluate long-term investments. **Capital investment analysis** (or *capital budgeting*) is the process by which management plans, evaluates, and controls investments in fixed assets. Capital investments involve the long-term commitment of funds and affect operations for many years. Thus, these investments must earn a reasonable rate of return, so that the business can meet its obligations to creditors and provide dividends to stockholders. Because capital investment decisions are some of the most important decisions that management makes, capital investment analysis must be carefully developed and implemented.

A capital investment program should encourage employees to submit proposals for capital investments. It should communicate to employees the long-range goals of the business, so that useful proposals are submitted. All reasonable proposals should be considered and evaluated with respect to economic costs and benefits. The program may reward employees whose proposals are accepted.

Methods of Evaluating Capital Investment Proposals

objective **2**

Evaluate capital investment proposals, using the following methods: average rate of return, cash payback, net present value, and internal rate of return.

Capital investment evaluation methods can be grouped into the following two categories:

1. Methods that do not use present values
2. Methods that use present values

Two methods that do not use present values are (1) the average rate of return method and (2) the cash payback method. Two methods that use present values are (1) the net present value method and (2) the internal rate of return method. These methods consider the time value of money. The **time value of money concept** recognizes that an amount of cash invested today will earn income and therefore has value over time.

Management often uses a combination of methods in evaluating capital investment proposals. Each method has advantages and disadvantages. In addition, some of the computations are complex. Computers, however, can perform the computations quickly and easily. Computers can also be used to analyze the impact of changes in key estimates in evaluating capital investment proposals.

METHODS THAT IGNORE PRESENT VALUE

The average rate of return and the cash payback methods are easy to use. These methods are often initially used to screen proposals. Management normally sets minimum standards for accepting proposals, and those not meeting these standards are dropped from further consideration. If a proposal meets the minimum standards, it is often subject to further analysis.

The methods that ignore present value are often useful in evaluating capital investment proposals that have relatively short useful lives. In such cases, the timing of the cash flows is less important.

Average Rate of Return Method The **average rate of return**, sometimes called the *accounting rate of return*, is a measure of the average income as a percent of the average investment in fixed assets. The average rate of return is determined by using the following equation:

A CFO survey of capital investment analysis methods used by large U.S. companies reported the following:

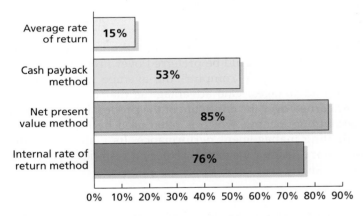

Percentage of Respondents Reporting the Use of the Method as "Always" or "Often"

Average rate of return: 15%
Cash payback method: 53%
Net present value method: 85%
Internal rate of return method: 76%

Source: Patricia A. Ryan and Glenn P. Ryan, "Capital Budgeting Practices of the Fortune 1000: How Have Things Changed?" *Journal of Business and Management* (Winter 2002).

$$\text{Average Rate of Return} = \frac{\text{Estimated Average Annual Income}}{\text{Average Investment}}$$

The numerator is the average of the annual income expected to be earned from the investment over the investment life, after deducting depreciation. The denominator is the average book value over the investment life. Thus, if straight-line depreciation and no residual value are assumed, the average investment over the useful life is equal to one-half of the original cost.[1]

---

1 The average investment is the midpoint of the depreciable cost of the asset. Since a fixed asset is never depreciated below its residual value, this midpoint is determined by adding the original cost of the asset to the estimated residual value and dividing by 2.

To illustrate, assume that management is considering the purchase of a machine at a cost of $500,000. The machine is expected to have a useful life of four years, with no residual value, and to yield total income of $200,000. The estimated average annual income is therefore $50,000 ($200,000/4), and the average investment is $250,000 [($500,000 + $0 residual value)/2]. Thus, the average rate of return on the average investment is 20%, computed as follows:

$$\text{Average Rate of Return} = \frac{\text{Estimated Average Annual Income}}{\text{Average Investment}}$$

$$\text{Average Rate of Return} = \frac{\$200,000/4}{(\$500,000 + \$0)/2} = 20\%$$

The average rate of return of 20% should be compared with the minimum rate for such investments. If the average rate of return equals or exceeds the minimum rate, the machine should be purchased.

When several capital investment proposals are considered, the proposals can be ranked by their average rates of return. The higher the average rate of return, the more desirable the proposal. For example, assume that management is considering two capital investment proposals and has computed the following average rates of return:

	Proposal A	Proposal B
Estimated average annual income	$ 30,000	$ 36,000
Average investment	$120,000	$180,000
Average rate of return:		
$30,000/$120,000	25%	
$36,000/$180,000		20%

If only the average rate of return is considered, Proposal A, with an average rate of return of 25%, would be preferred over Proposal B.

In addition to being easy to compute, the average rate of return method has several advantages. One advantage is that it includes the amount of income earned over the entire life of the proposal. In addition, it emphasizes accounting income, which is often used by investors and creditors in evaluating management performance. Its main disadvantage is that it does not directly consider the expected cash flows from the proposal and the timing of these cash flows.

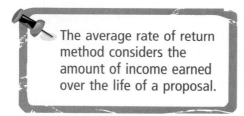

The average rate of return method considers the amount of income earned over the life of a proposal.

Example Exercise 10-1   objective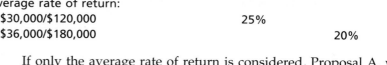

Determine the average rate of return for a project that is estimated to yield total income of $273,600 over three years, has a cost of $690,000, and has a $70,000 residual value.

Follow My Example 10-1

Estimated average annual income $91,200 ($273,600/3 years)
Average investment $380,000 ($690,000 + $70,000)/2
Average rate of return   24% ($91,200/$380,000)

For Practice: PE 10-1A, PE 10-1B

Cash Payback Method   Cash flows are important because cash can be reinvested. Very simply, the capital investment uses cash and must therefore return cash in the future in order to be successful.

The expected period of time that will pass between the date of an investment and the complete recovery in cash (or equivalent) of the amount invested is the **cash payback period**. To simplify the analysis, the revenues and expenses other than depreciation related to operating fixed assets are assumed to be all in the form of cash. The excess of the cash flowing in from revenue over the cash flowing out for expenses is termed *net cash flow*. The time required for the net cash flow to equal the initial outlay for the fixed asset is the payback period.

To illustrate, assume that the proposed investment in a fixed asset with an eight-year life is $200,000. The annual cash revenues from the investment are $50,000, and the annual cash expenses are $10,000. Thus, the annual net cash flow is expected to be $40,000 ($50,000 − $10,000). The estimated cash payback period for the investment is five years, computed as follows:

$$\frac{\$200,000}{\$40,000} = 5\text{-year cash payback period}$$

In this illustration, the annual net cash flows are equal ($40,000 per year). If these annual net cash flows are *not* equal, the cash payback period is determined by adding the annual net cash flows until the cumulative sum equals the amount of the proposed investment. To illustrate, assume that for a proposed investment of $400,000, the annual net cash flows and the cumulative net cash flows over the proposal's six-year life are as follows:

Year	Net Cash Flow	Cumulative Net Cash Flow
1	$ 60,000	$ 60,000
2	80,000	140,000
3	105,000	245,000
4	155,000	400,000
5	100,000	500,000
6	90,000	590,000

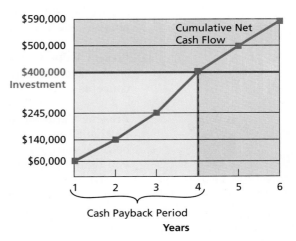

The cumulative net cash flow at the end of the fourth year equals the amount of the investment, $400,000. Thus, the payback period is four years.

If the amount of the proposed investment had been $450,000, the cash payback period would occur during the fifth year. Since $100,000 of net cash flow is expected during the fifth year, the additional $50,000 needed to cover the total investment of $450,000 would occur approximately half way through the fifth year ($50,000/$100,000). Thus, the cash payback period would be 4½ years.[2]

The cash payback method is widely used in evaluating proposals for investments in new projects. A short payback period is desirable, because the sooner the cash is recovered, the sooner it becomes available for reinvestment in other projects. In addition, there is less possibility of losses from economic conditions, out-of-date assets, and other unavoidable risks when the payback period is short. The cash payback period is also important to bankers and other creditors who may be depending upon net cash flow for repaying debt related to the capital investment. The sooner the cash is recovered, the sooner the debt or other liabilities can be paid. Thus, the cash payback method is especially useful to managers whose primary concern is liquidity.

One of the disadvantages of the cash payback method is that it ignores cash flows occurring after the payback period. In addition, the cash payback method does not use present value concepts in valuing cash flows occurring in different periods. In the next section, we will review present value concepts and introduce capital investment methods that use present value.

---

2 Unless otherwise stated, we assume that the net cash flows are received uniformly throughout the year.

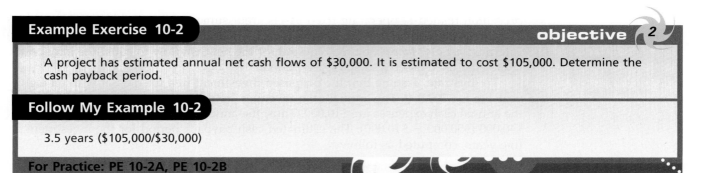

Example Exercise 10-2

objective 2

A project has estimated annual net cash flows of $30,000. It is estimated to cost $105,000. Determine the cash payback period.

Follow My Example 10-2

3.5 years ($105,000/$30,000)

For Practice: PE 10-2A, PE 10-2B

PRESENT VALUE METHODS

An investment in fixed assets may be viewed as acquiring a series of net cash flows over a period of time. The period of time over which these net cash flows will be received may be an important factor in determining the value of an investment. Present value methods use both the amount and the timing of net cash flows in evaluating an investment. Before illustrating how these methods are used in capital investment analysis, we will review basic present value concepts.[3]

Present Value Concepts   **Present value concepts** can be divided into the *present value of an amount* and the *present value of an annuity*. We describe and illustrate these two concepts next.

Present value concepts can also be used to evaluate personal finances. For example, the Heritage Foundation compared the present value of social security contributions of a 35-year-old average earner with the present value of social security benefits. Using an interest rate of 6%, the present value of the social security benefits is $300,000 less than the present value of the contributions. For a younger worker or a higher-salary earner, the difference is even greater.

Present Value of an Amount   If you were given the choice, would you prefer to receive $1 now or $1 three years from now? You should prefer to receive $1 now, because you could invest the $1 and earn interest for three years. As a result, the amount you would have after three years would be greater than $1.

To illustrate, assume that on January 1, 2008, you invest $1 in an account that earns 12% interest compounded annually. After one year, the $1 will grow to $1.12 ($1 × 1.12), because interest of 12¢ is added to the investment. The $1.12 earns 12% interest for the second year. Interest earning interest is called *compounding*. By the end of the second year, the investment has grown to $1.254 ($1.12 × 1.12). By the end of the third year, the investment has grown to $1.404 ($1.254 × 1.12). Thus, if money is worth 12%, you would be equally satisfied with $1 on January 1, 2008, or $1.404 three years later.

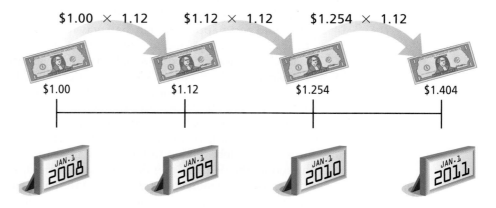

On January 1, 2008, what is the present value of $1.404 to be received on January 1, 2011? This is a present value question. The answer can be determined with the aid

---

3 Present value calculations were introduced in financial accounting courses in accounting for bond liabilities. Present value concepts are developed again here in order to reinforce that introduction.

of a present value of $1 table. For example, the partial table in Exhibit 1 indicates that the present value of $1 to be received three years hence, with earnings compounded at the rate of 12% a year, is 0.712. Multiplying 0.712 by $1.404 yields $1, which is the present value that started the compounding process.[4]

EXHIBIT 1

Partial Present Value of $1 Table

		Present Value of $1 at Compound Interest			
Year	6%	10%	12%	15%	20%
1	0.943	0.909	0.893	0.870	0.833
2	0.890	0.826	0.797	0.756	0.694
3	0.840	0.751	**0.712**	0.658	0.579
4	0.792	0.683	0.636	0.572	0.482
5	0.747	0.621	0.567	0.497	0.402
6	0.705	0.564	0.507	0.432	0.335
7	0.665	0.513	0.452	0.376	0.279
8	0.627	0.467	0.404	0.327	0.233
9	0.592	0.424	0.361	0.284	0.194
10	0.558	0.386	0.322	0.247	0.162

Present Value of an Annuity An **annuity** is a series of equal net cash flows at fixed time intervals. Annuities are very common in business. For example, monthly rental, salary, and bond interest cash flows are all examples of annuities. The **present value of an annuity** is the sum of the present values of each cash flow. That is, the present value of an annuity is the amount of cash that is needed today to yield a series of equal net cash flows at fixed time intervals in the future.

To illustrate, the present value of a $100 annuity for five periods at 12% could be determined by using the present value factors in Exhibit 1. Each $100 net cash flow could be multiplied by the present value of $1 at 12% factor for the appropriate period and summed to determine a present value of $360.50, as shown in the following timeline:

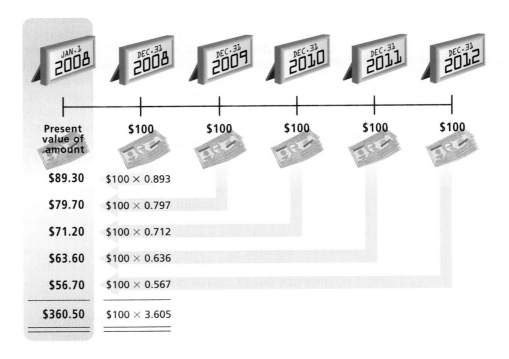

4 The present value factors in the table are rounded to three decimal places. More complete tables of present values are in Appendix A.

Using a present value of an annuity table is a simpler approach. Exhibit 2 is a partial table of present value of annuity factors.[5] These factors are merely the sum of the present value of $1 factors in Exhibit 1 for the number of annuity periods. Thus, 3.605 in the annuity table (Exhibit 2) is the sum of the five individual present value of $1 factors at 12%. Multiplying $100 by 3.605 yields the same amount ($360.50) that was determined in the preceding illustration by five successive multiplications.

EXHIBIT 2

Partial Present Value of an Annuity Table

	Present Value of an Annuity of $1 at Compound Interest				
Year	6%	10%	12%	15%	20%
1	0.943	0.909	0.893	0.870	0.833
2	1.833	1.736	1.690	1.626	1.528
3	2.673	2.487	2.402	2.283	2.106
4	3.465	3.170	3.037	2.855	2.589
5	4.212	3.791	3.605	3.353	2.991
6	4.917	4.355	4.111	3.785	3.326
7	5.582	4.868	4.564	4.160	3.605
8	6.210	5.335	4.968	4.487	3.837
9	6.802	5.759	5.328	4.772	4.031
10	7.360	6.145	5.650	5.019	4.192

A 55-year-old janitor won a $5 million lottery jackpot, payable in 21 annual installments of $240,245. Unfortunately, the janitor died after collecting only one payment. What happens to the remaining unclaimed payments? In this case, the lottery winnings were auctioned off for the benefit of the janitor's estate. The winning bid approximated the present value of the remaining cash flows, or about $2.1 million.

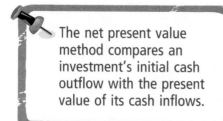

The net present value method compares an investment's initial cash outflow with the present value of its cash inflows.

Net Present Value Method   The **net present value method** analyzes capital investment proposals by comparing the initial cash investment with the present value of the net cash flows. It is sometimes called the *discounted cash flow method*. The interest rate (return) used in net present value analysis is the minimum desired rate of return set by management. This rate, sometimes termed the *hurdle rate*, is often based upon such factors as the nature of the business, the purpose of the investment, and the cost of securing funds for the investment. If the net present value of the cash flows expected from a proposed investment equals or exceeds the amount of the initial investment, the proposal is desirable.

To illustrate, assume a proposal to acquire $200,000 of equipment with an expected useful life of five years (no residual value) and a minimum desired rate of return of 10%. The present value of the net cash flow for each year is computed by multiplying the net cash flow for the year by the present value factor of $1 for that year. For example, the $70,000 net cash flow to be received on December 31, 2008, is multiplied by the present value of $1 for one year at 10% (0.909). Thus, the present value of the $70,000 is $63,630. Likewise, the $60,000 net cash flow on December 31, 2009, is multiplied by the present value of $1 for two years at 10% (0.826) to yield $49,560, and so on. The amount to be invested, $200,000, is then subtracted from the total present value of the net cash flows, $202,900, to determine the net present value, $2,900, as shown at the top of the following page. The net present value indicates that the proposal is expected to recover the investment and provide more than the minimum rate of return of 10%.

When capital investment funds are limited and the alternative proposals involve different amounts of investment, it is useful to prepare a ranking of the proposals by using a present value index. The **present value index** is calculated by dividing the total present value of the net cash flow by the amount to be invested. The present value index for the investment in the previous illustration is calculated as follows:

$$\text{Present Value Index} = \frac{\text{Total Present Value of Net Cash Flow}}{\text{Amount to Be Invested}}$$

$$= \frac{\$202,900}{\$200,000} = 1.0145$$

5 Expanded tables for the present value of an annuity are in Appendix A.

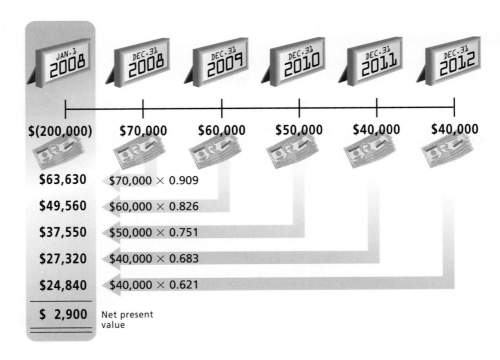

$(200,000) $70,000 $60,000 $50,000 $40,000 $40,000

$63,630 $70,000 × 0.909

$49,560 $60,000 × 0.826

$37,550 $50,000 × 0.751

$27,320 $40,000 × 0.683

$24,840 $40,000 × 0.621

$ 2,900   Net present value

If a business is considering three alternative proposals and has determined their net present values, the present value index for each proposal is as follows:

	Proposal A	Proposal B	Proposal C
Total present value of net cash flow ..	$107,000	$86,400	$86,400
Amount to be invested	100,000	80,000	90,000
Net present value	$ 7,000	$ 6,400	$ (3,600)
Present value index	1.07 ($107,000/$100,000)	1.08 ($86,400/$80,000)	0.96 ($86,400/$90,000)

A project will have a present value index greater than one when the net present value is positive. This is the case for Proposals A and B. When the net present value is negative, the present value index will be less than one, as is the case for Proposal C.

Although Proposal A has the largest net present value, the present value indices indicate that it is not as desirable as Proposal B. That is, Proposal B returns $1.08 present value per dollar invested, whereas Proposal A returns only $1.07. Proposal B requires an investment of $80,000, compared to an investment of $100,000 for Proposal A. Management should consider the possible use of the $20,000 difference between Proposal A and Proposal B investments before making a final decision.

An advantage of the net present value method is that it considers the time value of money. A disadvantage is that the computations are more complex than those for the methods that ignore present value. However, the use of spreadsheet software can simplify these computations. In addition, the net present value method assumes that the cash received from the proposal during its useful life can be reinvested at the rate of return used in computing the present value of the proposal. Because of changing economic conditions, this assumption may not always be reasonable.

Example Exercise 10-3   objective 2

A project has estimated annual net cash flows of $50,000 for seven years and is estimated to cost $240,000. Assume a minimum acceptable rate of return of 12%. Using Exhibit 2, determine (a) the net present value of the project and (b) the present value index, rounded to two decimal places.

(continued)

Follow My Example 10-3

a.   ($11,800)   [($50,000 × 4.564) − $240,000]
b.   0.95   ($228,200/$240,000)

For Practice: PE 10-3A, PE 10-3B

Internal Rate of Return Method   The **internal rate of return (IRR) method** uses present value concepts to compute the rate of return from the net cash flows expected from capital investment proposals. This method is sometimes called the *time-adjusted rate of return method*. It is similar to the net present value method, in that it focuses on the present value of the net cash flows. However, the internal rate of return method starts with the net cash flows and works in reverse to determine the rate of return expected from the proposal.

To illustrate, assume that management is evaluating a proposal to acquire equipment costing $33,530. The equipment is expected to provide annual net cash flows of $10,000 per year for five years. If we assume a rate of return of 12%, we can calculate the present value of the net cash flows, using the present value of an annuity table in Exhibit 2. These calculations are shown in Exhibit 3.

EXHIBIT 3

Net Present Value Analysis at 12%

Annual net cash flow (at the end of each of five years)	$10,000
Present value of an annuity of $1 at 12% for 5 years (Exhibit 2)	× 3.605
Present value of annual net cash flows	$36,050
Less amount to be invested	33,530
Net present value	$ 2,520

In Exhibit 3, the $36,050 present value of the cash inflows, based on a 12% rate of return, is greater than the $33,530 to be invested. Therefore, the internal rate of return must be greater than 12%. Through trial-and-error procedures, the rate of return that equates the $33,530 cost of the investment with the present value of the net cash flows is determined to be 15%, as shown below.

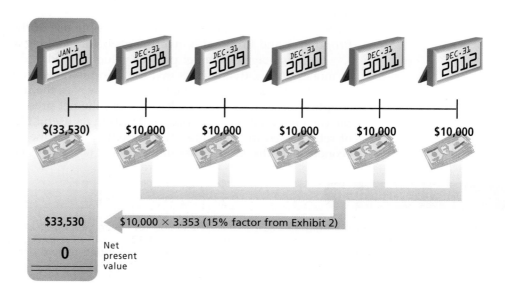

Such trial-and-error procedures are time consuming. However, when equal annual net cash flows are expected from a proposal, as in the illustration, the calculations are simplified by using the following steps:[6]

1. Determine a present value factor for an annuity of $1 by dividing the amount to be invested by the equal annual net cash flows, as follows:

$$\text{Present Value Factor for an Annuity of \$1} = \frac{\text{Amount to Be Invested}}{\text{Equal Annual Net Cash Flows}}$$

2. In the present value of an annuity of $1 table, locate the present value factor determined in step (1). First locate the number of years of expected useful life of the investment in the Year column, and then proceed horizontally across the table until you find the present value factor computed in step (1).
3. Identify the internal rate of return by the heading of the column in which the present value factor in step (2) is located.

To illustrate, assume that management is considering a proposal to acquire equipment costing $97,360. The equipment is expected to provide equal annual net cash flows of $20,000 for seven years. The present value factor for an annuity of $1 is 4.868, calculated as follows:

Present Value Factor for an Annuity of $1

$$= \frac{\text{Amount to Be Invested}}{\text{Equal Annual Net Cash Flows}}$$

$$= \frac{\$97,360}{\$20,000} = 4.868$$

For a period of seven years, the partial present value of an annuity of $1 table indicates that the factor 4.868 is related to a percentage of 10%, as shown below. Thus, 10% is the internal rate of return for this proposal.

Present Value of an Annuity of $1 at Compound Interest

Year	6%	10%	12%
1	0.943	0.909	0.893
2	1.833	1.736	1.690
3	2.673	2.487	2.402
4	3.465	3.170	3.037
5	4.212	3.791	3.605
6	4.917	4.355	4.111
7	5.582	4.868	4.564
8	6.210	5.335	4.968
9	6.802	5.759	5.328
10	7.360	6.145	5.650

If the minimum acceptable rate of return is 10%, then the proposed investment should be considered acceptable. When several proposals are considered, management often ranks the proposals by their internal rates of return. The proposal with the highest rate is considered the most desirable.

---

6 Equal annual net cash flows are assumed in order to simplify the illustration. If the annual net cash flows are not equal, the calculations are more complex, but the basic concepts are the same.

REAL WORLD

The minimum acceptable rate of return for Owens Corning is 18%; for General Electric Company, it is 20%. The CFO of Owens Corning states, "I'm here to challenge anyone—even the CEO—who gets emotionally attached to a project that doesn't reach our benchmark."

The primary advantage of the internal rate of return method is that the present values of the net cash flows over the entire useful life of the proposal are considered. In addition, by determining a rate of return for each proposal, all proposals are compared on a common basis. The primary disadvantage of the internal rate of return method is that the computations are more complex than for some of the other methods. However, spreadsheet software programs have internal rate of return functions that simplify the calculation. Also, like the net present value method, this method assumes that the cash received from a proposal during its useful life will be reinvested at the internal rate of return. Because of changing economic conditions, this assumption may not always be reasonable.

Example Exercise 10-4

objective **2**

A project is estimated to cost $208,175 and provide annual net cash flows of $55,000 for six years. Determine the internal rate of return for this project, using Exhibit 2.

Follow My Example 10-4

15%   [($208,175/$55,000) = 3.785, the present value of an annuity factor for six periods at 15%, from Exhibit 2]

For Practice: PE 10-4A, PE 10-4B

Business Connections

REAL WORLD

PANERA BREAD STORE RATE OF RETURN

Panera Bread owns, operates, and franchises bakery-cafes throughout the United States. A recent annual report to the Securities and Exchange Commission (SEC Form 10-K) disclosed the following information about an average company-owned store:

Operating profit	$317,000
Depreciation	75,000
Investment	905,000

Assume that the operating profit and depreciation will remain unchanged for the next 10 years. Assume operating profit plus depreciation approximates annual net cash flows, and that the investment salvage value will be zero. The average rate of return and internal rate of return can then be estimated. The average rate of return on a company-owned store is:

$$\frac{\$317,000}{\$905,000/2} = 70.1\%$$

The internal rate of return is calculated by first determining the present value of an annuity of $1:

$$\text{Present value of an annuity of \$1:} \quad \frac{\$905,000}{\$317,000 + \$75,000} = 2.31$$

For a period of three years, this factor implies an internal rate of return near 15% (from Exhibit 2). However, if we more realistically assumed these cash flows for 10 years, Panera's company-owned stores generate an estimated internal rate of return of approximately 42% (from a spreadsheet calculation). Clearly, both investment evaluation methods indicate a highly successful business.

© PHILLIP NEALY/PHOTODISC/GETTY IMAGES

Factors that Complicate Capital Investment Analysis

In the preceding discussion, we described four widely used methods of evaluating capital investment proposals. In practice, additional factors may have an impact on the outcome of a capital investment decision. In the following paragraphs, we discuss some of the most important of these factors: the federal income tax, unequal lives of alternative proposals, leasing, uncertainty, changes in price levels, and qualitative factors.

INCOME TAX

In many cases, the impact of the federal income tax on capital investment decisions can be material. For example, in determining depreciation for federal income tax purposes, useful lives that are much shorter than the actual useful lives are often used. Also, depreciation can be calculated by methods that approximate the double-declining-balance method. Thus, depreciation for tax purposes often exceeds the depreciation for financial statement purposes in the early years of an asset's use. The tax reduction in these early years is offset by higher taxes in the later years, so that accelerated depreciation does not result in a long-run saving in taxes. However, the timing of the cash outflows for income taxes can have a significant impact on capital investment analysis.[7]

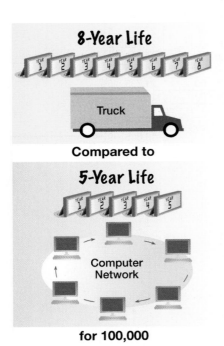

8-Year Life

Truck

Compared to

5-Year Life

Computer Network

for 100,000

UNEQUAL PROPOSAL LIVES

In the preceding discussion, the illustrations of the methods of analyzing capital investment proposals were based on the assumption that alternative proposals had the same useful lives. In practice, however, alternative proposals may have unequal lives. To illustrate, assume that alternative investments, a truck and a computer network, are being compared. The truck has a useful life of eight years, and the computer network has a useful life of five years. Each proposal requires an initial investment of $100,000, and the company desires a rate of return of 10%. The expected cash flows and net present value of each alternative are shown in Exhibit 4. Because of the unequal useful lives of the two proposals, however, the net present values in Exhibit 4 are not comparable.

To make the proposals comparable for the analysis, they can be adjusted to end at the same time. This can be done by assuming that the truck is to be sold at the end of five years. The residual value of the truck must be estimated at the end of five years, and this value must then be included as a cash flow at that date. Both proposals will then cover five years, and net present value analysis can be used to compare the two proposals over the same five-year period. If the truck's estimated residual value is $40,000 at the end of year 5, the net present value for the truck exceeds the net present value for the computers by $1,835 ($18,640 − $16,805), as shown in Exhibit 5. Therefore, the truck may be viewed as the more attractive of the two proposals.

Project 1 requires an original investment of $50,000. The project will yield cash flows of $12,000 per year for seven years. Project 2 has a calculated net present value of $8,900 over a five-year life. Project 1 could be sold at the end of five years for a price of $30,000. (a) Determine the net present value of Project 1 over a five-year life with salvage value assuming a minimum rate of return of 12%. (b) Which project provides the greatest net present value?

(continued)

---

7 The impact of income taxes on capital investment analysis is described and illustrated in advanced textbooks.

Follow My Example 10-5

Project 1

a.   Present value of $12,000 per year at 12% for 5 years $43,260 [$12,000 × 3.605 (Exhibit 2, 12%, 5 years)]
     Present value of $30,000 at 12% at the end of 5 years   17,010 [$30,000 × 0.567 (Exhibit 1, 12%, 5 years)]
     Total present value of Project 1 $60,270
     Total cost of Project 1   50,000
     Net present value of Project 1 $10,270

b.   Project 1—$10,270 is greater than the net present value of Project 2, $8,900.

For Practice: PE 10-5A, PE 10-5B

EXHIBIT 4   **Net Present Value Analysis—Unequal Lives of Proposals**

	A	B	C	D	
			Truck		
	Year	Present Value of $1 at 10%	Net Cash Flow	Present Value of Net Cash Flow	
1	1	0.909	$ 30,000	$ 27,270	1
2	2	0.826	30,000	24,780	2
3	3	0.751	25,000	18,775	3
4	4	0.683	20,000	13,660	4
5	5	0.621	15,000	9,315	5
6	6	0.564	15,000	8,460	6
7	7	0.513	10,000	5,130	7
8	8	0.467	10,000	4,670	8
9	Total		$155,000	$112,060	9
10					10
11	Amount to be invested			100,000	11
12	Net present value			$ 12,060	12

	A	B	C	D	
			Computer Network		
	Year	Present Value of $1 at 10%	Net Cash Flow	Present Value of Net Cash Flow	
1	1	0.909	$ 30,000	$ 27,270	1
2	2	0.826	30,000	24,780	2
3	3	0.751	30,000	22,530	3
4	4	0.683	30,000	20,490	4
5	5	0.621	35,000	21,735	5
6	Total		$155,000	$116,805	6
7					7
8	Amount to be invested			100,000	8
9	Net present value			$ 16,805	9

EXHIBIT 5

Net Present Value Analysis—Equalized Lives of Proposals

	A	B	C	D	
		Truck—Revised to 5-Year Life			
	Year	Present Value of $1 at 10%	Net Cash Flow	Present Value of Net Cash Flow	
1	1	0.909	$ 30,000	$ 27,270	1
2	2	0.826	30,000	24,780	2
3	3	0.751	25,000	18,775	3
4	4	0.683	20,000	13,660	4
5	5	0.621	15,000	9,315	5
6	5 (Residual				6
7	value)	0.621	40,000	24,840	7
8	Total		$160,000	$118,640	8
9					9
10	Amount to be invested			100,000	10
11	Net present value			$ 18,640	11

Truck NPV
greater than
Computer Network
NPV
by $1,835

LEASE VERSUS CAPITAL INVESTMENT

Leasing fixed assets has become common in many industries. For example, hospitals often lease diagnostic and other medical equipment. Leasing allows a business to use fixed assets without spending large amounts of cash to purchase them. In addition, management may believe that a fixed asset has a high risk of becoming obsolete. This risk may be reduced by leasing rather than purchasing the asset. Also, the *Internal Revenue Code* allows the lessor (the owner of the asset) to pass tax deductions on to the lessee (the party leasing the asset). These provisions of the tax law have made leasing assets more attractive. For example, a company that pays $50,000 per year for leasing a $200,000 fixed asset with a life of eight years is permitted to deduct from taxable income the annual lease payments.

In many cases, before a final decision is made, management should consider leasing assets instead of purchasing them. Normally, leasing assets is more costly than purchasing because the lessor must include in the rental price not only the costs associated with owning the assets but also a profit. Nevertheless, using the methods of evaluating capital investment proposals, management should consider whether it is more profitable to lease rather than purchase an asset.

Merck & Co., Inc., a major pharmaceutical company, includes uncertainty in analyzing drugs under research and development. A single hit would pay for the investment costs of many failures. Management uses a technique in probability theory, called *Monte Carlo analysis*, which shows that the drugs under development could be very profitable.

UNCERTAINTY

All capital investment analyses rely on factors that are uncertain. For example, the estimates related to revenues, expenses, and cash flows are uncertain. The long-term nature of capital investments suggests that some estimates are likely to involve uncertainty. Errors in one or more of the estimates could lead to incorrect decisions.

CHANGES IN PRICE LEVELS

In performing investment analysis, management must be concerned about changes in price levels. Price levels may change due to **inflation**, which occurs when general price levels are rising. Thus, while general prices are rising, the returns on an investment must exceed the rising price level, or else the cash returned on the investment becomes less valuable over time.

Price levels may also change for foreign investments as the result of currency exchange rates. **Currency exchange rates** are the rates at which currency in another country can be exchanged for U.S. dollars. If the amount of local dollars that can be exchanged for one U.S. dollar increases, then the local currency is said to be weakening to the dollar. Thus, if a company made an investment in another country where the local currency was weakening, it would adversely impact the return on that investment as expressed in U.S. dollars. This is because the expected amount of local currency returned on the investment would purchase fewer U.S. dollars.[8]

Management should attempt to anticipate future price levels and consider their effects on the estimates used in capital investment analyses. Changes in anticipated price levels could significantly affect the analyses.

QUALITATIVE CONSIDERATIONS

Some benefits of capital investments are qualitative in nature and cannot be easily estimated in dollar terms. If management does not consider these qualitative considerations, the quantitative analyses may suggest rejecting a worthy investment.

Qualitative considerations in capital investment analysis are most appropriate for strategic investments. Strategic investments are those that are designed to affect a company's long-term ability to generate profits. Strategic investments often have many uncertainties and intangible benefits. Unlike capital investments that are designed to cut costs, strategic investments have very few "hard" savings. Instead, they may affect future revenues, which are difficult to estimate. An example of a strategic investment is IBM's decision to develop molecular and atomic level nanotechnology

---

8 Further discussion on accounting for foreign currency transactions is available on the companion Web site at www.thomsonedu.com/accounting/warren.

Integrity, Objectivity, and Ethics in Business

ETHICS

ASSUMPTION FUDGING

The results of any capital budgeting analysis depend on many subjective estimates, such as the cash flows, discount rate, time period, and total investment amount. The results of the analysis should be used to either support or reject a project. Capital budgeting should not be used to justify an assumed net present value. That is, the analyst should not work backwards, filling in assumed numbers that will produce the desired net present value. Such a reverse approach reduces the credibility of the entire process.

for enhancing information technology. IBM's investment is justified more on the strategic potential of nanotechnology than on any economic analysis of cash flows.

Qualitative considerations that may influence capital investment analysis include product quality, manufacturing flexibility, employee morale, manufacturing productivity, and market opportunity. Many of these qualitative factors may be as important, if not more important, than the results of quantitative analysis.

Capital Rationing

objective **4**

Diagram the capital rationing process.

Funding for capital projects may be obtained from issuing bonds or stock or from operating cash. **Capital rationing** is the process by which management allocates these funds among competing capital investment proposals. In this process, management often uses a combination of the methods described in this chapter. Exhibit 6 portrays the capital rationing decision process.

In capital rationing, alternative proposals are initially screened by establishing minimum standards for the cash payback and the average rate of return. The proposals that survive this screening are further analyzed, using the net present value and internal rate of return methods. Throughout the capital rationing process, qualitative factors related to each proposal should also be considered. For example, the acquisition of new, more efficient equipment that eliminates several jobs could lower employee morale to a level that could decrease overall plant productivity. Alternatively, new equipment might improve the quality of the product and thus increase consumer satisfaction and sales.

The final steps in the capital rationing process are ranking the proposals according to management's criteria, comparing the proposals with the funds available, and selecting the proposals to be funded. Funded proposals are included in the *capital expenditures budget* to aid the planning and financing of operations. Unfunded proposals may be reconsidered if funds later become available.

EXHIBIT 6 | Capital Rationing Decision Process

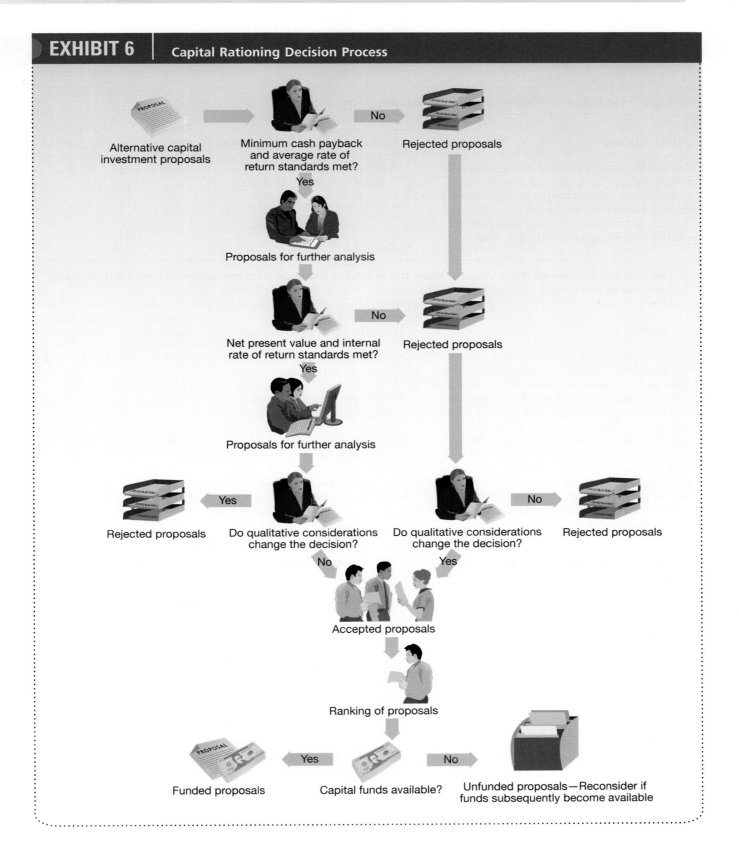

Alternative capital investment proposals

Minimum cash payback and average rate of return standards met?

No → Rejected proposals

Yes

Proposals for further analysis

Net present value and internal rate of return standards met?

No → Rejected proposals

Yes

Proposals for further analysis

Rejected proposals ← Yes — Do qualitative considerations change the decision?

Do qualitative considerations change the decision? — No → Rejected proposals

No — Accepted proposals — Yes

Ranking of proposals

Funded proposals ← Yes — Capital funds available? — No → Unfunded proposals—Reconsider if funds subsequently become available

At a Glance ⬎

1. Explain the nature and importance of capital investment analysis.

Key Points	Key Learning Outcomes	Example Exercises	Practice Exercises
Capital investment analysis is the process by which management plans, evaluates, and controls investments involving fixed assets. Capital investment analysis is important to a business because such investments affect profitability for a long period of time.	• Describe the purpose of capital investment analysis.		

2. Evaluate capital investment proposals, using the following methods: average rate of return, cash payback, net present value, and internal rate of return.

Key Points	Key Learning Outcomes	Example Exercises	Practice Exercises
The average rate of return method measures the expected profitability of an investment in fixed assets. The expected period of time that will pass between the date of an investment and the complete recovery in cash (or equivalent) of the amount invested is the cash payback period. The net present value method uses present values to compute the net present value of the cash flows expected from a proposal. The internal rate of return method uses present values to compute the rate of return from the net cash flows expected from capital investment proposals.	• Compute the average rate of return of a project.	10-1	10-1A, 10-1B
	• Compute the cash payback period of a project.	10-2	10-2A, 10-2B
	• Compute the net present value of a project.	10-3	10-3A, 10-3B
	• Compute the internal rate of return of a project.	10-4	10-4A, 10-4B

3. List and describe factors that complicate capital investment analysis.

Key Points	Key Learning Outcomes	Example Exercises	Practice Exercises
Factors that may complicate capital investment analysis include the impact of the federal income tax, unequal lives of alternative proposals, leasing, uncertainty, changes in price levels, and qualitative considerations.	• Describe the impact of income taxes in capital investment analysis.		
	• Evaluate projects with unequal lives.	10-5	10-5A, 10-5B
	• Describe leasing versus capital investment.		
	• Describe uncertainty, changes in price levels, and qualitative considerations in capital investment analysis.		

4. Diagram the capital rationing process.			
Key Points	**Key Learning Outcomes**	**Example Exercises**	**Practice Exercises**
Capital rationing refers to the process by which management allocates available investment funds among competing capital investment proposals. A diagram of the capital rationing process appears in Exhibit 6.	• Define *capital rationing*. • Diagram the capital rationing process.		

Key Terms

annuity (395)
average rate of return (391)
capital investment analysis (390)
capital rationing (404)
cash payback period (392)

currency exchange rate (403)
inflation (403)
internal rate of return (IRR) method (398)
net present value method (396)

present value concept (394)
present value index (396)
present value of an annuity (395)
time value of money concept (391)

Illustrative Problem

The capital investment committee of Hopewell Company is currently considering two investments. The estimated income from operations and net cash flows expected from each investment are as follows:

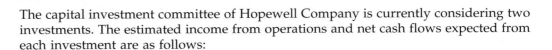

	Truck		Equipment	
Year	**Income from Operations**	**Net Cash Flow**	**Income from Operations**	**Net Cash Flow**
1	$ 6,000	$ 22,000	$13,000	$ 29,000
2	9,000	25,000	10,000	26,000
3	10,000	26,000	8,000	24,000
4	8,000	24,000	8,000	24,000
5	11,000	27,000	3,000	19,000
	$44,000	$124,000	$42,000	$122,000

Each investment requires $80,000. Straight-line depreciation will be used, and no residual value is expected. The committee has selected a rate of 15% for purposes of the net present value analysis.

Instructions
1. Compute the following:
   a. The average rate of return for each investment.
   b. The net present value for each investment. Use the present value of $1 table appearing in this chapter.
2. Why is the net present value of the equipment greater than the truck, even though its average rate of return is less?
3. Prepare a summary for the capital investment committee, advising it on the relative merits of the two investments.

(continued)

Solution

1. a. Average rate of return for the truck:

$$\frac{\$44{,}000 \div 5}{(\$80{,}000 + \$0) \div 2} = 22\%$$

Average rate of return for the equipment:

$$\frac{\$42{,}000 \div 5}{(\$80{,}000 + \$0) \div 2} = 21\%$$

b. Net present value analysis:

Year	Present Value of $1 at 15%	Net Cash Flow Truck	Net Cash Flow Equipment	Present Value of Net Cash Flow Truck	Present Value of Net Cash Flow Equipment
1	0.870	$ 22,000	$ 29,000	$19,140	$25,230
2	0.756	25,000	26,000	18,900	19,656
3	0.658	26,000	24,000	17,108	15,792
4	0.572	24,000	24,000	13,728	13,728
5	0.497	27,000	19,000	13,419	9,443
Total		$124,000	$122,000	$82,295	$83,849
Amount to be invested				80,000	80,000
Net present value				$ 2,295	$ 3,849

2. The equipment has a lower average rate of return than the truck because the equipment's total income from operations for the five years is $42,000, which is $2,000 less than the truck's. Even so, the net present value of the equipment is greater than that of the truck, because the equipment has higher cash flows in the early years.
3. Both investments exceed the selected rate established for the net present value analysis. The truck has a higher average rate of return, but the equipment offers a larger net present value. Thus, if only one of the two investments can be accepted, the equipment would be the more attractive.

Self-Examination Questions
(Answers at End of Chapter)

1. Methods of evaluating capital investment proposals that ignore present value include:
   A. average rate of return.
   B. cash payback.
   C. both A and B.
   D. neither A nor B.

2. Management is considering a $100,000 investment in a project with a five-year life and no residual value. If the total income from the project is expected to be $60,000 and recognition is given to the effect of straight-line depreciation on the investment, the average rate of return is:
   A. 12%.   C. 60%.
   B. 24%.   D. 75%.

3. The expected period of time that will elapse between the date of a capital investment and the complete recovery of the amount of cash invested is called the:

   A. average rate of return period.
   B. cash payback period.
   C. net present value period.
   D. internal rate of return period.

4. A project that will cost $120,000 is estimated to generate cash flows of $25,000 per year for eight years. What is the net present value of the project, assuming an 11% required rate of return? (Use the present value tables in Appendix A.)
   A. ($38,214)   C. $55,180
   B. $8,653   D. $75,000

5. A project is estimated to generate cash flows of $40,000 per year for 10 years. The cost of the project is $226,009. What is the internal rate of return for this project?
   A. 8%   C. 12%
   B. 10%   D. 14%

Eye Openers

1. What are the principal objections to the use of the average rate of return method in evaluating capital investment proposals?
2. Discuss the principal limitations of the cash payback method for evaluating capital investment proposals.
3. Why would the average rate of return differ from the internal rate of return on the same project?
4. What information does the cash payback period ignore that is included by the net present value method?
5. Your boss has suggested that a one-year payback period is the same as a 100% average rate of return. Do you agree?
6. Why would the cash payback method understate the attractiveness of a project with a large salvage value?
7. Why would the use of the cash payback period for analyzing the financial performance of theatrical releases from a motion picture production studio be supported over the net present value method?
8. A net present value analysis used to evaluate a proposed equipment acquisition indicated a $7,900 net present value. What is the meaning of the $7,900 as it relates to the desirability of the proposal?
9. Two projects have an identical net present value of $9,000. Are both projects equal in desirability?
10. What are the major disadvantages of the use of the net present value method of analyzing capital investment proposals?
11. What are the major disadvantages of the use of the internal rate of return method of analyzing capital investment proposals?
12. What provision of the Internal Revenue Code is especially important to consider in analyzing capital investment proposals?
13. What method can be used to place two capital investment proposals with unequal useful lives on a comparable basis?
14. What are the major advantages of leasing a fixed asset rather than purchasing it?
15. Give an example of a qualitative factor that should be considered in a capital investment analysis related to acquiring automated factory equipment.
16. Monsanto Company, a large chemical and fibers company, invested $37 million in state-of-the-art systems to improve process control, laboratory automation, and local area network (LAN) communications. The investment was not justified merely on cost savings but was also justified on the basis of qualitative considerations. Monsanto management viewed the investment as a critical element toward achieving its vision of the future. What qualitative and quantitative considerations do you believe Monsanto would have considered in its strategic evaluation of these investments?

Practice Exercises

PE 10-1A
Average rate of return
obj. 2

Determine the average rate of return for a project that is estimated to yield total income of $234,000 over four years, has a cost of $450,000, and has a $50,000 residual value.

PE 10-1B
Average rate of return
obj. 2

Determine the average rate of return for a project that is estimated to yield total income of $72,000 over three years, has a cost of $125,000, and has a $25,000 residual value.

PE 10-2A
Cash payback period
obj. 2

A project has estimated annual net cash flows of $150,000. It is estimated to cost $885,000. Determine the cash payback period.

PE 10-2B
Cash payback period
obj. 2

A project has estimated annual net cash flows of $27,200. It is estimated to cost $68,000. Determine the cash payback period.

PE 10-3A
Net present value
obj. 2

A project has estimated annual net cash flows of $65,000 for six years and is estimated to cost $265,000. Assume a minimum acceptable rate of return of 10%. Using Exhibit 2, determine (1) the net present value of the project and (2) the present value index, rounded to two decimal places.

PE 10-3B
Net present value
obj. 2

A project has estimated annual net cash flows of $22,000 for four years and is estimated to cost $70,000. Assume a minimum acceptable rate of return of 12%. Using Exhibit 2, determine (1) the net present value of the project and (2) the present value index, rounded to two decimal places.

PE 10-4A
Internal rate of return
obj. 2

A project is estimated to cost $175,665 and provide annual net cash flows of $35,000 for 10 years. Determine the internal rate of return for this project, using Exhibit 2.

PE 10-4B
Internal rate of return
obj. 2

A project is estimated to cost $745,200 and provide annual net cash flows of $120,000 for eight years. Determine the internal rate of return for this project, using Exhibit 2.

PE 10-5A
Net present value—unequal lives
obj. 3

Project 1 requires an original investment of $80,000. The project will yield cash flows of $14,000 per year for eight years. Project 2 has a calculated net present value of $5,000 over a five-year life. Project 1 could be sold at the end of five years for a price of $50,000. (a) Determine the net present value of Project 1 over a five-year life with salvage value assuming a minimum rate of return of 10%. (b) Which project provides the greatest net present value?

PE 10-5B
Net present value—unequal lives
obj. 3

Project A requires an original investment of $35,000. The project will yield cash flows of $8,000 per year for seven years. Project B has a calculated net present value of $1,000 over a five-year life. Project A could be sold at the end of five years for a price of $20,000. (a) Determine the net present value of Project A over a five-year life with salvage value assuming a minimum rate of return of 15%. (b) Which project provides the greatest net present value?

Exercises

EX 10-1
Average rate of return
obj. 2

✓ *Testing equipment, 10%*

The following data are accumulated by Green Mountain Testing Services Inc. in evaluating two competing capital investment proposals:

	Testing Equipment	Centrifuge
Amount of investment	$34,000	$40,000
Useful life	6 years	8 years
Estimated residual value	0	0
Estimated total income over the useful life	$10,200	$14,000

Determine the expected average rate of return for each proposal.

EX 10-2
Average rate of return—cost savings
obj. 2

International Fabricators Inc. is considering an investment in equipment that will replace direct labor. The equipment has a cost of $85,000, with a $5,000 residual value and a 10-year life. The equipment will replace one employee who has an average wage of $23,000 per year. In addition, the equipment will have operating and energy costs of $6,000 per year.

Determine the average rate of return on the equipment, giving effect to straight-line depreciation on the investment.

EX 10-3

Average rate of return—new product

obj. 2

✓ *Average annual income, $216,000*

Airwave Communications Inc. is considering an investment in new equipment that will be used to manufacture a PDA (personal data assistant). The PDA is expected to generate additional annual sales of 4,800 units at $350 per unit. The equipment has a cost of $910,000, residual value of $50,000, and a 10-year life. The equipment can only be used to manufacture the PDA. The cost to manufacture the PDA is shown below.

Cost per unit:	
Direct labor	$ 52.00
Direct materials	195.00
Factory overhead (including depreciation)	58.00
Total cost per unit	$305.00

Determine the average rate of return on the equipment.

EX 10-4

Calculate cash flows

obj. 2

✓ *Year 1: ($62,725)*

Gardeneer Inc. is planning to invest $184,000 in a new garden tool that is expected to generate additional sales of 7,500 units at $38 each. The $184,000 investment includes $54,000 for initial launch-related expenses and $130,000 for equipment that has a 10-year life and a $17,500 residual value. Selling expenses related to the new product are expected to be 6% of sales revenue. The cost to manufacture the product includes the following per-unit costs:

Direct labor	$ 6.00
Direct materials	11.75
Fixed factory overhead—depreciation	1.50
Variable factory overhead	1.80
Total	$21.05

Determine the net cash flows for the first year of the project, years 2–9, and for the last year of the project.

EX 10-5

Cash payback period

obj. 2

✓ *Proposal 1: 5 years*

First Union Bank Corporation is evaluating two capital investment proposals for a drive-up ATM kiosk, each requiring an investment of $300,000 and each with an eight-year life and expected total net cash flows of $480,000. Location 1 is expected to provide equal annual net cash flows of $60,000, and Location 2 is expected to have the following unequal annual net cash flows:

Year 1	$90,000	Year 5	$45,000
Year 2	80,000	Year 6	45,000
Year 3	65,000	Year 7	45,000
Year 4	65,000	Year 8	45,000

Determine the cash payback period for both proposals.

EX 10-6

Cash payback method

obj. 2

✓ *a. Cosmetics: 4 years*

Family Care Products Company is considering an investment in one of two new product lines. The investment required for either product line is $600,000. The net cash flows associated with each product are as follows:

Year	Liquid Soap	Cosmetics
1	$120,000	$165,000
2	120,000	155,000
3	120,000	140,000
4	120,000	140,000
5	120,000	110,000
6	120,000	90,000
7	120,000	80,000
8	120,000	80,000
Total	$960,000	$960,000

a. Recommend a product offering to Family Care Products Company, based on the cash payback period for each product line.

b. ⟶ Why is one product line preferred over the other, even though they both have the same total net cash flows through eight periods?

EX 10-7
Net present value method

obj. 2

✓ *a. NPV ($7,700)*

The following data are accumulated by Zadok Company in evaluating the purchase of $370,000 of equipment, having a four-year useful life:

	Net Income	Net Cash Flow
Year 1	$67,500	$160,000
Year 2	47,500	140,000
Year 3	(12,500)	80,000
Year 4	(12,500)	80,000

a. Assuming that the desired rate of return is 12%, determine the net present value for the proposal. Use the table of the present value of $1 appearing in Exhibit 1 of this chapter.
b. ▭▭▶ Would management be likely to look with favor on the proposal? Explain.

EX 10-8
Net present value method

obj. 2

✓ *a. $21*

Metro-Goldwyn-Mayer Studios Inc. (MGM) is a major producer and distributor of theatrical and television filmed entertainment. Regarding theatrical films, MGM states, "Our feature films are exploited through a series of sequential domestic and international distribution channels, typically beginning with theatrical exhibition. Thereafter, feature films are first made available for home video generally six months after theatrical release; for pay television, one year after theatrical release; and for syndication, approximately three to five years after theatrical release."

Assume that MGM releases a film during early 2009 at a cost of $115 million, and releases it halfway through the year. During the last half of 2009, the film earns revenues of $140 million at the box office. The film requires $45 million of advertising during the release. One year later, by the end of 2010, the film is expected to earn MGM net cash flows from home video sales of $36 million. By the end of 2011, the film is expected to earn MGM $19 million from pay TV; and by the end of 2012, the film is expected to earn $4 million from syndication.

a. Determine the net present value of the film as of the beginning of 2009 if the desired rate of return is 20%. To simplify present value calculations, assume all annual net cash flows occur at the end of each year. Use the table of the present value of $1 appearing in Exhibit 1 of this chapter. Round to the nearest whole million dollars.
b. ▭▭▶ Under the assumptions provided here, is the film expected to be financially successful?

EX 10-9
Net present value method—annuity

obj. 2

✓ *a. $50,000*

Maddox Excavation Company is planning an investment of $205,000 for a bulldozer. The bulldozer is expected to operate for 1,600 hours per year for five years. Customers will be charged $95 per hour for bulldozer work. The bulldozer operator is paid an hourly wage of $25 per hour. The bulldozer is expected to require annual maintenance costing $14,000. The bulldozer uses fuel that is expected to cost $30 per hour of bulldozer operation.

a. Determine the equal annual net cash flows from operating the bulldozer.
b. Determine the net present value of the investment, assuming that the desired rate of return is 10%. Use the table of present values of an annuity of $1 in the chapter. Round to the nearest dollar.
c. ▭▭▶ Should Maddox invest in the bulldozer, based on this analysis?

EX 10-10
Net present value— unequal lives

objs. 2, 3

✓ *Net present value, Apartment Complex, $117,500*

Blue Ridge Development Company has two competing projects: an apartment complex and an office building. Both projects have an initial investment of $720,000. The net cash flows estimated for the two projects are as follows:

	Net Cash Flow	
Year	Apartment Complex	Office Building
1	$240,000	$280,000
2	210,000	280,000
3	210,000	265,000
4	160,000	265,000
5	150,000	
6	120,000	
7	90,000	
8	60,000	

The estimated residual value of the apartment complex at the end of year 4 is $420,000.

Determine which project should be favored, comparing the net present values of the two projects and assuming a minimum rate of return of 15%. Use the table of present values in the chapter.

EX 10-11
Net present value method

obj. 2

✔ *a. Net investment, $1,693,000*

IHOP Corp. franchises breakfast-oriented restaurants throughout North America. The average development costs for a new restaurant were reported by IHOP as follows:

Land	$ 667,000
Building	800,000
Equipment	341,000
Site improvements	185,000
Total	$1,993,000

IHOP develops and owns the restaurant properties. IHOP indicates that the franchisee pays an initial franchise fee of $300,000 for a newly developed restaurant. IHOP also receives revenues from the franchisee as follows: (1) a royalty equal to 4.5% of the restaurant's sales; (2) income from the leasing of the restaurant and related equipment; and (3) revenue from the sale of certain proprietary products, primarily pancake mixes.

IHOP reported that franchise operators earned annual revenues averaging $1,500,000 per restaurant. Assume that the net cash flows received by IHOP for lease payments and sale of proprietary products (items 2 and 3 above) average $200,000 per year per restaurant, for 10 years. Assume further that the franchise operator can purchase the property for $700,000 at the end of the lease term.

Determine IHOP's:

a. Net investment (development cost less initial franchise fee) to develop a restaurant.
b. Net present value for a new restaurant, assuming a 10-year life, no change in annual revenues, and a 12% desired rate of return. Use the present value tables appearing in Exhibits 1 and 2 in this chapter.

EX 10-12
Net present value method

obj. 2

✔ *a. $95,950,000*

Carnival Corporation has recently placed into service some of the largest cruise ships in the world. One of these ships, the *Carnival Glory*, can hold up to 3,000 passengers and cost $530 million to build. Assume the following additional information:

- The average occupancy rate for the new ship is estimated to be 85% of capacity.
- There will be 300 cruise days per year.
- The variable expenses per passenger are estimated to be $80 per cruise day.
- The revenue per passenger is expected to be $310 per cruise day.
- The fixed expenses for running the ship, other than depreciation, are estimated to be $80,000,000 per year.
- The ship has a service life of 10 years, with a salvage value of $90,000,000 at the end of 10 years.

a. Determine the annual net cash flow from operating the cruise ship.
b. Determine the net present value of this investment, assuming a 12% minimum rate of return. Use the present value tables provided in the chapter in determining your answer.
c. Assume that Carnival Corp. decided to increase its price so that the revenue increased to $320 per passenger per cruise day. Would this allow Carnival Corp. to earn a 15% rate of return on the cruise ship investment, assuming no change in any of the other assumptions? Use the present value tables provided in the chapter in determining your answer.

EX 10-13
Present value index

obj. 2

✔ *Location A, 0.95*

Drive By Doughnuts has computed the net present value for capital expenditure locations A and B, using the net present value method. Relevant data related to the computation are as follows:

	Location A	Location B
Total present value of net cash flow	$306,280	$177,660
Amount to be invested	322,400	164,500
Net present value	$ (16,120)	$ 13,160

Determine the present value index for each proposal.

EX 10-14
Net present value method and present value index
obj. 2
✔ *b. Packing Machine, 1.09*

MVP Sporting Goods Company is considering an investment in one of two machines. The sewing machine will increase productivity from sewing 120 baseballs per hour to sewing 180 per hour. The contribution margin is $0.80 per baseball. Assume that any increased production of baseballs can be sold. The second machine is an automatic packing machine for the golf ball line. The packing machine will reduce packing labor cost. The labor cost saved is equivalent to $24 per hour. The sewing machine will cost $354,300, have an eight-year life, and will operate for 1,750 hours per year. The packing machine will cost $148,300, have an eight-year life, and will operate for 1,500 hours per year. MVP seeks a minimum rate of return of 15% on its investments.

a. Determine the net present value for the two machines. Use the table of present values of an annuity of $1 in the chapter. Round to the nearest dollar.
b. Determine the present value index for the two machines. Round to two decimal places.
c. ▭▭▭▶ If MVP has sufficient funds for only one of the machines and qualitative factors are equal between the two machines, in which machine should it invest?

EX 10-15
Average rate of return, cash payback period, net present value method
obj. 2
✔ *b. 5 years*

Southern Rail Inc. is considering acquiring equipment at a cost of $442,500. The equipment has an estimated life of 10 years and no residual value. It is expected to provide yearly net cash flows of $88,500. The company's minimum desired rate of return for net present value analysis is 12%.
    Compute the following:

a. The average rate of return, giving effect to straight-line depreciation on the investment.
b. The cash payback period.
c. The net present value. Use the table of the present value of an annuity of $1 appearing in this chapter. Round to the nearest dollar.

EX 10-16
Payback period, net present value analysis and qualitative considerations
objs. 2, 3

The plant manager of O'Brien Equipment Company is considering the purchase of a new robotic assembly plant. The new robotic line will cost $1,250,000. The manager believes that the new investment will result in direct labor savings of $250,000 per year for 10 years.

a. What is the payback period on this project?
b. What is the net present value, assuming a 10% rate of return?
c. ▭▭▭▶ What else should the manager consider in the analysis?

EX 10-17
Internal rate of return method
obj. 2
✔ *a. 4.487*

The internal rate of return method is used by Timberframe Renovations Inc. in analyzing a capital expenditure proposal that involves an investment of $62,818 and annual net cash flows of $14,000 for each of the eight years of its useful life.

a. Determine a present value factor for an annuity of $1 which can be used in determining the internal rate of return.
b. Using the factor determined in part (a) and the present value of an annuity of $1 table appearing in this chapter, determine the internal rate of return for the proposal.

EX 10-18
Internal rate of return method
obj. 2

IBM recently saved $250 million over three years by implementing supply chain software that reduced the cost of components used in its manufacture of computers. If we assume that the savings occurred equally over the three years and the cost of implementing the new software was $175,500,000, what would be the internal rate of return for this investment? Use the present value of an annuity of $1 table found in Exhibit 2 in determining your answer.

EX 10-19
Internal rate of return method—two projects
obj. 2

Southwest Chip Company is considering two possible investments: a delivery truck or a bagging machine. The delivery truck would cost $39,918 and could be used to deliver an additional 36,250 bags of taquitos chips per year. Each bag of chips can be sold for a contribution margin of $0.40. The delivery truck operating expenses, excluding depreciation,

✓ *a. Delivery truck, 10%*

are $0.35 per mile for 18,000 miles per year. The bagging machine would replace an old bagging machine, and its net investment cost would be $49,920. The new machine would require three fewer hours of direct labor per day. Direct labor is $16 per hour. There are 250 operating days in the year. Both the truck and the bagging machine are estimated to have seven-year lives. The minimum rate of return is 11%. However, Southwest has funds to invest in only one of the projects.

a. Compute the internal rate of return for each investment. Use the table of present values of an annuity of $1 in the chapter.
b. Provide a memo to management with a recommendation.

EX 10-20
Net present value method and internal rate of return method
obj. 2

✓ *a. ($6,606)*

Buckeye Healthcare Corp. is proposing to spend $96,030 on an eight-year project that has estimated net cash flows of $18,000 for each of the eight years.

a. Compute the net present value, using a rate of return of 12%. Use the table of present values of an annuity of $1 in the chapter.
b. Based on the analysis prepared in part (a), is the rate of return (1) more than 12%, (2) 12%, or (3) less than 12%? Explain.
c. Determine the internal rate of return by computing a present value factor for an annuity of $1 and using the table of the present value of an annuity of $1 presented in the text.

EX 10-21
Identify error in capital investment analysis calculations
obj. 2

Integrated Technologies Inc. is considering the purchase of automated machinery that is expected to have a useful life of four years and no residual value. The average rate of return on the average investment has been computed to be 25%, and the cash payback period was computed to be 4.5 years.

 Do you see any reason to question the validity of the data presented? Explain.

Problems Series A

PR 10-1A
Average rate of return method, net present value method, and analysis
obj. 2

✓ *1. a. 45.7%*

The capital investment committee of Estate Landscaping Company is considering two capital investments. The estimated income from operations and net cash flows from each investment are as follows:

Year	Greenhouse Income from Operations	Greenhouse Net Cash Flow	Skid Loader Income from Operations	Skid Loader Net Cash Flow
1	$16,000	$ 30,000	$26,000	$ 40,000
2	16,000	30,000	21,000	35,000
3	16,000	30,000	16,000	30,000
4	16,000	30,000	11,000	25,000
5	16,000	30,000	6,000	20,000
	$80,000	$150,000	$80,000	$150,000

Each project requires an investment of $70,000. Straight-line depreciation will be used, and no residual value is expected. The committee has selected a rate of 12% for purposes of the net present value analysis.

Instructions
1. Compute the following:
   a. The average rate of return for each investment. Round to one decimal place.
   b. The net present value for each investment. Use the present value of $1 table appearing in this chapter.
2. Prepare a brief report for the capital investment committee, advising it on the relative merits of the two investments.

PR 10-2A
Cash payback period, net present value method, and analysis
obj. 2

✓ *1. b. Plant Expansion, $104,410*

Unique Boutique Inc. is considering two investment projects. The estimated net cash flows from each project are as follows:

Year	Plant Expansion	Retail Store Expansion
1	$ 280,000	$ 260,000
2	260,000	260,000
3	230,000	250,000
4	260,000	250,000
5	270,000	280,000
Total	$1,300,000	$1,300,000

Each project requires an investment of $770,000. A rate of 15% has been selected for the net present value analysis.

Instructions
1. Compute the following for each project:
   a. Cash payback period.
   b. The net present value. Use the present value of $1 table appearing in this chapter.
2. ▭▭▭▶ Prepare a brief report advising management on the relative merits of each project.

PR 10-3A
Net present value method, present value index, and analysis
obj. 2

✓ *2. Railcars, 0.97*

Continental Railroad Company wishes to evaluate three capital investment proposals by using the net present value method. Relevant data related to the proposals are summarized as follows:

	Route Expansion	Acquire Railcars	New Maintenance Yard
Amount to be invested	$830,000	$480,000	$410,000
Annual net cash flows:			
Year 1	450,000	245,000	215,000
Year 2	400,000	220,000	205,000
Year 3	370,000	190,000	200,000

Instructions
1. Assuming that the desired rate of return is 20%, prepare a net present value analysis for each proposal. Use the present value of $1 table appearing in this chapter.
2. Determine a present value index for each proposal. Round to two decimal places.
3. ▭▭▭▶ Which proposal offers the largest amount of present value per dollar of investment? Explain.

PR 10-4A
Net present value method, internal rate of return method, and analysis
obj. 2

✓ *1. a. Generating unit, $191,750*

The management of Genco Utilities Inc. is considering two capital investment projects. The estimated net cash flows from each project are as follows:

Year	Generating Unit	Distribution Network Expansion
1	$650,000	$180,000
2	650,000	180,000
3	650,000	180,000
4	650,000	180,000

The generating unit requires an investment of $2,060,500, while the distribution network expansion requires an investment of $546,660. No residual value is expected from either project.

Instructions
1. Compute the following for each project:
   a. The net present value. Use a rate of 6% and the present value of an annuity of $1 table appearing in this chapter.
   b. A present value index. Round to two decimal places.
2. Determine the internal rate of return for each project by (a) computing a present value factor for an annuity of $1 and (b) using the present value of an annuity of $1 table appearing in this chapter.

3. ➤ What advantage does the internal rate of return method have over the net present value method in comparing projects?

PR 10-5A
Evaluate alternative capital investment decisions

objs. **2, 3**

✓1. Project II, $72,626

The investment committee of Safe Hands Insurance Co. is evaluating two projects. The projects have different useful lives, but each requires an investment of $225,000. The estimated net cash flows from each project are as follows:

	Net Cash Flows	
Year	Project I	Project II
1	$70,000	$98,000
2	70,000	98,000
3	70,000	98,000
4	70,000	98,000
5	70,000	
6	70,000	

The committee has selected a rate of 12% for purposes of net present value analysis. It also estimates that the residual value at the end of each project's useful life is $0, but at the end of the fourth year, Project I's residual value would be $150,000.

Instructions
1. For each project, compute the net present value. Use the present value of an annuity of $1 table appearing in this chapter. (Ignore the unequal lives of the projects.)
2. For each project, compute the net present value, assuming that Project I is adjusted to a four-year life for purposes of analysis. Use the present value of $1 table appearing in this chapter.
3. ➤ Prepare a report to the investment committee, providing your advice on the relative merits of the two projects.

PR 10-6A
Capital rationing decision involving four proposals

objs. **2, 4**

✓5. Proposal B, 1.18

Madison Capital Group is considering allocating a limited amount of capital investment funds among four proposals. The amount of proposed investment, estimated income from operations, and net cash flow for each proposal are as follows:

	Investment	Year	Income from Operations	Net Cash Flow
Proposal A:	$540,000	1	$ 42,000	$150,000
		2	42,000	150,000
		3	42,000	150,000
		4	(18,000)	90,000
		5	(18,000)	90,000
			$ 90,000	$630,000
Proposal B:	$250,000	1	$ 50,000	$100,000
		2	40,000	90,000
		3	30,000	80,000
		4	15,000	65,000
		5	15,000	65,000
			$150,000	$400,000
Proposal C:	$640,000	1	$ 92,000	$220,000
		2	82,000	210,000
		3	82,000	210,000
		4	62,000	190,000
		5	32,000	160,000
			$350,000	$990,000
Proposal D:	$310,000	1	$ 68,000	$130,000
		2	38,000	100,000
		3	(2,000)	60,000
		4	(2,000)	60,000
		5	(2,000)	60,000
			$100,000	$410,000

The company's capital rationing policy requires a maximum cash payback period of three years. In addition, a minimum average rate of return of 12% is required on all projects. If the preceding standards are met, the net present value method and present value indexes are used to rank the remaining proposals.

Instructions
1. Compute the cash payback period for each of the four proposals.
2. Giving effect to straight-line depreciation on the investments and assuming no estimated residual value, compute the average rate of return for each of the four proposals. Round to one decimal place.
3. Using the following format, summarize the results of your computations in parts (1) and (2). By placing a check mark in the appropriate column at the right, indicate which proposals should be accepted for further analysis and which should be rejected.

Proposal	Cash Payback Period	Average Rate of Return	Accept for Further Analysis	Reject
A				
B				
C				
D				

4. For the proposals accepted for further analysis in part (3), compute the net present value. Use a rate of 12% and the present value of $1 table appearing in this chapter. Round to the nearest dollar.
5. Compute the present value index for each of the proposals in part (4). Round to two decimal places.
6. Rank the proposals from most attractive to least attractive, based on the present values of net cash flows computed in part (4).
7. Rank the proposals from most attractive to least attractive, based on the present value indexes computed in part (5).
8. ▭▭▶ Based upon the analyses, comment on the relative attractiveness of the proposals ranked in parts (6) and (7).

Problems Series B

PR 10-1B
Average rate of return method, net present value method, and analysis

obj. 2

✓ 1.a. 15.9%

The capital investment committee of Triple C Trucking Inc. is considering two investment projects. The estimated income from operations and net cash flows from each investment are as follows:

Year	Warehouse		Parcel Tracking Technology	
	Income from Operations	Net Cash Flow	Income from Operations	Net Cash Flow
1	$ 46,000	$162,000	$ 19,000	$135,000
2	46,000	162,000	29,000	145,000
3	46,000	162,000	54,000	170,000
4	46,000	162,000	54,000	170,000
5	46,000	162,000	74,000	190,000
Total	$230,000	$810,000	$230,000	$810,000

Each project requires an investment of $580,000. Straight-line depreciation will be used, and no residual value is expected. The committee has selected a rate of 12% for purposes of the net present value analysis.

Instructions
1. Compute the following:
   a. The average rate of return for each investment. Round to one decimal place.
   b. The net present value for each investment. Use the present value of $1 table appearing in this chapter.
2. ▭▭▶ Prepare a brief report for the capital investment committee, advising it on the relative merits of the two projects.

PR 10-2B

Cash payback period, net present value method, and analysis

obj. 2

✓ *1. b. Home & Garden, $92,360*

Family Life Publications Inc. is considering two new magazine products. The estimated net cash flows from each product are as follows:

Year	Home & Garden	Today's Teen
1	$230,000	$160,000
2	210,000	280,000
3	190,000	200,000
4	50,000	40,000
5	40,000	40,000
Total	$720,000	$720,000

Each product requires an investment of $440,000. A rate of 15% has been selected for the net present value analysis.

Instructions

1. Compute the following for each project:
   a. Cash payback period.
   b. The net present value. Use the present value of $1 table appearing in this chapter.
2. ▭▭▷ Prepare a brief report advising management on the relative merits of each of the two products.

PR 10-3B

Net present value method, present value index, and analysis

obj. 2

✓ *2. Branch office expansion, 0.98*

First Security Bancorp Inc. wishes to evaluate three capital investment projects by using the net present value method. Relevant data related to the projects are summarized as follows:

	Branch Office Expansion	Computer System Upgrade	Install Internet Bill-Pay
Amount to be invested	$505,000	$375,000	$640,000
Annual net cash flows:			
Year 1	250,000	210,000	335,000
Year 2	235,000	190,000	320,000
Year 3	215,000	180,000	315,000

Instructions

1. Assuming that the desired rate of return is 20%, prepare a net present value analysis for each project. Use the present value of $1 table appearing in this chapter.
2. Determine a present value index for each project. Round to two decimal places.
3. ▭▭▷ Which project offers the largest amount of present value per dollar of investment? Explain.

PR 10-4B

Net present value method, internal rate of return method, and analysis

obj. 2

✓ *1. a. Radio station, $50,400*

The management of Horizon Media Inc. is considering two capital investment projects. The estimated net cash flows from each project are as follows:

Year	Radio Station	TV Station
1	$160,000	$450,000
2	160,000	450,000
3	160,000	450,000
4	160,000	450,000

The radio station requires an investment of $456,800, while the TV station requires an investment of $1,366,650. No residual value is expected from either project.

Instructions

1. Compute the following for each project:
   a. The net present value. Use a rate of 10% and the present value of an annuity of $1 table appearing in this chapter.
   b. A present value index. Round to two decimal places.
2. Determine the internal rate of return for each project by (a) computing a present value factor for an annuity of $1 and (b) using the present value of an annuity of $1 table appearing in this chapter.
3. ▭▭▷ What advantage does the internal rate of return method have over the net present value method in comparing projects?

PR 10-5B
*Evaluate alternative
capital investment
decisions*

objs. 2, 3

✓1. Site B, $150,470

The investment committee of Mr. Bob Restaurants Inc. is evaluating two restaurant sites. The sites have different useful lives, but each requires an investment of $445,000. The estimated net cash flows from each site are as follows:

	Net Cash Flows	
Year	Site A	Site B
1	$170,000	$230,000
2	170,000	230,000
3	170,000	230,000
4	170,000	230,000
5	170,000	
6	170,000	

The committee has selected a rate of 20% for purposes of net present value analysis. It also estimates that the residual value at the end of each restaurant's useful life is $0, but at the end of the fourth year, Site A's residual value would be $340,000.

Instructions
1. For each site, compute the net present value. Use the present value of an annuity of $1 table appearing in this chapter. (Ignore the unequal lives of the projects.)
2. For each site, compute the net present value, assuming that Site A is adjusted to a four-year life for purposes of analysis. Use the present value of $1 table appearing in this chapter.
3. ▭▬► Prepare a report to the investment committee, providing your advice on the relative merits of the two sites.

PR 10-6B
*Capital rationing decision
involving four proposals*

objs. 2, 4

✓5. Proposal B, 1.26

Horizon Communications Inc. is considering allocating a limited amount of capital investment funds among four proposals. The amount of proposed investment, estimated income from operations, and net cash flow for each proposal are as follows:

	Investment	Year	Income from Operations	Net Cash Flow
Proposal A:	$680,000	1	$ 74,000	$210,000
		2	74,000	210,000
		3	74,000	210,000
		4	14,000	150,000
		5	14,000	150,000
			$250,000	$930,000
Proposal B:	$155,000	1	$ 29,000	$ 60,000
		2	64,000	95,000
		3	9,000	40,000
		4	(1,000)	30,000
		5	(11,000)	20,000
			$ 90,000	$245,000
Proposal C:	$281,250	1	$ 18,750	$ 75,000
		2	18,750	75,000
		3	18,750	75,000
		4	18,750	75,000
		5	(6,250)	50,000
			$ 68,750	$350,000
Proposal D:	$260,000	1	$ 38,000	$ 90,000
		2	38,000	90,000
		3	28,000	80,000
		4	28,000	80,000
		5	23,000	75,000
			$155,000	$415,000

The company's capital rationing policy requires a maximum cash payback period of three years. In addition, a minimum average rate of return of 12% is required on all projects. If the preceding standards are met, the net present value method and present value indexes are used to rank the remaining proposals.

Instructions
1. Compute the cash payback period for each of the four proposals.
2. Giving effect to straight-line depreciation on the investments and assuming no estimated residual value, compute the average rate of return for each of the four proposals. Round to one decimal place.
3. Using the following format, summarize the results of your computations in parts (1) and (2). By placing a check mark in the appropriate column at the right, indicate which proposals should be accepted for further analysis and which should be rejected.

Proposal	Cash Payback Period	Average Rate of Return	Accept for Further Analysis	Reject
A				
B				
C				
D				

4. For the proposals accepted for further analysis in part (3), compute the net present value. Use a rate of 10% and the present value of $1 table appearing in this chapter. Round to the nearest dollar.
5. Compute the present value index for each of the proposals in part (4). Round to two decimal places.
6. Rank the proposals from most attractive to least attractive, based on the present values of net cash flows computed in part (4).
7. Rank the proposals from most attractive to least attractive, based on the present value indexes computed in part (5). Round to two decimal places.
8. Based upon the analyses, comment on the relative attractiveness of the proposals ranked in parts (6) and (7).

Special Activities

SA 10-1
Ethics and professional conduct in business

ETHICS

Elisa McRae was recently hired as a cost analyst by Medlab Medical Supplies Inc. One of Elisa's first assignments was to perform a net present value analysis for a new warehouse. Elisa performed the analysis and calculated a present value index of 0.75. The plant manager, I. M. Madd, is very intent on purchasing the warehouse because he believes that more storage space is needed. I. M. Madd asks Elisa into his office and the following conversation takes place.

I. M.: Elisa, you're new here, aren't you?

Elisa: Yes, sir.

I. M.: Well, Elisa, let me tell you something. I'm not at all pleased with the capital investment analysis that you performed on this new warehouse. I need that warehouse for my production. If I don't get it, where am I going to place our output?

Elisa: Hopefully with the customer, sir.

I. M.: Now don't get smart with me.

Elisa: No, really, I was being serious. My analysis does not support constructing a new warehouse. The numbers don't lie, the warehouse does not meet our investment return targets. In fact, it seems to me that purchasing a warehouse does not add much value to the business. We need to be producing product to satisfy customer orders, not to fill a warehouse.

I. M.: Listen, you need to understand something. The headquarters people will not allow me to build the warehouse if the numbers don't add up. You know as well as I that many assumptions go into your net present value analysis. Why don't you relax some of your assumptions so that the financial savings will offset the cost?

Elisa: I'm willing to discuss my assumptions with you. Maybe I overlooked something.

I. M.: Good. Here's what I want you to do. I see in your analysis that you don't project greater sales as a result of the warehouse. It seems to me, if we can store more goods, then we will have more to sell. Thus, logically, a larger warehouse translates into more sales. If you incorporate this into your analysis, I think you'll see that the numbers will work out. Why don't you work it through and come back with a new analysis. I'm really counting on you on this one. Let's get off to a good start together and see if we can get this project accepted.

⟶ What is your advice to Elisa?

SA 10-2
Personal investment analysis

A Masters of Accountancy degree at Mid-State University would cost $15,000 for an additional fifth year of education beyond the bachelor's degree. Assume that all tuition is paid at the beginning of the year. A student considering this investment must evaluate the present value of cash flows from possessing a graduate degree versus holding only the undergraduate degree. Assume that the average student with an undergraduate degree is expected to earn an annual salary of $45,000 per year (assumed to be paid at the end of the year) for 10 years. Assume that the average student with a graduate Masters of Accountancy degree is expected to earn an annual salary of $57,000 per year (assumed to be paid at the end of the year) for nine years after graduation. Assume a minimum rate of return of 10%.

1. Determine the net present value of cash flows from an undergraduate degree. Use the present value tables provided in this chapter.
2. Determine the net present value of cash flows from a Masters of Accountancy degree, assuming no salary is earned during the graduate year of schooling.
3. ⟶ What is the net advantage or disadvantage of pursuing a graduate degree under these assumptions?

SA 10-3
Changing prices

Global Products Inc. invested $1,000,000 to build a plant in a foreign country. The labor and materials used in production are purchased locally. The plant expansion was estimated to produce an internal rate of return of 20% in U.S. dollar terms. Due to a currency crisis, the currency exchange rate between the local currency and the U.S. dollar doubled from two local units per U.S. dollar to four local units per U.S. dollar.

a. Assume that the plant produced and sold product in the local economy. Explain what impact this change in the currency exchange rate would have on the project's internal rate of return.
b. Assume that the plant produced product in the local economy but exported the product back to the United States for sale. Explain what impact the change in the currency exchange rate would have on the project's internal rate of return under this assumption.

SA 10-4
Qualitative issues in investment analysis

The following are some selected quotes from senior executives:

CEO, Worthington Industries *(a high technology steel company):* "We try to find the best technology, stay ahead of the competition, and serve the customer. . . . We'll make any investment that will pay back quickly . . . but if it is something that we really see as a must down the road, payback is not going to be that important."

Chairman of Amgen Inc. *(a biotech company):* "You cannot really run the numbers, do net present value calculations, because the uncertainties are really gigantic . . . You decide on a project you want to run, and then you run the numbers [as a reality check on your assumptions]. Success in a business like this is much more dependent on tracking rather than on predicting, much more dependent on seeing results over time, tracking and adjusting and readjusting, much more dynamic, much more flexible."

Chief Financial Officer of Merck & Co., Inc. *(a pharmaceutical company):* ". . . at the individual product level—the development of a successful new product requires on the order of $230 million in R&D, spread over more than a decade—discounted cash flow style analysis does not become a factor until development is near the point of manufacturing scale-up effort. Prior to that point, given the uncertainties associated with new product development, it would be lunacy in our business to decide that we know exactly what's going to happen to a product once it gets out."

⟶ Explain the role of capital investment analysis for these companies.

SA 10-5
Analyze cash flows

You are considering an investment of $300,000 in either Project A or Project B for West Coast Studios Inc. In discussing the two projects with an advisor, you decided that, for the risk involved, an average rate of return of 12% on the cash investment would be required. For this purpose, you estimated the following economic factors for the projects:

	Project A	Project B
Useful life	4 years	4 years
Residual value	0	0
Net income:		
Year 1	$ 80,000	$ 40,000
2	65,000	55,000
3	55,000	73,000
4	40,000	79,200
	$240,000	$247,200

	Project A	Project B
Net cash flows:		
Year 1	$155,000	$115,000
2	140,000	130,000
3	130,000	148,000
4	115,000	154,200
	$540,000	$547,200

Although the average rate of return exceeded 12% on both projects, you have tentatively decided to invest in Project B because the rate was higher for Project B. You noted that the total cash flow from Project B is $547,200, which exceeds that of Project A by $7,200.

1. Determine the average rate of return for both projects.
2. ▐▬▬▶ Why is the timing of cash flows important in evaluating capital investments? Calculate the net present value of the two projects at a minimum rate of return of 12% to demonstrate the importance of net cash flows and their timing to these two projects. Round to the nearest dollar.

SA 10-6
Capital investment analysis

Internet Project

Group Project

In one group, find a local business, such as a copy shop, that rents time on desktop computers for an hourly rate. Determine the hourly rate. In the other group, determine the price of a mid-range desktop computer at **http://www.dell.com**. Combine this information from the two groups and perform a capital budgeting analysis. Assume that one student will use the computer for 35 hours per semester for the next three years. Also assume that the minimum rate of return is 10%. Use the interest tables in Appendix A in performing your analysis. (*Hint:* Use the appropriate present value factor for 5% compounded for six semiannual periods.) Does your analysis support the student purchasing the computer?

Answers to Self-Examination Questions

1. **C** Methods of evaluating capital investment proposals that ignore the time value of money are categorized as methods that ignore present value. This category includes the average rate of return method (answer A) and the cash payback method (answer B).

2. **B** The average rate of return is 24% (answer B), determined by dividing the expected average annual earnings by the average investment, as follows:

$$\frac{\$60,000/5}{(\$100,000 + 0)/2} = 24\%$$

3. **B** Of the four methods of analyzing proposals for capital investments, the cash payback period (answer B) refers to the expected period of time required to recover the amount of cash to be invested. The average rate of return (answer A) is a measure of the anticipated profitability of a proposal. The net present value method (answer C) reduces the expected future net cash flows originating from a proposal to their present values. The internal rate of return method (answer D) uses present value concepts to compute the rate of return from the net cash flows expected from the investment.

4. **B**   The net present value is determined as follows:

Present value of $25,000 for 8 years at 11%
($25,000 × 5.14612)	$128,653
Less project cost	120,000
Net present value	$ 8,653

5. **C**   The internal rate of return for this project is determined by solving for the present value of an annuity factor that when multiplied by $40,000 will equal $226,009. By division, the factor is:

$$\frac{\$226,009}{\$40,000} = 5.65022$$

In Appendix A on pp. A-4 and A-5, scan along the $n = 10$ years row until finding the 5.65022 factor. The column for this factor is 12%.

chapter 11

Cost Allocation and Activity-Based Costing

© LINDSAY PIERCE/THE DAILY TIMES/ASSOCIATED PRESS

objectives

After studying this chapter, you should be able to:

1 *Identify three methods used for allocating factory overhead costs to products.*

2 *Use a single plantwide factory overhead rate for product costing.*

3 *Use multiple production department factory overhead rates for product costing.*

4 *Use activity-based costing for product costing.*

5 *Use activity-based costing to allocate selling and administrative expenses to products.*

6 *Use activity-based costing in a service business.*

Cold Stone Creamery

Have you ever had to request service repairs on an appliance at your home? The repair person may arrive and take five minutes to replace a part, yet the bill may indicate a charge for a minimum amount that is more than five minutes of work. Why might the service person have a minimum charge just for showing up? The answer is that the service person must charge for the time and expense of coming to your house. In a sense, the bill reflects two elements of service: the cost of coming to your house and the cost of providing the repair. The first portion of the cost reflects the time required to "set up" the job, while the second part of the cost reflects the cost of performing the repair. Notice that the setup charge will be the same, whether the repairs take five minutes or five hours. In contrast, the second portion of the bill reflects the actual repair performed that varies with the time on the job.

Like the repair person, companies must be careful to cost their products and services to reflect the different activities involved in producing the product. Otherwise, the cost of products and services may be distorted and lead to improper management decisions. For example, Cold Stone Creamery, a chain of super premium ice cream shops, uses activity-based costing to determine the cost of its ice cream products, such as cones, mixings, cakes, frozen yogurt, smoothies, and sorbets. The cost of activities, such as scooping and mixing, are added to the cost of the ingredients to determine the total cost to prepare each product. As stated by Cold Stone's president, "it only makes sense to have the price you pay for the product be reflective of the activities involved in making it for you."

In this chapter, we will explain and illustrate three different methods of allocating factory overhead to products. In addition, we will explain how product cost distortions can result from improper factory overhead allocation. We will end the chapter by describing activity-based costing for selling and administrative expenses and illustrating its use in service businesses.

Product Costing Allocation Methods

objective 1

Identify three methods used for allocating factory overhead costs to products.

How does Nissan Motor Company determine if its *Xterra* SUV is a profitable product? First, it needs to determine the revenues earned from selling the cars. Most companies have accounting systems that trace revenues to individual product lines. In addition, however, Nissan needs to subtract the cost of manufacturing *Xterra* SUVs in order to determine the profit from *Xterra* sales. Nissan's cost accounting system provides this cost information. Determining the cost of the *Xterra*, or any other product, is termed **product costing**.

We introduced product costing in the job order costing chapter. We stated that product costs consist of direct materials, direct labor, and factory overhead. The direct materials and direct labor are direct to the product. However, factory overhead is often indirect to products and must be allocated. In this chapter we will illustrate three different factory overhead allocation approaches: (1) the single plantwide factory overhead rate method, (2) the multiple production department factory overhead rate method, and (3) the activity-based costing method.

Three Factory Overhead Allocation Methods

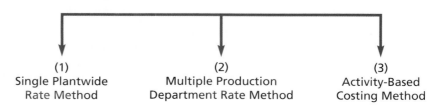

(1)	(2)	(3)
Single Plantwide Rate Method	Multiple Production Department Rate Method	Activity-Based Costing Method

How does an accountant know which method to use? In this chapter we will illustrate each of the three methods and identify the conditions favoring each method. Managers should be concerned about which method is selected because the method of allocation determines the accuracy of the resulting product cost. Accurate product costs support management decisions, such as determining product mix, establishing product price, or determining whether or not to emphasize a product line. For example, after implementing a more accurate factory overhead cost allocation system, a senior manager at Kraft Foods remarked, "I expect to see that there are some products we definitely should not be manufacturing and some other products that we should be committing many more resources to. . . . [The cost system] should affect our long-term decisions on which businesses Kraft should be in."[1] Thus, factory overhead allocation is not just necessary for financial reporting purposes, but it also contributes to management decision making.

Single Plantwide Factory Overhead Rate Method

objective 2

Use a single plantwide factory overhead rate for product costing.

As we discussed in a previous chapter, companies may use a predetermined factory overhead rate to allocate factory overhead costs to products. Under the **single plantwide factory overhead rate method**, all of the factory overhead is allocated to all the products, using only one rate.

To illustrate, assume that Ruiz Company manufactures two products, snowmobiles and lawnmowers. Both products are manufactured in a single factory. In addition, there is $1,600,000 of factory overhead budgeted for the period. The factory overhead consists of factory and equipment depreciation, factory power, factory supplies, and indirect labor.

Under the single plantwide factory overhead rate method, the $1,600,000 budgeted factory overhead is applied to all products by using one rate. This rate is computed by dividing the total budgeted factory overhead cost by the total budgeted (estimated) plantwide allocation base as follows:

$$\text{Single Plantwide Factory Overhead Rate} = \frac{\text{Total Budgeted Factory Overhead Cost}}{\text{Total Budgeted Plantwide Allocation Base}}$$

REAL WORLD

Many professional service companies use a single overhead rate in determining their prices and job profitability. For example, medical, legal, and accounting services develop hourly rates that will provide a profit after covering labor and overhead.

The budgeted allocation base is a measure of operating activity in the factory. Common allocation bases would include direct labor hours, direct labor dollars, and machine hours.

Assume that Ruiz Company allocates factory overhead to the two products on the basis of budgeted direct labor hours. The total budgeted direct labor hours can be determined by multiplying the budgeted manufacturing volume by the direct labor hours per unit. Ruiz Company plans to manufacture 1,000 units of each product. Assume that snowmobiles and lawnmowers both require 10 direct labor hours per unit to manufacture. The total budgeted plantwide direct labor hours is 20,000, as shown below.

Snowmobile: 1,000 units × 10 direct labor hours = 10,000 direct labor hours
Lawnmower: 1,000 units × 10 direct labor hours = <u>10,000</u>
<u>20,000</u> direct labor hours

---

1 R. Cooper, R. S. Kaplan, L. S. Maisel, E. Morrissey, and R. M. Oehm, *Implementing Activity-Based Cost Management: Moving from Analysis to Action* (Institute of Management Accountants, 1992), p. 269.

The single plantwide factory overhead rate is $80 per direct labor hour, determined as follows:

$$\text{Single Plantwide Factory Overhead Rate} = \frac{\$1,600,000}{20,000 \text{ direct labor hours}}$$

$$= \$80 \text{ per direct labor hour}$$

This plantwide rate of $80 per direct labor hour can be used to allocate factory overhead to each product, as shown below.

	Single Plantwide Factory Overhead Rate	×	Direct Labor Hours per Unit	=	Factory Overhead Cost per Unit
Snowmobile:	$80 per direct labor hour	×	10 direct labor hours	=	$800
Lawnmower:	$80 per direct labor hour	×	10 direct labor hours	=	$800

The factory overhead allocated to each unit of product is the same. This is because each product used the same number of direct labor hours.

The effects of using the single plantwide factory overhead rate method are summarized for Ruiz Company in Exhibit 1.

Many military contractors use a single plantwide rate for allocating factory overhead costs to products, such as jet fighters. This approach is satisfactory when all products in the plant are manufactured under cost plus profit margin contracts to a single customer, such as the Department of Defense. However, cost distortions can still occur. This is one reason why government contractors sometimes make "$200 flashlights" that could be purchased at the local hardware store for $5.

EXHIBIT 1

Single Plantwide Factory Overhead Rate Method—Ruiz Company

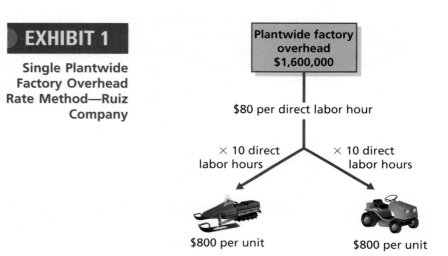

Plantwide factory overhead $1,600,000

$80 per direct labor hour

× 10 direct labor hours

× 10 direct labor hours

$800 per unit

$800 per unit

The greatest advantage of the single plantwide overhead rate method is that it is simple and inexpensive to apply in practice. Using a plantwide rate, we assume that the factory overhead costs are consumed in the same way by all products. For example, for Ruiz Company, we assume that all factory overhead can be accurately allocated to the two products based on the total number of direct labor hours consumed by each product. For companies that manufacture one or very few products, this assumption may be true. However, if the company manufactures many different types of products that consume factory overhead costs in different ways, then the assumption may not be true. In such a situation, a single plantwide rate may not accurately allocate factory overhead to the products. A solution may be to use multiple production department factory overhead rates, which we illustrate in the next section.

Example Exercise 11-1

objective 2

The total factory overhead for Morris Company is budgeted for the year at $650,000. Morris manufactures two office furniture products: a credenza and desk. The credenza and desk each require four direct labor hours to manufacture. Each product is budgeted for 5,000 units of production for the year. Determine (a) the total number of budgeted direct labor hours for the year, (b) the single plantwide factory overhead rate, and (c) the factory overhead allocated per unit for each product using the single plantwide factory overhead rate.

Follow My Example 11-1

a. Credenza: 5,000 units × 4 direct labor hours = 20,000 direct labor hours
    Desk: 5,000 units × 4 direct labor hours =   20,000
                                                     40,000 direct labor hours

b. Single plantwide factory overhead rate: $650,000/40,000 dlh = $16.25 per dlh
c. Credenza: $16.25 per direct labor hour × 4 dlh per unit = $65/unit
    Desk: $16.25 per direct labor hour × 4 dlh per unit = $65/unit

For Practice: PE 11-1A, PE 11-1B

Integrity, Objectivity, and Ethics in Business

ETHICS

FRAUD AGAINST YOU AND ME

The U.S. government makes a wide variety of purchases. Two of the largest are health care purchases under Medicare and military equipment. The purchase price for these and other items is often determined by the cost plus some profit. The cost is often the sum of direct costs plus allocated overhead. Due to the complexity of determining cost, government agencies review the amount charged for products and services. In the event of disagreement between the contractor and the government, the U.S. government may sue the contractor under the False Claims Act, which provides for three times the government's damages plus civil penalties. For example, Serono, a major pharmaceutical company, agreed to pay $704 million to settle a recent fraud case under the False Claims Act involving allegations of kickbacks to doctors and pharmacies for prescribing and recommending Serostim®, an AIDS-related drug.

Multiple Production Department Factory Overhead Rate Method

objective 3

Use multiple production department factory overhead rates for product costing.

When production departments *differ significantly* in their manufacturing processes, factory overhead costs are likely to be incurred differently in each department. For example, a fabrication department that uses equipment may require more depreciation, power, and maintenance than would an assembly department that uses people. In addition, different products may consume the factory overhead from each production department in different proportions. For example, some products may use more of the fabrication department, while others use more of the assembly department. Under these conditions, the factory overhead costs may be more accurately allocated using multiple production department factory overhead rates.

The **multiple production department factory overhead rate method** uses different rates for each production department to allocate factory overhead to products. This is in contrast to the single plantwide rate method, which uses only one rate to allocate plantwide factory overhead to the products. Exhibit 2 illustrates how these two methods differ.

EXHIBIT 2

Comparison of Single Plantwide Rate and Multiple Production Department Rate Methods

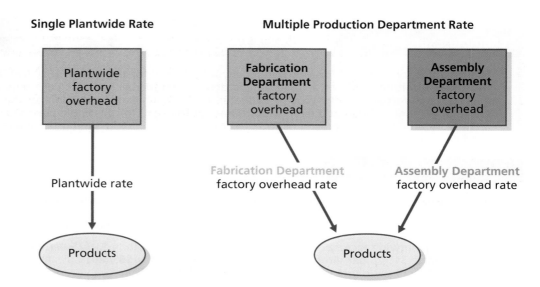

To illustrate the multiple production department factory overhead rate method, we will continue with the Ruiz Company example introduced in the previous section. Assume that Ruiz Company has two production departments, Fabrication and Assembly. Also assume that the budgeted factory overhead associated with the Fabrication Department is $1,030,000 and with the Assembly Department is $570,000.[2] The Fabrication Department has nearly twice the factory overhead of the Assembly Department because of the additional machinery-related factory overhead, such as power, equipment depreciation, and factory supplies. Note that the sum of the budgeted factory overhead in the two production departments of $1,600,000 ($1,030,000 + $570,000), equals the budgeted plantwide factory overhead.

Production Department Factory Overhead Rates and Allocation

A company may use different allocation bases for different departments. For example, a machine-intensive department may use machine hours as an allocation base, and a labor-intensive department may use labor hours as an allocation base. However, in situations where one employee operates one machine, machine hours and labor hours will be equal and will yield the same allocation results.

The **production department factory overhead rates** are determined by dividing the budgeted production department factory overhead by the budgeted allocation base for each department. For Ruiz Company, direct labor hours are used as the allocation base for each production department. Each production department uses 10,000 direct labor hours. Thus, the factory overhead rates for the two departments are determined as follows:

$$\text{Fabrication Department Factory Overhead Rate} = \frac{\$1,030,000}{10,000 \text{ dlh}}$$

$$= \$103 \text{ per direct labor hour}$$

$$\text{Assembly Department Factory Overhead Rate} = \frac{\$570,000}{10,000 \text{ dlh}}$$

$$= \$57 \text{ per direct labor hour}$$

---

2 The factory overhead is allocated to production departments by using methods that are discussed in advanced texts.

Recall that each product requires ten direct labor hours. We will now assume some additional information about these hours. The snowmobile requires eight direct labor hours in the Fabrication Department and two direct labor hours in the Assembly Department. The lawnmower requires two direct labor hours in the Fabrication Department and eight in the Assembly Department.

Factory overhead is allocated to each product by multiplying the direct labor hours used by each product in each department by the production department factory overhead rate. Exhibit 3 shows this process for Ruiz Company.

EXHIBIT 3   **Allocating Factory Overhead to Products—Ruiz Company**

	Allocation-Base Usage per Unit	×	Production Department Factory Overhead Rate	=	Allocated Factory Overhead per Unit of Product
Snowmobile					
Fabrication Department	8 direct labor hours	×	$103 per dlh	=	$824
Assembly Department	2 direct labor hours	×	$ 57 per dlh	=	114
Total factory overhead cost per snowmobile					$938
Lawnmower					
Fabrication Department	2 direct labor hours	×	$103 per dlh	=	$206
Assembly Department	8 direct labor hours	×	$ 57 per dlh	=	456
Total factory overhead cost per lawnmower					$662

The multiple production department rate allocation method for Ruiz Company is summarized in Exhibit 4. You should note that the production department factory overhead rates are not the same for each department. The Fabrication Department is more expensive in terms of factory overhead per direct labor hour than is the Assembly Department. In addition, the snowmobile uses more Fabrication Department direct labor hours than does the lawnmower. As a result, the total overhead allocated to each snowmobile is greater than that allocated to each lawnmower.

EXHIBIT 4

Multiple Production Department Rate Method—Ruiz Company

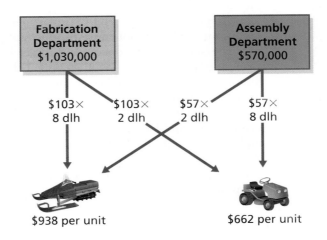

DISTORTION IN PRODUCT COSTS—SINGLE PLANTWIDE VERSUS MULTIPLE PRODUCTION DEPARTMENT FACTORY OVERHEAD RATES

For Ruiz Company, the following table shows the difference in the factory overhead per unit for each product, using the single plantwide and the multiple production department factory overhead rate methods:

	Factory Overhead Cost per Unit	
	Single Plantwide Rate	**Multiple Production Department Rates**
Snowmobile	$800	$938
Lawnmower	800	662

Which method is correct? In this case, the single plantwide factory overhead rate distorts the product cost by averaging the differences between the high factory overhead costs in the Fabrication Department and the low factory overhead costs in the Assembly Department. Using the single plantwide rate, we assume that all factory overhead is directly related to a single allocation base representing the entire plant. In many plants, this assumption is not realistic. Thus, using a single plantwide rate may result in product cost distortion.

In general, the following conditions may indicate that a single plantwide factory overhead rate will lead to distorted product costs:

> The single plantwide factory overhead rate distorts product cost by averaging high and low factory overhead costs.

Condition 1: Differences in production department factory overhead rates. There are significant differences in the factory overhead rates across different production departments. That is, some departments have high rates, while others have low rates.

and

Condition 2: Differences in the ratios of allocation-base usage. The products require different ratios of allocation base-usage across the departments.

Exhibit 5 illustrates both conditions for Ruiz Company. Condition 1 exists because the factory overhead rate for the Fabrication Department is $103 per direct labor hour, while the rate for the Assembly Department is only $57 per direct labor hour. This condition, by itself, will not cause product cost distortion. However, Condition 2 also exists. The snowmobile consumes 8 direct labor hours in the Fabrication Department, while the lawnmower consumes only 2 direct labor hours (8:2 ratio). The opposite is the case in the Assembly Department (2:8 ratio). Since both conditions exist, the product costs calculated using the single plantwide factory overhead rate are distorted. If Ruiz Company used the $800 product cost to determine its pricing strategy for both products, it would likely *underprice* the snowmobile and *overprice* the lawnmower. Eventually, Ruiz might be shut out of the lawnmower business due to this pricing error. If Ruiz used the multiple production department factory overhead rate approach, however, its product costs would be more accurate, and thus it would have a better starting point for making pricing decisions.

EXHIBIT 5

Conditions for Product Cost Distortion—Ruiz Company

| Fabrication Department | Assembly Department |

Condition 1: Differences in production department factory overhead rates

$103 per direct labor hour

$57 per direct labor hour

Condition 2: Differences in the ratios of allocation-base usage

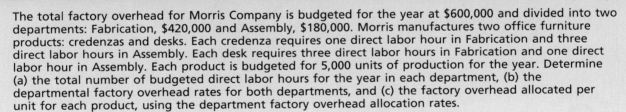

| 8 direct labor hours | 2 direct labor hours |
| 2 direct labor hours | 8 direct labor hours |

Example Exercise 11-2

objective **3**

The total factory overhead for Morris Company is budgeted for the year at $600,000 and divided into two departments: Fabrication, $420,000 and Assembly, $180,000. Morris manufactures two office furniture products: credenzas and desks. Each credenza requires one direct labor hour in Fabrication and three direct labor hours in Assembly. Each desk requires three direct labor hours in Fabrication and one direct labor hour in Assembly. Each product is budgeted for 5,000 units of production for the year. Determine (a) the total number of budgeted direct labor hours for the year in each department, (b) the departmental factory overhead rates for both departments, and (c) the factory overhead allocated per unit for each product, using the department factory overhead allocation rates.

Follow My Example 11-2

a. Fabrication: (5,000 credenzas × 1 dlh) + (5,000 desks × 3 dlh) = 20,000 direct labor hours
   Assembly: (5,000 credenzas × 3 dlh) + (5,000 desks × 1 dlh) = 20,000 direct labor hours
b. Fabrication Department rate: $420,000/20,000 direct labor hours = $21.00 per dlh
   Assembly Department rate: $180,000/20,000 direct labor hours = $9.00 per dlh

c. Credenza:

Fabrication Department	1 dlh × $21.00 = $21.00
Assembly Department	3 dlh × $ 9.00 = 27.00
Total factory overhead per credenza	$48.00

Desk:

Fabrication Department	3 dlh × $21.00 = $63.00
Assembly Department	1 dlh × $ 9.00 = 9.00
Total factory overhead per desk	$72.00

For Practice: PE 11-2A, PE 11-2B

Activity-Based Costing Method

In today's more complex manufacturing systems, product costs may still be distorted when multiple production department factory overhead rates are used. One way to avoid this distortion is by using the **activity-based costing (ABC) method**. This approach allocates factory overhead more accurately than does the multiple production department rate method.

The activity-based costing method uses cost of activities to determine product costs. Under this method, factory overhead costs are initially accounted for in **activity cost pools**. These cost pools are related to a given activity, such as machine usage, inspections, moving, production setups, and engineering activities. In contrast, when multiple production department factory overhead rates are used, factory overhead costs are first accounted for in production departments. Exhibit 6 illustrates how these two approaches compare.

EXHIBIT 6 **Multiple Production Department Factory Overhead Rate Method vs. Activity-Based Costing**

Multiple Production Department Factory Overhead Rate Method

Production Department Factory Overhead   Production Department Factory Overhead

Production Department Rates

Products

Activity-Based Costing

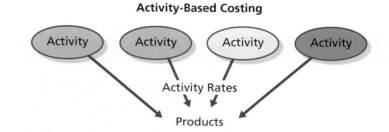

Activity   Activity   Activity   Activity

Activity Rates

Products

Another term for "setup" is "changeover." This term is often used in continuous process industries. Often, machine characteristics are changed while the process continues running ("on the fly"). Such changeovers are still costly, however, because the machines will make low-quality product for a period of time during the changeover.

To illustrate the activity-based costing method, assume that Ruiz Company has five activities. Two activities are the fabrication and assembly production activities. We now call these *activities*, rather than *departments*, because the factory overhead costs in these pools are more closely related to their activity bases than under the multiple department factory overhead rate method.

Ruiz has three additional activities, which are described below.

- *Setup*—the activity of changing the characteristics of a machine to prepare for manufacturing a different product. Often, a production run requires a **setup**. For example, changing a stamping machine from stamping the body for a snowmobile to stamping the body for a lawnmower would require stopping the machine and changing the die. The work associated with changing the die is a setup activity.

- *Quality control inspection*—the activity of inspecting the product for defects. For example, a snowmobile inspection may require the snowmobile to be run for several hours and then be disassembled to test for component strength, fit, and function.

- *Engineering changes*—the activity of processing changes in product design characteristics. An **engineering change order (ECO)** initiates an administrative process to change the design of a product. For example, to change the type of blade assembled in a lawnmower would require an engineering change order.

We will assume the following budgeted factory overhead associated with each activity:

Activity Cost Pool	Amount
Fabrication	$ 530,000
Assembly	70,000
Setup	480,000
Quality control inspection	312,000
Engineering changes	208,000
Total budgeted factory overhead	$1,600,000

The U.S. Postal Service has initiated a new activity-based costing system, called PostalOne!, which will track the real costs associated with processing and delivering each class of mail.

The total budgeted factory overhead to be allocated is still $1,600,000. However, the budgeted factory overhead has now been divided into activity cost pools. The costs in the fabrication and assembly pools are less than the costs in the production departments from the previous section because the production departments included costs that were not closely related to fabrication and assembly activities. These costs, which total $1,000,000 ($480,000 + $312,000 + $208,000), are now related to their own activity pools, namely setup, quality control inspection, and engineering changes.

ACTIVITY RATES AND ALLOCATION

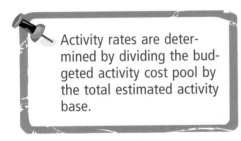

Activity rates are determined by dividing the budgeted activity cost pool by the total estimated activity base.

The activity cost pools are assigned to products, using factory overhead rates for each activity. These rates are often called **activity rates** because they are related to activities. Activity rates are determined by dividing the cost budgeted for each activity pool by the estimated activity base for that pool. We use the term **activity base**, rather than allocation base, since the base is related to an activity cost pool. For example, the activity rate for the setup activity would be determined by dividing the setup budgeted cost pool by the number of estimated setups. Setup cost would be related to a product by multiplying the setup activity rate by the number of setups used by that particular product.

To determine each activity-base quantity, assume the following additional information about the snowmobiles and lawnmowers for Ruiz Company:

- *Snowmobiles:* Ruiz Company estimates that the total production for snowmobiles will be 1,000 units. Snowmobiles are a new product for Ruiz Company, and the engineers are still tinkering with design changes. Thus, there are 12 engineering change orders estimated for the period. In addition, the snowmobile production run is expected to be set up 100 times during the period, or 10 units per production run (1,000 units total production/100 setups). For quality control purposes, 100 snowmobiles (10% of total production) will be inspected.

- *Lawnmowers:* Ruiz Company estimates that the total production for lawnmowers will also be 1,000 units. Lawnmowers are a mature and stable product that has been produced by Ruiz Company for many years. Thus, Ruiz Company expects the lawnmower to have only four engineering changes for the period. Due to its long history of successful production of lawnmowers, Ruiz expects fewer quality problems; thus, only four lawnmowers (0.4% of production) will be quality-control inspected. In addition, the lawnmower production run is expected to be set up 20 times during the period, or 50 units per production run (1,000 units total production/20 setups).

The estimated **activity-base usage quantities** are the total activity-base quantities related to each product. These quantities reflect differences with respect to using setup, quality control inspection, and engineering change activities, as we noted in the preceding paragraphs. In addition, each product uses different amounts of direct labor hours in the fabrication and assembly activities, as we noted in an earlier section. The estimated activity-base usage quantities for all 1,000 units of production for each product are shown in Exhibit 7.

| EXHIBIT 7 | Estimated Activity-Base Usage Quantities—Ruiz Company |

			Activities		
Products	Fabrication	Assembly	Setup	Quality Control Inspections	Engineering Changes
Snowmobile	8,000 dlh	2,000 dlh	100 setups	100 inspections	12 ECOs
Lawnmower	2,000	8,000	20	4	4
Total activity base	10,000 dlh	10,000 dlh	120 setups	104 inspections	16 ECOs

The activity rates for each activity can now be determined by dividing the budgeted activity cost pool by the total estimated activity base from Exhibit 7. These activity rates are shown in Exhibit 8.

| EXHIBIT 8 | Activity Rates—Ruiz Company |

Activity	Budgeted Activity Cost Pool	/	Estimated Activity Base	=	Activity Rate
Fabrication	$530,000	/	10,000 direct labor hours	=	$53 per direct labor hour
Assembly	$ 70,000	/	10,000 direct labor hours	=	$7 per direct labor hour
Setup	$480,000	/	120 setups	=	$4,000 per setup
Quality control inspections	$312,000	/	104 inspections	=	$3,000 per inspection
Engineering changes	$208,000	/	16 engineering changes	=	$13,000 per engineering change order

The product costs for the snowmobile and lawnmower are computed by multiplying the activity rate by the related activity-base quantity for each product. The total of these costs for each product is the total factory overhead cost for that product. This amount is divided by the total number of units of that product budgeted for manufacture in the period. This result, as shown in Exhibit 9, is the factory overhead cost per unit.

EXHIBIT 9	Activity-Based Product Cost Calculations

	A	B	C	D	E	F	G	H	I	J	K	L	
				Snowmobile						Lawnmower			
	Activity	Activity-Base Usage	×	Activity Rate	=	Activity Cost		Activity-Base Usage	×	Activity Rate	=	Activity Cost	
1	Fabrication	8,000 dlh		$53/dlh		$ 424,000		2,000 dlh		$53/dlh		$106,000	1
2	Assembly	2,000 dlh		$7/dlh		14,000		8,000 dlh		$7/dlh		56,000	2
3	Setup	100 setups		$4,000/setup		400,000		20 setups		$4,000/setup		80,000	3
4	Quality control												4
5	inspections	100 inspections		$3,000/insp.		300,000		4 inspections		$3,000/insp.		12,000	5
6	Engineering												6
7	changes	12 ECOs		$13,000/ECO		156,000		4 ECOs		$13,000/ECO		52,000	7
8	Total factory												8
9	overhead cost					$1,294,000						$306,000	9
10	Budgeted units												10
11	of production					/ 1,000						/ 1,000	11
12	Factory overhead												12
13	cost per unit					$ 1,294						$ 306	13

The activity-based costing method for Ruiz Company is summarized in Exhibit 10. Compare Exhibit 10 with Exhibit 4. In both exhibits, multiple rates are used. In Exhibit 4, production department factory overhead costs were allocated to products on the basis of the production department factory overhead rates. In contrast, under activity-based costing, the activity cost pools are allocated to the products on the basis of each activity's own unique activity rate.

DISTORTION IN PRODUCT COSTS—MULTIPLE PRODUCTION DEPARTMENT FACTORY OVERHEAD RATE METHOD VERSUS ACTIVITY-BASED COSTING

The factory overhead costs per unit for Ruiz Company across all three allocation methods are shown below.

Factory Overhead Cost per Unit— Three Cost Allocation Methods			
	Single Plantwide Rate	Multiple Production Department Rates	Activity-Based Costing
Snowmobile	$800	$938	$1,294
Lawnmower	800	662	306

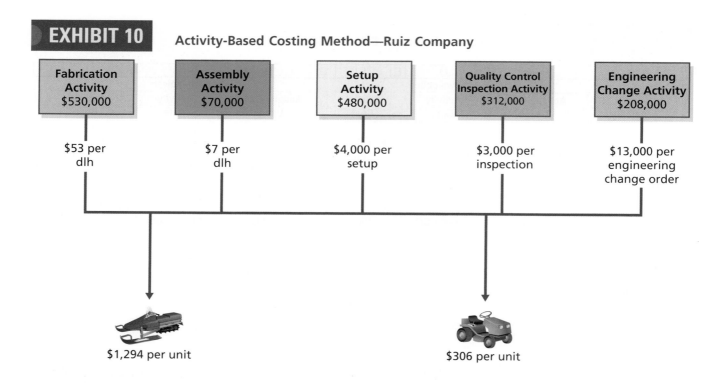

EXHIBIT 10   Activity-Based Costing Method—Ruiz Company

Fabrication Activity $530,000	Assembly Activity $70,000	Setup Activity $480,000	Quality Control Inspection Activity $312,000	Engineering Change Activity $208,000
$53 per dlh	$7 per dlh	$4,000 per setup	$3,000 per inspection	$13,000 per engineering change order

$1,294 per unit

$306 per unit

As you can see, the activity-based costing method produced different product costs from the multiple department factory overhead rate method. What caused these differences, and which method is more accurate? The answer lies in how the $1,000,000 of setup, quality control, and engineering change activities were treated. Under the multiple production department factory overhead rate method, this factory overhead was included in the production department factory overhead and allocated to products on the basis of direct labor hours. However, each product did *not* consume *activities* in proportion to its direct labor hours. Namely, the snowmobile consumed a larger portion of the setup, quality control inspection, and engineering change activities, even though each product consumed 10,000 labor hours. As a result, activity-based costing allocates more of this factory overhead cost to the snowmobile and less to the lawnmower than did the multiple production department factory overhead rate method. In summary, the activity-based costing method provided the most accurate product costs because activities were consumed in different proportions than the direct labor used in the two products.

THE DANGERS OF PRODUCT COST DISTORTION

Product cost distortion can lead to bad management decisions, and bad decisions can lead to business disasters. To illustrate, ArvinMeritor, Inc., conducted an activity-based costing study after one of its best-selling axles had begun losing market share. The study found that incorrect factory overhead cost allocations had "overcosted" its highest-volume axle by roughly 20%, while underestimating the cost of low-volume axles by as much as 40%. Since the sales prices were based on these estimated costs, ArvinMeritor had underpriced its low-volume axles and overpriced its high-volume axles. As a result, competitors had begun to attract customers away from ArvinMeritor's best-selling, high-volume axles. Without the activity-based costing analysis, ArvinMeritor could well have discovered that it was gradually being forced out of the high-volume axle business—not by choice, but because of inaccurate product costing and bad pricing decisions.

Example Exercise 11-3 objective 4

The total factory overhead for Morris Company is budgeted for the year at $600,000, divided into four activity pools: fabrication, $300,000; assembly, $120,000; setup, $100,000; and material handling $80,000. Morris manufactures two office furniture products: a credenza and desk. The activity-base usage quantities for each product by each activity are as follows:

	Fabrication	Assembly	Setup	Material Handling
Credenza	5,000 dlh	15,000 dlh	30 setups	50 moves
Desk	15,000	5,000	220	350
	20,000 dlh	20,000 dlh	250 setups	400 moves

Each product is budgeted for 5,000 units of production for the year. Determine (a) the activity rates for each activity and (b) the activity-based factory overhead per unit for each product.

Follow My Example 11-3

a. Fabrication: $300,000/20,000 direct labor hours = $15 per dlh
   Assembly: $120,000/20,000 direct labor hours = $6 per dlh
   Setup: $100,000/250 setups = $400 per setup
   Material handling: $80,000/400 moves = $200 per moveb.

	A	B	C	D	E	F	G	H	I	J	K	L	
		Credenza						Desk					
		Activity-Base		Activity		Activity		Activity-Base		Activity		Activity	
	Activity	Usage	×	Rate	=	Cost		Usage	×	Rate	=	Cost	
1	Fabrication	5,000 dlh		$15 per dlh		$ 75,000		15,000 dlh		$15 per dlh		$225,000	1
2	Assembly	15,000 dlh		$6 per dlh		90,000		5,000 dlh		$6 per dlh		30,000	2
3	Setup	30 setups		$400/setup		12,000		220 setups		$400/setup		88,000	3
4	Moves	50 moves		$200/move		10,000		350 moves		$200/move		70,000	4
5	Total					$187,000						$413,000	5
6	Budgeted units					/ 5,000						/ 5,000	6
7	Factory overhead												7
8	per unit					$ 37.40						$ 82.60	8

For Practice: PE 11-3A, PE 11-3B

Activity-Based Costing for Selling and Administrative Expenses

objective 5

Use activity-based costing to allocate selling and administrative expenses to products.

Generally accepted accounting principles require that selling and administrative expenses be treated as period expenses on the income statement prepared for external users. However, accountants may allocate selling and administrative expenses to products in preparing product profitability reports for management. A traditional method is to allocate selling and administrative expenses to the products based on product sales volumes. However, products may consume activities in ways that are unrelated to their sales volumes. When this occurs, activity-based costing may provide a more accurate allocation approach.

To illustrate, assume that Abacus Company has two products, Ipso and Facto. Both products have the same total sales volume. However, both products are not the same in terms of how they consume selling and administrative activities. Exhibit 11 identifies some of these differences.

EXHIBIT 11

Selling and
Administrative
Activity Product
Differences

Selling and Administrative Activities	Ipso	Facto
Post-sale technical support	Product is easy to use by the customer.	Product requires specialized training in order to be used by the customer.
Order writing	Product requires no technical information from the customer.	Product requires detailed technical information from the customer.
Promotional support	Product requires no promotional effort.	Product requires extensive promotional effort.
Order entry	Product is purchased in large volumes per order.	Product is purchased in small volumes per order.
Customer return processing	Product has few customer returns.	Product has many customer returns.
Shipping document preparation	Product is shipped domestically.	Product is shipped internationally, requiring customs and export documents.
Shipping and handling	Product is not hazardous.	Product is hazardous, requiring specialized shipping and handling.
Field service	Product has few warranty claims.	Product has many warranty claims.

REAL WORLD

ExxonMobil Corporation has analyzed the cost of its selling and administrative activities to better determine the cost of its lubrication products. In addition, the activity information helped ExxonMobil discover the relative costs of serving customers directly versus through distributors. Examples of selling and administrative activities used in its activity-based costing analysis included sales, maintenance, engineering calls, distributor calls, order taking, market research, and advertising.

If the selling and administrative expenses of Abacus Company were allocated on the basis of sales volumes, both products would be allocated the same amount, since they both have the same sales volume. Does this seem correct? Should both products have the same selling and administrative expenses? No, they should not. Ipso is much less complex and hence less expensive than Facto. The activity-based costing approach would allocate the selling and administrative activities to each product based on its individual differences in consuming these activities. For example, assume that the field service activity of Abacus Company had a budgeted cost of $150,000. Additionally, assume that 100 warranty claims were estimated for the period. Using warranty claims as an activity base, the cost per warranty claim would be $1,500 per warranty claim, computed as follows:

$150,000 field service activity cost/100 claims = $1,500 per warranty claim

Assume that Ipso had 10 warranty claims and Facto had 90 warranty claims. The field service activity would be allocated to each product as follows:

Ipso: 10 warranty claims × $1,500 per warranty claim = $15,000
Facto: 90 warranty claims × $1,500 per warranty claim = $135,000

Allocating selling and administrative expenses using activity-based costing would result in more accurate product profitability reports for Abacus Company management.

For some companies, selling and administrative expenses may be more related to *customer* behaviors than to differences in products. That is, some customers may demand more service and selling activities than other customers. In such cases, activity-based cost reports can be developed to show the impact of these differences on customer profitability. For example, a recent survey of manufacturers (suppliers) indicated that Wal-Mart has earned the distinction of being the easiest, and often most profitable, retailer with which to do business.[3] In the next section, we will see how service companies can also use activity-based costing to evaluate their costs in serving customers.

Example Exercise 11-4   objective **5**

Converse Company manufactures and sells LCD display products. Converse uses activity-based costing to determine the cost of the customer return processing and the shipping activity. The customer return processing activity has an activity rate of $90 per return, and the shipping activity has an activity rate of $15 per shipment. Converse shipped 4,000 units of LCD Model A1 in 2,200 shipments (some shipments are more than one unit). There were 200 returns. Determine the (a) total and (b) per-unit customer return processing and shipping activity cost for Model A1.

Follow My Example 11-4

a. Return activity: 200 returns × $90 per return = $18,000
    Shipping activity: 2,200 shipments × $15 per shipment =   33,000

    Total activity cost $51,000

b. $12.75 per unit ($51,000/4,000 units)

For Practice: PE 11-4A, PE 11-4B

Activity-Based Costing in Service Businesses

objective **6**

Use activity-based costing in a service business.

Owens & Minor, a medical distributor, used activity-based costing information to price distribution services to customers, based on the number of orders and the number of items per order.

Service companies have a need to determine the cost of services in order to make pricing, promoting, and other decisions with regard to service offerings. Many service companies find that single and multiple department overhead rate methods may lead to distortions similar to those of manufacturing firms. Thus, many service companies are now using activity-based costing for determining the cost of providing services to customers.

To illustrate activity-based costing for a service company, assume that Hopewell Hospital uses an activity-based costing system to determine how hospital overhead is allocated to patients. Hopewell Hospital first determines the activity cost pools and then allocates the activity cost pools to patients, using activity rates. We will assume that the activities of Hopewell Hospital include admitting, radiological testing, operating room, pathological testing, and dietary and laundry. Each activity cost pool has an estimated activity base measuring the output of the activity. The cost of activities is allocated to patients by multiplying the activity rate by the number of activity-base usage quantities consumed by each patient. Exhibit 12 illustrates the activity-based costing method for Hopewell Hospital.

Each activity rate shown in Exhibit 12 is determined by dividing the budgeted activity cost pool by the estimated activity-base quantity. To illustrate, assume that the radiological testing activity cost pool budget is $960,000, and the total estimated activity-base quantity is 3,000 images. The activity rate of $320 per image is calculated as follows:

$$\text{Radiological Testing Activity Rate} = \frac{\$960,000}{3,000 \text{ images}} = \$320 \text{ per image}$$

---

3 As reported in Jerry Useem, "One Nation Under Wal-Mart" Fortune, February 18, 2003.

Integrity, Objectivity, and Ethics in Business

ETHICS

UNIVERSITY AND COMMUNITY PARTNERSHIP—LEARNING YOUR ABC'S

Students at Harvard's Kennedy School of Government joined with the city of Sommerville, Massachusetts, in building an activity-based cost system for the city. The students volunteered several hours a week in four-person teams, interviewing city officials within 18 departments. The students were able to determine activity costs, such as the cost to fill a pothole, processing a building permit, or responding to a four-alarm fire. Their study will be used by the city in forming the 2006 city budget. As stated by some of the students participating on this project: "It makes sense to use the resources of the university for community building. ...Real-world experience is a tremendous thing to have in your back pocket. We learned from the mayor and the fire chief, who are seasoned professionals in their own right."

Source: Kennedy School Bulletin, Spring 2005, "Easy as A-B-C: Students take on the Sommerville Budget Overhaul."

> **EXHIBIT 12**   Activity-Based Costing Method—Hopewell Hospital

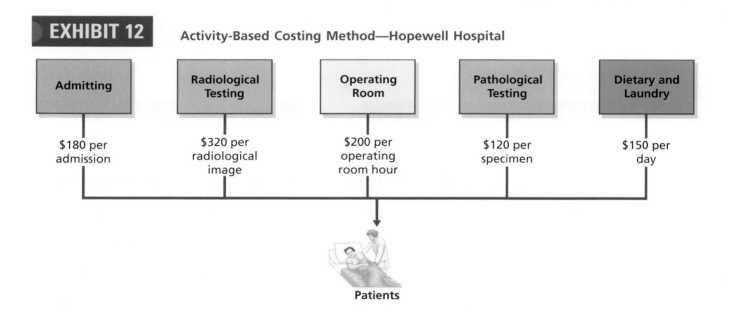

The activity rates for the other activities would be determined in a similar manner. These activity rates are used to allocate costs to patients. To illustrate, assume that Mia Wilson was a patient of the hospital. The hospital overhead cost associated with services (activities) performed for Mia Wilson is determined by multiplying the activity-base quantity for Mia Wilson's stay in the hospital by the activity rate. The sum of the costs across the activities is the total hospital overhead cost of services performed for Mia Wilson. These calculations are shown below.

	A	B	C	D	E	F	
		Patient Name: Mia Wilson					
	Activity	Activity-Base Usage	×	Activity Rate	=	Activity Cost	
1	Admitting	1 admission		$180/admission		$ 180	1
2	Radiological testing	2 images		$320/image		640	2
3	Operating room	4 hours		$200/hour		800	3
4	Pathological testing	1 specimen		$120/specimen		120	4
5	Dietary and laundry	7 days		$150/day		1,050	5
6	Total					$2,790	6

The patient activity costs can be combined with the direct costs, such as drugs and supplies, and reported with the revenues earned for each patient in a customer profitability report. A partial customer profitability report for Hopewell Hospital is shown in Exhibit 13.

The report in Exhibit 13 can be used by the administrators to guide decisions on pricing or service delivery. For example, there was a large loss on services provided to Brian Birini. Further investigation might reveal that services provided to Birini were out of line with what would be allowed for reimbursement by the insurance company. As a result, future losses could be avoided by lobbying for a higher insurance reimbursement or aligning the services closer to the revenues allowed by the insurance company.

EXHIBIT 13

Customer Profitability Report

Hopewell Hospital
Customer (Patient) Profitability Report
For the Period Ending December 31, 2008

	Adcock, Kim	Birini, Brian	Conway, Don	Wilson, Mia
Revenues	$9,500	$21,400	$5,050	$3,300
Less: Patient costs:				
Drugs and supplies	$ 400	$ 1,000	$ 300	$ 200
Admitting	180	180	180	180
Radiological testing	1,280	2,560	1,280	640
Operating room	2,400	6,400	1,600	800
Pathological testing	240	600	120	120
Dietary and laundry	4,200	14,700	1,050	1,050
Total patient costs	$8,700	$25,440	$4,530	$2,990
Income from operations	$ 800	$ (4,040)	$ 520	$ 310

Example Exercise 11-5   objective **6**

The Metro Radiology Clinic uses activity-based costing to determine the cost of servicing patients. There are three activity pools: patient administration, imaging, and diagnostic services. The activity rates associated with each activity pool are $45 per patient visit, $320 per X-ray image, and $450 per diagnosis. Julie Campbell went to the clinic and had two X-rays, each of which was read and interpreted by a doctor. Determine the total activity-based cost of Campbell's visit.

Follow My Example 11-5

Imaging	$ 640	(2 images × $320)
Diagnosis	900	(2 diagnoses × $450)
Patient administration	45	(1 visit × $45)
Total activity cost	$1,585	

For Practice: PE 11-5A, PE 11-5B

Business Connections

REAL WORLD

FINDING THE RIGHT NICHE

Businesses often attempt to divide a market into its unique characteristics, called market segmentation. Once a market segment is identified, product, price, promotion, and location strategies are tailored to fit that market. This is a better approach for many products and services than following a "one size fits all" strategy. Activity-based costing can be used to help tailor organizational effort toward different segments. For example, Fidelity Investments uses activity-based costing to tailor its sales and marketing strategies to different wealth segments. Thus, a higher wealth segment could rely on personal sales activities, while less wealthy segments would rely on less costly sales activities, such as mass mail. The following table lists popular forms of segmentation and their common characteristics:

Form of Segmentation	Characteristics
Demographic	Age, education, gender, income, race
Geographic	Region, city, country
Psychographic	Lifestyle, values, attitudes
Benefit	Benefits provided
Volume	Light vs. heavy use

Examples for each of these forms of segmentation are as follows:

Demographic: Fidelity Investments tailors sales and marketing strategies to different wealth segments.
Geographic: Pro sports teams offer merchandise in their home cities.
Psychographic: The Body Shop markets all-natural beauty products to consumers who value cosmetic products that have not been animal-tested.
Benefit: Cold Stone Creamery sells a premium ice cream product with customized toppings.
Volume: Delta Air Lines provides additional benefits, such as class upgrades, free air travel, and boarding priority, to its frequent fliers.

© PAUL CONNORS/FIDELITY INVESTMENTS/FEATURE PHOTO SERVICE (NEWSCOM)

At a Glance ↘

....

1. Identify three methods used for allocating factory overhead costs to products.

Key Points	Key Learning Outcomes	Example Exercises	Practice Exercises
There are three basic cost allocation methods used for determining the cost of products: the single plantwide factory overhead rate method, the multiple production department factory overhead rate method, and the activity-based costing method.	• List the three primary methods for allocating factory overhead costs to products.		

2. Use a single plantwide factory overhead rate for product costing.

Key Points	Key Learning Outcomes	Example Exercises	Practice Exercises
A single plantwide factory overhead rate can be used to allocate all plant overhead to all products. The single plantwide factory overhead rate is simple to apply, but it can lead to significant product cost distortions.	• Compute the single plantwide factory overhead rate and use this rate to allocate factory overhead costs to products. • Identify the conditions that favor the use of a single plantwide factory overhead rate for allocating factory overhead costs to products.	**11-1**	11-1A, 11-1B

3. Use multiple production department factory overhead rates for product costing.

Key Points	Key Learning Outcomes	Example Exercises	Practice Exercises
Product costing using multiple production department factory overhead rates requires identifying the factory overhead associated with the production departments. Using these rates will result in greater accuracy than using single plantwide factory overhead rates when: 1. There are significant differences in the factory overhead rates across different production departments. and 2. The products require different ratios of allocation-base usage in each production department.	• Compute multiple production department overhead rates and use these rates to allocate factory overhead costs to products. • Identify and describe the two conditions that favor the use of multiple production department factory overhead rates for allocating factory overhead costs to products as compared to the single plantwide factory overhead rate method.	**11-2**	11-2A, 11-2B

(continued)

4. Use activity-based costing for product costing.

Key Points	Key Learning Outcomes	Example Exercises	Practice Exercises
Activity-based costing requires factory overhead to be budgeted to activity cost pools. The activity cost pools are allocated to products by multiplying activity rates by the activity-base quantity consumed for each product. Using activity rates rather than multiple production department factory overhead rates may result in more accurate product costs when products consume activities in ratios that are unrelated to their departmental allocation bases.	• Compute activity rates and use these rates to allocate factory overhead costs to products. • Identify the conditions that favor the use of activity-based rates for allocating factory overhead costs to products, as compared to the other two methods of cost allocation. • Compare the three factory overhead allocation methods and describe the causes of cost allocation distortion.	11-3	11-3A, 11-3B

5. Use activity-based costing to allocate selling and administrative expenses to products.

Key Points	Key Learning Outcomes	Example Exercises	Practice Exercises
Selling and administrative expenses can be allocated to products for management profit reporting, using activity-based costing. The traditional approach to allocating selling and administrative expenses is by the relative sales volumes of the products. Activity-based costing would be preferred when the products use selling and administrative activities in ratios that are unrelated to their sales volumes.	• Compute selling and administrative activity rates and use these rates to allocate selling and administrative expenses to either a product or customer. • Identify the conditions that would favor the use of activity-based costing for allocating selling and administrative expenses.	11-4	11-4A, 11-4B

6. Use activity-based costing in a service business.

Key Points	Key Learning Outcomes	Example Exercises	Practice Exercises
Activity-based costing may be applied in service settings to determine the cost of individual service offerings. Service costs are determined by multiplying activity rates by the amount of activity-base quantities consumed by the customer using the service offering. Such information can support service pricing and profitability analysis.	• Compute activity rates for service offerings and use these rates to allocate indirect costs to either a service product line or a customer. • Prepare a customer profitability report using the cost of activities. • Describe how activity-based cost information can be used in a service business for improved decision making.	11-5	11-5A, 11-5B

Key Terms

activity base (435)
activity cost pools (434)
activity rate (435)
activity-base usage quantity (435)
activity-based costing (ABC)
  method (434)

engineering change order (ECO)
  (434)
multiple production department
  factory overhead rate method
  (429)
product costing (426)

production department factory
  overhead rates (430)
setup (434)
single plantwide factory overhead
  rate method (427)

Illustrative Problem

Hammer Company plans to use activity-based costing to determine its product costs. It presently uses a single plantwide factory overhead rate for allocating factory overhead to products, based on direct labor hours. The total factory overhead cost is as follows:

Department	Factory Overhead
Production Support	$1,225,000
Production (factory overhead only)	175,000
Total cost	$1,400,000

The company determined that it performed four major activities in the Production Support Department. These activities, along with their budgeted costs, are as follows:

Production Support Activities	Budgeted Cost
Setup	$ 428,750
Production control	245,000
Quality control	183,750
Materials management	367,500
Total	$1,225,000

Hammer Company estimated the following activity-base usage quantities and units produced for each of its three products:

Products	Number of Units	Direct Labor Hrs.	Setups	Production Orders	Inspections	Material Requisitions
TV	10,000	25,000	80	80	35	320
Computer	2,000	10,000	40	40	40	400
Cell phone	50,000	140,000	5	5	0	30
Total cost	62,000	175,000	125	125	75	750

Instructions

1. Determine the factory overhead cost per unit for the TV, computer, and cell phone under the single plantwide factory overhead rate method. Use direct labor hours as the activity base.
2. Determine the factory overhead cost per unit for the TV, computer, and cell phone under activity-based costing.
3. Which method provides more accurate product costing? Why?

Solution

1. Single Plantwide Factory Overhead Rate $= \dfrac{\$1,400,000}{175,000 \text{ direct labor hours}}$

$= \$8$ per direct labor hour

Factory overhead cost per unit:

	TV	Computer	Cell Phone
Number of direct labor hours	25,000	10,000	140,000
Single plantwide factory overhead rate	× $8/dlh	× $8/dlh	× $8/dlh
Total factory overhead	$200,000	$ 80,000	$1,120,000
Number of units	/ 10,000	/ 2,000	/ 50,000
Cost per unit	$ 20.00	$ 40.00	$ 22.40

2. Under activity-based costing, an activity rate must be determined for each activity pool:

Activity	Activity Cost Pool Budget	/	Estimated Activity Base	=	Activity Rate
Setup	$428,750	/	125 setups	=	$3,430 per setup
Production control	$245,000	/	125 production orders	=	$1,960 per production order

Activity	Activity Cost Pool Budget	/	Estimated Activity Base	=	Activity Rate
Quality control	$183,750	/	75 inspections	=	$2,450 per inspection
Materials management	$367,500	/	750 requisitions	=	$490 per requisition
Production	$175,000	/	175,000 direct labor hours	=	$1 per direct labor hour

These activity rates can be used to determine the activity-based factory overhead cost per unit as follows:

TV

Activity	Activity-Base Usage	×	Activity Rate	=	Activity Cost
Setup	80 setups	×	$3,430	=	$274,400
Production control	80 production orders	×	$1,960	=	156,800
Quality control	35 inspections	×	$2,450	=	85,750
Materials management	320 requisitions	×	$490	=	156,800
Production	25,000 direct labor hrs.	×	$1	=	25,000
Total factory overhead					$698,750
Unit volume					/ 10,000
Factory overhead cost per unit					$ 69.88

Computer

Activity	Activity-Base Usage	×	Activity Rate	=	Activity Cost
Setup	40 setups	×	$3,430	=	$137,200
Production control	40 production orders	×	$1,960	=	78,400
Quality control	40 inspections	×	$2,450	=	98,000
Materials management	400 requisitions	×	$490	=	196,000
Production	10,000 direct labor hrs.	×	$1	=	10,000
Total factory overhead					$519,600
Unit volume					/ 2,000
Factory overhead cost per unit					$ 259.80

Cell phone

Activity	Activity-Base Usage	×	Activity Rate	=	Activity Cost
Setup	5 setups	×	$3,430	=	$ 17,150
Production control	5 production orders	×	$1,960	=	9,800
Quality control	0 inspections	×	$2,450	=	0
Materials management	30 requisitions	×	$490	=	14,700
Production	140,000 direct labor hrs.	×	$1	=	140,000
Total factory overhead					$181,650
Unit volume					/ 50,000
Factory overhead cost per unit					$ 3.63

3. Activity-based costing is more accurate, compared to the single plantwide factory over-head rate method. Activity-based costing properly shows that the cell phone is actually less expensive to make, while the other two products are more expensive to make. The reason is that the single plantwide factory overhead rate method fails to account for activity costs correctly. The setup, production control, quality control, and materials management activities are all performed on products in rates that are different from their volumes. For example, the computer requires many of these activities relative to its actual unit volume. The computer requires 40 setups over a volume of 2,000 units (average production run size = 50 units), while the cell phone has only 5 setups over 50,000 units (average production run size = 10,000 units). Thus, the computer requires greater support costs relative to the cell phone.

The cell phone requires minimum activity support because it is scheduled in large batches and requires no inspections (has high quality) and few requisitions. The other two products exhibit the opposite characteristics.

Self-Examination Questions

(Answers at End of Chapter)

1. Which of the following statements is most accurate?
   A. The single plantwide factory overhead rate method will usually provide management with accurate product costs.
   B. Activity-based costing can be used by management to determine accurate profitability for each product.
   C. The multiple production department factory overhead rate method will usually result in more product cost distortion than the single plantwide factory overhead rate method.
   D. Generally accepted accounting principles require activity-based costing methods for inventory valuation.

2. San Madeo Company had the following factory overhead costs:
Power	$120,000
Indirect labor	60,000
Equipment depreciation	500,000

   The factory is budgeted to work 20,000 direct labor hours in the upcoming period. San Madeo uses a single plantwide factory overhead rate based on direct labor hours. What is the overhead cost per unit associated with Product M, if Product M uses 6 direct labor hours per unit in the factory?
   A. $34   C. $204
   B. $54   D. $150

3. Which of the following activity bases would best be used to allocate setup activity to products?
   A. Number of inspections
   B. Direct labor hours
   C. Direct machine hours
   D. Number of production runs

4. Production Department 1 (PD1) and Production Department 2 (PD2) had factory overhead budgets of $26,000 and $48,000, respectively. Each department was budgeted for 5,000 direct labor hours of production activity. Product T required 5 direct labor hours in PD1 and 2 direct labor hours in PD2. What is the factory overhead cost associated with a unit of Product T, assuming that factory overhead is allocated using the multiple production department rate method?
   A. $26.00   C. $45.20
   B. $40.40   D. $58.40

5. The following activity rates are associated with moving rail cars by train:
   $4 per gross ton mile
   $50 per rail car switch
   $200 per rail car

   A train with 20 rail cars traveled 100 miles. Each rail car carried 10 tons of product. Each rail car was switched 2 times. What is the total cost of moving this train?
   A. $5,400   C. $44,100
   B. $10,000   D. $86,000

Eye Openers

1. How does a company use product costing?
2. Why would it be appropriate for a company that builds aircraft carriers for the Navy to use a single overhead rate?
3. Why would management be concerned about the accuracy of product costs?
4. Why is the sum of product costs under alternative factory overhead cost allocation methods equal?
5. Why would a manufacturing company with multiple production departments still prefer to use a single plantwide overhead rate?
6. How do the multiple production department and the single plantwide factory overhead rate methods differ?
7. How are multiple production department factory overhead rates determined?
8. How is the allocation base for a production department selected?
9. Under what two conditions would the multiple production department factory overhead rate method provide more accurate product costs than the single plantwide factory overhead rate method?
10. How does activity-based costing differ from the multiple production department factory overhead rate method?
11. Shipping, selling, marketing, sales order processing, return processing, and advertising activities can be related to products by using activity-based costing. Would allocating these activities to products for financial statement reporting be acceptable according to GAAP?
12. What would happen to net income if the activities noted in Eye Opener 11 were allocated to products for financial statement reporting and the inventory increased?
13. Under what circumstances might the activity-based costing method provide more accurate product costs than the multiple production department factory overhead rate method?
14. When might activity-based costing be preferred over using a relative amount of product sales in allocating selling and administrative expenses to products?
15. How can activity-based costing be used in service companies?
16. How would a telecommunications company use activity-based costing in conducting profit analysis?

Practice Exercises

PE 11-1A
Single plantwide overhead rate and allocation
obj. 2

The total factory overhead for Goldstein Company is budgeted for the year at $270,000. Goldstein manufactures two types of men's pants: jeans and khakis. The jeans and khakis each require 0.2 direct labor hour for manufacture. Each product is budgeted for 15,000 units of production for the year. Determine (a) the total number of budgeted direct labor hours for the year, (b) the single plantwide factory overhead rate, and (c) the factory overhead allocated per unit for each product using the single plantwide factory overhead rate.

PE 11-1B
Single plantwide factory overhead rate and allocation
obj. 2

The total factory overhead for Kell Marine Company is budgeted for the year at $800,000. Kell Marine manufactures two types of boats: a speedboat and bass boat. The speedboat and bass boat each require 5 direct labor hours for manufacture. Each product is budgeted for 200 units of production for the year. Determine (a) the total number of budgeted direct labor hours for the year, (b) the single plantwide factory overhead rate, and (c) the factory overhead allocated per unit for each product using the single plantwide factory overhead rate.

PE 11-2A
Multiple production department factory overhead rates and allocation
obj. 3

The total factory overhead for Goldstein Company is budgeted for the year at $270,000, divided into two departments: Cutting, $90,000, and Sewing, $180,000. Goldstein manufactures two types of men's pants: jeans and khakis. The jeans require 0.04 direct labor hour in Cutting and 0.16 direct labor hour in Sewing. The khakis require 0.16 direct labor hour in Cutting and 0.04 direct labor hour in Sewing. Each product is budgeted for 15,000 units of production for the year. Determine (a) the total number of budgeted direct labor hours for the year in each department, (b) the departmental factory overhead rates for both departments, and (c) the factory overhead allocated per unit for each product using the department factory overhead allocation rates.

PE 11-2B
Multiple production department factory overhead rates and allocation
obj. 3

The total factory overhead for Kell Marine Company is budgeted for the year at $800,000, divided into two departments: Fabrication, $550,000, and Assembly, $250,000. Kell Marine manufactures two types of boats: speedboats and bass boats. The speedboats require 1.5 direct labor hours in Fabrication and 3.5 direct labor hours in Assembly. The bass boat require 3.5 direct labor hours in Fabrication and 1.5 direct labor hours in Assembly. Each product is budgeted for 200 units of production for the year. Determine (a) the total number of budgeted direct labor hours for the year in each department, (b) the departmental factory overhead rates for both departments, and (c) the factory overhead allocated per unit for each product using the department factory overhead allocation rates.

PE 11-3A
Activity-based rates and allocation
obj. 4

The total factory overhead for Goldstein Company is budgeted for the year at $270,000, divided into four activity pools: cutting, $75,000; sewing, $60,000; setup, $85,000; and inspection, $50,000. Goldstein manufactures two types of men's pants: jeans and khakis. The activity-base usage quantities for each product by each activity are as follows:

	Cutting	Sewing	Setup	Inspection
Jeans	600 dlh	2,400 dlh	1,600 setups	3,500 inspections
Khakis	2,400	600	400	500
	3,000 dlh	3,000 dlh	2,000 setups	4,000 inspections

Each product is budgeted for 15,000 units of production for the year. Determine (a) the activity rates for each activity and (b) the activity-based factory overhead per unit for each product.

PE 11-3B
Activity-based rates and allocation
obj. 4

The total factory overhead for Kell Marine Company is budgeted for the year at $800,000, divided into four activity pools: fabrication, $300,000; assembly, $150,000; setup, $140,000; and inspection, $210,000. Kell Marine manufactures two types of boats: a speedboat and bass boat. The activity-base usage quantities for each product by each activity are as follows:

	Fabrication	Assembly	Setup	Inspection
Speedboat	300 dlh	700 dlh	50 setups	100 inspections
Bass boat	700	300	90	400
	1,000 dlh	1,000 dlh	140 setups	500 inspections

Each product is budgeted for 200 units of production for the year. Determine (a) the activity rates for each activity and (b) the activity-based factory overhead per unit for each product.

PE 11-4A
Activity-based costing—selling and administrative expenses
obj. 5

Gemini Company manufactures and sells shoes. Gemini uses activity-based costing to determine the cost of the sales order processing and the shipping activity. The sales order processing activity has an activity rate of $18 per sales order, and the shipping activity has an activity rate of $24 per shipment. Gemini sold 40,000 units of walking shoes, which consisted of 5,000 orders and 3,000 shipments. Determine (a) the total and (b) the per-unit sales order processing and shipping activity cost for walking shoes.

PE 11-4B
Activity-based costing—selling and administrative expenses
obj. 5

Playtyme Company manufactures and sells outdoor play equipment. Playtyme uses activity-based costing to determine the cost of the sales order processing and the customer return activity. The sales order processing activity has an activity rate of $32 per sales order, and the customer return activity has an activity rate of $85 per return. Gemini sold 2,000 swing sets, which consisted of 500 orders and 40 returns. Determine (a) the total and (b) the per-unit sales order processing and customer return activity cost for swing sets.

PE 11-5A
Activity-based costing—service business
obj. 6

National Bancorp uses activity-based costing to determine the cost of servicing customers. There are three activity pools: teller transaction processing, check processing, and ATM transaction processing. The activity rates associated with each activity pool are $2.40 per teller transaction, $0.18 per canceled check, and $0.90 per ATM transaction. Jacob Ferris had 5 teller transactions, 65 canceled checks, and 12 ATM transactions during the month. Determine the total monthly activity-based cost for servicing Ferris during the month.

PE 11-5B
Activity-based costing—service business
obj. 6

Comfort Suites Hotel uses activity-based costing to determine the cost of servicing customers. There are three activity pools: guest check-in, room cleaning, and meal service. The activity rates associated with each activity pool are $5.80 per guest check-in, $18.60 per room cleaning, and $2.75 per served meal (not including food). Maurice Dee visited the hotel for a 3-night stay. Dee had four meals in the hotel during his visit. Determine the total activity-based cost for servicing Dee for this visit.

Exercises

EX 11-1
Single plantwide factory overhead rate
obj. 2

Spacely Company's Fabrication Department incurred $130,000 of factory overhead cost in producing gears and sprockets. The two products consumed a total of 5,000 direct machine hours. Of that amount, sprockets consumed 2,100 direct machine hours.
Determine the total amount of factory overhead that should be allocated to sprockets.

EX 11-2
Single plantwide factory overhead rate
obj. 2

✓ a. $32 per direct labor hour

River City Band Instruments Inc. makes three musical instruments: trumpets, tubas, and trombones. The budgeted factory overhead cost is $156,800. Factory overhead is allocated to the three products on the basis of direct labor hours. The products have the following budgeted production volume and direct labor hours per unit:

	Budgeted Production Volume	Direct Labor Hours per Unit
Trumpets	2,800 units	0.6
Tubas	700	1.8
Trombones	1,400	1.4

a. Determine the single plantwide factory overhead rate.
b. Use the factory overhead rate in (a) to determine the amount of total and per-unit factory overhead allocated to each of the three products.

EX 11-3
Single plantwide factory overhead rate
obj. 2

✓ a. $58 per processing hour

Snappy Snack Food Company manufactures three types of snack foods: tortilla chips, potato chips, and pretzels. The company has budgeted the following costs for the upcoming period:

Factory depreciation	$115,500
Indirect labor	336,600
Factory electricity	43,400
Indirect materials	72,900
Selling expenses	171,000
Administrative expenses	92,800
Total costs	$832,200

Factory overhead is allocated to the three products on the basis of processing hours. The products had the following production budget and processing hours per case:

	Budgeted Production Volume (Cases)	Processing Hours per Case
Tortilla chips	16,000	0.14
Potato chips	34,000	0.18
Pretzels	12,000	0.12
Total	62,000	

a. Determine the single plantwide factory overhead rate.
b. Use the factory overhead rate in (a) to determine the amount of total and per-case factory overhead allocated to each of the three products under generally accepted accounting principles.

EX 11-4
Product costs and product profitability reports, using a single plantwide factory overhead rate

obj. 2

✓ *c. Pistons gross profit, $13,500*

Flint Engine Parts Inc. (FEP) produces three products—pistons, valves, and cams—for the heavy equipment industry. FEP has a very simple production process and product line and uses a single plantwide factory overhead rate to allocate overhead to the three products. The factory overhead rate is based on direct labor hours. Information about the three products for 2009 is as follows:

	Budgeted Volume (Units)	Direct Labor Hours per Unit	Price per Unit	Direct Materials per Unit
Pistons	5,000	0.40	$45.00	$25.50
Valves	15,000	0.18	12.80	4.60
Cams	2,500	0.14	32.00	18.40

The estimated direct labor rate is $22 per direct labor hour. Beginning and ending inventories are negligible and are, thus, assumed to be zero. The budgeted factory overhead for FEP is $101,000.

a. Determine the plantwide factory overhead rate.
b. Determine the factory overhead and direct labor cost per unit for each product.
c. Use the information above to construct a budgeted gross profit report by product line for the year ended December 31, 2009. Include the gross profit as a percent of sales in the last line of your report, rounded to one decimal place.
d. What does the report in (c) indicate to you?

EX 11-5
Multiple production department factory overhead rate method

obj. 3

✓ *b. Small glove, $5.80 per unit*

Golden Glove Company produces three types of gloves: small, medium, and large. A glove pattern is first stenciled onto leather in the Pattern Department. The stenciled patterns are then sent to the Cut and Sew Department, where the final glove is cut and sewed together. Golden uses the multiple production department factory overhead rate method of allocating factory overhead costs. Its factory overhead costs were budgeted as follows:

Pattern Department overhead	$100,000
Cut and Sew Department overhead	350,000
Total	$450,000

The direct labor estimated for each production department was as follows:

Pattern Department	2,500 direct labor hours
Cut and Sew Department	5,000
Total	7,500 direct labor hours

Direct labor hours are used to allocate the production department overhead to the products. The direct labor hours per unit for each product for each production department were obtained from the engineering records as follows:

Production Departments	Small Glove	Medium Glove	Large Glove
Pattern Department	0.04	0.05	0.07
Cut and Sew Department	0.06	0.09	0.08
Direct labor hours per unit	0.10	0.14	0.15

a. Determine the two production department factory overhead rates.
b. Use the two production department factory overhead rates to determine the factory overhead per unit for each product.

EX 11-6

Single plantwide and multiple production department factory overhead rate methods and product cost distortion

objs. 2, 3

✓ b. Portable computer, $348 per unit

Orange Computer Company manufactures a desktop and portable computer through two production departments, Assembly and Testing. Presently, the company uses a single plantwide factory overhead rate for allocating factory overhead to the two products. However, management is considering using the multiple production department factory overhead rate method. The following factory overhead was budgeted for Orange:

Assembly Department	$ 420,000
Testing Department	740,000
Total	$1,160,000

Direct machine hours were estimated as follows:

Assembly Department	6,000 hours
Testing Department	4,000
Total	10,000 hours

In addition, the direct machine hours (dmh) used to produce a unit of each product in each department were determined from engineering records, as follows:

	Desktop	Portable
Assembly Department	0.90 dmh	1.80 dmh
Testing Department	0.60	1.20
Total machine hours per unit	1.50 dmh	3.00 dmh

a. Determine the per-unit factory overhead allocated to the desktop and portable computers under the single plantwide factory overhead rate method, using direct machine hours as the allocation base.
b. Determine the per-unit factory overhead allocated to the desktop and portable computers under the multiple production department factory overhead rate method, using direct machine hours as the allocation base for each department.
c. Recommend to management a product costing approach, based on your analyses in (a) and (b). Support your recommendation.

EX 11-7

Single plantwide and multiple production department factory overhead rate methods and product cost distortion

objs. 2, 3

✓ b. Diesel engine, $874 per unit

The management of Power Torque Engines Inc. manufactures gasoline and diesel engines through two production departments, Fabrication and Assembly. Management needs accurate product cost information in order to guide product strategy. Presently, the company uses a single plantwide factory overhead rate for allocating factory overhead to the two products. However, management is considering using the multiple production department factory overhead rate method. The following factory overhead was budgeted for Power Torque:

Fabrication Department factory overhead	$620,000
Assembly Department factory overhead	325,000
Total	$945,000

Direct labor hours were estimated as follows:

Fabrication Department	5,000 hours
Assembly Department	5,000
Total	10,000 hours

In addition, the direct labor hours (dlh) used to produce a unit of each product in each department were determined from engineering records, as follows:

Production Departments	Gasoline Engine	Diesel Engine
Fabrication Department	2 dlh	6 dlh
Assembly Department	6	2
Direct labor hours per unit	8 dlh	8 dlh

a. Determine the per-unit factory overhead allocated to the gasoline and diesel engines under the single plantwide factory overhead rate method, using direct labor hours as the activity base.
b. Determine the per-unit factory overhead allocated to the gasoline and diesel engines under the multiple production department factory overhead rate method, using direct labor hours as the activity base for each department.
c. Recommend to management a product costing approach, based on your analyses in (a) and (b). Support your recommendation.

EX 11-8
Identifying activity bases in an activity-based cost system
obj. **4**

Eden Foods Inc. uses activity-based costing to determine product costs. For each activity listed in the left column, match an appropriate activity base from the right column. You may use items in the activity base list more than once or not at all.

Activity	Activity Base
Accounting reports	Engineering change orders
Customer return processing	Kilowatt hours used
Electric power	Number of customer orders
Human resources	Number of customer returns
Inventory control	Number of customers
Invoice and collecting	Number of direct labor hours
Machine depreciation	Number of inventory transactions
Materials handling	Number of inspections
Order shipping	Number of machine hours
Payroll	Number of material moves
Production control	Number of payroll checks processed
Production setup	Number of production orders
Purchasing	Number of purchase orders
Quality control	Number of accounting reports
	Number of setups

EX 11-9
Product costs using activity rates
obj. **4**
✔ b. $52,200

E-gift Inc. sells china and flatware over the Internet. For the next period, the budgeted cost of the sales order processing activity is $115,200, and 12,800 sales orders are estimated to be processed.

a. Determine the activity rate of the sales order processing activity.
b. Determine the amount of sales order processing cost that china would receive if it had 5,800 sales orders.

EX 11-10
*Product costs using
activity rates*

obj. **4**

✔ *Treadmill activity cost
per unit, $51.98*

Lifeway Equipment Company manufactures stationary bicycles and treadmills. The products are produced in its Fabrication and Assembly production departments. In addition to production activities, several other activities are required to produce the two products. These activities and their associated activity rates are as follows:

Activity	Activity Rate
Fabrication	$28 per machine hour
Assembly	$9 per direct labor hour
Setup	$40 per setup
Inspecting	$26 per inspection
Production scheduling	$19 per production order
Purchasing	$13 per purchase order

The activity-base usage quantities and units produced for each product were as follows:

Activity Base	Stationary Bicycle	Treadmill
Machine hours	1,960	1,120
Direct labor hours	462	184
Setups	59	19
Inspections	683	425
Production orders	64	14
Purchase orders	211	130
Units produced	900	900

Use the activity rate and usage information to calculate the total activity cost and activity cost per unit for each product.

EX 11-11
*Activity rates and
product costs using
activity-based costing*

obj. **4**

✔ *b. Dining room lighting
fixtures, $56.00 per unit*

Nordic Night Inc. manufactures entry and dining room lighting fixtures. Five activities are used in manufacturing the fixtures. These activities and their associated activity cost pools and activity bases are as follows:

Activity	Activity Cost Pool (Budgeted)	Activity Base
Casting	$286,000	Machine hours
Assembly	161,000	Direct labor hours
Inspecting	27,600	Number of inspections
Setup	78,000	Number of setups
Materials handling	36,000	Number of loads

Corporate records were obtained to estimate the amount of activity to be used by the two products. The estimated activity-base usage quantities and units produced are provided in the table below.

Activity Base	Entry	Dining	Total
Machine hours	6,000	5,000	11,000
Direct labor hours	4,600	6,900	11,500
Number of inspections	1,700	600	2,300
Number of setups	240	60	300
Number of loads	780	220	1,000
Units produced	8,282	4,595	12,877

a. Determine the activity rate for each activity.
b. Use the activity rates in (a) to determine the total and per-unit activity costs associated with each product.

EX 11-12
*Activity cost pools,
activity rates, and
product costs using
activity-based costing*

obj. 4

✓ b. Oven, $74.00 per unit

Master Chef Inc. is estimating the activity cost associated with producing ovens and refrigerators. The indirect labor can be traced into four separate activity pools, based on time
records provided by the employees. The budgeted activity cost and activity base information are provided as follows:

Activity	Activity Pool Cost	Activity Base
Procurement	$159,300	Number of purchase orders
Scheduling	10,000	Number of production orders
Materials handling	32,000	Number of moves
Product development	26,400	Number of engineering changes
Total cost	$227,700	

The estimated activity-base usage and unit information for Master Chef's two product
lines was determined from corporate records as follows:

	Number of Purchase Orders	Number of Production Orders	Number of Moves	Number of Engineering Changes	Units
Ovens	800	260	480	140	1,850
Refrigerators	550	140	320	80	1,816
Totals	1,350	400	800	220	3,666

a. Determine the activity rate for each activity cost pool.
b. Determine the activity-based cost per unit of each product.

EX 11-13
*Activity-based costing
and product cost
distortion*

objs. 2, 4

✓ c. CD, $3.91

Storage Devices Inc. is considering a change to activity-based product costing. The company produces two products, compact disks (CDs) and data cartridges, in a single production department. The production department is estimated to require 5,000 direct labor hours.
The total indirect labor is budgeted to be $460,000.
    Time records from indirect labor employees revealed that they spent 40% of their time
setting up production runs and 60% of their time supporting actual production.
    The following information about CDs and data cartridges was determined from the
corporate records:

	Number of Setups	Direct Labor Hours	Units
CDs	500	2,500	50,000
Data cartridges	1,100	2,500	50,000
Total	1,600	5,000	100,000

a. Determine the indirect labor cost per unit allocated to CDs and data cartridges under a
single plantwide factory overhead rate system using the direct labor hours as the allocation base.
b. Determine the activity pools and activity rates for the indirect labor under activity-based
costing. Assume two activity pools—one for setup and the other for production support.
c. Determine the activity cost per unit for indirect labor allocated to each product under
activity-based costing.
d. Why are the per-unit allocated costs in (a) different from the per-unit activity cost assigned to the products in (c)?

EX 11-14
*Multiple production
department factory
overhead rate method*

obj. 3

✓ b. Blender, $17.00 per unit

Gourmet Assistant Appliance Company manufactures small kitchen appliances. The product line consists of blenders and toaster ovens. Gourmet Assistant presently uses the multiple production department factory overhead rate method. The factory overhead is as follows:

Assembly Department	$225,000
Test and Pack Department	150,000
Total	$375,000

The direct labor information for the production of 10,000 units of each product is as follows:

	Assembly Department	Test and Pack Department
Blender	400 dlh	1,100 dlh
Toaster oven	1,100	400
Total	1,500 dlh	1,500 dlh

Gourmet Assistant used direct labor hours to allocate production department factory overhead to products.

a. Determine the two production department factory overhead rates.
b. Determine the total factory overhead and the factory overhead per unit allocated to each product.

EX 11-15

Activity-based costing and product cost distortion

obj. 4

✓ *b. Blender, $19.25 per unit*

The management of Gourmet Assistant Appliance Company in Exercise 11-14 has asked you to use activity-based costing to allocate factory overhead costs to the two products. You have determined that $60,000 of factory overhead from each of the production departments can be associated with setup activity ($120,000 in total). Company records indicate that blenders required 330 setups, while the toaster ovens required only 150 setups. Each product has a production volume of 10,000 units.

a. Determine the three activity rates (assembly, test and pack, and setup).
b. Determine the total factory overhead and factory overhead per unit allocated to each product.

EX 11-16

Single plantwide rate and activity-based costing

objs. 2, 4

✓ *a. Low, Col. C., 143.7%*

Whirlpool Corporation conducted an activity-based costing study of its Evansville, Indiana, plant in order to identify its most profitable products. Assume that we select three representative refrigerators (out of 333): one low-, one medium-, and one high-volume refrigerator. Additionally, we assume the following activity-base information for each of the three refrigerators:

Three Representative Refrigerators	Number of Machine Hours	Number of Setups	Number of Sales Orders	Number of Units
Refrigerator—Low Volume	28	21	39	140
Refrigerator—Medium Volume	284	18	145	1,350
Refrigerator—High Volume	865	12	123	4,500

Prior to conducting the study, the factory overhead allocation was based on a single machine hour rate. The machine hour rate was $220 per hour. After conducting the activity-based costing study, assume that three activities were used to allocate the factory overhead. The new activity rate information is assumed to be as follows:

	Machining Activity	Setup Activity	Sales Order Processing Activity
Activity rate	$190	$350	$60

a. Complete the following table, using the single machine hour rate to determine the per-unit factory overhead for each refrigerator (Column A) and the three activity-based rates to determine the activity-based factory overhead per unit (Column B). Finally, compute the percent change in per-unit allocation from the single to activity-based rate methods (Column C). Round to one decimal place.

Product Volume Class	Column A Single Rate Overhead Allocation per Unit	Column B ABC Overhead Allocation per Unit	Column C Percent Change in Allocation (Col. B − Col. A)/Col. A
Low			
Medium			
High			

b. Why is the traditional overhead rate per machine hour greater under the single rate method than under the activity-based method?

c. Interpret Column C in your table from part (a).

EX 11-17

Evaluating selling and administrative cost allocations

obj. 5

Productivity Plus Furniture Company has two major product lines with the following characteristics:

Commercial office furniture: Few large orders, little advertising support, shipments in full truckloads, and low handling complexity

Home office furniture: Many small orders, large advertising support, shipments in partial truckloads, and high handling complexity

The company produced the following profitability report for management:

Productivity Plus Furniture Company
Product Profitability Report
For the Year Ended December 31, 2008

	Commercial Office Furniture	Home Office Furniture	Total
Revenue	$3,600,000	$1,800,000	$5,400,000
Cost of goods sold	1,500,000	700,000	2,200,000
Gross profit	$2,100,000	$1,100,000	$3,200,000
Selling and administrative expenses	1,200,000	600,000	1,800,000
Income from operations	$ 900,000	$ 500,000	$1,400,000

The selling and administrative expenses are allocated to the products on the basis of relative sales dollars.

Evaluate the accuracy of this report and recommend an alternative approach.

EX 11-18

Construct and interpret a product profitability report, allocating selling and administrative expenses

obj. 5

✓b. Generators operating profit-to-sales, 21%

Portable Power Equipment Company manufactures power equipment. Portable Power has two primary products—generators and air compressors. The following report was prepared by the controller for Portable Power's senior marketing management:

	Generators	Air Compressors	Total
Revenue	$1,750,000	$970,000	$2,720,000
Cost of goods sold	1,312,500	727,500	2,040,000
Gross profit	$ 437,500	$242,500	$ 680,000
Selling and administrative expenses			293,100
Income from operations			$ 386,900

The marketing management team was concerned that the selling and administrative expenses were not traced to the products. Marketing management believed that some products consumed larger amounts of selling and administrative expense than did other products. To verify this, the controller was asked to prepare a complete product profitability report, using activity-based costing.

The controller determined that selling and administrative expenses consisted of two activities: sales order processing and post-sale customer service. The controller was able to determine the activity base and activity rate for each activity, as shown below.

Activity	Activity Base	Activity Rate
Sales order processing	Sales orders	$100 per sales order
Post-sale customer service	Service requests	$320 per customer service request

The controller determined the following additional information about each product:

	Generators	Air Compressors
Number of sales orders	444	791
Number of service requests	80	450

a. Determine the activity cost of each product for sales order processing and post-sale customer service activities.

b. Use the information in (a) to prepare a complete product profitability report dated for the year ended December 31, 2008. Calculate the gross profit to sales and the income from operations to sales percentages for each product.

c. Interpret the product profitability report. How should management respond to the report?

EX 11-19
Activity-based costing and customer profitability

obj. 6

✓ a. Customer 1, $2,308

Square D Company manufactures power distribution equipment for commercial customers, such as hospitals and manufacturers. Activity-based costing was used to determine customer profitability. Customer service activities were assigned to individual customers, using the following assumed customer service activities, activity base, and activity rate:

Customer Service Activity	Activity Base	Activity Rate
Bid preparation	Number of bid requests	$140/request
Shipment	Number of shipments	$26/shipment
Support standard items	Number of standard items ordered	$48/std. item
Support nonstandard items	Number of nonstandard items ordered	$120/nonstd. item

Assume that the company had the following gross profit information for three representative customers:

	Customer 1	Customer 2	Customer 3
Revenue	$17,500	$26,250	$42,000
Cost of goods sold	9,100	12,600	26,040
Gross profit	$ 8,400	$13,650	$15,960
Gross profit as a percent of sales	48%	52%	38%

The administrative records indicated that the activity-base usage quantities for each customer were as follows:

Activity Base	Customer 1	Customer 2	Customer 3
Number of bid requests	6	20	8
Number of shipments	22	34	16
Number of standard items ordered	35	48	52
Number of nonstandard items ordered	25	50	15

a. Prepare a customer profitability report dated for the year ended December 31, 2008, showing (1) the income from operations after customer service activities and (2) the income from operations after customer service activities as a percent of sales. Prepare the report with a column for each customer. Round percentages to the nearest whole percent.

b. Interpret the table in part (a).

EX 11-20
Activity-based costing for a hospital

obj. 6

✓ a. Patient Malone, $6,495

Mercy Hospital plans to use activity-based costing to assign hospital indirect costs to the care of patients. The hospital has identified the following activities and activity rates for the hospital indirect costs:

Activity	Activity Rate
Room and meals	$165 per day
Radiology	$250 per image
Pharmacy	$45 per physician order
Chemistry lab	$85 per test
Operating room	$680 per operating room hour

The records of two representative patients were analyzed, using the activity rates. The activity information associated with the two patients is as follows:

	Patient Malone	Patient Talbot
Number of days	8 days	4 days
Number of images	5 images	3 images
Number of physician orders	6 orders	2 orders
Number of tests	7 tests	3 tests
Number of operating room hours	4.5 hours	2 hours

a. Determine the activity cost associated with each patient.
b. Why is the total activity cost different for the two patients?

EX 11-21
*Activity-based costing in
an insurance company*

objs. 5, 6

✓ a. Auto, $840,375

Sentinel Insurance Company carries three major lines of insurance: auto, workers' compensation, and homeowners. The company has prepared the following report for 2009:

Sentinel Insurance Company
Product Profitability Report
For the Year Ended December 31, 2009

	Auto	Workers' Compensation	Homeowners
Premium revenue	$6,000,000	$5,000,000	$7,000,000
Less estimated claims	4,200,000	3,500,000	4,900,000
Underwriting income	$1,800,000	$1,500,000	$2,100,000
Underwriting income as a percent of premium revenue	30%	30%	30%

Management is concerned that the administrative expenses may make some of the insurance lines unprofitable. However, the administrative expenses have not been allocated to the insurance lines. The controller has suggested that the administrative expenses could be assigned to the insurance lines using activity-based costing. The administrative expenses are comprised of five activities. The activities and their rates are as follows:

	Activity Rates
New policy processing	$170 per new policy
Cancellation processing	$260 per cancellation
Claim audits	$550 per claim audit
Claim disbursements processing	$115 per disbursement
Premium collection processing	$50 per premium collected

Activity-base usage data for each line of insurance was retrieved from the corporate records and is shown below.

	Auto	Workers' Comp.	Homeowners
Number of new policies	1,200	1,400	3,100
Number of canceled policies	500	180	1,650
Number of audited claims	350	120	710
Number of claim disbursements	375	150	740
Number of premiums collected	7,800	1,600	12,000

a. Complete the product profitability report through the administrative activities. Determine the income from operations as a percent of premium revenue, rounded to one decimal place.
b. Interpret the report.

Problems Series A

PR 11-1A
Single plantwide factory overhead rate

obj. 2

✓ 1. b. $166 per machine hour

Custom Car Accessory Company manufactures three chrome-plated products—automobile bumpers, valve covers, and wheels. These products are manufactured in two production departments (Stamping and Plating). The factory overhead for Custom Car is $996,000.

The three products consume both machine hours and direct labor hours in the two production departments as follows:

	Direct Labor Hours	Machine Hours
Stamping Department		
Automobile bumpers	500	780
Valve covers	460	710
Wheels	740	910
	1,700	2,400
Plating Department		
Automobile bumpers	210	1,100
Valve covers	240	930
Wheels	250	1,570
	700	3,600
Total	2,400	6,000

Instructions
1. Determine the single plantwide factory overhead rate, using each of the following allocation bases: (a) direct labor hours and (b) machine hours.
2. Determine the product factory overhead costs, using (a) the direct labor hour plantwide factory overhead rate and (b) the machine hour plantwide factory overhead rate.

PR 11-2A
Multiple production department factory overhead rates

obj. 3

✓ 2. Wheels, $433,825

The management of Custom Car Accessory Company, described in Problem 11-1A, now plans to use the multiple production department factory overhead rate method. The total factory overhead associated with each department is as follows:

Stamping Department	$663,000
Plating Department	333,000
Total	$996,000

Instructions
1. Determine the multiple production department factory overhead rates, using direct labor hours for the Stamping Department and machine hours for the Plating Department.
2. Determine the product factory overhead costs, using the multiple production department rates in (1).

PR 11-3A
Activity-based and department rate product costing and product cost distortions

objs. 3, 4

✓ 4. Snowboards, $455,500 and $18.22

Mountain Jam Sports Inc. manufactures two products: snowboards and skis. The factory overhead incurred is as follows:

Indirect labor	$ 480,000
Cutting Department	350,000
Finishing Department	260,000
Total	$1,090,000

The activity base associated with the two production departments is direct labor hours. The indirect labor can be assigned to two different activities as follows:

Activity	Activity Cost Pool	Activity Base
Production control	$150,000	Number of production runs
Materials handling	330,000	Number of moves
Total	$480,000	

The activity-base usage quantities and units produced for the two products are shown below.

	Number of Production Runs	Number of Moves	Direct Labor Hours—Cutting	Direct Labor Hours—Finishing	Units Produced
Snowboards	60	2,000	3,500	1,500	25,000
Skis	340	4,000	1,500	3,500	25,000
Total	400	6,000	5,000	5,000	50,000

Instructions

1. Determine the factory overhead rates under the multiple production department rate method. Assume that indirect labor is associated with the production departments, so that the total factory overhead is $650,000 and $440,000 for the Cutting and Finishing departments, respectively.
2. Determine the total and per-unit factory overhead costs allocated to each product, using the multiple production department overhead rates in (1).
3. Determine the activity rates, assuming that the indirect labor is associated with activities rather than with the production departments.
4. Determine the total and per-unit cost assigned to each product under activity-based costing.
5. Explain the difference in the per-unit overhead allocated to each product under the multiple production department factory overhead rate and activity-based costing methods.

PR 11-4A
Activity-based product costing
obj. 4

✔2. Newsprint total activity cost, $405,595

Georgia Forest Paper Company manufactures three products (computer paper, newsprint, and specialty paper) in a continuous production process. Senior management has asked the controller to conduct an activity-based costing study. The controller identified the amount of factory overhead required by the critical activities of the organization as follows:

Activity	Activity Cost Pool
Production	$ 763,200
Setup	255,000
Moving	27,200
Shipping	90,000
Product engineering	37,000
Total	$1,172,400

The activity bases identified for each activity are as follows:

Activity	Activity Base
Production	Machine hours
Setup	Number of setups
Moving	Number of moves
Shipping	Number of customer orders
Product engineering	Number of test runs

The activity-base usage quantities and units produced for the three products were determined from corporate records and are as follows:

	Machine Hours	Number of Setups	Number of Moves	Number of Customer Orders	Number of Test Runs	Units
Computer paper	1,080	130	290	440	90	1,200
Newsprint	1,350	60	130	135	20	1,500
Specialty paper	450	310	430	625	140	500
Total	2,880	500	850	1,200	250	3,200

Each product requires 0.9 machine hour per unit.

Instructions

1. Determine the activity rate for each activity.
2. Determine the total and per-unit activity cost for all three products. Round to the nearest cent.
3. Why aren't the activity unit costs equal across all three products since they require the same machine time per unit?

PR 11-5A
Allocating selling and administrative expenses using activity-based costing

obj. 5

✓ *3. Mid-States University income from operations, ($58,300)*

Cool Zone Inc. manufactures cooling units for commercial buildings. The price and cost of goods sold for each unit are as follows:

Price	$120,000 per unit
Cost of goods sold	85,000
Gross profit	$ 35,000 per unit

In addition, the company incurs selling and administrative expenses of $477,700. The company wishes to assign these costs to its three major customers, Mid-States University, Celebrity Arena, and Hope Hospital. These expenses are related to three major nonmanufacturing activities: customer service, project bidding, and engineering support. The engineering support is in the form of engineering changes that are placed by the customer to change the design of a product. The activity cost pool and activity bases associated with these activities are:

Activity	Activity Cost Pool	Activity Base
Customer service	$209,000	Number of service requests
Project bidding	147,200	Number of bids
Engineering support	121,500	Number of customer design changes
Total costs	$477,700	

Activity-base usage and unit volume information for the three customers is as follows:

	Mid-States University	Celebrity Arena	Hope Hospital	Total
Number of service requests	110	35	45	190
Number of bids	14	12	20	46
Number of customer design changes	75	25	35	135
Unit volume	5	10	15	30

Instructions

1. Determine the activity rates for each of the three nonmanufacturing activity pools.
2. Determine the activity costs allocated to the three customers, using the activity rates in (1).
3. Construct customer profitability reports for the three customers dated for the year ended December 31, 2009, using the activity costs in (2). The reports should disclose the gross profit and income from operations associated with each customer.
4. Provide recommendations to management, based on the profitability reports in (3).

PR 11-6A
Product costing and decision analysis for a hospital

obj. 6

✓ *3. Procedure B excess, $263,250*

Nightingale Healthcare Inc. wishes to determine its product costs. Nightingale offers a variety of medical procedures (operations) that are considered its "products." The overhead has been separated into three major activities. The annual estimated activity costs and activity bases are provided below.

Activity	Activity Pool Cost	Activity Base
Scheduling and admitting	$ 207,000	Number of patients
Housekeeping	2,064,000	Number of patient days
Nursing	2,310,000	Weighted care unit
Total costs	$4,581,000	

Total "patient days" are determined by multiplying the number of patients by the average length of stay in the hospital. A weighted care unit (wcu) is a measure of nursing effort used to care for patients. There were 140,000 weighted care units estimated for the year. In addition, Mercy estimated 4,600 patients and 17,200 patient days for the year. (The average patient is expected to have a a little less than a four-day stay in the hospital.)

During a portion of the year, Nightingale collected patient information for three selected procedures, as shown below.

	Activity-Base Usage
Procedure A	
Number of patients	210
Average length of stay	× 5 days
Patient days	1,050
Weighted care units	15,000
Procedure B	
Number of patients	500
Average length of stay	× 4 days
Patient days	2,000
Weighted care units	4,500
Procedure C	
Number of patients	900
Average length of stay	× 3 days
Patient days	2,700
Weighted care units	19,000

Private insurance reimburses the hospital for these activities at a fixed daily rate of $300 per patient day for all three procedures.

Instructions
1. Determine the activity rates.
2. Determine the activity cost for each procedure.
3. Determine the excess or deficiency of reimbursements over activity cost.
4. Interpret your results.

Problems Series B

PR 11-1B
Single plantwide factory overhead rate

obj. 2

✓ 1. b. $228 per machine hour

Morningside Dairy Company manufactures three products—whole milk, skim milk, and cream—in two production departments, Blending and Packing. The factory overhead for Morningside Dairy is $684,000.

The three products consume both machine hours and direct labor hours in the two production departments as follows:

	Direct Labor Hours	Machine Hours
Blending Department		
Whole milk	270	820
Skim milk	290	760
Cream	215	290
	775	1,870
Packing Department		
Whole milk	355	460
Skim milk	520	490
Cream	150	180
	1,025	1,130
Total	1,800	3,000

Instructions
1. Determine the single plantwide factory overhead rate, using each of the following allocation bases: (a) direct labor hours and (b) machine hours.
2. Determine the product factory overhead costs, using (a) the direct labor hour plantwide factory overhead rate and (b) the machine hour plantwide factory overhead rate.

PR 11-2B
Multiple production department factory overhead rates

obj. **3**

✔ 2. Cream, $105,000

The management of Morningside Dairy Company, described in Problem 11-1B, now plans to use the multiple production department factory overhead rate method. The total factory overhead associated with each department is as follows:

Blending Department	$561,000
Packing Department	123,000
Total	$684,000

Instructions
1. Determine the multiple production department factory overhead rates, using machine hours for the Blending Department and direct labor hours for the Packing Department.
2. Determine the product factory overhead costs, using the multiple production department rates in (1).

PR 11-3B
Activity-based and department rate product costing and product cost distortions

objs. **3, 4**

✔ 4. CD players, $478,000 and $47.80

Soundwave Audio Inc. manufactures two products: receivers and CD players. The factory overhead incurred is as follows:

Indirect labor	$ 560,000
Subassembly Department	420,000
Final Assembly Department	350,000
Total	$1,330,000

The activity base associated with the two production departments is direct labor hours. The indirect labor can be assigned to two different activities as follows:

Activity	Activity Cost Pool	Activity Base
Setup	$360,000	Number of setups
Quality control	200,000	Number of inspections
Total	$560,000	

The activity-base usage quantities and units produced for the two products are shown below.

	Number of Setups	Number of Inspections	Direct Labor Hours— Subassembly	Direct Labor Hours— Final Assembly	Units Produced
Receivers	200	1,000	600	400	10,000
CD Players	40	250	400	600	10,000
Total	240	1,250	1,000	1,000	20,000

Instructions
1. Determine the factory overhead rates under the multiple production department rate method. Assume that indirect labor is associated with the production departments, so that the total factory overhead is $700,000 and $630,000 for the Subassembly and Final Assembly Departments, respectively.
2. Determine the total and per-unit factory overhead costs allocated to each product, using the multiple production department overhead rates in (1).
3. Determine the activity rates, assuming that the indirect labor is associated with activities rather than with the production departments.
4. Determine the total and per-unit cost assigned to each product under activity-based costing.
5. Explain the difference in the per-unit overhead allocated to each product under the multiple production department factory overhead rate and activity-based costing methods.

PR 11-4B
*Activity-based product
costing*

obj. 4

✓ *2. Brown sugar total
activity cost, $529,600*

Caribbean Sugar Company manufactures three products (white sugar, brown sugar, and powdered sugar) in a continuous production process. Senior management has asked the controller to conduct an activity-based costing study. The controller identified the amount of factory overhead required by the critical activities of the organization as follows:

Activity	Activity Cost Pool
Production	$ 600,000
Setup	450,000
Inspection	172,000
Shipping	260,000
Customer service	74,000
Total	$1,556,000

The activity bases identified for each activity are as follows:

Activity	Activity Base
Production	Machine hours
Setup	Number of setups
Inspection	Number of inspections
Shipping	Number of customer orders
Customer service	Number of customer service requests

The activity-base usage quantities and units produced for the three products were determined from corporate records and are as follows:

	Machine Hours	Number of Setups	Number of Inspections	Number of Customer Orders	Number of Customer Service Requests	Units
White sugar	3,840	100	200	800	40	9,600
Brown sugar	1,600	150	300	2,200	250	4,000
Powdered sugar	2,560	150	500	1,000	110	6,400
Total	8,000	400	1,000	4,000	400	20,000

Each product requires 0.4 machine hour per unit.

Instructions
1. Determine the activity rate for each activity.
2. Determine the total and per-unit activity cost for all three products. Round to the nearest cent.
3. Why aren't the activity unit costs equal across all three products since they require the same machine time per unit?

PR 11-5B
*Allocating selling and
administrative expenses
using activity-based
costing*

obj. 5

✓ *3. Office Warehouse,
income from operations,
$119,510*

Z-Rox Inc. manufactures office copiers, which are sold to retailers. The price and cost of goods sold for each copier are as follows:

Price	$450 per unit
Cost of goods sold	365
Gross profit	$ 85 per unit

In addition, the company incurs selling and administrative expenses of $228,160. The company wishes to assign these costs to its three major retail customers, Office Warehouse, General Office Supply, and Office-to-Go. These expenses are related to its three major non-manufacturing activities: customer service, sales order processing, and advertising support. The advertising support is in the form of advertisements that are placed by Z-Rox Inc. to support the retailer's sale of Z-Rox copiers to consumers. The activity cost pool and activity bases associated with these activities are:

Activity	Activity Cost Pool	Activity Base
Customer service	$ 61,200	Number of service requests
Sales order processing	39,560	Number of sales orders
Advertising support	127,400	Number of ads placed
Total activity cost	$228,160	

Activity-base usage and unit volume information for the three customers is as follows:

	Office Warehouse	General Office Supply	Office-to-Go	Total
Number of service requests	50	10	180	240
Number of sales orders	240	100	520	860
Number of ads placed	20	15	105	140
Unit volume	1,900	1,900	1,900	5,700

Instructions

1. Determine the activity rates for each of the three nonmanufacturing activity pools.
2. Determine the activity costs allocated to the three customers, using the activity rates in (1).
3. Construct customer profitability reports for the three customers, dated for the year ended December 31, 2008, using the activity costs in (2). The reports should disclose the gross profit and income from operations associated with each customer.
4. Provide recommendations to management, based on the profitability reports in (3).

PR 11-6B
Product costing and decision analysis for a passenger airline

obj. 6

✓ *3. Flight 102 income from operations, $8,357*

Up and Away Airline provides passenger airline service, using small jets. The airline connects four major cities: Atlanta, Cincinnati, Chicago, and Los Angeles. The company expects to fly 125,000 miles during a month. The following costs are budgeted for a month:

Fuel	$1,040,000
Ground personnel	766,000
Crew salaries	628,000
Depreciation	342,000
Total costs	$2,776,000

Up and Away management wishes to assign these costs to individual flights in order to gauge the profitability of its service offerings. The following activity bases were identified with the budgeted costs:

Airline Cost	Activity Base
Fuel, crew, and depreciation costs	Number of miles flown
Ground personnel	Number of arrivals and departures at an airport

The size of the company's ground operation in each city is determined by the size of the workforce. The following monthly data are available from corporate records for each terminal operation:

Terminal City	Ground Personnel Cost	Number of Arrivals/Departures
Atlanta	$264,000	320
Cincinnati	98,800	130
Chicago	133,500	150
Los Angeles	269,700	290
Total	$766,000	890

Three recent representative flights have been selected for the profitability study. Their characteristics are as follows:

	Description	Miles Flown	Number of Passengers	Ticket Price per Passenger
Flight 101	Atlanta to LA	1,850	23	$1,700
Flight 102	Chicago to Atlanta	600	29	680
Flight 103	Atlanta to Cincinnati	350	14	475

Instructions
1. Determine the fuel, crew, and depreciation cost per mile flown.
2. Determine the cost per arrival or departure by terminal city.
3. Use the information in (1) and (2) to construct a profitability report for the three flights.
4. Evaluate flight profitability by determining the break-even number of passengers required for each flight. Round to the nearest whole number.

Special Activities

SA 11-1
Ethics and professional conduct in business

The controller of Accent Systems Inc. devised a new costing system based on tracing the cost of activities to products. The controller was able to measure post-manufacturing activities, such as selling, promotional, and distribution activities, and allocate these activities to products in order to have a more complete view of the company's product costs. This effort produced better strategic information about the relative profitability of product lines. In addition, the controller used the same product cost information for inventory valuation on the financial statements. Surprisingly, the controller discovered that the company's reported net income was larger under this scheme than under the traditional costing approach.
Why was the net income larger, and how would you react to the controller's action?

SA 11-2
Identifying product cost distortion

King Soda Company manufactures soft drinks. Information about two products is as follows:

	Volume	Sales Price per Case	Gross Profit per Case
Jamaican Punch	10,000 cases	$30	$12
King Kola	800,000 cases	30	12

It is known that both products have the same direct materials and direct labor costs per case. King Soda allocates factory overhead to products by using a single plantwide factory overhead rate, based on direct labor cost. Additional information about the two products is as follows:

Jamaican Punch: Requires extensive process preparation and sterilization prior to processing. The ingredients are from Jamaica, requiring complex import controls. The formulation is complex, and it is thus difficult to maintain quality. Lastly, the product is sold in small (less than full truckload) orders.
King Kola: Requires minor process preparation and sterilization prior to processing. The ingredients are acquired locally. The formulation is simple, and it is easy to maintain quality. Lastly, the product is sold in large bulk (full truckload) orders.

Explain the product profitability report in light of the additional data.

SA 11-3
Activity-based costing

Acordia, Inc., is an insurance brokerage company that classified insurance products as either "easy" or "difficult." Easy and difficult products were defined as follows:

Easy: Electronic claims, few inquiries, mature product
Difficult: Paper claims, complex claims to process, many inquiries, a new product with complex options

The company originally allocated processing and service expenses on the basis of revenue. Under this traditional allocation approach, the product profitability report revealed the following:

	Easy Product	Difficult Product	Total
Revenue	$600	$400	$1,000
Processing and service expenses	420	280	700
Income from operations	$180	$120	$ 300
Operating income margin	30%	30%	30%

Acordia decided to use activity-based costing to allocate the processing and service expenses. The following activity-based costing analysis of the same data illustrates a much different profit picture for the two types of products.

	Easy Product	Difficult Product	Total
Revenue	$600	$ 400	$1,000
Processing and service expenses	183	517	700
Income from operations	$417	$(117)	$ 300
Operating income margin	70%	(29%)	30%

Explain why the activity-based profitability report reveals different information from the traditional sales allocation report.

Source: Dan Patras and Kevin Clancy, "ABC in the Service Industry: Product Line Profitability at Acordia, Inc." As Easy as ABC Newsletter, Issue 12, Spring 1993.

SA 11-4
Using a product profitability report to guide strategic decisions

The controller of Audio Eclipse Inc. prepared the following product profitability report for management, using activity-based costing methods for allocating both the factory overhead and the marketing expenses. As such, the controller has confidence in the accuracy of this report. In addition, the controller interviewed the vice president of marketing, who indicated that the floor loudspeakers were an older product that was highly recognized in the marketplace. The ribbon loudspeakers were a new product that was recently launched. The ribbon loudspeakers are a new technology that have no competition in the marketplace, and it is hoped that they will become an important future addition to the company's product portfolio. Initial indications are that the product is well received by customers. The controller believes that the manufacturing costs for all three products are in line with expectations.

	Floor Loudspeakers	Bookshelf Loudspeakers	Ribbon Loudspeakers	Totals
Sales	$8,000,000	$50,000,000	$25,000,000	$83,000,000
Less cost of goods sold	5,200,000	25,000,000	24,000,000	54,200,000
Gross profit	$2,800,000	$25,000,000	$ 1,000,000	$28,800,000
Less marketing expenses	3,200,000	5,000,000	600,000	8,800,000
Income from operations	$ (400,000)	$20,000,000	$ 400,000	$20,000,000

1. Calculate the gross profit and income from operations to sales ratios for each product.
2. Write a memo using the product profitability report and the calculations in (1) to make recommendations to management with respect to strategies for the three products.

SA 11-5
Product cost distortion

Orlando Ortega, president of Tower Tech Inc., was reviewing the product profitability reports with the controller, Tameka Dorr. The following conversation took place:

Orlando: I've been reviewing the product profitability reports. Our high-volume calculator, the T-100, appears to be unprofitable, while some of our lower-volume specialty calculators in the T-900 series appear to be very profitable. These results do not make sense to me. How are the product profits determined?

Tameka: First, we identify the revenues associated with each product line. This information comes directly from our sales order system and is very accurate. Next, we identify the direct materials and direct labor associated with making each of the calculators. Again, this information is very accurate. The final cost that must be considered is the factory overhead. Factory overhead is allocated to the products, based on the direct labor hours used to assemble the calculator.

Orlando: What about distribution, promotion, and other post-manufacturing costs that can be associated with the product?

Tameka: According to generally accepted accounting principles, we expense them in the period that they are incurred and do not treat them as product costs.

Orlando: Another thing, you say that you allocate factory overhead according to direct labor hours. Yet I know that the T-900 series specialty products have very low volumes but require extensive engineering, testing, and materials management effort. They are our newer, more complex products. It seems that these sources of factory overhead will end up being allocated to the T-100 line because it is the high-volume and therefore high direct labor hour product. Yet the T-100 line is easy to make and requires very little support from our engineering, testing, and materials management personnel.

Tameka: I'm not too sure. I do know that our product costing approach is similar to that used by many different types of companies. I don't think we could all be wrong.

Is Orlando Ortega's concern valid, and how might Tameka Dorr redesign the cost allocation system to address Ortega's concern?

SA 11-6
Allocating bank administrative costs

Banks have a variety of products, such as savings accounts, checking accounts, certificates of deposit (CDs), and loans. Assume that you were assigned the task of determining the administrative costs of "savings accounts" as a complete product line. What are some of the activities associated with savings accounts? In answering this question, consider the activities that you might perform with your savings account. For each activity, what would be an activity base that could be used to allocate the activity cost to the savings account product line?

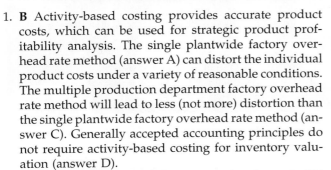

Answers to Self-Examination Questions

1. **B** Activity-based costing provides accurate product costs, which can be used for strategic product profitability analysis. The single plantwide factory overhead rate method (answer A) can distort the individual product costs under a variety of reasonable conditions. The multiple production department factory overhead rate method will lead to less (not more) distortion than the single plantwide factory overhead rate method (answer C). Generally accepted accounting principles do not require activity-based costing for inventory valuation (answer D).

2. **C** The single plantwide factory overhead rate is $34 per hour (answer A), determined as $680,000/20,000 hours. This rate is multiplied by 6 direct labor hours per unit of Product M to determine the correct overhead per unit of $204. The total overhead should be

used in the numerator in determining the overhead rate, not just power and indirect labor (answer B) or equipment depreciation (answer D).

3. **D** The number of production runs best relates the activity cost of setup to the products. Number of inspections, direct labor hours, and direct machine hours (answers A, B, and C) will likely have very little logical association with the costs incurred in setting up production runs.

4. **C** PD1 rate: $26,000/5,000 dlh = $5.20 per dlh
   PD2 rate: $48,000/5,000 dlh = $9.60 per dlh
   Product T: (5 dlh × $5.20) + (2 dlh × $9.60) = $45.20

5. **D** (100 miles × 20 cars × 10 tons × $4) + ($200 × 20 cars) + (20 cars × 2 switches × $50) = $80,000 + $4,000 + $2,000 = $86,000

chapter 12

Cost Management for Just-in-Time Environments

© BANANA STOCK/FIRST LIGHT

objectives

After studying this chapter, you should be able to:

1   *Compare and contrast just-in-time (JIT) manufacturing practices with traditional manufacturing practices.*

2   *Apply just-in-time manufacturing practices to a traditional manufacturing illustration.*

3   *Describe the implications of a just-in-time manufacturing philosophy on cost accounting and performance measurement systems.*

4   *Apply just-in-time practices to a nonmanufacturing setting.*

5   *Describe and illustrate activity analysis for improving operations.*

Precor

When you order the salad bar at the local restaurant, you are able to serve yourself at your own pace. There is no waiting for the waitress to take the order or for the cook to prepare the meal. You are able to move directly to the salad bar and select from various offerings. You might wish to have salad with lettuce, cole slaw, bacon bits, croutons, and salad dressing. The offerings are arranged in a row so that you can build your salad as you move down the salad bar.

Many manufacturers are producing each product directly to customer needs, in much the same way that the salad bar is designed to satisfy each customer's needs. Like customers at the salad bar, products move through a production process as they are built for each customer's unique needs. Such a process eliminates many sources of waste, which is why it is termed just in time.

Using just in time principles can dramatically improve performance. For example, Precor, a manufacturer of fitness equipment, used just-in-time principles to improve its manufacturing operations. Within three years, Precor improved on-time shipments from near 40% to above 90%, decreased direct labor costs by 30%, cut the number of suppliers from 3,000 to under 250, reduced inventory by 40%, and chiseled warranty claims by near 60%.

In this chapter, we will discuss the just-in-time philosophy and illustrate the managerial accounting principles and tools used in just-in-time environments. We will complete the chapter by discussing and illustrating the accounting for quality costs and process activity analysis.

Just-in-Time Principles

objective **1**

Compare and contrast just-in-time (JIT) manufacturing practices with traditional manufacturing practices.

The operating methods used by many companies are undergoing significant change. Companies are recognizing the need to produce products and services with high quality, low cost, and instant availability. Achieving these objectives requires a change in the methods of manufacturing products and delivering services. One approach reflecting these changes is the just-in-time philosophy. **Just-in-time (JIT)**, sometimes called *short-cycle* or *lean* **manufacturing**, focuses on reducing time, cost, and poor quality within manufacturing and nonmanufacturing processes.

We will first discuss just-in-time principles within a manufacturing setting. Exhibit 1 lists some of the just-in-time manufacturing principles and the traditional manufacturing principles. In the following paragraphs, we briefly discuss each of the just-in-time principles. We will then address the accounting implications of these principles.

REDUCING INVENTORY

Just-in-time manufacturing views inventory as wasteful and unnecessary, and thus attempts to reduce or eliminate inventory. Under traditional manufacturing, inventory hides underlying production problems. For example, inventory is often used to maintain sales and production levels during various production interruptions, such as machine breakdowns, manufacturing schedule changes, transportation delays, and unexpected scrap and rework. An important focus in just-in-time manufacturing is to remove these production problems so that the materials, work in process, and finished goods inventory levels can be reduced or eliminated.

The role of inventory can be explained by referring to a river. Inventory is the water in a river, while the rocks at the bottom of the river are the production problems. When the water level is high, all the rocks at the

Issue	Just-in-Time Manufacturing	Traditional Manufacturing
Inventory	Reduces inventory.	Increases inventory to protect against process problems.
Lead time	Reduces lead time.	Increases lead time to protect against uncertainty.
Setup time	Reduces setup time.	Disregards setup time as an improvement priority.
Production layout	Emphasizes product-oriented layout.	Emphasizes process-oriented layout.
Role of the employee	Emphasizes team-oriented employee involvement.	Emphasizes work of individuals, following manager instructions.
Production scheduling policy	Emphasizes pull manufacturing.	Emphasizes push manufacturing.
Quality	Emphasizes zero defects.	Tolerates defects.
Suppliers and customers	Emphasizes supply chain management.	Treats suppliers and customers as "arm's-length," independent entities.

bottom of the river are hidden. That is, inventory hides the production problems. However, as the water level drops, the rocks become exposed, one by one. Reducing inventory reveals production problems. Once these problems are fixed, the "water level" can be reduced even further to expose more "rocks" for elimination until an efficient, effective production process is achieved.

Integrity, Objectivity, and Ethics in Business

ETHICS

THE INVENTORY SHIFT

Some managers take a shortcut to reducing inventory by shifting inventory to their suppliers. With this tactic, the hard work of improving processes is avoided. Enlightened managers realize that such tactics often have short-lived savings. Suppliers will eventually increase their prices to compensate for the additional inventory holding costs, thus resulting in no savings. Therefore, shifting a problem doesn't eliminate a problem.

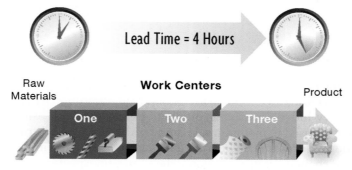

Lead Time = 4 Hours

Raw Materials   **Work Centers**   Product

One   Two   Three

Production Process

REDUCING LEAD TIMES

Lead time, sometimes called *throughput time,* is a measure of the time that elapses between starting a unit of product into the beginning of a process and completing the unit of product. As shown in the illustration, if a product begins the process at 1:00 P.M. and is completed at 5:00 P.M., the lead time is four hours.

Reducing lead times can be an objective for products manufactured in the plant or any other item that is produced through a process. For example, lead times could be reduced for processing sales orders, invoices, insurance applications, or hospital patients.

The total lead time can be divided into value-added and non-value-added time portions, as shown in Exhibit 2. **Value-added lead time** is the time required to actually manufacture a unit of a product. It is the conver-

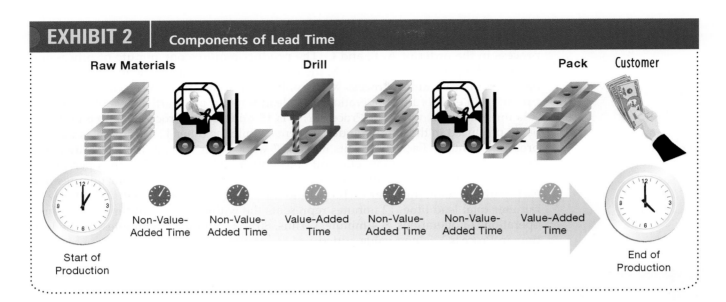

EXHIBIT 2 | **Components of Lead Time**

Raw Materials — Drill — Pack — Customer

Start of Production — Non-Value-Added Time — Non-Value-Added Time — Value-Added Time — Non-Value-Added Time — Non-Value-Added Time — Value-Added Time — End of Production

sion time for a unit. For example, value-added lead time would include the time to drill and pack parts for shipment. The **value-added ratio** is the ratio of the value-added lead time to the total lead time. **Non-value-added lead time** is the time that a unit of product sits in inventories or moves unnecessarily. Non-value-added lead time occurs in poor production processes. In a well-functioning process, the product should spend very little time waiting in inventory, because inventory is at a minimum. The product should also spend little time moving, because operations are sequenced closely.

Just-in-time manufacturing reduces or eliminates non-value-added time, thereby reducing the cost and improving the speed of production. Reducing non-value-added lead time is often directly related to reducing inventory. Organizations that use many work in process inventory locations may discover that the value-added ratio can be as little as 5% of the total lead time.

REDUCING SETUP TIME

As we introduced in the previous chapter, a *setup* is the effort required to prepare an operation for a new production run. For example, a beverage company's bottling line would need to be cleaned between flavor changes. If setups are long and expensive, the production run (*batch*) must be large in order to recover the setup cost. Large batches increase inventory, and larger inventories add to lead time. Exhibit 3 is a diagram of the relationship between setup times and lead time.

EXHIBIT 3 | **Relationship between Setup Times and Lead Time**

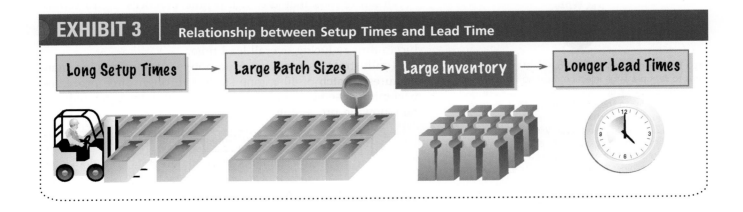

Long Setup Times → Large Batch Sizes → Large Inventory → Longer Lead Times

Exhibit 4 illustrates the impact of batch sizes on lead times, using a product that is manufactured in two identical processes (X and Y) that require three operations in each process in the order of A, B, and C. The product requires one minute of processing inside each operation. In Process X, the batch size is one unit, while in Process Y, the batch size is five units. Process X has only three units in process—one unit being produced in each of three operations. The lead time for any particular unit in Process X is three minutes, while for Process Y, it is 15 minutes. In Process Y, three units are being produced in the operating departments, while the other 12 are stored as work in process inventory. Each unit waits its "turn" while other units in the batch are being processed. At each operation, one unit takes five minutes to complete the operation— four minutes waiting its "turn" and one minute in production. The four minutes that each part "waits its turn" at each operation is called *within-batch wait time*. Of the 15 minutes total lead time, 12 minutes represents the within-batch wait time for all three operations (3 operations × 4 minutes). Thus, 80% (12 minutes/15 minutes) of the lead time in Process Y is non-value-added.

EXHIBIT 4   Impact of Batch Sizes on Lead Times

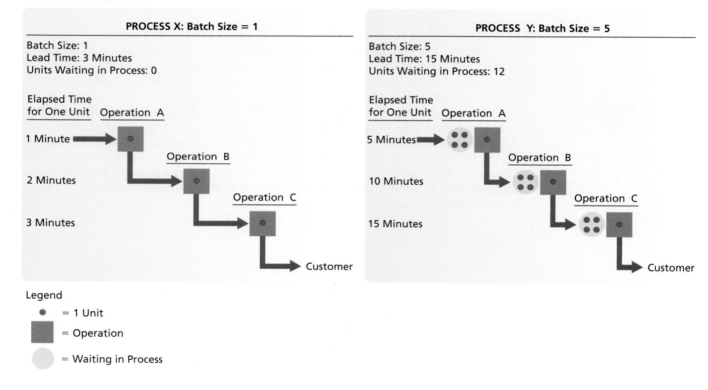

Legend

● = 1 Unit

■ = Operation

● = Waiting in Process

Tech Industries required five hours and 84 separate steps to set up a large injection molding machine. A videotape of the setup showed that the operator climbed a ladder to the top of the machine 35 times, walked around the machine 37 times, and left the area for tools 12 times, for over 3,000 yards of walking. The improvement team reorganized the setup so that the operator climbed the machine only seven times, walked around the machine 12 times, and never left the area for tools. These improvements reduced the number of process steps from 84 to 19 and the setup time from five hours to one hour.

Organizations that use just-in-time practices try to reduce setup times in order to reduce the batch size. Once batch sizes are reduced, the work in process inventory and wait time are reduced, thus reducing overall lead time.

To illustrate, assume that Automotive Components Inc. manufactures a batch of 40 engine starters through three processes: machining, assembly, and testing. Each unit in the batch requires the following processing times:

Processing Time per Unit

Machining	6 minutes
Assembly	10
Testing	8
Total	24 minutes

After machining, it takes 10 minutes to move the machined batch to assembly. It then takes 15 minutes to move the assembled batch to testing. The lead time can be analyzed as follows:

	Lead Times	Percent of Total
Value-added lead time	24 minutes	2.5%
Non-value-added lead time:		
Within-batch wait time [24 min. × (40 − 1)]	936	95.0
Move time (10 min. + 15 min.)	25	2.5
Total lead time	985 minutes	100.0%

The value-added time is the sum of the machining, assembly, and testing processing times per unit, or 24 (6 + 10 + 8) minutes. The within-batch wait time is the time for the units that are not being processed to wait their turn. This is equal to one minus the batch size, or 39 units, multiplied by the amount of processing time per unit, or 936 minutes [(40 − 1) × 24 minutes]. The total non-value-added time of 961 minutes is the sum of the within-batch time of 936 minutes plus the move time of 25 minutes.

Approximately 97.5% of the lead time is consumed by non-value-added waiting and moving. How could Automotive Components improve its lead time performance? First, it could reduce setups so that the batch size could be reduced to one piece, termed *one-piece flow*. Second, it could move the processes closer to each other so that the move time is eliminated. With these two steps, the total lead time would approach the value-added lead time.

Business Connections

ELIMINATING NONVALUE TIME ON THE B-2 STEALTH BOMBER

Northrop Grumman is a defense contractor that designs, develops, and manufactures a wide variety of defense electronics and systems, aerospace management systems, precision weapons, marine systems, logistic systems, and automation and information systems. Along with other projects, Northrop provides systems for the F-16 and F-22 fighter aircraft, the Longbow Apache helicopter, and the B-2 Stealth Bomber.

In an attempt to improve its manufacturing operations, Northrop videotaped a mechanic in its Palmdale, California plant, whose job was to apply approximately 70 feet of tape to the B-2 bomber. The mechanic walked away from the airplane 26 times and took three hours to gather the necessary chemicals, hoses, gauges, and other material needed just to start, and the total job took 8.4 hours. The diagram on the left shows the path of the mechanic in performing this job.

By designing prepackaged kits for the job, the mechanic did not have to leave the plane at all, and the total time to perform the job dropped to 1.62 hours. The diagram on the right shows the path of the mechanic using the prepackaged kits.

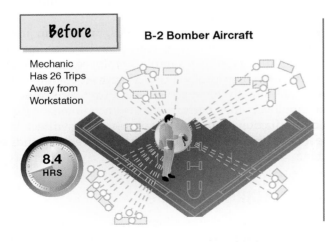

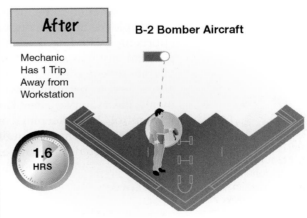

Source: Andrew Pollack, "Aerospace Gets Japan's Message," *The New York Times*, March 9, 1999.

Example Exercise 12-1

objective 1

The Helping Hands glove company manufactures gloves in the cutting and assembly process. Gloves are manufactured in 50-glove batch sizes. The cutting time is 4 minutes per glove. The assembly time is 6 minutes per glove. It takes 12 minutes to move a batch of gloves from cutting to assembly.

a. Compute the value-added, non-value-added, and total lead time of this process.
b. Compute the value-added ratio. Round to one decimal.

Follow My Example 12-1

a. Value-added lead time: 10 min.   (4 min. + 6 min.)
    Non-value-added lead time:
        Within-batch wait time   490   [10 min. × (50 − 1)]
        Move time   12
    Total lead time   512 min.

b. Value-added ratio: $\dfrac{10 \text{ min.}}{512 \text{ min.}} = 2.0\%$

For Practice: PE 12-1A, PE 12-1B

Sony has organized a small team of four employees to completely assemble a camcorder, doing everything from soldering to testing. The new line reduces assembly time from 70 minutes to 15 minutes per camera. "There is no future in conventional conveyor lines. They are a tool that conforms to the person with the least ability," states a Sony representative.

Kenney Manufacturing Company, a manufacturer of window shades, estimated that 50% of its window shade process was non-value-added. By using pull manufacturing and changing the line layout, it was able to reduce inventory by 82% and lead time by 84%.

EMPHASIZING PRODUCT-ORIENTED LAYOUT

Organizing work around products is called a **product-oriented layout** (or *product cells*), while organizing work around processes is called a **process-oriented layout**. Just-in-time methods favor organizing work around products rather than processes. Organizing work around products reduces the amount of materials movement, coordination between operations, and work in process inventory. As a result, lead time and production costs are reduced.

For example, Yamaha manufactures its musical instruments in a product-oriented layout. It has a unique process for trumpets, horns, saxophones, clarinets, and flutes. These processes are broken into subprocesses for each of the unique elements of the product. For a trumpet, Yamaha uses subprocesses to make the bell, valve casings, valve pistons, tubing, and mouthpieces.

EMPHASIZING EMPLOYEE INVOLVEMENT

Employee involvement is a management approach that grants employees the responsibility and authority to make decisions about operations, rather than relying solely on management instructions. This decision-making authority requires accounting and other information to be made available to all employees.

Employee involvement uses teams organized in product cells, rather than just the efforts of isolated, individual employees. Such employee teams can be *cross-trained* to perform any operation within the product cell. For example, employees learn how to operate several different machines within their product cell. Moreover, team members are trained to perform functions traditionally handled by centralized service departments. For example, direct labor employees may perform their own maintenance, quality control, housekeeping, and production improvement work. When direct labor employees perform such indirect functions, the distinction between direct and indirect labor cost becomes less important.

EMPHASIZING PULL MANUFACTURING

Another important just-in-time principle is to produce items only as they are needed by the customer. This principle is called **pull manufacturing** (or *make to order*). In pull manufacturing, the status of the next operation determines when products are moved or produced. If the next operation is busy, then production stops so that material does not pile up in front of the busy operation. If the next operation is ready, then product can be produced or moved to that operation.

The system that accomplishes pull manufacturing is often called *kanban*, which is Japanese for "cards." Electronic cards or containers signal production quantities to be filled by the feeder operation. The cards link the customer back through each stage of production. When a consumer purchases a product, a card triggers assembly of a replacement product, which in turn triggers cards to manufacture the components required for the assembly. This creates a flow of parts and products that move to the drumbeat of customer demand.

In contrast, the traditional approach is to schedule production based on forecasted customer requirements. This principle is called **push manufacturing** (or *make to stock*). In push manufacturing, product is released for manufacturing without reference to line status but according to a production schedule. The schedule "pushes" product to inventory ahead of known customer demand. As a result, manufacturers using push manufacturing will generally have more inventory than will manufacturers using pull manufacturing. As stated by one consultant, "If your manufacturing operations are still set up around guessing demand, you will forever be in a loop of producing and holding the wrong items and not having enough of what the customer actually wants."[1]

EMPHASIZING ZERO DEFECTS

Ford Motor Company's Cleveland Engine Site earned Ford's best overall warranty results by engaging its employees in a six-sigma system.

Just-in-time manufacturing practices include eliminating poor quality. Poor quality results in scrapped product, fixing product made wrong the first time (termed *rework*), and warranty costs. In addition to these direct costs, poor quality also causes disruptions in the production process, additional recordkeeping for scrap, inspection effort, and bad will from dissatisfied customers. One of the methods used to improve the quality of products and processes is six-sigma. **Six-sigma** is a widely adopted improvement system developed by Motorola Corporation.[2] The system consists of five steps: define, measure, analyze, improve, and control (DMAIC). Motorola has claimed over $17 billion in savings since six-sigma was adopted. Six-sigma is now used by thousands of organizations worldwide.

EMPHASIZING SUPPLY CHAIN MANAGEMENT

Supply chain management is the coordination and control of materials, services, information, and finances as they move in a process from the supplier, through the manufacturer, wholesaler, and retailer to the consumer. Supply chain management involves developing long-term customer/supplier agreements with supply chain partners. Such partnering encourages supply chain partners to commit to delivering products with the right quality, at the right cost, at the right time. Supply chain management often involves improving partner operations by employing just-in-time principles. Thus, the just-in-time approach does not stop within the four walls of the factory but extends to the supply chain partner operations as well. Toyota Motor is famous for its willingness to work with supply chain partners in developing its just-in-time capabilities.

Supply chains that embrace just-in-time principles use electronic data interchange, radio frequency identification devices (RFID), and the Internet to improve the information flows between suppliers and customers. **Electronic data interchange (EDI)** is a method of using computers to electronically communicate orders, relay information, and make or receive payments from one organization to another. **Radio frequency identification devices (RFID)** are electronic tags (chips) placed on or embedded within products that can be read by radio waves that allow instant monitoring of product location. The Internet allows customers and suppliers to link their business planning

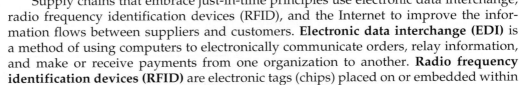

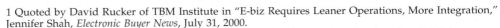

1 Quoted by David Rucker of TBM Institute in "E-biz Requires Leaner Operations, More Integration," Jennifer Shah, *Electronic Buyer News*, July 31, 2000.
2 The term "six-sigma" refers to a statistical property whereby a process has less than 3.4 defects per one million items.

and control systems through enterprise resource planning systems. **Enterprise resource planning (ERP)** systems are integrated business and information systems used by companies to plan and control both internal and supply chain operations. The result is an effective and efficient supply chain that operates from raw materials to the final consumer.

Applying a Just-in-Time Approach to Anderson Metal Fabricators

objective **2**

Apply just-in-time manufacturing practices to a traditional manufacturing illustration.

To illustrate just-in-time manufacturing principles, we will assume that Anderson Metal Fabricators (AMF) makes two types of metal covers, large and small, for electronic test equipment. Metal covers are made by stamping a pattern of the cover from sheet steel, much like a cookie cutter stamps cookies out of dough. The stamped patterns are then sent through a punching operation, which punches holes on the pattern for fasteners. The last operation is the forming operation, where the pattern is bent into a cover and fasteners are attached.

TRADITIONAL OPERATIONS—AMF

Exhibit 5 illustrates the plant layout of AMF as a traditional manufacturer. The facility is divided into three major production departments: Stamping, Punching, and Forming. This is an example of the process-oriented layout found in many traditional manufacturing operations. AMF has many machines in each department. Within each department, partially completed products are stored in work in process inventory, waiting to be worked on by the next department. The Maintenance and Tooling Department is in a centralized location within the plant. Customers order product from the finished goods inventory. Departments receive their production schedules and work instructions based on forecasted demand, which is an example of push manufacturing.

Following the traditional approach, AMF's purchasing function attempts to supply the correct amount of raw materials according to production schedules. Extra raw materials are ordered "just in case" a shipment is missed, delayed, or incorrect. Likewise, uncertainty about the final output of any department, because of machine break-

EXHIBIT 5

Traditional Operations—AMF

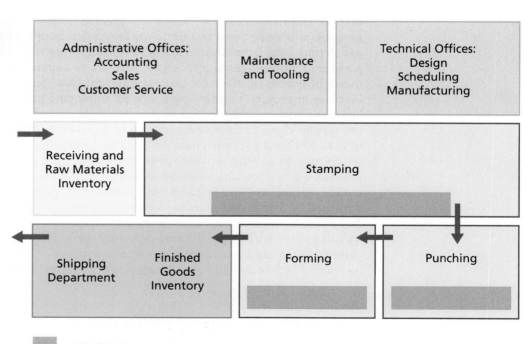

= Work in Process Areas

downs, scrap, rework, or production inefficiency, causes managers to increase work in process inventory. For example, the large work in process inventory in the Stamping Department keeps the Punching Department from running out of stampings when the stamping machines break down. Finally, the machines within AMF's departments must be set up to change production between the small and large covers.

JUST-IN-TIME OPERATIONS—AMF

The management of AMF wishes to introduce a new product, the medium-size metal cover. Unfortunately, the existing production capacity and space will not support the increased production. As a result, AMF management has decided to use just-in-time principles in order to better utilize the existing productive capacity and space.

Exhibit 6 illustrates the just-in-time operations for AMF. To apply just-in-time principles, management revised the department structure. Rather than organizing the production departments around the various operational processes, they are now organized around the three product lines (small, medium, and large covers). This product-oriented layout was accomplished by taking the machines and the people in each of the old departments and separating them into three product production cells. For example, the Stamping Department machines were separated to form the first position in three separate product cells.

EXHIBIT 6

Just-in-Time Operations—AMF

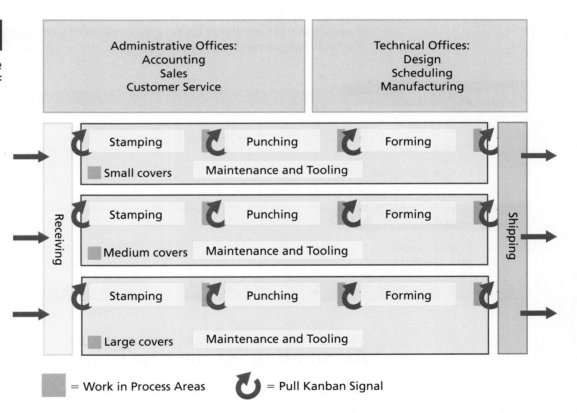

= Work in Process Areas   = Pull Kanban Signal

Since each product has its own product cell, there is no longer any need for setups. For example, the medium cover line has no setups because only medium covers are manufactured in this cell. Eliminating setup time releases productive capacity to make the medium covers. In addition, the operations within a product cell are positioned physically close to each other in order to minimize move time. The close physical distance between each machine allows materials to be transferred between each operation in small batches, using kanban signals.

The Maintenance and Tooling Department was decentralized. Each product cell now includes a maintenance and tooling function. This allows equipment to be repaired more quickly, since the parts, tools, and personnel are physically closer to the problem.

The materials, work in process, and finished goods inventory storage space is reduced significantly. Eliminating the wasted space used for inventory provides room for producing the medium covers. Thus, AMF is able to expand production without investing in new facilities.

AMF orders raw materials only as they are needed for production. In the just-in-time environment, trucks often arrive daily or even more frequently, with just enough raw materials to last until the next shipment arrives. The raw materials are received directly by the various product cells, without inspection, because suppliers guarantee zero defects through supplier partnering.

Minimal work in process inventory exists between the product cells because of employee involvement to reduce the mistakes and errors within the process. Thus, AMF's employees have improved quality, while reducing machine failures, scrap, and rework. Normally, small work in process inventory levels would cause AMF to risk a loss in productivity through unexpected manufacturing stoppages. However, the process improvements will allow AMF's production to continue without risk of shutdown, even with reduced inventory. As a result of these improvements, the non-value-added lead time has been significantly reduced.

Operations do not produce product just to remain busy and improve machine utilization. In pull manufacturing, operations respond only to customer orders. As a result, all operations within a cell operate at the same pace. This practice avoids a buildup of work in process inventory from "out-running" slower operations. If customer demand slows, then the production pace will also be slowed to match the demand. Employees can then use the extra time to work on improving the process or to move to other cells where product demand is high.

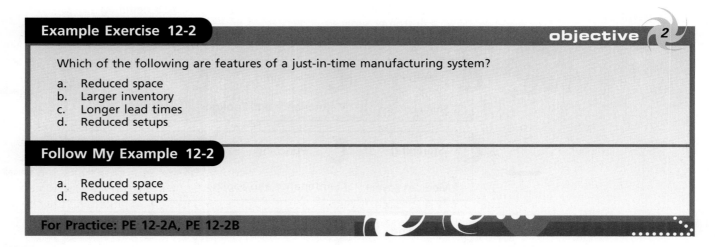

Example Exercise 12-2   objective 2

Which of the following are features of a just-in-time manufacturing system?

a. Reduced space
b. Larger inventory
c. Longer lead times
d. Reduced setups

Follow My Example 12-2

a. Reduced space
d. Reduced setups

For Practice: PE 12-2A, PE 12-2B

Accounting for Just-in-Time Operations

objective 3

Describe the implications of a just-in-time manufacturing philosophy on cost accounting and performance measurement systems.

In just-in-time operations, the accounting system will have the characteristics listed below.[3] Each of these characteristics is described in the following paragraphs.

■ *Fewer transactions.* The accounting system is simpler because there are fewer transactions to record.

■ *Combined accounts.* All in-process work is combined with raw materials to form a new account, **Raw and In Process (RIP) Inventory**, while the direct labor becomes part of the conversion cost.

■ *Nonfinancial performance measures.* There is a greater emphasis on nonfinancial performance measures.

3 A good summary of just-in-time implications for accounting can be found in Brian H. Maskell and Bruce L. Baggaley, "Lean Accounting: What's It All About?" *Target* (First Issue, 2006) pp. 35–43.

- *Direct tracing of overhead.* Indirect labor is directly assigned to product production cells, requiring less factory overhead allocation to products.

FEWER TRANSACTIONS

At Caterpillar, Inc., traditional plant layouts required a transmission assembly to travel as much as 10 miles as it moved to different operations. Its progress was tracked by more than 1,000 pieces of paper. Caterpillar then reorganized its work flows, using just-in-time approaches. As a result, the transmission assembly travel distance was reduced to 200 feet, with an average of 10 pieces of paper used to track each transmission.

The traditional process cost accounting system accumulates the cost incurred in a department and then transfers this cost to the next department. Thus, materials are recorded into and out of work in process inventories as production moves through the factory. Recording the flow of costs through a plant in this way leads to control of departmental costs. However, since each department has transactions flowing in and out, the traditional cost accounting system has many transactions to record, accumulate, correct, and report. This adds cost, complexity, and delay in reporting accounting information.

In the just-in-time production process, the need for accounting cost control is much less, because lower inventories make problems much more visible on the factory floor. That is, managers don't need an accounting report to indicate problems, since any problems are immediately visible to them. Thus, the accounting system can be simplified by eliminating the accumulation and transfer of costs as products move through the production process. Such simplification is termed **backflush accounting**. In backflush accounting, costs are transferred from combined material and conversion cost accounts directly to finished production without transferring costs through intermediate departmental work in process accounts. We illustrate the use of combined accounts in this way in the next section.

COMBINED ACCOUNTS

Since the just-in-time manufacturer attempts to eliminate inventory, including raw materials, there is no need for a separate materials account. For example, GM's Saturn plant has receiving areas all around the perimeter of its factory. In this way, raw materials can be delivered by trucks to a receiving area that is located near the point of use on the assembly line. Thus, there is no need for a separate materials inventory location or a materials account, since materials are introduced immediately into production. Many just-in-time manufacturers debit all materials and conversion costs to *Raw and In Process Inventory* and thus combine materials and work in process costs in one account.

The direct labor cost classification is often not used by just-in-time manufacturers. This is because the employees in product cells perform many tasks, some of which could be classified as direct, such as performing operations, and some as indirect, such as performing inspections. From an accounting perspective, the product cell labor cost is combined with other cell overhead costs to form the total product cell conversion cost.

To illustrate these accounting concepts, assume that the annual budgeted conversion cost for AMF's medium-cover product cell is $2,400,000. These costs will support 1,920 planned hours of production. The cell conversion cost rate is determined by dividing the annual budgeted conversion cost by the planned production hours to yield $1,250 per hour, as shown below. This rate is similar to a predetermined factory overhead rate, except that it includes all conversion costs in the numerator.

$$\text{Budgeted Cell Conversion Cost Rate} = \frac{\$2,400,000 \text{ budgeted conversion cost}}{1,920 \text{ planned production hours}}$$

$$= \$1,250 \text{ per hour}$$

The medium-cover product cell is expected to require 0.02 hour of manufacturing time per unit. Thus, the conversion cost is estimated to be $25 per unit, as shown below.

0.02 hour per unit × $1,250 conversion cost per hour = $25 conversion cost per unit

To illustrate the recording of transactions in AMF's just-in-time operations, assume that the following selected transactions occurred during April:

Transaction	Journal Entry		Comment

1. Steel coil is purchased for producing 8,000 medium covers. The purchase cost was $120,000, or $15 per unit.	Raw and In Process Inventory
	  Accounts Payable
	    To record materials purchases.
		120,000
		
		   120,000
			Note that the materials purchased are debited to the combined account, Raw and In Process Inventory. A separate materials account is not used, because materials are received directly in the product cells, rather than in an inventory location.

2. Conversion costs are applied to 8,000 medium covers at a rate of $25 per cover.	Raw and In Process Inventory
	  Conversion Costs
	    To record applied conversion
	    costs of the medium-cover
	    line.
		200,000
		
		   200,000
			The raw and in process inventory account is used to accumulate the applied cell conversion costs during the period. The credit to conversion costs is similar to the treatment of applied factory overhead.

3. All 8,000 medium covers were completed in the cell. The raw and in process inventory account is reduced by the $15 per-unit materials cost and the $25 per-unit conversion cost.	Finished Goods Inventory
	  Raw and In Process Inventory
	    To transfer the cost of
	    completed units to finished
	    goods.
		320,000
		
		   320,000
			Materials ($15 × 8,000 units) $120,000
			Conversion ($25 × 8,000 units) 200,000
			  Total $320,000
			
			After the cost of the completed units is transferred from the raw and in process inventory account, the account's balance is zero. There are no units left in process within the cell.[4] This is a backflush transaction.

4. Of the 8,000 units completed, 7,800 were sold and shipped to customers at $70 per unit, leaving 200 finished units in stock. Thus, the finished goods inventory account has a balance of $8,000 (200 × $40). Even though AMF is now a just-in-time manufacturer, a small number of customer orders were not shipped at the end of the month.	Accounts Receivable
	  Sales
	    To record sales.
	
	Cost of Goods Sold
	  Finished Goods
	    To record cost of goods sold.
		546,000
		
		   546,000
		
		312,000
		
		   312,000
			Units sold 7,800
			Conversion and materials costs
			  per unit × $40
			Transferred to cost of goods sold $312,000

Example Exercise 12-3

objective 3

The budgeted conversion costs for a just-in-time cell are $142,500 for 1,900 production hours. Each unit produced by the cell requires 10 minutes of cell process time. During the month, 1,050 units are manufactured in the cell. The estimated materials cost is $46 per unit. Provide the following journal entries:

a. Materials are purchased to produce 1,100 units.
b. Conversion costs are applied to 1,050 units of production.
c. 1,030 units are placed into finished goods.

Follow My Example 12-3

a. Raw and In Process Inventory 50,600*
    Accounts Payable   50,600
    *$46 per unit × 1,100 units

b. Raw and In Process Inventory 13,125*
    Conversion Costs   13,125
    *[($142,500/1,900 hours) × (10 min./60 min.)] = $12.50 per unit; $12.50 × 1,050 units = $13,125

c. Finished Goods Inventory 60,255*
    Raw and In Process Inventory   60,255
    *($46.00 + $12.50) × 1,030 units

For Practice: PE 12-3A, PE 12-3B

---

4 The actual conversion cost per unit may be different from the budgeted conversion cost per unit due to cell inefficiency, improvements in processing methods, or excess scrap. These deviations from the budgeted cost can be accounted for as cost variances, as illustrated in more advanced texts.

NONFINANCIAL PERFORMANCE MEASURES

Just-in-time manufacturing frequently relies on nonfinancial measures to guide short-term operational performance. A **nonfinancial measure** is operating information that has not been stated in dollar terms. Examples of nonfinancial measures of performance include lead time, the value-added ratio, setup time, the number of production line stops, the number of units scrapped, and deviations from scheduled production. A survey of manufacturing firms revealed the following use of nonfinancial measures:[5]

Measure	Percent of Respondents of High Quality Manufacturers	Just-in-Time Principle Addressed by the Performance Measure
Product defects	94.9%	Improving quality
Labor productivity	82.1	Improving lead time
Material usage	79.4	Improving quality
Customer satisfaction	76.9	Improving quality
Inventory levels	76.9	Reducing inventory
Manufacturing cycle time	64.1	Improving lead time
Employee satisfaction	61.5	Involving employees
Time to fill customer orders	59.0	Improving lead time
Setup efficiency	35.9	Improving setups

Nonfinancial measures are used for day-to-day decision making because nonfinancial data can often be provided much more quickly than can accounting data. Accounting data must first be translated into dollars and then summarized, whereas nonfinancial data need not be stated in dollar terms. Periodic nonfinancial measures give product cell employees instant feedback that can be used to improve the process. Traditional accounting data are much better suited for guiding longer-term operational decisions and trade-off analyses, while nonfinancial measures can provide timely and focused operational information. Most companies use a combination of both types of information. A company will often term its combined measures *KPI's*, or *key performance indicators*.

DIRECT TRACING OF OVERHEAD

Just-in-time practices often assign many indirect tasks to a specific product cell. For example, an individual from the Maintenance Department may be assigned to AMF's medium-cover cell and cross-trained to perform other operations. Thus, the salary of this person is directly attributed to the medium-cover product line.

In a traditional facility, the maintenance person is part of the Maintenance Department and is not assigned to a particular product line. Thus, the accounting system must allocate the cost of maintenance services to product lines. Allocating such costs is not necessary when the indirect employees are assigned to a product cell in a just-in-time environment.

Just-in-Time for Nonmanufacturing Processes

objective **4**

Apply just-in-time practices to a nonmanufacturing setting.

Just-in-time principles also apply for service and administrative processes, such as hospitals, banks, insurance companies, hotels, transportation providers, sales order processes, and other nonmanufacturing settings. In nonmanufacturing processes, either information or the customer is often the "product" of the process. For example,

5 Chee Chow and Wim A. Vander Stede, "The Use and Usefulness of Nonfinancial Performance Measures," *Management Accounting Quarterly* (Spring 2006), pp. 1–8.

ITW Paslode, a manufacturer of specialty tools, used just-in-time principles to reduce steps in the sales order process by 86% and improve delivery time by 80%.

just-in-time principles can be used on processes for insurance applications, product designs, sales orders, hospital patients, and university students. To illustrate, the process used by a typical hospital to treat patients is illustrated in Exhibit 7.

The Admitting Department first admits the patient. This takes some time as patient information is collected and insurance is verified. The admitted patient is then transported to a room where a variety of tests may be performed prior to a surgical procedure. These tests often require the patient to be moved to the testing location, as in the case of an X ray, or for specimens to be moved to centralized chemistry labs, as in the case of blood workups. In addition, drugs are ordered from the central pharmacy to be delivered to the patient's floor for nurse administration. Each of these processes consumes time as the patient, specimen, test result, and drug order are moved to the respective departments for processing. In each of the centralized departments, any one patient's requirements must wait its turn behind all the other patients before processing can be completed. Again, this also consumes time. As a result, an average patient's time in the hospital is longer than it needs to be.

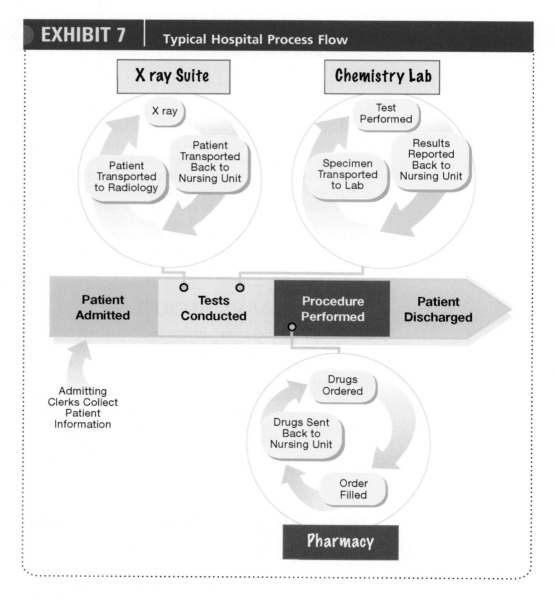

EXHIBIT 7 | **Typical Hospital Process Flow**

Alternatively, Exhibit 8 illustrates a just-in-time hospital layout. There are a number of distinct features in Exhibit 8, compared to Exhibit 7. First, patients with common health problems are placed together on a floor in the hospital. Second, many centralized services are distributed to each of the floors, so that each floor has its own miniphar-

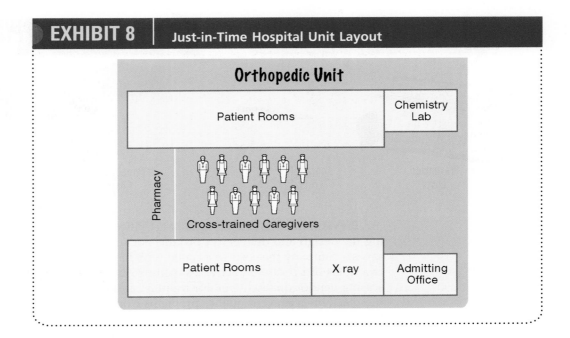

EXHIBIT 8 | Just-in-Time Hospital Unit Layout

Orthopedic Unit

Patient Rooms

Chemistry Lab

Pharmacy

Cross-trained Caregivers

Patient Rooms

X ray

Admitting Office

macy, X ray suite, chemistry lab, and admitting office. Patients are served where they are, rather than having to move around the hospital. These two features are similar to the product-oriented layout in manufacturing. Third, "cross-trained" generalists in the nursing units replace specialists in the centralized departments. This provides much greater flexibility in responding to patient needs and provides faster response times.

A just-in-time hospital process will reduce the "inventory" of orders, results, patients, and drugs that will be moving through the system waiting to be processed. As a result, the lead time to process orders and tests will be decreased, reducing the average stay in the hospital. The quality of the patient's experience should be better, since the same group of caregivers serves the patient from admittance to discharge. The experience of the caregivers should be better, since they are able to work as a team in providing patient services. Lastly, the overall cost of patient care should decline as the hospital achieves greater efficiency while maintaining patient care standards.

Activity Analysis

objective **5**

Describe and illustrate activity analysis for improving operations.

In this chapter, we have discussed how businesses use just-in-time operating principles to eliminate wasted time, cost, and poor quality. In doing so, JIT improves operations. Another method used for improving operations is activity analysis. An **activity analysis** determines the cost of activities based on an analysis of employee effort and other records. An activity analysis can be used to determine (1) the costs of quality, (2) the cost of value-added and non-value-added activities, and (3) the cost of processes.

COSTS OF QUALITY USING ACTIVITY ANALYSIS

The level of business competition is increasing in many industries. As a result, businesses must emphasize product, service, and process quality in order to succeed. Businesses concerned with providing high-quality products, services, and processes are motivated to reduce the total costs of quality. The **costs of quality** are costs incurred by the firm to "control" or "fail to control" quality. The costs of quality can be determined from an activity analysis. Such an analysis can be used to classify the costs of "control quality" further into prevention and appraisal costs. Likewise, the "costs of failing to control quality" can be classified further into internal failure and external failure costs. These classifications can be presented as follows:

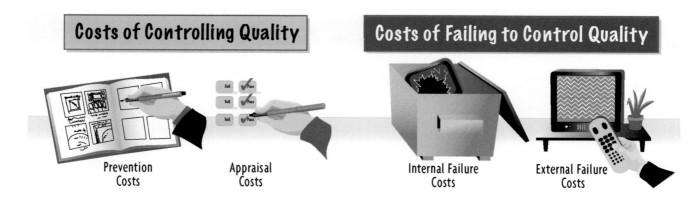

Costs of Controlling Quality		Costs of Failing to Control Quality	
Prevention Costs	Appraisal Costs	Internal Failure Costs	External Failure Costs

Prevention costs are the costs of activities that prevent defects from occurring during the design and delivery of products or services. Preventing defects from occurring saves a company the costs associated with handling, disposing, and recording of scrap. Examples of prevention activities include quality engineering, design engineering, assessing vendor quality, operator training, and preventive machine maintenance. All of these activities prevent quality problems from occurring and, as such, are investments in future quality.

Appraisal costs are the costs of activities that detect, measure, evaluate, and inspect products and processes to ensure that they meet customer needs. Appraisal costs are most often related to inspection and testing activities. Appraisal costs do not fundamentally change the amount of poor quality produced—only the amount of poor quality that "slips out the door." Thus, appraisal activities are a less permanent method of improving quality than are prevention activities.

Internal failure costs are the costs associated with defects discovered by a business before the product or service is delivered to the consumer. These costs include the cost of scrap and rework, which are recorded by the accounting system. However, in addition to obvious costs related to internal failure, there are also costs related to lost equipment time from producing scrap, supervision to move, record, and dispose of scrap, procurement time to repurchase parts that arrive defective, and inventory produced to protect against possible lost production from scrap.

External failure costs are the costs incurred after defective units or services have been delivered to consumers. These costs are "external" because the defects are discovered while the consumer is using the products or services. External failure costs include the cost of activities related to field repairs, recalls, warranty work, correcting invoice errors, and processing returned merchandise. More importantly, external failure costs also include the cost of lost customer goodwill. Although this cost is difficult to measure, some believe it is the largest cost in the quality equation. It has been reported that every dissatisfied customer tells at least ten people about an unhappy experience with a product, so the impact of a failure extends far beyond the single event.

THE RELATIONSHIP BETWEEN THE COSTS OF QUALITY

Exhibit 9 shows the relationship between the costs of quality. As the graph indicates, the prevention and appraisal costs increase as the percentage of good units produced increases. This is because additional costs are needed for designing products and processes that will produce high-quality products. The internal and external failure costs decline with increases in the percentage of good units produced. This is because the costs from scrap, warranty work, and other failure costs go down as quality improves. The total cost line is the sum of both the prevention/appraisal cost and internal/external failure cost lines.

The best level of quality is the one that minimizes the total quality costs. In Exhibit 9, this level is at (or near) 100% quality! The reason for this result is that the costs of appraisal and prevention grow moderately as quality increases. However, the costs of internal and external failure drop much more dramatically as quality increases. That is, when more effort is given to prevention and appraisal, internal and external failure costs decrease markedly.

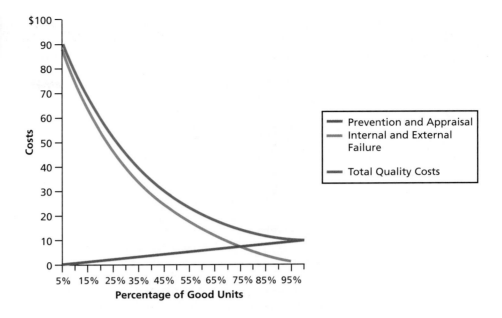

EXHIBIT 9

The Relationship between the Costs of Quality

PARETO CHART OF QUALITY COSTS

An activity analysis quantifies the costs of quality in dollar terms. To illustrate, assume that Gifford Company has performed an activity analysis of quality costs, whose results are shown in Exhibit 10. This exhibit lists the activities, the dollar amount associated with each activity, and the quality cost classification of each activity.

EXHIBIT 10

Quality Control Activity Analysis— Gifford Company

Quality Control Activities	Activity Cost	Quality Cost Classification
Design engineering	$ 55,000	Prevention
Disposing of rejected materials	160,000	Internal Failure
Finished goods inspection	140,000	Appraisal
Materials inspection	70,000	Appraisal
Preventive maintenance	80,000	Prevention
Processing returned materials	150,000	External Failure
Disposing of scrap	195,000	Internal Failure
Assessing vendor quality	45,000	Prevention
Rework	380,000	Internal Failure
Warranty work	225,000	External Failure
Total activity cost	$1,500,000	

Managers want information displayed so that the important problems or issues can be identified quickly. One method of reporting information is the **Pareto chart**. A Pareto chart is a bar chart that shows the totals of an attribute for a number of categories. The categories are ranked and displayed left to right, so that the largest total attribute is on the left and the smallest total is on the right. To illustrate, Exhibit 11 shows a Pareto chart for the quality control activities in Exhibit 10.

In Exhibit 11, the vertical axis is dollars, the attribute in which management is interested. Examples of other attributes that could be used on the vertical axis of a Pareto chart are number of defects, number of orders, time, cost savings, or any other numerical characteristic.

The horizontal axis represents categories for which data are reported. In Exhibit 11, the horizontal axis is categorized according to the ten quality cost activities. The horizontal axis of a Pareto chart could show types of defects, products, customers, employees, or other categories for which data are reported.

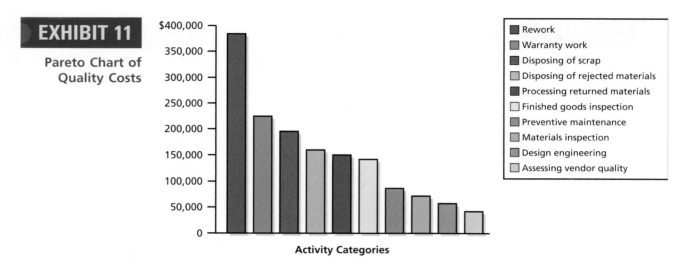

EXHIBIT 11

Pareto Chart of
Quality Costs

The categories on the horizontal axis are ranked from the one with the largest total on the left to the one with the smallest total on the right. Thus, the largest bar on the left in Exhibit 11 is the most expensive quality cost activity—rework. The second largest bar is the second most expensive quality cost activity—warranty work, and so on. The Pareto chart gives the manager a visual tool for identifying the most important categories on which to focus efforts. In this case, rework and warranty work would be high-priority improvement items.

COST OF QUALITY REPORT

In addition to a Pareto chart, the costs of quality from the activity analysis can be summarized in a cost of quality report. A **cost of quality report** identifies the total activity cost associated with each quality cost classification and the percentage of total quality costs associated with each classification. In addition, cost of quality reports will often provide the percentage of each quality cost classification to sales. Exhibit 12 is a cost of quality report for Gifford Company, based on assumed sales of $5,000,000 for the period.

EXHIBIT 12

Cost of Quality
Report—Gifford
Company

	Gifford Company Cost of Quality Report		
Quality Cost Classification	Quality Cost	Percent of Total Quality Cost	Percent of Total Sales
Prevention	$ 180,000	12.00%	3.6%
Appraisal	210,000	14.00	4.2
Internal failure	735,000	49.00	14.7
External failure	375,000	25.00	7.5
Total	$1,500,000	100.00%	30.0%

As you can see, 12% of the total quality cost is the cost of preventing quality problems and 14% is the cost of appraisal activities, while the remaining 74% is for internal and external failures. In addition, internal and external failure-related costs are equal to 22.2% of sales. Gifford Company is not spending a sufficient amount of money in prevention and appraisal activities, while the amount of money spent on internal and external failure activities is too high. This information can be used by Gifford Company to improve quality by focusing on prevention and appraisal activities and thus reducing internal and external failure costs and total quality costs.

Example Exercise 12-4

objective 5

A quality control activity analysis indicated the following four activity costs of an administrative department:

Verifying the accuracy of a form	$ 50,000
Responding to customer complaints	100,000
Correcting errors in forms	75,000
Redesigning forms to reduce errors	25,000
Total	$250,000

Sales are $2,000,000. Prepare a cost of quality report.

Follow My Example 12-4

Cost of Quality Report

Quality Cost Classification	Quality Cost	Percent of Total Quality Cost	Percent of Total Sales
Prevention	$ 25,000	10%	1.25%
Appraisal	50,000	20	2.50
Internal failure	75,000	30	3.75
External failure	100,000	40	5.00
Total	$250,000	100%	12.50%

For Practice: PE 12-4A, PE 12-4B

Bank One, a large regional bank, performed a quality control activity analysis. The analysis indicated the following percentage of costs allocated to each classification:

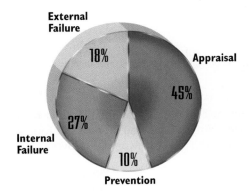

External Failure 18%

Appraisal 45%

Internal Failure 27%

Prevention 10%

As a result of this study, Bank One was able to justify greater investments in prevention activities to improve customer service at lower operating costs.

VALUE-ADDED/NON-VALUE-ADDED ACTIVITY ANALYSIS

In the preceding section, the quality control activities of Gifford Company were classified as prevention, appraisal, internal failure, and external failure costs. Alternatively, activities may be classified as value-added and non-value-added. A **value-added activity** is one that is necessary to meet customer requirements. A **non-value-added activity** is *not* required by the customer but exists because of mistakes, errors, omissions, and other process failures. To illustrate, Exhibit 13 shows the value-added and non-value-added classification for the quality control activities for Gifford Company.[6]

As you can see, the internal and external failure costs are classified as non-value-added, while the prevention and appraisal costs are classified as value-added.[7] A summary of the value-added and non-value-added activities can be developed to show the percentage of the value-added and non-value-added costs to the total costs, as follows:

Classification	Amount	Percent
Value-added	$ 390,000	26%
Non-value-added	1,110,000	74
Total	$1,500,000	100%

For Gifford Company, 74% of the studied activities are non-value-added. This information should further motivate management to make improvements to reduce non-valued-added activities.

6 We use the quality control activities for illustrating the value-added and non-value-added activities in this section. However, a value-added/non-value-added activity analysis can be done for any activity in a business, not just quality control activities.

7 Some believe that appraisal costs are non-value-added. They argue that if the product had been made correctly, then no inspection would be required. We will take a less strict view and assume that appraisal costs are value-added.

EXHIBIT 13

Value-Added/
Non-Value-Added
Quality Control
Activities

Quality Control Activities	Activity Cost	Classification
Design engineering	$ 55,000	Value-added
Disposing of rejected materials	160,000	Non-value-added
Finished goods inspection	140,000	Value-added
Materials inspection	70,000	Value-added
Preventive maintenance	80,000	Value-added
Processing returned materials	150,000	Non-value-added
Disposing of scrap	195,000	Non-value-added
Assessing vendor quality	45,000	Value-added
Rework	380,000	Non-value-added
Warranty work	225,000	Non-value-added
Total activity cost	$1,500,000	

ACTIVITY ANALYSIS FOR PROCESSES

Activity analysis can also be used to evaluate the cost of business processes. A **process** is a sequence of activities that converts an input into an output. That is, a process is a set of activities linked together by common inputs and outputs. Examples of common business processes include procurement, product development, manufacturing, distribution, and sales order fulfillment. Exhibit 14 shows a simplified sales order fulfillment process for Masters Company. This process converts a customer order (the input) into a product received by the customer (the output) through a series of four activities.

EXHIBIT 14 | Sales Order Fulfillment Process

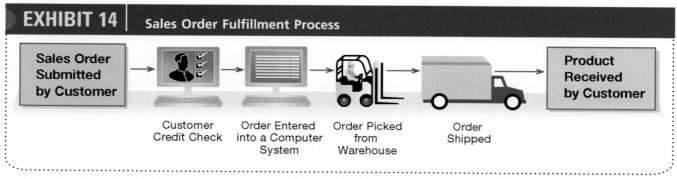

Sales Order Submitted by Customer → Customer Credit Check → Order Entered into a Computer System → Order Picked from Warehouse → Order Shipped → Product Received by Customer

*Operators driving forklifts receive a list of orders, drive to stacking locations within the warehouse, pick the orders, and then transport them back to an area to prepare for shipment.

An activity analysis can be used to determine the cost of the activities of this process. To illustrate, assume that an activity analysis determined that the cost of the four activities in the Masters Company sales order fulfillment process was as follows:

Sales Order Fulfillment Activities	Activity Cost	Percent of Total Process Cost
Customer credit check	$14,400	18%
Order entering	9,600	12
Order picking	36,000	45
Order shipping	20,000	25
Total sales order fulfillment process cost	$80,000	100%

The total cost of performing the sales order fulfillment process is $80,000. The order picking activity represents 45% of the total process cost. If we assume that 10,000 sales orders were submitted and eventually shipped through this process, the process could be calculated to average $8 per shipped order ($80,000/10,000 shipped orders).

Management can use process cost information to support cost improvement activity. For example, assume that Masters Company management set a cost improvement target of $6 per shipped order. A $2 reduction per shipped order would require this process to be improved by either eliminating unnecessary or wasteful work or improving processing method efficiency. In this case, Masters Company determines that cost can be improved by eliminating unnecessary credit check work and by improving the picking activity efficiency.

Specifically, management determines that not all customer orders need to go through credit check, just the new orders from new customers. If Masters assumes that the process will ship 10,000 orders during the next period, it is estimated that this change would require the credit check activity to process only 2,500 sales orders, or 25% of the total. In addition, management introduces a more efficient warehouse product layout. This layout reduces the cost of picking orders by 35%. The cost savings from these two efforts and their impact on the cost of the sales order fulfillment process can be evaluated as follows:

Activity	Activity Cost Prior to Improvement	Activity Cost After Improvement	Activity Cost Savings
Customer credit check	$14,400	$ 3,600[1]	$10,800
Order entering	9,600	9,600	0
Order picking	36,000	23,400[2]	12,600
Order shipping	20,000	20,000	0
Total sales order fulfillment process cost	$80,000	$56,600	$23,400
Cost per shipped order (total divided by 10,000 orders shipped)	$8.00	$5.66	

[1]$14,400 × 25%
[2]$36,000 × 65%

Management's improvement activities would generate a savings of $23,400 during a period in which 10,000 sales orders are shipped.[8] This savings would reduce the cost from $8.00 to $5.66 per sales order shipped, thus exceeding management's improvement target.

More complex analyses can be performed by integrating activity-based process analysis into the budgeting system. In this way, process activity costs could be segregated into fixed and variable costs, and thus planned and controlled, using flexible budgets as discussed in a previous chapter. The use of activity-based process analysis in this way is discussed in advanced managerial accounting texts.

Example Exercise 12-5 objective 5

Mason Company incurred an activity cost of $120,000 for inspecting 50,000 units of production. Management determined that the inspecting objectives could be met without inspecting every unit. Therefore, rather than inspecting 50,000 units of production, the inspection activity was limited to 20% of the production. Determine the inspection activity cost per unit on 50,000 units of total production both before and after the improvement.

Follow My Example 12-5

Inspection activity before improvement: $120,000/50,000 units = $2.40 per unit
Inspection activity after improvement: ($120,000 × 20%)/50,000 units = $0.48 per unit

For Practice: PE 12-5A, PE 12-5B

8 This analysis assumes that the activity costs are variable to the inputs and outputs of the process. While this is likely true for processes primarily using labor, such as a sales order fulfillment process, other types of processes may have significant fixed costs that would not change with changes of inputs and outputs.

At a Glance

1. Compare and contrast just-in-time (JIT) manufacturing practices with traditional manufacturing practices.

Key Points	Key Learning Outcomes	Example Exercises	Practice Exercises
Just-in-time emphasizes reduced lead time, a product-oriented production layout, a team-oriented work environment, setup time reduction, pull manufacturing, high quality, and supplier and customer partnering in order to improve the supply chain.	• Identify the characteristics of a just-in-time manufacturing environment and compare it to traditional approaches. • Describe the relationship between setup time, batch size, inventory, and lead time. • Compute lead time and the value-added ratio.	12-1	12-1A, 12-1B

2. Apply just-in-time manufacturing practices to a traditional manufacturing illustration.

Key Points	Key Learning Outcomes	Example Exercises	Practice Exercises
The just-in-time philosophy was illustrated for Anderson Metal Fabricators (AMF). In the illustration, AMF was able to add a new product line without increasing the size of its facility. This was done by using just-in-time principles to eliminate the space normally used for inventory. This space could now be used for producing the new product line.	• Describe how just-in-time principles are applied to a manufacturing setting.	12-2	12-2A, 12-2B

3. Describe the implications of a just-in-time manufacturing philosophy on cost accounting and performance measurement systems.

Key Points	Key Learning Outcomes	Example Exercises	Practice Exercises
The just-in-time philosophy has implications for cost accounting. The cost accounting system will have fewer transactions, will combine the materials and work in process accounts, and will account for direct labor as a part of cell conversion cost. Just-in-time will use nonfinancial reporting measures and result in more direct tracing of factory overhead to product cells.	• Identify the implications of the just-in-time philosophy for cost accounting. • Prepare just-in-time journal entries for material purchases, application of cell conversion cost, and transfer of cell costs to finished goods. • Describe nonfinancial performance measures.	12-3	12-3A, 12-3B

4. Apply just-in-time practices to a nonmanufacturing setting.

Key Points	Key Learning Outcomes	Example Exercises	Practice Exercises
Just-in-time principles can be used in service businesses and administrative processes. For example, hospitals are removing delays in serving patients by improving admission, testing, and recovery processes. This is accomplished by designing product-focused hospital units that use cross-trained caregivers in the delivery of hospital care.	• Illustrate the use of just-in-time principles in a nonmanufacturing setting, such as a hospital.		

5. Describe and illustrate activity analysis for improving operations.

Key Points	Key Learning Outcomes	Example Exercises	Practice Exercises
Companies use activity analysis to identify the costs of quality, which include prevention, appraisal, internal failure, and external failure costs. The quality cost activities may be reported on a Pareto chart, which visually highlights the most expensive quality cost categories. In addition, the quality costs can be summarized in a quality cost report by each of the four major classifications. An alternative method for categorizing activities is by value-added and non-value-added classifications. An activity analysis can also be used to determine the cost of processes. Process costs can be improved by either improving processing methods or eliminating unnecessary or wasteful work.	• Define the costs of quality. • Define and prepare a Pareto chart. • Prepare a cost of quality report. • Identify value-added and non-value-added activity costs. • Use a process activity analysis to measure process improvement.	12-4 12-5	12-4A, 12-4B 12-5A, 12-5B

Key Terms

activity analysis (487)
appraisal costs (488)
backflush accounting (483)
cost of quality report (490)
costs of quality (487)
electronic data interchange (EDI) (479)
employee involvement (478)
enterprise resource planning (ERP) systems (480)
external failure costs (488)
internal failure costs (488)

just-in-time (JIT) manufacturing (473)
lead time (474)
nonfinancial measure (485)
non-value-added activity (491)
non-value-added lead time (475)
Pareto chart (489)
prevention costs (488)
process (492)
process-oriented layout (478)
product-oriented layout (478)
pull manufacturing (478)

push manufacturing (479)
radio frequency identification devices (RFID) (479)
Raw and In Process (RIP) Inventory (482)
six-sigma (479)
supply chain management (479)
value-added activity (491)
value-added lead time (474)
value-added ratio (475)

Illustrative Problem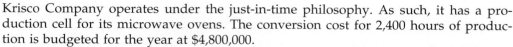

Krisco Company operates under the just-in-time philosophy. As such, it has a production cell for its microwave ovens. The conversion cost for 2,400 hours of production is budgeted for the year at $4,800,000.

During January, 2,000 microwave ovens were started and completed. Each oven requires six minutes of cell processing time. The materials cost for each oven is $100.

Instructions

1. Determine the budgeted cell conversion cost per hour.
2. Determine the manufacturing cost per unit.
3. Journalize the entry to record the costs charged to the production cell in January.
4. Journalize the entry to record the costs transferred to finished goods.

Solution

1. Budgeted Cell Conversion Cost Rate $= \dfrac{\$4,800,000}{2,400 \text{ hours}} = \$2,000$ per cell hour

2.
Materials	$100 per unit
Conversion cost [($2,000 per hour/60 min.) × 6 min.]	200
Total	$300 per unit

3.
1	Raw and In Process Inventory	200 0 0 0 00	
2	Accounts Payable		200 0 0 0 00
3	To record materials costs.		
4	(2,000 units × $100 per unit).		
5			
6	Raw and In Process Inventory	400 0 0 0 00	
7	Conversion Costs		400 0 0 0 00
8	To record conversion costs.		
9	(2,000 units × $200 per unit).		
10			
4. 11	Finished Goods (2,000 × $300 per unit)	600 0 0 0 00	
12	Raw and In Process Inventory		600 0 0 0 00
13	To record finished production.		

Self-Examination Questions

(Answers at End of Chapter)

1. Which of the following is not a characteristic of the just-in-time philosophy?
   A. Product-oriented layout
   B. Push manufacturing (make to stock)
   C. Short lead times
   D. Reducing setup time as a critical improvement priority

2. Accounting in a just-in-time environment is best described as:
   A. more complex.
   B. focused on direct labor.
   C. providing detailed variance reports.
   D. providing less transaction control.

3. The product cell for Dynah Company has budgeted conversion costs of $420,000 for the year. The cell is planned to be available 2,100 hours for production. Each unit requires $12.50 of materials cost. The cell started and completed 700 units. The cell process time for the product is 15 minutes per unit. What is the cost debited to finished goods for the period?
   A. $8,750   C. $43,750
   B. $35,000   D. $140,000

4. In-process inspection activities are an example of what type of quality cost?
   A. Prevention
   B. Appraisal
   C. Internal failure
   D. External failure

5. A Pareto chart is used to display:
   A. a ranking of attribute totals, by category, in the form of a bar chart.
   B. important trends in the form of a line chart.
   C. percentage information in the form of a pie chart.
   D. a listing of attribute totals, by category, in a table.

Eye Openers

1. What is the benefit of just-in-time processing?
2. What are some examples of non-value-added lead time?
3. Why is a product-oriented layout preferred by just-in-time manufacturers over a process-oriented layout?
4. How is setup time related to lead time?
5. Why do just-in-time manufacturers favor pull or "make to order" manufacturing?
6. Why would a just-in-time manufacturer strive to produce zero defects?
7. How is supply chain management different from traditional supplier and customer relationships?
8. Why does accounting in a just-in-time environment result in fewer transactions?
9. Why is a "raw and in process inventory" account used by just-in-time manufacturers, rather than separately reporting materials and work in process?
10. Why is the direct labor cost category eliminated in many just-in-time environments?
11. How does accounting under a just-in-time environment provide less transaction control?
12. What are some possible explanations for the actual conversion cost per unit being greater than the budgeted cost per unit in a just-in-time production cell?
13. What just-in-time principles might a hospital use?
14. What is the benefit of an activity analysis?
15. How does a Pareto chart assist management?
16. What is the benefit of identifying non-value-added activities?
17. What ways can the cost of a process be improved?

Practice Exercises

PE 12-1A
Lead time computation and analysis
obj. 1

The Winterscape Ski company manufactures skis in the finishing and assembly process. Skis are manufactured in 35-ski batch sizes. The finishing time is 18 minutes per ski. The assembly time is 12 minutes per ski. It takes 9 minutes to move a batch of skis from finishing to assembly.

a. Compute the value-added, non-value-added, and total lead time of this process.
b. Compute the value-added ratio. Round to one decimal.

PE 12-1B
Lead time computation and analysis
obj. 1

The Fashion Jean company manufactures jeans in the cutting and sewing process. Jeans are manufactured in 60-jean batch sizes. The cutting time is 8 minutes per jean. The sewing time is 15 minutes per jean. It takes 18 minutes to move a batch of jeans from cutting to sewing.

a. Compute the value-added, non-value-added, and total lead time of this process.
b. Compute the value-added ratio. Round to one decimal.

PE 12-2A
Identify just-in-time benefits
obj. 2

Which of the following are features of a just-in-time manufacturing system?

a. Centralized maintenance areas
b. Smaller batch sizes
c. Employee involvement
d. Push scheduling

PE 12-2B
Identify just-in-time benefits
obj. 2

Which of the following are features of a just-in-time manufacturing system?

a. Production pace matches demand
b. Centralized work in process inventory locations
c. Less wasted movement of material and people
d. Receive raw materials directly to manufacturing cells

PE 12-3A
Just-in-time journal entries
obj. 3

The budgeted conversion costs for a just-in-time cell are $1,927,000 for 2,050 production hours. Each unit produced by the cell requires 12 minutes of cell process time. During the month, 850 units are manufactured in the cell. The estimated materials cost are $1,450 per unit. Provide the following journal entries:

a. Materials are purchased to produce 870 units.
b. Conversion costs are applied to 850 units of production.
c. 840 units are placed into finished goods.

PE 12-3B
Just-in-time journal entries
obj. 3

The budgeted conversion costs for a just-in-time cell are $270,000 for 1,800 production hours. Each unit produced by the cell requires 24 minutes of cell process time. During the month, 370 units are manufactured in the cell. The estimated materials cost are $95 per unit. Provide the following journal entries:

a. Materials are purchased to produce 400 units.
b. Conversion costs are applied to 370 units of production.
c. 350 units are placed into finished goods.

PE 12-4A
Cost of quality report
obj. 5

A quality control activity analysis indicated the following four activity costs of a manufacturing department:

Rework	$ 12,000
Inspecting incoming raw materials	30,000
Warranty work	3,000
Process improvement effort	105,000
Total	$150,000

Sales are $1,000,000. Prepare a cost of quality report.

PE 12-4B
Cost of quality report
obj. 5

A quality control activity analysis indicated the following four activity costs of a hotel:

Inspecting cleanliness of rooms	$ 90,000
Processing lost customer reservations	495,000
Rework incorrectly prepared room service meal	45,000
Employee training	270,000
Total	$900,000

Sales are $6,000,000. Prepare a cost of quality report.

PE 12-5A
Process activity analysis
obj. 5

Tudor Company incurred an activity cost of $360,000 for inspecting 60,000 units of production. Management determined that the inspecting objectives could be met without inspecting every unit. Therefore, rather than inspecting 60,000 units of production, the inspection activity was limited to 25% of the production. Determine the inspection activity cost per unit on 60,000 units of total production both before and after the improvement.

PE 12-5B
Process activity analysis
obj. 5

Stuart Company incurred an activity cost of $45,000 for inspecting 5,000 units of production. Management determined that the inspecting objectives could be met without inspecting every unit. Therefore, rather than inspecting 5,000 units of production, the inspection activity was limited to a random selection of 500 units out of the 5,000 units of production. Determine the inspection activity cost per unit on 5,000 units of total production both before and after the improvement.

Exercises

EX 12-1
Just-in-time principles
obj. 1

The chief executive officer (CEO) of Lordsland Inc. has just returned from a management seminar describing the benefits of the just-in-time philosophy. The CEO issued the following statement after returning from the conference:

This company will become a just-in-time manufacturing company. Presently, we have too much inventory. To become just-in-time we need to eliminate the excess inventory. Therefore, I want all employees to begin reducing inventories until we are just-in-time. Thank you for your cooperation.

How would you respond to the CEO's statement?

EX 12-2
Just-in-time as a strategy
obj. 1

The American textile industry has moved much of its operations offshore in the pursuit of lower labor costs. Textile imports have risen from 2% of all textile production in 1962 to over 60% in 2006. Offshore manufacturers make long runs of standard mass-market apparel items. These are then brought to the United States in container ships, requiring significant time between original order and delivery. As a result, retail customers must accurately forecast market demands for imported apparel items.

Assuming that you work for a U.S.-based textile company, how would you recommend responding to the low-cost imports?

EX 12-3
Lead time reduction—service company
objs. 1, 4

Homeguard Insurance Company takes ten days to make payments on insurance claims. Claims are processed through three departments: Data Input, Claims Audit, and Claims Adjustment. The three departments are on different floors, approximately one hour apart from each other. Claims are processed in batches of 100. Each batch of 100 claims moves through the three departments on a wheeled cart. Management is concerned about customer dissatisfaction caused by the long lead time for claim payments.

How might this process be changed so that the lead time could be reduced significantly?

EX 12-4
Just-in-time principles
obj. 1

Celestial Shirt Company manufactures various styles of men's casual wear. Shirts are cut and assembled by a workforce that is paid by piece rate. This means that they are paid according to the amount of work completed during a period of time. To illustrate, if the piece rate is $0.10 per sleeve assembled, and the worker assembles 700 sleeves during the day, then the worker would be paid $70 (700 × $0.10) for the day's work.

The company is considering adopting a just-in-time manufacturing philosophy by organizing work cells around various types of products and employing pull manufacturing. However, no change is expected in the compensation policy. On this point, the manufacturing manager stated the following:

"Piecework compensation provides an incentive to work fast. Without it, the workers will just goof off and expect a full day's pay. We can't pay straight hourly wages—at least not in this industry."

How would you respond to the manufacturing manager's comments?

EX 12-5
Lead time analysis
obj. 1

Kiddie Kuddles Inc. manufactures toy stuffed animals. The direct labor time required to cut, sew, and stuff a toy is 12 minutes per unit. The company makes two types of stuffed toys—a lion and a bear. The lion is assembled in lot sizes of 50 units per batch, while the bear is assembled in lot sizes of 5 units per batch. Since each product has direct labor time of 12 minutes per unit, management has determined that the lead time for each product is 12 minutes.

Is management correct? What are the lead times for each product?

EX 12-6
Reduce setup time
obj. 1

Compressor Inc. has analyzed the setup time on its computer-controlled lathe. The setup requires changing the type of fixture that holds a part. The average setup time has been 200 minutes, consisting of the following steps:

Turn off machine and remove fixture from lathe	10 minutes
Go to tool room with fixture	30
Record replacement of fixture to tool room	15
Return to lathe	30
Clean lathe	25
Return to tool room	30
Record withdrawal of new fixture from tool room	20
Return to lathe	30
Install new fixture and turn on machine	10
Total setup time	200 minutes

a. ▭▭▭▶ Why should management be concerned about improving setup time?

b. ▭▭▭▶ What do you recommend to Compressor Inc. for improving setup time?

c. How much time would be required for a setup, using your suggestion in (b)?

EX 12-7
Calculate lead time
obj. 1

Madison Machining Company machines metal parts for the automotive industry. Under the traditional manufacturing approach, the parts are machined through two processes: milling and finishing. Parts are produced in batch sizes of 90 parts. A part requires 6 minutes in milling and 8 minutes in finishing. The move time between the two operations for a complete batch is 10 minutes.

Under the just-in-time philosophy, the part is produced in a cell that includes both the milling and finishing operations. The operating time is unchanged; however, the batch size is reduced to 5 parts and the move time is eliminated.

Determine the value-added, non-value-added, total lead time, and the value-added ratio under the traditional and just-in-time manufacturing methods. Round whole percentages to one decimal place.

EX 12-8
Calculate lead time
obj. 1

Mercury Memories Inc. is considering a new just-in-time product cell. The present manufacturing approach produces a product in four separate steps. The production batch sizes are 45 units. The process time for each step is as follows:

Process Step 1	6 minutes
Process Step 2	4 minutes
Process Step 3	15 minutes
Process Step 4	9 minutes

The time required to move each batch between steps is 20 minutes. In addition, the time to move raw materials to Process Step 1 is also 20 minutes, and the time to move completed units from Process Step 4 to finished goods inventory is 20 minutes.

The new just-in-time layout will allow the company to reduce the batch sizes from 45 units to 4 units. The time required to move each batch between steps and the inventory locations will be reduced to 3 minutes. The processing time in each step will stay the same.

Determine the value-added, non-value-added, total lead times, and the value-added ratio under the present and proposed production approaches. Round whole percentages to one decimal place.

EX 12-9
Lead time calculation—doctor's office
objs. 1, 4

✓ b. 140 minutes

Mi Chen caught the flu and needed to see the doctor. Chen called to set up an appointment and was told to come in at 1:00 p.m. Chen arrived at the doctor's office promptly at 1:00 p.m. The waiting room had 12 other people in it. Patients were admitted from the waiting room in FIFO (first-in, first-out) order at a rate of five minutes per patient. After waiting until her turn, a nurse finally invited Chen to an examining room. Once in the examining room, Chen waited another 15 minutes before a nurse arrived to take some basic readings (temperature, blood pressure). The nurse needed five minutes to collect the clinical information. After the nurse left, Chen waited 15 additional minutes before the doctor arrived. The doctor arrived and diagnosed the flu and provided a prescription for antibiotics. This took the doctor 10 minutes. Before leaving the doctor's office, Chen waited 10 minutes at the business office to pay for the office visit.

Chen spent 5 minutes walking next door to fill the prescription at the pharmacy. There were five people in front of Chen, each person requiring 8 minutes to fill and purchase his or her prescription. Chen finally arrived home 22 minutes after paying for her prescription.

a. What time does Chen arrive home?
b. How much of the total elapsed time from 1:00 p.m. until when Chen arrived home was non-value-added time?
c. Why does the doctor require patients to wait so long for service?

EX 12-10
Suppy chain management
obj. 1

The following is an excerpt from a recent article discussing supplier relationships with the Big Three North American automakers.

"The Big Three select suppliers on the basis of lowest price and annual price reductions," said Neil De Koker, president of the Original Equipment Suppliers Association. "They look globally for the lowest parts prices from the lowest cost countries," De Koker said. "There is little trust and respect. Collaboration is missing." Japanese auto makers want long-term supplier relationships. They select suppliers as a person would a mate. The Big Three are quick to beat down prices with methods such as electronic auctions or rebidding work to a competitor. The Japanese are equally tough on price but are committed to maintaining supplier continuity. "They work with you to arrive at a competitive price, and they are willing to pay because they want long-term partnering," said Carl Code, a vice president at Ernie Green Industries. "They [Honda and Toyota] want suppliers to make enough money to stay in business, grow and bring them innovation." The Big Three's supply chain model is not much different from the one set by Henry Ford. In 1913, he set up the system of independent supplier firms operating at arm's length on short-term contracts. One consequence of the Big Three's low-price-at-all-costs mentality is that suppliers are reluctant to offer them their cutting-edge technology out of fear the contract will be resourced before the research and development costs are recouped.

a. Contrast the Japanese supply chain model with that of the Big Three.
b. Why might a supplier prefer the Japanese model?
c. What benefits might accrue to the Big Three by adopting the Japanese supply chain practices?

Source: Robert Sherefkin and Amy Wilson, "Suppliers Prefer Japanese Business Model," *Rubber & Plastics News*, March 17, 2003, Vol. 24, No. 11.

EX 12-11
Employee involvement
obj. 1

Quickie Designs Inc. uses teams in the manufacture of lightweight wheelchairs. Two features of its team approach are team hiring and peer reviews. Under team hiring, the team recruits, interviews, and hires new team members from within the organization. Using peer reviews, the team evaluates each member of the team with regard to quality, knowledge, teamwork, goal performance, attendance, and safety. These reviews provide feedback to the team member for improvement.

How do these two team approaches differ from using managers to hire and evaluate employees?

EX 12-12
Accounting issues in a just-in-time environment
obj. 3

Vision Electronics Company has recently implemented a just-in-time manufacturing approach. A production department manager has approached the controller with the following comments:

I am very upset with our accounting system now that we have implemented our new just-in-time manufacturing methods. It seems as if all I'm doing is paperwork. Our product is moving so fast through the manufacturing process that the paperwork can hardly keep up. For example, it just doesn't make sense to me to fill out daily labor reports. The employees are assigned to complete cells, performing many different tasks. I can't keep up with direct labor reports on each individual task. I thought we were trying to eliminate waste. Yet the information requirements of the accounting system are slowing us down and adding to overall lead time. Moreover, I'm still getting my monthly variance reports. I don't think that these are necessary. I have nonfinancial performance measures that are more timely than these reports. Besides, the employees don't really understand accounting variances. How about giving some information that I can really use?

What accounting system changes would you suggest in light of the production department manager's criticisms?

EX 12-13

Just-in-time journal entries

obj. 3

✓ b. $78

Wave Media Inc. uses a just-in-time strategy to manufacture DVD players. The company manufactures DVDs through a single product cell. The budgeted conversion cost for the year is $998,400 for 1,920 production hours. Each unit requires 9 minutes of cell process time. During March, 1,100 DVDs are manufactured in the cell. The materials cost per unit is $70. The following summary transactions took place during March:

1. Materials are purchased for March production.
2. Conversion costs were applied to production.
3. 1,100 DVDs are assembled and placed in finished goods.
4. 1,050 DVDs are sold for $250 per unit.

a. Determine the budgeted cell conversion cost per hour.
b. Determine the budgeted cell conversion cost per unit.
c. Journalize the summary transactions (1)–(4) for March.

EX 12-14

Just-in-time journal entries

obj. 3

✓ a. $60

Glowstream Inc. manufactures lighting fixtures, using just-in-time manufacturing methods. Style BB-01 has a materials cost per unit of $24. The budgeted conversion cost for the year is $120,000 for 2,000 production hours. A unit of Style BB-01 requires 15 minutes of cell production time. The following transactions took place during June:

1. Materials were acquired to assemble 650 Style BB-01 units for June.
2. Conversion costs were applied to 650 Style BB-01 units of production.
3. 640 units of Style BB-01 were completed in June.
4. 630 units of Style BB-01 were sold in June for $65 per unit.

a. Determine the budgeted cell conversion cost per hour.
b. Determine the budgeted cell conversion cost per unit.
c. Journalize the summary transactions (1)–(4) for June.

EX 12-15

Just-in-time journal entries

obj. 3

Allendale Audio Company manufactures audio speakers. Each speaker requires $68 per unit of direct materials. The speaker manufacturing assembly cell includes the following estimated costs for the period:

Speaker assembly cell estimated costs:	
Cell labor	$33,100
Cell depreciation	5,900
Cell supplies	2,200
Cell power	1,300
Total cell costs for the period	$42,500

The operating plan calls for 170 operating hours for the period. Each speaker requires 18 minutes of cell process time. The unit selling price for each speaker is $260. During the period, the following transactions occurred:

1. Purchased materials to produce 600 speaker units.
2. Applied conversion costs to production of 570 speaker units.
3. Completed and transferred 560 speaker units to finished goods.
4. Sold 540 speaker units.

There were no inventories at the beginning of the period.

a. Journalize the summary transactions (1)–(4) for the period.
b. Determine the ending balance for raw and in-process inventory and finished goods inventory.

EX 12-16

Just-in-time—fast-food restaurant

obj. 4

The management of Mister Burger fast-food franchise wants to provide hamburgers quickly to customers. It has been using a process by which precooked hamburgers are prepared and placed under hot lamps. These hamburgers are then sold to customers. In this process, every customer receives the same type of hamburger and dressing (ketchup, onions, mustard). If a customer wants something different, then a "special order" must be cooked to the customer's requirements. This requires the customer to wait several minutes, which often slows down the service line. Mister Burger has been receiving more and more special orders from customers, which has been slowing service down considerably.

a. ▬▬▶ How would you describe the present Mister Burger service delivery system?

b. ▬▬▶ How might you use just-in-time principles to provide customers quick service, yet still allow them to custom order their burgers?

EX 12-17
Pareto chart
obj. 5

Integrity Memory Circuits Inc. manufactures RAM memory chips for personal computers. An activity analysis was conducted, and the following activity costs were identified with the manufacture and sale of memory chips:

Activities	Activity Cost
Correct shipment errors	$108,000
Disposing of scrap	126,000
Emergency equipment maintenance	81,000
Employee training	27,000
Final inspection	103,500
Inspecting incoming materials	27,000
Preventive equipment maintenance	22,500
Processing customer returns	90,000
Scrap reporting	36,000
Supplier development	18,000
Warranty claims	261,000
Total	$900,000

Prepare a Pareto chart of these activities.

EX 12-18
Cost of quality report
obj. 5

✓ *a. Appraisal, 14.5% of total costs*

a. Using the information in Exercise 12-17, prepare a cost of quality report. Assume that the sales for the period were $4,500,000.

b. ▬▬▶ Interpret the cost of quality report.

EX 12-19
Pareto chart for a service company
obj. 5

Countrywide Cable Company provides cable TV and Internet service to the local community. The activities and activity costs of Countrywide Cable are identified as follows:

Activities	Activity Cost
Billing error correction	$ 30,000
Cable signal testing	108,000
Reinstalling service (installed incorrectly the first time)	78,000
Repairing satellite equipment	12,000
Repairing underground cable connections to the customer	24,000
Replacing old technology cable with higher quality cable	132,000
Replacing old technology signal switches with higher quality switches	144,000
Responding to customer home repair requests	42,000
Training employees	30,000
Total	$600,000

Prepare a Pareto chart of these activities.

EX 12-20
Cost of quality and value-added/non-value-added reports
obj. 5

✓ *a. External failure, 29% of total costs*

a. Using the activity data in Exercise 12-19, prepare a cost of quality report. Assume that sales are $2,000,000. Round percentages to one decimal place.

b. Using the activity data in Exercise 12-19, prepare a value-added/non-value-added analysis.

c. ▬▬▶ Interpret the information in (a) and (b).

EX 12-21

Process activity analysis

objs. 4, 5

✓ b. $40 per claim
payment

Metropolitan Insurance Company has a process for making payments on insurance claims as follows:

An activity analysis revealed that the cost of these activities was as follows:

Receiving claim	$ 30,000
Adjusting claim	130,000
Paying claim	40,000
Total	$200,000

This process includes only the cost of processing the claim payments, not the actual amount of the claim payments. The adjusting activity involves verifying and estimating the amount of the claim.

The process received, adjusted, and paid 5,000 claims during the period. All claims were treated identically in this process.

To improve the cost of this process, management has determined that claims should be segregated into two categories. Claims under $1,000 and claims greater than $1,000: claims under $1,000 would not be adjusted but would be accepted upon the insured's evidence of claim. Claims above $1,000 would be adjusted. It is estimated that 65% of the claims are under $1,000 and would thus be paid without adjustment. It is also estimated that the additional effort to segregate claims would add 12% to the "receiving claim" activity cost.

a. Develop a table showing the percent of activity cost to the total process cost for the claim payment activities.
b. Determine the average total process cost per claim payment, assuming 5,000 total claims.
c. Prepare a table showing the changes in the activity costs as a result of the changes proposed by management.
d. Estimate the average cost per claim payment, assuming that the changes proposed by management are enacted for 5,000 total claims.

EX 12-22

Process activity analysis

obj. 5

✓ b. $20 per payment

The procurement process for Baker Company includes a series of activities that transforms a materials requisition into a vendor check. The process begins with a request for materials. The requesting department prepares and sends a materials request form to the Purchasing Department. The Purchasing Department then places a request for a quote to vendors. Vendors prepare bids in response to the request for a quote. A vendor is selected based on the lowest bid. A purchase order to the low-bid vendor is prepared. The vendor delivers the materials to the company, whereupon a receiving ticket is prepared. Payment to the vendor is authorized if the materials request form, receiving ticket, and vendor invoice are in agreement. These three documents fail to agree 45% of the time, initiating effort to reconcile the differences. Once the three documents agree, a check is issued. The process can be diagrammed as follows:

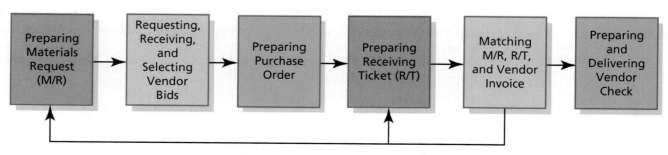

Correcting Reconciliation Differences

An activity analysis indicated the following activity costs with this process:

Preparing materials request	$ 40,000
Requesting, receiving, and selecting vendor bids	120,000
Preparing purchase order	25,000
Preparing receiving ticket	35,000
Matching M/R, R/T, and invoice	50,000
Correcting reconciliation differences	180,000
Preparing and delivering vendor payment	50,000
Total process activity cost	$500,000

On average, the process handles 25,000 individual requests for materials that result in 25,000 individual payments to vendors.

Management proposes to improve this process in two ways. First, the Purchasing Department will develop a preapproved vendor list for which orders can be placed without a request for quote. It is expected that this will reduce the need for requesting and receiving vendor bids by 75%. Second, additional training and standardization will be provided to reduce errors introduced into the materials requisition form and receiving tickets. It is expected that this will reduce the number of reconciliations from 45% to 15%, over an average of 25,000 payments.

a. Develop a table showing the percent of individual activity cost to the total process cost for the procurement activities.
b. Determine the average total process cost per vendor payment, assuming 25,000 payments.
c. Prepare a table showing the improvements in the activity costs as a result of the changes proposed by management.
d. Estimate the average cost per vendor payment, assuming that the changes proposed by management are enacted for 25,000 total payments.

Problems Series A

PR 12-1A
Just-in-time principles
obj. 1
✓ 3. $0.20 per pound

Safety Glow Co. manufactures light bulbs. Safety Glow's purchasing policy requires that the purchasing agents place each quarter's purchasing requirements out for bid. This is because the Purchasing Department is evaluated solely by its ability to get the lowest purchase prices. The lowest cost bidder receives the order for the next quarter (90 working days).

To make its bulb products, Safety Glow requires 24,300 pounds of glass per quarter. Safety Glow received two glass bids for the second quarter, as follows:

- *Continental Glass Company:* $20.00 per pound of glass. Delivery schedule: 27,000 pounds at the beginning of April to last for 3 months.
- *Emory Glass Company:* $20.15 per pound of glass. Delivery schedule: 300 pounds per working day (90 days in the quarter).

Safety Glow accepted Continental Glass Company's bid because it was the low-cost bid.

Instructions
1. ▭▭▶ Comment on Safety Glow's purchasing policy.
2. ▭▭▶ What are the additional (hidden) costs, beyond price, of Continental Glass Company's bid? Why weren't these costs considered?
3. Considering just inventory financing costs, what is the additional cost per pound of Continental Glass Company's bid if the cost of money is 8%? (*Hint:* Determine the average value of glass inventory held for the quarter and multiply by the quarterly interest charge.)

PR 12-2A
Lead time
obj. **1**

✓1. Total wait time,
1,843 minutes

Soundwave Audio Company manufactures electronic stereo equipment. The manufacturing process includes printed circuit (PC) card assembly, final assembly, testing, and shipping. In the PC card assembly operation, a number of individuals are responsible for assembling electronic components into printed circuit boards. Each operator is responsible for soldering components according to a given set of instructions. Operators work on batches of 50 printed circuit boards. Each board requires 6 minutes of assembly time. After each batch is completed, the operator moves the assembled cards to the final assembly area. This move takes 10 minutes to complete.

The final assembly for each stereo unit requires 18 minutes and is also done in batches of 50 units. A batch of 50 stereos is moved into the test building, which is across the street. The move takes 15 minutes. Before conducting the test, the test equipment must be set up for the particular stereo model. The test setup requires 30 minutes. The units wait while the setup is performed. In the final test, the 50-unit batch is tested one at a time. Each test requires 5 minutes. The completed batch, after all testing, is sent to shipping for packaging and final shipment to customers. A complete batch of 50 units is sent from final assembly to shipping. The Shipping Department is located next to final assembly. Thus, there is no move time between these two operations. Packaging and labeling requires 8 minutes per unit.

Instructions
1. Determine the amount of value-added and non-value-added lead time and the value-added ratio in this process for an average stereo unit in a batch of 50 units. Round percentages to one decimal place. Categorize the non-value-added time into wait and move time.
2. ▭▭▷ How could this process be improved so as to reduce the amount of waste in the process?

PR 12-3A
Just-in-time accounting
obj. **3**

✓4. Raw and In Process
Inventory, $4,075

Display Labs Inc. manufactures and assembles automobile instrument panels for both Yamura Motors and Detroit Motors. The process consists of a just-in-time product cell for each customer's instrument assembly. The data that follow concern only the Yamura just-in-time cell.

For the year, Display Labs Inc. budgeted the following costs for the Yamura production cell:

Conversion Cost Categories	Budget
Labor	$610,000
Supplies	84,000
Utilities	26,000
Total	$720,000

Display Labs Inc. plans 2,500 hours of production for the Yamura cell for the year. The materials cost is $115 per instrument assembly. Each assembly requires 25 minutes of cell assembly time. There was no June 1 inventory for either Raw and In Process Inventory or Finished Goods Inventory.

The following summary events took place in the Yamura cell during June:

a. Electronic parts and wiring were purchased to produce 515 instrument assemblies in June.
b. Conversion costs were applied for the production of 500 units in June.
c. 490 units were started and completed and transferred to finished goods in June.
d. 475 units were shipped to customers at a price of $400 per unit.

Instructions
1. Determine the budgeted cell conversion cost per hour.
2. Determine the budgeted cell conversion cost per unit.
3. Journalize the summary transactions (a) through (d).
4. Determine the ending balance in Raw and In Process Inventory and Finished Goods Inventory.
5. ▭▭▷ How does the accounting in a JIT environment differ from traditional accounting?

PR 12-4A
Pareto chart and cost of quality report—municipality

objs. 4, 5

✔ 3. Non-value-added, 61.5%

The administrator of elections for the city of Maryville has been asked to perform an activity analysis of its optical scanning center. The optical scanning center reads voter forms into the computer. The result of the activity analysis is summarized as follows:

Activities	Activity Cost
Correcting errors identified by election commission	$ 38,400
Correcting jams	57,600
Correcting scan errors	33,600
Loading	12,000
Logging-in control codes (for later reconciliation)	14,400
Program scanner	7,200
Rerunning job due to scan reading errors	18,000
Scanning	31,200
Verifying scan accuracy via reconciling totals	12,000
Verifying scanner accuracy with test run	15,600
Total	$240,000

Instructions
1. Prepare a Pareto chart of the department activities.
2. Use the activity cost information to determine the percentages of total department costs that are prevention, appraisal, internal failure, external failure, and not costs of quality. Round percentages to one decimal place.
3. Determine the percentages of the total department costs that are value- and non-value-added. Round percentages to one decimal place.
4. Interpret the information.

Problems Series B

PR 12-1B
Just-in-time principles

obj. 1

✔ 3. $3.25 per frame

Hawg Wild Motorcycle Company manufactures a variety of motorcycles. Hawg's purchasing policy requires that the purchasing agents place each quarter's purchasing requirements out for bid. This is because the Purchasing Department is evaluated solely by its ability to get the lowest purchase prices. The lowest cost bidder receives the order for the next quarter (90 days). To make its motorcycles, Hawg Wild requires 7,200 frames per quarter. Hawg Wild received two frame bids for the third quarter, as follows:

- *Forever Frames, Inc.:* $262 per frame. Delivery schedule: 80 frames per working day (90 days in the quarter).
- *Iron Horse Frames Inc.:* $260 per frame. Delivery schedule: 7,200 (80 frames × 90 days) frames at the beginning of July to last for three months.

  Hawg Wild accepted Iron Horse Frames Inc.'s bid because it was the low-cost bid.

Instructions
1. Comment on Hawg Wild's purchasing policy.
2. What are the additional (hidden) costs, beyond price, of Iron Horse Frames Inc.'s bid? Why weren't these costs considered?
3. Considering just inventory financing costs, what is the additional cost per frame of Iron Horse Frames Inc.'s bid if the cost of money is 10%? (*Hint:* Determine the average value of frame inventory held for the quarter and multiply by the quarterly interest charge.)

PR 12-2B
Lead time

obj. 1

Kitchenware Appliance Company manufactures home kitchen appliances. The manufacturing process includes stamping, final assembly, testing, and shipping. In the stamping operation, a number of individuals are responsible for stamping the steel outer surface of the appliance. The stamping operation is set up prior to each run. A run of 80 stampings is completed after each setup. A setup requires 100 minutes. The parts wait for the setup to be completed before stamping begins. Each stamping requires 4 minutes of operating time.

✓ 1. Total wait time,
3,418 minutes

After each batch is completed, the operator moves the stamped covers to the final assembly area. This move takes 12 minutes to complete.

The final assembly for each appliance unit requires 20 minutes and is also done in batches of 80 appliance units. The batch of 80 appliance units is moved into the test building, which is across the street. The move takes 24 minutes. In the final test, the 80-unit batch is tested one at a time. Each test requires 6 minutes. The completed units are sent to shipping for packaging and final shipment to customers. A complete batch of 80 units is sent from final assembly to shipping. The Shipping Department is located next to final assembly. Thus, there is no move time between these two operations. Packaging and shipment labeling requires 12 minutes per unit.

Instructions

1. Determine the amount of value-added and non-value-added lead time and the value-added ratio in this process for an average kitchen appliance in a batch of 80 units. Round percentages to one decimal place. Categorize the non-value-added time into wait and move time.
2. ▭▭▸ How could this process be improved so as to reduce the amount of waste in the process?

PR 12-3B
Just-in-time accounting

obj. **3**

✓ 4. Raw and In Process
Inventory, $2,100

Telecom Technologies Inc. manufactures and assembles two major types of telephone assemblies—a desk phone and a mobile phone. The process consists of a just-in-time cell for each product. The data that follow concern only the mobile phone just-in-time cell.

For the year, Telecom Technologies Inc. budgeted the following costs for the mobile phone production cell:

Conversion Cost Categories	Budget
Labor	$100,000
Supplies	38,000
Utilities	12,000
Total	$150,000

Telecom plans 3,000 hours of production for the mobile phone cell for the year. The materials cost is $75 per unit. Each assembly requires 18 minutes of cell assembly time. There was no October 1 inventory for either Raw and In Process Inventory or Finished Goods Inventory.

The following summary events took place in the mobile phone cell during October:

a. Electronic parts were purchased to produce 840 mobile phone assemblies in October.
b. Conversion costs were applied for 830 units of production in October.
c. 815 units were completed and transferred to finished goods in October.
d. 810 units were shipped to customers at a price of $210 per unit.

Instructions

1. Determine the budgeted cell conversion cost per hour.
2. Determine the budgeted cell conversion cost per unit.
3. Journalize the summary transactions (a) through (d).
4. Determine the ending balance in Raw and In Process Inventory and Finished Goods Inventory.
5. ▭▭▸ How does the accounting in a JIT environment differ from traditional accounting?

PR 12-4B
*Pareto chart and cost of quality report—
manufacturing company*

obj. **5**

✓ 3. Non-value-added,
38%

The president of Cardio-Care Exercise Equipment Inc. has been concerned about the growth in costs over the last several years. The president asked the controller to perform an activity analysis to gain a better insight into these costs. The activity analysis revealed the following:

Activity	Activity Cost
Correcting invoice errors	$ 18,000
Disposing of incoming materials with poor quality	22,500
Disposing of scrap	49,500
Expediting late production	54,000
Final inspection	31,500
Inspecting incoming materials	9,000
Inspecting work in process	45,000
Preventive machine maintenance	31,500
Producing product	162,000
Responding to customer quality complaints	27,000
Total	$450,000

The production process is complicated by quality problems, requiring the production manager to expedite production and dispose of scrap.

Instructions

1. Prepare a Pareto chart of the company activities.
2. Use the activity cost information to determine the percentages of total costs that are prevention, appraisal, internal failure, external failure, and not costs of quality.
3. Determine the percentages of total costs that are value- and non-value-added.
4. Interpret the information.

Special Activities

SA 12-1
Ethics and professional conduct in business

ETHICS

In August, Apollo Company introduced a new performance measurement system in manufacturing operations. One of the new performance measures was lead time. The lead time was determined by tagging a random sample of items with a log sheet throughout the month. This log sheet recorded the time that the item started and the time that it ended production, as well as all steps in between. The controller collected the log sheets and calculated the average lead time of the tagged products. This number was reported to central management and was used to evaluate the performance of the plant manager. The plant was under extreme pressure to reduce lead time because of poor lead time results reported in June.

The following memo was intercepted by the controller.

Date: September 1
To: Hourly Employees
From: Plant Manager

During last month, you noticed that some of the products were tagged with a log sheet. This sheet records the time that a product enters production and the time that it leaves production. The difference between these two times is termed the "lead time." Our plant is evaluated on improving lead time. From now on, I ask all of you to keep an eye out for the tagged items. When you receive a tagged item, it is to receive special attention. Work on that item first, and then immediately move it to the next operation. Under no circumstances should tagged items wait on any other work that you have. Naturally, report accurate information. I insist that you record the correct times on the log sheet as the product goes through your operations.

 How should the controller respond to this discovery?

SA 12-2
Just-in-time principles

Winter Comfort Inc. manufactures electric space heaters. While the CEO, Kevin Cross, is visiting the production facility, the following conversation takes place with the plant manager, Alicia Alvarez:

Kevin: As I walk around the facility, I can't help noticing all the materials inventories. What's going on?

Alicia: I have found our suppliers to be very unreliable in meeting their delivery commitments. Thus, I keep a lot of materials on hand so as to not risk running out and shutting down production.

Kevin: Not only do I see a lot of materials inventory, but there also seems to be a lot of finished goods inventory on hand. Why is this?

Alicia: As you know, I am evaluated on maintaining a low cost per unit. The one way that I am able to reduce my unit costs is by producing as many space heaters as possible. This allows me to spread my fixed costs over a larger base. When orders are down, the excess production builds up as inventory, as we are seeing now. But don't worry—I'm really keeping our unit costs down this way.

Kevin: I'm not so sure. It seems that this inventory must cost us something.

Alicia: Not really. I'll eventually use the materials and we'll eventually sell the finished goods. By keeping the plant busy, I'm using our plant assets wisely. This is reflected in the low unit costs that I'm able to maintain.

➤ If you were Kevin Cross, how would you respond to Alicia Alvarez? What recommendations would you provide Alicia Alvarez?

SA 12-3
Just-in-time principles

Zenith Concepts Inc. prepared the following performance graphs for the prior year:

Total Manufacturing Lead Time

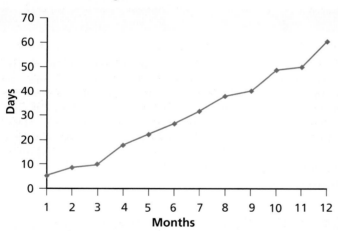

Percent of Sales Orders Filled on Time

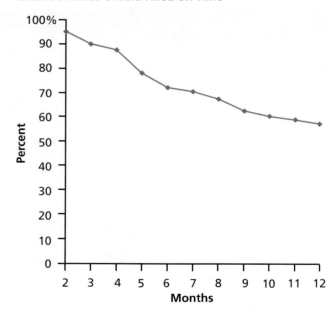

Total Inventory Dollars (in 000s)

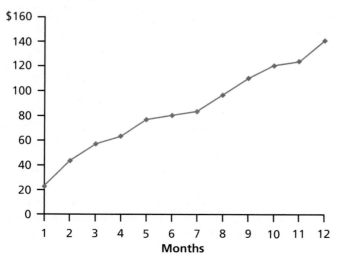

▱▱▱▱▸ What do these charts appear to indicate?

SA 12-4
Value-added and non-value-added activity costs

Midland Company prepared the following factory overhead report from its general ledger:

Indirect labor	$500,000
Fringe benefits	60,000
Supplies	110,000
Depreciation	230,000
Total	$900,000

The management of Midland Company was dissatisfied with this report and asked the controller to prepare an activity analysis of the same information. This activity analysis was as follows:

Processing sales orders	$198,000	22%
Disposing scrap	189,000	21
Expediting work orders	153,000	17
Producing parts	135,000	15
Resolving supplier quality problems	108,000	12
Reissuing corrected purchase orders	81,000	9
Expediting customer orders	36,000	4
Total	$900,000	100%

▱▱▱▱▸ Interpret the activity analysis by identifying value-added and non-value-added activity costs. How does the activity cost report differ from the general ledger report?

SA 12-5
Lead time

Group Project

In groups of two to four people, visit a sit-down restaurant and do a lead time study. If more than one group chooses to visit the same restaurant, choose different times for your visits. Note the time when you walk in the door of the restaurant and the time when you walk out the door after you have eaten. The difference between these two times is the total lead time of your restaurant experience. While in the restaurant, determine the time spent on non-value-added time, such as wait time, and the time spent on value-added eating time. Note the various activities and the time required to perform each activity during your visit to the restaurant. Compare your analyses, identifying possible reasons for differences in the times recorded by groups that visited the same restaurant.

Answers to Self-Examination Questions

1. **B** The just-in-time philosophy embraces a product-oriented layout (answer A), making lead times short (answer C), and reducing setup times (answer D). Pull manufacturing, the opposite of push manufacturing (answer B), is also a just-in-time principle.
2. **D** Accounting in a just-in-time environment should not be complex (answer A), not focus on direct labor (answer B) because it is combined with other conversion costs, and not provide detailed variance reporting (answer C) because of a higher reliance on nonfinancial performance measures. However, the just-in-time accounting environment will have fewer transaction control features than the traditional system (answer D).
3. **C** $420,000\2,100 hours = $200 per hour
$200 per hour × 0.25 hour = $50 per unit
700 units × ($50 + $12.50) = $43,750

4. **B** Appraisal costs (answer B) are the costs of inspecting and testing activities, which include detecting, measuring, evaluating, and auditing products and processes. Prevention (answer A) activities are incurred to prevent defects from occurring during the design and delivery of products or services. Internal failure costs (answer C) are associated with defects that are discovered by the organization before the product or service is delivered to the consumer. External failure costs (answer D) are the costs incurred after defective units or service have been delivered to consumers.
5. **A** A Pareto chart is a bar chart that ranks attribute totals by category (answer A). A line chart (answer B), a pie chart (answer C), and a table listing (answer D) are other ways of displaying information, but they are not Pareto charts.

Statement of Cash Flows

© ELAINE THOMPSON/ASSOCIATED PRESS

objectives

After studying this chapter, you should be able to:

1 *Summarize the types of cash flow activities reported in the statement of cash flows.*

2 *Prepare a statement of cash flows, using the indirect method.*

3 *Prepare a statement of cash flows, using the direct method.*

Jones Soda Co.

Suppose you were to receive $100 as a result of some event. Would it make a difference what the event was? Yes, it would! If you received $100 for your birthday, then it's a gift. If you received $100 as a result of working part time for a week, then it's the result of your effort. If you received $100 as a loan, then it's money that you will have to pay back in the future. If you received $100 as a result of selling your CD player, then it's the result of giving up something tangible. Thus, the same $100 received can be associated with different types of events, and these events have different meanings to you. You would much rather receive a $100 gift than take out a $100 loan. Likewise, company stakeholders would also view events such as these differently.

Companies are required to report information about the events causing a change in cash over a period of time. This information is reported in the statement of cash flows. One such company is Jones Soda Co. Jones began in the late 1980s as an alternative beverage company, known for its customer provided labels, unique flavors, and support for extreme sports. You have probably seen Jones Soda at Barnes & Noble, Panera Bread, or Starbucks, or maybe sampled some of its unique flavors, such as Fufu Berry®, Blue Bubblegum®, or Lemon Drop®. As with any company, cash is important to Jones Soda. Without cash, Jones would be unable to expand its brands, distribute its product, support extreme sports, or provide a return for its owners. Thus, its managers are concerned about the sources and uses of cash.

In previous chapters, we have used the income statement, balance sheet, retained earnings statement, and other information to analyze the effects of management decisions on a business's financial position and operating performance. In this chapter, we focus on the events causing a change in cash by presenting the preparation and use of the statement of cash flows.

Reporting Cash Flows

objective **1**

Summarize the types of cash flow activities reported in the statement of cash flows.

The statement of cash flows is one of the basic financial statements of a business. The **statement of cash flows** reports a firm's major cash inflows and outflows for a period.[1] It provides useful information about a firm's ability to generate cash from operations, maintain and expand its operating capacity, meet its financial obligations, and pay dividends. As a result, it is used by managers in evaluating past operations and in planning future investing and financing activities. It is also used by investors, creditors, and others in assessing a firm's profit potential. In addition, it is a basis for assessing the firm's ability to pay its maturing debt.

The statement of cash flows reports cash flows by three types of activities:

1. **Cash flows from operating activities** are cash flows from transactions that affect net income. Examples of such transactions include the purchase and sale of merchandise by a retailer.
2. **Cash flows from investing activities** are cash flows from transactions that affect the investments in noncurrent assets. Examples of such transactions include the sale and purchase of fixed assets, such as equipment and buildings.
3. **Cash flows from financing activities** are cash flows from transactions that affect the debt and equity of the business. Examples of such transactions include issuing or retiring equity and debt securities.

---

1 As used in this chapter, *cash* refers to cash and cash equivalents. Examples of cash equivalents include short-term, highly liquid investments, such as money market funds, certificates of deposit, and commercial paper.

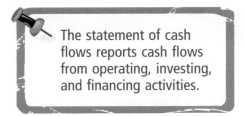

The statement of cash flows reports cash flows from operating, investing, and financing activities.

The cash flows from operating activities are normally presented first, followed by the cash flows from investing activities and financing activities. The total of the net cash flow from these activities is the net increase or decrease in cash for the period. The cash balance at the beginning of the period is added to the net increase or decrease in cash, resulting in the cash balance at the end of the period. The ending cash balance on the statement of cash flows equals the cash reported on the balance sheet. Exhibit 1 illustrates a simple statement of cash flows that is reproduced from Chapter 1 (Exhibit 6) for NetSolutions.

EXHIBIT 1

Statement of Cash Flows—NetSolutions

NetSolutions
Statement of Cash Flows
For the Month Ended November 30, 2007

Cash flows from operating activities:		
Cash received from customers	$ 7,500	
Deduct cash payments for expenses and		
payments to creditors	4,600	
Net cash flow from operating activities		$ 2,900
Cash flows from investing activities:		
Cash payments for purchase of land		(20,000)
Cash flows from financing activities:		
Cash received from issuing stock	$25,000	
Deduct cash dividends	2,000	
Net cash flow provided by financing activities		23,000
Net cash flow and November 30, 2007, cash balance		$ 5,900

We have not discussed the statement of cash flows since introducing the statement in Chapter 1. We did this because a more complete understanding of operating, investing, and financing activities is helpful prior to developing and interpreting this statement. Previous chapters have introduced and described these activities so that you now have a foundation for the discussion that follows.

Exhibit 2 shows the major sources and uses of cash according to the three cash flow activities reported in the statement of cash flows. A *source* of cash causes the cash flow to increase, also called a *cash inflow*. For example, in Exhibit 1, the $25,000 cash received from issuing stock is a financing activity that is a source of cash. A *use* of cash causes cash flow to decrease, also called a *cash outflow*. In Exhibit 1, Net-Solutions' $20,000 cash payment for purchase of land is a use of cash. By reporting cash flows by operating, investing, and financing activities, significant relationships within and among the activities can be evaluated. For example, the cash receipts from issuing bonds can be related to repayments of borrowings when both are reported as financing activities. Also, the impact of each of the three activities (operating, investing, and financing) on cash flows can be identified. This allows investors and creditors to evaluate the effects of a firm's profits on cash flows and its ability to generate cash flows for dividends and for paying debts.

CASH FLOWS FROM OPERATING ACTIVITIES

The most important cash flows of a business often relate to operating activities. There are two alternative methods for reporting cash flows from operating activities in the statement of cash flows. These methods are (1) the direct method and (2) the indirect method.

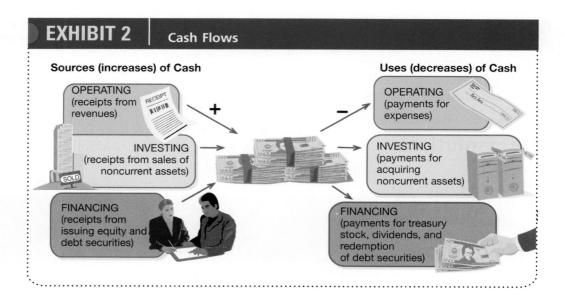

EXHIBIT 2 | Cash Flows

Sources (increases) of Cash

OPERATING (receipts from revenues)

INVESTING (receipts from sales of noncurrent assets)

FINANCING (receipts from issuing equity and debt securities)

Uses (decreases) of Cash

OPERATING (payments for expenses)

INVESTING (payments for acquiring noncurrent assets)

FINANCING (payments for treasury stock, dividends, and redemption of debt securities)

Cash Flows from Operating Activities

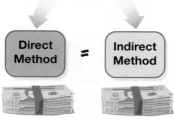

Direct Method = Indirect Method

The **direct method** reports the sources of operating cash and the uses of operating cash. The major source of operating cash is cash received from customers. The major uses of operating cash include cash paid to suppliers for merchandise and services and cash paid to employees for wages. The difference between these operating cash receipts and cash payments is the net cash flow from operating activities. The direct method is illustrated in Exhibit 1 for NetSolutions.

The primary advantage of the direct method is that it reports the sources and uses of operating cash flows in the statement of cash flows. Its primary disadvantage is that the necessary data may not be readily available and may be costly to gather.

The **indirect method** reports the operating cash flows by beginning with net income and adjusting it for revenues and expenses that do not involve the receipt or payment of cash. In other words, accrual net income is adjusted to determine the net amount of cash flows from operating activities.

A major advantage of the indirect method is that it focuses on the differences between net income and cash flows from operations. Thus, it shows the relationship between the income statement, the balance sheet, and the statement of cash flows. Because the data are readily available, the indirect method is normally less costly to use than the direct method. Because of these advantages, over 99% of all firms use the indirect method to report cash flows from operations.[2] We have not discussed the indirect method until this point, because it assumes an understanding of the accrual accounting concepts discussed in the prior chapters.

Exhibit 3 illustrates the cash flows from operating activities section of the statement of cash flows under the direct and indirect methods. Both statements are for NetSolutions for the month ended November 2007. The methods show the same amount of net cash flow from operating activities, regardless of the method. We will illustrate both methods in detail later in this chapter.

The Walt Disney Company recently invested $1.4 billion in parks, resorts, and other properties, including the development of Hong Kong Disneyland.

CASH FLOWS FROM INVESTING ACTIVITIES

Cash inflows from investing activities normally arise from selling fixed assets, investments, and intangible assets. Cash outflows normally include payments to acquire fixed assets, investments, and intangible assets.

---

2 *Accounting Trends & Techniques*, AICPA, 2005 edition.

| EXHIBIT 3 | Cash Flow from Operations: Direct and Indirect Methods—NetSolutions |

Direct Method (from Exhibit 1)

Cash flows from operating activities:	
Cash received from customers	$7,500
Deduct cash payments for expenses and payments to creditors	4,600
Net cash flow from operating activities	$2,900

Indirect Method

Cash flows from operating activities:	
Net income	$3,050
Add increase in accounts payable	400
	$3,450
Deduct increase in supplies	550
Net cash flow from operating activities	$2,900

the same

Cash flows from investing activities are reported on the statement of cash flows by first listing the cash inflows. The cash outflows are then presented. If the inflows are greater than the outflows, *net cash flow provided by investing activities* is reported. If the inflows are less than the outflows, *net cash flow used for investing activities* is reported.

The cash flows from investing activities section in the statement of cash flows for NetSolutions from Exhibit 1 is shown below.

Cash flows from investing activities:
Cash payments for purchase of land . . . . $(20,000)

CASH FLOWS FROM FINANCING ACTIVITIES

Cash inflows from financing activities normally arise from issuing debt or equity securities. Examples of such inflows include issuing bonds, notes payable, and preferred and common stocks. Cash outflows from financing activities include paying cash dividends, repaying debt, and acquiring treasury stock.

Cash flows from financing activities are reported on the statement of cash flows by first listing the cash inflows. The cash outflows are then presented. If the inflows are greater than the outflows, *net cash flow provided by financing activities* is reported. If the inflows are less than the outflows, *net cash flow used for financing activities* is reported.

The cash flows from financing activities section in the statement of cash flows for NetSolutions from Exhibit 1 is shown below.

Cash flows from financing activities:
Cash received from issuing stock $25,000
Deduct cash dividends   2,000
Net cash flow provided by financing activities $23,000

NONCASH INVESTING AND FINANCING ACTIVITIES

A business may enter into investing and financing activities that do not directly involve cash. For example, it may issue common stock to retire long-term debt. Such a transaction does not have a direct effect on cash. However, the transaction does eliminate the need for future cash payments to pay interest and retire the bonds. Thus, because of their future effect on cash flows, such transactions should be reported to readers of the financial statements.

When noncash investing and financing transactions occur during a period, their effect is reported in a separate schedule. This schedule usually appears at the bottom of the statement of cash flows. For example, in such a schedule Google recently disclosed the issuance of over $25 million in common stock for business acquisitions. Other examples of noncash investing and financing transactions include acquiring fixed assets by issuing bonds or capital stock and issuing common stock in exchange for convertible preferred stock.

Business Connections

REAL WORLD

TOO MUCH CASH!

Is it possible to have too much cash? Clearly, most of us would answer no. However, a business views cash differently than an individual. Naturally, a business needs cash to develop and launch new products, expand markets, purchase plant and equipment, and acquire other businesses. However, some businesses have built up huge cash balances beyond even these needs. For example, both Microsoft Corporation and Dell Inc. have accumulated billions of dollars in cash and temporary investments, totaling in excess of 60% of their total assets. Such large cash balances can lower the return on total assets. As stated by one analyst, "When a company sits on cash (which earns 1% or 2%) and leaves equity outstanding . . . , it is tantamount to taking a loan at 15% and investing in a passbook savings account that earns 2%—it destroys value." So while having too much cash is a good problem to have, companies like Microsoft, Cisco Systems, Inc., IBM, Apple Computer Inc., and Dell are under pressure to pay dividends or repurchase common stock. For example, Microsoft recently declared a $32 billion special dividend to return cash to its shareholders.

NO CASH FLOW PER SHARE

The term *cash flow per share* is sometimes reported in the financial press. Often, the term is used to mean "cash flow from operations per share." Such reporting may be misleading to users of the financial statements. For example, users might interpret cash flow per share as the amount available for dividends. This would not be the case if most of the cash generated by operations is required for repaying loans or for reinvesting in the business. Users might also think that cash flow per share is equivalent or perhaps superior to earnings per share. For these reasons, the financial statements, including the statement of cash flows, should not report cash flow per share.

Example Exercise 13-1

objective **1**

Identify whether each of the following would be reported as an operating, investing, or financing activity in the statement of cash flows.

a. Purchase of patent
b. Payment of cash dividend
c. Disposal of equipment

d. Cash sales
e. Purchase of treasury stock
f. Payment of wages expense

Follow My Example 13-1

a. Investing
b. Financing
c. Investing

d. Operating
e. Financing
f. Operating

For Practice: PE 13-1A, PE 13-1B

Statement of Cash Flows—The Indirect Method

objective **2**

Prepare a statement of cash flows, using the indirect method.

The indirect method of reporting cash flows from operating activities is normally less costly and more efficient than the direct method. In addition, when the direct method is used, the indirect method must also be used in preparing a supplemental reconciliation of net income with cash flows from operations. The 2005 edition of *Accounting Trends & Techniques* reported that 99% of the companies surveyed used the indirect method. For these reasons, we will first discuss the indirect method of preparing the statement of cash flows.

To collect the data for the statement of cash flows, all the cash receipts and cash payments for a period could be analyzed. However, this procedure is expensive and time consuming. A more efficient approach is to analyze the changes in the noncash balance sheet accounts. The logic of this approach is that a change in any balance sheet account (including cash) can be analyzed in terms of changes in the other balance sheet accounts. To illustrate, the accounting equation is rewritten below to focus on the cash account.

$$\text{Assets} = \text{Liabilities} + \text{Stockholders' Equity}$$
$$\text{Cash} + \text{Noncash Assets} = \text{Liabilities} + \text{Stockholders' Equity}$$
$$\text{Cash} = \text{Liabilities} + \text{Stockholders' Equity} - \text{Noncash Assets}$$

Any change in the cash account results in a change in one or more noncash balance sheet accounts. That is, if the cash account changes, then a liability, stockholders' equity, or noncash asset account must also change.

Additional data are also obtained by analyzing the income statement accounts and supporting records. For example, since the net income or net loss for the period is closed to *Retained Earnings*, a change in the retained earnings account can be partially explained by the net income or net loss reported on the income statement.

There is no order in which the noncash balance sheet accounts must be analyzed. However, it is usually more efficient to analyze the accounts in the reverse order in which they appear on the balance sheet. Thus, the analysis of retained earnings provides the starting point for determining the cash flows from operating activities, which is the first section of the statement of cash flows.

The comparative balance sheet for Rundell Inc. on December 31, 2008 and 2007, is used to illustrate the indirect method. This balance sheet is shown in Exhibit 4. Selected ledger accounts and other data are presented as needed.[3]

RETAINED EARNINGS

The comparative balance sheet for Rundell Inc. shows that retained earnings increased $80,000 during the year. Analyzing the entries posted to the retained earnings account indicates how this change occurred. The retained earnings account for Rundell Inc. is shown below.

ACCOUNT *Retained Earnings*		**Debit**	**Credit**	Balance Debit	Balance Credit	**ACCOUNT NO.**
Date	Item	Debit	Credit	Debit	Credit	
2008 Jan. 1	Balance				202 300 00	
Dec. 31	Net income		108 000 00		310 300 00	
31	Cash dividends	28 000 00			282 300 00	

The retained earnings account must be carefully analyzed because some of the entries to retained earnings may not affect cash. For example, a decrease in retained earnings resulting from issuing a stock dividend does not affect cash. Such transactions are not reported on the statement of cash flows.

For Rundell Inc., the retained earnings account indicates that the $80,000 change resulted from net income of $108,000 and cash dividends declared of $28,000. The effect of each of these items on cash flows is discussed in the following sections.

CASH FLOWS FROM OPERATING ACTIVITIES—INDIRECT METHOD

The net income of $108,000 reported by Rundell Inc. normally is not equal to the amount of cash generated from operations during the period. This is because net income is determined using the accrual method of accounting.

---

3 An appendix that discusses using a spreadsheet (work sheet) as an aid in assembling data for the statement of cash flows is presented at the end of this chapter. This appendix illustrates the use of this spreadsheet in reporting cash flows from operating activities using the indirect method.

EXHIBIT 4

Comparative
Balance Sheet

Rundell Inc.
Comparative Balance Sheet
December 31, 2008 and 2007

Assets	2008	2007	Increase Decrease*
Cash.	$ 97,500	$ 26,000	$ 71,500
Accounts receivable (net).	74,000	65,000	9,000
Inventories.	172,000	180,000	8,000*
Land.	80,000	125,000	45,000*
Building.	260,000	200,000	60,000
Accumulated depreciation—building.	(65,300)	(58,300)	7,000
Total assets.	$618,200	$537,700	$ 80,500
Liabilities			
Accounts payable (merchandise			
creditors).	$ 43,500	$ 46,700	$ 3,200*
Accrued expenses payable			
(operating expenses).	26,500	24,300	2,200
Income taxes payable.	7,900	8,400	500*
Dividends payable.	14,000	10,000	4,000
Bonds payable.	100,000	150,000	50,000*
Total liabilities.	$191,900	$239,400	$ 47,500*
Stockholders' Equity			
Common stock ($2 par).	$ 24,000	$ 16,000	$ 8,000
Paid-in capital in excess of par.	120,000	80,000	40,000
Retained earnings.	282,300	202,300	80,000
Total stockholders' equity.	$426,300	$298,300	$128,000
Total liabilities and stockholders' equity. . . .	$618,200	$537,700	$ 80,500

Under the accrual method of accounting, revenues and expenses are recorded at different times from when cash is received or paid. For example, merchandise may be sold on account and the cash received at a later date. Likewise, insurance expense represents the amount of insurance expired during the period. The premiums for the insurance may have been paid in a prior period.

Under the indirect method, these differences are used to reconcile the net income to cash flows from operating activities. The typical adjustments to net income under the indirect method are reported in the statement of cash flows, as shown in Exhibit 5.[4]

In practice, the list of adjustments often begins with expenses that do not affect cash. Common examples are depreciation of fixed assets and amortization of intangible assets. Thus, in Exhibit 5, these two items are *added* to net income in determining cash flows from operating activities.

Typically, the next adjustments to net income are for gains and losses from disposal of assets. These adjustments arise because cash flows from operating activities should not include investing or financing transactions. For example, assume that land costing $50,000 was sold for $90,000 (a gain of $40,000). The sale should be reported as an investing activity: "Cash receipts from the sale of land, $90,000." However, the $40,000 gain on the disposal of the land is included in net income on the income statement. Thus, the $40,000 gain is *deducted* from net income in determining cash flows from operations to

---

4 Other items that also require adjustments to net income to obtain cash flows from operating activities include amortization of bonds payable discounts (add), losses on debt retirement (add), amortization of bonds payable premium (deduct), and gains on retirement of debt (deduct).

EXHIBIT 5		Increase (Decrease)
Adjustments to Net Income (Loss) Using the Indirect Method	Net income (loss)	$ XXX
	Adjustments to reconcile net income to net cash flow from operating activities:	
	Depreciation of fixed assets	XXX
	Amortization of intangible assets	XXX
	Losses on disposal of assets	XXX
	Gains on disposal of assets	(XXX)
	Changes in current operating assets and liabilities:	
	Increases in noncash current operating assets	(XXX)
	Decreases in noncash current operating assets	XXX
	Increases in current operating liabilities	XXX
	Decreases in current operating liabilities	(XXX)
	Net cash flow from operating activities	$ XXX or $(XXX)

Subtract	Add
Increases in accounts receivable	Decreases in accounts receivable
Increases in inventory	Decreases in inventory
Increases in prepaid expenses	Decreases in prepaid expenses
Decreases in accounts payable	Increases in accounts payable
Decreases in accrued expenses payable	Increases in accrued expenses payable

avoid "double counting" the cash flow from the gain. Likewise, losses from the disposal of fixed assets are *added* to net income in determining cash flows from operations.

Net income is also adjusted for changes in noncash current assets and current liabilities that support operations. Under the indirect method, these items are often listed last as "changes in current operating assets and liabilities." Under this heading, current assets are listed first, followed by current liabilities. Changes in noncash current assets and current liabilities are the result of revenue or expense transactions that may or may not affect cash flow. For example, a sale of $10,000 on account increases accounts receivable by $10,000. However, cash is not affected. Thus, the increase in accounts receivable of $10,000 between two balance sheet dates is *deducted* from net income in arriving at cash flows from operating activities. In contrast, a decrease in accounts receivable indicates the collection of cash that may have been reported as revenues in a prior period. Thus, a decrease in accounts receivable is added to net income in arriving at cash flows from operating activities.

Similar adjustments to net income are required for the changes in the other current asset and liability accounts supporting operations, such as inventory, prepaid expenses, accounts payable, and other accrued expenses. The direction of the adjustment is shown at the bottom of Exhibit 5. For example, an increase in accounts payable from the beginning to the end of the period would be added to net income in determining cash flows from operating activities.

The effect of dividends payable, though a current liability, is not included in the operating activity section of the statement of cash flows. Dividends payable is omitted from Exhibit 5 because dividends are not an operating activity that affects net income. Later in the chapter, we will discuss how dividends are reported in the statement of cash flows as a part of financing activities. In the following paragraphs, we will discuss each of the adjustments that convert Rundell Inc.'s net income to "Cash flows from operating activities."

Depreciation The comparative balance sheet in Exhibit 4 indicates that Accumulated Depreciation—Building increased by $7,000. As shown at the top of the following page, this account indicates that depreciation for the year was $7,000 for the building.

ACCOUNT *Accumulated Depreciation—Building*					ACCOUNT NO.	
					Balance	
Date	Item	Debit	Credit	Debit	Debit	Credit
2008 Jan. 1	Balance					58 3 0 0 00
Dec. 31	Depreciation for year		7 0 0 0 00			65 3 0 0 00

The $7,000 of depreciation expense reduced net income but did not require an outflow of cash. Thus, the $7,000 is added to net income in determining cash flows from operating activities, as follows:

Cash flows from operating activities:
Net income $108,000
Add depreciation   7,000 $115,000

Gain on Sale of Land　The ledger or income statement of Rundell Inc. indicates that the sale of land resulted in a gain of $12,000. As we discussed previously, the sale proceeds, which include the gain and the carrying value of the land, are included in cash flows from investing activities.[5] The gain is also included in net income. Thus, to avoid double reporting, the gain of $12,000 is deducted from net income in determining cash flows from operating activities, as shown below.

Cash flows from operating activities:
Net income $108,000
Deduct gain on sale of land   12,000

Example Exercise 13-2   objective 2

Omni Corporation's accumulated depreciation increased by $12,000, while patents decreased by $3,400 between balance sheet dates. There were no purchases or sales of depreciable or intangible assets during the year. In addition, the income statement showed a gain of $4,100 from the sale of land. Reconcile a net income of $50,000 to net cash flow from operating activities.

Follow My Example 13-2

Net income $50,000
Adjustments to reconcile net income to net cash flow from operating activities:
　Depreciation   12,000
　Amortization   3,400
　Gain from sale of land . . . .   (4,100)
Net cash flow from operating activities $61,300

For Practice: PE 13-2A, PE 13-2B

Changes in Current Operating Assets and Liabilities　As shown in Exhibit 5, decreases in noncash current assets and increases in current liabilities are added to net income. In contrast, increases in noncash current assets and decreases in current liabilities are deducted from net income. The current asset and current liability accounts of Rundell Inc. are as follows:

---

5 The reporting of the proceeds (cash flows) from the sale of land as part of investing activities is discussed later in this chapter.

Accounts	December 31		Increase Decrease*
	2008	2007	
Accounts receivable (net)	$ 74,000	$ 65,000	$9,000
Inventories	172,000	180,000	8,000*
Accounts payable (merchandise creditors)	43,500	46,700	3,200*
Accrued expenses payable (operating expenses) ..	26,500	24,300	2,200
Income taxes payable	7,900	8,400	500*

Continental Airlines had a net loss of $363 million but a positive cash flow from operating activities of $373 million. This difference was mostly due to $414 million of depreciation expenses and $417 million from changes in operating assets and liabilities.

As discussed previously, the $9,000 increase in *accounts receivable* indicates that the sales on account during the year are $9,000 more than collections from customers on account. The amount reported as sales on the income statement therefore includes $9,000 that did not result in a cash inflow during the year. Thus, $9,000 is deducted from net income.

The $8,000 decrease in *inventories* indicates that the merchandise sold exceeds the cost of the merchandise purchased by $8,000. The amount deducted as cost of merchandise sold on the income statement therefore includes $8,000 that did not require a cash outflow during the year. Thus, $8,000 is added to net income.

The $3,200 decrease in *accounts payable* indicates that the amount of cash payments for merchandise exceeds the merchandise purchased on account by $3,200. The amount reported on the income statement for cost of merchandise sold therefore excludes $3,200 that required a cash outflow during the year. Thus, $3,200 is deducted from net income.

The $2,200 increase in *accrued expenses payable* indicates that the amount incurred during the year for operating expenses exceeds the cash payments by $2,200. The amount reported on the income statement for operating expenses therefore includes $2,200 that did not require a cash outflow during the year. Thus, $2,200 is added to net income.

The $500 decrease in *income taxes payable* indicates that the amount paid for taxes exceeds the amount incurred during the year by $500. The amount reported on the income statement for income tax therefore is less than the amount paid by $500. Thus, $500 is deducted from net income.

Example Exercise 13-3

objective **2**

Victor Corporation's comparative balance sheet for current assets and liabilities was as follows:

	Dec. 31, 2009	Dec. 31, 2008
Accounts receivable	$ 6,500	$ 4,900
Inventory	12,300	15,000
Accounts payable	4,800	5,200
Dividends payable	5,000	4,000

Adjust net income of $70,000 for changes in operating assets and liabilities to arrive at cash flows from operating activities.

Follow My Example 13-3

Net income	$70,000
Adjustments to reconcile net income to net cash flow from operating activities:	
Changes in current operating assets and liabilities:	
Increase in accounts receivable	(1,600)
Decrease in inventory	2,700
Decrease in accounts payable	(400)
Net cash flow from operating activities	$70,700

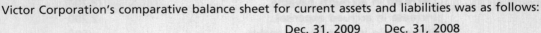

For Practice: PE 13-3A, PE 13-3B

Integrity, Objectivity, and Ethics in Business

CREDIT POLICY AND CASH FLOW

One would expect customers to pay for products and services sold on account. Unfortunately, that is not always the case. Collecting accounts receivable efficiently is the key to turning a current asset into positive cash flow. Most entrepreneurs would rather think about the exciting aspects of their business—such as product development, marketing, sales, and advertising—rather than credit collection. This can be a mistake. Hugh McHugh of Overhill Flowers, Inc., decided that he would have no more trade accounts after dealing with Christmas orders that weren't paid for until late February, or sometimes not paid at all. As stated by one collection service, "One thing business owners always tell me is that they never thought about [collections] when they started their own business." To small business owners, the collected receivable is often their paycheck, so it pays to pay attention.

Source: Paulette Thomas, "Making Them Pay: The Last Thing Most Entrepreneurs Want to Think About Is Bill Collection; It Should Be One of the First Things," *The Wall Street Journal*, September 19, 2005, p. R6.

Reporting Cash Flows from Operating Activities We have now presented all the necessary adjustments to convert the net income to cash flows from operating activities for Rundell Inc. These adjustments are summarized in Exhibit 6 for the statement of cash flows.

EXHIBIT 6   Cash Flows from Operating Activities—Indirect Method

Cash flows from operating activities:	
Net income	$108,000
Adjustments to reconcile net income to net cash flow from operating activities:	
Depreciation	7,000
Gain on sale of land	(12,000)
Changes in current operating assets and liabilities:	
Increase in accounts receivable	(9,000)
Decrease in inventory	8,000
Decrease in accounts payable	(3,200)
Increase in accrued expenses	2,200
Decrease in income taxes payable	(500)
Net cash flow from operating activities	$100,500

Example Exercise 13-4   objective 2

Omicron Inc. reported the following data:

Net income	$120,000
Depreciation expense	12,000
Loss on disposal of equipment	15,000
Increase in accounts receivable	5,000
Decrease in accounts payable	2,000

Prepare the cash flows from operating activities section of the statement of cash flows using the indirect method.

(continued)

Follow My Example 13-4

Cash flows from operating activities:	
Net income	$120,000
Adjustments to reconcile net income to net cash flow from operating activities:	
Depreciation	12,000
Loss from disposal of equipment	15,000
Changes in current operating assets and liabilities:	
Increase in accounts receivable	(5,000)
Decrease in accounts payable	(2,000)
Net cash flow from operating activities	$140,000

For Practice: PE 13-4A, PE 13-4B

CASH FLOWS USED FOR PAYMENT OF DIVIDENDS

According to the retained earnings account of Rundell Inc., shown earlier in the chapter, cash dividends of $28,000 were declared during the year. However, the dividends payable account, shown below, indicates that dividends of only $24,000 were paid during the year.

ACCOUNT *Dividends Payable*   **ACCOUNT NO.**

Date		Item	Debit	Credit	Balance Debit	Balance Credit
2008 Jan.	1	Balance				10 0 0 0 00
	10	Cash paid	10 0 0 0 00		—	—
June	20	Dividends declared		14 0 0 0 00		14 0 0 0 00
July	10	Cash paid	14 0 0 0 00		—	—
Dec.	20	Dividends declared		14 0 0 0 00		14 0 0 0 00

The $24,000 of dividend payments represents a cash outflow that is reported in the financing activities section as follows:

Cash flows from financing activities:	
Cash paid for dividends	$24,000

COMMON STOCK

The common stock account increased by $8,000, and the paid-in capital in excess of par—common stock account increased by $40,000, as shown below. These increases result from issuing 4,000 shares of common stock for $12 per share.

XM Satellite Radio has had negative cash flows from operations for most of its young corporate life. However, it has been able to grow by obtaining cash from the sale of common stock and issuing debt. Investors are willing to purchase the common stock and debt on the belief that XM will have a very profitable future as satellite radio matures.

ACCOUNT *Common Stock*   **ACCOUNT NO.**

Date		Item	Debit	Credit	Balance Debit	Balance Credit
2008 Jan.	1	Balance				16 0 0 0 00
Nov.	1	4,000 shares issued for cash		8 0 0 0 00		24 0 0 0 00

ACCOUNT *Paid-In Capital in Excess of Par—Common Stock*   **ACCOUNT NO.**

Date		Item	Debit	Credit	Balance Debit	Balance Credit
2008 Jan.	1	Balance				80 0 0 0 00
Nov.	1	4,000 shares issued for cash		40 0 0 0 00		120 0 0 0 00

This cash inflow is reported in the financing activities section as follows:

Cash flows from financing activities:
Cash received from sale of common stock $48,000

BONDS PAYABLE

The bonds payable account decreased by $50,000, as shown below. This decrease results from retiring the bonds by a cash payment for their face amount.

ACCOUNT Bonds Payable				ACCOUNT NO.		
					Balance	
Date	Item	Debit	Credit	Debit	Credit
2008 Jan. 1	Balance				150 0 0 0 00
June 30	Retired by payment of cash				
	at face amount	50 0 0 0 00			100 0 0 0 00

This cash outflow is reported in the financing activities section as follows:

Cash flows from financing activities:
Cash paid to retire bonds payable $50,000

BUILDING

The building account increased by $60,000, and the accumulated depreciation—building account increased by $7,000, as shown below.

ACCOUNT Building				ACCOUNT NO.		
					Balance	
Date	Item	Debit	Credit	Debit	Credit
2008 Jan. 1	Balance			200 0 0 0 00	
Dec. 27	Purchased for cash	60 0 0 0 00		260 0 0 0 00	

ACCOUNT Accumulated Depreciation—Building				ACCOUNT NO.		
					Balance	
Date	Item	Debit	Credit	Debit	Credit
2008 Jan. 1	Balance				58 3 0 0 00
Dec. 31	Depreciation for the year		7 0 0 0 00		65 3 0 0 00

The purchase of a building for cash of $60,000 is reported as an outflow of cash in the investing activities section, as follows:

Cash flows from investing activities:
Cash paid for purchase of building $60,000

The credit in the accumulated depreciation—building account, shown earlier, represents depreciation expense for the year. This depreciation expense of $7,000 on the building has already been considered as an addition to net income in determining cash flows from operating activities, as reported in Exhibit 6.

LAND

The $45,000 decline in the land account resulted from two separate transactions, as shown below.

ACCOUNT *Land*				ACCOUNT NO.		
				Balance		
Date	Item	Debit	Credit	Debit	Credit	
2008 Jan. 1	Balance			125 000 00		
June 8	Sold for $72,000 cash		60 000 00	65 000 00		
Oct. 12	Purchased for $15,000 cash	15 000 00		80 000 00		

The first transaction is the sale of land with a cost of $60,000 for $72,000 in cash. The $72,000 proceeds from the sale are reported in the investing activities section, as follows:

Cash flows from investing activities:
    Cash received from sale of land (includes
        $12,000 gain reported in net income) $72,000

The proceeds of $72,000 include the $12,000 gain on the sale of land and the $60,000 cost (book value) of the land. As shown in Exhibit 6, the $12,000 gain is also deducted from net income in the cash flows from operating activities section. This is necessary so that the $12,000 cash inflow related to the gain is not included twice as a cash inflow.

The second transaction is the purchase of land for cash of $15,000. This transaction is reported as an outflow of cash in the investing activities section, as follows:

Cash flows from investing activities:
    Cash paid for purchase of land $15,000

Example Exercise 13-5   objective **2**

Alpha Corporation purchased land for $125,000. Later in the year, the company sold land with a book value of $165,000 for $200,000. How are the effects of these transactions reported on the statement of cash flows?

Follow My Example 13-5

The gain on sale of land is deducted from net income as shown below:
    Gain on sale of land . . . . $ (35,000)

The purchase and sale of land is reported as part of cash flows from investing activities as shown below:
    Cash received for sale of land   200,000
    Cash paid for purchase of land . . . .   (125,000)

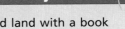

For Practice: PE 13-5A, PE 13-5B

PREPARING THE STATEMENT OF CASH FLOWS

The statement of cash flows for Rundell Inc. is prepared from the data assembled and analyzed above, using the indirect method. Exhibit 7 shows the statement of cash flows prepared by Rundell Inc. The statement indicates that the cash position increased by $71,500 during the year. The most significant increase in net cash flows, $100,500, was from operating activities. The most significant use of cash, $26,000, was for financing activities.

EXHIBIT 7	Rundell Inc.

Statement of Cash Flows—Indirect Method

Rundell Inc.
Statement of Cash Flows
For the Year Ended December 31, 2008

Cash flows from operating activities:			
Net income		$108,000	
Adjustments to reconcile net income to net cash flow from operating activities:			
Depreciation		7,000	
Gain on sale of land		(12,000)	
Changes in current operating assets and liabilities:			
Increase in accounts receivable		(9,000)	
Decrease in inventory		8,000	
Decrease in accounts payable		(3,200)	
Increase in accrued expenses.		2,200	
Decrease in income taxes payable		(500)	
Net cash flow from operating activities			$100,500
Cash flows from investing activities:			
Cash from sale of land		$ 72,000	
Less: Cash paid to purchase land	$15,000		
Cash paid for purchase of building	60,000	75,000	
Net cash flow used for investing activities			(3,000)
Cash flows from financing activities:			
Cash received from sale of common stock		$ 48,000	
Less: Cash paid to retire bonds payable	$50,000		
Cash paid for dividends	24,000	74,000	
Net cash flow used for financing activities			(26,000)
Increase in cash			$ 71,500
Cash at the beginning of the year			26,000
Cash at the end of the year			$ 97,500

Statement of Cash Flows—The Direct Method

objective **3**

Prepare a statement of cash flows, using the direct method.

As we discussed previously, the manner of reporting cash flows from investing and financing activities is the same under the direct and indirect methods. In addition, the direct method and the indirect method will report the same amount of cash flows from operating activities. However, the methods differ in how the cash flows from operating activities data are obtained, analyzed, and reported.

To illustrate the direct method, we will use the comparative balance sheet and the income statement for Rundell Inc. In this way, we can compare the statement of cash flows under the direct method and the indirect method.

Exhibit 8 shows the changes in the current asset and liability account balances for Rundell Inc. The income statement in Exhibit 8 shows additional data for Rundell Inc.

The direct method reports cash flows from operating activities by major classes of operating cash receipts and operating cash payments. The difference between the major classes of total operating cash receipts and total operating cash payments is the net cash flow from operating activities.

CASH RECEIVED FROM CUSTOMERS

The $1,180,000 of sales for Rundell Inc. is reported by using the accrual method. To determine the cash received from sales to customers, the $1,180,000 must be adjusted.

EXHIBIT 8

Balance Sheet and
Income Statement
Data for Direct
Method

Rundell Inc.
Schedule of Changes in Current Accounts

Accounts	December 31 2008	2007	Increase Decrease*
Cash	$ 97,500	$ 26,000	$71,500
Accounts receivable (net)	74,000	65,000	9,000
Inventories	172,000	180,000	8,000*
Accounts payable (merchandise creditors)	43,500	46,700	3,200*
Accrued expenses payable (operating expenses) . .	26,500	24,300	2,200
Income taxes payable	7,900	8,400	500*
Dividends payable	14,000	10,000	4,000

Rundell Inc.
Income Statement
For the Year Ended December 31, 2008

Sales		$1,180,000
Cost of merchandise sold		790,000
Gross profit		$ 390,000
Operating expenses:		
Depreciation expense	$ 7,000	
Other operating expenses	196,000	
Total operating expenses		203,000
Income from operations		$ 187,000
Other income:		
Gain on sale of land	$ 12,000	
Other expense:		
Interest expense	8,000	4,000
Income before income tax		$ 191,000
Income tax expense		83,000
Net income		$ 108,000

The adjustment necessary to convert the sales reported on the income statement to the cash received from customers is summarized below.

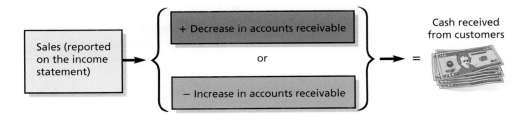

For Rundell Inc., the cash received from customers is $1,171,000, as shown below.

Sales	$1,180,000
Less increase in accounts receivable	9,000
Cash received from customers	$1,171,000

The additions to *accounts receivable* for sales on account during the year were $9,000 more than the amounts collected from customers on account. Sales reported on the income statement therefore included $9,000 that did not result in a cash inflow during the year. In other words, the increase of $9,000 in accounts receivable during 2008 indicates that sales on account exceeded cash received from customers by $9,000. Thus, $9,000 is deducted from sales to determine the cash received from customers. The $1,171,000 of cash received from customers is reported in the cash flows from operating activities section of the cash flow statement.

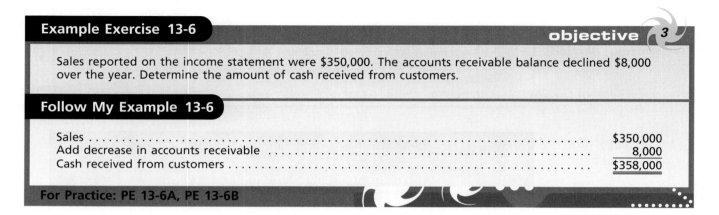

Example Exercise 13-6   objective 3

Sales reported on the income statement were $350,000. The accounts receivable balance declined $8,000 over the year. Determine the amount of cash received from customers.

Follow My Example 13-6

Sales	$350,000
Add decrease in accounts receivable	8,000
Cash received from customers	$358,000

For Practice: PE 13-6A, PE 13-6B

CASH PAYMENTS FOR MERCHANDISE

The $790,000 of cost of merchandise sold is reported on the income statement for Rundell Inc. using the accrual method. The adjustments necessary to convert the cost of merchandise sold to cash payments for merchandise during 2008 are summarized below.

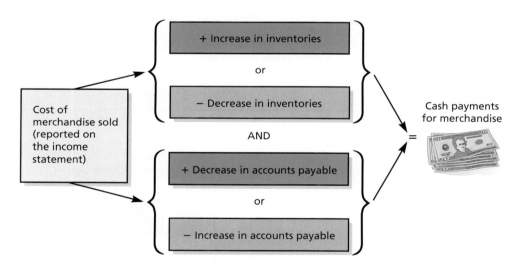

For Rundell Inc., the amount of cash payments for merchandise is $785,200, as determined below.

Cost of merchandise sold	$790,000
Deduct decrease in inventories	(8,000)
Add decrease in accounts payable	3,200
Cash payments for merchandise	$785,200

The $8,000 decrease in *inventories* indicates that the merchandise sold exceeded the cost of the merchandise purchased by $8,000. The amount reported on the income statement for cost of merchandise sold therefore includes $8,000 that did not require a cash outflow during the year. Thus, $8,000 is deducted from the cost of merchandise sold in determining the cash payments for merchandise.

The $3,200 decrease in *accounts payable* (merchandise creditors) indicates a cash outflow that is excluded from cost of merchandise sold. That is, the decrease in accounts payable indicates that cash payments for merchandise were $3,200 more than the purchases on account during 2008. Thus, $3,200 is added to the cost of merchandise sold in determining the cash payments for merchandise.

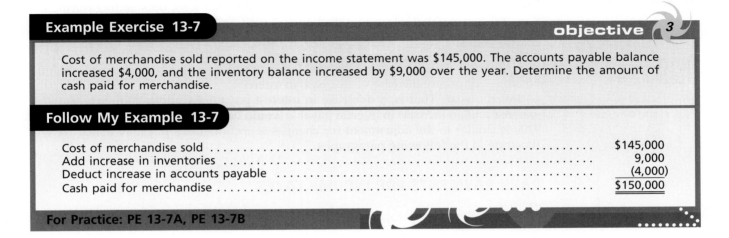

Example Exercise 13-7   **objective 3**

Cost of merchandise sold reported on the income statement was $145,000. The accounts payable balance increased $4,000, and the inventory balance increased by $9,000 over the year. Determine the amount of cash paid for merchandise.

Follow My Example 13-7

Cost of merchandise sold	$145,000
Add increase in inventories	9,000
Deduct increase in accounts payable	(4,000)
Cash paid for merchandise	$150,000

For Practice: PE 13-7A, PE 13-7B

CASH PAYMENTS FOR OPERATING EXPENSES

The $7,000 of depreciation expense reported on the income statement did not require a cash outflow. Thus, under the direct method, it is not reported on the statement of cash flows. The $196,000 reported for other operating expenses is adjusted to reflect the cash payments for operating expenses, as summarized below.

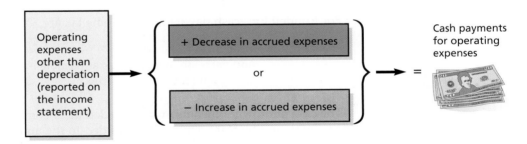

For Rundell Inc., the amount of cash payments for operating expenses is $193,800, determined as follows:

Operating expenses other than depreciation	$196,000
Deduct increase in accrued expenses	2,200
Cash payments for operating expenses	$193,800

The increase in *accrued expenses* (operating expenses) indicates that operating expenses include $2,200 for which there was no cash outflow (payment) during the year. That is, the increase in accrued expenses indicates that the cash payments for operating expenses were $2,200 less than the amount reported as an expense during the year. Thus, $2,200 is deducted from the operating expenses on the income statement in determining the cash payments for operating expenses.

GAIN ON SALE OF LAND

The income statement for Rundell Inc. in Exhibit 8 reports a gain of $12,000 on the sale of land. As we discussed previously, the gain is included in the proceeds from the sale of land, which is reported as part of the cash flows from investing activities.

INTEREST EXPENSE

The income statement for Rundell Inc. in Exhibit 8 reports interest expense of $8,000. The interest expense is related to the bonds payable that were outstanding during the year. We assume that interest on the bonds is paid on June 30 and December 31. Thus, $8,000 cash outflow for interest expense is reported on the statement of cash flows as an operating activity.

If interest payable had existed at the end of the year, the interest expense would be adjusted for any increase or decrease in interest payable from the beginning to the end of the year. That is, a decrease in interest payable would be added to interest expense and an increase in interest payable would be subtracted from interest expense. This is similar to the adjustment for changes in income taxes payable, which we will illustrate in the following paragraphs.

CASH PAYMENTS FOR INCOME TAXES

The adjustment to convert the income tax reported on the income statement to the cash basis is summarized below.

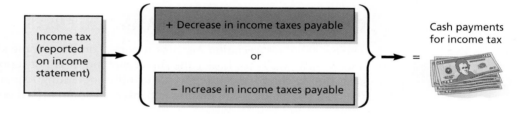

For Rundell Inc., cash payments for income tax are $83,500, determined as follows:

Income tax	$83,000
Add decrease in income taxes payable	500
Cash payments for income tax	$83,500

The cash outflow for income taxes exceeded the income tax deducted as an expense during the period by $500. Thus, $500 is added to the amount of income tax reported on the income statement in determining the cash payments for income tax.

REPORTING CASH FLOWS FROM OPERATING ACTIVITIES—DIRECT METHOD

Exhibit 9 is a complete statement of cash flows for Rundell Inc., using the direct method for reporting cash flows from operating activities. The portions of this statement that differ from the indirect method are highlighted in color. Exhibit 9 also includes the separate schedule reconciling net income and net cash flow from operating activities. This schedule must accompany the statement of cash flows when the direct method is used. This schedule is similar to the cash flows from operating activities section of the statement of cash flows prepared using the indirect method.

EXHIBIT 9

Statement of Cash Flows—Direct Method

Rundell Inc.
Statement of Cash Flows
For the Year Ended December 31, 2008

Cash flows from operating activities:			
Cash received from customers		$1,171,000	
Deduct: Cash payments for merchandise.	$785,200		
Cash payments for operating expenses. . . .	193,800		
Cash payments for interest	8,000		
Cash payments for income taxes	83,500	1,070,500	
Net cash flow from operating activities			$100,500
Cash flows from investing activities:			
Cash from sale of land		$ 72,000	
Less: Cash paid to purchase land	$ 15,000		
Cash paid for purchase of building	60,000	75,000	
Net cash flow used for investing activities			(3,000)
Cash flows from financing activities:			
Cash received from sale of common stock		$ 48,000	
Less: Cash paid to retire bonds payable	$ 50,000		
Cash paid for dividends	24,000	74,000	
Net cash flow used for financing activities			(26,000)
Increase in cash			$ 71,500
Cash at the beginning of the year			26,000
Cash at the end of the year			$ 97,500
Schedule Reconciling Net Income with Cash Flows from Operating Activities:			
Cash flows from operating activities:			
Net income			$108,000
Adjustments to reconcile net income to net cash flow from operating activities:			
Depreciation			7,000
Gain on sale of land			(12,000)
Changes in current operating assets and liabilities:			
Increase in accounts receivable			(9,000)
Decrease in inventory			8,000
Decrease in accounts payable			(3,200)
Increase in accrued expenses			2,200
Decrease in income taxes payable			(500)
Net cash flow from operating activities			$100,500

Financial Analysis and Interpretation

A valuable tool for evaluating the cash flows of a business is free cash flow. **Free cash flow** is a measure of operating cash flow available for corporate purposes after providing sufficient fixed asset additions to maintain current productive capacity and dividends. Thus, free cash flow can be calculated as follows:

Cash flow from operating activities	$XXX
Less: Investments in fixed assets to maintain current production	XXX
Free cash flow	$XXX

Analysts often use free cash flow, rather than cash flows from operating activities, to measure the financial strength of a business. Many high-technology firms must aggressively reinvest in new technology to remain competitive. This can reduce free cash flow. For example, Motorola Inc.'s free cash flow is less than 10% of the cash flow from operating activities. In contrast, The Coca-Cola Company's free cash flow is approximately 75% of the cash flow from operating activities. The top three nonfinancial companies with the largest free cash flows for a recent year were as follows:

	Free Cash Flow (in millions)
General Electric Company	$25,598
ExxonMobil Corporation	18,705
Microsoft Corporation	14,289

To illustrate, the cash flow from operating activities for Intuit Inc., the developer of TurboTax®, was $590 million in a recent fiscal year. The statement of cash flows indicated that the cash invested in property, plant, and equipment was $38 million. Assuming that the amount invested in property, plant, and equipment maintained existing operations, free cash flow would be calculated as follows (in millions):

Cash flow from operating activities	$590
Less: Investments in fixed assets to maintain current production	38
Free cash flow	$552

During this period, Intuit generated free cash flow in excess of $500 million, which was 94% of cash flows from operations and over 27% of sales.

Positive free cash flow is considered favorable. A company that has free cash flow is able to fund internal growth, retire debt, pay dividends, and enjoy financial flexibility. A company with no free cash flow is unable to maintain current productive capacity. Lack of free cash flow can be an early indicator of liquidity problems. As stated by one analyst, "Free cash flow gives the company firepower to reduce debt and ultimately generate consistent, actual income."[6]

Source: "CFO Free Cash Flow Scorecard," *CFO Magazine,* January 1, 2005.

Appendix

Spreadsheet (Work Sheet) for Statement of Cash Flows—The Indirect Method

A spreadsheet (work sheet) may be useful in assembling data for the statement of cash flows. Whether or not a spreadsheet (work sheet) is used, the concepts of cash flow and the statements of cash flows presented in this chapter are not affected. In this appendix, we will describe and illustrate use of the spreadsheet (work sheet) for the indirect method.

---

6 Jill Krutick, *Fortune,* March 30, 1998, p. 106.

We will use the data for Rundell Inc., presented in Exhibit 4, as a basis for illustrating the spreadsheet (work sheet) for the indirect method. The procedures used in preparing this spreadsheet (work sheet), shown in Exhibit 10, are outlined below.

1. List the title of each balance sheet account in the Accounts column. For each account, enter its balance as of December 31, 2007, in the first column and its balance as of December 31, 2008, in the last column. Place the credit balances in parentheses. The column totals should equal zero, since the total of the debits in a column should equal the total of the credits in a column.
2. Analyze the change during the year in each account to determine the net increase (decrease) in cash and the cash flows from operating activities, investing activities, financing activities, and the noncash investing and financing activities. Show the effect of the change on cash flows by making entries in the Transactions columns.

ANALYZING ACCOUNTS

An efficient method of analyzing cash flows is to determine the type of cash flow activity that led to changes in balance sheet accounts during the period. As we analyze each noncash account, we will make entries on the spreadsheet (work sheet) for specific types of cash flow activities related to the noncash accounts. After we have analyzed all the noncash accounts, we will make an entry for the increase (decrease) in cash during the period. These entries, however, are not posted to the ledger. They only aid in assembling the data on the spreadsheet.

The order in which the accounts are analyzed is unimportant. However, it is more efficient to begin with the retained earnings account and proceed upward in the account listing.

RETAINED EARNINGS

The spreadsheet (work sheet) shows a Retained Earnings balance of $202,300 at December 31, 2007, and $282,300 at December 31, 2008. Thus, Retained Earnings increased $80,000 during the year. This increase resulted from two factors: (1) net income of $108,000 and (2) declaring cash dividends of $28,000. To identify the cash flows by activity, we will make two entries on the spreadsheet. These entries also serve to account for or explain, in terms of cash flows, the increase of $80,000.

In closing the accounts at the end of the year, the retained earnings account was credited for the net income of $108,000. The $108,000 is reported on the statement of cash flows as "cash flows from operating activities." The following entry is made in the Transactions columns on the spreadsheet. This entry (1) accounts for the credit portion of the closing entry (to Retained Earnings) and (2) identifies the cash flow in the bottom portion of the spreadsheet.

(a)	Operating Activities—Net Income	108,000	
	Retained Earnings		108,000

In closing the accounts at the end of the year, the retained earnings account was debited for dividends declared of $28,000. The $28,000 is reported as a financing activity on the statement of cash flows. The following entry on the spreadsheet (1) accounts for the debit portion of the closing entry (to Retained Earnings) and (2) identifies the cash flow in the bottom portion of the spreadsheet.

(b)	Retained Earnings	28,000	
	Financing Activities—Declared Cash Dividends		28,000

The $28,000 of declared dividends will be adjusted later for the actual amount of cash dividends paid during the year.

EXHIBIT 10   End-of-Period Spreadsheet (Work Sheet) for Statement of Cash Flows—Indirect Method

	A	B	C	D	E	F	G	
		Rundell Inc.						
		End-of-Period Spreadsheet (Work Sheet) for Statement of Cash Flows						
		For the Year Ended December 31, 2008						
	Accounts	**Balance,**	**Transactions**				**Balance,**	
		Dec. 31, 2007	**Debit**			**Credit**	**Dec. 31, 2008**	
1	Cash	26,000	(o)	71,500			97,500	1
2	Accounts receivable (net)	65,000	(n)	9,000			74,000	2
3	Inventories	180,000			(m)	8,000	172,000	3
4	Land	125,000	(k)	15,000	(l)	60,000	80,000	4
5	Building	200,000	(j)	60,000			260,000	5
6	Accumulated depreciation—building	(58,300)			(i)	7,000	(65,300)	6
7	Accounts payable (merchandise creditors)	(46,700)	(h)	3,200			(43,500)	7
8	Accrued expenses payable (operating expenses)	(24,300)			(g)	2,200	(26,500)	8
9	Income taxes payable	(8,400)	(f)	500			(7,900)	9
10	Dividends payable	(10,000)			(e)	4,000	(14,000)	10
11	Bonds payable	(150,000)	(d)	50,000			(100,000)	11
12	Common stock	(16,000)			(c)	8,000	(24,000)	12
13	Paid-in capital in excess of par	(80,000)			(c)	40,000	(120,000)	13
14	Retained earnings	(202,300)	(b)	28,000	(a)	108,000	(282,300)	14
15	Totals	0		237,200		237,200	0	15
16	Operating activities:							16
17	Net income		(a)	108,000				17
18	Depreciation of building		(i)	7,000				18
19	Gain on sale of land				(l)	12,000		19
20	Increase in accounts receivable				(n)	9,000		20
21	Decrease in inventories		(m)	8,000				21
22	Decrease in accounts payable				(h)	3,200		22
23	Increase in accrued expenses		(g)	2,200				23
24	Decrease in income taxes payable				(f)	500		24
25	Investing activities:							25
26	Sale of land		(l)	72,000				26
27	Purchase of land				(k)	15,000		27
28	Purchase of building				(j)	60,000		28
29	Financing activities:							29
30	Issued common stock		(c)	48,000				30
31	Retired bonds payable				(d)	50,000		31
32	Declared cash dividends				(b)	28,000		32
33	Increase in dividends payable		(e)	4,000				33
34	Net increase in cash				(o)	71,500		34
35	Totals			249,200		249,200		35

OTHER ACCOUNTS

The entries for the other accounts are made in the spreadsheet in a manner similar to entries (a) and (b). A summary of these entries is as follows:

(c)	Financing Activities—Issued Common Stock	48,000	
	Common Stock		8,000
	Paid-In Capital in Excess of Par—Common Stock		40,000
(d)	Bonds Payable	50,000	
	Financing Activities—Retired Bonds Payable		50,000
(e)	Financing Activities—Increase in Dividends Payable	4,000	
	Dividends Payable		4,000
(f)	Income Taxes Payable	500	
	Operating Activities—Decrease in Income Taxes Payable		500

(g)	Operating Activities—Increase in Accrued Expenses	2,200	
	Accrued Expenses Payable		2,200
(h)	Accounts Payable	3,200	
	Operating Activities—Decrease in Accounts Payable		3,200
(i)	Operating Activities—Depreciation of Building	7,000	
	Accumulated Depreciation—Building		7,000
(j)	Building	60,000	
	Investing Activities—Purchase of Building		60,000
(k)	Land	15,000	
	Investing Activities—Purchase of Land		15,000
(l)	Investing Activities—Sale of Land	72,000	
	Operating Activities—Gain on Sale of Land		12,000
	Land		60,000
(m)	Operating Activities—Decrease in Inventories	8,000	
	Inventories		8,000
(n)	Accounts Receivable	9,000	
	Operating Activities—Increase in Accounts Receivable		9,000
(o)	Cash	71,500	
	Net Increase in Cash		71,500

After we have analyzed all the balance sheet accounts and made the entries on the spreadsheet (work sheet), all the operating, investing, and financing activities are identified in the bottom portion of the spreadsheet. The accuracy of the spreadsheet entries is verified by the equality of each pair of the totals of the debit and credit Transactions columns.

PREPARING THE STATEMENT OF CASH FLOWS

The statement of cash flows prepared from the spreadsheet is identical to the statement in Exhibit 7. The data for the three sections of the statement are obtained from the bottom portion of the spreadsheet.

At a Glance

1. Summarize the types of cash flow activities reported in the statement of cash flows.

Key Points	Key Learning Outcomes	Example Exercises	Practice Exercises
The statement of cash flows reports cash receipts and cash payments by three types of activities: operating activities, investing activities, and financing activities. Investing and financing for a business may be affected by transactions that do not involve cash. The effect of such transactions should be reported in a separate schedule accompanying the statement of cash flows.	• Classify transactions that either provide or use cash into either operating, investing, or financing activities.	**13-1**	13-1A, 13-1B

(continued)

2. Prepare a statement of cash flows, using the indirect method.

Key Points	Key Learning Outcomes	Example Exercises	Practice Exercises
The changes in the noncash balance sheet accounts are used to develop the statement of cash flows, beginning with the cash flows from operating activities.			
Determine the cash flows from operating activities using the indirect method by adjusting net income for expenses that do not require cash and for gains and losses from disposal of fixed assets.	• Adjust net income for noncash expenses and gains and losses from asset disposals under the indirect method.	**13-2**	13-2A, 13-2B
Determine the cash flows from operating activities using the indirect method by adjusting net income for changes in current operating assets and liabilities.	• Adjust net income for changes in current operating assets and liabilities under the indirect method.	**13-3**	13-3A, 13-3B
Report cash flows from operating activities under the indirect method.	• Prepare the cash flows from operating activities under the indirect method in proper form.	**13-4**	13-4A, 13-4B
Report investing and financing activities on the statement of cash flows.	• Prepare the remainder of the statement of cash flows by reporting investing and financing activities.	**13-5**	13-5A, 13-5B

3. Prepare a statement of cash flows, using the direct method.

Key Points	Key Learning Outcomes	Example Exercises	Practice Exercises
The direct method reports cash flows from operating activities by major classes of operating cash receipts and cash payments. The difference between the major classes of total operating cash receipts and total operating cash payments is the net cash flow from operating activities. The investing and financing activities sections of the statement are the same as under the indirect method.	• Prepare the cash flows from operating activities and the remainder of the statement of cash flows under the direct method.	**13-6** **13-7**	13-6A, 13-6B 13-7A, 13-7B

Key Terms

cash flows from financing activities (514)
cash flows from investing activities (514)

cash flows from operating activities (514)
direct method (516)
free cash flow (534)

indirect method (516)
statement of cash flows (514)

Illustrative Problem

The comparative balance sheet of Dowling Company for December 31, 2008 and 2007, is as follows:

Dowling Company
Comparative Balance Sheet
December 31, 2008 and 2007

Assets	2008	2007
Cash	$ 140,350	$ 95,900
Accounts receivable (net)	95,300	102,300
Inventories	165,200	157,900
Prepaid expenses	6,240	5,860
Investments (long-term)	35,700	84,700
Land	75,000	90,000
Buildings	375,000	260,000
Accumulated depreciation—buildings	(71,300)	(58,300)
Machinery and equipment	428,300	428,300
Accumulated depreciation—machinery and equipment	(148,500)	(138,000)
Patents	58,000	65,000
Total assets	$1,159,290	$1,093,660

Liabilities and Stockholders' Equity		
Accounts payable (merchandise creditors)	$ 43,500	$ 46,700
Accrued expenses (operating expenses)	14,000	12,500
Income taxes payable	7,900	8,400
Dividends payable	14,000	10,000
Mortgage note payable, due 2019	40,000	0
Bonds payable	150,000	250,000
Common stock, $30 par	450,000	375,000
Excess of issue price over par—common stock	66,250	41,250
Retained earnings	373,640	349,810
Total liabilities and stockholders' equity	$1,159,290	$1,093,660

The income statement for Dowling Company is shown below.

Dowling Company
Income Statement
For the Year Ended December 31, 2008

Sales		$1,100,000
Cost of merchandise sold		710,000
Gross profit		$ 390,000
Operating expenses:		
Depreciation expense	$ 23,500	
Patent amortization	7,000	
Other operating expenses	196,000	
Total operating expenses		226,500
Income from operations		$ 163,500
Other income:		
Gain on sale of investments	$ 11,000	
Other expense:		
Interest expense	26,000	(15,000)
Income before income tax		$ 148,500
Income tax expense		50,000
Net income		$ 98,500

An examination of the accounting records revealed the following additional information applicable to 2008:

a. Land costing $15,000 was sold for $15,000.
b. A mortgage note was issued for $40,000.
c. A building costing $115,000 was constructed.
d. 2,500 shares of common stock were issued at 40 in exchange for the bonds payable.
e. Cash dividends declared were $74,670.

Instructions

1. Prepare a statement of cash flows, using the indirect method of reporting cash flows from operating activities.
2. Prepare a statement of cash flows, using the direct method of reporting cash flows from operating activities.

Solution

1.

Dowling Company
Statement of Cash Flows—Indirect Method
For the Year Ended December 31, 2008

Cash flows from operating activities:			
Net income		$ 98,500	
Adjustments to reconcile net income to net cash flow from operating activities:			
Depreciation		23,500	
Amortization of patents		7,000	
Gain on sale of investments		(11,000)	
Changes in current operating assets and liabilities:			
Decrease in accounts receivable		7,000	
Increase in inventories		(7,300)	
Increase in prepaid expenses		(380)	
Decrease in accounts payable		(3,200)	
Increase in accrued expenses		1,500	
Decrease in income taxes payable		(500)	
Net cash flow from operating activities			$115,120
Cash flows from investing activities:			
Cash received from sale of:			
Investments	$60,000		
Land	15,000	$ 75,000	
Less: Cash paid for construction of building		115,000	
Net cash flow used for investing activities			(40,000)
Cash flows from financing activities:			
Cash received from issuing mortgage note payable		$ 40,000	
Less: Cash paid for dividends		70,670	
Net cash flow used for financing activities			(30,670)
Increase in cash			$ 44,450
Cash at the beginning of the year			95,900
Cash at the end of the year			$140,350
Schedule of Noncash Investing and Financing Activities:			
Issued common stock to retire bonds payable			$100,000

2.

Dowling Company			
Statement of Cash Flows—Direct Method			
For the Year Ended December 31, 2008			

Cash flows from operating activities:

Cash received from customers[1]		$1,107,000	
Deduct: Cash paid for merchandise[2]	$720,500		
Cash paid for operating expenses[3]	194,880		
Cash paid for interest expense	26,000		
Cash paid for income tax[4]	50,500	991,880	
Net cash flow from operating activities			$115,120

Cash flows from investing activities:

Cash received from sale of:

Investments	$ 60,000		
Land	15,000	$ 75,000	
Less: Cash paid for construction of building . . .		115,000	
Net cash flow used for investing activities			(40,000)

Cash flows from financing activities:

Cash received from issuing mortgage note payable		$ 40,000	
Less: Cash paid for dividends[5]		70,670	
Net cash flow used for financing activities			(30,670)
Increase in cash			$ 44,450
Cash at the beginning of the year			95,900
Cash at the end of the year			$140,350

Schedule of Noncash Investing and
Financing Activities:

Issued common stock to retire bonds payable . .			$100,000

Schedule Reconciling Net Income with Cash Flows
from Operating Activities[6]

Computations:
[1]$1,100,000 + $7,000 = $1,107,000
[2]$710,000 + $3,200 + $7,300 = $720,500
[3]$196,000 + $380 − $1,500 = $194,880
[4]$50,000 + $500 = $50,500

[5]$74,670 + $10,000 − $14,000 = $70,670
[6]The content of this schedule is the same as the operating activities section of part (1) of this solution and is not reproduced here for the sake of brevity.

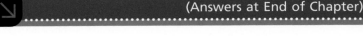

Self-Examination Questions

(Answers at End of Chapter)

1. An example of a cash flow from an operating activity is:
   A. receipt of cash from the sale of stock.
   B. receipt of cash from the sale of bonds.
   C. payment of cash for dividends.
   D. receipt of cash from customers on account.

2. An example of a cash flow from an investing activity is:
   A. receipt of cash from the sale of equipment.
   B. receipt of cash from the sale of stock.
   C. payment of cash for dividends.
   D. payment of cash to acquire treasury stock.

3. An example of a cash flow from a financing activity is:
   A. receipt of cash from customers on account.
   B. receipt of cash from the sale of equipment.

   C. payment of cash for dividends.
   D. payment of cash to acquire land.

4. Which of the following methods of reporting cash flows from operating activities adjusts net income for revenues and expenses not involving the receipt or payment of cash?
   A. Direct method
   B. Purchase method
   C. Reciprocal method
   D. Indirect method

5. The net income reported on the income statement for the year was $55,000, and depreciation of fixed assets for the year was $22,000. The balances of the current asset and current liability accounts at the beginning and end of the year are shown at the top of the following page.

	End	Beginning
Cash	$ 65,000	$ 70,000
Accounts receivable	100,000	90,000
Inventories	145,000	150,000
Prepaid expenses	7,500	8,000
Accounts payable		
(merchandise creditors)	51,000	58,000

The total amount reported for cash flows from operating activities in the statement of cash flows, using the indirect method, is:

A. $33,000.   C. $65,500.

B. $55,000.   D. $77,000.

Eye Openers

1. What is the principal disadvantage of the direct method of reporting cash flows from operating activities?
2. What are the major advantages of the indirect method of reporting cash flows from operating activities?
3. A corporation issued $300,000 of common stock in exchange for $300,000 of fixed assets. Where would this transaction be reported on the statement of cash flows?
4. a. What is the effect on cash flows of declaring and issuing a stock dividend?
   b. Is the stock dividend reported on the statement of cash flows?
5. A retail business, using the accrual method of accounting, owed merchandise creditors (accounts payable) $290,000 at the beginning of the year and $315,000 at the end of the year. How would the $25,000 increase be used to adjust net income in determining the amount of cash flows from operating activities by the indirect method? Explain.
6. If salaries payable was $75,000 at the beginning of the year and $60,000 at the end of the year, should $15,000 be added to or deducted from income to determine the amount of cash flows from operating activities by the indirect method? Explain.
7. A long-term investment in bonds with a cost of $75,000 was sold for $84,000 cash. (a) What was the gain or loss on the sale? (b) What was the effect of the transaction on cash flows? (c) How should the transaction be reported in the statement of cash flows if cash flows from operating activities are reported by the indirect method?
8. A corporation issued $4,000,000 of 20-year bonds for cash at 105. How would the transaction be reported on the statement of cash flows?
9. Fully depreciated equipment costing $65,000 was discarded. What was the effect of the transaction on cash flows if (a) $12,000 cash is received, (b) no cash is received?
10. For the current year, Bearings Company decided to switch from the indirect method to the direct method for reporting cash flows from operating activities on the statement of cash flows. Will the change cause the amount of net cash flow from operating activities to be (a) larger, (b) smaller, or (c) the same as if the indirect method had been used? Explain.
11. Name five common major classes of operating cash receipts or operating cash payments presented on the statement of cash flows when the cash flows from operating activities are reported by the direct method.
12. In a recent annual report, eBay Inc. reported that during the year it issued stock of $128 million for acquisitions. How would this be reported on the statement of cash flows?

Practice Exercises

PE 13-1A
Classifying cash flows
obj. 1

Identify whether each of the following would be reported as an operating, investing, or financing activity in the statement of cash flows.

a. Issuance of bonds payable
b. Collection of accounts receivable
c. Purchase of investments

d. Disposal of equipment
e. Payment for selling expenses
f. Cash sales

PE 13-1B
Classifying cash flows
obj. 1

Identify whether each of the following would be reported as an operating, investing, or financing activity in the statement of cash flows.

a. Payment for administrative expenses
b. Retirement of bonds payable
c. Purchase of land

d. Issuance of common stock
e. Cash received from customers
f. Payment of accounts payable

PE 13-2A
Adjustments to net income—indirect method
obj. 2

Zale Corporation's accumulated depreciation—equipment increased by $8,000, while patents decreased by $5,200 between balance sheet dates. There were no purchases or sales of depreciable or intangible assets during the year. In addition, the income statement showed a loss of $6,000 from the sale of investments. Reconcile a net income of $90,000 to net cash flow from operating activities.

PE 13-2B
Adjustments to net income—indirect method
obj. 2

Nordic Corporation's accumulated depreciation—furniture increased by $3,500, while patents decreased by $1,800 between balance sheet dates. There were no purchases or sales of depreciable or intangible assets during the year. In addition, the income statement showed a gain of $12,500 from the sale of land. Reconcile a net income of $125,000 to net cash flow from operating activities.

PE 13-3A
Changes in current operating assets and liabilities—indirect method
obj. 2

Sage Corporation's comparative balance sheet for current assets and liabilities was as follows:

	Dec. 31, 2008	Dec. 31, 2007
Accounts receivable	$12,000	$14,000
Inventory	9,000	6,500
Accounts payable	8,500	7,200
Dividends payable	24,000	26,000

Adjust net income of $110,000 for changes in operating assets and liabilities to arrive at cash flows from operating activities.

PE 13-3B
Changes in current operating assets and liabilities—indirect method
obj. 2

Lanier Corporation's comparative balance sheet for current assets and liabilities was as follows:

	Dec. 31, 2008	Dec. 31, 2007
Accounts receivable	$32,500	$25,000
Inventory	69,000	48,000
Accounts payable	51,500	32,000
Dividends payable	15,000	16,400

Adjust net income of $290,000 for changes in operating assets and liabilities to arrive at cash flows from operating activities.

PE 13-4A
Reporting cash flows from operating activities—indirect method
obj. 2

Texas Holdem Inc. reported the following data:

Net income	$85,000
Depreciation expense	14,000
Gain on disposal of equipment	10,500
Decrease in accounts receivable	6,000
Decrease in accounts payable	1,800

Prepare the cash flows from operating activities section of the statement of cash flows using the indirect method.

PE 13-4B
Reporting cash flows from operating activities—indirect method
obj. 2

Pier Inc. reported the following data:

Net income	$150,000
Depreciation expense	25,000
Loss on disposal of equipment	14,300
Increase in accounts receivable	9,400
Increase in accounts payable	4,300

Prepare the cash flows from operating activities section of the statement of cash flows using the indirect method.

PE 13-5A
Reporting land transactions on the statement of cash flows
obj. 2

Gamma Corporation purchased land for $200,000. Later in the year, the company sold land with a book value of $105,000 for $90,000. How are the effects of these transactions reported on the statement of cash flows?

PE 13-5B
Reporting land transactions on the statement of cash flows
obj. 2

Sunrise Corporation purchased land for $500,000. Later in the year, the company sold land with a book value of $320,000 for $375,000. How are the effects of these transactions reported on the statement of cash flows?

PE 13-6A
Cash received from customers—direct method
obj. 3

Sales reported on the income statement were $623,000. The accounts receivable balance increased $48,000 over the year. Determine the amount of cash received from customers.

PE 13-6B
Cash received from customers—direct method
obj. 3

Sales reported on the income statement were $58,400. The accounts receivable balance decreased $2,100 over the year. Determine the amount of cash received from customers.

PE 13-7A
Cash payments for merchandise—direct method
obj. 3

Cost of merchandise sold reported on the income statement was $568,000. The accounts payable balance decreased $28,000, and the inventory balance decreased by $39,000 over the year. Determine the amount of cash paid for merchandise.

PE 13-7B
Cash payments for merchandise—direct method
obj. 3

Cost of merchandise sold reported on the income statement was $111,000. The accounts payable balance increased $5,700, and the inventory balance increased by $8,400 over the year. Determine the amount of cash paid for merchandise.

Exercises

EX 13-1
Cash flows from operating activities—net loss
obj. 1

On its income statement for a recent year, Northwest Airlines Corporation reported a net *loss* of $862 million from operations. On its statement of cash flows, it reported $271 million of cash flows from operating activities.

➤ Explain this apparent contradiction between the loss and the positive cash flows.

EX 13-2
Effect of transactions on cash flows
obj. 1

✓ b. Cash receipt, $36,000

State the effect (cash receipt or payment and amount) of each of the following transactions, considered individually, on cash flows:

a. Sold 5,000 shares of $30 par common stock for $90 per share.
b. Sold equipment with a book value of $42,500 for $36,000.
c. Purchased land for $250,000 cash.
d. Purchased 5,000 shares of $30 par common stock as treasury stock at $60 per share.
e. Sold a new issue of $100,000 of bonds at 98.
f. Paid dividends of $1.50 per share. There were 40,000 shares issued and 5,000 shares of treasury stock.

g. Retired $500,000 of bonds, on which there was $2,500 of unamortized discount, for $500,500.
h. Purchased a building by paying $40,000 cash and issuing a $90,000 mortgage note payable.

EX 13-3
Classifying cash flows
obj. 1

Identify the type of cash flow activity for each of the following events (operating, investing, or financing):

a. Issued preferred stock.
b. Net income.
c. Sold equipment.
d. Purchased treasury stock.
e. Purchased buildings.
f. Purchased patents.

g. Issued bonds.
h. Issued common stock.
i. Sold long-term investments.
j. Paid cash dividends.
k. Redeemed bonds.

EX 13-4
Cash flows from operating activities—indirect method
obj. 2

Indicate whether each of the following would be added to or deducted from net income in determining net cash flow from operating activities by the indirect method:

a. Gain on retirement of long-term debt
b. Increase in merchandise inventory
c. Amortization of patent
d. Decrease in accounts receivable
e. Depreciation of fixed assets
f. Decrease in prepaid expenses
g. Decrease in salaries payable

h. Increase in notes receivable due in 90 days from customers
i. Decrease in accounts payable
j. Loss on disposal of fixed assets
k. Increase in notes payable due in 90 days to vendors

EX 13-5
Cash flows from operating activities—indirect method
obj. 2
✓ *Net cash flow from operating activities, $111,700*

The net income reported on the income statement for the current year was $92,000. Depreciation recorded on store equipment for the year amounted to $18,600. Balances of the current asset and current liability accounts at the beginning and end of the year are as follows:

	End of Year	Beginning of Year
Cash	$46,700	$44,200
Accounts receivable (net)	32,300	31,100
Merchandise inventory	54,800	56,700
Prepaid expenses	4,000	3,500
Accounts payable (merchandise creditors)	46,000	42,900
Wages payable	21,400	23,600

Prepare the cash flows from operating activities section of the statement of cash flows, using the indirect method.

EX 13-6
Cash flows from operating activities—indirect method
objs. 1, 2
✓ *a. Cash flows from operating activities, $203,100*

The net income reported on the income statement for the current year was $165,300. Depreciation recorded on equipment and a building amounted to $46,700 for the year. Balances of the current asset and current liability accounts at the beginning and end of the year are as follows:

	End of Year	Beginning of Year
Cash	$ 42,000	$ 43,500
Accounts receivable (net)	65,400	69,200
Inventories	125,900	115,100
Prepaid expenses	5,800	6,400
Accounts payable (merchandise creditors)	61,400	64,200
Salaries payable	8,300	8,000

a. Prepare the cash flows from operating activities section of the statement of cash flows, using the indirect method.
b. If the direct method had been used, would the net cash flow from operating activities have been the same? Explain.

EX 13-7
Cash flows from operating activities—indirect method
objs. 1, 2

The income statement disclosed the following items for 2008:

Depreciation expense	$ 24,500
Gain on disposal of equipment	10,200
Net income	186,000

Balances of the current assets and current liability accounts changed between December 31, 2007, and December 31, 2008, as follows:

Accounts receivable	$4,400
Inventory	2,000*
Prepaid insurance	800*
Accounts payable	2,700*
Income taxes payable	900
Dividends payable	500

*Decrease

Prepare the cash flows from operating activities section of the statement of cash flows, using the indirect method.

EX 13-8
Determining cash payments to stockholders
obj. 2

The board of directors declared cash dividends totaling $120,000 during the current year. The comparative balance sheet indicates dividends payable of $35,000 at the beginning of the year and $30,000 at the end of the year. What was the amount of cash payments to stockholders during the year?

EX 13-9
Reporting changes in equipment on statement of cash flows
obj. 2

An analysis of the general ledger accounts indicates that office equipment, which cost $60,000 and on which accumulated depreciation totaled $15,000 on the date of sale, was sold for $41,000 during the year. Using this information, indicate the items to be reported on the statement of cash flows.

EX 13-10
Reporting changes in equipment on statement of cash flows
obj. 2

An analysis of the general ledger accounts indicates that delivery equipment, which cost $45,000 and on which accumulated depreciation totaled $32,000 on the date of sale, was sold for $15,000 during the year. Using this information, indicate the items to be reported on the statement of cash flows.

EX 13-11
Reporting land transactions on statement of cash flows
obj. 2

On the basis of the details of the following fixed asset account, indicate the items to be reported on the statement of cash flows:

ACCOUNT *Land*   ACCOUNT NO.

Date		Item	Debit	Credit	Balance	
					Debit	Credit
2008						
Jan.	1	Balance			900,000	
Feb.	5	Purchased for cash	400,000		1,300,000	
Oct.	30	Sold for $365,000		250,000	1,050,000	

EX 13-12
Reporting stockholders' equity items on statement of cash flows
obj. 2

On the basis of the following stockholders' equity accounts, indicate the items, exclusive of net income, to be reported on the statement of cash flows. There were no unpaid dividends at either the beginning or the end of the year.

ACCOUNT *Common Stock, $10 par*   ACCOUNT NO.

Date		Item	Debit	Credit	Balance	
					Debit	Credit
2008						
Jan.	1	Balance, 70,000 shares				700,000
Feb.	11	16,000 shares issued for cash		160,000		860,000
June	30	4,100-share stock dividend		41,000		901,000

ACCOUNT *Paid-In Capital in Excess of Par—Common Stock*   ACCOUNT NO.

2008					
Jan.	1	Balance			140,000
Feb.	11	16,000 shares issued for cash		336,000	476,000
June	30	Stock dividend		102,500	578,500

ACCOUNT *Retained Earnings*   ACCOUNT NO.

2008					
Jan.	1	Balance			1,000,000
June	30	Stock dividend	143,500		856,500
Dec.	30	Cash dividend	124,000		732,500
	31	Net income		630,000	1,362,500

EX 13-13
Reporting land acquisition for cash and mortgage note on statement of cash flows
obj. 2

On the basis of the details of the following fixed asset account, indicate the items to be reported on the statement of cash flows:

ACCOUNT *Land*   ACCOUNT NO.

	Date	Item	Debit	Credit	Balance Debit	Balance Credit
2008						
Jan.	1	Balance			160,000	
Feb.	10	Purchased for cash	326,000		486,000	
Nov.	20	Purchased with long-term mortgage note	400,000		886,000	

EX 13-14
Reporting issuance and retirement of long-term debt
obj. 2

On the basis of the details of the following bonds payable and related discount accounts, indicate the items to be reported in the financing section of the statement of cash flows, assuming no gain or loss on retiring the bonds:

ACCOUNT *Bonds Payable*   ACCOUNT NO.

	Date	Item	Debit	Credit	Balance Debit	Balance Credit
2008						
Jan.	1	Balance				150,000
Jan.	3	Retire bonds	70,000			80,000
July	30	Issue bonds		350,000		430,000

ACCOUNT *Discount on Bonds Payable*   ACCOUNT NO.

	Date	Item	Debit	Credit	Balance Debit	Balance Credit
2008						
Jan.	1	Balance			12,000	
Jan.	3	Retire bonds		5,600	6,400	
July	30	Issue bonds	20,000		26,400	
Dec.	31	Amortize discount		1,600	24,800	

EX 13-15
Determining net income from net cash flow from operating activities
obj. 2

Emerald Golf Inc. reported a net cash flow from operating activities of $86,700 on its statement of cash flows for the year ended December 31, 2008. The following information was reported in the cash flows from operating activities section of the statement of cash flows, using the indirect method:

Decrease in income taxes payable	$2,000
Decrease in inventories	5,600
Depreciation	8,500
Gain on sale of investments	3,400
Increase in accounts payable	1,200
Increase in prepaid expenses	700
Increase in accounts receivable	4,300

Determine the net income reported by Emerald Golf Inc. for the year ended December 31, 2008.

EX 13-16
Cash flows from operating activities—indirect method

obj. 2

✓ *Net cash flow used in operating activities, ($773)*

Selected data derived from the income statement and balance sheet of Jones Soda Co. for a recent year are as follows:

Income statement data (in thousands):

Net earnings	$1,330
Depreciation expense	193
Stock-based compensation expense (noncash)	20

Balance sheet data (in thousands):

Increase in accounts receivable	$1,328
Increase in inventory	1,550
Increase in prepaid expenses	124
Increase in accounts payable	686

a. Prepare the cash flows from operating activities section of the statement of cash flows using the indirect method for Jones Soda Co. for the year.
b. Interpret your results in part (a).

EX 13-17
Statement of cash flows—indirect method

obj. 2

✓ *Net cash flow from operating activities, $50*

The comparative balance sheet of Alliance Structures Inc. for December 31, 2008 and 2007, is as follows (amounts in thousands):

	Dec. 31, 2008	Dec. 31, 2007
Assets		
Cash	$ 90	$ 23
Accounts receivable (net)	30	27
Inventories	24	21
Land	35	55
Equipment	32	22
Accumulated depreciation—equipment	(9)	(5)
Total	$202	$143
Liabilities and Stockholders' Equity		
Accounts payable (merchandise creditors)	$ 17	$ 10
Dividends payable	1	—
Common stock, $1 par	6	3
Paid-in capital in excess of par—common stock	30	10
Retained earnings	148	120
Total	$202	$143

The following additional information is taken from the records (all amounts in thousands):

a. Land was sold for $15.
b. Equipment was acquired for cash.
c. There were no disposals of equipment during the year.
d. The common stock was issued for cash.
e. There was a $40 credit to Retained Earnings for net income.
f. There was a $12 debit to Retained Earnings for cash dividends declared.

Prepare a statement of cash flows, using the indirect method of presenting cash flows from operating activities.

EX 13-18
Statement of cash flows—indirect method

obj. 2

List the errors you find in the following statement of cash flows. The cash balance at the beginning of the year was $83,600. All other amounts are correct, except the cash balance at the end of the year.

Whole Life Nutrition Products Inc.
Statement of Cash Flows
For the Year Ended December 31, 2008

Cash flows from operating activities:			
Net income		$123,400	
Adjustments to reconcile net income to net cash flow from operating activities:			
Depreciation		35,000	
Gain on sale of investements		6,000	
Changes in current operating assets and liabilities:			
Increase in accounts receivable		9,500	
Increase in inventories		(12,300)	
Increase in accounts payable		(3,700)	
Decrease in accrued expenses		(900)	
Net cash flow from operating activities			$157,000
Cash flows from investing activities:			
Cash received from sale of investments		$ 85,000	
Less: Cash paid for purchase of land	$ 90,000		
Cash paid for purchase of equipment	150,100	240,100	
Net cash flow used for investing activities			(155,100)
Cash flows from financing activities:			
Cash received from sale of common stock		$107,000	
Cash paid for dividends		45,000	
Net cash flow provided by financing activities			152,000
Increase in cash			$153,900
Cash at the end of the year			105,300
Cash at the beginning of the year			$259,200

EX 13-19
Cash flows from operating activities—direct method
obj. 3
✓ *a. $471,000*

The cash flows from operating activities are reported by the direct method on the statement of cash flows. Determine the following:

a. If sales for the current year were $450,000 and accounts receivable decreased by $21,000 during the year, what was the amount of cash received from customers?
b. If income tax expense for the current year was $35,000 and income tax payable decreased by $3,100 during the year, what was the amount of cash payments for income tax?

EX 13-20
Cash paid for merchandise purchases
obj. 3

The cost of merchandise sold for Kohl's Corporation for a recent year was $8,639 million. The balance sheet showed the following current account balances (in millions):

	Balance, End of Year	Balance, Beginning of Year
Merchandise inventories	$2,238	$1,947
Accounts payable	830	705

Determine the amount of cash payments for merchandise.

EX 13-21
Determining selected amounts for cash flows from operating activities—direct method
obj. 3
✓ *b. $59,900*

Selected data taken from the accounting records of Extravaganza Inc. for the current year ended December 31 are as follows:

	Balance, December 31	Balance, January 1
Accrued expenses (operating expenses)	$ 4,300	$ 4,700
Accounts payable (merchandise creditors)	32,100	35,400
Inventories	59,500	64,700
Prepaid expenses	2,500	3,000

During the current year, the cost of merchandise sold was $345,000, and the operating expenses other than depreciation were $60,000. The direct method is used for presenting the cash flows from operating activities on the statement of cash flows.

Determine the amount reported on the statement of cash flows for (a) cash payments for merchandise and (b) cash payments for operating expenses.

EX 13-22
Cash flows from operating activities—direct method

obj. 3

✓ *Net cash flow from operating activities, $87,200*

The income statement of Country Kitchen Bakeries Inc. for the current year ended June 30 is as follows:

Sales		$456,000
Cost of merchandise sold		259,000
Gross profit		$197,000
Operating expenses:		
Depreciation expense	$35,000	
Other operating expenses	92,400	
Total operating expenses		127,400
Income before income tax		$ 69,600
Income tax expense		19,300
Net income		$ 50,300

Changes in the balances of selected accounts from the beginning to the end of the current year are as follows:

	Increase Decrease*
Accounts receivable (net)	$10,500*
Inventories	3,500
Prepaid expenses	3,400*
Accounts payable (merchandise creditors)	7,200*
Accrued expenses (operating expenses)	1,100
Income tax payable	2,400*

Prepare the cash flows from operating activities section of the statement of cash flows, using the direct method.

EX 13-23
Cash flows from operating activities—direct method

obj. 3

✓ *Net cash flow from operating activities, $47,600*

The income statement for Wholly Bagel Company for the current year ended June 30 and balances of selected accounts at the beginning and the end of the year are as follows:

Sales		$184,000
Cost of merchandise sold		67,000
Gross profit		$117,000
Operating expenses:		
Depreciation expense	$14,500	
Other operating expenses	49,000	
Total operating expenses		63,500
Income before income tax		$ 53,500
Income tax expense		15,400
Net income		$ 38,100

	End of Year	Beginning of Year
Accounts receivable (net)	$14,800	$12,900
Inventories	38,100	33,100
Prepaid expenses	6,000	6,600
Accounts payable (merchandise creditors)	27,900	25,900
Accrued expenses (operating expenses)	7,900	8,600
Income tax payable	1,500	1,500

Prepare the cash flows from operating activities section of the statement of cash flows, using the direct method.

EX 13-24
Free cash flow

Mediterranean Tile Company has cash flows from operating activities of $120,000. Cash flows used for investments in property, plant, and equipment totaled $45,000, of which 60% of this investment was used to replace existing capacity.

Determine the free cash flow for Mediterranean Tile Company.

EX 13-25
Free cash flow

The financial statements for Williams-Sonoma, Inc., are provided in Appendix B at the end of the text.

Determine the free cash flow for the year ended January 29, 2006. Assume that 70% of purchases of property and equipment were for new store openings, and the remaining was for remodeling and updating existing stores.

Problems Series A

PR 13-1A
Statement of cash flows—indirect method

obj. 2

✓ *Net cash flow from operating activities, $72,200*

The comparative balance sheet of Oak and Tile Flooring Co. for June 30, 2008 and 2007, is as follows:

	June 30, 2008	June 30, 2007
Assets		
Cash	$ 34,700	$ 23,500
Accounts receivable (net)	101,600	92,300
Inventories	146,300	142,100
Investments	0	50,000
Land	145,000	0
Equipment	215,000	175,500
Accumulated depreciation	(48,600)	(41,300)
	$594,000	$442,100
Liabilities and Stockholders' Equity		
Accounts payable (merchandise creditors)	$100,900	$ 95,200
Accrued expenses (operating expenses)	15,000	13,200
Dividends payable	12,500	10,000
Common stock, $1 par	56,000	50,000
Paid-in capital in excess of par—common stock	220,000	100,000
Retained earnings	189,600	173,700
	$594,000	$442,100

The following additional information was taken from the records of Oak and Tile Flooring Co.:

a. Equipment and land were acquired for cash.
b. There were no disposals of equipment during the year.
c. The investments were sold for $45,000 cash.
d. The common stock was issued for cash.
e. There was a $65,900 credit to Retained Earnings for net income.
f. There was a $50,000 debit to Retained Earnings for cash dividends declared.

Instructions
Prepare a statement of cash flows, using the indirect method of presenting cash flows from operating activities.

PR 13-2A
Statement of cash flows—indirect method

obj. 2

The comparative balance sheet of Portable Luggage Company at December 31, 2008 and 2007, is as follows:

✓ *Net cash flow from operating activities, $221,700*

	Dec. 31, 2008	Dec. 31, 2007
Assets		
Cash	$ 175,900	$ 143,200
Accounts receivable (net)	264,100	235,000
Inventories	352,300	405,800
Prepaid expenses	12,500	10,000
Land	120,000	120,000
Buildings	680,000	450,000
Accumulated depreciation—buildings	(185,000)	(164,500)
Machinery and equipment	310,000	310,000
Accumulated depreciation—machinery & equipment	(85,000)	(76,000)
Patents	42,500	48,000
	$1,687,300	$1,481,500
Liabilities and Stockholders' Equity		
Accounts payable (merchandise creditors)	$ 332,300	$ 367,900
Dividends payable	13,000	10,000
Salaries payable	30,200	34,600
Mortgage note payable, due 2015	90,000	—
Bonds payable	—	154,000
Common stock, $1 par	24,000	20,000
Paid-in capital in excess of par—common stock	200,000	50,000
Retained earnings	997,800	845,000
	$1,687,300	$1,481,500

An examination of the income statement and the accounting records revealed the following additional information applicable to 2008:

a. Net income, $204,800.
b. Depreciation expense reported on the income statement: buildings, $20,500; machinery and equipment, $9,000.
c. Patent amortization reported on the income statement, $5,500.
d. A building was constructed for $230,000.
e. A mortgage note for $90,000 was issued for cash.
f. 4,000 shares of common stock were issued at $38.50 in exchange for the bonds payable.
g. Cash dividends declared, $52,000.

Instructions

Prepare a statement of cash flows, using the indirect method of presenting cash flows from operating activities.

PR 13-3A
Statement of cash flows—indirect method

obj. 2

✓ *Net cash flow from operating activities, $4,100*

The comparative balance sheet of Reston Supply Co. at December 31, 2008 and 2007, is as follows:

	Dec. 31, 2008	Dec. 31, 2007
Assets		
Cash	$ 45,500	$ 51,200
Accounts receivable (net)	106,700	92,400
Inventories	139,200	131,200
Prepaid expenses	2,800	4,000
Land	150,000	210,000
Buildings	300,000	150,000
Accumulated depreciation—buildings	(60,200)	(55,500)
Equipment	100,100	80,300
Accumulated depreciation—equipment	(20,200)	(24,500)
	$763,900	$639,100
Liabilities and Stockholders' Equity		
Accounts payable (merchandise creditors)	$ 90,000	$ 95,600
Income tax payable	4,000	3,200
Bonds payable	50,000	0
Common stock, $1 par	33,000	30,000
Paid-in capital in excess of par—common stock	180,000	120,000
Retained earnings	406,900	390,300
	$763,900	$639,100

The noncurrent asset, noncurrent liability, and stockholders' equity accounts for 2008 are as follows:

ACCOUNT *Land*   **ACCOUNT NO.**

Date		Item	Debit	Credit	Balance	
					Debit	Credit
2008						
Jan.	1	Balance			210,000	
Apr.	20	Realized $69,000 cash from sale		60,000	150,000	

ACCOUNT *Buildings*   **ACCOUNT NO.**

2008						
Jan.	1	Balance			150,000	
Apr.	20	Acquired for cash	150,000		300,000	

ACCOUNT *Accumulated Depreciation—Buildings*   **ACCOUNT NO.**

2008						
Jan.	1	Balance				55,500
Dec.	31	Depreciation for year		4,700		60,200

ACCOUNT *Equipment*   **ACCOUNT NO.**

2008						
Jan.	1	Balance			80,300	
	26	Discarded, no salvage		10,000	70,300	
Aug.	11	Purchased for cash	29,800		100,100	

ACCOUNT *Accumulated Depreciation—Equipment*   **ACCOUNT NO.**

2008						
Jan.	1	Balance				24,500
	26	Equipment discarded	10,000			14,500
Dec.	31	Depreciation for year		5,700		20,200

ACCOUNT *Bonds Payable*   **ACCOUNT NO.**

2008						
May	1	Issued 20-year bonds		50,000		50,000

ACCOUNT *Common Stock, $1 par*   **ACCOUNT NO.**

2008						
Jan.	1	Balance				30,000
Dec.	7	Issued 3,000 shares of common stock for $21 per share		3,000		33,000

ACCOUNT *Paid-In Capital in Excess of Par—Common Stock*   **ACCOUNT NO.**

2008						
Jan.	1	Balance				120,000
Dec.	7	Issued 3,000 shares of common stock for $21 per share		60,000		180,000

ACCOUNT *Retained Earnings*   **ACCOUNT NO.**

2008						
Jan.	1	Balance				390,300
Dec.	31	Net income		28,600		418,900
	31	Cash dividends	12,000			406,900

Instructions

Prepare a statement of cash flows, using the indirect method of presenting cash flows from operating activities.

PR 13-4A
Statement of cash flows—direct method

obj. 3

✓*Net cash flow from operating activities, $107,900*

The comparative balance sheet of Green Earth Lawn and Garden Inc. for December 31, 2008 and 2009, is as follows:

	Dec. 31, 2009	Dec. 31, 2008
Assets		
Cash	$ 137,900	$142,300
Accounts receivable (net)	206,800	190,500
Inventories	290,500	284,100
Investments	0	90,000
Land	200,000	0
Equipment	255,000	205,000
Accumulated depreciation	(100,300)	(76,700)
	$ 989,900	$835,200
Liabilities and Stockholders' Equity		
Accounts payable (merchandise creditors)	$ 224,900	$201,400
Accrued expenses (operating expenses)	14,100	16,500
Dividends payable	21,000	19,000
Common stock, $1 par	10,000	8,000
Paid-in capital in excess of par—common stock	200,000	100,000
Retained earnings	519,900	490,300
	$ 989,900	$835,200

The income statement for the year ended December 31, 2009, is as follows:

Sales		$940,000
Cost of merchandise sold		489,300
Gross profit		$450,700
Operating expenses:		
Depreciation expense	$ 23,600	
Other operating expenses	278,900	
Total operating expenses		302,500
Operating income		$148,200
Other income:		
Gain on sale of investments		32,000
Income before income tax		$180,200
Income tax expense		62,300
Net income		$117,900

The following additional information was taken from the records:

a. Equipment and land were acquired for cash.
b. There were no disposals of equipment during the year.
c. The investments were sold for $122,000 cash.
d. The common stock was issued for cash.
e. There was a $88,300 debit to Retained Earnings for cash dividends declared.

Instructions
Prepare a statement of cash flows, using the direct method of presenting cash flows from operating activities.

PR 13-5A
Statement of cash flows—direct method applied to PR 14-1A

obj. 3

✓*Net cash flow from operating activities, $72,200*

The comparative balance sheet of Oak and Tile Flooring Co. for June 30, 2008 and 2007, is as follows:

	June 30, 2008	June 30, 2007
Assets		
Cash	$ 34,700	$ 23,500
Accounts receivable (net)	101,600	92,300
Inventories	146,300	142,100
Investments	0	50,000
Land	145,000	0
Equipment	215,000	175,500
Accumulated depreciation	(48,600)	(41,300)
	$594,000	$442,100

Liabilities and Stockholders' Equity

Accounts payable (merchandise creditors)	$100,900	$ 95,200
Accrued expenses (operating expenses)	15,000	13,200
Dividends payable	12,500	10,000
Common stock, $1 par	56,000	50,000
Paid-in capital in excess of par—common stock	220,000	100,000
Retained earnings	189,600	173,700
	$594,000	$442,100

The income statement for the year ended June 30, 2008, is as follows:

Sales		$963,400
Cost of merchandise sold		662,100
Gross profit		$301,300
Operating expenses:		
Depreciation expense	$ 7,300	
Other operating expenses	195,000	
Total operating expenses		202,300
Operating income		$ 99,000
Other expenses:		
Loss on sale of investments		(5,000)
Income before income tax		$ 94,000
Income tax expense		28,100
Net income		$ 65,900

The following additional information was taken from the records:

a. Equipment and land were acquired for cash.
b. There were no disposals of equipment during the year.
c. The investments were sold for $45,000 cash.
d. The common stock was issued for cash.
e. There was a $50,000 debit to Retained Earnings for cash dividends declared.

Instructions
Prepare a statement of cash flows, using the direct method of presenting cash flows from operating activities.

Problems Series B

PR 13-1B
Statement of cash flows—indirect method

obj. 2

✓ *Net cash flow from operating activities, $61,900*

The comparative balance sheet of Gold Medal Sporting Goods Inc. for December 31, 2008 and 2007, is shown as follows:

	Dec. 31, 2008	Dec. 31, 2007
Assets		
Cash	$ 391,100	$ 366,200
Accounts receivable (net)	142,400	130,600
Inventories	401,100	385,700
Investments	0	150,000
Land	205,000	0
Equipment	440,700	345,700
Accumulated depreciation—equipment	(104,000)	(92,500)
	$1,476,300	$1,285,700
Liabilities and Stockholders' Equity		
Accounts payable (merchandise creditors)	$ 267,800	$ 253,100
Accrued expenses (operating expenses)	26,400	32,900
Dividends payable	15,000	12,000
Common stock, $10 par	80,000	60,000
Paid-in capital in excess of par—common stock	300,000	175,000
Retained earnings	787,100	752,700
	$1,476,300	$1,285,700

The following additional information was taken from the records:

a. The investments were sold for $175,000 cash.
b. Equipment and land were acquired for cash.
c. There were no disposals of equipment during the year.
d. The common stock was issued for cash.
e. There was a $94,400 credit to Retained Earnings for net income.
f. There was a $60,000 debit to Retained Earnings for cash dividends declared.

Instructions

Prepare a statement of cash flows, using the indirect method of presenting cash flows from operating activities.

PR 13-2B
Statement of cash flows—indirect method

obj. 2

✓ *Net cash flow from operating activities, $108,500*

The comparative balance sheet of Air Glide Athletic Apparel Co. at December 31, 2008 and 2007, is as follows:

	Dec. 31, 2008	Dec. 31, 2007
Assets		
Cash	$ 45,800	$ 56,200
Accounts receivable (net)	70,200	75,600
Merchandise inventory	100,500	93,500
Prepaid expenses	4,200	3,000
Equipment	204,700	167,800
Accumulated depreciation—equipment	(53,400)	(41,300)
	$372,000	$354,800
Liabilities and Stockholders' Equity		
Accounts payable (merchandise creditors)	$ 78,200	$ 74,300
Mortgage note payable	0	105,000
Common stock, $1 par	15,000	10,000
Paid-in capital in excess of par—common stock	180,000	100,000
Retained earnings	98,800	65,500
	$372,000	$354,800

Additional data obtained from the income statement and from an examination of the accounts in the ledger for 2008 are as follows:

a. Net income, $81,300.
b. Depreciation reported on the income statement, $26,100.
c. Equipment was purchased at a cost of $50,900, and fully depreciated equipment costing $14,000 was discarded, with no salvage realized.
d. The mortgage note payable was not due until 2011, but the terms permitted earlier payment without penalty.
e. 5,000 shares of common stock were issued at $17 for cash.
f. Cash dividends declared and paid, $48,000.

Instructions

Prepare a statement of cash flows, using the indirect method of presenting cash flows from operating activities.

PR 13-3B
Statement of cash flows—indirect method

obj. 2

✓ *Net cash flow from operating activities, ($68,400)*

The comparative balance sheet of Rise N' Shine Juice Co. at December 31, 2008 and 2007, is as follows:

	Dec. 31, 2008	Dec. 31, 2007
Assets		
Cash	$ 392,300	$ 412,300
Accounts receivable (net)	354,200	325,600
Inventories	542,100	497,000
Prepaid expenses	12,500	15,000
Land	135,000	205,000
Buildings	625,000	385,000
Accumulated depreciation—buildings	(174,600)	(163,400)
Equipment	218,900	194,300
Accumulated depreciation—equipment	(60,400)	(67,800)
	$2,045,000	$1,803,000

Liabilities and Stockholders' Equity

Accounts payable (merchandise creditors)	$ 394,200	$ 409,500
Bonds payable	115,000	0
Common stock, $1 par	58,000	50,000
Paid-in capital in excess of par—common stock	400,000	240,000
Retained earnings	1,077,800	1,103,500
	$2,045,000	$1,803,000

The noncurrent asset, noncurrent liability, and stockholders' equity accounts for 2008 are as follows:

ACCOUNT *Land* **ACCOUNT NO.**

Date		Item	Debit	Credit	Balance Debit	Balance Credit
2008						
Jan.	1	Balance			205,000	
Apr.	20	Realized $64,000 cash from sale		70,000	135,000	

ACCOUNT *Buildings* **ACCOUNT NO.**

Date		Item	Debit	Credit	Balance Debit	Balance Credit
2008						
Jan.	1	Balance			385,000	
Apr.	20	Acquired for cash	240,000		625,000	

ACCOUNT *Accumulated Depreciation—Buildings* **ACCOUNT NO.**

Date		Item	Debit	Credit	Balance Debit	Balance Credit
2008						
Jan.	1	Balance				163,400
Dec.	31	Depreciation for year		11,200		174,600

ACCOUNT *Equipment* **ACCOUNT NO.**

Date		Item	Debit	Credit	Balance Debit	Balance Credit
2008						
Jan.	1	Balance			194,300	
	26	Discarded, no salvage		20,000	174,300	
Aug.	11	Purchased for cash	44,600		218,900	

ACCOUNT *Accumulated Depreciation—Equipment* **ACCOUNT NO.**

Date		Item	Debit	Credit	Balance Debit	Balance Credit
2008						
Jan.	1	Balance				67,800
	26	Equipment discarded	20,000			47,800
Dec.	31	Depreciation for year		12,600		60,400

ACCOUNT *Bonds Payable* **ACCOUNT NO.**

Date		Item	Debit	Credit	Balance Debit	Balance Credit
2008						
May	1	Issued 20-year bonds		115,000		115,000

ACCOUNT *Common Stock, $1 par* **ACCOUNT NO.**

Date		Item	Debit	Credit	Balance Debit	Balance Credit
2008						
Jan.	1	Balance				50,000
Dec.	7	Issued 8,000 shares of common stock for $21 per share		8,000		58,000

ACCOUNT *Paid-In Capital in Excess of Par—Common Stock* **ACCOUNT NO.**

Date		Item	Debit	Credit	Balance Debit	Balance Credit
2008						
Jan.	1	Balance				240,000
Dec.	7	Issued 8,000 shares of common stock for $21 per share		160,000		400,000

(continued)

		ACCOUNT *Retained Earnings*			ACCOUNT NO.	

Date		Item	Debit	Credit	Balance	
					Debit	Credit
2008						
Jan.	1	Balance				1,103,500
Dec.	31	Net loss	11,700			1,091,800
	31	Cash dividends	14,000			1,077,800

Instructions

Prepare a statement of cash flows, using the indirect method of presenting cash flows from operating activities.

PR 13-4B
Statement of cash flows—direct method

obj. 3

✓ *Net cash flow from operating activities, $193,600*

The comparative balance sheet of Home and Hearth Inc. for December 31, 2009 and 2008, is as follows:

	Dec. 31, 2009	Dec. 31, 2008
Assets		
Cash	$ 402,100	$ 424,600
Accounts receivable (net)	354,200	342,100
Inventories	631,900	614,200
Investments	0	150,000
Land	325,000	0
Equipment	550,000	425,000
Accumulated depreciation	(152,700)	(125,300)
	$2,110,500	$1,830,600
Liabilities and Stockholders' Equity		
Accounts payable (merchandise creditors)	$ 482,400	$ 467,800
Accrued expenses (operating expenses)	39,600	44,200
Dividends payable	5,500	4,000
Common stock, $1 par	24,000	20,000
Paid-in capital in excess of par—common stock	260,000	120,000
Retained earnings	1,299,000	1,174,600
	$2,110,500	$1,830,600

The income statement for the year ended December 31, 2009, is as follows:

Sales		$3,745,700
Cost of merchandise sold		1,532,500
Gross profit		$2,213,200
Operating expenses:		
Depreciation expense	$ 27,400	
Other operating expenses	1,936,800	
Total operating expenses		1,964,200
Operating income		$ 249,000
Other expense:		
Loss on sale of investments		(40,000)
Income before income tax		$ 209,000
Income tax expense		63,000
Net income		$ 146,000

The following additional information was taken from the records:

a. Equipment and land were acquired for cash.
b. There were no disposals of equipment during the year.
c. The investments were sold for $110,000 cash.
d. The common stock was issued for cash.
e. There was a $21,600 debit to Retained Earnings for cash dividends declared.

Instructions

Prepare a statement of cash flows, using the direct method of presenting cash flows from operating activities.

PR 13-5B
Statement of cash flows—direct method applied to PR 14-1B

obj. 3

✓ *Net cash flow from operating activities, $61,900*

The comparative balance sheet of Gold Medal Sporting Goods Inc. for December 31, 2008 and 2007, is as follows:

	Dec. 31, 2008	Dec. 31, 2007
Assets		
Cash	$ 391,100	$ 366,200
Accounts receivable (net)	142,400	130,600
Inventories	401,100	385,700
Investments	0	150,000
Land	205,000	0
Equipment	440,700	345,700
Accumulated depreciation—equipment	(104,000)	(92,500)
	$1,476,300	$1,285,700
Liabilities and Stockholders' Equity		
Accounts payable (merchandise creditors)	$ 267,800	$ 253,100
Accrued expenses (operating expenses)	26,400	32,900
Dividends payable	15,000	12,000
Common stock, $10 par	80,000	60,000
Paid-in capital in excess of par—common stock	300,000	175,000
Retained earnings	787,100	752,700
	$1,476,300	$1,285,700

The income statement for the year ended December 31, 2008, is as follows:

Sales		$1,632,500
Cost of merchandise sold		908,300
Gross profit		$ 724,200
Operating expenses:		
Depreciation expense	$ 11,500	
Other operating expenses	609,000	
Total operating expenses		620,500
Operating income		$ 103,700
Other income:		
Gain on sale of investments		25,000
Income before income tax		$ 128,700
Income tax expense		34,300
Net income		$ 94,400

The following additional information was taken from the records:

a. The investments were sold for $175,000 cash.
b. Equipment and land were acquired for cash.
c. There were no disposals of equipment during the year.
d. The common stock was issued for cash.
e. There was a $60,000 debit to Retained Earnings for cash dividends declared.

Instructions

Prepare a statement of cash flows, using the direct method of presenting cash flows from operating activities.

Special Activities

SA 13-1
Ethics and professional conduct in business

ETHICS

Linda Stern, president of Venician Fashions Inc., believes that reporting operating cash flow per share on the income statement would be a useful addition to the company's just completed financial statements. The following discussion took place between Linda Stern and Venician Fashions' controller, Ben Trotter, in January, after the close of the fiscal year.

Linda: I have been reviewing our financial statements for the last year. I am disappointed that our net income per share has dropped by 10% from last year. This is not going to look good to our shareholders. Isn't there anything we can do about this?

Ben: What do you mean? The past is the past, and the numbers are in. There isn't much that can be done about it. Our financial statements were prepared according to generally accepted accounting principles, and I don't see much leeway for significant change at this point.

Linda: No, no. I'm not suggesting that we "cook the books." But look at the cash flow from operating activities on the statement of cash flows. The cash flow from operating activities has increased by 20%. This is very good news—and, I might add, useful information. The higher cash flow from operating activities will give our creditors comfort.

Ben: Well, the cash flow from operating activities is on the statement of cash flows, so I guess users will be able to see the improved cash flow figures there.

Linda: This is true, but somehow I feel that this information should be given a much higher profile. I don't like this information being "buried" in the statement of cash flows. You know as well as I do that many users will focus on the income statement. Therefore, I think we ought to include an operating cash flow per share number on the face of the income statement—someplace under the earnings per share number. In this way users will get the complete picture of our operating performance. Yes, our earnings per share dropped this year, but our cash flow from operating activities improved! And all the information is in one place where users can see and compare the figures. What do you think?

Ben: I've never really thought about it like that before. I guess we could put the operating cash flow per share on the income statement, under the earnings per share. Users would really benefit from this disclosure. Thanks for the idea—I'll start working on it.

Linda: Glad to be of service.

➤ How would you interpret this situation? Is Ben behaving in an ethical and professional manner?

SA 13-2
Using the statement of cash flows

You are considering an investment in a new start-up company, Aspen Technologies Inc., an Internet service provider. A review of the company's financial statements reveals a negative retained earnings. In addition, it appears as though the company has been running a negative cash flow from operating activities since the company's inception.

➤ How is the company staying in business under these circumstances? Could this be a good investment?

SA 13-3
Analysis of cash flow from operations

The Retailing Division of Bargain Buyer Inc. provided the following information on its cash flow from operations:

Net income	$ 450,000
Increase in accounts receivable	(540,000)
Increase in inventory	(600,000)
Decrease in accounts payable	(90,000)
Depreciation	100,000
Cash flow from operating activities	$(680,000)

The manager of the Retailing Division provided the accompanying memo with this report:

From: Senior Vice President, Retailing Division

I am pleased to report that we had earnings of $450,000 over the last period. This resulted in a return on invested capital of 10%, which is near our targets for this division. I have been aggressive in building the revenue volume in the division. As a result, I am happy to report that we have increased the number of new credit card customers as a result of an aggressive marketing campaign. In addition, we have found some excellent merchandise opportunities. Some of our suppliers have made some of their apparel merchandise available at a deep discount. We have purchased as much of these goods as possible in order to improve profitability. I'm also happy to report that our vendor payment problems have improved. We are nearly caught up on our over-due payables balances.

➤ Comment on the senior vice president's memo in light of the cash flow information.

SA 13-4
Analysis of statement of cash flows

Jabari Daniels is the president and majority shareholder of Cabinet Craft Inc., a small retail store chain. Recently, Daniels submitted a loan application for Cabinet Craft Inc. to Montvale National Bank. It called for a $200,000, 9%, 10-year loan to help finance the construction of a building and the purchase of store equipment, costing a total of $250,000, to enable Cabinet Craft Inc. to open a store in Montvale. Land for this purpose was acquired last year. The bank's loan officer requested a statement of cash flows in addition to the most recent income statement, balance sheet, and retained earnings statement that Daniels had submitted with the loan application.

As a close family friend, Daniels asked you to prepare a statement of cash flows. From the records provided, you prepared the following statement:

Cabinet Craft Inc.
Statement of Cash Flows
For the Year Ended December 31, 2008

Cash flows from operating activities:		
Net income	$ 94,500	
Adjustments to reconcile net income to net cash flow from operating activities:		
Depreciation	26,000	
Gain on sale of investments	(8,000)	
Changes in current operating assets and liabilities:		
Decrease in accounts receivable	5,000	
Increase in inventories	(12,000)	
Increase in accounts payable	8,500	
Decrease in accrued expenses	(1,200)	
Net cash flow from operating activities		$112,800
Cash flows from investing activities:		
Cash received from investments sold	$ 50,000	
Less cash paid for purchase of store equipment	(30,000)	
Net cash flow provided by investing activities		20,000
Cash flows from financing activities:		
Cash paid for dividends	$ 35,000	
Net cash flow used for financing activities		(35,000)
Increase in cash		$ 97,800
Cash at the beginning of the year		34,800
Cash at the end of the year		$132,600
Schedule of Noncash Financing and Investing Activities:		
Issued common stock for land		$ 75,000

After reviewing the statement, Daniels telephoned you and commented, "Are you sure this statement is right?" Daniels then raised the following questions:

1. "How can depreciation be a cash flow?"
2. "Issuing common stock for the land is listed in a separate schedule. This transaction has nothing to do with cash! Shouldn't this transaction be eliminated from the statement?"

(continued)

3. "How can the gain on sale of investments be a deduction from net income in determining the cash flow from operating activities?"

4. "Why does the bank need this statement anyway? They can compute the increase in cash from the balance sheets for the last two years."

After jotting down Daniels' questions, you assured him that this statement was "right." However, to alleviate Daniels' concern, you arranged a meeting for the following day.

a. How would you respond to each of Daniels' questions?
b. Do you think that the statement of cash flows enhances the chances of Cabinet Craft Inc. receiving the loan? Discuss.

SA 13-5
Statement of cash flows

Group Project

Internet Project

This activity will require two teams to retrieve cash flow statement information from the Internet. One team is to obtain the most recent year's statement of cash flows for Johnson & Johnson, and the other team the most recent year's statement of cash flows for AMR Corp. (American Airlines).

The statement of cash flows is included as part of the annual report information that is a required disclosure to the Securities and Exchange Commission (SEC). The SEC, in turn, provides this information online through its EDGAR service. EDGAR (Electronic Data Gathering, Analysis, and Retrieval) is the electronic archive of financial statements filed with the Securities and Exchange Commission (SEC). SEC documents can be retrieved using the EdgarScan service from PricewaterhouseCoopers at **http://edgarscan.pwcglobal.com**.

To obtain annual report information, type in a company name in the appropriate space. EdgarScan will list the reports available to you for the company you've selected. Select the most recent annual report filing, identified as a 10-K or 10-K405. EdgarScan provides an outline of the report, including the separate financial statements. You can double-click the income statement and balance sheet for the selected company into an Excel™ spreadsheet for further analysis.

As a group, compare the two statements of cash flows.

a. How are Johnson & Johnson and AMR similar or different regarding cash flows?
b. Compute and compare the free cash flow for each company, assuming additions to property, plant, and equipment replace current capacity.

Answers to Self-Examination Questions

1. **D** Cash flows from operating activities affect transactions that enter into the determination of net income, such as the receipt of cash from customers on account (answer D). Receipts of cash from the sale of stock (answer A) and the sale of bonds (answer B) and payments of cash for dividends (answer C) are cash flows from financing activities.

2. **A** Cash flows from investing activities include receipts from the sale of noncurrent assets, such as equipment (answer A), and payments to acquire noncurrent assets. Receipts of cash from the sale of stock (answer B) and payments of cash for dividends (answer C) and to acquire treasury stock (answer D) are cash flows from financing activities.

3. **C** Payment of cash for dividends (answer C) is an example of a financing activity. The receipt of cash from customers on account (answer A) is an operating activity. The receipt of cash from the sale of equipment (answer B) is an investing activity. The payment of cash to acquire land (answer D) is an example of an investing activity.

4. **D** The indirect method (answer D) reports cash flows from operating activities by beginning with net income and adjusting it for revenues and expenses not involving the receipt or payment of cash.

5. **C** The cash flows from operating activities section of the statement of cash flows would report net cash flow from operating activities of $65,500, determined as follows:

Cash flows from operating activities:		
Net income		$ 55,000
Adjustments to reconcile net income		
to net cash flow from operating activities:		
Depreciation		22,000
Changes in current operating assets		
and liabilities:		
Increase in accounts receivable		(10,000)
Decrease in inventories		5,000
Decrease in prepaid expenses		500
Decrease in accounts payable		(7,000)
Net cash flow from operating activities		$65,500

Financial Statement Analysis

© CHITOSE SUZUKI/ASSOCIATED PRESS

objectives

After studying this chapter, you should be able to:

1 *List basic financial statement analytical procedures.*

2 *Apply financial statement analysis to assess the solvency of a business.*

3 *Apply financial statement analysis to assess the profitability of a business.*

4 *Describe the contents of corporate annual reports.*

Williams-Sonoma, Inc.

During a recent year, Williams-Sonoma, Inc., reported revenues of over $3.1 billion and net income of over $190 million. The common stock of Williams-Sonoma is traded on the New York Stock Exchange (symbol WSM) and closed on February 17, 2006, at $39.80 per share. Based upon current market values, Williams-Sonoma is worth almost $4.6 billion. Do you wish you could have invested in Williams-Sonoma 15 years ago?

Williams-Sonoma is a specialty retailer in the United States, well-known for its home furnishings. The company began in 1956, when owner Chuck Williams opened a store selling restaurant-quality cookware from France in Sonoma, California. The business expanded quickly, and Williams soon moved his store to Sutter Street in San Francisco. From there, the company expanded into catalogs, the Internet, and additional brands, such as Pottery Barn.

The success of Williams-Sonoma shows that reputation and the popularity of a company's product are important indicators of success. However, these are not the *only* factors that determine a company's success. A business needs to combine product offerings with proper financial, marketing, and sales

strategies to be successful. Clearly, Williams-Sonoma has accomplished this. If you had invested in its common stock back in 1990, the stock price would have risen from $3 per share to nearly $40 per share today.

How, then, should you select companies in which to invest? Like any significant purchase, you should do some research to guide your investment decision. If you were buying a car, for example, you might go to Edmunds.com to obtain reviews, ratings, prices, specifications, options, and fuel economy across a number of vehicle alternatives. In deciding whether to invest in a company, you can use financial analysis to gain insight into a company's past performance and future prospects. This chapter describes and illustrates common financial data that can be analyzed to assist you in making investment decisions such as whether or not to invest in Williams-Sonoma stock. The contents of corporate annual reports are also discussed.

Source: Walter Nicholls, "The 90-Year-Old Pioneer Behind Williams-Sonoma," *The Seattle Times*, October 5, 2005.

Basic Analytical Procedures

objective **1**

List basic financial statement analytical procedures.

The basic financial statements provide much of the information users need to make economic decisions about businesses. In this chapter, we illustrate how to perform a complete analysis of these statements by integrating individual analytical measures.

Analytical procedures may be used to compare items on a current statement with related items on earlier statements. For example, cash of $150,000 on the current balance sheet may be compared with cash of $100,000 on the balance sheet of a year earlier. The current year's cash may be expressed as 1.5 or 150% of the earlier amount, or as an increase of 50% or $50,000.

Analytical procedures are also widely used to examine relationships within a financial statement. To illustrate, assume that cash of $50,000 and inventories of $250,000 are included in the total assets of $1,000,000 on a balance sheet. In relative terms, the cash balance is 5% of the total assets, and the inventories are 25% of the total assets.

In this chapter, we will illustrate a number of common analytical measures. The measures are not ends in themselves. They are only guides in evaluating financial and operating data. Many other factors, such as trends in the industry and general economic conditions, should also be considered.

HORIZONTAL ANALYSIS

The percentage analysis of increases and decreases in related items in comparative financial statements is called **horizontal analysis**. The amount of each item on the most recent statement is compared with the related item on one or more earlier statements. The amount of increase or decrease in the item is listed, along with the percent of increase or decrease.

Horizontal analysis may compare two statements. In this case, the earlier statement is used as the base. Horizontal analysis may also compare three or more statements. In this case, the earliest date or period may be used as the base for comparing all later dates or periods. Alternatively, each statement may be compared to the immediately preceding statement. Exhibit 1 is a condensed comparative balance sheet for two years for Lincoln Company, with horizontal analysis.

EXHIBIT 1

Comparative Balance Sheet—Horizontal Analysis

Lincoln Company
Comparative Balance Sheet
December 31, 2008 and 2007

			Increase (Decrease)	
	2008	**2007**	**Amount**	**Percent**
Assets				
Current assets	$ 550,000	$ 533,000	$ 17,000	3.2%
Long-term investments	95,000	177,500	(82,500)	(46.5%)
Property, plant, and				
equipment (net)	444,500	470,000	(25,500)	(5.4%)
Intangible assets	50,000	50,000	—	—
Total assets	$1,139,500	$1,230,500	$ (91,000)	(7.4%)
Liabilities				
Current liabilities	$ 210,000	$ 243,000	$ (33,000)	(13.6%)
Long-term liabilities	100,000	200,000	(100,000)	(50.0%)
Total liabilities	$ 310,000	$ 443,000	$(133,000)	(30.0%)
Stockholders' Equity				
Preferred 6% stock, $100 par . . .	$ 150,000	$ 150,000	—	—
Common stock, $10 par	500,000	500,000	—	—
Retained earnings	179,500	137,500	$ 42,000	30.5%
Total stockholders' equity	$ 829,500	$ 787,500	$ 42,000	5.3%
Total liabilities and				
stockholders' equity	$1,139,500	$1,230,500	$ (91,000)	(7.4%)

We cannot fully evaluate the significance of the various increases and decreases in the items shown in Exhibit 1 without additional information. Although total assets at the end of 2008 were $91,000 (7.4%) less than at the beginning of the year, liabilities were reduced by $133,000 (30%), and stockholders' equity increased $42,000 (5.3%). It appears that the reduction of $100,000 in long-term liabilities was achieved mostly through the sale of long-term investments.

The balance sheet in Exhibit 1 may be expanded to include the details of the various categories of assets and liabilities. An alternative is to present the details in separate schedules. Exhibit 2 is a supporting schedule with horizontal analysis.

The decrease in accounts receivable may be due to changes in credit terms or improved collection policies. Likewise, a decrease in inventories during a period of increased sales may indicate an improvement in the management of inventories.

EXHIBIT 2

Comparative Schedule of Current Assets— Horizontal Analysis

Lincoln Company Comparative Schedule of Current Assets December 31, 2008 and 2007				
			Increase (Decrease)	
	2008	2007	Amount	Percent
Cash	$ 90,500	$ 64,700	$ 25,800	39.9%
Marketable securities	75,000	60,000	15,000	25.0%
Accounts receivable (net)	115,000	120,000	(5,000)	(4.2%)
Inventories	264,000	283,000	(19,000)	(6.7%)
Prepaid expenses	5,500	5,300	200	3.8%
Total current assets	$550,000	$533,000	$ 17,000	3.2%

The changes in the current assets in Exhibit 2 appear favorable. This assessment is supported by the 24.8% increase in net sales shown in Exhibit 3.

EXHIBIT 3

Comparative Income Statement— Horizontal Analysis

Lincoln Company Comparative Income Statement For the Years Ended December 31, 2008 and 2007				
			Increase (Decrease)	
	2008	2007	Amount	Percent
Sales	$1,530,500	$1,234,000	$296,500	24.0%
Sales returns and allowances . . .	32,500	34,000	(1,500)	(4.4%)
Net sales	$1,498,000	$1,200,000	$298,000	24.8%
Cost of goods sold	1,043,000	820,000	223,000	27.2%
Gross profit	$ 455,000	$ 380,000	$ 75,000	19.7%
Selling expenses	$ 191,000	$ 147,000	$ 44,000	29.9%
Administrative expenses	104,000	97,400	6,600	6.8%
Total operating expenses	$ 295,000	$ 244,400	$ 50,600	20.7%
Income from operations	$ 160,000	$ 135,600	$ 24,400	18.0%
Other income	8,500	11,000	(2,500)	(22.7%)
	$ 168,500	$ 146,600	$ 21,900	14.9%
Other expense (interest)	6,000	12,000	(6,000)	(50.0%)
Income before income tax	$ 162,500	$ 134,600	$ 27,900	20.7%
Income tax expense	71,500	58,100	13,400	23.1%
Net income	$ 91,000	$ 76,500	$ 14,500	19.0%

An increase in net sales may not have a favorable effect on operating performance. The percentage increase in Lincoln Company's net sales is accompanied by a greater percentage increase in the cost of goods (merchandise) sold.[1] This has the effect of reducing gross profit as a percentage of sales. Selling expenses increased significantly, and administrative expenses increased slightly. Overall, operating expenses increased by 20.7%, whereas gross profit increased by only 19.7%.

The increase in income from operations and in net income is favorable. However, a study of the expenses and additional analyses and comparisons should be made before reaching a conclusion as to the cause.

Exhibit 4 illustrates a comparative retained earnings statement with horizontal analysis. It reveals that retained earnings increased 30.5% for the year. The increase is due to net income of $91,000 for the year, less dividends of $49,000.

---

1 The term *cost of goods sold* is often used in practice in place of *cost of merchandise sold*. Such usage is followed in this chapter.

EXHIBIT 4

Comparative Retained
Earnings Statement—
Horizontal Analysis

Lincoln Company
Comparative Retained Earnings Statement
December 31, 2008 and 2007

	2008	2007	Increase (Decrease) Amount	Increase (Decrease) Percent
Retained earnings, January 1.....	$137,500	$100,000	$37,500	37.5%
Net income for the year.........	91,000	76,500	14,500	19.0%
Total........................	$228,500	$176,500	$52,000	29.5%
Dividends:				
On preferred stock..........	$ 9,000	$ 9,000	—	—
On common stock...........	40,000	30,000	$10,000	33.3%
Total........................	$ 49,000	$ 39,000	$10,000	25.6%
Retained earnings, December 31 ...	$179,500	$137,500	$42,000	30.5%

Example Exercise 14-1   **objective 1**

The comparative cash and accounts receivable balances for a company are provided below.

	2008	2007
Cash	$62,500	$50,000
Accounts receivable (net)	74,400	80,000

Based on this information, what is the amount and percentage of increase or decrease that would be shown in a balance sheet with horizontal analysis?

Follow My Example 14-1

Cash $12,500 increase ($62,500 − $50,000), or 25%
Accounts receivable $5,600 decrease ($74,400 − $80,000), or −7%

For Practice: PE 14-1A, PE 14-1B

VERTICAL ANALYSIS

A percentage analysis may also be used to show the relationship of each component to the total within a single statement. This type of analysis is called **vertical analysis**. Like horizontal analysis, the statements may be prepared in either detailed or condensed form. In the latter case, additional details of the changes in individual items may be presented in supporting schedules. In such schedules, the percentage analysis may be based on either the total of the schedule or the statement total. Although vertical analysis is limited to an individual statement, its significance may be improved by preparing comparative statements.

In vertical analysis of the balance sheet, each asset item is stated as a percent of the total assets. Each liability and stockholders' equity item is stated as a percent of the total liabilities and stockholders' equity. Exhibit 5 is a condensed comparative balance sheet with vertical analysis for Lincoln Company.

The major percentage changes in Lincoln Company's assets are in the current asset and long-term investment categories. Current assets increased from 43.3% to 48.3% of total assets, and long-term investments decreased from 14.4% to 8.3% of total assets. In the Liabilities and Stockholders' Equity sections of the balance sheet, the greatest percentage changes are in long-term liabilities and retained earnings. Stockholders' equity increased from 64% to 72.8% of total liabilities and stockholders' equity in 2008. There is a comparable decrease in liabilities.

EXHIBIT 5

Comparative Balance
Sheet—Vertical
Analysis

Lincoln Company
Comparative Balance Sheet
December 31, 2008 and 2007

	2008 Amount	2008 Percent	2007 Amount	2007 Percent
Assets				
Current assets	$ 550,000	48.3%	$ 533,000	43.3%
Long-term investments	95,000	8.3	177,500	14.4
Property, plant, and				
equipment (net)	444,500	39.0	470,000	38.2
Intangible assets	50,000	4.4	50,000	4.1
Total assets	$1,139,500	100.0%	$1,230,500	100.0%
Liabilities				
Current liabilities	$ 210,000	18.4%	$ 243,000	19.7%
Long-term liabilities	100,000	8.8	200,000	16.3
Total liabilities	$ 310,000	27.2%	$ 443,000	36.0%
Stockholders' Equity				
Preferred 6% stock, $100 par	$ 150,000	13.2%	$ 150,000	12.2%
Common stock, $10 par	500,000	43.9	500,000	40.6
Retained earnings	179,500	15.7	137,500	11.2
Total stockholders' equity	$ 829,500	72.8%	$ 787,500	64.0%
Total liabilities and				
stockholders' equity	$1,139,500	100.0%	$1,230,500	100.0%

In a vertical analysis of the income statement, each item is stated as a percent of net sales. Exhibit 6 is a condensed comparative income statement with vertical analysis for Lincoln Company.

EXHIBIT 6

Comparative Income
Statement—Vertical
Analysis

Lincoln Company
Comparative Income Statement
For the Years Ended December 31, 2008 and 2007

	2008 Amount	2008 Percent	2007 Amount	2007 Percent
Sales	$1,530,500	102.2%	$1,234,000	102.8%
Sales returns and allowances	32,500	2.2	34,000	2.8
Net sales	$1,498,000	100.0%	$1,200,000	100.0%
Cost of goods sold	1,043,000	69.6	820,000	68.3
Gross profit	$ 455,000	30.4%	$ 380,000	31.7%
Selling expenses	$ 191,000	12.8%	$ 147,000	12.3%
Administrative expenses	104,000	6.9	97,400	8.1
Total operating expenses	$ 295,000	19.7%	$ 244,400	20.4%
Income from operations	$ 160,000	10.7%	$ 135,600	11.3%
Other income	8,500	0.6	11,000	0.9
	$ 168,500	11.3%	$ 146,600	12.2%
Other expense (interest).	6,000	0.4	12,000	1.0
Income before income tax	$ 162,500	10.9%	$ 134,600	11.2%
Income tax expense	71,500	4.8	58,100	4.8
Net income	$ 91,000	6.1%	$ 76,500	6.4%

The percentages of gross profit and net income to sales for a recent fiscal year for Target and Wal-Mart are shown below.

	Target	Wal-Mart
Gross profit to sales	31.2%	22.9%
Net income to sales	6.8%	3.6%

Wal-Mart has a significantly lower gross profit margin percentage than does Target, which is likely due to Wal-Mart's aggressive pricing strategy. However, Target's gross profit margin advantage shrinks when comparing the net income to sales ratio. Target must have larger selling and administrative expenses to sales than does Wal-Mart. Even so, Target's net income to sales is still 3.2 percentage points better than Wal-Mart's net income to sales.

We must be careful when judging the significance of differences between percentages for the two years. For example, the decline of the gross profit rate from 31.7% in 2007 to 30.4% in 2008 is only 1.3 percentage points. In terms of dollars of potential gross profit, however, it represents a decline of approximately $19,500 (1.3% × $1,498,000).

COMMON-SIZE STATEMENTS

Horizontal and vertical analyses with both dollar and percentage amounts are useful in assessing relationships and trends in financial conditions and operations of a business. Vertical analysis with both dollar and percentage amounts is also useful in comparing one company with another or with industry averages. Such comparisons are easier to make with the use of common-size statements. In a **common-size statement**, all items are expressed in percentages.

Common-size statements are useful in comparing the current period with prior periods, individual businesses, or one business with industry percentages. Industry data are often available from trade associations and financial information services. Exhibit 7 is a comparative common-size income statement for two businesses.

Exhibit 7 indicates that Lincoln Company has a slightly higher rate of gross profit than Madison Corporation. However, this advantage is more than offset by Lincoln Company's higher percentage of selling and administrative expenses. As a result, the income from operations of Lincoln Company is 10.7% of net sales, compared with 14.4% for Madison Corporation—an unfavorable difference of 3.7 percentage points.

EXHIBIT 7

Common-Size Income Statement

Lincoln Company and Madison Corporation
Condensed Common-Size Income Statement
For the Year Ended December 31, 2008

	Lincoln Company	Madison Corporation
Sales	102.2%	102.3%
Sales returns and allowances	2.2	2.3
Net sales	100.0%	100.0%
Cost of goods sold	69.6	70.0
Gross profit	30.4%	30.0%
Selling expenses	12.8%	11.5%
Administrative expenses	6.9	4.1
Total operating expenses	19.7%	15.6%
Income from operations	10.7%	14.4%
Other income	0.6	0.6
	11.3%	15.0%
Other expense (interest)	0.4	0.5
Income before income tax	10.9%	14.5%
Income tax expense	4.8	5.5
Net income	6.1%	9.0%

OTHER ANALYTICAL MEASURES

In addition to the preceding analyses, other relationships may be expressed in ratios and percentages. Often, these items are taken from the financial statements and thus are a type of vertical analysis. Comparing these items with items from earlier periods is a type of horizontal analysis.

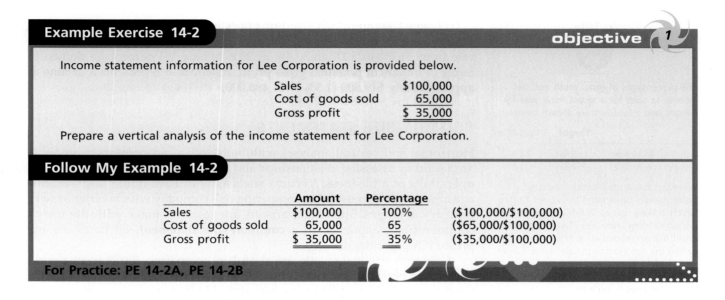

Example Exercise 14-2   objective 1

Income statement information for Lee Corporation is provided below.

Sales	$100,000
Cost of goods sold	65,000
Gross profit	$ 35,000

Prepare a vertical analysis of the income statement for Lee Corporation.

Follow My Example 14-2

	Amount	Percentage	
Sales	$100,000	100%	($100,000/$100,000)
Cost of goods sold	65,000	65	($65,000/$100,000)
Gross profit	$ 35,000	35%	($35,000/$100,000)

For Practice: PE 14-2A, PE 14-2B

Solvency Analysis

objective 2

Apply financial statement analysis to assess the solvency of a business.

Some aspects of a business's financial condition and operations are of greater importance to some users than others. However, all users are interested in the ability of a business to pay its debts as they are due and to earn income. The ability of a business to meet its financial obligations (debts) is called **solvency**. The ability of a business to earn income is called **profitability**.

The factors of solvency and profitability are interrelated. A business that cannot pay its debts on a timely basis may experience difficulty in obtaining credit. A lack of available credit may, in turn, lead to a decline in the business's profitability. Eventually, the business may be forced into bankruptcy. Likewise, a business that is less profitable than its competitors is likely to be at a disadvantage in obtaining credit or new capital from stockholders.

In the following paragraphs, we discuss various types of financial analyses that are useful in evaluating the solvency of a business. In the next section, we discuss various types of profitability analyses. The examples in both sections are based on Lincoln Company's financial statements presented earlier. In some cases, data from Lincoln Company's financial statements of the preceding year and from other sources are also used. These historical data are useful in assessing the past performance of a business and in forecasting its future performance. The results of financial analyses may be even more useful when they are compared with those of competing businesses and with industry averages.

Two popular printed sources for industry ratios are *Annual Statement Studies* from Robert Morris Associates and *Industry Norms & Key Business Ratios* from Dun's Analytical Services. Online analysis is available from Zacks Investment Research site or Market Guide's site, both of which are linked to the text's Web site at **www.thomson edu.com/accounting/warren**.

Solvency analysis focuses on the ability of a business to pay or otherwise satisfy its current and noncurrent liabilities. It is normally assessed by examining balance sheet relationships, using the following major analyses:

1. Current position analysis
2. Accounts receivable analysis
3. Inventory analysis
4. The ratio of fixed assets to long-term liabilities
5. The ratio of liabilities to stockholders' equity
6. The number of times interest charges are earned

CURRENT POSITION ANALYSIS

To be useful in assessing solvency, a ratio or other financial measure must relate to a business's ability to pay or otherwise satisfy its liabilities. Using measures to assess a

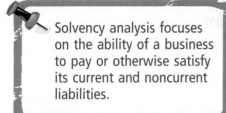

Solvency analysis focuses on the ability of a business to pay or otherwise satisfy its current and noncurrent liabilities.

business's ability to pay its current liabilities is called *current position analysis*. Such analysis is of special interest to short-term creditors.

An analysis of a firm's current position normally includes determining the working capital, the current ratio, and the quick ratio. The current and quick ratios are most useful when analyzed together and compared to previous periods and other firms in the industry.

Working Capital The excess of the current assets of a business over its current liabilities is called *working capital*. The working capital is often used in evaluating a company's ability to meet currently maturing debts. It is especially useful in making monthly or other period-to-period comparisons for a company. However, amounts of working capital are difficult to assess when comparing companies of different sizes or in comparing such amounts with industry figures. For example, working capital of $250,000 may be adequate for a small kitchenware store, but it would be inadequate for all of Williams-Sonoma, Inc.

Current Ratio Another means of expressing the relationship between current assets and current liabilities is the **current ratio**. This ratio is sometimes called the *working capital ratio* or *bankers' ratio*. The ratio is computed by dividing the total current assets by the total current liabilities. For Lincoln Company, working capital and the current ratio for 2008 and 2007 are as follows:

	2008	2007
a. Current assets	$550,000	$533,000
b. Current liabilities	210,000	243,000
Working capital (a − b)	$340,000	$290,000
Current ratio (a/b)	2.6	2.2

REAL WORLD

Microsoft Corporation maintains a high current ratio—4.7 for a recent year. Microsoft's stable and profitable software business has allowed it to develop a strong cash position coupled with no short-term notes payable.

The current ratio is a more reliable indicator of solvency than is working capital. To illustrate, assume that as of December 31, 2008, the working capital of a competitor is much greater than $340,000, but its current ratio is only 1.3. Considering these facts alone, Lincoln Company, with its current ratio of 2.6, is in a more favorable position to obtain short-term credit than the competitor, which has the greater amount of working capital.

Quick Ratio The working capital and the current ratio do not consider the makeup of the current assets. To illustrate the importance of this consideration, the current position data for Lincoln Company and Jefferson Corporation as of December 31, 2008, are as follows:

	Lincoln Company	Jefferson Corporation
Current assets:		
Cash	$ 90,500	$ 45,500
Marketable securities	75,000	25,000
Accounts receivable (net)	115,000	90,000
Inventories	264,000	380,000
Prepaid expenses	5,500	9,500
a. Total current assets	$550,000	$550,000
b. Current liabilities	210,000	210,000
Working capital (a − b)	$340,000	$340,000
Current ratio (a/b)	2.6	2.6

Both companies have a working capital of $340,000 and a current ratio of 2.6. But the ability of each company to pay its current debts is significantly different. Jefferson Corporation has more of its current assets in inventories. Some of these inventories must be sold and the receivables collected before the current liabilities can be paid in full. Thus, a large amount of time may be necessary to convert these inventories into cash. Declines in market prices and a reduction in demand could also impair its ability to pay current liabilities. In contrast, Lincoln Company has cash and current assets (marketable securities and accounts receivable) that can generally be converted to cash rather quickly to meet its current liabilities.

A ratio that measures the "instant" debt-paying ability of a company is called the **quick ratio** or *acid-test ratio*. It is the ratio of the total quick assets to the total current liabilities. **Quick assets** are cash and other current assets that can be quickly converted to cash. Quick assets normally include cash, marketable securities, and receivables. The quick ratio data for Lincoln Company are as follows:

	2008	2007
Quick assets:		
Cash	$ 90,500	$ 64,700
Marketable securities	75,000	60,000
Accounts receivable (net)	115,000	120,000
a. Total quick assets	$280,500	$244,700
b. Current liabilities	$210,000	$243,000
Quick ratio (a/b)	1.3	1.0

Example Exercise 14-3   objective 2

The following items are reported on a company's balance sheet:

Cash	$300,000
Marketable securities	100,000
Accounts receivable (net)	200,000
Inventory	200,000
Accounts payable	400,000

Determine (a) the current ratio and (b) the quick ratio.

Follow My Example 14-3

a. Current Ratio = Current Assets/Current Liabilities
Current Ratio = ($300,000 + $100,000 + $200,000 + $200,000)/$400,000
Current Ratio = 2.0

b. Quick Ratio = Quick Assets/Current Liabilities
Quick Ratio = ($300,000 + $100,000 + $200,000)/$400,000
Quick Ratio = 1.5

For Practice: PE 14-3A, PE 14-3B

ACCOUNTS RECEIVABLE ANALYSIS

The size and makeup of accounts receivable change constantly during business operations. Sales on account increase accounts receivable, whereas collections from customers decrease accounts receivable. Firms that grant long credit terms usually have larger accounts receivable balances than those granting short credit terms. Increases or decreases in the volume of sales also affect the balance of accounts receivable.

It is desirable to collect receivables as promptly as possible. The cash collected from receivables improves solvency. In addition, the cash generated by prompt collections from customers may be used in operations for such purposes as purchasing merchandise in large quantities at lower prices. The cash may also be used for payment of dividends to stockholders or for other investing or financing purposes. Prompt collection also lessens the risk of loss from uncollectible accounts.

Accounts Receivable Turnover   The relationship between sales and accounts receivable may be stated as the **accounts receivable turnover**. This ratio is computed by dividing net sales by the average net accounts receivable.[2] It is desirable to base the average on monthly balances, which allows for seasonal changes in sales. When such data are not available, it may be necessary to use the average of the accounts receivable balance at the beginning and the end of the year. If there are trade notes receivable as well as accounts, the two may be combined. The accounts receivable turnover data for Lincoln Company are as follows.

	2008	2007
a. Net sales	$1,498,000	$1,200,000
Accounts receivable (net):		
Beginning of year	$ 120,000	$ 140,000
End of year	115,000	120,000
Total	$ 235,000	$ 260,000
b. Average accounts receivable (Total/2)	$ 117,500	$ 130,000
Accounts receivable turnover (a/b)	12.7	9.2

The increase in the accounts receivable turnover for 2008 indicates that there has been an improvement in the collection of receivables. This may be due to a change in the granting of credit or in collection practices or both.

Number of Days' Sales in Receivables   Another measure of the relationship between sales and accounts receivable is the **number of days' sales in receivables**. This ratio is computed by dividing the average accounts receivable by the average daily sales. Average daily sales is determined by dividing net sales by 365 days. The number of days' sales in receivables is computed for Lincoln Company as follows:

	2008	2007
a. Average accounts receivable (Total/2)	$ 117,500	$ 130,000
Net sales	$1,498,000	$1,200,000
b. Average daily sales (Sales/365)	$4,104	$3,288
Number of days' sales in		
receivables (a/b)	28.6	39.5

The number of days' sales in receivables is an estimate of the length of time (in days) the accounts receivable have been outstanding. Comparing this measure with the credit terms provides information on the efficiency in collecting receivables. For example, assume that the number of days' sales in receivables for Grant Inc. is 40. If Grant Inc.'s credit terms are n/45, then its collection process appears to be efficient. On the other hand, if Grant Inc.'s credit terms are n/30, its collection process does not appear to be efficient. A comparison with other firms in the same industry and with prior years also provides useful information. Such comparisons may indicate efficiency of collection procedures and trends in credit management.

---

2 If known, *credit* sales should be used in the numerator. Because credit sales are not normally known by external users, we use net sales in the numerator.

Example Exercise 14-4   objective 2

A company reports the following:

Net sales	$960,000
Average accounts receivable (net)	48,000

Determine (a) the accounts receivable turnover and (b) the number of days' sales in receivables. Round to one decimal place.

Follow My Example 14-4

a.   Accounts Receivable Turnover = Sales/Average Accounts Receivable
     Accounts Receivable Turnover = $960,000/$48,000
     Accounts Receivable Turnover = 20.0

b.   Number of Days' Sales in Receivables = Average Accounts Receivable/Average Daily Sales
     Number of Days' Sales in Receivables = $48,000/($960,000/365) = $48,000/$2,630
     Number of Days' Sales in Receivables = 18.3 days

For Practice: PE 14-4A, PE 14-4B

INVENTORY ANALYSIS

A business should keep enough inventory on hand to meet the needs of its customers and its operations. At the same time, however, an excessive amount of inventory reduces solvency by tying up funds. Excess inventories also increase insurance expense, property taxes, storage costs, and other related expenses. These expenses further reduce funds that could be used elsewhere to improve operations. Finally, excess inventory also increases the risk of losses because of price declines or obsolescence of the inventory. Two measures that are useful for evaluating the management of inventory are the inventory turnover and the number of days' sales in inventory.

Inventory Turnover   The relationship between the volume of goods (merchandise) sold and inventory may be stated as the **inventory turnover**. It is computed by dividing the cost of goods sold by the average inventory. If monthly data are not available, the average of the inventories at the beginning and the end of the year may be used. The inventory turnover for Lincoln Company is computed as follows:

	2008	2007
a. Cost of goods sold	$1,043,000	$820,000
Inventories:		
Beginning of year	$ 283,000	$311,000
End of year	264,000	283,000
Total	$ 547,000	$594,000
b. Average inventory (Total/2)	$ 273,500	$297,000
Inventory turnover (a/b)	3.8	2.8

The inventory turnover improved for Lincoln Company because of an increase in the cost of goods sold and a decrease in the average inventories. Differences across inventories, companies, and industries are too great to allow a general statement on what is a good inventory turnover. For example, a firm selling food should have a higher turnover than a firm selling furniture or jewelry. Likewise, the perishable foods department of a supermarket should have a higher turnover than the soaps and cleansers department. However, for each business or each department within a business, there is a reasonable turnover rate. A turnover lower than this rate could mean that inventory is not being managed properly.

Number of Days' Sales in Inventory Another measure of the relationship between the cost of goods sold and inventory is the **number of days' sales in inventory**. This measure is computed by dividing the average inventory by the average daily cost of goods sold (cost of goods sold divided by 365). The number of days' sales in inventory for Lincoln Company is computed as follows:

	2008	2007
a. Average inventory (Total/2)	$ 273,500	$297,000
Cost of goods sold	$1,043,000	$820,000
b. Average daily cost of goods sold (COGS/365 days)	$2,858	$2,247
Number of days' sales in inventory (a/b)	95.7	132.2

The number of days' sales in inventory is a rough measure of the length of time it takes to acquire, sell, and replace the inventory. For Lincoln Company, there is a major improvement in the number of days' sales in inventory during 2008. However, a comparison with earlier years and similar firms would be useful in assessing Lincoln Company's overall inventory management.

Example Exercise 14-5   objective 2

A company reports the following:

Cost of goods sold $560,000
Average inventory   112,000

Determine (a) the inventory turnover and (b) the number of days' sales in inventory. Round to one decimal place.

Follow My Example 14-5

a. Inventory Turnover = Cost of Goods Sold/Average Inventory
Inventory Turnover = $560,000/$112,000
Inventory Turnover = 5.0

b. Number of Days' Sales in Inventory = Average Inventory/Average Daily Cost of Goods Sold
Number of Days' Sales in Inventory = $112,000/($560,000/365) = $112,000/$1,534
Number of Days' Sales in Inventory = 73.0 days

For Practice: PE 14-5A, PE 14-5B

RATIO OF FIXED ASSETS TO LONG-TERM LIABILITIES

Long-term notes and bonds are often secured by mortgages on fixed assets. The **ratio of fixed assets to long-term liabilities** is a solvency measure that indicates the margin of safety of the noteholders or bondholders. It also indicates the ability of the business to borrow additional funds on a long-term basis. The ratio of fixed assets to long-term liabilities for Lincoln Company is as follows:

	2008	2007
a. Fixed assets (net)	$444,500	$470,000
b. Long-term liabilities	$100,000	$200,000
Ratio of fixed assets to long-term liabilities (a/b)	4.4	2.4

The major increase in this ratio at the end of 2008 is mainly due to liquidating one-half of Lincoln Company's long-term liabilities. If the company needs to borrow additional funds on a long-term basis in the future, it is in a strong position to do so.

RATIO OF LIABILITIES TO STOCKHOLDERS' EQUITY

REAL WORLD

The ratio of liabilities to stock-holders' equity varies across industries. For example, recent annual reports of some selected companies showed the following ratio of liabilities to stock-holders' equity:

Continental Airlines	66.8
Procter & Gamble	2.5
Circuit City Stores, Inc.	0.8

The airline industry generally uses more debt financing than the consumer product or retail industries. Thus, the airline in-dustry is generally considered more risky.

Claims against the total assets of a business are divided into two groups: (1) claims of creditors and (2) claims of owners. The relationship between the total claims of the creditors and owners—the **ratio of liabilities to stockholders' equity**—is a solvency measure that indicates the margin of safety for creditors. It also indicates the ability of the business to withstand adverse business conditions. When the claims of creditors are large in relation to the equity of the stockholders, there are usually significant in-terest payments. If earnings decline to the point where the company is unable to meet its interest payments, the business may be taken over by the creditors.

The relationship between creditor and stockholder equity is shown in the vertical analysis of the balance sheet. For example, the balance sheet of Lincoln Company in Exhibit 5 indicates that on December 31, 2008, liabilities represented 27.2% and stock-holders' equity represented 72.8% of the total liabilities and stockholders' equity (100.0%). Instead of expressing each item as a percent of the total, this relationship may be expressed as a ratio of one to the other, as follows:

	2008	2007
a. Total liabilities	$310,000	$443,000
b. Total stockholders' equity	$829,500	$787,500
Ratio of liabilities to stockholders' equity (a/b)	0.4	0.6

The balance sheet of Lincoln Company shows that the major factor affecting the change in the ratio was the $100,000 decrease in long-term liabilities during 2008. The ratio at the end of both years shows a large margin of safety for the creditors.

Example Exercise 14-6   objective 2

The following information was taken from Acme Company's balance sheet:

Fixed assets (net)	$1,400,000
Long-term liabilities	400,000
Total liabilities	560,000
Total stockholders' equity	1,400,000

Determine the company's (a) ratio of fixed assets to long-term liabilities and (b) ratio of liabilities to total stockholders' equity.

Follow My Example 14-6

a.   Ratio of Fixed Assets to Long-Term Liabilities = Fixed Assets/Long-Term Liabilities
     Ratio of Fixed Assets to Long-Term Liabilities = $1,400,000/$400,000
     Ratio of Fixed Assets to Long-Term Liabilities = 3.5

b.   Ratio of Liabilities to Total Stockholders' Equity = Total Liabilities/Total Stockholders' Equity
     Ratio of Liabilities to Total Stockholders' Equity = $560,000/$1,400,000
     Ratio of Liabilities to Total Stockholders' Equity = 0.4

For Practice: PE 14-6A, PE 14-6B

NUMBER OF TIMES INTEREST CHARGES EARNED

Corporations in some industries, such as airlines, normally have high ratios of debt to stockholders' equity. For such corporations, the relative risk of the debtholders is normally measured as the **number of times interest charges are earned**, sometimes called the *fixed charge coverage ratio*, during the year. The higher the ratio, the lower the risk that interest payments will not be made if earnings decrease. In other words, the higher the ratio, the greater the assurance that interest payments will be made on a continuing basis. This measure also indicates the general financial strength of the busi-ness, which is of interest to stockholders and employees as well as creditors.

The amount available to meet interest charges is not affected by taxes on income. This is because interest is deductible in determining taxable income. Thus, the number of times interest charges are earned for Lincoln Company is computed as shown below, rounded to one decimal place.

	2008	2007
Income before income tax	$162,500	$134,600
a. Add interest expense	6,000	12,000
b. Amount available to meet interest charges	$168,500	$146,600
Number of times interest charges earned (b/a)	28.1	12.2

These calculations indicate Lincoln Company has very high coverage of its interest charges for both years. Analysis such as this can also be applied to dividends on preferred stock. In such a case, net income is divided by the amount of preferred dividends to yield the *number of times preferred dividends are earned*. This measure indicates the risk that dividends to preferred stockholders may not be paid.

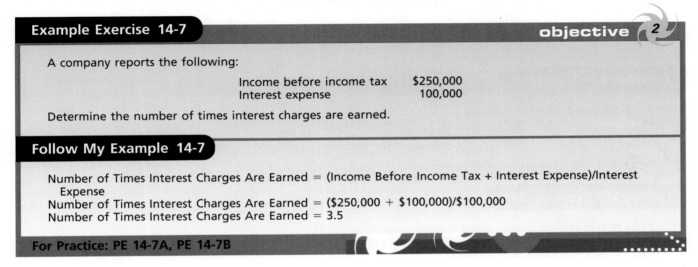

Example Exercise 14-7   objective 2

A company reports the following:

Income before income tax	$250,000
Interest expense	100,000

Determine the number of times interest charges are earned.

Follow My Example 14-7

Number of Times Interest Charges Are Earned = (Income Before Income Tax + Interest Expense)/Interest Expense
Number of Times Interest Charges Are Earned = ($250,000 + $100,000)/$100,000
Number of Times Interest Charges Are Earned = 3.5

For Practice: PE 14-7A, PE 14-7B

Profitability Analysis

objective 3

Apply financial statement analysis to assess the profitability of a business.

The ability of a business to earn profits depends on the effectiveness and efficiency of its operations as well as the resources available to it. Profitability analysis, therefore, focuses primarily on the relationship between operating results as reported in the income statement and resources available to the business as reported in the balance sheet. Major analyses used in assessing profitability include the following:

1. Ratio of net sales to assets
2. Rate earned on total assets
3. Rate earned on stockholders' equity
4. Rate earned on common stockholders' equity
5. Earnings per share on common stock
6. Price-earnings ratio
7. Dividends per share
8. Dividend yield

> Profitability analysis focuses on the relationship between operating results and the resources available to a business.

RATIO OF NET SALES TO ASSETS

The ratio of net sales to assets is a profitability measure that shows how effectively a firm utilizes its assets. For example, two competing businesses have equal amounts of assets. If the sales of one are twice the sales of the other, the business with the higher sales is making better use of its assets.

In computing the ratio of net sales to assets, any long-term investments are excluded from total assets, because such investments are unrelated to normal operations involving the sale of goods or services. Assets may be measured as the total at the end of the year, the average at the beginning and end of the year, or the average of monthly totals. The basic data and the computation of this ratio for Lincoln Company are as follows:

	2008	2007
a. Net sales	$1,498,000	$1,200,000
Total assets (excluding long-term investments):		
Beginning of year	$1,053,000	$1,010,000
End of year	1,044,500	1,053,000
Total	$2,097,500	$2,063,000
b. Average (Total/2)	$1,048,750	$1,031,500
Ratio of net sales to assets (a/b)	1.4	1.2

This ratio improved during 2008, primarily due to an increase in sales volume. A comparison with similar companies or industry averages would be helpful in assessing the effectiveness of Lincoln Company's use of its assets.

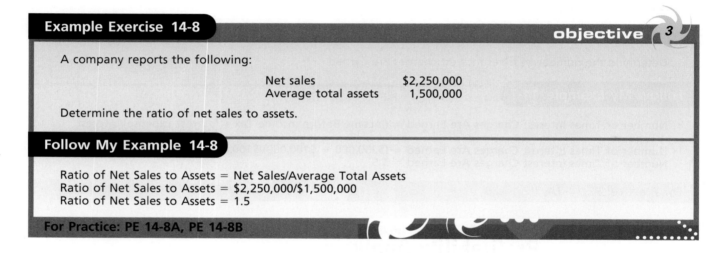

Example Exercise 14-8   **objective** 3

A company reports the following:

Net sales	$2,250,000
Average total assets	1,500,000

Determine the ratio of net sales to assets.

Follow My Example 14-8

Ratio of Net Sales to Assets = Net Sales/Average Total Assets
Ratio of Net Sales to Assets = $2,250,000/$1,500,000
Ratio of Net Sales to Assets = 1.5

For Practice: PE 14-8A, PE 14-8B

RATE EARNED ON TOTAL ASSETS

The **rate earned on total assets** measures the profitability of total assets without considering how the assets are financed. This rate is therefore not affected by whether the assets are financed primarily by creditors or stockholders.

The rate earned on total assets is computed by adding interest expense to net income and dividing this sum by the average total assets. Adding interest expense to net income eliminates the effect of whether the assets are financed by debt or equity. The rate earned by Lincoln Company on total assets is computed as follows:

	2008	2007
Net income	$ 91,000	$ 76,500
Plus interest expense	6,000	12,000
a. Total	$ 97,000	$ 88,500
Total assets:		
Beginning of year	$1,230,500	$1,187,500
End of year	1,139,500	1,230,500
Total	$2,370,000	$2,418,000
b. Average (Total/2)	$1,185,000	$1,209,000
Rate earned on total assets (a/b)	8.2%	7.3%

The rate earned on total assets of Lincoln Company during 2008 improved over that of 2007. A comparison with similar companies and industry averages would be useful in evaluating Lincoln Company's profitability on total assets.

Sometimes it may be desirable to compute the *rate of income from operations to total assets*. This is especially true if significant amounts of nonoperating income and expense are reported on the income statement. In this case, any assets related to the nonoperating income and expense items should be excluded from total assets in computing the rate. In addition, using income from operations (which is before tax) has the advantage of eliminating the effects of any changes in the tax structure on the rate of earnings. When evaluating published data on rates earned on assets, you should be careful to determine the exact nature of the measure that is reported.

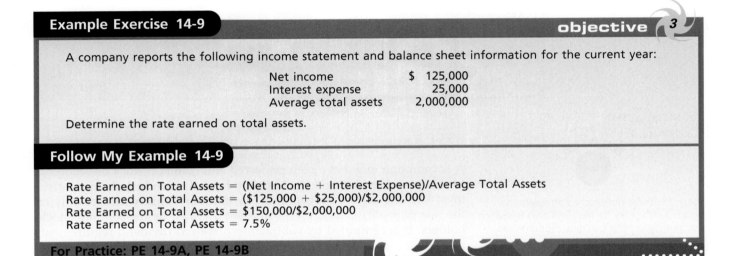

Example Exercise 14-9   objective ③

A company reports the following income statement and balance sheet information for the current year:

Net income	$ 125,000
Interest expense	25,000
Average total assets	2,000,000

Determine the rate earned on total assets.

Follow My Example 14-9

Rate Earned on Total Assets = (Net Income + Interest Expense)/Average Total Assets
Rate Earned on Total Assets = ($125,000 + $25,000)/$2,000,000
Rate Earned on Total Assets = $150,000/$2,000,000
Rate Earned on Total Assets = 7.5%

For Practice: PE 14-9A, PE 14-9B

RATE EARNED ON STOCKHOLDERS' EQUITY

Another measure of profitability is the **rate earned on stockholders' equity**. It is computed by dividing net income by average total stockholders' equity. In contrast to the rate earned on total assets, this measure emphasizes the rate of income earned on the amount invested by the stockholders.

The total stockholders' equity may vary throughout a period. For example, a business may issue or retire stock, pay dividends, and earn net income. If monthly amounts are not available, the average of the stockholders' equity at the beginning and the end of the year is normally used to compute this rate. For Lincoln Company, the rate earned on stockholders' equity is computed as follows:

	2008	2007
a. Net income	$ 91,000	$ 76,500
Stockholders' equity:		
Beginning of year	$ 787,500	$ 750,000
End of year	829,500	787,500
Total	$1,617,000	$1,537,500
b. Average (Total/2)	$ 808,500	$ 768,750
Rate earned on stockholders' equity (a/b)	11.3%	10.0%

The rate earned by a business on the equity of its stockholders is usually higher than the rate earned on total assets. This occurs when the amount earned on assets acquired with creditors' funds is more than the interest paid to creditors. This difference in the rate on stockholders' equity and the rate on total assets is called **leverage**.

Lincoln Company's rate earned on stockholders' equity for 2008, 11.3%, is greater than the rate of 8.2% earned on total assets. The leverage of 3.1% (11.3% − 8.2%) for 2008 compares favorably with the 2.7% (10.0% − 7.3%) leverage for 2007. Exhibit 8 shows the 2008 and 2007 leverages for Lincoln Company.

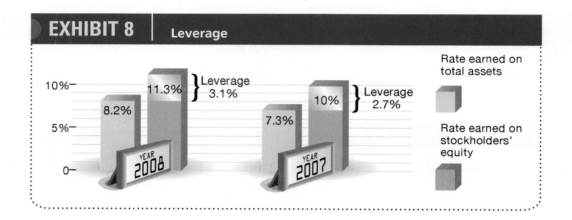

EXHIBIT 8 | Leverage

The approximate rates earned on assets and stockholders' equity for Molson Coors Brewing Company and Anheuser-Busch Companies, Inc., for a recent fiscal year are shown below.

	Molson Coors	Anheuser-Busch
Rate earned on assets	4%	15%
Rate earned on stockholders' equity	12%	83%

Anheuser-Busch has been more profitable and has benefited from a greater use of leverage than has Molson Coors.

RATE EARNED ON COMMON STOCKHOLDERS' EQUITY

A corporation may have both preferred and common stock outstanding. In this case, the common stockholders have the residual claim on earnings. The **rate earned on common stockholders' equity** focuses only on the rate of profits earned on the amount invested by the common stockholders. It is computed by subtracting preferred dividend requirements from the net income and dividing by the average common stockholders' equity.

Lincoln Company has $150,000 of 6% nonparticipating preferred stock outstanding on December 31, 2008 and 2007. Thus, the annual preferred dividend requirement is $9,000 ($150,000 × 6%). The common stockholders' equity equals the total stockholders' equity, including retained earnings, less the par of the preferred stock ($150,000). The basic data and the rate earned on common stockholders' equity for Lincoln Company are as follows:

	2008	2007
Net income	$ 91,000	$ 76,500
Preferred dividends	9,000	9,000
a. Remainder—identified with common stock	$ 82,000	$ 67,500
Common stockholders' equity:		
Beginning of year	$ 637,500	$ 600,000
End of year	679,500	637,500
Total	$1,317,000	$1,237,500
b. Average (Total/2)	$ 658,500	$ 618,750
Rate earned on common stockholders' equity (a/b)	12.5%	10.9%

The rate earned on common stockholders' equity differs from the rates earned by Lincoln Company on total assets and total stockholders' equity. This occurs if there are borrowed funds and also preferred stock outstanding, which rank ahead of the common shares in their claim on earnings. Thus, the concept of leverage, as we discussed in the preceding section, can also be applied to the use of funds from the sale of preferred stock as well as borrowing. Funds from both sources can be used in an attempt to increase the return on common stockholders' equity.

Example Exercise 14-10   objective **3**

A company reports the following:

Net income	$ 125,000
Preferred dividends	5,000
Average stockholders' equity	1,000,000
Average common stockholders' equity	800,000

Determine (a) the rate earned on stockholders' equity and (b) the rate earned on common stockholders' equity.

Follow My Example 14-10

a. Rate Earned on Stockholders' Equity = Net Income/Average Stockholders' Equity
    Rate Earned on Stockholders' Equity = $125,000/$1,000,000
    Rate Earned on Stockholders' Equity = 12.5%

b. Rate Earned on Common Stockholders' Equity = (Net Income − Preferred Dividends)/Average
                                                  Common Stockholders' Equity
    Rate Earned on Common Stockholders' Equity = ($125,000 − $5,000)/$800,000
    Rate Earned on Common Stockholders' Equity = 15%

For Practice: PE 14-10A, PE 14-10B

EARNINGS PER SHARE ON COMMON STOCK

One of the profitability measures often quoted by the financial press is **earnings per share (EPS) on common stock**. It is also normally reported in the income statement in corporate annual reports. If a company has issued only one class of stock, the earnings per share is computed by dividing net income by the number of shares of stock outstanding. If preferred and common stock are outstanding, the net income is first reduced by the amount of preferred dividend requirements.

The data on the earnings per share of common stock for Lincoln Company are as follows:

	2008	2007
Net income	$91,000	$76,500
Preferred dividends	9,000	9,000
a. Remainder—identified with common stock	$82,000	$67,500
b. Shares of common stock outstanding	50,000	50,000
Earnings per share on common stock (a/b)	$1.64	$1.35

PRICE-EARNINGS RATIO

Another profitability measure quoted by the financial press is the **price-earnings (P/E) ratio** on common stock. The price-earnings ratio is an indicator of a firm's future earnings prospects. It is computed by dividing the market price per share of common stock at a specific date by the annual earnings per share. To illustrate, assume that the market prices per common share are $41 at the end of 2008 and $27 at the end of 2007. The price-earnings ratio on common stock of Lincoln Company is computed as follows:

	2008	2007
Market price per share of common stock	$41.00	$27.00
Earnings per share on common stock	÷ 1.64	÷ 1.35
Price-earnings ratio on common stock	25	20

The price-earnings ratio indicates that a share of common stock of Lincoln Company was selling for 20 times the amount of earnings per share at the end of 2007. At the end of 2008, the common stock was selling for 25 times the amount of earnings per share.

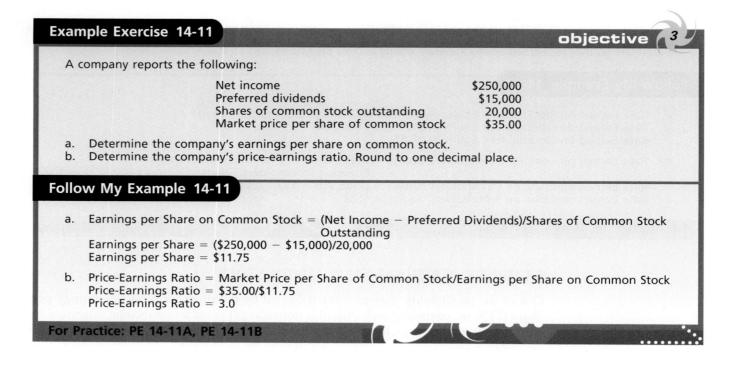

Example Exercise 14-11   objective **3**

A company reports the following:

Net income	$250,000
Preferred dividends	$15,000
Shares of common stock outstanding	20,000
Market price per share of common stock	$35.00

a. Determine the company's earnings per share on common stock.
b. Determine the company's price-earnings ratio. Round to one decimal place.

Follow My Example 14-11

a. Earnings per Share on Common Stock = (Net Income − Preferred Dividends)/Shares of Common Stock Outstanding
   Earnings per Share = ($250,000 − $15,000)/20,000
   Earnings per Share = $11.75

b. Price-Earnings Ratio = Market Price per Share of Common Stock/Earnings per Share on Common Stock
   Price-Earnings Ratio = $35.00/$11.75
   Price-Earnings Ratio = 3.0

For Practice: PE 14-11A, PE 14-11B

DIVIDENDS PER SHARE AND DIVIDEND YIELD

The dividend per share, dividend yield, and P/E ratio of a common stock are normally quoted on the daily listing of stock prices in *The Wall Street Journal* and on Yahoo!'s finance Web site.

Since the primary basis for dividends is earnings, dividends per share and earnings per share on common stock are commonly used by investors in assessing alternative stock investments. The dividends per share for Lincoln Company were $0.80 ($40,000/50,000 shares) for 2008 and $0.60 ($30,000/50,000 shares) for 2007.

Dividends per share can be reported with earnings per share to indicate the relationship between dividends and earnings. Comparing these two per share amounts indicates the extent to which the corporation is retaining its earnings for use in operations. Exhibit 9 shows these relationships for Lincoln Company.

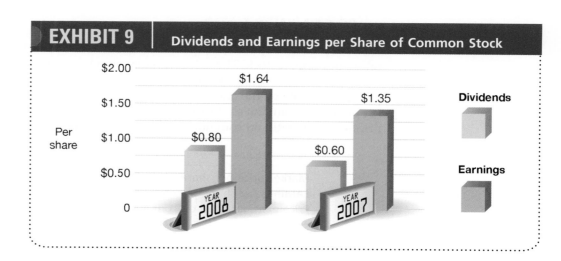

EXHIBIT 9 | **Dividends and Earnings per Share of Common Stock**

The **dividend yield** on common stock is a profitability measure that shows the rate of return to common stockholders in terms of cash dividends. It is of special interest to investors whose main investment objective is to receive current returns (dividends) on an investment rather than an increase in the market price of the investment. The dividend yield is computed by dividing the annual dividends paid per share of common stock by the market price per share on a specific date. To illustrate, assume that the market price was $41 at the end of 2008 and $27 at the end of 2007. The dividend yield on common stock of Lincoln Company is as follows:

	2008	2007
Dividends per share of common stock	$ 0.80	$ 0.60
Market price per share of common stock	÷ 41.00	÷ 27.00
Dividend yield on common stock	2.0%	2.2%

SUMMARY OF ANALYTICAL MEASURES

Exhibit 10 presents a summary of the analytical measures that we have discussed. These measures can be computed for most medium-size businesses. Depending on the specific business being analyzed, some measures might be omitted or additional measures could be developed. The type of industry, the capital structure, and the diversity of the business's operations usually affect the measures used. For example, analysis for an airline might include revenue per passenger mile and cost per available seat as measures. Likewise, analysis for a hotel might focus on occupancy rates.

Percentage analyses, ratios, turnovers, and other measures of financial position and operating results are useful analytical measures. They are helpful in assessing a business's past performance and predicting its future. They are not, however, a substitute for sound judgment. In selecting and interpreting analytical measures, conditions peculiar to a business or its industry should be considered. In addition, the influence of the general economic and business environment should be considered.

In determining trends, the interrelationship of the measures used in assessing a business should be carefully studied. Comparable indexes of earlier periods should also be studied. Data from competing businesses may be useful in assessing the efficiency of operations for the firm under analysis. In making such comparisons, however, the effects of differences in the accounting methods used by the businesses should be considered.

EXHIBIT 10   Summary of Analytical Measures

	Method of Computation	Use
Solvency measures:		
Working Capital	Current Assets − Current Liabilities	To indicate the ability to meet currently maturing obligations
Current Ratio	$\dfrac{\text{Current Assets}}{\text{Current Liabilities}}$	
Quick Ratio	$\dfrac{\text{Quick Assets}}{\text{Current Liabilities}}$	To indicate instant debt-paying ability
Accounts Receivable Turnover	$\dfrac{\text{Net Sales}}{\text{Average Accounts Receivable}}$	To assess the efficiency in collecting receivables and in the management of credit
Numbers of Days' Sales in Receivables	$\dfrac{\text{Average Accounts Receivable}}{\text{Average Daily Sales}}$	
Inventory Turnover	$\dfrac{\text{Cost of Goods Sold}}{\text{Average Inventory}}$	To assess the efficiency in the management of inventory
Number of Days' Sales in Inventory	$\dfrac{\text{Average Inventory}}{\text{Average Daily Cost of Goods Sold}}$	
Ratio of Fixed Assets to Long-Term Liabilities	$\dfrac{\text{Fixed Assets (net)}}{\text{Long-Term Liabilities}}$	To indicate the margin of safety to long-term creditors
Ratio of Liabilities to Stockholders' Equity	$\dfrac{\text{Total Liabilities}}{\text{Total Stockholders' Equity}}$	To indicate the margin of safety to creditors
Number of Times Interest Charges Earned	$\dfrac{\text{Income Before Income Tax + Interest Expense}}{\text{Interest Expense}}$	To assess the risk to debtholders in terms of number of times interest charges were earned
Profitability measures:		
Ratio of Net Sales to Assets	$\dfrac{\text{Net Sales}}{\text{Average Total Assets (excluding long-term investments)}}$	To assess the effectiveness in the use of assets
Rate Earned on Total Assets	$\dfrac{\text{Net Income + Interest Expense}}{\text{Average Total Assets}}$	To assess the profitability of the assets
Rate Earned on Stockholders' Equity	$\dfrac{\text{Net Income}}{\text{Average Total Stockholders' Equity}}$	To assess the profitability of the investment by stockholders
Rate Earned on Common Stockholders' Equity	$\dfrac{\text{Net Income − Preferred Dividends}}{\text{Average Common Stockholders' Equity}}$	To assess the profitability of the investment by common stockholders
Earnings per Share on Common Stock	$\dfrac{\text{Net Income − Preferred Dividends}}{\text{Shares of Common Stock Outstanding}}$	
Price-Earnings Ratio	$\dfrac{\text{Market Price per Share of Common Stock}}{\text{Earnings per Share of Common Stock}}$	To indicate future earnings prospects, based on the relationship between market value of common stock and earnings
Dividends per Share of Common Stock	$\dfrac{\text{Dividends}}{\text{Shares of Common Stock Outstanding}}$	To indicate the extent to which earnings are being distributed to common stockholders
Dividend Yield	$\dfrac{\text{Dividends per Share of Common Stock}}{\text{Market Price per Share of Common Stock}}$	To indicate the rate of return to common stockholders in terms of dividends

Integrity, Objectivity, and Ethics in Business

ETHICS

ONE BAD APPLE

A recent survey by *CFO* magazine reported that 47% of chief financial officers have been pressured by the chief executive officer to use questionable accounting. In addition, only 38% of those surveyed feel less pressure to use aggressive accounting today than in years past, while 20% believe there is more pressure. Perhaps more troublesome is the chief financial officers' confidence in the quality of financial information, with only 27% being "very confident" in the quality of financial information presented by public companies.

Source: D. Durfee, "It's Better (and Worse) Than You Think," *CFO*, May 3, 2004.

Corporate Annual Reports

objective 4

Describe the contents of corporate annual reports.

Public corporations are required to issue annual reports to their stockholders and other interested parties. Such reports summarize the corporation's operating activities for the past year and plans for the future. There are many variations in the order and form for presenting the major sections of annual reports. However, one section of the annual report is devoted to the financial statements, including the accompanying notes. In addition, annual reports usually include the following sections:

1. Management discussion and analysis
2. Report on adequacy of internal control
3. Report on fairness of financial statements

In the following paragraphs, we describe these sections. Each section, as well as the financial statements, is illustrated in the annual report for Williams-Sonoma, Inc., in Appendix B.

MANAGEMENT DISCUSSION AND ANALYSIS

A required disclosure in the annual report filed with the Securities and Exchange Commission is the **Management's Discussion and Analysis (MD&A)**. The MD&A provides critical information in interpreting the financial statements and assessing the future of the company.

The MD&A includes an analysis of the results of operations and discusses management's opinion about future performance. It compares the prior year's income statement with the current year's to explain changes in sales, significant expenses, gross profit, and income from operations. For example, an increase in sales may be explained by referring to higher shipment volume or stronger prices.

The MD&A also includes an analysis of the company's financial condition. It compares significant balance sheet items between successive years to explain changes in liquidity and capital resources. In addition, the MD&A discusses significant risk exposure.

A new subsection of the MD&A required by the Sarbanes-Oxley Act must now include a section describing any "off-balance-sheet" arrangements. Such arrangements are discussed in advanced accounting courses.

REPORT ON ADEQUACY OF INTERNAL CONTROL

The Sarbanes-Oxley Act of 2002 requires management to provide a report stating their responsibility for establishing and maintaining internal control. In addition, the report must state management's conclusion concerning the effectiveness of internal controls over financial reporting. The act also requires a public accounting firm to examine and verify management's conclusions regarding internal control. Thus, public companies must provide two reports, one by management and one by a public accounting firm, certifying the management report as accurate. In some situations, the auditor may combine these reports into a single report. The combined report for Williams-Sonoma, Inc., is included in the annual report in Appendix B.

REPORT ON FAIRNESS OF FINANCIAL STATEMENTS

In addition to a public accounting firm's internal control report, all publicly held corporations are also required to have an independent audit (examination) of their financial statements. For the financial statements of most companies, the CPAs who conduct the audit render an opinion on the fairness of the statements. An opinion stating that the financial statements fairly represent the financial condition of a public company is said to be an unqualified, or "clean," opinion. The Independent Auditors' Report for Williams-Sonoma, Inc., is an unqualified opinion.

Business Connections

REAL WORLD

INVESTING STRATEGIES

How do people make investment decisions? Investment decisions, like any major purchase, must meet the needs of the buyer. For example, if you have a family of five and are thinking about buying a new car, you probably wouldn't buy a two-seat sports car. It just wouldn't meet your objectives or fit your lifestyle. Alternatively, if you are a young single person, a minivan might not meet your immediate needs. Investors buy stocks in the same way, buying stocks that match their investment style and their financial needs. Two common approaches are value and growth investing.

Value Investing

Value investors search for undervalued stocks. That is, the investor tries to find companies whose value is not reflected in their stock price. These are typically quiet, "boring" companies with excellent financial performance that are temporarily out of favor in the stock market. This investment approach assumes that the stock's price will eventually rise to match the company's value. The most successful investor of all time, Warren Buffett, uses this approach almost exclusively. Naturally, the key to successful value investing is to accurately determine a stock's value. This will often include analyzing a company's financial ratios, as discussed in this chapter, compared to target ratios and industry norms. For example,

the stock of Darden Restaurants, the operator of restaurant chains including Olive Garden and Red Lobster, was selling for $18.35 on May 25, 2003, a value relative to its earnings per share of $1.36. Over the next three years, the company's stock price more than doubled, reaching $41.44 on February 17, 2006.

Growth Investing

The growth investor tries to identify companies that have the potential to grow sales and earnings through new products, markets, or opportunities. Growth companies are often newer companies that are still unproven but that possess unique technologies or capabilities. The strategy is to purchase these companies before their potential becomes obvious, hoping to profit from relatively large increases in the company's stock price. This approach, however, carries the risk that the growth may not occur. Growth investors use many of the ratios discussed in this chapter to identify high-potential growth companies. For example, in March 2003, Research in Motion Limited, maker of the popular BlackBerry® handheld mobile device, reported earnings per share of −$0.96, and the company's stock price was trading near $5 per share. In the following two years, the company's sales increased by 340%, earnings increased to $1.14 per share, and the company's stock price rose above $75 per share.

At a Glance ↘

1. List basic financial statement analytical procedures.			
Key Points	**Key Learning Outcomes**	**Example Exercises**	**Practice Exercises**
The basic financial statements provide much of the information users need to make economic decisions. Analytical procedures are used to compare items on a current financial statement with related items on earlier statements, or to examine relationships within a financial statement.	• Prepare a horizontal analysis from a company's financial statements. • Prepare a vertical analysis from a company's financial statements.	14-1	14-1A, 14-1B
	• Prepare common-size financial statements.	14-2	14-2A, 14-2B

2. Apply financial statement analysis to assess the solvency of a business.			
Key Points	**Key Learning Outcomes**	**Example Exercises**	**Practice Exercises**
All users of financial statements are interested in the ability of a business to pay its debts (solvency) and earn income (profitability). Solvency and profitability are interrelated. Solvency analysis is normally assessed by examining the following balance sheet relationships: (1) current position analysis, (2) accounts receivable analysis, (3) inventory analysis, (4) the ratio of fixed assets to long-term liabilities, (5) the ratio of liabilities to stockholders' equity, and (6) the number of times interest charges are earned.	• Determine working capital. • Calculate and interpret the current ratio.	14-3	14-3A, 14-3B
	• Calculate and interpret the quick ratio.	14-3	14-3A, 14-3B
	• Calculate and interpret accounts receivable turnover.	14-4	14-4A, 14-4B
	• Calculate and interpret number of days' sales in receivables.	14-4	14-4A, 14-4B
	• Calculate and interpret inventory turnover.	14-5	14-5A, 14-5B
	• Calculate and interpret number of days' sales in inventory.	14-5	14-5A, 14-5B
	• Calculate and interpret the ratio of fixed assets to long-term liabilities.	14-6	14-6A, 14-6B
	• Calculate and interpret the ratio of liabilities to stockholders' equity.	14-6	14-6A, 14-6B
	• Calculate and interpret the number of times interest charges are earned.	14-7	14-7A, 14-7B

(continued)

3. Apply financial statement analysis to assess the profitability of a business.

Key Points	Key Learning Outcomes	Example Exercises	Practice Exercises
Profitability analysis focuses mainly on the relationship between operating results (income statement) and resources available (balance sheet). Major analyses include (1) the ratio of net sales to assets, (2) the rate earned on total assets, (3) the rate earned on stockholders' equity, (4) the rate earned on common stockholders' equity, (5) earnings per share on common stock, (6) the price-earnings ratio, (7) dividends per share, and (8) dividend yield.	• Calculate and interpret the ratio of net sales to assets.	**14-8**	14-8A, 14-8B
	• Calculate and interpret the rate earned on total assets.	**14-9**	14-9A, 14-9B
	• Calculate and interpret the rate earned on stockholders' equity.	**14-10**	14-10A, 14-10B
	• Calculate and interpret the rate earned on common stockholders' equity.	**14-10**	14-10A, 14-10B
	• Calculate and interpret the earnings per share on common stock.	**14-11**	14-11A, 14-11B
	• Calculate and interpret the price-earnings ratio.	**14-11**	14-11A, 14-11B
	• Calculate and interpret the dividends per share and dividend yield.		
	• Describe the uses and limitations of analytical measures.		

4. Describe the contents of corporate annual reports.

Key Points	Key Learning Outcomes	Example Exercises	Practice Exercises
Corporations normally issue annual reports to their stockholders and other interested parties. Such reports summarize the corporation's operating activities for the past year and plans for the future.	• Describe the elements of a corporate annual report.		

Key Terms

accounts receivable turnover (573)
common-size statement (569)
current ratio (571)
dividend yield (583)
earnings per share (EPS) on common stock (581)
horizontal analysis (564)
inventory turnover (574)
leverage (579)
Management's Discussion and Analysis (MD&A) (585)
number of days' sales in inventory (575)

number of days' sales in receivables (573)
number of times interest charges are earned (576)
price-earnings (P/E) ratio (581)
profitability (570)
quick assets (572)
quick ratio (572)
rate earned on common stockholders' equity (580)
rate earned on stockholders' equity (579)
rate earned on total assets (578)

ratio of fixed assets to long-term liabilities (575)
ratio of liabilities to stockholders' equity (576)
solvency (570)
vertical analysis (567)

Illustrative Problem

Rainbow Paint Co.'s comparative financial statements for the years ending December 31, 2008 and 2007, are as follows. The market price of Rainbow Paint Co.'s common stock was $30 on December 31, 2007, and $25 on December 31, 2008.

Rainbow Paint Co.
Comparative Income Statement
For the Years Ended December 31, 2008 and 2007

	2008	2007
Sales	$5,125,000	$3,257,600
Sales returns and allowances	125,000	57,600
Net sales	$5,000,000	$3,200,000
Cost of goods sold	3,400,000	2,080,000
Gross profit	$1,600,000	$1,120,000
Selling expenses	$ 650,000	$ 464,000
Administrative expenses	325,000	224,000
Total operating expenses	$ 975,000	$ 688,000
Income from operations	$ 625,000	$ 432,000
Other income	25,000	19,200
	$ 650,000	$ 451,200
Other expense (interest)	105,000	64,000
Income before income tax	$ 545,000	$ 387,200
Income tax expense	300,000	176,000
Net income	$ 245,000	$ 211,200

Rainbow Paint Co.
Comparative Retained Earnings Statement
For the Years Ended December 31, 2008 and 2007

	2008	2007
Retained earnings, January 1	$723,000	$581,800
Add net income for year	245,000	211,200
Total	$968,000	$793,000
Deduct dividends:		
On preferred stock	$ 40,000	$ 40,000
On common stock	45,000	30,000
Total	$ 85,000	$ 70,000
Retained earnings, December 31	$883,000	$723,000

(continued)

Rainbow Paint Co.
Comparative Balance Sheet
December 31, 2008 and 2007

	2008	2007
Assets		
Current assets:		
Cash	$ 175,000	$ 125,000
Marketable securities	150,000	50,000
Accounts receivable (net)	425,000	325,000
Inventories	720,000	480,000
Prepaid expenses	30,000	20,000
Total current assets	$1,500,000	$1,000,000
Long-term investments.	250,000	225,000
Property, plant, and equipment (net)	2,093,000	1,948,000
Total assets	$3,843,000	$3,173,000
Liabilities		
Current liabilities	$ 750,000	$ 650,000
Long-term liabilities:		
Mortgage note payable, 10%, due 2011	$ 410,000	—
Bonds payable, 8%, due 2014	800,000	$ 800,000
Total long-term liabilities	$1,210,000	$ 800,000
Total liabilities	$1,960,000	$1,450,000
Stockholders' Equity		
Preferred 8% stock, $100 par	$ 500,000	$ 500,000
Common stock, $10 par	500,000	500,000
Retained earnings	883,000	723,000
Total stockholders' equity	$1,883,000	$1,723,000
Total liabilities and stockholders' equity	$3,843,000	$3,173,000

Instructions

Determine the following measures for 2008:

1. Working capital
2. Current ratio
3. Quick ratio
4. Accounts receivable turnover
5. Number of days' sales in receivables
6. Inventory turnover
7. Number of days' sales in inventory
8. Ratio of fixed assets to long-term liabilities
9. Ratio of liabilities to stockholders' equity
10. Number of times interest charges earned
11. Number of times preferred dividends earned
12. Ratio of net sales to assets
13. Rate earned on total assets
14. Rate earned on stockholders' equity
15. Rate earned on common stockholders' equity
16. Earnings per share on common stock
17. Price-earnings ratio
18. Dividends per share of common stock
19. Dividend yield

Solution
(Ratios are rounded to the nearest single digit after the decimal point.)

1. Working capital: $750,000
   $1,500,000 − $750,000

2. Current ratio: 2.0
   $1,500,000/$750,000

3. Quick ratio: 1.0
   $750,000/$750,000

4. Accounts receivable turnover: 13.3
   $5,000,000/[($425,000 + $325,000)/2]

5. Number of days' sales in receivables: 27.4 days
   $5,000,000/365 = $13,699
   $375,000/$13,699

6. Inventory turnover: 5.7
   $3,400,000/[($720,000 + $480,000)/2]

7. Number of days' sales in inventory: 64.4 days
   $3,400,000/365 = $9,315
   $600,000/$9,315

8. Ratio of fixed assets to long-term liabilities: 1.7
   $2,093,000/$1,210,000

9. Ratio of liabilities to stockholders' equity: 1.0
   $1,960,000/$1,883,000

10. Number of times interest charges earned: 6.2
    ($545,000 + $105,000)/$105,000

11. Number of times preferred dividends earned: 6.1
    $245,000/$40,000

12. Ratio of net sales to assets: 1.5
    $5,000,000/[($3,593,000 + $2,948,000)/2]

13. Rate earned on total assets: 10.0%
    ($245,000 + $105,000)/[($3,843,000 + $3,173,000)/2]

14. Rate earned on stockholders' equity: 13.6%
    $245,000/[($1,883,000 + $1,723,000)/2]

15. Rate earned on common stockholders' equity: 15.7%
    ($245,000 − $40,000)/[($1,383,000 + $1,223,000)/2]

16. Earnings per share on common stock: $4.10
    ($245,000 − $40,000)/50,000

17. Price-earnings ratio: 6.1
    $25/$4.10

18. Dividends per share of common stock: $0.90
    $45,000/50,000 shares

19. Dividend yield: 3.6%
    $0.90/$25

Self-Examination Questions

(Answers at End of Chapter)

1. What type of analysis is indicated by the following?

	Amount	Percent
Current assets	$100,000	20%
Property, plant, and equipment	400,000	80
Total assets	$500,000	100%

A. Vertical analysis
B. Horizontal analysis
C. Profitability analysis
D. Contribution margin analysis

2. Which of the following measures indicates the ability of a firm to pay its current liabilities?
A. Working capital
B. Current ratio
C. Quick ratio
D. All of the above

3. The ratio determined by dividing total current assets by total current liabilities is:
A. current ratio.
B. working capital ratio.
C. bankers' ratio.
D. all of the above.

4. The ratio of the quick assets to current liabilities, which indicates the "instant" debt-paying ability of a firm, is the:
A. current ratio.
B. working capital ratio.
C. quick ratio.
D. bankers' ratio.

5. A measure useful in evaluating efficiency in the management of inventories is the:
A. working capital ratio.
B. quick ratio.
C. number of days' sales in inventory.
D. ratio of fixed assets to long-term liabilities.

Eye Openers

1. What is the difference between horizontal and vertical analysis of financial statements?
2. What is the advantage of using comparative statements for financial analysis rather than statements for a single date or period?
3. The current year's amount of net income (after income tax) is 20% larger than that of the preceding year. Does this indicate an improved operating performance? Discuss.
4. How would you respond to a horizontal analysis that showed an expense increasing by over 80%?
5. How would the current and quick ratios of a service business compare?
6. For Lindsay Corporation, the working capital at the end of the current year is $8,000 less than the working capital at the end of the preceding year, reported as follows:

	Current Year	Preceding Year
Current assets:		
Cash, marketable securities, and receivables	$35,000	$36,000
Inventories	55,000	42,000
Total current assets	$90,000	$78,000
Current liabilities	50,000	30,000
Working capital	$40,000	$48,000

Has the current position improved? Explain.
7. Why would the accounts receivable turnover ratio be different between Wal-Mart and Procter & Gamble?
8. A company that grants terms of n/45 on all sales has a yearly accounts receivable turnover, based on monthly averages, of 5. Is this a satisfactory turnover? Discuss.
9. a. Why is it advantageous to have a high inventory turnover?
   b. Is it possible for the inventory turnover to be too high? Discuss.
   c. Is it possible to have a high inventory turnover and a high number of days' sales in inventory? Discuss.
10. What do the following data taken from a comparative balance sheet indicate about the company's ability to borrow additional funds on a long-term basis in the current year as compared to the preceding year?

	Current Year	Preceding Year
Fixed assets (net)	$300,000	$300,000
Total long-term liabilities	100,000	120,000

11. a. How does the rate earned on total assets differ from the rate earned on stockholders' equity?
    b. Which ratio is normally higher? Explain.
12. a. Why is the rate earned on stockholders' equity by a thriving business ordinarily higher than the rate earned on total assets?
    b. Should the rate earned on common stockholders' equity normally be higher or lower than the rate earned on total stockholders' equity? Explain.
13. The net income (after income tax) of Choi Inc. was $15 per common share in the latest year and $60 per common share for the preceding year. At the beginning of the latest year, the number of shares outstanding was doubled by a stock split. There were no other changes in the amount of stock outstanding. What were the earnings per share in the preceding year, adjusted for comparison with the latest year?
14. The price-earnings ratio for the common stock of Cotter Company was 10 at December 31, the end of the current fiscal year. What does the ratio indicate about the selling price of the common stock in relation to current earnings?
15. Why would the dividend yield differ significantly from the rate earned on common stockholders' equity?
16. Favorable business conditions may bring about certain seemingly unfavorable ratios, and unfavorable business operations may result in apparently favorable ratios. For example, Trivec Company increased its sales and net income substantially for the current year, yet the current ratio at the end of the year is lower than at the beginning of the year. Discuss some possible causes of the apparent weakening of the current position, while sales and net income have increased substantially.

Practice Exercises

PE 14-1A
Horizontal analysis
obj. 1

The comparative marketable securities and inventory balances for a company are provided below.

	2008	2007
Marketable securities	$68,200	$55,000
Inventory	63,700	65,000

Based on this information, what is the amount and percentage of increase or decrease that would be shown in a balance sheet with horizontal analysis?

PE 14-1B
Horizontal analysis
obj. 1

The comparative accounts payable and long-term debt balances of a company are provided below.

	2008	2007
Accounts payable	$141,600	$120,000
Long-term debt	150,000	125,000

Based on this information, what is the amount and percentage of increase or decrease that would be shown in a balance sheet with horizontal analysis?

PE 14-2A
Common-size financial statements
obj. 1

Income statement information for Washburn Corporation is provided below.

Sales	$400,000
Cost of goods sold	340,000
Gross profit	$ 60,000

Prepare a vertical analysis of the income statement for Washburn Corporation.

PE 14-2B
Common-size financial statements
obj. 1

Income statement information for Lewis Corporation is provided below.

Sales	$250,000
Gross profit	100,000
Net income	50,000

Prepare a vertical analysis of the income statement for Lewis Corporation.

PE 14-3A
Current position analysis
obj. 2

The following items are reported on a company's balance sheet:

Cash	$125,000
Marketable securities	40,000
Accounts receivable (net)	30,000
Inventory	120,000
Accounts payable	150,000

Determine (a) the current ratio and (b) the quick ratio. Round to one decimal place.

PE 14-3B
Current position analysis
obj. 2

The following items are reported on a company's balance sheet:

Cash	$275,000
Marketable securities	200,000
Accounts receivable (net)	625,000
Inventory	300,000
Accounts payable	800,000

Determine (a) the current ratio and (b) the quick ratio. Round to one decimal place.

PE 14-4A
Accounts receivable analysis
obj. 2

A company reports the following:

Net sales	$450,000
Average accounts receivable (net)	37,500

Determine (a) the accounts receivable turnover and (b) the number of days' sales in receivables. Round to one decimal place.

PE 14-4B
Accounts receivable analysis
obj. 2

A company reports the following:

Net sales	$225,000
Average accounts receivable (net)	25,000

Determine (a) the accounts receivable turnover and (b) the number of days' sales in receivables. Round to one decimal place.

PE 14-5A
Inventory analysis
obj. 2

A company reports the following:

Cost of goods sold	$465,000
Average inventory	71,500

Determine (a) the inventory turnover and (b) the number of days' sales in inventory. Round to one decimal place.

PE 14-5B
Inventory analysis
obj. 2

A company reports the following:

Cost of goods sold	$330,000
Average inventory	55,000

Determine (a) the inventory turnover and (b) the number of days' sales in inventory. Round to one decimal place.

PE 14-6A
Ratio of fixed assets to long-term liabilities and ratio of liabilities to stockholders' equity
obj. 2

The following information was taken from Straub Company's balance sheet:

Fixed assets (net)	$700,000
Long-term liabilities	218,750
Total liabilities	235,000
Total stockholders' equity	940,000

Determine the company's (a) ratio of fixed assets to long-term liabilities and (b) ratio of liabilities to stockholders' equity.

PE 14-6B
Ratio of fixed assets to long-term liabilities and ratio of liabilities to stockholders' equity
obj. 2

The following information was taken from Tristar Company's balance sheet:

Fixed assets (net)	$900,000
Long-term liabilities	625,000
Total liabilities	850,000
Total stockholders' equity	500,000

Determine the company's (a) ratio of fixed assets to long-term liabilities and (b) ratio of liabilities to stockholders' equity.

PE 14-7A
Number of times interest charges are earned
obj. 2

A company reports the following:

Income before income tax	$375,000
Interest expense	120,000

Determine the number of times interest charges are earned.

PE 14-7B
Number of times interest charges are earned
obj. 2

A company reports the following:

Income before income tax	$625,000
Interest expense	160,000

Determine the number of times interest charges are earned.

PE 14-8A
Ratio of net sales to assets
obj. 3

A company reports the following:

Net sales	$1,170,000
Average total assets	650,000

Determine the ratio of net sales to assets.

PE 14-8B
Ratio of net sales to assets
obj. 3

A company reports the following:

Net sales	$1,520,000
Average total assets	950,000

Determine the ratio of net sales to assets.

PE 14-9A
Rate earned on total assets
obj. 3

A company reports the following income statement and balance sheet information for the current year:

Net income	$ 225,000
Interest expense	20,000
Average total assets	3,250,000

Determine the rate earned on total assets.

PE 14-9B
Rate earned on total assets
obj. 3

A company reports the following income statement and balance sheet information for the current year:

Net income	$ 115,000
Interest expense	10,000
Average total assets	1,250,000

Determine the rate earned on total assets.

PE 14-10A
Rate earned on stockholders' equity and rate earned on common stockholders' equity
obj. 3

A company reports the following:

Net income	$ 225,000
Preferred dividends	20,000
Average stockholders' equity	1,750,000
Average common stockholders' equity	1,000,000

Determine (a) the rate earned on stockholders' equity and (b) the rate earned on common stockholders' equity. Round to one decimal place.

PE 14-10B
Rate earned on stockholders' equity and rate earned on common stockholders' equity
obj. 3

A company reports the following:

Net income	$115,000
Preferred dividends	10,000
Average stockholders' equity	850,000
Average common stockholders' equity	750,000

Determine (a) the rate earned on stockholders' equity and (b) the rate earned on common stockholders' equity.

PE 14-11A
Earnings per share on common stock and price-earnings ratio
obj. 3

A company reports the following:

Net income	$115,000
Preferred dividends	$15,000
Shares of common stock outstanding	20,000
Market price per share of common stock	$65.00

a. Determine the company's earnings per share on common stock.
b. Determine the company's price-earnings ratio.

PE 14-11B
Earnings per share on common stock and price-earnings ratio
obj. 3

A company reports the following:

Net income	$525,000
Preferred dividends	$25,000
Shares of common stock outstanding	50,000
Market price per share of common stock	$75.00

a. Determine the company's earnings per share on common stock.
b. Determine the company's price-earnings ratio.

Exercises

EX 14-1
Vertical analysis of income statement
obj. 1

✓ a. 2008 net income: $37,500; 5% of sales

Revenue and expense data for Jazz-Tech Communications Co. are as follows:

	2008	2007
Sales	$750,000	$600,000
Cost of goods sold	450,000	312,000
Selling expenses	120,000	126,000
Administrative expenses	105,000	84,000
Income tax expense	37,500	30,000

a. Prepare an income statement in comparative form, stating each item for both 2008 and 2007 as a percent of sales. Round to one decimal place.

b. ▭▭▭▶ Comment on the significant changes disclosed by the comparative income statement.

EX 14-2
Vertical analysis of income statement
obj. 1

✓ *a. Fiscal year 2004 income from continuing operations, 26.7% of revenues*

The following comparative income statement (in thousands of dollars) for the fiscal years 2003 and 2004 was adapted from the annual report of Speedway Motorsports, Inc., owner and operator of several major motor speedways, such as the Atlanta, Texas, and Las Vegas Motor Speedways.

	Fiscal Year 2004	Fiscal Year 2003
Revenues:		
Admissions	$156,718	$150,253
Event-related revenue	137,074	127,055
NASCAR broadcasting revenue	110,016	90,682
Other operating revenue	42,711	36,539
Total revenue	$446,519	$404,529
Expenses and other:		
Direct expense of events	$ 81,432	$ 77,962
NASCAR purse and sanction fees	78,473	69,691
Other direct expenses	102,053	101,408
General and administrative	65,152	58,698
Total expenses and other	$327,110	$307,759
Income from continuing operations	$119,409	$ 96,770

a. Prepare a comparative income statement for fiscal years 2003 and 2004 in vertical form, stating each item as a percent of revenues. Round to one decimal place.

b. ▭▭▭▶ Comment on the significant changes.

EX 14-3
Common-size income statement
obj. 1

✓ *a. Jaribo net income: $85,000; 6.8% of sales*

Revenue and expense data for the current calendar year for Jaribo Communications Company and for the communications industry are as follows. The Jaribo Communications Company data are expressed in dollars. The communications industry averages are expressed in percentages.

	Jaribo Communications Company	Communications Industry Average
Sales	$1,265,000	101.0%
Sales returns and allowances	15,000	1.0
Cost of goods sold	450,000	41.0
Selling expenses	525,000	38.0
Administrative expenses	143,750	10.5
Other income	22,500	1.2
Other expense (interest)	18,750	1.7
Income tax expense	50,000	4.0

a. Prepare a common-size income statement comparing the results of operations for Jaribo Communications Company with the industry average. Round to one decimal place.

b. ▭▭▭▶ As far as the data permit, comment on significant relationships revealed by the comparisons.

EX 14-4
Vertical analysis of balance sheet
obj. 1

Balance sheet data for the Dover Hot Tub Company on December 31, the end of the fiscal year, are shown at the top of the following page.

✓ *Retained earnings,*
Dec. 31, 2008, 47.5%

	2008	2007
Current assets	$768,000	$250,000
Property, plant, and equipment	336,000	650,000
Intangible assets	96,000	100,000
Current liabilities	270,000	175,000
Long-term liabilities	300,000	255,000
Common stock	60,000	70,000
Retained earnings	570,000	500,000

Prepare a comparative balance sheet for 2008 and 2007, stating each asset as a percent of total assets and each liability and stockholders' equity item as a percent of the total liabilities and stockholders' equity. Round to one decimal place.

EX 14-5
Horizontal analysis of the income statement
obj. **1**

✓ *a. Net income decrease,*
53.3%

Income statement data for Web-pics Company for the years ended December 31, 2008 and 2007, are as follows:

	2008	2007
Sales	$117,000	$150,000
Cost of goods sold	56,000	70,000
Gross profit	$ 61,000	$ 80,000
Selling expenses	$ 36,000	$ 37,500
Administrative expenses	12,500	10,000
Total operating expenses	$ 48,500	$ 47,500
Income before income tax	$ 12,500	$ 32,500
Income tax expense	2,000	10,000
Net income	$ 10,500	$ 22,500

a. Prepare a comparative income statement with horizontal analysis, indicating the increase (decrease) for 2008 when compared with 2007. Round to one decimal place.
b. ▭▭▭▶ What conclusions can be drawn from the horizontal analysis?

EX 14-6
Current position analysis
obj. **2**

✓ *a. 2008 working capital,*
$1,265,000

The following data were taken from the balance sheet of Outdoor Suppliers Company:

	Dec. 31, 2008	Dec. 31, 2007
Cash	$325,000	$300,000
Marketable securities	270,000	256,000
Accounts and notes receivable (net)	440,000	430,000
Inventories	675,000	557,000
Prepaid expenses	130,000	81,000
Accounts and notes payable (short-term)	425,000	450,000
Accrued liabilities	150,000	130,000

a. Determine for each year (1) the working capital, (2) the current ratio, and (3) the quick ratio. Round ratios to one decimal place.
b. ▭▭▭▶ What conclusions can be drawn from these data as to the company's ability to meet its currently maturing debts?

EX 14-7
Current position analysis
obj. **2**

✓ *a. (1) Dec. 25, 2004,*
current ratio, 1.2

PepsiCo, Inc., the parent company of Frito-Lay snack foods and Pepsi beverages, had the following current assets and current liabilities at the end of two recent years:

	Dec. 31, 2005 (in millions)	Dec. 25, 2004 (in millions)
Cash and cash equivalents	$1,716	$1,280
Short-term investments, at cost	3,166	2,165
Accounts and notes receivable, net	3,261	2,999
Inventories	1,693	1,541
Prepaid expenses and other current assets	618	654
Short-term obligations	2,889	1,054
Accounts payable and other current liabilities	5,971	5,999
Income taxes payable	546	99

a. Determine the (1) current ratio and (2) quick ratio for both years. Round to one decimal place.

b. What conclusions can you draw from these data?

EX 14-8
Current position analysis
obj. 2

The bond indenture for the 20-year, 11% debenture bonds dated January 2, 2007, required working capital of $560,000, a current ratio of 1.5, and a quick ratio of 1.2 at the end of each calendar year until the bonds mature. At December 31, 2008, the three measures were computed as follows:

1. Current assets:

Cash	$190,000	
Marketable securities	95,000	
Accounts and notes receivable (net)	171,000	
Inventories	20,000	
Prepaid expenses	4,500	
Intangible assets	55,000	
Property, plant, and equipment	65,000	
Total current assets (net)		$600,500
Current liabilities:		
Accounts and short-term notes payable	$250,000	
Accrued liabilities	150,000	
Total current liabilities		400,000
Working capital		$200,500

2. Current Ratio = 1.50 ($600,500/$400,000)
3. Quick Ratio = 2.04 ($511,000/$250,000)

a. List the errors in the determination of the three measures of current position analysis.

b. Is the company satisfying the terms of the bond indenture?

EX 14-9
Accounts receivable analysis
obj. 2

✓ *a. Accounts receivable turnover, 2008, 6.9*

The following data are taken from the financial statements of Creekside Technology Inc. Terms of all sales are 2/10, n/60.

	2008	2007	2006
Accounts receivable, end of year	$ 75,452	$ 85,500	$81,624
Monthly average accounts receivable (net)	78,261	80,645	—
Net sales	540,000	500,000	—

a. Determine for each year (1) the accounts receivable turnover and (2) the number of days' sales in receivables. Round to nearest dollar and one decimal place.

b. What conclusions can be drawn from these data concerning accounts receivable and credit policies?

EX 14-10
Accounts receivable analysis
obj. 2

REAL WORLD

✓ *a. (1) May's accounts receivable turnover, 7.1*

The May Department Stores Company (Marshall Field's, Hecht's, Lord & Taylor) and Federated Department Stores, Inc. (Macy's and Bloomingdale's) are two of the largest department store chains in the United States. Both companies offer credit to their customers through their own credit card operations. Information from the financial statements for both companies for two recent years is as follows (all numbers are in millions):

	May	Federated
Merchandise sales	$14,441	$15,630
Credit card receivables—beginning	2,294	3,418
Credit card receivables—ending	1,788	3,213

a. Determine the (1) accounts receivable turnover and (2) the number of days' sales in receivables for both companies. Round to one decimal place.

b. Compare the two companies with regard to their credit card policies.

EX 14-11
Inventory analysis
obj. 2

✓ a. Inventory turnover, current year, 7.5

The following data were extracted from the income statement of Clear View Systems Inc.:

	Current Year	Preceding Year
Sales	$756,000	$950,760
Beginning inventories	67,200	44,000
Cost of goods sold	492,000	528,200
Ending inventories	64,000	67,200

a. Determine for each year (1) the inventory turnover and (2) the number of days' sales in inventory. Round to nearest dollar and one decimal place.

b. ▭▭▭► What conclusions can be drawn from these data concerning the inventories?

EX 14-12
Inventory analysis
obj. 2

REAL WORLD

✓ a. Dell inventory turnover, 88.2

Dell Inc. and Hewlett-Packard Company (HP) compete with each other in the personal computer market. Dell's strategy is to assemble computers to customer orders, rather than for inventory. Thus, for example, Dell will build and deliver a computer within four days of a customer entering an order on a Web page. Hewlett-Packard, on the other hand, builds some computers prior to receiving an order, then sells from this inventory once an order is received. Below is selected financial information for both companies from a recent year's financial statements (in millions):

	Dell Inc.	Hewlett-Packard Company
Sales	$55,908	$86,696
Cost of goods sold	45,620	66,440
Inventory, beginning of period	459	7,071
Inventory, end of period	576	6,877

a. Determine for both companies (1) the inventory turnover and (2) the number of days' sales in inventory. Round to one decimal place.

b. ▭▭▭► Interpret the inventory ratios by considering Dell's and Hewlett-Packard's operating strategies.

EX 14-13
Ratio of liabilities to stockholders' equity and number of times interest charges earned
obj. 2

✓ a. Ratio of liabilities to stockholders' equity, Dec. 31, 2008, 0.5

The following data were taken from the financial statements of Quality Construction Inc. for December 31, 2008 and 2007:

	December 31, 2008	December 31, 2007
Accounts payable	$ 240,000	$ 224,000
Current maturities of serial bonds payable	320,000	320,000
Serial bonds payable, 10%, issued 2004, due 2014	1,600,000	1,920,000
Common stock, $1 par value	160,000	160,000
Paid-in capital in excess of par	800,000	800,000
Retained earnings	3,404,800	2,560,000

The income before income tax was $844,800 and $537,600 for the years 2008 and 2007, respectively.

a. Determine the ratio of liabilities to stockholders' equity at the end of each year. Round to one decimal place.

b. Determine the number of times the bond interest charges are earned during the year for both years. Round to one decimal place.

c. ▭▭▭► What conclusions can be drawn from these data as to the company's ability to meet its currently maturing debts?

EX 14-14
Ratio of liabilities to stockholders' equity and number of times interest charges earned
obj. 2

Hasbro and Mattel, Inc., are the two largest toy companies in North America. Condensed liabilities and stockholders' equity from a recent balance sheet are shown for each company as follows:

✓a. Hasbro, 1.0

	Hasbro	Mattel, Inc.
Current liabilities	$1,148,611,000	$1,727,171,000
Long-term debt	302,698,000	400,000,000
Deferred liabilities	149,627,000	243,509,000
Total liabilities	$1,600,936,000	$2,370,680,000
Shareholders' equity:		
Common stock, $0.50 par value	$ 104,847,000	$ 441,369,000
Additional paid-in capital	380,745,000	1,594,332,000
Retained earnings	1,721,209,000	1,093,288,000
Accumulated other comprehensive loss and other equity items	82,290,000	(269,828,000)
Treasury stock, at cost	(649,367,000)	(473,349,000)
Total stockholders' equity	$1,639,724,000	$2,385,812,000
Total liabilities and stockholders' equity	$3,240,660,000	$4,756,492,000

The income from operations and interest expense from the income statement for both companies were as follows:

	Hasbro	Mattel, Inc.
Income from operations	$293,012,000	$730,817,000
Interest expense	31,698,000	77,764,000

a. Determine the ratio of liabilities to stockholders' equity for both companies. Round to one decimal place.
b. Determine the number of times interest charges are earned for both companies. Round to one decimal place.
c. ▭▭▭▶ Interpret the ratio differences between the two companies.

EX 14-15
Ratio of liabilities to stockholders' equity and ratio of fixed assets to long-term liabilities

obj. 2

✓a. H.J. Heinz, 3.1

Recent balance sheet information for two companies in the food industry, H.J. Heinz Company and The Hershey Company, are as follows (in thousands of dollars):

	H.J. Heinz	Hershey
Net property, plant, and equipment	$2,163,938	$1,659,138
Current liabilities	2,587,068	1,518,223
Long-term debt	4,121,984	942,755
Other liabilities (pensions, deferred taxes)	1,266,093	813,182
Stockholders' equity	2,602,573	1,021,076

a. Determine the ratio of liabilities to stockholders' equity for both companies. Round to one decimal place.
b. Determine the ratio of fixed assets to long-term liabilities for both companies. Round to one decimal place.
c. ▭▭▭▶ Interpret the ratio differences between the two companies.

EX 14-16
Ratio of net sales to assets

obj. 3

✓a. YRC Worldwide, 1.9

Three major segments of the transportation industry are motor carriers, such as YRC Worldwide; railroads, such as Union Pacific; and transportation arrangement services, such as C.H. Robinson Worldwide Inc. Recent financial statement information for these three companies is shown as follows (in thousands of dollars):

	YRC Worldwide	Union Pacific	C.H. Robinson Worldwide
Net sales	$6,767,485	$12,215,000	$4,341,538
Average total assets	3,545,199	34,041,500	994,423

a. Determine the ratio of net sales to assets for all three companies. Round to one decimal place.
b. ▭▭▭▶ Assume that the ratio of net sales to assets for each company represents their respective industry segment. Interpret the differences in the ratio of net sales to assets in terms of the operating characteristics of each of the respective segments.

EX 14-17
Profitability ratios

obj. **3**

✓ *a. Rate earned on total assets, 2008, 11.6%*

The following selected data were taken from the financial statements of Berry Group Inc. for December 31, 2008, 2007, and 2006:

	December 31, 2008	December 31, 2007	December 31, 2006
Total assets	$1,160,000	$1,040,000	$880,000
Notes payable (10% interest)	150,000	150,000	150,000
Common stock	360,000	360,000	360,000
Preferred $8 stock, $100 par			
(no change during year)	160,000	160,000	160,000
Retained earnings	426,900	327,200	205,000

The 2008 net income was $112,500, and the 2007 net income was $135,000. No dividends on common stock were declared between 2006 and 2008.

a. Determine the rate earned on total assets, the rate earned on stockholders' equity, and the rate earned on common stockholders' equity for the years 2007 and 2008. Round to one decimal place.
b. ▬▬▶ What conclusions can be drawn from these data as to the company's profitability?

EX 14-18
Profitability ratios

obj. **3**

REAL WORLD

✓ *a. 2005 rate earned on total assets, 6.0%*

Ann Taylor Retail, Inc., sells professional women's apparel through company-owned retail stores. Recent financial information for Ann Taylor is provided below (all numbers in thousands):

	Fiscal Year Ended	
	Jan. 28, 2006	Jan. 29, 2005
Net income	$81,872	$63,276
Interest expense	2,083	3,641

	Jan. 28, 2006	Jan. 29, 2005	Jan. 31, 2004
Total assets	$1,492,906	$1,327,338	$1,256,397
Total stockholders' equity	1,034,482	926,744	818,856

Assume the apparel industry average rate earned on total assets is 8.2%, and the average rate earned on stockholders' equity is 16.7% for fiscal 2005.

a. Determine the rate earned on total assets for Ann Taylor for the fiscal years ended January 28, 2006, and January 29, 2005. Round to one digit after the decimal place.
b. Determine the rate earned on stockholders' equity for Ann Taylor for the fiscal years ended January 28, 2006, and January 29, 2005. Round to one decimal place.
c. ▬▬▶ Evaluate the two-year trend for the profitability ratios determined in (a) and (b).
d. ▬▬▶ Evaluate Ann Taylor's profit performance relative to the industry.

EX 14-19
Six measures of solvency or profitability

objs. **2, 3**

✓ *c. Ratio of net sales to assets, 1.5*

The following data were taken from the financial statements of Bendax Enterprises Inc. for the current fiscal year. Assuming that long-term investments totaled $240,000 throughout the year and that total assets were $2,525,000 at the beginning of the year, determine the following: (a) ratio of fixed assets to long-term liabilities, (b) ratio of liabilities to stockholders' equity, (c) ratio of net sales to assets, (d) rate earned on total assets, (e) rate earned on stockholders' equity, and (f) rate earned on common stockholders' equity. Round to one decimal place.

Property, plant, and equipment (net)		$1,200,000
Liabilities:		
Current liabilities	$ 60,000	
Mortgage note payable, 8%, issued 1997, due 2013	825,000	
Total liabilities		$ 885,000

Stockholders' equity:

Preferred $9 stock, $100 par (no change during year) ...		$ 250,000
Common stock, $20 par (no change during year)		800,000

Retained earnings:

Balance, beginning of year	$600,000		
Net income	216,000	$816,000	
Preferred dividends	$ 22,500		
Common dividends	57,600	80,100	
Balance, end of year			735,900
Total stockholders' equity			$1,785,900
Net sales			$3,600,000
Interest expense			$ 66,000

EX 14-20
Six measures of solvency or profitability
objs. 2, 3
✓ *d. Price-earnings ratio, 16.1*

The balance sheet for Chaney Resources Inc. at the end of the current fiscal year indicated the following:

Bonds payable, 10% (issued in 1995, due in 2015)	$2,250,000
Preferred $25 stock, $200 par	500,000
Common stock, $10 par	2,500,000

   Income before income tax was $625,000, and income taxes were $175,000 for the current year. Cash dividends paid on common stock during the current year totaled $125,000. The common stock was selling for $25 per share at the end of the year. Determine each of the following: (a) number of times bond interest charges are earned, (b) number of times preferred dividends are earned, (c) earnings per share on common stock, (d) price-earnings ratio, (e) dividends per share of common stock, and (f) dividend yield. Round to one decimal place except earnings per share, which should be rounded to two decimal places.

EX 14-21
Earnings per share, price-earnings ratio, dividend yield
obj. 3
✓ *b. Price-earnings ratio, 14.8*

The following information was taken from the financial statements of Royer Medical Inc. for December 31 of the current fiscal year:

Common stock, $5 par value (no change during the year)	$1,500,000
Preferred $5 stock, $50 par (no change during the year)	450,000

   The net income was $450,000, and the declared dividends on the common stock were $75,000 for the current year. The market price of the common stock is $20 per share.
   For the common stock, determine (a) the earnings per share, (b) the price-earnings ratio, (c) the dividends per share, and (d) the dividend yield. Round to one decimal place except earnings per share, which should be rounded to two decimal places.

EX 14-22
Earnings per share
obj. 3
✓ *b. Earnings per share on common stock, $3.00*

The net income reported on the income statement of Ground Hog Co. was $1,250,000. There were 250,000 shares of $40 par common stock and 50,000 shares of $10 preferred stock outstanding throughout the current year. The income statement included two extraordinary items: a $360,000 gain from condemnation of land and a $235,000 loss arising from flood damage, both after applicable income tax. Determine the per share figures for common stock for (a) income before extraordinary items and (b) net income.

EX 14-23
Price-earnings ratio; dividend yield
obj. 3

The table below shows the stock price, earnings per share, and dividends per share for three companies as of February 10, 2006:

	Price	Earnings per Share	Dividends per Share
Bank of America Corporation	$44.47	$4.15	$2.00
eBay Inc.	41.60	0.78	0.00
The Coca-Cola Company	41.19	2.04	1.12

a. Determine the price-earnings ratio and dividend yield for the three companies. Round to one decimal place.
b. ➤ Explain the differences in these ratios across the three companies.

Problems Series A

PR 14-1A
Horizontal analysis for income statement
obj. **1**

✓ *1. Net sales, 25.1% increase*

For 2008, Doane Inc. reported its most significant increase in net income in years. At the end of the year, Jeff Newton, the president, is presented with the following condensed comparative income statement:

Doane Inc.
Comparative Income Statement
For the Years Ended December 31, 2008 and 2007

	2008	2007
Sales	$91,500	$73,200
Sales returns and allowances	1,440	1,200
Net sales	$90,060	$72,000
Cost of goods sold	50,400	42,000
Gross profit	$39,660	$30,000
Selling expenses	$16,560	$14,400
Administrative expenses	10,800	9,600
Total operating expenses	$27,360	$24,000
Income from operations	$12,300	$ 6,000
Other income	600	600
Income before income tax	$12,900	$ 6,600
Income tax expense	2,880	1,440
Net income	$10,020	$ 5,160

Instructions
1. Prepare a comparative income statement with horizontal analysis for the two-year period, using 2007 as the base year. Round to one decimal place.
2. ➤ To the extent the data permit, comment on the significant relationships revealed by the horizontal analysis prepared in (1).

PR 14-2A
Vertical analysis for income statement
obj. **1**

✓ *1. Net income, 2007, 8.0%*

For 2008, Dusan Water Supplies Inc. initiated a sales promotion campaign that included the expenditure of an additional $21,000 for advertising. At the end of the year, Ivana Novatna, the president, is presented with the following condensed comparative income statement:

Dusan Water Supplies Inc.
Comparative Income Statement
For the Years Ended December 31, 2008 and 2007

	2008	2007
Sales	$255,000	$214,000
Sales returns and allowances	5,000	4,000
Net sales	$250,000	$210,000
Cost of goods sold	142,500	121,800
Gross profit	$107,500	$ 88,200
Selling expenses	$100,000	$ 50,400
Administrative expenses	20,000	16,800
Total operating expenses	$120,000	$ 67,200
Income from operations	$ (12,500)	$ 21,000
Other income	6,250	4,200
Income before income tax	$ (6,250)	$ 25,200
Income tax expense (benefit)	(2,500)	8,400
Net income (loss)	$ (3,750)	$ 16,800

Instructions

1. Prepare a comparative income statement for the two-year period, presenting an analysis of each item in relationship to net sales for each of the years. Round to one decimal place.

2. ➤ To the extent the data permit, comment on the significant relationships revealed by the vertical analysis prepared in (1).

PR 14-3A
Effect of transactions on current position analysis

obj. 2

✓ *1. c. Quick ratio, 1.4*

Data pertaining to the current position of Tsali Industries, Inc., are as follows:

Cash	$195,000
Marketable securities	92,500
Accounts and notes receivable (net)	293,000
Inventories	357,500
Prepaid expenses	15,000
Accounts payable	295,000
Notes payable (short-term)	92,000
Accrued expenses	42,500

Instructions

1. Compute (a) the working capital, (b) the current ratio, and (c) the quick ratio. Round to one decimal place.

2. List the following captions on a sheet of paper:

Transaction   **Working Capital**   **Current Ratio**   **Quick Ratio**

Compute the working capital, the current ratio, and the quick ratio after each of the following transactions, and record the results in the appropriate columns. Consider each transaction separately and assume that only that transaction affects the data given above. Round to one decimal place.

a. Sold marketable securities at no gain or loss, $37,500.
b. Paid accounts payable, $84,000.
c. Purchased goods on account, $55,000.
d. Paid notes payable, $32,500.
e. Declared a cash dividend, $38,000.
f. Declared a common stock dividend on common stock, $21,500.
g. Borrowed cash from bank on a long-term note, $185,000.
h. Received cash on account, $93,500.
i. Issued additional shares of stock for cash, $175,000.
j. Paid cash for prepaid expenses, $15,000.

PR 14-4A
Nineteen measures of solvency and profitability

objs. 2, 3

✓ *9. Ratio of liabilities to stockholders' equity, 0.5*

The comparative financial statements of Triad Images Inc. are as follows. The market price of Triad Images Inc. common stock was $55 on December 31, 2008.

Triad Images Inc.
Comparative Retained Earnings Statement
For the Years Ended December 31, 2008 and 2007

	Dec. 31, 2008	Dec. 31, 2007
Retained earnings, January 1	$1,006,500	$ 781,500
Add net income for year	430,000	277,500
Total	$1,436,500	$1,059,000
Deduct dividends:		
On preferred stock	$ 12,500	$ 12,500
On common stock	40,000	40,000
Total	$ 52,500	$ 52,500
Retained earnings, December 31	$1,384,000	$1,006,500

(continued)

Triad Images Inc.
Comparative Income Statement
For the Years Ended December 31, 2008 and 2007

	2008	2007
Sales	$3,395,000	$3,062,500
Sales returns and allowances	35,000	22,500
Net sales	$3,360,000	$3,040,000
Cost of goods sold	1,500,000	1,437,500
Gross profit..	$1,860,000	$1,602,500
Selling expenses	$ 726,000	$ 718,750
Administrative expenses	486,000	475,000
Total operating expenses	$1,212,000	$1,193,750
Income from operations	$ 648,000	$ 408,750
Other income	48,000	37,500
	$ 696,000	$ 446,250
Other expense (interest)	98,000	50,000
Income before income tax	$ 598,000	$ 396,250
Income tax expense	168,000	118,750
Net income	$ 430,000	$ 277,500

Triad Images Inc.
Comparative Balance Sheet
December 31, 2008 and 2007

	Dec. 31, 2008	Dec. 31, 2007
Assets		
Current assets:		
Cash	$ 132,000	$ 120,000
Marketable securities	387,000	157,500
Accounts receivable (net)	260,000	196,500
Inventories	425,000	332,500
Prepaid expenses	27,500	35,000
Total current assets	$1,231,500	$ 841,500
Long-term investments	319,500	250,000
Property, plant, and equipment (net)	2,575,000	2,000,000
Total assets	$4,126,000	$3,091,500
Liabilities		
Current liabilities	$ 342,000	$ 285,000
Long-term liabilities:		
Mortgage note payable, 8%, due 2013	$ 600,000	—
Bonds payable, 10%, due 2017	500,000	$ 500,000
Total long-term liabilities	$1,100,000	$ 500,000
Total liabilities	$1,442,000	$ 785,000
Stockholders' Equity		
Preferred $2.50 stock, $100 par	$ 500,000	$ 500,000
Common stock, $20 par	800,000	800,000
Retained earnings	1,384,000	1,006,500
Total stockholders' equity	$2,684,000	$2,306,500
Total liabilities and stockholders' equity	$4,126,000	$3,091,500

Instructions

Determine the following measures for 2008, rounding to one decimal place:

1. Working capital
2. Current ratio
3. Quick ratio
4. Accounts receivable turnover
5. Number of days' sales in receivables
6. Inventory turnover
7. Number of days' sales in inventory
8. Ratio of fixed assets to long-term liabilities

9. Ratio of liabilities to stockholders' equity
10. Number of times interest charges earned
11. Number of times preferred dividends earned
12. Ratio of net sales to assets
13. Rate earned on total assets
14. Rate earned on stockholders' equity
15. Rate earned on common stockholders' equity
16. Earnings per share on common stock
17. Price-earnings ratio
18. Dividends per share of common stock
19. Dividend yield

PR 14-5A
Solvency and profitability trend analysis

objs. 2, 3

Shore Company has provided the following comparative information:

	2008	2007	2006	2005	2004
Net income	$ 42,000	$ 70,000	$ 140,000	$ 210,000	$ 210,000
Interest expense	142,800	133,000	119,000	112,000	105,000
Income tax expense	12,600	21,000	42,000	63,000	63,000
Total assets (ending balance)	2,240,000	2,100,000	1,890,000	1,680,000	1,400,000
Total stockholders' equity (ending balance)	812,000	770,000	700,000	560,000	350,000
Average total assets	2,170,000	1,995,000	1,785,000	1,540,000	1,260,000
Average stockholders' equity	791,000	735,000	630,000	455,000	315,000

You have been asked to evaluate the historical performance of the company over the last five years.

Selected industry ratios have remained relatively steady at the following levels for the last five years:

	2004–2008
Rate earned on total assets	14%
Rate earned on stockholders' equity	20%
Number of times interest charges earned	3.0
Ratio of liabilities to stockholders' equity	2.0

Instructions
1. Prepare four line graphs with the ratio on the vertical axis and the years on the horizontal axis for the following four ratios (rounded to one decimal place):
   a. Rate earned on total assets
   b. Rate earned on stockholders' equity
   c. Number of times interest charges earned
   d. Ratio of liabilities to stockholders' equity
   Display both the company ratio and the industry benchmark on each graph. That is, each graph should have two lines.
2. Prepare an analysis of the graphs in (1).

Problems Series B

PR 14-1B
Horizontal analysis for income statement

obj. 1

For 2008, Phoenix Technology Company reported its most significant decline in net income in years. At the end of the year, Hai Chow, the president, is presented with the following condensed comparative income statement:

✓ 1. Net sales, 11.8%
increase

Phoenix Technology Company
Comparative Income Statement
For the Years Ended December 31, 2008 and 2007

	2008	2007
Sales	$385,000	$343,200
Sales returns and allowances	4,800	3,200
Net sales	$380,200	$340,000
Cost of goods sold	180,000	144,000
Gross profit	$200,200	$196,000
Selling expenses	$ 87,400	$ 76,000
Administrative expenses	30,000	24,000
Total operating expenses	$117,400	$100,000
Income from operations	$ 82,800	$ 96,000
Other income	1,600	1,600
Income before income tax	$ 84,400	$ 97,600
Income tax expense	36,800	32,000
Net income	$ 47,600	$ 65,600

Instructions

1. Prepare a comparative income statement with horizontal analysis for the two-year period, using 2007 as the base year. Round to one decimal place.
2. ▰▰▰▶ To the extent the data permit, comment on the significant relationships revealed by the horizontal analysis prepared in (1).

PR 14-2B
*Vertical analysis for
income statement*
obj. 1

✓ 1. Net income, 2008,
20.0%

For 2008, Acedia Technology Company initiated a sales promotion campaign that included the expenditure of an additional $10,000 for advertising. At the end of the year, Gordon Kincaid, the president, is presented with the following condensed comparative income statement:

Acedia Technology Company
Comparative Income Statement
For the Years Ended December 31, 2008 and 2007

	2008	2007
Sales	$755,000	$676,000
Sales returns and allowances	5,000	6,000
Net sales	$750,000	$670,000
Cost of goods sold	292,500	274,700
Gross profit	$457,500	$395,300
Selling expenses	$172,500	$160,800
Administrative expenses	82,500	80,400
Total operating expenses	$255,000	$241,200
Income from operations	$202,500	$154,100
Other income	7,500	6,700
Income before income tax	$210,000	$160,800
Income tax expense	60,000	53,600
Net income	$150,000	$107,200

Instructions

1. Prepare a comparative income statement for the two-year period, presenting an analysis of each item in relationship to net sales for each of the years. Round to one decimal place.
2. ▰▰▰▶ To the extent the data permit, comment on the significant relationships revealed by the vertical analysis prepared in (1).

PR 14-3B
*Effect of transactions on
current position analysis*
obj. 2

✓ 1. b. Current ratio, 2.1

Data pertaining to the current position of Spruce Pine Medical Company are as follows:

Cash	$384,000
Marketable securities	176,000
Accounts and notes receivable (net)	608,000
Inventories	792,000
Prepaid expenses	48,000
Accounts payable	624,000
Notes payable (short-term)	240,000
Accrued expenses	80,000

Instructions

1. Compute (a) the working capital, (b) the current ratio, and (c) the quick ratio. Round to one decimal place.
2. List the following captions on a sheet of paper:

Transaction	Working Capital	Current Ratio	Quick Ratio

Compute the working capital, the current ratio, and the quick ratio after each of the following transactions, and record the results in the appropriate columns. Consider each transaction separately and assume that only that transaction affects the data given above. Round to one decimal place.

a. Sold marketable securities at no gain or loss, $65,000.
b. Paid accounts payable, $90,000.
c. Purchased goods on account, $120,000.
d. Paid notes payable, $65,000.
e. Declared a cash dividend, $32,500.
f. Declared a common stock dividend on common stock, $34,000.
g. Borrowed cash from bank on a long-term note, $160,000.
h. Received cash on account, $125,000.
i. Issued additional shares of stock for cash, $425,000.
j. Paid cash for prepaid expenses, $16,000.

PR 14-4B
Nineteen measures of solvency and profitability

objs. 2, 3

✓ 5. Number of days' sales in receivables, 50.8

The comparative financial statements of Dental Innovations Inc. are as follows. The market price of Dental Innovations Inc. common stock was $15 on December 31, 2008.

Dental Innovations Inc.
Comparative Retained Earnings Statement
For the Years Ended December 31, 2008 and 2007

	Dec. 31, 2008	Dec. 31, 2007
Retained earnings, January 1	$265,000	$ 31,000
Add net income for year	321,500	244,000
Total	$586,500	$275,000
Deduct dividends:		
On preferred stock	$ 10,000	$ 5,000
On common stock	7,000	5,000
Total	$ 17,000	$ 10,000
Retained earnings, December 31	$569,500	$265,000

Dental Innovations Inc.
Comparative Income Statement
For the Years Ended December 31, 2008 and 2007

	2008	2007
Sales	$1,055,000	$966,000
Sales returns and allowances	5,000	6,000
Net sales	$1,050,000	$960,000
Cost of goods sold	300,000	312,000
Gross profit	$ 750,000	$648,000
Selling expenses	$ 202,500	$220,000
Administrative expenses	146,250	132,000
Total operating expenses	$ 348,750	$352,000
Income from operations	$ 401,250	$296,000
Other income	15,000	12,000
	$ 416,250	$308,000
Other expense (interest)	64,000	40,000
Income before income tax	$ 352,250	$268,000
Income tax expense	30,750	24,000
Net income	$ 321,500	$244,000

(continued)

Dental Innovations Inc.
Comparative Balance Sheet
December 31, 2008 and 2007

	Dec. 31, 2008	Dec. 31, 2007
Assets		
Current assets:		
Cash	$ 165,000	$ 101,500
Marketable securities	335,000	205,500
Accounts receivable (net)	160,000	132,000
Inventories	67,500	41,500
Prepaid expenses	27,000	14,500
Total current assets	$ 754,500	$ 495,000
Long-term investments	310,000	160,000
Property, plant, and equipment (net)	950,000	610,000
Total assets	$2,014,500	$1,265,000
Liabilities		
Current liabilities	$ 225,000	$ 200,000
Long-term liabilities:		
Mortgage note payable, 10%, due 2013	$ 240,000	—
Bonds payable, 8%, due 2017	500,000	$ 500,000
Total long-term liabilities	$ 740,000	$ 500,000
Total liabilities	$ 965,000	$ 700,000
Stockholders' Equity		
Preferred $2.50 stock, $50 par	$ 200,000	$ 100,000
Common stock, $10 par	280,000	200,000
Retained earnings	569,500	265,000
Total stockholders' equity	$1,049,500	$ 565,000
Total liabilities and stockholders' equity	$2,014,500	$1,265,000

Instructions

Determine the following measures for 2008, rounding to one decimal place:

1. Working capital
2. Current ratio
3. Quick ratio
4. Accounts receivable turnover
5. Number of days' sales in receivables
6. Inventory turnover
7. Number of days' sales in inventory
8. Ratio of fixed assets to long-term liabilities
9. Ratio of liabilities to stockholders' equity
10. Number of times interest charges earned
11. Number of times preferred dividends earned
12. Ratio of net sales to assets
13. Rate earned on total assets
14. Rate earned on stockholders' equity
15. Rate earned on common stockholders' equity
16. Earnings per share on common stock
17. Price-earnings ratio
18. Dividends per share of common stock
19. Dividend yield

PR 14-5B

Solvency and profitability trend analysis

objs. 2, 3

Van DeKamp Company has provided the following comparative information:

	2008	2007	2006	2005	2004
Net income	$1,815,000	$1,200,000	$ 900,000	$ 600,000	$ 450,000
Interest expense	271,800	234,000	202,500	162,000	135,000
Income tax expense	635,250	420,000	315,000	210,000	157,500
Total assets (ending balance)	9,035,000	6,800,000	5,250,000	3,900,000	3,000,000
Total stockholders' equity (ending balance)	6,015,000	4,200,000	3,000,000	2,100,000	1,500,000
Average total assets	7,917,500	6,025,000	4,575,000	3,450,000	2,700,000
Average stockholders' equity	5,107,500	3,600,000	2,550,000	1,800,000	1,350,000

You have been asked to evaluate the historical performance of the company over the last five years.

Selected industry ratios have remained relatively steady at the following levels for the last five years:

	2004–2008
Rate earned on total assets	13%
Rate earned on stockholders' equity	20%
Number of times interest charges earned	4.0
Ratio of liabilities to stockholders' equity	1.3

Instructions

1. Prepare four line graphs with the ratio on the vertical axis and the years on the horizontal axis for the following four ratios (rounded to one decimal place):
   a. Rate earned on total assets
   b. Rate earned on stockholders' equity
   c. Number of times interest charges earned
   d. Ratio of liabilities to stockholders' equity
   Display both the company ratio and the industry benchmark on each graph. That is, each graph should have two lines.
2. Prepare an analysis of the graphs in (1).

Williams-Sonoma, Inc., Problem

FINANCIAL STATEMENT ANALYSIS

The financial statements for Williams-Sonoma, Inc., are presented in Appendix B at the end of the text. The following additional information (in thousands) is available:

Accounts receivable at February 1, 2004	$ 31,573
Inventories at February 1, 2004	404,100
Total assets at February 1, 2004	1,470,735
Stockholders' equity at February 1, 2004	804,591

Instructions

1. Determine the following measures for the fiscal years ended January 29, 2006, and January 30, 2005, rounding to one decimal place.
   a. Working capital
   b. Current ratio
   c. Quick ratio
   d. Accounts receivable turnover
   e. Number of days' sales in receivables
   f. Inventory turnover
   g. Number of days' sales in inventory
   h. Ratio of liabilities to stockholders' equity
   i. Ratio of net sales to average total assets
   j. Rate earned on average total assets
   k. Rate earned on average common stockholders' equity
   l. Price-earnings ratio, assuming that the market price was $40.62 per share on January 29, 2006, and $34.53 on January 30, 2005.
   m. Percentage relationship of net income to net sales
2. What conclusions can be drawn from these analyses?

Special Activities

SA 14-1
Analysis of financing corporate growth

Assume that the president of Ice Mountain Brewery made the following statement in the Annual Report to Shareholders:

"The founding family and majority shareholders of the company do not believe in using debt to finance future growth. The founding family learned from hard experience during Prohibition and the Great Depression that debt can cause loss of flexibility and eventual loss of corporate control. The company will not place itself at such risk. As such, all future growth will be financed either by stock sales to the public or by internally generated resources."

➤ As a public shareholder of this company, how would you respond to this policy?

SA 14-2
Receivables and inventory turnover

Roan Mountain Fitness Company has completed its fiscal year on December 31, 2008. The auditor, Steve Berry, has approached the CFO, Tony Brubaker, regarding the year-end receivables and inventory levels of Roan Mountain Fitness. The following conversation takes place:

Steve: We are beginning our audit of Roan Mountain Fitness and have prepared ratio analyses to determine if there have been significant changes in operations or financial position. This helps us guide the audit process. This analysis indicates that the inventory turnover has decreased from 4.5 to 2.1, while the accounts receivable turnover has decreased from 10 to 6. I was wondering if you could explain this change in operations.

Tony: There is little need for concern. The inventory represents computers that we were unable to sell during the holiday buying season. We are confident, however, that we will be able to sell these computers as we move into the next fiscal year.

Steve: What gives you this confidence?

Tony: We will increase our advertising and provide some very attractive price concessions to move these machines. We have no choice. Newer technology is already out there, and we have to unload this inventory.

Steve: . . . and the receivables?

Tony: As you may be aware, the company is under tremendous pressure to expand sales and profits. As a result, we lowered our credit standards to our commercial customers so that we would be able to sell products to a broader customer base. As a result of this policy change, we have been able to expand sales by 35%.

Steve: Your responses have not been reassuring to me.

Tony: I'm a little confused. Assets are good, right? Why don't you look at our current ratio? It has improved, hasn't it? I would think that you would view that very favorably.

➤ Why is Steve concerned about the inventory and accounts receivable turnover ratios and Tony's responses to them? What action may Steve need to take? How would you respond to Tony's last comment?

SA 14-3
Vertical analysis

The condensed income statements through income from operations for Dell Inc. and Apple Computer, Inc., are reproduced below for recent fiscal years (numbers in millions of dollars).

	Dell Inc.	Apple Computer, Inc.
Sales (net)	$55,908	$13,931
Cost of sales	45,958	9,888
Gross profit	$ 9,950	$ 4,043
Selling, general, and administrative expenses	$ 5,140	$ 1,859
Research and development	463	534
Operating expenses	$ 5,603	$ 2,393
Income from operations	$ 4,347	$ 1,650

⬛▬▶ Prepare comparative common-size statements, rounding percents to one decimal place. Interpret the analyses.

SA 14-4
Profitability and stockholder ratios

REAL WORLD

Ford Motor Company is the second largest automobile and truck manufacturer in the United States. In addition to manufacturing motor vehicles, Ford also provides vehicle-related financing, insurance, and leasing services. Historically, people purchase automobiles when the economy is strong and delay automobile purchases when the economy is faltering. For this reason, Ford is considered a cyclical company. This means that when the economy does well, Ford usually prospers, and when the economy is down, Ford usually suffers.

The following information is available for three recent years (in millions except per-share amounts):

	2005	2004	2003
Net income (loss)	$2,024	$3,487	$495
Preferred dividends	$0	$0	$0
Shares outstanding for computing earnings per share	1,846	1,830	1,832
Cash dividend per share	$0.40	$0.40	$0.40
Average total assets	$287,669	$308,032	$293,678
Average stockholders' equity	$14,501	$13,848	$8,532
Average stock price per share	$11.22	$14.98	$11.95

1. Calculate the following ratios for each year:
   a. Rate earned on total assets
   b. Rate earned on stockholders' equity
   c. Earnings per share
   d. Dividend yield
   e. Price-earnings ratio
2. What is the ratio of average liabilities to average stockholders' equity for 2005?
3. ⬛▬▶ Why does Ford have so much leverage?
4. ⬛▬▶ Explain the direction of the dividend yield and price-earnings ratio in light of Ford's profitability trend.

SA 14-5
Projecting financial statements

REAL WORLD

Internet Project

Go to Microsoft Corporation's Web site at **http://www.microsoft.com** and click on the "Investor Relations" area under "About Microsoft." Select the menu item "Stock Info and Analysis." Select the "What-if?" tool. With this tool, use horizontal and vertical information to create a full-year projection of the Microsoft income statement. Make the following assumptions:

Revenue growth	12%
Cost of goods sold as a percent of revenue	15%
Research and development growth	10%
Sales and marketing as a percent of sales	18%
General and administrative as a percent of sales	6%
Tax rate	32%
Diluted shares outstanding	12,000

SA 14-6
Comprehensive profitability and solvency analysis

REAL WORLD

Marriott International, Inc., and Hilton Hotels Corporation are two major owners and managers of lodging and resort properties in the United States. Abstracted income statement information for the two companies is as follows for a recent year:

(continued)

	Marriott (in millions)	Hilton (in millions)
Operating profit before other expenses and interest	$ 477	$ 658
Other income (expenses)	318	(19)
Interest expense	(99)	(274)
Income before income taxes	$ 696	$ 365
Income tax expense	100	127
Net income	$ 596	$ 238

Balance sheet information is as follows:

	Marriott (in millions)	Hilton (in millions)
Total liabilities	$4,587	$5,674
Total stockholders' equity	4,081	2,568
Total liabilties and stockholders' equity	$8,668	$8,242

The average liabilities, stockholders' equity, and total assets were as follows:

	Marriott	Hilton
Average total liabilities	$4,210	$5,809
Average total stockholders' equity	3,960	2,404
Average total assets	8,423	8,213

1. Determine the following ratios for both companies (round to one decimal place after the whole percent):
   a. Rate earned on total assets
   b. Rate earned on total stockholders' equity
   c. Number of times interest charges are earned
   d. Ratio of liabilities to stockholders' equity
2. ➤ Analyze and compare the two companies, using the information in (1).

Answers to Self-Examination Questions

1. **A** Percentage analysis indicating the relationship of the component parts to the total in a financial statement, such as the relationship of current assets to total assets (20% to 100%) in the question, is called vertical analysis (answer A). Percentage analysis of increases and decreases in corresponding items in comparative financial statements is called horizontal analysis (answer B). An example of horizontal analysis would be the presentation of the amount of current assets in the preceding balance sheet, along with the amount of current assets at the end of the current year, with the increase or decrease in current assets between the periods expressed as a percentage. Profitability analysis (answer C) is the analysis of a firm's ability to earn income. Contribution margin analysis (answer D) is discussed in a later managerial accounting chapter.

2. **D** Various solvency measures, categorized as current position analysis, indicate a firm's ability to meet currently maturing obligations. Each measure contributes to the analysis of a firm's current position and is most useful when viewed with other measures and when compared with similar measures for other periods and for other firms. Working capital (answer A) is the excess of current assets over current liabilities; the current ratio (answer B) is the ratio of current assets to current liabilities; and the quick ratio (answer C) is the ratio of the sum of cash, receivables, and marketable securities to current liabilities.

3. **D** The ratio of current assets to current liabilities is usually called the current ratio (answer A). It is sometimes called the working capital ratio (answer B) or bankers' ratio (answer C).

4. **C** The ratio of the sum of cash, receivables, and marketable securities (sometimes called quick assets) to current liabilities is called the quick ratio (answer C) or acid-test ratio. The current ratio (answer A), working capital ratio (answer B), and bankers' ratio (answer D) are terms that describe the ratio of current assets to current liabilities.

5. **C** The number of days' sales in inventory (answer C), which is determined by dividing the average inventory by the average daily cost of goods sold, expresses the relationship between the cost of goods sold and inventory. It indicates the efficiency in the management of inventory. The working capital ratio (answer A) indicates the ability of the business to meet currently maturing obligations (debt). The quick ratio (answer B) indicates the "instant" debt-paying ability of the business. The ratio of fixed assets to long-term liabilities (answer D) indicates the margin of safety for long-term creditors.

Appendices

Appendix A ● ● ● ● ● ● ● ● ● ● ● ● ● ● ● ● ● ●

Interest Tables

Present Value of $1 at Compound Interest Due in n Periods: $p_{\overline{n}|i} = \dfrac{1}{(1 + i)^n}$

$n \diagdown i$	5%	5.5%	6%	6.5%	7%	8%
1	0.95238	0.94787	0.94334	0.93897	0.93458	0.92593
2	0.90703	0.89845	0.89000	0.88166	0.87344	0.85734
3	0.86384	0.85161	0.83962	0.82785	0.81630	0.79383
4	0.82270	0.80722	0.79209	0.77732	0.76290	0.73503
5	0.78353	0.76513	0.74726	0.72988	0.71290	0.68058
6	0.74622	0.72525	0.70496	0.68533	0.66634	0.63017
7	0.71068	0.68744	0.66506	0.64351	0.62275	0.58349
8	0.67684	0.65160	0.62741	0.60423	0.58201	0.54027
9	0.64461	0.61763	0.59190	0.56735	0.54393	0.50025
10	0.61391	0.58543	0.55840	0.53273	0.50835	0.46319
11	0.58468	0.55491	0.52679	0.50021	0.47509	0.42888
12	0.55684	0.52598	0.49697	0.46968	0.44401	0.39711
13	0.53032	0.49856	0.46884	0.44102	0.41496	0.36770
14	0.50507	0.47257	0.44230	0.41410	0.38782	0.34046
15	0.48102	0.44793	0.41726	0.38883	0.36245	0.31524
16	0.45811	0.42458	0.39365	0.36510	0.33874	0.29189
17	0.43630	0.40245	0.37136	0.34281	0.31657	0.27027
18	0.41552	0.38147	0.35034	0.32189	0.29586	0.25025
19	0.39573	0.36158	0.33051	0.30224	0.27651	0.23171
20	0.37689	0.34273	0.31180	0.28380	0.25842	0.21455
21	0.35894	0.32486	0.29416	0.26648	0.24151	0.19866
22	0.34185	0.30793	0.27750	0.25021	0.22571	0.18394
23	0.32557	0.29187	0.26180	0.23494	0.21095	0.17032
24	0.31007	0.27666	0.24698	0.22060	0.19715	0.15770
25	0.29530	0.26223	0.23300	0.20714	0.18425	0.14602
26	0.28124	0.24856	0.21981	0.19450	0.17211	0.13520
27	0.26785	0.23560	0.20737	0.18263	0.16093	0.12519
28	0.25509	0.22332	0.19563	0.17148	0.15040	0.11591
29	0.24295	0.21168	0.18456	0.16101	0.14056	0.10733
30	0.23138	0.20064	0.17411	0.15119	0.13137	0.09938
31	0.22036	0.19018	0.16426	0.14196	0.12277	0.09202
32	0.20987	0.18027	0.15496	0.13329	0.11474	0.08520
33	0.19987	0.17087	0.14619	0.12516	0.10724	0.07889
34	0.19036	0.16196	0.13791	0.11752	0.10022	0.07304
35	0.18129	0.15352	0.13010	0.11035	0.09366	0.06764
40	0.14205	0.11746	0.09722	0.08054	0.06678	0.04603
45	0.11130	0.08988	0.07265	0.05879	0.04761	0.03133
50	0.08720	0.06877	0.05429	0.04291	0.03395	0.02132

Present Value of \$1 at Compound Interest Due in n Periods: $p_{\bar{n}\backslash i} = \dfrac{1}{(1+i)^n}$

$n \backslash i$	9%	10%	11%	12%	13%	14%
1	0.91743	0.90909	0.90090	0.89286	0.88496	0.87719
2	0.84168	0.82645	0.81162	0.79719	0.78315	0.76947
3	0.77218	0.75132	0.73119	0.71178	0.69305	0.67497
4	0.70842	0.68301	0.65873	0.63552	0.61332	0.59208
5	0.64993	0.62092	0.59345	0.56743	0.54276	0.51937
6	0.59627	0.56447	0.53464	0.50663	0.48032	0.45559
7	0.54703	0.51316	0.48166	0.45235	0.42506	0.39964
8	0.50187	0.46651	0.43393	0.40388	0.37616	0.35056
9	0.46043	0.42410	0.39092	0.36061	0.33288	0.30751
10	0.42241	0.38554	0.35218	0.32197	0.29459	0.26974
11	0.38753	0.35049	0.31728	0.28748	0.26070	0.23662
12	0.35554	0.31863	0.28584	0.25668	0.23071	0.20756
13	0.32618	0.28966	0.25751	0.22917	0.20416	0.18207
14	0.29925	0.26333	0.23199	0.20462	0.18068	0.15971
15	0.27454	0.23939	0.20900	0.18270	0.15989	0.14010
16	0.25187	0.21763	0.18829	0.16312	0.14150	0.12289
17	0.23107	0.19784	0.16963	0.14564	0.12522	0.10780
18	0.21199	0.17986	0.15282	0.13004	0.11081	0.09456
19	0.19449	0.16351	0.13768	0.11611	0.09806	0.08295
20	0.17843	0.14864	0.12403	0.10367	0.08678	0.07276
21	0.16370	0.13513	0.11174	0.09256	0.07680	0.06383
22	0.15018	0.12285	0.10067	0.08264	0.06796	0.05599
23	0.13778	0.11168	0.09069	0.07379	0.06014	0.04911
24	0.12640	0.10153	0.08170	0.06588	0.05323	0.04308
25	0.11597	0.09230	0.07361	0.05882	0.04710	0.03779
26	0.10639	0.08390	0.06631	0.05252	0.04168	0.03315
27	0.09761	0.07628	0.05974	0.04689	0.03689	0.02908
28	0.08955	0.06934	0.05382	0.04187	0.03264	0.02551
29	0.08216	0.06304	0.04849	0.03738	0.02889	0.02237
30	0.07537	0.05731	0.04368	0.03338	0.02557	0.01963
31	0.06915	0.05210	0.03935	0.02980	0.02262	0.01722
32	0.06344	0.04736	0.03545	0.02661	0.02002	0.01510
33	0.05820	0.04306	0.03194	0.02376	0.01772	0.01325
34	0.05331	0.03914	0.02878	0.02121	0.01568	0.01162
35	0.04899	0.03558	0.02592	0.01894	0.01388	0.01019
40	0.03184	0.02210	0.01538	0.01075	0.00753	0.00529
45	0.02069	0.01372	0.00913	0.00610	0.00409	0.00275
50	0.01345	0.00852	0.00542	0.00346	0.00222	0.00143

Present Value of Ordinary Annuity of $1 per Period: $p_{\overline{n}|i} = \dfrac{1 - \dfrac{1}{(1 + i)^n}}{i}$

n \ i	5%	5.5%	6%	6.5%	7%	8%
1	0.95238	0.94787	0.94340	0.93897	0.93458	0.92593
2	1.85941	1.84632	1.83339	1.82063	1.80802	1.78326
3	2.72325	2.69793	2.67301	2.64848	2.62432	2.57710
4	3.54595	3.50515	3.46511	3.42580	3.38721	3.31213
5	4.32948	4.27028	4.21236	4.15568	4.10020	3.99271
6	5.07569	4.99553	4.91732	4.84101	4.76654	4.62288
7	5.78637	5.68297	5.58238	5.48452	5.38923	5.20637
8	6.46321	6.33457	6.20979	6.08875	5.97130	5.74664
9	7.10782	6.95220	6.80169	6.65610	6.51523	6.24689
10	7.72174	7.53763	7.36009	7.18883	7.02358	6.71008
11	8.30641	8.09254	7.88688	7.68904	7.49867	7.13896
12	8.86325	8.61852	8.38384	8.15873	7.94269	7.53608
13	9.39357	9.11708	8.85268	8.59974	8.35765	7.90378
14	9.89864	9.58965	9.29498	9.01384	8.74547	8.22424
15	10.37966	10.03758	9.71225	9.40267	9.10791	8.55948
16	10.83777	10.46216	10.10590	9.76776	9.44665	8.85137
17	11.27407	10.86461	10.47726	10.11058	9.76322	9.12164
18	11.68959	11.24607	10.82760	10.43247	10.05909	9.37189
19	12.08532	11.60765	11.15812	10.73471	10.33560	9.60360
20	12.46221	11.95038	11.46992	11.01851	10.59401	9.81815
21	12.82115	12.27524	11.76408	11.28498	10.83553	10.01680
22	13.16300	12.58317	12.04158	11.53520	11.06124	10.20074
23	13.48857	12.87504	12.30338	11.77014	11.27219	10.37106
24	13.79864	13.15170	12.55036	11.99074	11.46933	10.52876
25	14.09394	13.41393	12.78336	12.19788	11.65358	10.67478
26	14.37518	13.66250	13.00317	12.39237	11.82578	10.80998
27	14.64303	13.89810	13.21053	12.57500	11.98671	10.93516
28	14.89813	14.12142	13.40616	12.74648	12.13711	11.05108
29	15.14107	14.33310	13.59072	12.90749	12.27767	11.15841
30	15.37245	14.53375	13.76483	13.05868	12.40904	11.25778
31	15.59281	14.72393	13.92909	13.20063	12.53181	11.34980
32	15.80268	14.90420	14.08404	13.33393	12.64656	11.43500
33	16.00255	15.07507	14.23023	13.45909	12.75379	11.51389
34	16.19290	15.23703	14.36814	13.57661	12.85401	11.58693
35	16.37420	15.39055	14.49825	13.68696	12.94767	11.65457
40	17.15909	16.04612	15.04630	14.14553	13.33171	11.92461
45	17.77407	16.54773	15.45583	14.48023	13.60552	12.10840
50	18.25592	16.93152	15.76186	14.72452	13.80075	12.23348

Present Value of Ordinary Annuity of $1 per Period: $p_{\bar{n}|i} = \dfrac{1 - \dfrac{1}{(1+i)^n}}{i}$

n \ i	9%	10%	11%	12%	13%	14%
1	0.91743	0.90909	0.90090	0.89286	0.88496	0.87719
2	1.75911	1.73554	1.71252	1.69005	1.66810	1.64666
3	2.53130	2.48685	2.44371	2.40183	2.36115	2.32163
4	3.23972	3.16986	3.10245	3.03735	2.97447	2.91371
5	3.88965	3.79079	3.69590	3.60478	3.51723	3.43308
6	4.48592	4.35526	4.23054	4.11141	3.99755	3.88867
7	5.03295	4.86842	4.71220	4.56376	4.42261	4.28830
8	5.53482	5.33493	5.14612	4.96764	4.79677	4.63886
9	5.99525	5.75902	5.53705	5.32825	5.13166	4.94637
10	6.41766	6.14457	5.88923	5.65022	5.42624	5.21612
11	6.80519	6.49506	6.20652	5.93770	5.68694	5.45273
12	7.16072	6.81369	6.49236	6.19437	5.91765	5.66029
13	7.48690	7.10336	6.74987	6.42355	6.12181	5.84236
14	7.78615	7.36669	6.96187	6.62817	6.30249	6.00207
15	8.06069	7.60608	7.19087	6.81086	6.46238	6.14217
16	8.31256	7.82371	7.37916	6.97399	6.60388	6.26506
17	8.54363	8.02155	7.54879	7.11963	6.72909	6.37286
18	8.75562	8.20141	7.70162	7.24967	6.83991	6.46742
19	8.95012	8.36492	7.83929	7.36578	6.93797	6.55037
20	9.12855	8.51356	7.96333	7.46944	7.02475	6.62313
21	9.29224	8.64869	8.07507	7.56200	7.10155	6.68696
22	9.44242	8.77154	8.17574	7.64465	7.16951	6.74294
23	9.58021	8.88322	8.26643	7.71843	7.22966	6.79206
24	9.70661	8.98474	8.34814	7.78432	7.28288	6.83514
25	9.82258	9.07704	8.42174	7.84314	7.32998	6.87293
26	9.92897	9.16094	8.48806	7.89566	7.37167	6.90608
27	10.02658	9.23722	8.54780	7.94255	7.40856	6.93515
28	10.11613	9.30657	8.60162	7.98442	7.44120	6.96066
29	10.19828	9.36961	8.65011	8.02181	7.47009	6.98304
30	10.27365	9.42691	8.69379	8.05518	7.49565	7.00266
31	10.34280	9.47901	8.73315	8.08499	7.51828	7.01988
32	10.40624	9.52638	8.76860	8.11159	7.53830	7.03498
33	10.46444	9.56943	8.80054	8.13535	7.55602	7.04823
34	10.51784	9.60858	8.82932	8.15656	7.57170	7.05985
35	10.56682	9.64416	8.85524	8.17550	7.58557	7.07005
40	10.75736	9.77905	8.95105	8.24378	7.63438	7.10504
45	10.88118	9.86281	9.00791	8.28252	7.66086	7.12322
50	10.96168	9.91481	9.04165	8.30450	7.67524	7.13266

WILLIAMS-SONOMA, INC.

2005 ANNUAL REPORT

Annual Meeting of Shareholders
May 23, 2006

ITEM 8. FINANCIAL STATEMENTS AND SUPPLEMENTARY DATA

Williams-Sonoma, Inc.
Consolidated Statements of Earnings

	Fiscal Year Ended		
Dollars and shares in thousands, except per share amounts	Jan. 29, 2006	Jan. 30, 2005	Feb. 1, 2004
Net revenues	$3,538,947	$3,136,931	$2,754,368
Cost of goods sold	2,103,465	1,865,786	1,643,791
Gross margin	1,435,482	1,271,145	1,110,577
Selling, general and administrative expenses	1,090,392	961,176	855,790
Interest income	(5,683)	(1,939)	(873)
Interest expense	1,975	1,703	22
Earnings before income taxes	348,798	310,205	255,638
Income taxes	133,932	118,971	98,427
Net earnings	$ 214,866	$ 191,234	$ 157,211
Basic earnings per share	$ 1.86	$ 1.65	$ 1.36
Diluted earnings per share	$ 1.81	$ 1.60	$ 1.32
Shares used in calculation of earnings per share:			
Basic	115,616	116,159	115,583
Diluted	118,427	119,347	119,016

See Notes to Consolidated Financial Statements.

38

Williams-Sonoma, Inc.
Consolidated Balance Sheets

Dollars and shares in thousands, except per share amounts	Jan. 29, 2006	Jan. 30, 2005
ASSETS		
Current assets		
Cash and cash equivalents	$ 360,982	$ 239,210
Accounts receivable (less allowance for doubtful accounts of $168 and $217)	51,020	42,520
Merchandise inventories – net	520,292	452,421
Prepaid catalog expenses	53,925	53,520
Prepaid expenses	31,847	38,018
Deferred income taxes	57,267	39,015
Other assets	7,831	9,061
Total current assets	1,083,164	873,765
Property and equipment – net	880,305	852,412
Other assets (less accumulated amortization of $679 and $2,066)	18,151	19,368
Total assets	$1,981,620	$1,745,545
LIABILITIES AND SHAREHOLDERS' EQUITY		
Current liabilities		
Accounts payable	$ 196,074	$ 173,781
Accrued salaries, benefits and other	93,434	86,767
Customer deposits	172,775	148,535
Income taxes payable	83,589	72,052
Current portion of long-term debt	18,864	23,435
Other liabilities	25,656	17,587
Total current liabilities	590,392	522,157
Deferred rent and lease incentives	218,254	212,193
Long-term debt	14,490	19,154
Deferred income tax liabilities	18,455	21,057
Other long-term obligations	14,711	13,322
Total liabilities	856,302	787,883
Commitments and contingencies – See Note L		
Shareholders' equity		
Preferred stock, $.01 par value, 7,500 shares authorized, none issued	—	—
Common stock, $.01 par value, 253,125 shares authorized, 114,779 shares issued and outstanding at January 29, 2006; 115,372 shares issued and outstanding at January 30, 2005	1,148	1,154
Additional paid-in capital	325,146	286,720
Retained earnings	791,329	664,619
Accumulated other comprehensive income	7,695	5,169
Total shareholders' equity	1,125,318	957,662
Total liabilities and shareholders' equity	$1,981,620	$1,745,545

See Notes to Consolidated Financial Statements.

Form 10-K

Williams-Sonoma, Inc.
Consolidated Statements of Shareholders' Equity

Dollars and shares in thousands	Common Stock		Additional Paid-in Capital	Retained Earnings	Accumulated Other Comprehensive Income (Loss)	Deferred Stock-Based Compensation	Total Shareholders' Equity	Comprehensive Income
	Shares	Amount						
Balance at February 2, 2003	114,317	$1,143	$196,259	$446,837	$ (11)	$(250)	$ 643,978	
Net earnings	—	—	—	157,211	—	—	157,211	$157,211
Foreign currency translation adjustment and related tax effect	—	—	—	—	3,298	—	3,298	3,298
Exercise of stock options and related tax effect	3,295	33	59,516	—	—	—	59,549	
Repurchase and retirement of common stock	(1,785)	(18)	(3,450)	(56,227)	—	—	(59,695)	
Amortization of deferred stock-based compensation	—	—	—	—	—	250	250	
Comprehensive income								$160,509
Balance at February 1, 2004	115,827	1,158	252,325	547,821	3,287	—	804,591	
Net earnings	—	—	—	191,234	—	—	191,234	$191,234
Foreign currency translation adjustment	—	—	—	—	1,882	—	1,882	1,882
Exercise of stock options and related tax effect	1,818	18	39,257	—	—	—	39,275	
Repurchase and retirement of common stock	(2,273)	(22)	(4,862)	(74,436)	—	—	(79,320)	
Comprehensive income								$193,116
Balance at January 30, 2005	115,372	1,154	286,720	664,619	5,169	—	957,662	
Net earnings	—	—	—	214,866	—	—	214,866	$214,866
Foreign currency translation adjustment	—	—	—	—	2,526	—	2,526	2,526
Exercise of stock options and related tax effect	1,829	18	43,727	—	—	—	43,745	
Repurchase and retirement of common stock	(2,422)	(24)	(5,741)	(88,156)	—	—	(93,921)	
Stock-based compensation expense	—	—	440	—	—	—	440	
Comprehensive income								$217,392
Balance at January 29, 2006	114,779	$1,148	$325,146	$791,329	$7,695	$ —	$1,125,318	

See Notes to Consolidated Financial Statements.

Williams-Sonoma, Inc.
Consolidated Statements of Cash Flows

	Fiscal Year Ended		
Dollars in thousands	Jan. 29, 2006	Jan. 30, 2005	Feb. 1, 2004
Cash flows from operating activities:			
Net earnings	$ 214,866	$ 191,234	$ 157,211
Adjustments to reconcile net earnings to net cash provided by operating activities:			
Depreciation and amortization	123,199	111,624	99,534
Loss on disposal/impairment of assets	12,050	1,080	2,353
Amortization of deferred lease incentives	(24,909)	(22,530)	(19,513)
Deferred income taxes	(20,791)	(6,254)	(6,472)
Tax benefit from exercise of stock options	15,743	13,085	20,429
Stock-based compensation expense	440	—	250
Other	—	335	—
Changes in:			
Accounts receivable	(6,829)	(10,900)	2,796
Merchandise inventories	(67,474)	(48,017)	(82,196)
Prepaid catalog expenses	(405)	(15,056)	(3,302)
Prepaid expenses and other assets	9,032	(19,702)	(15,161)
Accounts payable	14,365	17,773	(11,358)
Accrued salaries, benefits and other	15,950	9,955	(1,020)
Customer deposits	24,066	32,273	23,014
Deferred rent and lease incentives	27,661	42,080	34,800
Income taxes payable	11,409	7,457	7,986
Net cash provided by operating activities	348,373	304,437	209,351
Cash flows from investing activities:			
Purchases of property and equipment	(151,788)	(181,453)	(211,979)
Net cash used in investing activities	(151,788)	(181,453)	(211,979)
Cash flows from financing activities:			
Proceeds from bond issuance	—	15,000	—
Repayments of long-term obligations	(9,235)	(9,789)	(7,610)
Proceeds from exercise of stock options	28,002	26,190	39,120
Repurchase of common stock	(93,921)	(79,320)	(59,695)
Credit facility costs	(654)	(288)	(41)
Net cash used in financing activities	(75,808)	(48,207)	(28,226)
Effect of exchange rates on cash and cash equivalents	995	523	1,269
Net increase (decrease) in cash and cash equivalents	121,772	75,300	(29,585)
Cash and cash equivalents at beginning of year	239,210	163,910	193,495
Cash and cash equivalents at end of year	$ 360,982	$ 239,210	$ 163,910
Supplemental disclosure of cash flow information:			
Cash paid during the year for:			
Interest[1]	$ 3,352	$ 3,585	$ 2,367
Income taxes	130,766	105,910	79,184
Non-cash investing and financing activities:			
Assets acquired under capital lease obligations	—	—	1,275
Consolidation of Memphis-based distribution facilities:			
Fixed assets assumed	—	—	19,512
Long-term debt assumed	—	—	18,223
Other long-term liabilities assumed	—	—	1,289

[1] *Interest paid, net of capitalized interest, was $2.2 million, $1.9 million and $0.2 million in fiscal 2005, 2004 and 2003, respectively.*

See Notes to Consolidated Financial Statements.

Williams-Sonoma, Inc.
Notes to Consolidated Financial Statements

Note A: Summary of Significant Accounting Policies

We are a specialty retailer of products for the home. The retail segment of our business sells our products through our six retail store concepts (Williams-Sonoma, Pottery Barn, Pottery Barn Kids, Hold Everything, West Elm and Williams-Sonoma Home). The direct-to-customer segment of our business sells similar products through our eight direct-mail catalogs (Williams-Sonoma, Pottery Barn, Pottery Barn Kids, Pottery Barn Bed + Bath, PBteen, Hold Everything, West Elm and Williams-Sonoma Home) and six e-commerce websites (williams-sonoma.com, potterybarn.com, potterybarnkids.com, pbteen.com, westelm.com and holdeverything.com). The catalogs reach customers throughout the U.S., while the six retail concepts currently operate 570 stores in 43 states, Washington, D.C. and Canada.

In January 2006, we decided to transition the merchandising strategies of our Hold Everything brand into our other existing brands by the end of fiscal 2006. In connection with this transition, we incurred a pre-tax charge of approximately $13,500,000, or $0.07 per diluted share, in the fourth quarter of fiscal 2005. These costs primarily included the initial asset impairment and lease termination costs associated with the shutdown of the Hold Everything retail stores, the asset impairment of the e-commerce website, and the write-down of impaired merchandise inventories. Of this pre-tax charge, approximately $4,500,000 is included in cost of goods sold and approximately $9,000,000 is included in selling, general, and administrative expenses. We expect to incur an additional after-tax charge of $0.03 per diluted share in the first half of fiscal 2006.

Significant intercompany transactions and accounts have been eliminated.

Fiscal Year

Our fiscal year ends on the Sunday closest to January 31, based on a 52/53-week year. Fiscal years 2005, 2004 and 2003 ended on January 29, 2006 (52 weeks), January 30, 2005 (52 weeks) and February 1, 2004 (52 weeks), respectively. The Company's next 53-week fiscal year will be fiscal 2007, ending on February 3, 2008.

Use of Estimates

The preparation of financial statements in accordance with accounting principles generally accepted in the United States of America requires us to make estimates and assumptions that affect the reported amounts of assets, liabilities, revenues and expenses and related disclosures of contingent assets and liabilities. These estimates and assumptions are evaluated on an on-going basis and are based on historical experience and various other factors that we believe to be reasonable under the circumstances. Actual results could differ from these estimates.

Cash Equivalents

Cash equivalents include highly liquid investments with an original maturity of three months or less. Our policy is to invest in high-quality, short-term instruments to achieve maximum yield while maintaining a level of liquidity consistent with our needs. Book cash overdrafts issued but not yet presented to the bank for payment are reclassified to accounts payable.

Allowance for Doubtful Accounts

A summary of activity in the allowance for doubtful accounts is as follows:

Dollars in thousands	Fiscal 2005	Fiscal 2004	Fiscal 2003
Balance at beginning of year	$217	$207	$ 64
Provision for loss on accounts receivable	(49)	10	143
Accounts written off	—	—	—
Balance at end of year	$168	$217	$207

Merchandise Inventories

Merchandise inventories, net of an allowance for excess quantities and obsolescence, are stated at the lower of cost (weighted average method) or market. We estimate a provision for damaged, obsolete, excess and slow-moving inventory based on inventory aging reports and specific identification. We generally reserve, based on inventory aging reports, for 50% of the cost of all inventory between one and two years old and 100% of the cost of all inventory over two years old. If actual obsolescence is different from our estimate, we will adjust our provision accordingly. Specific reserves are also recorded in the event the cost of the inventory exceeds the fair market value. In addition, on a monthly basis, we estimate a reserve for expected shrinkage at the concept and channel level based on historical shrinkage factors and our current inventory levels. Actual shrinkage is recorded at year-end based on the results of our physical inventory count and can vary from our estimates due to such factors as changes in operations within our distribution centers, the mix of our inventory (which ranges from large furniture to small tabletop items) and execution against loss prevention initiatives in our stores, off-site storage locations, and our third party transportation providers.

Approximately 63%, 62% and 61% of our merchandise purchases in fiscal 2005, fiscal 2004 and fiscal 2003, respectively, were foreign-sourced, primarily from Asia and Europe.

Prepaid Catalog Expenses

Prepaid catalog expenses consist of third party incremental direct costs, including creative design, paper, printing, postage and mailing costs for all of our direct response catalogs. Such costs are capitalized as prepaid catalog expenses and are amortized over their expected period of future benefit. Such amortization is based upon the ratio of actual revenues to the total of actual and estimated future revenues on an individual catalog basis. Estimated future revenues are based upon various factors such as the total number of catalogs and pages circulated, the probability and magnitude of consumer response and the assortment of merchandise offered. Each catalog is generally fully amortized over a six to nine month period, with the majority of the amortization occurring within the first four to five months. Prepaid catalog expenses are evaluated for realizability on a monthly basis by comparing the carrying amount associated with each catalog to the estimated probable remaining future profitability (remaining net revenues less merchandise cost of goods sold, selling expenses and catalog related-costs) associated with that catalog. If the catalog is not expected to be profitable, the carrying amount of the catalog is impaired accordingly. Catalog advertising expenses were $321,610,000, $278,169,000 and $250,337,000 in fiscal 2005, fiscal 2004 and fiscal 2003, respectively.

Property and Equipment

Property and equipment is stated at cost. Depreciation is computed using the straight-line method over the estimated useful lives of the assets below. Any reduction in the estimated lives would result in higher depreciation expense in a given period for the related assets.

Leasehold improvements	Shorter of estimated useful life or lease term (generally 3 – 22 years)
Fixtures and equipment	2 – 20 years
Buildings and building improvements	12 – 40 years
Capitalized software	2 – 10 years
Corporate aircraft	20 years (20% salvage value)
Capital leases	Shorter of estimated useful life or lease term (generally 4 – 5 years)

Internally developed software costs are capitalized in accordance with the American Institute of Certified Public Accountants Statement of Position 98-1, "Accounting for the Costs of Computer Software Developed or Obtained for Internal Use."

Interest costs related to assets under construction, including software projects, are capitalized during the construction or development period. We capitalized interest costs of $1,200,000, $1,689,000 and $2,142,000 in fiscal 2005, fiscal 2004 and fiscal 2003, respectively.

For any store closures where a lease obligation still exists, we record the estimated future liability associated with the rental obligation on the date the store is closed in accordance with Statement of Financial Accounting Standards ("SFAS") No. 146, "Accounting for Costs Associated with Exit or Disposal Activities." However, most store closures occur upon the lease expiration.

We review the carrying value of all long-lived assets for impairment whenever events or changes in circumstances indicate that the carrying value of an asset may not be recoverable. In accordance with SFAS No. 144, "Accounting for the Impairment or Disposal of Long-Lived Assets," we review for impairment all stores for which current cash flows from operations are negative, or the construction costs are significantly in excess of the amount originally expected. Impairment results when the carrying value of the assets exceeds the undiscounted future cash flows over the life of the lease. Our estimate of undiscounted future cash flows over the lease term (typically 5 to 22 years) is based upon our experience, historical operations of the stores and estimates of future store profitability and economic conditions. The future estimates of store profitability and economic conditions require estimating such factors as sales growth, employment rates, lease escalations, inflation on operating expenses and the overall economics of the retail industry for up to 20 years in the future, and are therefore subject to variability and difficult to predict. If a long-lived asset is found to be impaired, the amount recognized for impairment is equal to the difference between the carrying value and the asset's fair value. The fair value is estimated based upon future cash flows (discounted at a rate that approximates our weighted average cost of capital) or other reasonable estimates of fair market value.

Lease Rights and Other Intangible Assets
Lease rights, representing costs incurred to acquire the lease of a specific commercial property, are recorded at cost in other assets and are amortized over the lives of the respective leases. Other intangible assets include fees associated with the acquisition of our credit facility and are recorded at cost in other assets and amortized over the life of the facility.

Self-Insured Liabilities
We are primarily self-insured for workers' compensation, employee health benefits and product and general liability claims. We record self-insurance liabilities based on claims filed, including the development of those claims, and an estimate of claims incurred but not yet reported. Factors affecting this estimate include future inflation rates, changes in severity, benefit level changes, medical costs and claim settlement patterns. Should a different amount of claims occur compared to what was estimated, or costs of the claims increase or decrease beyond what was anticipated, reserves may need to be adjusted accordingly. We determine our workers' compensation liability and general liability claims reserves based on an actuarial analysis. Reserves for self-insurance liabilities are recorded within accrued salaries, benefits and other on our consolidated balance sheet.

Customer Deposits
Customer deposits are primarily comprised of unredeemed gift certificates and merchandise credits and deferred revenue related to undelivered merchandise. We maintain a liability for unredeemed gift certificates and merchandise credits until the earlier of redemption, escheatment or seven years. After seven years, the remaining unredeemed gift certificate or merchandise credit liability is relieved and recorded within selling, general and administrative expenses.

Deferred Rent and Lease Incentives
For leases that contain fixed escalations of the minimum annual lease payment during the original term of the lease, we recognize rental expense on a straight-line basis over the lease term, including the construction period, and record the difference between rent expense and the amount currently payable as deferred rent. Any rental expense incurred during the construction period is capitalized as a leasehold improvement within property and equipment and depreciated over the lease term. Deferred lease incentives include construction allowances received from landlords, which are amortized on a straight-line basis over the lease term, including the construction period. Beginning in fiscal 2006, in accordance with Financial Accounting Standards Board

44

("FASB") Staff Position ("FSP") FAS 13-1, "Accounting for Rental Costs Incurred During a Construction Period," we will expense any rental costs incurred during the construction period.

Contingent Liabilities
Contingent liabilities are recorded when it is determined that the outcome of an event is expected to result in a loss that is considered probable and reasonably estimable.

Fair Value of Financial Instruments
The carrying values of cash and cash equivalents, accounts receivable, investments, accounts payable and debt approximate their estimated fair values.

Revenue Recognition
We recognize revenues and the related cost of goods sold (including shipping costs) at the time the products are received by customers in accordance with the provisions of Staff Accounting Bulletin ("SAB") No. 101, "Revenue Recognition in Financial Statements" as amended by SAB No. 104, "Revenue Recognition." Revenue is recognized for retail sales (excluding home-delivered merchandise) at the point of sale in the store and for home-delivered merchandise and direct-to-customer sales when the merchandise is delivered to the customer. Discounts provided to customers are accounted for as a reduction of sales. We record a reserve for estimated product returns in each reporting period. Shipping and handling fees charged to the customer are recognized as revenue at the time the products are delivered to the customer.

Sales Returns Reserve
Our customers may return purchased items for an exchange or refund. We record a reserve for estimated product returns, net of cost of goods sold, based on historical return trends together with current product sales performance. If actual returns, net of cost of goods sold, are different than those projected by management, the estimated sales returns reserve will be adjusted accordingly. A summary of activity in the sales returns reserve is as follows:

Dollars in thousands	Fiscal 2005[1]	Fiscal 2004[1]	Fiscal 2003[1]
Balance at beginning of year	$ 13,506	$ 12,281	$ 10,292
Provision for sales returns	243,807	215,715	182,829
Actual sales returns	(243,631)	(214,490)	(180,840)
Balance at end of year	$ 13,682	$ 13,506	$ 12,281

[1]*Amounts are shown net of cost of goods sold.*

Vendor Allowances
We may receive allowances or credits from vendors for volume rebates. In accordance with Emerging Issues Task Force ("EITF") 02-16, "Accounting by a Customer (Including a Reseller) for Certain Consideration Received from a Vendor," our accounting policy is to treat such volume rebates as an offset to the cost of the product or services provided at the time the expense is recorded. These allowances and credits received are primarily recorded in cost of goods sold or in selling, general and administrative expenses.

Foreign Currency Translation
The functional currency of our Canadian subsidiary is the Canadian dollar. Assets and liabilities are translated into U.S. dollars using the current exchange rates in effect at the balance sheet date, while revenues and expenses are translated at the average exchange rates during the period. The resulting translation adjustments are recorded as other comprehensive income within shareholders' equity. Gains and losses resulting from foreign currency transactions have not been significant and are included in selling, general and administrative expenses.

Financial Instruments

As of January 29, 2006, we have 14 retail stores in Canada, which expose us to market risk associated with foreign currency exchange rate fluctuations. As necessary, we have utilized 30-day foreign currency contracts to minimize any currency remeasurement risk associated with intercompany assets and liabilities of our Canadian subsidiary. These contracts are accounted for by adjusting the carrying amount of the contract to market and recognizing any gain or loss in selling, general and administrative expenses in each reporting period. We did not enter into any new foreign currency contracts during fiscal 2005 or fiscal 2004. Any gain or loss associated with these types of contracts in prior years was not material to us.

Income Taxes

Income taxes are accounted for using the asset and liability method. Under this method, deferred income taxes arise from temporary differences between the tax basis of assets and liabilities and their reported amounts in the consolidated financial statements. We record reserves for estimates of probable settlements of foreign and domestic tax audits. At any one time, many tax years are subject to audit by various taxing jurisdictions. The results of these audits and negotiations with taxing authorities may affect the ultimate settlement of these issues. Our effective tax rate in a given financial statement period may be materially impacted by changes in the mix and level of earnings.

Earnings Per Share

Basic earnings per share is computed as net earnings divided by the weighted average number of common shares outstanding for the period. Diluted earnings per share is computed as net earnings divided by the weighted average number of common shares outstanding for the period plus common stock equivalents, consisting of shares subject to stock options and other stock compensation awards.

Stock-Based Compensation

We account for stock options and awards granted to employees using the intrinsic value method in accordance with Accounting Principles Board Opinion No. 25, "Accounting for Stock Issued to Employees." No compensation expense has been recognized in the consolidated financial statements for stock options, as we grant all stock options with an exercise price equal to the market price of our common stock at the date of grant, however, stock compensation expense is recognized in the consolidated financial statements for restricted stock unit awards. SFAS No. 123, "Accounting for Stock-Based Compensation," as amended by SFAS No. 148, "Accounting for Stock-Based Compensation – Transition and Disclosure," however, requires the disclosure of pro forma net earnings and earnings per share as if we had adopted the fair value method. Under SFAS No. 123, the fair value of stock-based awards to employees is calculated through the use of option pricing models. These models require subjective assumptions, including future stock price volatility and expected time to exercise, which affect the calculated values. Our calculations are based on a single option valuation approach, and forfeitures are recognized as they occur.

The following table illustrates the effect on net earnings and earnings per share as if we had applied the fair value recognition provisions of SFAS No. 123, as amended by SFAS No. 148, to all of our stock-based compensation arrangements.

	Fiscal Year Ended		
Dollars in thousands, except per share amounts	Jan. 29, 2006	Jan. 30, 2005	Feb. 1, 2004
Net earnings, as reported	$214,866	$191,234	$157,211
Add: Stock-based employee compensation expense included in reported net earnings, net of related tax effect	273	—	154
Deduct: Total stock-based employee compensation expense determined under fair value method for all awards, net of related tax effect	(16,788)	(17,059)	(16,780)
Pro forma net earnings	$198,351	$174,175	$140,585
Basic earnings per share			
As reported	$ 1.86	$ 1.65	$ 1.36
Pro forma	1.72	1.50	1.22
Diluted earnings per share			
As reported	$ 1.81	$ 1.60	$ 1.32
Pro forma	1.69	1.47	1.16

The fair value of each option grant was estimated on the date of the grant using the Black-Scholes option-pricing model with the following weighted average assumptions:

	Fiscal Year Ended		
	Jan. 29, 2006	Jan. 30, 2005	Feb. 1, 2004
Dividend yield	—	—	—
Volatility	59.2%	60.1%	63.9%
Risk-free interest rate	4.3%	3.9%	3.4%
Expected term (years)	6.5	6.8	6.7

In January 2006, we issued 840,000 restricted stock units of our common stock to certain employees. Fifty percent of the restricted stock units will vest on January 31, 2010, and the remaining fifty percent will vest on January 31, 2011 based upon the employees' continued employment throughout the vesting period. Accordingly, total compensation expense (based upon the fair market value of $42.18 on the issue date) of $35,431,000 will be recognized on a straight-line basis over the vesting period. In fiscal 2005, we recognized approximately $440,000 of compensation expense related to these restricted stock units.

During fiscal 2001, we entered into employment agreements with certain executive officers. All stock-based compensation expense related to these agreements was fully recognized as of our first quarter ended May 4, 2003. We recognized approximately zero, zero and $250,000 of stock-based compensation expense related to these employment agreements in fiscal 2005, fiscal 2004 and fiscal 2003, respectively.

New Accounting Pronouncements
In December 2004, the FASB issued SFAS No. 123R, "Share Based Payment." SFAS No. 123R will require us to measure and record compensation expense in our consolidated financial statements for all employee share-based compensation awards using a fair value method. In addition, the adoption of SFAS No. 123R requires additional accounting and disclosure related to the income tax and cash flow effects resulting from share-based payment arrangements. We expect to adopt this Statement using the modified prospective application transition method beginning in the first quarter of fiscal 2006. We anticipate the adoption of this Statement to result in a reduction to our diluted earnings per share of approximately $0.19 for fiscal 2006.

In March 2005, the FASB issued FASB Interpretation No. ("FIN") No. 47, "Accounting for Conditional Asset Retirement Obligations – An Interpretation of FASB Statement No. 143," which requires an entity to recognize a liability for the fair value of a conditional asset retirement obligation when incurred if the liability's fair value can be reasonably estimated. We adopted the provisions of FIN 47 as of January 29, 2006. The adoption of this Interpretation did not have a material impact on our consolidated financial position, results of operations or cash flows.

In October 2005, the FASB issued FSP No. FAS 13-1, "Accounting for Rental Costs Incurred during a Construction Period," which requires us, beginning on January 30, 2006, to expense all rental costs associated with our operating leases that are incurred during a construction period. Prior to this date, rental costs incurred during the construction period were capitalized until the store opening date. We anticipate the adoption of this Staff Position to result in a reduction to our diluted earnings per share of approximately $0.03 for fiscal 2006.

In September 2005, the EITF issued EITF No. 05-6, "Determining the Amortization Period for Leasehold Improvements Purchased after Lease Inception or Acquired in a Business Combination," which requires us to amortize leasehold improvements that are placed in service significantly after the beginning of a lease term over the shorter of the useful life of the assets, or a term that includes required lease periods and renewals that are deemed to be reasonably assumed at the date the leasehold improvement is purchased. This EITF did not have a material impact on our consolidated financial position, results of operations or cash flows.

Reclassifications
Certain items in the fiscal 2004 and fiscal 2003 consolidated financial statements have been reclassified to conform to the fiscal 2005 presentation.

Note B: Property and Equipment

Property and equipment consists of the following:

Dollars in thousands	Jan. 29, 2006	Jan. 30, 2005
Leasehold improvements	$ 651,498	$ 600,249
Fixtures and equipment	437,243	398,826
Land and buildings	131,484	131,471
Capitalized software	145,407	132,614
Corporate systems projects in progress[1]	98,398	77,077
Corporate aircraft	48,677	48,618
Construction in progress[2]	31,501	8,063
Capital leases	11,920	11,920
Total	1,556,128	1,408,838
Accumulated depreciation and amortization	(675,823)	(556,426)
Property and equipment – net	$ 880,305	$ 852,412

[1]*Corporate systems projects in progress is primarily comprised of a new merchandising, inventory management and order management system currently under development.*
[2]*Construction in progress is primarily comprised of leasehold improvements and furniture and fixtures related to new, unopened retail stores.*

Note C: Borrowing Arrangements

Long-term debt consists of the following:

Dollars in thousands	Jan. 29, 2006	Jan. 30, 2005
Senior notes	—	$ 5,716
Obligations under capital leases	$ 3,458	5,673
Memphis-based distribution facilities obligation	15,696	17,000
Industrial development bonds	14,200	14,200
Total debt	33,354	42,589
Less current maturities	18,864	23,435
Total long-term debt	$14,490	$19,154

Senior Notes

In August, 2005, we repaid the remaining outstanding balance of $5,716,000 on our unsecured senior notes, with interest payable semi-annually at 7.2% per annum.

Capital Leases

Our $3,458,000 of capital lease obligations consist primarily of in-store computer equipment leases with a term of 60 months. The in-store computer equipment leases include an early purchase option at 54 months for $2,496,000, which is approximately 25% of the acquisition cost. We have an end of lease purchase option to acquire the equipment at the greater of fair market value or 15% of the acquisition cost.

Subsequent to year-end, we exercised the early purchase option on three of these leases and expect to exercise this option on the remaining computer equipment leases during fiscal 2006.

See Note F for a discussion on our bond-related debt pertaining to our Memphis-based distribution facilities.

Industrial Development Bonds

In June 2004, in an effort to utilize tax incentives offered to us by the state of Mississippi, we entered into an agreement whereby the Mississippi Business Finance Corporation issued $15,000,000 in long-term variable rate industrial development bonds, the proceeds, net of debt issuance costs, of which were loaned to us to finance the acquisition and installation of leasehold improvements and equipment located in our newly leased Olive Branch distribution center (the "Mississippi Debt Transaction"). The bonds are marketed through a remarketing agent and are secured by a letter of credit issued under our $300,000,000 line of credit facility. The bonds mature on June 1, 2024. The bond rate resets each week based upon current market rates. The rate in effect at January 29, 2006 was 4.5%.

The bond agreement allows for each bondholder to tender their bonds to the trustee for repurchase, on demand, with seven days advance notice. In the event the remarketing agent fails to remarket the bonds, the trustee will draw upon the letter of credit to fund the purchase of the bonds. As of January 29, 2006, $14,200,000 remained outstanding on these bonds and was classified as current debt. The bond proceeds are restricted for use in the acquisition and installation of leasehold improvements and equipment located in our Olive Branch, Mississippi facility. As of January 29, 2006, we had acquired and installed $14,700,000 of leasehold improvements and equipment associated with the facility.

The aggregate maturities of long-term debt at January 29, 2006 were as follows:

Dollars in thousands

Fiscal 2006[1]	$18,864
Fiscal 2007	1,668
Fiscal 2008	1,584
Fiscal 2009	1,438
Fiscal 2010	1,462
Thereafter	8,338
Total	$33,354

[1]*Includes $14.2 million related to the Mississippi Debt Transaction classified as current debt.*

Credit Facility
As of January 29, 2006, we have a credit facility that provides for a $300,000,000 unsecured revolving line of credit that may be used for loans or letters of credit and contains certain financial covenants, including a maximum leverage ratio (funded debt adjusted for lease and rent expense to EBITDAR), and a minimum fixed charge coverage ratio. Prior to August 22, 2009, we may, upon notice to the lenders, request an increase in the credit facility of up to $100,000,000, to provide for a total of $400,000,000 of unsecured revolving credit. The credit facility contains events of default that include, among others, non-payment of principal, interest or fees, inaccuracy of representations and warranties, violation of covenants, bankruptcy and insolvency events, material judgments, cross defaults to certain other indebtedness and events constituting a change of control. The occurrence of an event of default will increase the applicable rate of interest by 2.0% and could result in the acceleration of our obligations under the credit facility, and an obligation of any or all of our U.S. subsidiaries to pay the full amount of our obligations under the credit facility. The credit facility matures on February 22, 2010, at which time all outstanding borrowings must be repaid and all outstanding letters of credit must be cash collateralized.

We may elect interest rates calculated at Bank of America's prime rate (or, if greater, the average rate on overnight federal funds plus one-half of one percent) or LIBOR plus a margin based on our leverage ratio. No amounts were borrowed under the credit facility during fiscal 2005 or fiscal 2004. However, as of January 29, 2006, $36,073,000 in issued but undrawn standby letters of credit were outstanding under the credit facility. The standby letters of credit were issued to secure the liabilities associated with workers' compensation, other insurance programs and certain debt transactions. As of January 29, 2006, we were in compliance with our financial covenants under the credit facility.

Letter of Credit Facilities
We have three unsecured commercial letter of credit reimbursement facilities for an aggregate of $145,000,000, each of which expires on September 9, 2006. As of January 29, 2006, an aggregate of $105,260,000 was outstanding under the letter of credit facilities. Such letters of credit represent only a future commitment to fund inventory purchases to which we had not taken legal title as of January 29, 2006. The latest expiration possible for any future letters of credit issued under the agreements is February 6, 2007.

Interest Expense
Interest expense was $1,975,000 (net of capitalized interest of $1,200,000), $1,703,000 (net of capitalized interest of $1,689,000), and $22,000 (net of capitalized interest of $2,142,000) for fiscal 2005, fiscal 2004 and fiscal 2003, respectively.

Note D: Income Taxes

The components of earnings before income taxes, by tax jurisdiction, are as follows:

	Fiscal Year Ended		
Dollars in thousands	Jan. 29, 2006	Jan. 30, 2005	Feb. 1, 2004
United States	$ 337,468	$ 303,986	$ 252,119
Foreign	11,330	6,219	3,519
Total earnings before income taxes	$ 348,798	$ 310,205	$ 255,638

The provision for income taxes consists of the following:

	Fiscal Year Ended		
Dollars in thousands	Jan. 29, 2006	Jan. 30, 2005	Feb. 1, 2004
Current payable			
Federal	$ 131,242	$ 105,096	$ 87,194
State	19,002	17,642	15,640
Foreign	4,479	2,487	2,065
Total current	154,723	125,225	104,899
Deferred			
Federal	(18,912)	(6,168)	(3,587)
State	(1,538)	(70)	(2,015)
Foreign	(341)	(16)	(870)
Total deferred	(20,791)	(6,254)	(6,472)
Total provision	$ 133,932	$ 118,971	$ 98,427

Except where required by U.S. tax law, no provision was made for U.S. income taxes on the cumulative undistributed earnings of our Canadian subsidiary, as we intend to utilize those earnings in the Canadian operations for an indefinite period of time and do not intend to repatriate such earnings.

Accumulated undistributed earnings of our Canadian subsidiary were approximately $13,440,000 as of January 29, 2006. It is currently not practical to estimate the tax liability that might be payable if these foreign earnings were repatriated.

A reconciliation of income taxes at the federal statutory corporate rate to the effective rate is as follows:

	Fiscal Year Ended		
	Jan. 29, 2006	Jan. 30, 2005	Feb. 1, 2004
Federal income taxes at the statutory rate	35.0%	35.0%	35.0%
State income tax rate, less federal benefit	3.4%	3.4%	3.5%
Total	38.4%	38.4%	38.5%

51

Significant components of our deferred tax accounts are as follows:

Dollars in thousands	Jan. 29, 2006	Jan. 30, 2005
Deferred tax asset (liability)		
Current:		
Compensation	$ 15,362	$ 14,667
Inventory	11,580	11,357
Accrued liabilities	14,186	13,725
Customer deposits	36,079	19,342
Deferred catalog costs	(20,696)	(20,540)
Other	756	464
Total current	57,267	39,015
Non-current:		
Depreciation	(11,559)	(18,634)
Deferred rent	8,683	8,275
Deferred lease incentives	(16,506)	(11,595)
Other	927	897
Total non-current	(18,455)	(21,057)
Total	$ 38,812	$ 17,958

Note E: Accounting for Leases

Operating Leases

We lease store locations, warehouses, corporate facilities, call centers and certain equipment under operating and capital leases for original terms ranging generally from 3 to 22 years. Certain leases contain renewal options for periods up to 20 years. The rental payment requirements in our store leases are typically structured as either minimum rent, minimum rent plus additional rent based on a percentage of store sales if a specified store sales threshold is exceeded, or rent based on a percentage of store sales if a specified store sales threshold or contractual obligations of the landlord have not been met.

We have an operating lease for a 1,002,000 square foot retail distribution facility located in Olive Branch, Mississippi. The lease has an initial term of 22.5 years, expiring January 2022, with two optional five-year renewals. The lessor, an unrelated party, is a limited liability company. The construction and expansion of the distribution facility was financed by the original lessor through the sale of $39,200,000 Taxable Industrial Development Revenue Bonds, Series 1998 and 1999, issued by the Mississippi Business Finance Corporation. The bonds are collateralized by the distribution facility. As of January 29, 2006, approximately $31,249,000 was outstanding on the bonds. During fiscal 2005, we made annual rental payments of approximately $3,753,000, plus applicable taxes, insurance and maintenance expenses.

We have an operating lease for an additional 1,103,000 square foot retail distribution facility located in Olive Branch, Mississippi. The lease has an initial term of 22.5 years, expiring January 2023, with two optional five-year renewals. The lessor, an unrelated party, is a limited liability company. The construction of the distribution facility was financed by the original lessor through the sale of $42,500,000 Taxable Industrial Development Revenue Bonds, Series 1999, issued by the Mississippi Business Finance Corporation. The bonds are collateralized by the distribution facility. As of January 29, 2006, approximately $34,396,000 was outstanding on the bonds. During fiscal 2005, we made annual rental payments of approximately $4,181,000, plus applicable taxes, insurance and maintenance expenses.

In December 2003, we entered into an agreement to lease 780,000 square feet of a distribution facility located in Olive Branch, Mississippi. The lease has an initial term of six years, with two optional two-year renewals. The agreement includes an option to lease an additional 390,000 square feet of the same distribution center. We exercised this option during fiscal 2005, however, as of January 29, 2006, we had not occupied this space. During fiscal 2005, we made annual rental payments of approximately $1,927,000, plus applicable taxes, insurance and maintenance expenses.

On February 2, 2004, we entered into an agreement to lease 781,000 square feet of a distribution center located in Cranbury, New Jersey. The lease has an initial term of seven years, with three optional five-year renewals. The agreement requires us to lease an additional 219,000 square feet of the facility in the event the current tenant vacates the premises. As of January 29, 2006, the current tenant had not yet vacated the premises. During fiscal 2005, we made annual rental payments of approximately $3,339,000, plus applicable taxes, insurance and maintenance expenses.

On August 18, 2004, we entered into an agreement to lease a 500,000 square foot distribution facility located in Memphis, Tennessee. The lease has an initial term of four years, with one optional three-year and nine-month renewal. During fiscal 2005, we made annual rental payments of approximately $913,000, plus applicable taxes, insurance and maintenance expenses.

Total rental expense for all operating leases was as follows:

	Fiscal Year Ended		
Dollars in thousands	Jan. 29, 2006	Jan. 30, 2005	Feb. 1, 2004[1]
Minimum rent expense	$ 119,440	$ 110,618	$ 101,377
Contingent rent expense	33,529	26,724	21,796
Less: Sublease rental income	(62)	(59)	(90)
Total rent expense	$ 152,907	$ 137,283	$ 123,083

[1]*Includes rent expense for our Memphis-based distribution facilities which were consolidated by us on February 1, 2004. See Note F.*

The aggregate minimum annual rental payments under noncancelable operating leases (excluding the Memphis-based distribution facilities) in effect at January 29, 2006 were as follows:

Dollars in thousands	Minimum Lease Commitments[1]
Fiscal 2006	$ 178,846
Fiscal 2007	176,891
Fiscal 2008	170,041
Fiscal 2009	160,569
Fiscal 2010	149,092
Thereafter	672,358
Total	$ 1,507,797

[1]*Projected payments include only those amounts that are fixed and determinable as of the reporting date.*

Note F: Consolidation of Memphis-Based Distribution Facilities

Our Memphis-based distribution facilities include an operating lease entered into in July 1983 for a distribution facility in Memphis, Tennessee. The lessor is a general partnership ("Partnership 1") comprised of W. Howard Lester, Chairman of the Board of Directors and a significant shareholder, and James A. McMahan, a Director Emeritus and a significant shareholder. Partnership 1 does not have operations separate from the leasing of this distribution facility and does not have lease agreements with any unrelated third parties.

Partnership 1 financed the construction of this distribution facility through the sale of a total of $9,200,000 of industrial development bonds in 1983 and 1985. Annual principal payments and monthly interest payments are required through maturity in December 2010. The Partnership 1 industrial development bonds are collateralized by the distribution facility and the individual partners guarantee the bond repayments. As of January 29, 2006, $1,887,000 was outstanding under the Partnership 1 industrial development bonds.

During fiscal 2005, we made annual rental payments of approximately $618,000 plus interest on the bonds calculated at a variable rate determined monthly (3.5% in January 2006), applicable taxes, insurance and

Form 10-K

maintenance expenses. Although the current term of the lease expires in August 2006, we are obligated to renew the operating lease on an annual basis until these bonds are fully repaid.

Our other Memphis-based distribution facility includes an operating lease entered into in August 1990 for another distribution facility that is adjoined to the Partnership 1 facility in Memphis, Tennessee. The lessor is a general partnership ("Partnership 2") comprised of W. Howard Lester, James A. McMahan and two unrelated parties. Partnership 2 does not have operations separate from the leasing of this distribution facility and does not have lease agreements with any unrelated third parties.

Partnership 2 financed the construction of this distribution facility and related addition through the sale of a total of $24,000,000 of industrial development bonds in 1990 and 1994. Quarterly interest and annual principal payments are required through maturity in August 2015. The Partnership 2 industrial development bonds are collateralized by the distribution facility and require us to maintain certain financial covenants. As of January 29, 2006, $13,809,000 was outstanding under the Partnership 2 industrial development bonds.

During fiscal 2005, we made annual rental payments of approximately $2,600,000, plus applicable taxes, insurance and maintenance expenses. This operating lease has an original term of 15 years expiring in August 2006, with three optional five-year renewal periods. We are, however, obligated to renew the operating lease on an annual basis until these bonds are fully repaid.

As of February 1, 2004, the Company adopted FIN 46R, which requires existing unconsolidated variable interest entities to be consolidated by their primary beneficiaries if the entities do not effectively disperse risks among parties involved. The two partnerships described above qualify as variable interest entities under FIN 46R due to their related party relationship and our obligation to renew the leases until the bonds are fully repaid. Accordingly, the two related party variable interest entity partnerships from which we lease our Memphis-based distribution facilities were consolidated by us as of February 1, 2004. As of January 29, 2006, the consolidation resulted in increases to our consolidated balance sheet of $18,250,000 in assets (primarily buildings), $15,696,000 in debt, and $2,554,000 in other long-term liabilities. Consolidation of these partnerships did not have an impact on our net income. However, the interest expense associated with the partnerships' debt, shown as occupancy expense in fiscal 2003, is now recorded as interest expense. In fiscal 2005 and fiscal 2004, this interest expense approximated $1,462,000 and $1,525,000, respectively.

Note G: Earnings Per Share

The following is a reconciliation of net earnings and the number of shares used in the basic and diluted earnings per share computations:

Dollars and amounts in thousands, except per share amounts	Net Earnings	Weighted Average Shares	Per-Share Amount
2005			
Basic	$214,866	115,616	$1.86
Effect of dilutive stock options	—	2,811	
Diluted	$214,866	118,427	$1.81
2004			
Basic	$191,234	116,159	$1.65
Effect of dilutive stock options	—	3,188	
Diluted	$191,234	119,347	$1.60
2003			
Basic	$157,211	115,583	$1.36
Effect of dilutive stock options	—	3,433	
Diluted	$157,211	119,016	$1.32

Options with an exercise price greater than the average market price of common shares for the period were 320,000 in fiscal 2005, 196,000 in fiscal 2004 and 436,000 in fiscal 2003 and were not included in the computation of diluted earnings per share, as their inclusion would be anti-dilutive.

Note H: Common Stock

Authorized preferred stock consists of 7,500,000 shares at $0.01 par value of which none was outstanding during fiscal 2005 or fiscal 2004. Authorized common stock consists of 253,125,000 shares at $0.01 par value. Common stock outstanding at the end of fiscal 2005 and fiscal 2004 was 114,779,000 and 115,372,000 shares, respectively. Our Board of Directors is authorized to issue stock options for up to the total number of shares authorized and remaining available for grant under each plan.

In May 2005, our Board of Directors authorized a stock repurchase program to acquire up to 2,000,000 additional shares of our outstanding common stock. During the fourth quarter of fiscal 2005, we repurchased and retired 780,800 shares at a weighted average cost of $41.70 per share and a total cost of approximately $32,556,000. During fiscal 2005, we repurchased and retired a total of 2,422,300 shares at a weighted average cost of $38.77 per share and a total cost of approximately $93,921,000. As of fiscal year-end, the remaining authorized number of shares eligible for repurchase was 20,000. During the first quarter of fiscal 2006, we repurchased and retired these shares at a weighted average cost of $38.84 per share and a total cost of approximately $777,000, which completed all stock repurchase programs previously authorized by our Board of Directors.

In March 2006, our Board of Directors authorized a stock repurchase program to acquire up to an additional 2,000,000 shares of our outstanding common stock. Stock repurchases under this program may be made through open market and privately negotiated transactions at times and in such amounts as management deems appropriate. The timing and actual number of shares repurchased will depend on a variety of factors, including price, corporate and regulatory requirements, capital availability, and other market conditions. The stock repurchase program does not have an expiration date and may be limited or terminated at any time without prior notice.

Prior to March 2006, we had never declared or paid a cash dividend on our common stock. In March 2006, our Board of Directors authorized the initiation of a quarterly cash dividend. The quarterly dividend will be initiated at $0.10 per common share, payable on May 24, 2006, to shareholders of record as of the close of business on April 26, 2006. The aggregate quarterly dividend is estimated at approximately $11,500,000 based on the current number of common shares outstanding. The indicated annual cash dividend, subject to capital availability, is $0.40 per common share, or approximately $46,000,000 in fiscal 2006 based on the current number of common shares outstanding.

Note I: Stock Compensation

Our 1993 Stock Option Plan, as amended (the "1993 Plan"), provides for grants of incentive and nonqualified stock options up to an aggregate of 17,000,000 shares. Stock options may be granted under the 1993 Plan to key employees and Board members of the company and any parent or subsidiary. Annual grants are limited to options to purchase 200,000 shares on a per person basis under this plan. All stock option grants made under the 1993 Plan have a maximum term of ten years, except incentive stock options issued to shareholders with greater than 10% of the voting power of all of our stock, which have a maximum term of five years. The exercise price of these options is not less than 100% of the fair market value of our stock on the date of the option grant or not less than 110% of such fair market value for an incentive stock option granted to a 10% shareholder. Options granted to employees generally vest over five years. Options granted to non-employee Board members generally vest in one year.

Our 2000 Nonqualified Stock Option Plan, as amended (the "2000 Plan"), provides for grants of nonqualified stock options up to an aggregate of 3,000,000 shares. Stock options may be granted under the 2000 Plan to employees who are not officers or Board members. Annual grants are not limited on a per person basis under this plan. All nonqualified stock option grants under the 2000 Plan have a maximum term of ten years with an exercise price of 100% of the fair value of the stock at the option grant date. Options granted to employees generally vest over five years.

Our Amended and Restated 2001 Long-Term Incentive Plan (the "2001 Plan") provides for grants of incentive stock options, nonqualified stock options, restricted stock awards and deferred stock awards up to an aggregate of 8,500,000 shares. Awards may be granted under the 2001 Plan to officers, employee and non-employee Board members of the company and any parent or subsidiary. Annual grants are limited to options to purchase 1,000,000 shares, 200,000 shares of restricted stock, and deferred stock awards of up to 200,000 shares on a per person basis. All stock option grants made under the 2001 Plan have a maximum term of ten years, except incentive stock options issued to 10% shareholders, which have a maximum term of five years. The exercise price of these stock options is not less than 100% of the fair market value of our stock on the date of the option grant or not less than 110% of such fair market value for an incentive stock option granted to a 10% shareholder. Options granted to employees generally vest over five years. Options granted to non-employee Board members generally vest in one year. Non-employee Board members automatically receive stock options on the date of their initial election to the Board and annually thereafter on the date of the annual meeting of shareholders (so long as they continue to serve as a non-employee Board member).

The following table reflects the aggregate activity under our stock option plans:

	Shares	Weighted Average Exercise Price
Balance at February 2, 2003	14,567,106	$14.77
Granted (weighted average fair value of $15.56)	1,596,075	24.37
Exercised	(3,294,478)	11.87
Canceled	(1,089,045)	18.07
Balance at February 1, 2004	11,779,658	16.58
Granted (weighted average fair value of $20.58)	1,626,811	32.57
Exercised	(1,817,308)	14.41
Canceled	(488,734)	20.81
Balance at January 30, 2005	11,100,427	19.08
Granted (weighted average fair value of $23.77)	1,754,990	39.07
Exercised	(1,829,082)	15.30
Canceled	(716,426)	26.81
Balance at January 29, 2006	10,309,909	22.63
Exercisable, February 1, 2004	5,077,371	$12.83
Exercisable, January 30, 2005	5,461,541	14.26
Exercisable, January 29, 2006	5,704,164	16.00

Options to purchase 2,424,858 shares were available for grant at January 29, 2006.

The following table summarizes information about stock options outstanding at January 29, 2006:

	Options Outstanding			Options Exercisable	
Range of exercise prices	Number Outstanding	Weighted Average Contractual Life (Years)	Weighted Average Exercise Price	Number Exercisable	Weighted Average Exercise Price
$ 4.50 – $ 9.50	1,651,008	2.71	$ 8.17	1,651,008	$ 8.17
$ 9.66 – $14.50	1,880,843	4.07	12.80	1,529,680	12.61
$15.00 – $22.47	2,006,335	5.68	19.56	1,282,100	18.26
$22.48 – $31.58	1,786,723	7.14	26.80	922,126	26.66
$32.01 – $43.85	2,985,000	8.82	36.39	319,250	32.92
$ 4.50 – $43.85	10,309,909	6.07	$22.63	5,704,164	$16.00

In January 2006, we issued 840,000 restricted stock units of our common stock to certain employees. Fifty percent of the restricted stock units will vest on January 31, 2010, and the remaining fifty percent will vest on January 31, 2011 based upon the employees' continued employment throughout the vesting period. As of January 29, 2006, 840,000 restricted stock units were outstanding.

56

Note J: Associate Stock Incentive Plan and Other Employee Benefits

We have a defined contribution retirement plan, the "Williams-Sonoma, Inc. Associate Stock Incentive Plan" (the "Plan"), for eligible employees, which is intended to be qualified under Internal Revenue Code Sections 401(a), 401(k) and 401(m). The Plan permits eligible employees to make salary deferral contributions in accordance with Internal Revenue Code Section 401(k) up to 15% of eligible compensation each pay period (4% for certain higher paid individuals). Employees designate the funds in which their contributions are invested. Each participant may choose to have his or her salary deferral contributions and earnings thereon invested in one or more investment funds, including investing in our company stock fund. Prior to November 1, 2005, all matching contributions were invested in our company stock fund. Effective November 1, 2005, participants were allowed to reallocate past matching contributions to one or more investment funds. Effective December 1, 2005, company contributions are invested in a similar manner as the participant's salary deferral contributions. Effective August 1, 2003, our matching contribution is equal to 50% of the participant's salary deferral contribution each pay period, taking into account only those contributions that do not exceed 6% of the participant's eligible pay for the pay period (4% for certain higher paid individuals). For the first five years of the participant's employment, all matching contributions generally vest at the rate of 20% per year of service, measuring service from the participant's hire date. Thereafter, all matching contributions vest immediately. Our contributions to the plan were $3,322,000 in fiscal 2005, $2,850,000 in fiscal 2004 and $3,540,000 in fiscal 2003.

We have a nonqualified executive deferred compensation plan that provides supplemental retirement income benefits for a select group of management and other certain highly compensated employees. This plan permits eligible employees to make salary and bonus deferrals that are 100% vested. We have an unsecured obligation to pay in the future the value of the deferred compensation adjusted to reflect the performance, whether positive or negative, of selected investment measurement options, chosen by each participant, during the deferral period. At January 29, 2006, $11,176,000 was included in other long-term obligations. Additionally, we have purchased life insurance policies on certain participants to potentially offset these unsecured obligations. The cash surrender value of these policies was $9,661,000 at January 29, 2006 and was included in other assets.

Note K: Financial Guarantees

We are party to a variety of contractual agreements under which we may be obligated to indemnify the other party for certain matters. These contracts primarily relate to our commercial contracts, operating leases, trademarks, intellectual property, financial agreements and various other agreements. Under these contracts, we may provide certain routine indemnifications relating to representations and warranties or personal injury matters. The terms of these indemnifications range in duration and may not be explicitly defined. Historically, we have not made significant payments for these indemnifications. We believe that if we were to incur a loss in any of these matters, the loss would not have a material effect on our financial condition or results of operations.

Note L: Commitments and Contingencies

On September 30, 2004, we entered into a five-year service agreement with IBM to host and manage certain aspects of our data center information technology infrastructure. The terms of the agreement require the payment of both fixed and variable charges over the life of the agreement. The variable charges are primarily based on CPU hours, storage capacity and support services that are expected to fluctuate throughout the term of the agreement.

Under the terms of the agreement, we are subject to a minimum charge over the five-year term of the agreement. This minimum charge is based on both a fixed and variable component calculated as a percentage of the total estimated service charges over the five-year term of the agreement. As of January 29, 2006, we estimate the remaining minimum charge to be approximately $21,000,000. The fixed component of this minimum charge will be paid annually not to exceed approximately $5,000,000, while the variable component will be based on usage. The agreement can be terminated at any time for cause and after 24 months for convenience. In the event the agreement is terminated for convenience, a graduated termination fee will be assessed based on the time period remaining in the contract term, not to exceed $9,000,000. During fiscal 2005, we recognized expense of approximately $12,000,000 relating to this agreement.

In addition, we are involved in lawsuits, claims and proceedings incident to the ordinary course of our business. These disputes, which are not currently material, are increasing in number as our business expands and our company grows larger. Litigation is inherently unpredictable. Any claims against us, whether meritorious or not, could be time consuming, result in costly litigation, require significant amounts of management time and result in the diversion of significant operational resources. The results of these lawsuits, claims and proceedings cannot be predicted with certainty. However, we believe that the ultimate resolution of these current matters will not have a material adverse effect on our consolidated financial statements taken as a whole.

Note M: Segment Reporting

We have two reportable segments, retail and direct-to-customer. The retail segment has six merchandising concepts which sell products for the home (Williams-Sonoma, Pottery Barn, Pottery Barn Kids, Hold Everything, West Elm and Williams-Sonoma Home). The six retail merchandising concepts are operating segments, which have been aggregated into one reportable segment, retail. The direct-to-customer segment has seven merchandising concepts (Williams-Sonoma, Pottery Barn, Pottery Barn Kids, PBteen, Hold Everything, West Elm and Williams-Sonoma Home) and sells similar products through our eight direct-mail catalogs (Williams-Sonoma, Pottery Barn, Pottery Barn Kids, Pottery Barn Bed + Bath, PBteen, Hold Everything, West Elm and Williams-Sonoma Home) and six e-commerce websites (williams-sonoma.com, potterybarn.com, potterybarnkids.com, pbteen.com, westelm.com and holdeverything.com). Management's expectation is that the overall economics of each of our major concepts within each reportable segment will be similar over time.

These reportable segments are strategic business units that offer similar home-centered products. They are managed separately because the business units utilize two distinct distribution and marketing strategies. It is not practicable for us to report revenue by product group.

We use earnings before unallocated corporate overhead, interest and taxes to evaluate segment profitability. Unallocated costs before income taxes include corporate employee-related costs, depreciation expense, other occupancy expense and administrative costs, primarily in our corporate systems, corporate facilities and other administrative departments. Unallocated assets include corporate cash and cash equivalents, the net book value of corporate facilities and related information systems, deferred income taxes and other corporate long-lived assets.

Income tax information by segment has not been included as taxes are calculated at a company-wide level and are not allocated to each segment.

Segment Information

Dollars in thousands	Retail[1]	Direct-to-Customer	Unallocated	Total
2005				
Net revenues	$2,032,907	$1,506,040	—	$3,538,947
Depreciation and amortization expense	84,045	17,566	$ 21,588	123,199
Earnings (loss) before income taxes[2]	278,057	232,023	(161,282)	348,798
Assets[3]	986,222	295,200	700,198	1,981,620
Capital expenditures	96,918	20,984	33,886	151,788
2004				
Net revenues	$1,810,979	$1,325,952	—	$3,136,931
Depreciation and amortization expense	76,667	16,174	$ 18,783	111,624
Earnings (loss) before income taxes	253,038	210,809	(153,642)	310,205
Assets[3]	910,924	279,579	555,042	1,745,545
Capital expenditures	90,027	40,894	50,532	181,453
2003				
Net revenues	$1,622,383	$1,131,985	—	$2,754,368
Depreciation and amortization expense	68,800	15,472	$ 15,262	99,534
Earnings (loss) before income taxes	231,512	172,266	(148,140)	255,638
Assets[3]	822,340	218,603	429,792	1,470,735
Capital expenditures	121,759	11,845	78,375	211,979

[1]Net revenues include $64.6 million, $50.1 million and $42.7 million in fiscal 2005, 2004 and 2003, respectively, related to our foreign operations.

[2]Includes $11.4 million, $2.0 million, and $0.1 million in the retail, direct-to-customer, and corporate unallocated segments, respectively, related to the transitioning of the merchandising strategies of our Hold Everything brand into our other existing brands.

[3]Includes $26.5 million, $23.1 million and $22.5 million of long-term assets in fiscal 2005, 2004 and 2003, respectively, related to our foreign operations.

Form 10-K

Glossary

A

absorption costing   The reporting of the costs of manufactured products, normally direct materials, direct labor, and factory overhead, as product costs. (172)

accounts receivable turnover   The relationship between net sales and accounts receivable, computed by dividing the net sales by the average net accounts receivable; measures how frequently during the year the accounts receivable are being converted to cash. (573)

activity analysis   The study of employee effort and other business records to determine the cost of activities. (487)

activity base (driver)   A measure of activity that is related to changes in cost. Used in analyzing and classifying cost behavior. Activity bases are also used in the denominator in calculating the predetermined factory overhead rate to assign overhead costs to cost objects. (45, 128, 435)

activity cost pools   Cost accumulations that are associated with a given activity, such as machine usage, inspections, moving, and production setups. (434)

activity rate   The cost of an activity per unit of activity base, determined by dividing the activity cost pool by the activity base. (435)

activity-base usage quantity   The amount of activity used by a particular product measured in activity-base terms. (435)

activity-based costing (ABC)   A cost allocation method that identifies activities causing the incurrence of costs and allocates these costs to products (or other cost objects), based upon activity drivers (bases). (46, 365, 434)

annuity   A series of equal cash flows at fixed intervals. (395)

appraisal costs   Costs to detect, measure, evaluate, and audit products and processes to ensure that they conform to customer requirements and performance standards. (488)

average rate of return   A method of evaluating capital investment proposals that focuses on the expected profitability of the investment. (391)

B

backflush accounting   Simplification of the accounting system by eliminating accumulation and transfer of costs as products move through production. (483)

balanced scorecard   A performance evaluation approach that incorporates multiple performance dimensions by combining financial and nonfinancial measures. (321)

bottleneck   A condition that occurs when product demand exceeds production capacity. (366)

break-even point   The level of business operations at which revenues and expired costs are equal. (136)

budget   An accounting device used to plan and control resources of operational departments and divisions. (220)

budget performance report   A report comparing actual results with budget figures. (269)

budgetary slack   Excess resources set within a budget to provide for uncertain events. (223)

C

capital expenditures budget   The budget summarizing future plans for acquiring plant facilities and equipment. (238)

capital investment analysis   The process by which management plans, evaluates, and controls long-term capital investments involving property, plant, and equipment. (390)

capital rationing   The process by which management plans, evaluates, and controls long-term capital investments involving fixed assets. (404)

cash budget   A budget of estimated cash receipts and payments. (235)

cash flows from financing activities   The section of the statement of cash flows that reports cash flows from transactions affecting the equity and debt of the business. (514)

cash flows from investing activities   The section of the statement of cash flows that reports cash flows from transactions affecting investments in noncurrent assets. (514)

cash flows from operating activities   The section of the statement of cash flows that reports the cash transactions affecting the determination of net income. (514)

cash payback period   The expected period of time that will elapse between the date of a capital expenditure and the complete recovery in cash (or equivalent) of the amount invested. (392)

common-size statement   A financial statement in which all items are expressed only in relative terms. (569)

continuous budgeting   A method of budgeting that provides for maintaining a twelve-month projection into the future. (224)

continuous process improvement   A management approach that is part of the overall total quality management philosophy. The approach requires all employees to constantly improve processes of which they are a part or for which they have managerial responsibility. (6)

contribution margin   Sales less variable costs and variable selling and administrative expenses. (134, 173)

contribution margin analysis   The systematic examination of the differences between planned and actual contribution margins. (187)

contribution margin ratio   The percentage of each sales dollar that is available to cover the fixed costs and provide an operating income. (134)

controllable cost   Cost that can be influenced (increased, decreased, or eliminated) by someone such as a manager or factory worker. (180)

controllable expenses   Costs that can be influenced by the decisions of a manager. (312)

controllable variance   The difference between the actual amount of variable factory overhead cost incurred and the amount of variable factory overhead budgeted for the standard product. (276)

controller   The chief management accountant of a division or other segment of a business. (4)

controlling A phase in the management process that consists of monitoring the operating results of implemented plans and comparing the actual results with the expected results. (6)

conversion costs The combination of direct labor and factory overhead costs. (11)

cost A payment of cash (or a commitment to pay cash in the future) for the purpose of generating revenues. (7)

cost accounting system A branch of managerial accounting concerned with accumulating manufacturing costs for financial reporting and decision-making purposes. (39)

cost allocation The process of assigning indirect cost to a cost object, such as a job. (45)

cost behavior The manner in which a cost changes in relation to its activity base (driver). (128)

cost center A decentralized unit in which the department or division manager has responsibility for the control of costs incurred and the authority to make decisions that affect these costs. (310)

cost object The object or segment of operations to which costs are related for management's use, such as a product or department. (8)

cost of goods manufactured The total cost of making and finishing a product. (14)

cost of goods sold budget A budget of the estimated direct materials, direct labor, and factory overhead consumed by sold products. (233)

cost of merchandise sold The cost that is reported as an expense when merchandise is sold. (14)

cost of production report A report prepared periodically by a processing department, summarizing (1) the units for which the department is accountable and the disposition of those units and (2) the costs incurred by the department and the allocation of those costs between completed and incomplete production. (92)

cost of quality report A report summarizing the costs, percent of total, and percent of sales by appraisal, prevention, internal failure, and external failure cost of quality categories. (490)

cost per equivalent unit The rate used to allocate costs between completed and partially completed production. (90)

cost price approach An approach to transfer pricing that uses cost as the basis for setting the transfer price. (326)

cost variance The difference between actual cost and the flexible budget at actual volumes. (266)

costs of quality The cost associated with controlling quality (prevention and appraisal) and failing to control quality (internal and external failure). (487)

cost-volume-profit analysis The systematic examination of the relationships among selling prices, volume of sales and production, costs, expenses, and profits. (134)

cost-volume-profit chart A chart used to assist management in understanding the relationships among costs, expenses, sales, and operating profit or loss. (141)

currency exchange rate The rate at which currency in another country can be exchanged for local currency. (403)

current ratio A financial ratio that is computed by dividing current assets by current liabilities. (571)

currently attainable standards Standards that represent levels of operation that can be attained with reasonable effort. (267)

D

decentralization The separation of a business into more manageable operating units. (308)

decision making A component inherent in the other management processes of planning, directing, controlling, and improving. (6)

differential analysis The area of accounting concerned with the effect of alternative courses of action on revenues and costs. (351)

differential cost The amount of increase or decrease in cost expected from a particular course of action compared with an alternative. (351)

differential revenue The amount of increase or decrease in revenue expected from a particular course of action as compared with an alternative. (350)

direct costs Costs that can be traced directly to a cost object. (8)

direct labor cost The wages of factory workers who are directly involved in converting materials into a finished product. (10)

direct labor rate variance The cost associated with the difference between the standard rate and the actual rate paid for direct labor used in producing a commodity. (273)

direct labor time variance The cost associated with the difference between the standard hours and the actual hours of direct labor spent producing a commodity. (273)

direct materials cost The cost of materials that are an integral part of the finished product. (9)

direct materials price variance The cost associated with the difference between the standard price and the actual price of direct materials used in producing a commodity. (271)

direct materials purchases budget A budget that uses the production budget as a starting point to budget materials purchases. (230)

direct materials quantity variance The cost associated with the difference between the standard quantity and the actual quantity of direct materials used in producing a commodity. (272)

direct method A method of reporting the cash flows from operating activities as the difference between the operating cash receipts and the operating cash payments. (516)

directing The process by which managers, given their assigned level of responsibilities, run day-to-day operations. (5)

dividend yield A ratio, computed by dividing the annual dividends paid per share of common stock by the market price per share at a specific date, that indicates the rate of return to stockholders in terms of cash dividend distributions. (583)

division A decentralized unit that is structured around a common function, product, customer, or geographical territory. (308)

DuPont formula An expanded expression of return on investment determined by multiplying the profit margin by the investment turnover. (317)

E

earnings per share (EPS) on common stock The profitability ratio of net income available to common shareholders to the number of common shares outstanding. (581)

electronic data interchange (EDI) An information technology that allows different business organizations to use computers to communicate orders, relay information, and make or receive payments. (479)

employee involvement A philosophy that grants employees the responsibility and authority to make their own decisions about their operations. (478)

engineering change order (ECO) A document that initiates a change in the specification or a product or process. (434)

enterprise resource planning (ERP) system An integrated business and information system used by companies to plan and control both internal and supply chain operations. (480)

equivalent units of production The number of production units that could have been completed within a given accounting period, given the resources consumed. (86)

external failure costs The costs incurred after defective units or services have been delivered to consumers. (488)

F

factory burden Another term for manufacturing overhead or factory overhead. (10)

factory overhead cost All of the costs of producing a product except for direct materials and direct labor. (10)

feedback Measures provided to operational employees or managers on the performance of subunits of the organization. These measures are used by employees to adjust a process or a behavior to achieve goals. *See* **management by exception**. (6)

financial accounting The branch of accounting that is concerned with recording transactions using generally accepted accounting principles (GAAP) for a business or other economic unit and with a periodic preparation of various statements from such records. (2)

finished goods inventory The direct materials costs, direct labor costs, and factory overhead costs of finished products that have not been sold. (14)

finished goods ledger The subsidiary ledger that contains the individual accounts for each kind of commodity or product produced. (50)

first-in, first-out (FIFO) method The method of inventory costing based on the assumption that the costs of merchandise sold should be charged against revenue in the order in which the costs were incurred. (84)

fixed costs Costs that tend to remain the same in amount, regardless of variations in the level of activity. (130)

flexible budget A budget that adjusts for varying rates of activity. (226)

free cash flow The amount of operating cash flow remaining after replacing current productive capacity and maintaining current dividends. (534)

G

goal conflict A condition that occurs when individual objectives conflict with organizational objectives. (223)

H

high-low method A technique that uses the highest and lowest total costs as a basis for estimating the variable cost per unit and the fixed cost component of a mixed cost. (132)

horizontal analysis Financial analysis that compares an item in a current statement with the same item in prior statements. (564)

I

ideal standards Standards that can be achieved only under perfect operating conditions, such as no idle time, no machine breakdowns, and no materials spoilage; also called theoretical standards. (267)

income from operations (operating income) Revenues less operating expenses and service department charges for a profit or investment center. (315)

indirect costs Costs that cannot be traced directly to a cost object. (8)

indirect method A method of reporting the cash flows from operating activities as the net income from operations adjusted for all deferrals of past cash receipts and payments and all accruals of expected future cash receipts and payments. (516)

inflation A period when prices in general are rising and the purchasing power of money is declining. (403)

internal failure costs The costs associated with defects that are discovered by the organization before the product or service is delivered to the consumer. (488)

internal rate of return (IRR) method A method of analysis of proposed capital investments that uses present value concepts to compute the rate of return from the net cash flows expected from the investment. (398)

inventory turnover The relationship between the volume of goods sold and inventory, computed by dividing the cost of goods sold by the average inventory. (574)

investment center A decentralized unit in which the manager has the responsibility and authority to make decisions that affect not only costs and revenues but also the fixed assets available to the center. (316)

investment turnover A component of the rate of return on investment, computed as the ratio of sales to invested assets. (317)

J

job cost sheet An account in the work in process subsidiary ledger in which the costs charged to a particular job order are recorded. (42)

job order cost system A type of cost accounting system that provides for a separate record of the cost of each particular quantity of product that passes through the factory. (39)

just-in-time (JIT) manufacturing A business philosophy that focuses on eliminating time, cost, and poor quality within manufacturing processes. (473)

just-in-time (JIT) processing A processing approach that focuses on eliminating time, cost, and poor quality within manufacturing and nonmanufacturing processes. (97)

L

lead time The elapsed time between starting a unit of product into the beginning of a process and its completion. (474)

leverage The amount of debt used by a firm to finance its assets; causes the rate earned on stockholders' equity to vary from the rate earned on total assets because the amount earned on assets acquired through the use of funds provided by creditors varies from the interest paid to these creditors. (579)

line department A unit that is directly involved in the basic objectives of an organization. (3)

M

management by exception The philosophy of managing which involves monitoring the operating results of implemented plans and comparing the expected results with the actual results. This feedback allows management to isolate significant variations for further investigation and possible remedial action. (6)

management process The five basic management functions of (1) planning, (2) directing, (3) controlling, (4) improving, and (5) decision making. (4)

Management's Discussion and Analysis (MD&A) An annual report disclosure that provides management's analysis of the results of operations and financial condition. (585)

managerial accounting The branch of accounting that uses both historical and estimated data in providing information that management uses in conducting daily operations, in planning future operations, and in developing overall business strategies. (3)

manufacturing cells A grouping of processes where employees are cross-trained to perform more than one function. (98)

manufacturing margin The variable cost of goods sold deducted from sales. (173)

manufacturing overhead Costs, other than direct materials and direct labor costs, that are incurred in the manufacturing process. (10)

margin of safety The difference between current sales revenue and the sales at the break-even point. (148)

market price approach An approach to transfer pricing that uses the price at which the product or service transferred could be sold to outside buyers as the transfer price. (323)

market segment A portion of business that can be assigned to a manager for profit responsibility. (182)

markup An amount that is added to a "cost" amount to determine product price. (360)

master budget The comprehensive budget plan linking all the individual budgets related to sales, cost of goods sold, operating expenses, projects, capital expenditures, and cash. (228)

materials inventory The cost of materials that have not yet entered into the manufacturing process. (13)

materials ledger The subsidiary ledger containing the individual accounts for each type of material. (42)

materials requisitions The form or electronic transmission used by a manufacturing department to authorize materials issuances from the storeroom. (42)

mixed cost A cost with both variable and fixed characteristics, sometimes called a semivariable or semifixed cost. (130)

multiple production department factory overhead rate method A method that allocated factory overhead to product by using factory overhead rates for each production department. (429)

N

negotiated price approach An approach to transfer pricing that allows managers of decentralized units to agree (negotiate) among themselves as to the transfer price. (324)

net present value method A method of analysis of proposed capital investments that focuses on the present value of the cash flows expected from the investments. (396)

noncontrollable costs Costs that cannot be influenced (increased, decreased, or eliminated) by someone such as a manager or factory worker. (180)

nonfinancial measure A performance measure that has not been stated in dollar terms. (485)

nonfinancial performance measure A performance measure expressed in units rather than dollars. (283)

non-value-added activities The cost of activities that are perceived as unnecessary from the customer's perspective and are thus candidates for elimination. (491)

non-value-added lead time The time that units wait in inventories, move unnecessarily, and wait during machine breakdowns. (475)

number of days' sales in inventory The relationship between the volume of sales and inventory, computed by dividing the inventory at the end of the year by the average daily cost of goods sold. (575)

number of days' sales in receivables The relationship between sales and accounts receivable, computed by dividing the net accounts receivable at the end of the year by the average daily sales. (573)

number of times interest charges are earned A ratio that measures creditor margin of safety for interest payments, calculated as income before interest and taxes divided by interest expense. (576)

O

objectives (goals) Developed in the planning stage, these reflect the direction and desired outcomes of certain courses of action. (5)

operating leverage A measure of the relative mix of a business's variable costs and fixed costs, computed as contribution margin divided by operating income. (147)

operational planning The development of short-term plans to achieve goals identified in a business's strategic plan. Sometimes called tactical planning. (5)

opportunity cost The amount of income forgone from an alternative to a proposed use of cash or its equivalent. (357)

overapplied factory overhead The amount of factory overhead applied in excess of the actual factory overhead costs incurred for production during a period. (46)

P

Pareto chart A bar chart that shows the totals of a particular attribute for a number of categories, ranked left to right from the largest to smallest totals. (489)

period costs Those costs that are used up in generating revenue during the current period and that are not involved in manufacturing a product, such as selling, general, and administratvie expenses. (11, 51)

planning A phase of the management process whereby objectives are outlined and courses of action determined. (5)

predetermined factory overhead rate The rate used to apply factory overhead costs to the goods manufactured. The rate is determined by dividing the budgeted overhead cost by the estimated activity usage at the beginning of the fiscal period. (45)

present value concept Cash to be received (or paid) in the future is not the equivalent of the same amount of money received at an earlier date. (394)

present value index An index computed by dividing the total present value of the net cash flow to be received from a proposed capital investment by the amount to be invested. (396)

present value of an annuity The sum of the present values of a series of equal cash flows to be received at fixed intervals. (395)

prevention costs Costs incurred to prevent defects from occurring during the design and delivery of products or services. (488)

price factor The effect of a difference in unit sales price or unit cost on the number of units sold. (187)

price-earnings (P/E) ratio The ratio of the market price per share of common stock, at a specific date, to the annual earnings per share. (581)

prime costs The combination of direct materials and direct labor costs. (11)

process A sequence of activities linked together for performing a particular task. (283, 492)

process cost system A type of cost system that accumulates costs for each of the various departments within a manufacturing facility. (40, 81)

process manufacturers Manufacturers that use large machines to process a continuous flow of raw materials through various stages of completion into a finished state. (80)

process-oriented layout Organizing work in a plant or administrative function around processes (tasks). (478)

product cost concept A concept used in applying the cost-plus approach to product pricing in which only the costs of manufacturing the product, termed the product cost, are included in the cost amount to which the markup is added. (363)

product costing Determining the cost of a product. (426)

product costs The three components of manufacturing cost: direct materials, direct labor, and factory overhead costs. (11)

production budget A budget of estimated unit production. (229)

production department factory overhead rates Rates determined by dividing the budgeted production department factory overhead by the budgeted allocation base for each department. (430)

product-oriented layout Organizing work in a plant or administrative function around products; sometimes referred to as product cells. (478)

profit center A decentralized unit in which the manager has the responsibility and the authority to make decisions that affect both costs and revenues (and thus profits). (312)

profit margin A component of the rate of return on investment, computed as the ratio of income from operations to sales. (317)

profit-volume chart A chart used to assist management in understanding the relationship between profit and volume. (143)

profitability The ability of a firm to earn income. (570)

pull manufacturing A just-in-time method wherein customer orders trigger the release of finished goods, which trigger production, which trigger release of materials from suppliers. (478)

push manufacturing Materials are released into production and work in process is released into finished goods in anticipation of future sales. (479)

Q

quantity factor The effect of a difference in the number of units sold, assuming no change in unit sales price or unit cost. (187)

quick assets Cash and other current assets that can be quickly converted to cash, such as marketable securities and receivables. (572)

quick ratio A financial ratio that measures the ability to pay current liabilities with quick assets (cash, marketable securities, accounts receivable). (572)

R

radio frequency identification devices (RFID) Electronic tags (chips) placed on or embedded within products that can be read by radio waves that allow instant monitoring of product location. (479)

rate earned on common stockholders' equity A measure of profitability computed by dividing net income, reduced by preferred dividend requirements, by common stockholders' equity. (580)

rate earned on stockholders' equity A measure of profitability computed by dividing net income by total stockholders' equity. (579)

rate earned on total assets A measure of the profitability of assets, without regard to the equity of creditors and stockholders in the assets. (578)

rate of return on investment (ROI) A measure of managerial efficiency in the use of investments in assets, computed as income from operations divided by invested assets. (317)

ratio of fixed assets to long-term liabilities A leverage ratio that measures the margin of safety of long-term creditors, calculated as the net fixed assets divided by the long-term liabilities. (575)

ratio of liabilities to stockholders' equity A comprehensive leverage ratio that measures the relationship of the claims of creditors to that stockholders' equity. (576)

Raw and In Process (RIP) Inventory The capitalized cost of direct materials purchases, labor, and overhead charged to the production cell. (482)

receiving report The form or electronic transmission used by the receiving personnel to indicate that materials have been received and inspected. (42)

relevant range The range of activity over which changes in cost are of interest to management. (128)

residual income The excess of divisional income from operations over a "minimum" acceptable income from operations. (320)

responsibility accounting The process of measuring and reporting operating data by areas of responsibility. (309)

responsibility center An organizational unit for which a manager is assigned responsibility over costs, revenues, or assets. (221)

S

sales budget One of the major elements of the income statement budget that indicates the quantity of estimated sales and the expected unit selling price. (229)

sales mix The relative distribution of sales among the various products available for sale. (146, 184)

service department charges The costs of services provided by an internal service department and transferred to a responsibility center. (313)

setup Changing the characteristics of a machine to produce a different product. (434)

single plantwide factory overhead rate method A method that allocates all factory overhead to products by using a single factory overhead rate. (427)

six-sigma A quality improvement process developed by Motorola Corporation consisting of five steps: define, measure, analyze, improve, and control (DMAIC). (479)

solvency The ability of a firm to pay its debts as they come due. (570)

staff department A unit that provides services, assistance, and advice to the departments with line or other staff responsibilities. (4)

standard cost A detailed estimate of what a product should cost. (266)

standard cost systems Accounting systems that use standards for each element of manufacturing cost entering into the finished product. (266)

statement of cost of goods manufactured The income statement of manufacturing companies. (15)

statement of cash flows A summary of the cash receipts and cash payments *for a specific period of time*, such as a month or a year. (514)

static budget A budget that does not adjust to changes in activity levels. (225)

strategic planning The development of a long-range course of action to achieve business goals. (5)

strategies The means by which business goals and objectives will be achieved. (5)

sunk cost A cost that is not affected by subsequent decisions. (350)

supply chain management The coordination and control of materials, services, information, and finances as they move in a process from supplier, through the manufacturer, wholesaler, and retailer to the consumer. (479)

T

target costing The target cost is determined by subtracting a desired profit from a market method determined price. The resulting target cost is used to motivate cost improvements in design and manufacture. (365)

theory of constraints (TOC) A manufacturing strategy that attempts to remove the influence of bottlenecks (constraints) on a process. (366)

time tickets The form on which the amount of time spent by each employee and the labor cost incurred for each individual job, or for factory overhead, are recorded. (43)

time value of money concept The concept that an amount of money invested today will earn income. (391)

total cost concept A concept used in applying the cost-plus approach to product pricing in which all the costs of manufacturing the product plus the selling and administrative expenses are included in the cost amount to which the markup is added. (361)

transfer price The price charged one decentralized unit by another for the goods or services provided. (323)

U

underapplied factory overhead The amount of actual factory overhead in excess of the factory overhead applied to production during a period. (46)

unit contribution margin The dollars available from each unit of sales to cover fixed costs and provide operating profits. (135)

V

value-added activities The cost of activities that are needed to meet customer requirements. (491)

value-added lead time The time required to manufacture a unit of product or other output. (474)

value-added ratio The ratio of the value-added lead time to the total lead time. (475)

variable cost concept A concept used in applying the cost-plus approach to product pricing in which only the variable costs are included in the cost amount to which the markup is added. (364)

variable costing The concept that considers the cost of products manufactured to be composed only of those manufacturing costs that increase or decrease as the volume of production rises or falls (direct materials, direct labor, and variable factory overhead). (133, 172)

variable costs Costs that vary in total dollar amount as the level of activity changes. (129)

vertical analysis An analysis that compares each item in a current statement with a total amount within the same statement. (567)

volume variance The difference between the budgeted fixed overhead at 100% of normal capacity and the standard fixed overhead for the actual production achieved during the period. (277)

W

whole units The number of units in production during a period, whether completed or not. (86)

work in process inventory The direct materials costs, the direct labor costs, and the applied factory overhead costs that have entered into the manufacturing process but are associated with products that have not been finished. (13)

Y

yield A measure of materials usage efficiency. (97)

Z

zero-based budgeting A concept of budgeting that requires all levels of management to start from zero and estimate budget data as if there had been no previous activities in their units. (224)

Subject Index • • • • • • • • • • • • • • • • • •

Jobs, 39
    assigning factory overhead to,
        illus., 47
Journal entries for process cost system, 94
Just-in-time (JIT) manufacturing
    def., 473
    vs. traditional manufacturing, operating principles of, *illus.*, 474
Just-in-time approach, applying, 480
Just-in-time for nonmanufacturing processes, 485
Just-in-time hospital unit layout, *illus.*, 487
Just-in-time operations, 481
    accounting for, 482
    illus., 481
Just-in-time principles, 473
Just-in-time processing (JIT), *def.*, 97
Just-in-time production line, *illus.*, 98

K

Kaizen costing, 267
Kanban, 479
Key performance indicators (KPI's), 485

L

Labor information and cost flows, *illus.*, 44
Land, 527
    gain on sale of, 522, 532
Lead time
    and setup times, relationship between, *illus.*, 475
    components of, *illus.*, 475
    def., 474
    non-value-added, 475
    impact of batch sizes on, *illus.*, 476
    reducing, 474
Lean manufacturing, 473
Lease or sell, 351
    differential analysis report, *illus.*, 352
Lease vs. capital investment, 402
Leverage
    def., 579
    illus., 580
Liabilities
    ratio of, to stockholders' equity, 576
    changes in current operating, 522
    ratio of fixed assets to long-term, 575
Line, 4
Line department, *def.*, 3
Load factor, 190
Long-term liabilities, ratio of fixed assets to, 575

M

Make or buy, 355
    differential analysis report, *illus.*, 356
Make to order, 178
Make to stock, 479
Management
    controlling function of, 221
    decisions and accounting reports, *illus.*, 181
    directing function of, 221
    planning function of, 220

use of variable costing and absorption costing by, 180
Management accountant in the organization, 3
Management by exception, *def.*, 68
Management process
    def., 4
    illus., 4
    managerial accounting in, 4
Management's Discussion and Analysis (MD&A), *def.*, 585
Managerial accounting, 2
    and financial accounting, differences between, 2
    def., 3
    illus., 3
    in management process, 4
    uses of, 18
Manufacturing business
    balance sheet for, 13
    financial statements for, 13
    job order cost systems for, 40
Manufacturing cells, *def.*, 98
Manufacturing company
    balance sheet presentation of inventory of, *illus.*, 14
    income statement for, 14, *illus.*, 17
Manufacturing costs, 9
    and inventories, *illus.*, 40
    flow of, *illus.*, 15, 41, 52
    schedule of payments for, *illus.*, 237
Manufacturing margin, *def.*, 173
Manufacturing operations
    illus., 7
    tour of, 7
Manufacturing overhead, *def.*, 10
MAP (minimum advertised price), 362
Margin of safety, *def.*, 148
Market price approach, *def.*, 323
Market segment
    analysis, service firm, 190
    analyzing, 182
    def., 182
    variable costing in analyzing, 182
Market segmentation, 444
Markup, *def.*, 360
Master budget, *def.*, 228
Material substitution variance, 278
Materials, 41
    equivalent units, 87
    information and cost flows, *illus.*, 41
    inventory, *def.*, 13
    ledger, *def.*, 42
    requisitions, *def.*, 42
Mathematical approach to cost-volume-profit analysis, 136
Merchandise, cash payments for, 530
Merchandise sold, cost of, 41, 566fn
Merchandising companies, balance sheet presentation of inventory of, *illus.*, 14
Method variance, 278
Mixed costs
    def., 130
    illus., 131
Monte Carlo analysis, 403
Movie business, making money in, 55
Multiple production department factory overhead rate method
    def., 429
    vs. activity-based costing, 437, *illus.*, 434

vs. single plantwide factory overhead rates, 432
Multiple production department rate and single plantwide rate methods, comparison of, *illus.*, 430
    illus., 431

N

Negotiated price approach, *def.*, 324
Net cash flow, 393
    provided by financing activities, 517
    provided by investing activities, 517
    used for financing activities, 517
    used for investing activities, 517
Net present value analysis
    at 12%, *illus.*, 398
    equalized lives of proposals, *illus.*, 402
    unequal lives of proposals, *illus.*, 402
Net present value method, *def.*, 396
Net sales to assets, ratio of, 577
Network business, 147
Noncash investing and financing activities, 517
Noncontrollable costs, *def.*, 180
Nonfinancial measure, *def.*, 485
Nonfinancial performance measures, 482, 485
    def., 283
Nonmanufacturing activities, direct labor standards for, 274
Nonmanufacturing processes, just-in-time for, 485
Nonvalue time, eliminating, 477
Non-value-added activity, *def.*, 491
Non-value-added lead time, *def.*, 475
Non-value-added/value-added quality control activities, *illus.*, 492
Normal standards, 267
Number of days' sales in inventory, *def.*, 575
Number of days' sales in receivables, *def.*, 573
Number of times interest charges are earned, *def.*, 576
Number of times preferred dividends are earned, 577

O

Objectives (goals), *def.*, 4
One-piece flow, 477
Operating activities
    cash flows from, 514, 515, 532, 519, *illus.*, 524
    reporting cash flows from, 524
Operating expenses, cash payments for, 531
Operating leverage, *def.*, 147
Operating principles of just-in-time vs. traditional manufacturing, *illus.*, 474
Operational planning, *def.*, 4
Operations
    accounting for just-in-time, 482
    cash flow from, direct and indirect methods, *illus.*, 517
    centralized and decentralized, 308
    just-in-time, *illus.*, 481
    tour of manufacturing, 7
    traditional, *illus.*, 480

Company Index ● ● ● ● ● ● ● ● ● ● ● ● ● ● ●

The Basics

1. Accounting Equation:

Assets = Liabilities + Owner's (Stockholders') Equity

2. T Account:

Account Title

Left Side debit	Right Side credit

3. Rules of Debit and Credit:

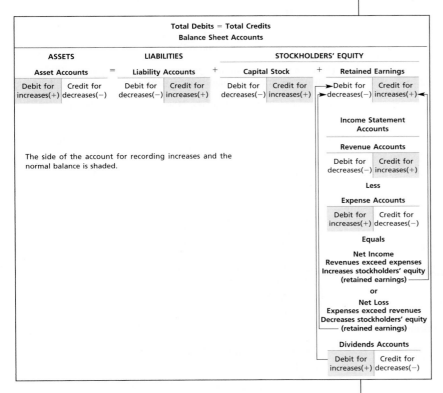

4. Analyzing and Recording Transactions:

1. Carefully read the description of the transaction to determine whether an asset, liability, capital stock, retained earnings, revenue, expense, or dividends account is affected by the transaction.
2. For each account affected by the transaction, determine whether the account increases or decreases.
3. Determine whether each increase or decrease should be recorded as a debit or a credit.
4. Record the transaction using a journal entry.
5. Periodically post journal entries to the accounts in the ledger.
6. Prepare an unadjusted trial balance at the end of the period.

5. Financial Statements:

INCOME STATEMENT
A summary of the revenue and expenses of a business entity for a specific period of time, such as a month or a year.

RETAINED EARNINGS STATEMENT
A summary of the changes in the retained earnings of a business entity that have occurred during a specific period of time, such as a month or a year.

BALANCE SHEET
A list of the assets, liabilities, and stockholders' equity of a business entity as of a specific date, usually at the close of the last day of a month or a year.

STATEMENT OF CASH FLOWS
A summary of the cash receipts and cash payments of a business entity for a specific period of time, such as a month or a year.

6. Accounting Cycle:

1. Transactions are analyzed and recorded in the journal.
2. Transactions are posted to the ledger.
3. An unadjusted trial balance is prepared.
4. Adjustment data are assembled and analyzed.
5. An optional end-of-period spreadsheet (work sheet) is prepared.
6. Adjusting entries are journalized and posted to the ledger.
7. An adjusted trial balance is prepared.
8. Financial statements are prepared.
9. Closing entries are journalized and posted to the ledger.
10. A post-closing trial balance is prepared.

7. Types of Adjusting Entries:

1. Prepaid expense (deferred expense)
2. Unearned revenue (deferred revenue)
3. Accrued revenue (accrued asset)
4. Accrued expense (accrued liability)
5. Depreciation expense

Each entry will always affect both balance sheet and income statement accounts.

8. Closing Entries:

1. Transfer revenue account balances to Income Summary.
2. Transfer expense account balances to Income Summary.
3. Transfer Income Summary balance to Retained Earnings.
4. Transfer dividends account balance to Retained Earnings.

9. Special Journals:

Providing services on account ⟶ recorded in ⟶ Revenue (sales) journal

Receipt of cash from any source ⟶ recorded in ⟶ Cash receipts journal

Purchase of items on account ⟶ recorded in ⟶ Purchases journal

Payments of cash for any purpose ⟶ recorded in ⟶ Cash payments journal

10. Shipping Terms:

	FOB Shipping Point	FOB Destination
Ownership (title) passes to buyer when merchandise is....................	delivered to freight carrier	delivered to buyer
Transportation costs are paid by	buyer	seller

11. Format for Bank Reconciliation:

Cash balance according to bank statement		$xxx
Add: Additions by company not on bank statement	$xx	
Bank errors	xx	xx
		$xxx
Deduct: Deductions by company not on bank statement	$xx	
Bank errors	xx	xx
Adjusted balance..		$xxx
Cash balance according to company's records		$xxx
Add: Additions by bank not recorded by company ..	$xx	
Company errors..	xx	xx
		$xxx
Deduct: Deductions by bank not recorded by company..	$xx	
Company errors..	xx	xx
Adjusted balance..		$xxx

12. Inventory Costing Methods:
1. First-in, First-out (FIFO)
2. Last-in, First-out (LIFO)
3. Average Cost

13. Interest Computations:

$$\text{Interest} = \text{Face Amount (or Principal)} \times \text{Rate} \times \text{Time}$$

14. Methods of Determining Annual Depreciation:

STRAIGHT-LINE: $\dfrac{\text{Cost} - \text{Estimated Residual Value}}{\text{Estimated Life}}$

DOUBLE-DECLINING-BALANCE: Rate* × Book Value at Beginning of Period

*Rate is commonly twice the straight-line rate (1/Estimated Life).

15. Adjustments to Net Income (Loss) Using the Indirect Method

	Increase (Decrease)
Net income (loss)	$ XXX
Adjustments to reconcile net income to net cash flow from operating activities:	
Depreciation of fixed assets	XXX
Amortization of intangible assets	XXX
Losses on disposal of assets	XXX
Gains on disposal of assets	(XXX)
Changes in current operating assets and liabilities:	
Increases in noncash current operating assets	(XXX)
Decreases in noncash current operating assets	XXX
Increases in current operating liabilities	XXX
Decreases in current operating liabilities	(XXX)
Net cash flow from operating activities	$ XXX
	or
	$(XXX)

16. Contribution Margin Ratio $= \dfrac{\text{Sales} - \text{Variable Costs}}{\text{Sales}}$

17. Break-Even Sales (Units) $= \dfrac{\text{Fixed Costs}}{\text{Unit Contribution Margin}}$

18. Sales (Units) $= \dfrac{\text{Fixed Costs} + \text{Target Profit}}{\text{Unit Contribution Margin}}$

19. Margin of Safety $= \dfrac{\text{Sales} - \text{Sales at Break-Even Point}}{\text{Sales}}$

20. Operating Leverage $= \dfrac{\text{Contribution Margin}}{\text{Income from Operations}}$

21. Variances

$\dfrac{\text{Direct Materials}}{\text{Price Variance}} = \dfrac{\text{Actual Price per Unit} -}{\text{Standard Price}} \times \dfrac{\text{Actual Quantity}}{\text{Used}}$

$\dfrac{\text{Direct Materials}}{\text{Quantity Variance}} = \dfrac{\text{Actual Quantity Used} -}{\text{Standard Quantity}} \times \dfrac{\text{Standard Price}}{\text{per Unit}}$

$\dfrac{\text{Direct Labor}}{\text{Rate Variance}} = \dfrac{\text{Actual Rate per Hour} -}{\text{Standard Rate}} \times \dfrac{\text{Actual Hours}}{\text{Worked}}$

$\dfrac{\text{Direct Labor}}{\text{Time Variance}} = \dfrac{\text{Actual Hours Worked} -}{\text{Standard Hours}} \times \dfrac{\text{Standard Rate}}{\text{per Hour}}$

$\begin{matrix}\text{Variable Factory} \\ \text{Overhead Controllable} \\ \text{Variance}\end{matrix} = \begin{matrix}\text{Actual} \\ \text{Factory} \\ \text{Overhead}\end{matrix} - \begin{matrix}\text{Budgeted Factory} \\ \text{Overhead for} \\ \text{Amount Produced}\end{matrix}$

$\begin{matrix}\text{Fixed Factory} \\ \text{Overhead Volume} \\ \text{Variance}\end{matrix} = \begin{matrix}\text{Budgeted Factory} \\ \text{Overhead for} \\ \text{Amount Produced}\end{matrix} - \begin{matrix}\text{Applied} \\ \text{Factory} \\ \text{Overhead}\end{matrix}$

22. Rate of Return on Investment (ROI) $= \dfrac{\text{Income from Operations}}{\text{Invested Assets}}$

Alternative ROI Computation:

$$\text{ROI} = \dfrac{\text{Income from Operations}}{\text{Sales}} \times \dfrac{\text{Sales}}{\text{Invested Assets}}$$

23. Capital Investment Analysis Methods:
1. Methods That Ignore Present Values:
   A. Average Rate of Return Method
   B. Cash Payback Method
2. Methods That Use Present Values:
   A. Net Present Value Method
   B. Internal Rate of Return Method

24. Average Rate of Return $= \dfrac{\text{Estimated Average Annual Income}}{\text{Average Investment}}$

25. Present Value Index $= \dfrac{\text{Total Present Value of Net Cash Flow}}{\text{Amount to Be Invested}}$

26. Present Value Factor for an Annuity of $1 $= \dfrac{\text{Amount to Be Invested}}{\text{Equal Annual Net Cash Flows}}$

Abbreviations and Acronyms Commonly Used in Business and Accounting

AAA	American Accounting Association
ABC	Activity-based costing
AICPA	American Institute of Certified Public Accountants
CIA	Certified Internal Auditor
CIM	Computer-integrated manufacturing
CMA	Certified Management Accountant
CPA	Certified Public Accountant
Cr.	Credit
Dr.	Debit
EFT	Electronic funds transfer
EPS	Earnings per share
FAF	Financial Accounting Foundation
FASB	Financial Accounting Standards Board
FEI	Financial Executives International
FICA tax	Federal Insurance Contributions Act tax
FIFO	First-in, first-out
FOB	Free on board
GAAP	Generally accepted accounting principles
GASB	Governmental Accounting Standards Board
GNP	Gross National Product
IMA	Institute of Management Accountants
IRC	Internal Revenue Code
IRS	Internal Revenue Service
JIT	Just-in-time
LIFO	Last-in, first-out
Lower of C or M	Lower of cost or market
MACRS	Modified Accelerated Cost Recovery System
n/30	Net 30
n/eom	Net, end-of-month
P/E Ratio	Price-earnings ratio
POS	Point of sale
ROI	Return on investment
SEC	Securities and Exchange Commission
TQC	Total quality control

Classification of Accounts

Account Title	Account Classification	Normal Balance	Financial Statement
Accounts Payable	Current liability	Credit	Balance sheet
Accounts Receivable	Current asset	Debit	Balance sheet
Accumulated Depreciation	Contra fixed asset	Credit	Balance sheet
Accumulated Depletion	Contra fixed asset	Credit	Balance sheet
Advertising Expense	Operating expense	Debit	Income statement
Allowance for Doubtful Accounts	Contra current asset	Credit	Balance sheet
Amortization Expense	Operating expense	Debit	Income statement
Bonds Payable	Long-term liability	Credit	Balance sheet
Building	Fixed asset	Debit	Balance sheet
Capital Stock	Stockholders' equity	Credit	Balance sheet
Cash	Current asset	Debit	Balance sheet
Cash Dividends	Stockholders' equity	Debit	Retained earnings statement
Cash Dividends Payable	Current liability	Credit	Balance sheet
Common Stock	Stockholders' equity	Credit	Balance sheet
Cost of Merchandise (Goods) Sold	Cost of merchandise (goods sold)	Debit	Income statement
Deferred Income Tax Payable	Current liability/Long-term liability	Credit	Balance sheet
Depletion Expense	Operating expense	Debit	Income statement
Discount on Bonds Payable	Long-term liability	Debit	Balance sheet
Dividend Revenue	Other income	Credit	Income statement
Dividends	Stockholders' equity	Debit	Retained earnings statement
Employees Federal Income Tax Payable	Current liability	Credit	Balance sheet
Equipment	Fixed asset	Debit	Balance sheet
Exchange Gain	Other income	Credit	Income statement
Exchange Loss	Other expense	Debit	Income statement
Factory Overhead (Overapplied)	Deferred credit	Credit	Balance sheet (interim)
Factory Overhead (Underapplied)	Deferred debit	Debit	Balance sheet (interim)
Federal Income Tax Payable	Current liability	Credit	Balance sheet
Federal Unemployment Tax Payable	Current liability	Credit	Balance sheet
Finished Goods	Current asset	Debit	Balance sheet
Gain on Disposal of Fixed Assets	Other income	Credit	Income statement
Gain on Redemption of Bonds	Other income	Credit	Income statement
Gain on Sale of Investments	Other income	Credit	Income statement
Goodwill	Intangible asset	Debit	Balance sheet
Income Tax Expense	Income tax	Debit	Income statement
Income Tax Payable	Current liability	Credit	Balance sheet
Insurance Expense	Operating expense	Debit	Income statement
Interest Expense	Other expense	Debit	Income statement
Interest Receivable	Current asset	Debit	Balance sheet
Interest Revenue	Other income	Credit	Income statement
Investment in Bonds	Investment	Debit	Balance sheet
Investment in Stocks	Investment	Debit	Balance sheet
Investment in Subsidiary	Investment	Debit	Balance sheet
Land	Fixed asset	Debit	Balance sheet
Loss on Disposal of Fixed Assets	Other expense	Debit	Income statement
Loss on Redemption of Bonds	Other expense	Debit	Income statement
Loss on Sale of Investments	Other expense	Debit	Income statement
Marketable Securities	Current asset	Debit	Balance sheet
Materials	Current asset	Debit	Balance sheet
...care Tax Payable	Current liability	Credit	Balance sheet

Account Title	Account Classification	Normal Balance	Financial Statement
Merchandise Inventory	Current asset/Cost of merchandise sold	Debit	Balance sheet/Income statement
Notes Payable	Current liability/Long-term liability	Credit	Balance sheet
Notes Receivable	Current asset/Investment	Debit	Balance sheet
Organizational Expenses	Operating expense	Debit	Income statement
Patents	Intangible asset	Debit	Balance sheet
Paid-In Capital from Sale of Treasury Stock	Stockholders' equity	Credit	Balance sheet
Paid-In Capital in Excess of Par (Stated Value)	Stockholders' equity	Credit	Balance sheet
Payroll Tax Expense	Operating expense	Debit	Income statement
Pension Expense	Operating expense	Debit	Income statement
Petty Cash	Current asset	Debit	Balance sheet
Premium on Bonds Payable	Long-term liability	Credit	Balance sheet
Prepaid Insurance	Current asset	Debit	Balance sheet
Prepaid Rent	Current asset	Debit	Balance sheet
Preferred Stock	Stockholders' equity	Credit	Balance sheet
Purchases	Cost of merchandise sold	Debit	Income statement
Purchases Discounts	Cost of merchandise sold	Credit	Income statement
Purchases Returns and Allowances	Cost of merchandise sold	Credit	Income statement
Rent Expense	Operating expense	Debit	Income statement
Rent Revenue	Other income	Credit	Income statement
Retained Earnings	Stockholders' equity	Credit	Balance sheet/Retained earnings statement
Salaries Expense	Operating expense	Debit	Income statement
Salaries Payable	Current liability	Credit	Balance sheet
Sales	Revenue from sales	Credit	Income statement
Sales Discounts	Revenue from sales	Debit	Income statement
Sales Returns and Allowances	Revenue from sales	Debit	Income statement
Sales Tax Payable	Current liability	Credit	Balance sheet
Sinking Fund Cash	Investment	Debit	Balance sheet
Sinking Fund Investments	Investment	Debit	Balance sheet
Social Security Tax Payable	Current liability	Credit	Balance sheet
State Unemployment Tax Payable	Current liability	Credit	Balance sheet
Stock Dividends	Stockholders' equity	Debit	Retained earnings statement
Stock Dividends Distributable	Stockholders' equity	Credit	Balance sheet
Supplies	Current asset	Debit	Balance sheet
Supplies Expense	Operating expense	Debit	Income statement
Transportation In	Cost of merchandise sold	Debit	Income statement
Transportation Out	Operating expense	Debit	Income statement
Treasury Stock	Stockholders' equity	Debit	Balance sheet
Uncollectible Accounts Expense	Operating expense	Debit	Income statement
Unearned Rent	Current liability	Credit	Balance sheet
Utilities Expense	Operating expense	Debit	Income statement
Vacation Pay Expense	Operating expense	Debit	Income statement
Vacation Pay Payable	Current liability/Long-term liability	Credit	Balance sheet
Work in Process	Current asset	Debit	Balance sheet